ECONOMICS OF
SOCIAL ISSUES

FOURTEENTH
EDITION

ECONOMICS OF SOCIAL ISSUES

Ansel M. Sharp
University of the South

Charles A. Register
Florida Atlantic University

Paul W. Grimes
Mississippi State University

Irwin
McGraw-Hill

Boston   Burr Ridge, IL   Dubuque, IA   Madison, WI   New York   San Francisco   St. Louis
Bangkok   Bogotá   Caracas   Lisbon   London   Madrid
Mexico City   Milan   New Delhi   Seoul   Singapore   Sydney   Taipei   Toronto

McGraw-Hill Higher Education

A Division of The **McGraw-Hill** Companies

Economics of Social Issues

Copyright © 2000, 1998, 1996, 1994, 1992, 1990, 1988, 1986, 1984, 1982, 1980, 1979, 1976, 1974 by The McGraw-Hill Companies, Inc. All rights reserved. Printed in the United States of America. Except as permitted under the United States Copyright Act of 1976, no part of this publication may be reproduced or distributed in any form or by any means, or stored in a data base or retrieval system, without the prior written permission of the publisher.

This book is printed on acid-free paper.

1 2 3 4 5 6 7 8 9 0 FGR FGR 9 0 9 8 7 6 5 4 3 2 1 0 9

ISBN 0-07-231598-9

Editorial director: Mike Junior	Designer: Suzanne Montazer
Publisher: Gary Burke	Cover concept: Chantal Guillemin
Executive editor: Paul Shensa	Cover designer: Amanda Kavanagh
Development editor: Chantal Guillemin	Cover illustrator: Richard Tuschman
Marketing manager: Nelson Black	Compositor: GAC Indianapolis
Project manager: Eva Strock	Typeface: Palatino
Production supervisor: Rich DeVitto	Printer: Quebecor Printing
Supplements coordinator: Louis Swaim	

Cover photo credits: President Clinton, AP/Wide World Photos; Mark McGuire, © Richard Anastasio

Library of Congress Cataloging-in-Publication Data

Sharp, Ansel Miree, 1924-
    Economics of social issues / Ansel M. Sharp, Charles A. Register,
Paul W. Grimes. — 15th ed.
      p.   cm.
    Includes index.
    ISBN 0-07-231598-9 (alk. paper)
    1. Economics. 2. Social problems. I. Register, Charles A.
II. Grimes, Paul W. III. Title
HB171.5. S5498   1999   99-29684
330—dc21   CIP

http://www.mhhe.com

Preface

Welcome to the fourteenth edition of *Economics of Social Issues*. With this edition, our textbook surpasses its twenty-fifth anniversary. Many things have changed since Richard Leftwich and Ansel Sharp first published *Economics of Social Issues* in 1974. Over the years, our selection of topics changed to match the important social issues of the times, one author retired and two new authors joined the team, competing textbooks entered the marketplace (but not all survived), and our publisher was acquired and merged with a larger corporation (not once, but twice). However, at least one thing has remained constant: our basic teaching objectives designed to produce economically literate citizens. These objectives are to (1) create student interest in the study of economics and (2) provide a framework of basic analytical tools useful in the understanding of social issues. To reach these objectives, we first introduce and discuss the important aspects of a contemporary social issue. Next, we develop the economic concepts and principles germane to the issue. Finally, we apply these principles to the issue in order to discover if there are ways that can help us resolve the issue. The issues throughout the text are arranged so that basic economic concepts are logically developed and an understanding of these concepts is reinforced through repeated use and application. However, enough flexibility is built in to give instructors the ability to experiment with different sequences of topics and chapters. As always, we carefully choose relevant social issues that not only stimulate classroom discussion but also lend themselves to helping students learn the important basic principles of economics.

New Features

Again, our primary goal throughout the revision process was to enhance the uniqueness of our pedagogical approach to teaching basic economic concepts while continuing to improve the overall quality of our final product. We feel we succeeded in doing this and hope that both our new and long-time users will agree.

The most apparent revision to this edition is the addition of a new chapter on Social Security and Medicare (Chapter 14). This new chapter replaces the previous editions' chapter on health care. The demise of the national health care reform movement and the increasing focus of public debate on our social insurance programs motivated this change. However, many of the important economic issues within the health care market have been retained in the new material concerning the Medicare program. Furthermore, the new material on Social Security allows instructors to introduce and reinforce a number of important economic concepts. The continuing headlines predicting the bankruptcy of the Social Security program should capture and maintain student interest in this chapter. Although this new chapter has been sequentially placed within the macroeconomics section of the book for instructors who wish to tie it in with the chapters concerning public finance, some instructors may wish to teach it earlier in order to reinforce and exemplify various market operations. The chapter has been written to make its placement in the teaching sequence as flexible as possible.

This is also the second edition in which a chapter on economic growth appears (Chapter 16). In recent years, economic growth has become a popular topic of social discourse and public debate due to its influence on our personal standard of living. We use economic growth to introduce students to concepts such as productivity and the business cycle. Although Chapter 16 is at the end of the book, some instructors may find it useful to draw material from it substantially earlier. For example, much of Chapter 16 could be used after completion of Chapter 2 in order to include long-run concepts of market functioning in your presentations.

Again in this edition, we approach the issue of achieving maximum social well-being from the marginal social benefits and costs perspective. This convention lets us more formally address the virtues of the market and consider in more depth the impact of social spillovers on well-being. Although this approach is woven into several chapters, it is most obvious in Chapter 5, where pollution is shown to create a divergence between marginal private and marginal social costs of production.

Other notable revisions in this edition include: a new section in Chapter 7 that analyzes the effects of the earned income tax credit on our poverty population, a strengthening of the discussion concerning antitrust issues in Chapter 8, a new section in Chapter 10 outlining the spread of common markets and trading blocks around the globe, a new discussion of the 1990s economic expansion and its effect on unemployment in Chapter 11, and a revised treatment in Chapter 13 of federal government budgets to account for our first surpluses in decades.

The end of each chapter includes an up-dated list of recommended World Wide Web sites relevant to the particular social issues discussed in that chapter. These cyberspace sites were chosen based on their content and ability to provide students with additional information or alternative points of view. Please visit our new Web site created and maintained by Margaret A. Ray and hosted by Irwin/McGraw-Hill. This site provides hyperlinks to each Web site listed at the end of each chapter as well as links to articles and information that supplement our textbook material. Furthermore, self-tests designed to enhance the resources found in our companion *Study Guide* are available to students. The URL for our Web site is **www.mhhe.com/economics/sharp.**

Many other minor changes and revisions, too numerous to list here, are found throughout the book. Of course, all the economic statistics and data were thoroughly updated and revised with the latest figures available at press time.

The Social Issues Pedagogy

To those instructors who are contemplating the adoption of a social issues approach to teaching economic principles, we would like to call your attention to the following research article: "The Social Issues Pedagogy vs. the Traditional Principles of Economics: An Empirical Examination," *The American Economist*, vol. 41, no. 1, Spring 1998. This paper was written by Paul along with Professor Paul S. Nelson of Northeast Louisiana University (NLU). It presents the results of a controlled experiment comparing the learning of NLU students enrolled in a social issues-oriented course that used a previous edition of this book with students who took traditional principles of economics courses and used a standard encyclopedic text. The results are encouraging in that no significant difference was found between students in the social issues course and students enrolled in the traditional macroeconomics principles course, after controlling for student demographic characteristics, prior experiences, and academic aptitude. Furthermore, the results strongly indicate that the students in the social issues course had a higher probability of course completion relative to those in the control group. In this era, in which student retention is becoming more important, we strongly believe that this result suggests an important positive spillover benefit of our pedagogical approach that those who design economics courses and curriculum should consider.

Acknowledgments

First, we would like to thank former author Richard H. Leftwich for all his contributions to past editions of this book. Much of the credit for the success of the social issues pedagogy belongs to him. The author team also extends its sincere appreciation to the author of the *Study Guide,* Margaret A. Ray of Mary Washington College, for her diligent work in revising and updating this important companion to our book. Margaret also gave insightful comments and suggestions throughout the textbook revision process. We also wish to thank her for applying her expertise in economic education to the development and maintenance of the Web site. Margaret's hard work proved instrumental in the establishment of this important enhancement of our efforts. We are convinced that Web site will prove invaluable to our readers.

Many of the features included in this edition are based on suggestions made to us in conversation or in writing by the following users or previous reviewers of our book:

Ugur Aker, *Hiram College*; John E. Altazan, *University of New Orleans*; Michael W. Babcock, *Kansas State University*; Walter Baumgartner, *State University of New York-College at Oneonta*; David Blanchard, *University of Wisconsin at Oshkosh*; Edward Cearny, *Coastal Carolina University*; Heather Campbell, *Arizona State University*; Harry L. Cook, *Southern Oregon State College*; Edward J. Deak, *Fairfield University*; James H. Dukes, *University of West Florida*; Allen Early, *West Texas State College*; Robert C. Eisenstadt, *Northeast Louisiana University*; Ed Ford, *University of South Florida*; Dan Fuller, *Weber State University*; Dan Gallagher, *St. Cloud State University*; James Gapinski, *Florida State University*; David E. R. Gay, *University of Arkansas*; Steven A. Greenlaw, *Mary Washington College*; George H. Hand, *Southern Illinois University*; Robert B. Harris, *Indiana University-Purdue University at Indianapolis*; Sydney Hicks, *Interfirst Bank of Dallas*; Doug Hodo, *University of Texas at San Antonio*; William W. Howard, *Phoenix College*; John Jambura, *Eastern Oregon State College*; William Kern, *Western Michigan University*; Barry Krissoff, *Western Michigan University*; Howard D. Leftwich, *Oklahoma Christian College*; E. Victor Maafo, *North Carolina Central University*; Thomas McCann, *Northeastern Louisiana University*; James McClain, *University of New Orleans*; Douglas NcNeil, *McNeese State University*; Jim Mangum, *Louisiana Technical College*; James Marsden, *University of Kentucky*; Charles Meyerding, *Inver Hills Community College*; Thomas Mitchell, *Southern Illinois University at Carbondale*; Jeff Moore, *University of Houston*; Clair E. Morris, *United States Naval Academy*; Roland Mullins, *Arkansas State University*; Dave Nagao, *Sacramento City College*; Ken Nair, *West Virginia Wesleyan University*; John Neal, *Lake-Sumter Community College*; Paul S. Nelson, *Northeast Louisiana University*; Thomas Parsons, *Massachusetts Bay Community College*; Wayne Plumly, *Valdosta State University*; Rose Rubin, *University of Memphis*; Michael Sattinger, *State University of New York at Albany*; John L. Scott, *Northeast Louisiana University*; Harold M. Seeberger, *Heidelberg College*; Robert Smith, *Louisiana State University*; John Somers, *Portland Community College*; Gary Stone, *Winthrop College*; Terry P. Sutton, *Southeast Missouri State University*;

Millicent Taylor, *Carson-Newman College;* Philip F. Warnken, *University of Missouri;* and Shiu-fang Yu, *Texas State University.*

In addition, our work significantly benefited from the comments and suggestions supplied to us by the following reviewers during the writing of the fourteenth edition:

John E. Altazan, *University of New Orleans;* Joe G. Baker, *Southern Utah University;* Louis E. Bauer, *Concordia University, Portland;* Dr. Lawrence P. Brunner, *Central Michigan University;* Donald Bumpass, *Sam Houston State University;* Daniel S. Chiremba, *Queens College of The City University of New York;* Elchanan Cohn, *University of South Carolina;* Douglas W. Copeland, *Johnson County Community College;* Bruce R. Domazlicky, *Southeast Missouri State University;* Dr. Douglas Dyer, *University of Central Texas;* Gregory Green, *Idaho State University;* Linda Hill, *Idaho State University;* Robert Kirk, *Indiana University-Purdue University at Indianapolis;* Joseph Krislov, *University of Kentucky;* Shohreh Majin, *Western Michigan University;* Margaret Malixi, *California State University, Bakersfield;* Lanse Minkler, *University of Connecticut at Storrs;* Thomas Mitchell, *Southern Illinois University at Carbondale;* Janie Phelps, *Mississippi State University;* Laurence Seidman, *University of Delaware;* Lee C. Spector, *Ball State University;* T. D. Stanley, *Hendrix College;* Gary Stone, *Winthrop University;* James M. Warner, *Gustavus Adolphus College;* Rudolph B. Wuilleumier, *Eastern Kentucky University;* Anthony Zambelli, J.D., *University of Redlands.*

Furthermore, a special appreciation is extended to Marybeth F. Grimes, Reference Librarian at Mississippi State University, for her expert help and research in identifying and compiling our lists of World Wide Web sites for each chapter. Thanks are also extended for her help in locating various economic data sources and updating our lists of recommended reading and citations.

We also wish to thank the employees of Irwin/McGraw-Hill for their expert help in preparing this edition, including Chantal Guillemin and our editor, Paul Shensa. Finally, thanks are extended to Patty Moran and Malinda Sutherland for editorial advice and assistance. We, however, are responsible for all errors of fact and theory.

Ansel M. Sharp

Charles A. Register

Paul W. Grimes

Contents

14 Social Security and Medicare: How Secure Is Our Safety Net for the Elderly? **384**

15 The Big National Debt: Is It Bad? **416**

16 Economic Growth: Why Is It So Important? **441**

CHAPTER 1

Human Misery

The Most Important Issue of Them All

Chapter Outline

Checklist of Economic Concepts

Labor resources
Capital resources
Technology
Production possibilities curve
Opportunity costs
Opportunity cost principle
Increasing opportunity costs
Gross domestic product, current dollar
Gross domestic product, real
Gross domestic product, real per capita
Gross domestic product, per capita
Price index numbers
Marginal social cost
Marginal social benefit
Cost-benefit analysis
Efficiency
Lesser developed countries
Developed countries
Social overhead capital

August 19, 1998. Two million North Koreans—nearly 10 percent of the population—may have died during three years of famine in North Korea, U.S. congressional aids said Wednesday.

Video footage brought back from the secretive communist country by a congressional staff delegation showed sickly, emaciated children, some with stick-thin bodies. One young child, too weak to sit up, had to be propped up in the corner in an orphanage. Older children filmed during the delegation's week-long visit appeared severely stunted by malnutrition.

To survive the persisting food shortages, North Koreans are eating weeds, grasses and corn stalks that are mashed into powder and sometimes with flour to make noodles or cakes. "The food shortage continues," said Mark Kirk, one of the bipartisan delegation's four members. "They are out of food. That's clear." Over the past three years, the famine has killed an estimated 300,000 to 800,000 people annually, with the number of deaths peaking in 1997, Kirk said. "Two million would be the highest possible estimate."

North Korea's food shortages were precipitated by two years of flooding followed by a drought last year that pushed the reclusive communist nation's inefficient collective farming system to the brink of collapse. The famine has left North Korea's 23 million people largely dependent on international aid. International food aid is clearly saving lives, and the international community is feeding nearly every child under the age of 7,[1] . . .

[1]Excerpt from report "Famine may have killed 2 million in North Korea," dated 8/19/99 from CNN.com. (*www.cnn.com/WORLD/asiapcf/9808/19/nkorea.famine/index.html*). Correspondent May Lee and The Associated Press, contributors. Reprinted with permission of Cable News Network, Inc. Nothing contained herein or granting of permission to reprint any of the above shall be deemed an endorsement of any kind of Licensee and/or any of its product, ideas or the views expressed herein.

World Poverty and Economics

Some two-thirds of the world's population go to sleep hungry at night. The World Bank estimates that perhaps as much as one-quarter of the world survives on no more than $1 per day. Outright famine regularly occurs in various parts of the world—recent examples being the mass starvation of an estimated 1 million people in Ethiopia during the drought of 1984–1985, the tragedy of Somalia in the early 1990s, and the current catastrophes occurring in both North Korea and the Sudan. Most of the hungry have no protection from the summer's heat or the winter's cold. They receive little or no medical care and live in unsanitary surroundings. Infant mortality is high and life expectancy is low. Whereas in the United States 9 infants out of each 1,000 live births die before reaching their first birthday, the rate explodes to well over 1 in 10 in places such as Ethiopia, Pakistan, and

Tanzania. At the opposite end of life, the typical Ethiopian can expect to die about 30 years earlier than his or her contemporary in the United States. Recognition that the misery of poverty is the lot of the largest part of the world's population leads us to ask the questions: Why is it so? What are the causes? How can it be alleviated? This in turn leads us directly into the province of economics. An assessment and an analysis of poverty problems require an explicit understanding of the very foundations of economic activity. In this section, we sketch out its fundamental aspects.

Our Insatiable Wants

Economic activity springs from human wants and desires. Human beings want the things necessary to keep them alive—food and protection from the elements of nature. We usually want a great many other things, too, and the fulfillment of these wants and desires is the end toward which economic activity is directed.

As nearly as we can tell, human wants in the aggregate are unlimited, or insatiable. This is true because once our basic needs are met, we desire variety in the way they are met—variety in foods, in housing, in clothing, and in entertainment. Additionally, as we look around, we see other people enjoying things that we do not have (digital audio equipment and home computers, for example), and we think that our level of well-being would be higher if we had those things, too. But most important, want-satisfying activity itself generates new wants. A new house generates wants for new furnishings—the old ones look shabby in the new setting. A college or university education opens the doors to wants that would never have existed if we had stayed on the farm or in the machine shop. To be sure, any one of us can saturate ourselves—temporarily, at least—with any one kind of good or service (like ice cream or beer), but almost all of us would like to have more than we have of almost everything and higher qualities of purchases than we now can obtain.

Our Limited Means

The fundamental economic problem is that the means available for satisfying wants are *scarce* or limited relative to the extent of the wants. The amounts and qualities of goods and services per year that an economic system can produce are limited because (1) the resources available to produce them cannot be increased by any great amount in any given year and (2) the technology available for production is subject to a limited degree of annual improvement.

An economy's *resources* are the ingredients that go into the making of goods (like automobiles) and services (like physical examinations). Production is similar to cooking. Resources (ingredients) are brought together; technology is used to process these resources in certain ways (mixing and cooking them); and finally a good or service results (a cake, perhaps). Some outputs of production processes are used directly to satisfy wants. Others become inputs for additional production processes. The resources available in an economy are usually divided into two broad classifications: (1) labor and (2) capital.

Labor resources refer to the physical and mental efforts of an economy's people that are available to produce goods and services.

Labor resources consist of all the efforts of mind and muscle that can be used in production processes. The ditchdigger's output along with that of the heart surgeon and the university professor is included. There are many kinds and grades of labor reserves; their main common characteristics is that they are human.

Capital resources refer to all nonhuman ingredients of production. Capital resources can be further divided into natural and man-made categories.

Capital resources consist of all the nonhuman ingredients that go into the production of goods and services. They include both natural and man-made ingredients of production. Ingredients such as land that is usable for agriculture or as space for production facilities, rivers, forests, and mineral deposits are all examples of natural capital resources. Man-made capital resources include factories and tools and machinery built up over time as well as semifinished materials such as sheets of steel and business inventories.

Resources are always scarce relative to the sum total of human wants. Consider the U.S. economy. The U.S. population is about 260 million. Most U.S. citizens want more things than they now have. Can the economy increase next year's production enough to fulfill all these wants? Obviously not. The labor force available from the present population cannot be increased substantially in either quantity or quality very quickly. Both may be increased over time by increasing the size of the population and through improving the education and training of the general population, but this increases total wants, too. The stocks of buildings, machines, tools, raw and semifinished materials, and usable land are not susceptible to rapid increases either; instead they are accumulated slowly over time.

Technology refers to the know-how and the means and methods of production available within an economy.

Technology refers to the known means and methods available for combining resources to produce goods and services. Given the quantities of an economy's labor and capital resources, the better its technology, the greater the annual volume of goods and services it can turn out. Usually improvements in technology in an economic system result from increasing the scope and depth of its educational processes and from an ample supply of capital that provides a laboratory for experimentation, practice, and the generation of new ideas.

The Capacity of the Economy to Produce

Gross Domestic Product.   The fundamental economic problem facing any society is scarcity: That is, in no society does there exist the resources necessary to produce enough goods and services to fully satisfy all wants and desires. In much of the world, scarcity translates directly into the type of grinding poverty that was described in the introduction to this chapter. And even in relatively wealthy countries like the United States and Canada, while scarcity results in abject poverty for comparatively small minorities of the overall populations, even those at the top of the income spectrums, no doubt, feel that their overall level of well-being could be enhanced by higher quantities and qualities of existing goods and services or by greater invention and innovation of new products. It is scarcity that forces each society to make economic choices as to how their resources can be "best" used. As a guiding principle, most economists define the best use of resources as that use which most fully satisfies wants and desires. Put slightly differently, throughout our analysis, we assume that the goal of an economic system is to minimize the effects of scarcity or, more positively, to maximize social well-being. A first step in determining how well an economy is doing relative to this goal is to ascertain how effectively the economy is translating its labor and capital resources into goods and services. To this end, we wish to quantify, in dollar terms, the production of goods and services within an economy. Our primary measure of production is *gross domestic product (GDP)*, which measures the total market value of all final goods and services produced within the economy during a specific time period.

Gross domestic product (GDP) measures the market value of all final goods and services produced within an economy during 1 year. GDP ignores the issue of whether the resources used for the production are domestically or foreign owned.

As is true with any type of accounting, the measurement of national production using GDP can be quite misleading unless we have a clear understanding of what is, and what is not, measured by GDP. First, it is essential to bear in mind that GDP is measured in terms of market values or market prices. As such, increases in GDP can come about either through increases in the production of goods and services or simply through increases in average prices. The impact of the two clearly have different effects on social well-being. Second, it is important to remember that GDP measures the total value of production taking place within a country, regardless of who might own the resources used in production. For example, even though Toyota Camrys are built with capital resources owned by a Japanese company, the fact that the cars are built in Kentucky causes them to be considered part of U.S. GDP. From the opposite perspective, Chevrolet Camaros, being built in Canada, are not considered part of U.S. GDP even though Chevrolet is a division of an American firm. Finally, since we hope to use GDP as a first approximation of how well an economy is doing in fulfilling the goal of maximizing well-being, it is important to note that GDP is a measure of the dollar value of production only, which indicates nothing about who actually benefits from that production. Sometimes in the popular press GDP is referred to as the "economic pie." And if one wishes to assess how well an economy is doing in satisfying wants and desires, it is essential to know the size of the pie that is available for consumption. Equally important, however, are the number of people the pie must be distributed among and how evenly the pie is distributed. We take up each of these issues in detail later in this chapter.

Production Possibilities.   Given an economy's available stocks of
resources and level of technology, the combinations of goods and services
that can compose its GDP are practically limitless. For simplicity, suppose
that it produces only two items—food and education—and that all its
resources are devoted to producing these two items. The curve *AE* in Figure 1–1, called the *production possibilities curve,* represents all the maximum
possible combinations of food and education that can be produced during
1 year. Thus, GDP might consist of 100 million tons of food per year if no
education is produced as shown by point *A,* or 100 million student-years
of education if no food is produced as shown by point *E.* Of course, there
is no reason to devote all resources to producing one or the other of the
two items, and thus a combination such as 90 million tons of food and
40 million student-years of education, as shown by point *B,* or any other
combination along *AE* is possible. Equally possible is a combination like *F,*

The **production possibilities curve** represents the
maximum   quantities   of
two goods and/or services
that an economy can pro-
duce when its resources are
used in the most efficient
way possible.

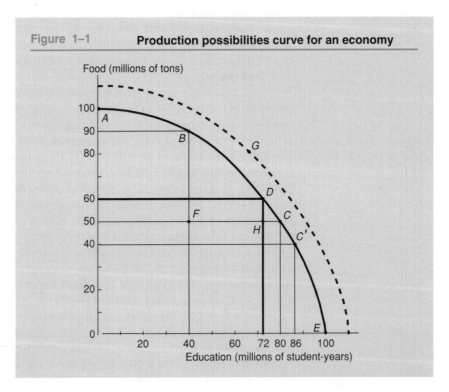

Figure 1–1   **Production possibilities curve for an economy**

Food (millions of tons)

Education (millions of student-years)

Curve *AE* shows all combinations of food and education that the economy's available resources and techniques of production can produce annually. Combinations
such as *F* imply unemployment of resources or inefficiency in production. Those
such as *G* are not attainable without economic growth.
    If the economy were originally producing combination *D,* and then moved to
combination *C,* the opportunity cost of the additional *HC* of education is the *HD* of
food that must be given up to produce it.

which yields a GDP of 50 million tons of food and 40 million student-years of education. This combination is clearly inefficient, however, because with the same stocks of resources and level of technology, the economy could produce up to 90 million tons of food without having to cut production of education below the 40 million student-year level. To be operating below the production possibilities curve indicates that either some of the economy's resources are not being used (called unemployment) or not being used to their fullest extent (called underemployment), or the economy is not using the best available technology. Operating below the curve would be of little consequence were it not for the fundamental economic problem of scarcity. That is, operating below the production possibilities curve makes an already difficult problem of scarcity worse.

Combinations of goods and services like G, lying above the production possibilities curve, while desirable, are not attainable given the economy's current stock of resources and level of technology. Over time, perhaps, production can be pressed to the higher level indicated by the dashed curve, but only if there is an increase in either the quality or quantity of productive resources or an improvement in the level of technology. Outward shifts in the production possibilities curve are a graphical depiction of economic growth. We address the requisites for such growth briefly later in this chapter, but the concept of economic growth will be considered in detail in Chapter 16.

The Opportunity Cost Principle.   Have you heard the expression, "There is no such thing as a free lunch"? Actually, this is a simple way of expressing one of the most important concepts in economics, the *opportunity cost principle*. Suppose the economy is producing combination D, containing 60 million tons of food and 72 million student-years of education. Now let the output of education be increased to 80 million student-years. What is the cost to society of the additional 8 million student-years of education? The opportunity cost principle embodies the often overlooked but obvious point: If society's resources are initially fully and efficiently used as is true at D, an increase in the production of one good or service can come about only if the production of another good or service is reduced. In this sense, the true cost or opportunity cost to society of the additional 8 million student-years of education is the 10 million tons of food that must be forgone. An economy's ability to produce is limited by its resources and technology, and so more of one product necessarily means less of another or others.

The downward slope of the production possibilities curve shows the opportunity cost principle or trade-off in production that exists when an economy is operating at maximum efficiency. A quick glance at the production possibilities curve further indicates that this trade-off of food for education is not constant, however. That is, while the move from D to C requires society to give up 10 million tons of food for the additional

The **opportunity cost principle** states that the true cost of producing an additional unit of a good or service is the value of other goods or services that must be given up to obtain it.

The concept of **increasing opportunity cost** indicates that as more of a particular good or service is produced, the cost in terms of other goods or services given up grows. This gives the production possibilities curve its bow shape.

8 million student-years of education, the next 10 million tons of food given up releases only enough resources to produce an additional 6 million student-years of education (shown as the move from C to C'). In opportunity cost terms, it is becoming more costly for the economy to shift production from food to education. It is this *increasing opportunity cost* of production that gives the production possibilities curve its convex or bowed-out shape.

The increase in opportunity costs as the economy concentrates more of its resources to producing education is due to the fact that all resources are not perfectly substitutable for one another. Suppose the economy is initially at point A on the production possibilities curve, producing only food, but then decides to produce some education as well. The cost in terms of forgone food is likely to be relatively low initially since the first resource to be taken out of production of food tend to be those resources that are least effective in producing food. That is, the first labor resources taken from food production will likely be those farmers and farm laborers who are not very good at farm life; the first land to be converted to school yards and university campuses is likely to be least fit for agricultural pursuits, and so on. As production of education is expanded further, resources of greater value in food production are increasingly drawn into educational pursuits, and thus, relatively more food must be given up. The same would be true with all resources—not simply labor and land. This is especially true in a modern and quite complex economy in which there is a high degree of specialization among many, if not most, productive resources. The more specialized and less easily substituted an economy's resources are, the more extreme will be the bow in its production possibilities curve.

Finally, consider how costs are measured abstractly in Figure 1–1. The increase in the output of education and the corresponding decrease in the production of food are represented as the movement from D to C; that is, HD of food is given up for HC of education. The ratio HD/HC, which is the approximate slope of the production possibilities curve between D and C, measures the (average) opportunity cost of a student-year of education in terms of food. Between D and C, this equals 10 million divided by 8 million, or simply 1¼ tons of food per student-year of education. And the same computation shows an opportunity cost increase to 1⅔ tons of food per student-year of education for the subsequent movement from C to C'.

The Optimal Combination of Goods and Services.   From the above we know that all combinations of food and education along the production possibilities curve AE in Figure 1–1 imply that the economy is producing as much of the two goods as possible, given its technology and scarce resources. But which of these combinations is best, or optimal? To answer this, recall that the primary goal we established for an economy was to maximize social well-being. Thus, the best combination is that which increases social well-being as much as possible. To see how we might, at least abstractly, arrive at this optimal combination, suppose that the economy is initially at combination A on the production possibilities curve, producing only food. What happens to well-being as the economy begins to move down the production possibilities curve toward point B and starts producing some education as well? In order for the shift to be consistent with the goal of increasing social well-being, the public must be better off and more satisfied after the shift than it had been before. To make this determination, first consider the negative side of the shift. With each successive student-year of education produced, a certain amount of food must be given up. We call this the opportunity cost of the additional unit of education or, in slightly different terms, the *marginal social cost (MSC)* of the education. On the positive side, however, the shift in production gives society access to newly produced education, and the enhanced social well-being from each successive student-year of education is called the *marginal social benefit (MSB)* of the new schooling.

To determine whether each successive student-year of education between A and B should be produced, *cost-benefit analysis* can be applied. In general terms, cost-benefit analysis indicates that expansion of an activity serves to enhance well-being when it yields greater benefits than costs. Applying cost-benefit analysis in this context, we can conclude that each additional student-year of education should be produced as long as its marginal social benefit is at least as great as its marginal social cost.

Movements along the production possibilities curve then can be evaluated based on a comparison of marginal social benefits and costs. Any movement for which $MSB > MSC$ of necessity improves social well-being, while the reverse would lead to falling well-being. With these tools we can get a better handle on the question of the optimal combination of goods and services. Suppose that for each successive student-year of education from A to B, social well-being is, in fact, enhanced since $MSB > MSC$. What about further movements down the curve? It might seem that if these first increments in the production of education yielded greater benefits than costs, why would this not continue to be true. Unfortunately, this will not be the case indefinitely because with each increase in the production of education and the corresponding fall in the production of food, the benefits of further shifts to education decline while the costs rise. From society's perspective, the greatest marginal benefit from education no doubt comes as the public moves from illiteracy to basic, functional literacy. Especially in modern society, if one is unable to read and do simple arithmetic, it is very difficult to make a significant contribution to GDP. Beyond basic literacy, while additional years of education clearly add to well-being, their addition is likely to be, on average, of declining value. Thus, as production is shifted from food to education, the greatest marginal value is found for the early increments in education. In other words, as more education is produced and consumed, the MSB from additional education falls.

Marginal social cost (MSC) is the true, or opportunity, cost borne by society when the production of a good or service is increased by one unit.

Marginal social benefit (MSB) is the true benefit to society of a one-unit increase in the production of a good or service.

Cost-benefit analysis is a technique for determining the optimal level of an economic activity. In general, an activity should be expanded so long as the expansion leads to greater benefits than costs.

On the cost side, recall that the production possibilities curve is bow-shaped due to the concept of increasing opportunity cost of production. In this context, as we expand the production of education, the value of the food that we must give up rises—that is, the *MSC* of education increases. As we move down the production possibilities curve, then, any gap between *MSB* and *MSC* that might initially exist tends to narrow. Once we reach the combination at which *MSB* = *MSC*, no further shifts in production will lead to increasing well-being. To go beyond this point would imply that we produced and consumed an increment in education which was not worth what it cost. Consequently, the optimal combination of goods and services is defined as that combination where the marginal social benefit of production just equals marginal social cost. How does a complex modern economy arrive at this combination of goods and services and the allocation of resources embodied in it? This question is the basis for Chapter 2.

Assessing Well-Being Using GDP

Adjusting GDP for Inflation.   GDP was not created to be used as a measure of overall well-being; rather, its primary use is simply as a gauge of the value of production that takes place within an economy. Before it can be used to roughly assess the overall well-being of a county's inhabitants, a number of adjustments must be made. First, when we are evaluating an economy's performance over time, we must take into account that an increase in GDP, far from indicating a general improvement in well-being, may simply come about due to an increase in the average level of prices—inflation. In an economy that produces only food and education, calculating GDP requires that the quantity of food produced be multiplied by the average price of food, making the same calculation for education and adding the total values together. Consequently, if we look at data for a series of years and find that GDP in dollar terms is rising, we cannot be certain whether the economy's production is increasing or whether average prices are rising. If the increase in GDP is due to increasing production, overall well-being may be increasing, but if the increase in GDP is due either entirely or predominately to inflation, overall well-being may be declining.

To see the effect of inflation on GDP, consider a very simplistic economy in which only one good, bread, is produced. Suppose that during 1998, the economy produces 1,000 loaves which are sold for $1 each. GDP for this economy in 1998 is simply $1,000 (1,000 times $1). Now suppose that during 1999 the economy continues to produce 1,000 loaves, but due to inflation each loaf sells for $2. GDP for 1999 is $2,000. Thus, between 1998 and 1999, GDP doubles even though the production of bread remains unchanged. The entire increase in GDP is due to inflation.

To correct for inflation, the entire series of GDP *numbers at price levels for each year* must be converted to a "base" year price level. Suppose we use 1998 as the base year and want to convert 1999 GDP to 1998 prices. The relationship between 1998 and 1999 can be depicted with price index numbers. In percentage terms, the price index for each year is calculated by dividing each year's price level (or average price level if more than one item is produced) by the price level that existed in the base year, then multiplying by 100, as in Table 1–1. Thus, the price index for 1998 is 100 (1998 price of $1 divided by the base year price, also 1998, of $1, then multiplying by 100). Likewise the price index for 1999 is 200, indicating that the average price in 1999 is 200 percent of the average for 1998. Once price index numbers are created for each year, the GDP data can be corrected for inflation by dividing each year's GDP in current dollars by that year's price index, after converting the index to decimal form. That is, 1998's inflation-corrected GDP is equal to its current dollar GDP of $1,000 divided by the 1998 price index, in decimals, of 1, or simply $1,000. Inflation-corrected GDP for 1999 is found in the same way and is also $1,000 since current dollar GDP in 1999 is $2,000 but the price index for the year is 2, in decimals. When current dollar GDP is corrected for inflation, the result is *real GDP.* In this example, while current dollar GDP doubles between 1998 and 1999, real GDP remains constant, reflecting the fact that production is unchanged. In this way, real GDP shows us what is happening over time to the economy's real production.

When GDP in current dollars is corrected for inflation, the result is **real GDP.** The correction requires dividing each year's GDP in current dollars by that year's price index, in decimal form.

Adjusting GDP for Population.   When we look at a series of GDP data, we must correct the series for the misleading effects of inflation. A second adjustment that must be made, regardless of whether we are considering a series of GDP data or simply one year's GDP, concerns the number of people that GDP must be spread among. That is, GDP in China is many times that of Switzerland, but since China's GDP must be spread between so many more people, the average level of well-being of the Swiss population is many times that of the Chinese population.

Table 1–1	Calculating real GDP using a price index			
	(1)	(2)	(3) GDP in Current Dollars	(4) Price Index Percentage and	(5) Real GDP (1998 Dollars)
Year	Production of Bread (Loaves)	Price of Bread	(1) × (2)	Decimal Forms	(3)/(4, in decimals)
1998	1,000	$1.00	$1,000	($1/$1) × 100 = 100 or 1.00	$1,000
1999	1,000	2.00	2,000	($2/$1) × 100 = 200 or 2.00	1,000

Adjusting GDP for differences in population requires that GDP be divided by the population of the country in question. But which GDP values, GDP in current prices or real GDP, should we use in the calculation? This depends on the data that we are analyzing. If we are looking at the performance of a single economy over time, the appropriate measure would be inflation-adjusted, or real GDP divided by the population, since prices are not likely to remain constant over time. This would be called *per capita real GDP*. Alternatively, if we are analyzing a country's GDP data for only 1 year, the appropriate measure would be GDP in current prices divided by the population, known simply as *per capita GDP*. For any one country, per capita real GDP for a series of years is indicative of whether or not the performance of the economy, in terms of the average well-being of its inhabitants, is improving. When our intent is to roughly compare differences in well-being between countries at one point in time, per capita GDP is most useful.

When real GDP is divided by population, the result is **per capita real GDP.** Alternatively, when GDP in current dollars is divided by population, the result is **per capita GDP.**

In Table 1–2 we track the performance of the U.S. economy for the period 1970 through 1997 as an example of how per capita real GDP is calculated and used to shed light on changes in potential well-being. Current dollar GDP is listed in column 2. The price index used is called the implicit price deflator and is found in column 3, in percentage terms. You will note that the price index uses 1992 as its base. Column 4 gives real GDP and is obtained by dividing column 2 by column 3, after converting the price index to decimals.

The first item of interest in Table 1–2 is the fact that real GDP declined during 1974, 1975, 1980, 1982, and 1991, even though current dollar GDP increased during each of these years. This indicates that while actual production was falling in these years, the falls in production were more than offset by price increases, and this reinforces the importance of adjusting current GDP for inflation. In each of these years, there were fewer goods and services available for consumption by the general public in the United States than had been available in the year prior. When this occurs, we say that the economy is in *recession*. Graphically, during the years 1974, 1975, 1980, 1982, and 1991, the U.S. economy operated below the production possibilities curve, indicating that the average well-being of the population was lower than its potential. A rough estimate of average well-being can be found by dividing real GDP by population, giving per capita real GDP, as in column 6. Here again we find declines during the recessionary years.

Table 1–3 reports data on population, GDP in current prices, and per capita GDP for selected countries in 1995 (ignore the other data in the table for now). Here, we use current dollar GDP rather than real GDP since we are considering only 1 year's data. To maintain consistency, GDP for all countries is converted to U.S. dollar values. We arbitrarily classify a country as lesser developed (LDC) if its per capita GDP is less than $5,000 per year and as developed (DC) if its per capita GDP is greater than this level.

(1) Year	(2) GDP, Current Dollars (Billions)	(3) Implicit Price Deflator	(4) GDP, Real 1992 Dollars (Billions)	(5) Population (Millions)	(6) GDP, Real per Capita (1992 Dollars)
1970	1,035.6	30.6	3,384.3	205.1	16,500.8
1971	1,125.4	32.2	3,495.0	207.7	16,827.3
1972	1,237.3	33.5	3,693.4	209.9	17,596.2
1973	1,382.6	35.4	3,905.6	211.9	18,431.6
1974	1,496.9	38.5	3,888.1	213.9	18,177.0
1975	1,630.6	42.2	3,864.0	216.0	17,888.8
1976	1,819.0	44.6	4,078.5	218.0	18,708.6
1977	2,026.9	47.4	4,276.2	220.2	19,419.4
1978	2,291.4	51.0	4,492.9	222.6	20,183.9
1979	2,557.5	55.3	4,624.8	225.1	20,545.4
1980	2,784.2	60.4	4,609.6	227.7	20,244.2
1981	3,115.9	65.9	4,728.2	229.8	20,575.4
1982	3,242.1	70.1	4,625.0	232.1	19,926.6
1983	3,514.5	73.1	4,807.8	235.5	20,415.3
1984	3,902.4	75.9	5,141.5	237.6	21,639.3
1985	4,180.7	78.4	5,332.5	239.3	22,283.9
1986	4,422.2	80.6	5,486.6	241.6	22,709.4
1987	4,692.3	83.1	5,646.6	243.8	23,160.7
1988	5,049.6	86.1	5,864.8	246.4	23,802.0
1989	5,438.7	89.7	6,063.2	248.8	24,369.8
1990	5,743.8	93.6	6,136.5	251.3	24,419.2
1991	5,916.7	97.3	6,080.9	252.7	24,063.6
1992	6,244.4	100.0	6,244.4	255.4	24,449.5
1993	6,558.1	102.4	6,404.4	258.1	24,813.6
1994	6,947.0	105.9	6,560.0	260.7	25,163.0
1995	7,269.6	107.5	6,762.4	263.0	25,712.5
1996	7,661.6	109.5	6,997.0	265.5	26,354.0
1997	8,110.9	111.6	7,267.8	267.6	27,159.2

Table 1–2   U.S. gross domestic product in current and real dollars, 1970–1997

Source: www.bea.doc.gov/ and www.frwebgate3.access.gpo.gov

Data of this sort provide direct insight into the economic problem of scarcity and allow for a rough international comparison of average well-being.

GDP in the United States during 1995 was roughly $6.9 trillion. That is, during 1995 there were about $7 trillion in goods and services available for consumption by the country's 260 million citizens. Dividing GDP by

Table 1–3   **Per capita real GDP and population, actual and growth rates; population density; and life expectancy (selected countries, 1985–1995)**

Country	Population Estimate 1995 (Millions)	Annual Rate of Population Increase (1990–1995)	Population Density per Square Kilometer (1995)	Per Capita GDP* (1995)	Percentage Annual Growth Rate of GDP (Constant Prices)	Life Expectancy at Birth, Latest Available Dates
Lesser developed						
Chile	14.2	1.5	19	4,160	6.1	72
Colombia	36.8	1.8	32	1,910	2.6	70
Egypt	57.8	2.0	58	790	1.1	63
El Salvador	5.6	2.2	267	1,610	2.8	67
Ethiopia	56.4	1.9	51	100	−0.3	49
India	929.4	1.8	283	340	3.2	62
Indonesia	193.3	1.6	101	980	6.0	64
Kenya	26.7	2.7	46	280	0.1	58
Mexico	91.8	1.9	47	3,320	0.1	72
Nigeria	111.3	2.9	121	260	1.2	53
Peru	23.8	2.0	19	2,310	−1.6	66
Philippines	68.6	2.2	229	1,050	1.5	66
South Africa	41.5	2.2	34	3,160	−1.1	64
Thailand	58.2	0.9	113	2,740	8.4	69
Venezuela	21.7	2.3	24	3,020	0.5	71
Zambia	9.0	2.9		400	−0.8	46
Average		2.1			1.9	63
Developed						
Canada	29.6	1.6	3	19,380	0.4	78
France	58.1	0.5	105	24,990	1.5	78
Germany†	81.9	0.6	229	27,510	1.1	76
Italy	57.2	0.2	190	19,020	1.8	78
Japan	125.2	0.3	331	39,640	2.9	80
Singapore	3.0	2.0	3,000	26,730	6.2	76
Sweden	8.8	0.6	20	23,750	−0.1	79
Switzerland	7.0	1.0	171	40,630	0.2	78
United Kingdom	58.5	0.3	238	18,700	1.4	77
United States	263.0	1.0	28	26,980	1.3	77
Average		0.8			1.7	78

*At market prices (U.S. dollars).

†Data are for unified Germany, except GDP and growth of GDP, which are for the Federal Republic of Germany before unification.

Source: World Bank, *World Development Report*, 1997, Tables 1, 1a, and 4.

the population yields a per capita GDP of $26,980. Thus, if U.S. national production were equally divided in 1995, each member of the public would have had about $27,000 of goods and services at his or her disposal. Compare this with the plight of the average citizen in an LDC. In Zambia, for example, the per capita GDP is only $400 per year. And poverty of this nature is not simply an isolated problem, but rather commonplace in much of the world. While scarcity is primarily a problem of not having all wants and desires satisfied in DCs, in much—or even most—of the world, scarcity translates into the type of grinding poverty noted in the introduction to this chapter. Finally, bear in mind that the problem of poverty that plagues much of the world is not simply an academic abstraction. Rather, as is pointed out in Table 1–3, it translates directly into early death. While an individual fortunate enough to be born in a DC in 1995 could count on an average life of 78 years, his counterpart born in an LDC would likely leave this life 15 years earlier.

Adjusting GDP for Distribution.   The data in Table 1–3 indicate that much of the world's population suffers from a degree of misery that is probably unintelligible to those of us living in DCs. Yet, even the dire circumstances reflected by the data understate the true extent of human misery that afflicts so many. This understatement is due to the fact that average measures of well-being such as per capita GDP fail to take into account the unequal distribution of GDP within a country. Consider again Zambia with its per capita GDP of $400. Clearly, life would seem to amount to mere subsistence for a Zambian earning only $400 per year. Yet, most Zambians would dearly love to earn this "average" amount of income. In Zambia, with its very limited GDP, the problem of human misery is greatly complicated by the very uneven distribution of GDP. While a fortunate few earn many times more than $400 per year, the majority of Zambians have annual incomes far below this average figure.

What is meant by the distribution of GDP, or the distribution of income as it is more commonly known, may be best understood by considering a simple example. Suppose that there are two economies, Alpha and Omega, each composed of five families, A through E. Further, suppose that in Alpha each of the families earns $2,000 per year, while in Omega families A through D have no income and family E earns $10,000 per year, as presented in Table 1–4. In each economy, then, the annual income for all families, or GDP, is $10,000 and the average income is $2,000. Do these facts suggest that the people of each economy are equally well off? Obviously not. Simply looking at averages is quite misleading in this case since, while GDP levels are the same, the distribution of GDP differs so markedly between the two countries.

In the real world, of course, it is unlikely that either the perfectly equal distribution of Alpha or the perfectly unequal distribution of Omega will exist. But with a little reflection on Table 1–4, a way of evaluating actual

Table 1–4	The distribution of income within an economy						
	Annual Income Family A	Annual Income Family B	Annual Income Family C	Annual Income Family D	Annual Income Family E	Annual Income of All Families	Average Annual Family Income
Alpha	$2,000	$2,000	$2,000	$2,000	$2,000	$10,000	$2,000
Omega	0	0	0	0	10,000	10,000	2,000

distributions of GDP becomes apparent. That is, why is the distribution of income in Alpha considered to be perfectly equal? The answer is straight-forward: Each of the five families controls the same share of Alpha's income ($2,000). Put differently, each of the five families represents one-fifth, or 20 percent, of Alpha's population, and at the same time, each of the five controls one-fifth, or 20 percent, of Alpha's GDP ($2,000/$10,000). Thus, perfect equality exists when each 20 percent "chunk" of an economy's families controls 20 percent of the economy's income.

How closely do existing economies come to perfect equality? Are there systematic differences in income distribution between LDCs and DCs? Answers to these questions are found in Table 1–5, which reports data on income distribution for selected LDCs and DCs. (You will note that, as is customary, Table 1–5 ranks each economy's families from poorest to richest rather than in randomly chosen 20 percent groups.)

To see the impact of the distribution of GDP on individual well-being, again consider Zambia. Recall that Zambia has a per capita GDP of $400, which was suggested to understate the degree of poverty felt by Zambians. If GDP were equally distributed, that is, if all Zambians earned $400 per year, then each 20 percent chunk of Zambian families would control approximately 20 percent of Zambian GDP. Yet, as Table 1–5 points out, this is not the case. As miserable as their plight would be with a perfectly equal distribution of income yielding a 20 percent share of GDP for the "poorest" families, in reality these families control only 3.9 percent of Zambian GDP. Thus, if the meager Zambian GDP were equally distributed, giving meaning to the per capita GDP value of $400, the families making up the poorest 20 percent grouping would find their income increasing by about a factor of 5 (rising from 3.9 to 20 percent).

This is not to suggest that all Zambians earn less than the average of $400. Such cannot be the case if the average is properly calculated. Table 1–5 indicates that while a majority of Zambian families are truly impoverished, some families are relatively rich. Note the share of Zambian

Table 1–5	The distribution of income in selected countries*				
	Total Income or GDP Controlled by Each Group of Families				
Country (Year of Study)	**Poorest 20 Percent**	**Second 20 Percent**	**Third 20 Percent**	**Fourth 20 Percent**	**Richest 20 Percent**
Lesser developed					
Chile (1994)	3.5%	6.6%	10.9%	18.1%	61%
Colombia (1991)	3.6	7.6	12.6	20.4	55.8
Egypt (1991)	8.7	12.5	16.3	21.4	41.1
El Salvador (1976–77)	5.5	10.0	14.8	22.4	47.3
India (1992)	8.5	12.1	15.8	21.1	42.6
Indonesia (1993)	8.7	12.3	16.3	22.1	40.7
Kenya (1992)	3.4	6.7	10.7	17	62.1
Mexico (1992)	4.1	7.8	12.5	20.2	55.3
Peru (1994)	4.9	9.2	14.1	21.4	50.4
Philippines (1988)	6.5	10.1	14.4	21.2	47.8
South Africa (1993)	3.3	5.8	9.8	17.7	63.3
Thailand (1992)	5.6	8.7	13.0	20.0	52.7
Venezuela (1990)	3.6	7.1	11.7	19.3	58.4
Zambia (1993)	3.9	8.0	13.8	23.8	50.4
Average	5.3	8.9	13.3	20.4	52.1
Developed					
Canada (1987)	5.7	11.8	17.7	24.6	40.2
France (1989)	5.6	11.8	17.2	23.5	41.9
Italy (1986)	6.8	12.0	16.7	23.5	41.0
Japan (1979)	8.7	13.2	17.5	23.1	37.5
Singapore (1982–83)	5.1	9.9	14.6	21.4	48.9
Sweden (1981)	8.0	13.2	17.4	24.5	36.9
Switzerland (1982)	5.2	11.7	16.4	22.1	44.6
United Kingdom (1988)	4.6	10.0	16.8	24.3	44.3
United States (1985)	4.7	11.0	17.4	25.0	41.9
West Germany (1988)	7.0	11.8	17.1	23.9	40.3
Average	6.1	11.6	16.9	23.6	41.8

*Ethiopia and Nigeria were omitted due to a lack of data.
Source: World Bank, *World Development Report,* 1997, Table 5.

GDP controlled by the richest 20 percent of families. The 50.4 percent share of national income controlled by this group indicates that the degree of human misery brought on by Zambia's extremely limited GDP is greatly worsened by the fact that this limited GDP is very unequally distributed.

Is this situation unique to Zambia? Unfortunately not. As the averages for the shares of GDP controlled by each group of families for the different countries indicate, the degree of income inequality in LDCs is much greater than in DCs. This is not to suggest that the DCs have distributions that approximate perfect equality. In fact, some may feel that the degree of income inequality that exists in DCs is unacceptably high. The importance of Table 1–5 is that the data indicate that the degree of inequality that exists appears to be significantly greater in LDCs than in DCs. Given this, it may be concluded that the degree of human misery reflected by average measures of well-being such as per capita GDP fails to describe accurately the misery suffered by much of the world's population.

Causes of Poverty and Requisites of Economic Growth

The economic roots of world poverty become reasonably clear from an examination of the foundations of economic analysis. In some cases, an economy may be operating to its potential, that is, operating on its production possibilities curve, and yet pervasive poverty is still the rule. Often mentioned as problems in this regard are pressures from the size and growth of an economy's population. Whether population pressures are the primary problem, when an economy's production possibilities are such that even achieving maximum output results in excessive poverty, remedial action must be directed toward economic growth. Pushing the production possibilities curve outward requires improvement in either the quality and quantity of a nation's labor and capital resources or an improvement in the overall level of technology—and occasionally an improvement in both. In other cases, poverty results from relatively inefficient production methods. Here remedies should be targeted toward returning the economy to its production possibilities curve. These topics are the focus for the rest of this book; we briefly introduce them here.

Quality of the Labor Force.   Almost without exception, LDCs have labor forces that are not very well educated and thus not very productive relative to DCs. For example, whereas the adult literacy rate in the United States approaches 99 percent, countries like Haiti and Ethiopia barely reach the 5 percent level. Education is the key to improvement in the quality of a country's labor force. As literacy rates increase, so do the possibilities for upgrading the skills of the labor force. A broad-based primary education system is a prerequisite for literacy, and literacy is, in turn, a basic foundation for economic growth. Beyond the primary level, secondary and higher education are important in improving labor force quality in that they develop workers who are more capable of problem solving and innovation. It is clear that the development of a comprehensive educational system is essential to providing rising living standards. It is equally clear that developing such a system is difficult in a society whose population lives close to, or at, a subsistence level.

Stock of Capital and Capital Accumulation.   Small amounts of available capital resources and, thus, low capital-to-labor ratios translate directly into low labor productivity and poverty. Countries with limited mineral deposits, meager supplies of tools and machinery, and poorly developed transportation and communications networks usually have low per capita GDPs. Capital accumulation is necessary if a country is to break out of a poverty prison. But capital accumulation requires that some of a country's annual output of consumer goods and services be sacrificed in favor of production of capital goods and development of resources. As is true with development of an educational system, this is particularly difficult when many of a country's citizens suffer from malnutrition or even starvation.

Technology.   A trip through the countryside and a visit to the industrial production sites in a poor country reveal very primitive techniques of production. Failure or inability to adapt to modern production techniques translates directly into low productivity and poverty. Unfortunately for LDCs, to some extent, technological development goes hand in hand with capital accumulation and the development of educational systems. High levels of technology are seldom developed in poor countries.

Efficiency.   In many poor countries, available resources are either not fully or efficiently used. Often, traditional ways of doing things block adaptation of new and efficient production techniques. For example, it is easy to find poor countries naturally endowed with potentially productive agricultural land but which, based on traditional tenure systems, hold the land in units too small to allow for maximum efficiency. In other countries, rigid wage systems make it uneconomical for potential employers to hire the entire labor force, leading to unemployment.

Population.   Are population pressures serious threats to living standards? Evidence on this issue is presented in Table 1–3. Consider first the issue of population and the density of population. Does the absolute level of a country's population or the density of it preclude a high level of well-being? The answer is "no" on both counts. While India is an example of an LDC with a very large population, the United States and Japan are examples of DCs with both high levels of well-being and relatively large populations. In addition, many of the LDCs listed in Table 1–3 have relatively small populations. As for the concentration of population, known as population density, consider Ethiopia and Singapore. Ethiopia, truly one of the most impoverished countries on earth, has a low 51 persons per square kilometer, while Singapore, with a per capita GDP many times that of

Ethiopia, is home to 3,000 people per square kilometer. Similar outcomes exist for the relatively wealthy and densely populated United States and Japan and for the relatively poor, less densely populated Zambia, Chile, and Argentina. Finally, what of pressures from population growth? The evidence is again clear: While it is true that the average level of population growth is higher in the LDCs, so also is the average level of GDP growth during the 1990s.

What may we then conclude with respect to the impact of population pressures on poverty? Perhaps the most defensible conclusion would be that while population pressures are not the fundamental cause of world poverty, excessive population growth does tend to complicate the problem of scarcity. At the very least, we know that if overall well-being is to increase, real GDP must grow more rapidly than the population.

Can Governments Help?

What, if anything, can governments do to help solve world poverty problems? Over the last few decades, populations have looked increasingly to their governments to solve their problems for them. Governments, in turn, have accepted more responsibility for solving the economic problems of their populations. Unfortunately, people often expect more of their governments than those governments can provide. And governments promise more than they are able to deliver.

Governments of LDCs

The single most important decision that government must make with respect to economic development concerns the extent to which economic decision making will be influenced by government. The options range from little or no government involvement to decision making based entirely on government dictate. As will be discussed in Chapter 2, the ongoing movement away from extreme government interference in economic decision making that is sweeping through Eastern Europe and, to a lesser but still significant degree, in countries such as China and Vietnam, indicates that economic development may be enhanced by reducing the economic role of government. Although it may seem paradoxical, the governments of many LDCs, rather than being vehicles for economic improvement, are burdens to development. In general, economic development tends to reach its potential when private parties, rather than government, are allowed to own economic resources and decide the use for those resources. Economists refer to this as *private property rights*. Equally important, resource owners must be allowed to reap the benefits of well-made decisions on resource use, and they must also be allowed to suffer the penalty of poorly made decisions. Governments of LDCs then would well serve the development interests of their people by making sure that their involvement in economic activity is limited to those areas where the economy, left to its own devices, clearly fails to achieve desired development goals. In this regard, the governments of LDCs should pursue policies that would improve the quality of the labor force, enhance capital accumulation, raise levels of technology, increase efficiency, and, perhaps, slow population growth. This is a tall order—more easily said than done.

In most countries where literacy rates are high, governments have assumed responsibilities for primary education. In many countries this responsibility has been extended to secondary and even to higher education. Insofar as it can, the government of an LDC would be well advised to emulate these countries. But universal education does not come easily or without cost. The establishment of an educational system is a slow, expensive task. Physical facilities must be built, and a corps of teachers must be trained. LDCs find it very difficult to divert resources from the provision of subsistence goods to the provision of education. The immediate opportunity cost of additional education is high for a hungry population.

Most government help in the capital accumulation process will be indirect rather than direct. Governments cannot create new capital resources directly, but they can establish an economic climate favorable to capital accumulation. They can pursue monetary and fiscal policies conducive to economic stability. They can enact tax laws that provide special incentives for capital accumulation. It is also important that those who engage in saving and investing in new capital equipment be allowed to reap the rewards for doing so. In many instances, capital accumulation is discouraged because revenue-hungry governments tax away the returns that accrue from it.

Social overhead capital refers to capital resources that are shared by the entire economy rather than used by one firm. Highways and communications networks are examples of social overhead capital.

Government officials in LDCs often speak glibly about such things as raising the levels of technology and increasing the operating efficiencies of their economies. One of the most positive things they can do in this respect is to press development of *social overhead capital* to the maximum extent that their resources will allow. Transportation networks and communications networks contribute greatly to efficiency. So do energy or power systems.

Sparked by governmental activities, some positive action appears to be under way in certain parts of the world concerning population control. In India, Thailand, and China, massive government educational efforts for birth control and family planning have been made. In India, voluntary sterilization of both men and women has been subsidized. In China, families are encouraged to have only one child and are heavily taxed for exceeding that number. In any case, during the past couple of decades trends in world population growth appear to have turned downward.

Governments of DCs

Since World War II, the economically advanced countries of the world have provided some economic assistance to LDCs, partly for humanitarian reasons and partly in hopes of obtaining ideological allegiance from the LDCs. There has been much rivalry between communist countries and those of the Western world. Some aid to LDCs has been channeled through the World Bank. At the same time, individual countries have conducted aid programs of their own. Basically, aid takes two forms: (1) loans and grants and (2) technical assistance.

Loans and grants generally are expected to help the recipient countries improve their labor forces, accumulate capital, improve their technological capabilities, and increase the efficiencies of their production processes. They are used to build educational facilities and for sanitary engineering purposes. They help construct power plants, cement plants, communications and transportation facilities, agricultural facilities, and the like. They are also used to import such things as fertilizer, raw and semifinished materials, industrial equipment, agricultural equipment, and spare parts.

Technical assistance helps in upgrading labor force skills and in advancing the technologies of the recipient countries. Much technical assistance is turned toward increasing the productivity of agricultural resources, improving educational systems, and raising standards of public health. In addition, advisors from the DCs often assist in getting industrial projects under way.

The World Bank is an organization through which DCs can jointly assist LDCs. It provides both low-interest loans from funds supplied by the DCs and technical assistance to low-income countries. Loans are made for a variety of projects, large and small, public and private. Bank officials require that the projects for which loans are made show every promise of paying off both the principal and the interest. The World Bank has been quite successful in this respect but has often been criticized as being too stingy with its loans.

Summary

Abject poverty is without question the major economic problem of the world. This has always been so, but it has become the focus of great concern for nations and for large numbers of persons in recent years. To understand its causes and achieve its possible alleviation, it is necessary to understand the nature of economics and economic activity.

Economic activity is generated by the wants of human beings, which seem to be insatiable in the aggregate. The means available in any economy for satisfying the wants of its population are scarce. They consist of the economy's resources—its labor and its capital—along with its available technology. The supplies of resources, together with the level of technology available, determine the maximum GDP that the country can produce to satisfy wants. Dividing a country's GDP by its population yields its per capita GDP, which is a rough measure of its citizens' average well-being. Further insight into actual well-being is achieved when the distribution of GDP is taken into account, as well.

The basic elements of economic activity and economic analysis provide insight into the causes of poverty. Poverty stems from low labor force qualities, little capital for labor to work with, low levels of technology, inefficiencies in the use of resources, and, in some instances, excessive rates of population growth. To break out of the poverty trap, a country must make progress in attacking some or all of the causes. But it is unlikely to make much progress unless it achieves a marked degree of political and economic stability.

Developed countries can and do assist LDCs as they strive to improve their economic lots. Aid takes two basic forms: (1) loans or grants and (2) technical assistance. Individual DCs have independent aid programs. They also engage in joint aid programs through such organizations as the World Bank.

Discussion Questions

1. GDP measures the total value of production within an economy during 1 year. What adjustments must be made in GDP before it can be used as a rough measure of social well-being?
2. Using a production possibilities curve, explain the opportunity cost principle.
3. Using a production possibilities curve, explain the concept of increasing opportunity costs.
4. Often it is blithely stated that "a country should pull itself up by its own bootstraps." From the standpoint of shifting the production possibilities curve outward, improving educational systems is an example of this. Referring to the data for LDCs in Table 1–3, discuss the practical problems of such a recommendation.
5. Production possibilities curves are typically assumed to be convex, or bowed out. Explain the economic implications of this shape.
6. Cost-benefit analysis is one of the most versatile tools in economic analysis. Suppose the end of the semester is approaching and you have to begin preparing for exams. Explain how you might use cost-benefit analysis to maximize your grade point average.
7. Make up an example that shows the GDP can increase even though real production is falling within an economy between 2 years.

8. If the goal of public spending is to shift the production possibilities curve of an economy outward, which of the following proposals would seem most likely to succeed: The purchase of a nuclear-powered aircraft carrier; a "hot meals" program for the elderly; a job training program for unemployed workers?

9. Suppose an economy produces only food and housing. Draw and explain the characteristics of its production possibilities curve. Show and explain the impact on the curve of (*a*) a new technology that improves food production only; (*b*) a new invention that improves both food and housing production.

10. Using the concepts of marginal social benefit and marginal social cost, explain how the optimal combination of goods can be determined in an economy that produces only two goods.

Additional Readings

Arnold, Guy. *The End of the Third World.* New York: St. Martin's Press, 1993.
Looks at the end of the Third World, beginning in the 1990s, emphasizing the economic implications for those countries.

Brue, Stanley L., and Donald R. Wentworth. "Mr. Malthus." In *Economic Scenes: Theory in Today's World.* Englewood Cliffs, NJ: Prentice-Hall, 1988, pp. 256–266.
Novel approach to summarizing the economics of population growth, resource scarcity, and economic growth.

Haggard, Stephan. *Developing Nations and the Politics of Global Integration.* Washington, DC: The Brookings Institution, 1995.
Focuses on East and Southeast Asia and Latin America's international trade policies.

Kincaid, A. Douglas, and Alejandro Portes, eds. *Comparative National Development: Society and Economy in the New Global Order.* Chapel Hill: University of North Carolina Press, 1994.
Group of essays that discusses international economic development.

Mittleman, James H., and Mustapha Kamal Pasha. *Out from Underdevelopment Revisited.* New York: St. Martin's Press, 1997.
Discusses underdevelopment of the Third World and strategies for development.

Salvatore, Dominick, ed. *World Population Trends and Their Impact on Economic Development.* Contributions in Economics and Economic History, number 82. New York: Greenwood Press, 1988.
Fourteen essays that cover economic development, migration, population growth, status of women, and other topics.

Van De Walle, Dominique, and Kimberly Nead, eds. *Public Spending and the Poor.* Baltimore: The Johns Hopkins University Press, 1995.
This book is an excellent analysis of the relations between public spending programs and the plight of the poor from an international perspective.

Wolff, Edward N. *Economics of Poverty, Inequality, and Discrimination.* Cincinnati: South-Western College Publishing, 1997.

Although most of this book deals explicitly with poverty in the United States, Chapter 3 is a thorough treatment of income inequality from an international perspective.

World Development Report. New York: Oxford University Press, annual.

Outstanding source for data on development issues. Includes data on income, population, life expectancy, health status, and educational attainment (as well as other topics) for well over 100 countries.

World Wide Web Resources

Economic Growth Resources
www.nuff.ox.ac.uk/economics/growth

Site includes links to statistical datasets, surveys, research papers, and other general matter related to economic growth and development.

The Hunger Project
www.igc.org/thp

In English, Spanish, French, and Japanese. The Hunger Project is an international organization dedicated to ending world hunger. Includes links to the organization's conference proceedings, reports, and speeches.

InterAction
www.interaction.org

InterAction is a coalition of over 150 nonprofit organizations, based in the United States, working to help the world's poor. The Web page includes a mission statement, a search engine, a list of publications, a calendar of events, and other topics.

United Nations Home Page
www.un.org

Provides information about many international topics, including human rights, economic and social development, and humanitarian affairs.

United Nations Capital Development Fund (UNCDF)
www.undp.org/uncdf/front.htm

UNCDF is administered by the United Nations Development Programme and works to reduce poverty in the least-developed countries. Provides links to their projects, news, and reports.

United Nations Children's Fund (UNICEF)
www.unicef.org

Text available in English, Spanish, and French. Provides links to its publications, a search engine, its gopher site, and *The State of the World's Children 1998.*

The World Bank Group
www.worldbank.org

The World Bank provides financing for economic development projects in the lesser developed countries. Topics include News, Publications, Topics in Development, Countries and Regions, Doing Business with the Bank, and About the World Bank Group.

2

Economic Systems, Resource Allocation, and Social Well-Being

Lessons from the Fall of the Soviet Union

Chapter Outline

Checklist of Economic Concepts

Moscow, February 8—In Nadezhda Shilyayeva's first-grade class, the words of the day are "profit" and "inventory." As the kindly teacher bounces her pointer along the curly blackboard script, her 26 students at School 139 sing the syllables in unison.

"Now what do we call the money left over in Misha's wallet after all his expenses are paid?" asked Miss Shilyayeva. "Profit!" shouted a pigtailed 7-year-old girl named Dasha. The teacher continued, "And why does Misha need this profit?"

Silence. Then a small voice ventured, "So he can"—a pause—"expand his store?"

"Excellent, Adrusha!" boomed the teacher's voice.

Ten years go, this kind of aggressive attempt to plant a seed of capitalism in her young students would have landed Miss Shilyayeva in the gulag. Today she is among a growing number of elementary school teachers in Russia who have seen the future and know that in order to survive it, her students will need to be able to compute interest rates.

"If we don't teach children about the market economy from an early age," said Miss Shilyayeva, 57, "they will end up like us. The older generation knew nothing about economics. We never gave it a thought. As a result, we are like blind kittens bumping into walls, looking for a way out."[1]

[1]Sarah Koenig, "In Russia, Teaching Tiny Capitalists to Compete," *The New York Times*, February 9, 1997, p. 3. Copyright©1997 by The New York times Co. Reprinted by permission.

As noted in Chapter 1, few decisions influence social well-being more directly and forcefully than choices concerning the way in which we organize our economies. The history of the Union of Soviet Socialist Republics (USSR) during this century clearly bears out this point. Although czarist Russia had taken the initial steps toward industrialization by the turn of the twentieth century, the country still lagged significantly behind the United States, Great Britain, and much of Europe. In fact, by the beginning of World War I, Russia, although very rich in economic resources, was the poorest of European countries. The economic development of Russia was to be unalterably changed, however, by the political events of the following decade. The Bolshevik revolution of 1917–1918, led by Vladimir Lenin, created the new USSR and ushered in an unprecedented period of economic experimentation and change. Most notably, by the end of the 1920s, Soviet strongman Joseph Stalin had essentially eliminated all vestiges of market-based resource allocation in favor of central planning. And this system remained in place, with only relatively minor changes, until the collapse from within of the USSR in 1991.

The Soviet experience causes us to ask first how resources are allocated in differing types of economies. Then, and more importantly, we will want to know how well each allocation mechanism serves the people of the economy. In doing so, we should be able to shed light on the issue of whether the fall of the USSR was related to its choice of economic organization.

Economic Systems

Within any country, organizational arrangements develop that serve as a framework within which economic decisions are made. In general terms, these organizational arrangements specify who determines what is produced with the country's scarce resources and who benefits from well-made decisions, as well as who suffers from poorly made decisions. It is important to stress from the beginning that the choice of organizational arrangement does not determine whether decision making and planning will occur but rather *who* will decide and plan. Historically, answers to this question range from private parties to a mix of private parties and the state, to the state entirely. The extent to which the state is involved in the economy is determined by the choice of an economic system, which can be thought of as falling on a continuum with the pure market economy at one extreme and the pure command economy at the other.

Pure Market Economy

The **pure market economy** is based on private ownership and control of resources, known as private property rights, and coordination of resource-use decisions through markets.

There are two essential elements of the *pure market economy:* (1) private ownership of the economy's resources, known as private property rights, and (2) *de*centralized decision making coordinated through markets. Within the pure market, or capitalist economy, private individuals, businesses, and combinations of the two are allowed, with minor interference, to engage in whatever voluntary exchanges they feel best maximize their well-being. If offered a job for $10 per hour, the individual may choose whether to accept it or turn it down depending on such factors as the value placed on his or her time and the availability of alternative sources of income. Similarly, a business owner decides whether to hire more or fewer workers, to seek more or less capital, and to increase or reduce production. The key is that within a pure market economy, choices surrounding the use of resources are left to private resource owners who are expected to make decisions that best suit their goals and aspirations. Once this myriad of decisions is made, coordination of the decisions takes place within markets. (Note the absence of any discussion of government in this process, with the implicit exception of legal enforcement of property rights.)

Pure Command Economy

The **pure command economy** is characterized by state ownership and/or control of resources and centralized resource-use decision making.

At the opposite end of the continuum of economic systems is the *pure command economy*. This economic system, also known as pure socialism, is everything capitalism is not. That is, the pure command economy is characterized by state ownership and/or control of economic resources and by centralized planning. Decisions concerning what and how to produce are made by central authorities through binding directives to producers (deals that are too good to refuse!). Given the centralization of decision making, alternative means of coordination of decisions such as reliance on markets is not necessary. And the resulting extremely expanded role of government should be obvious; who else can play the role of central planner?

Mixed Systems

Although examples of economies at or at least near the two extremes of pure market and pure command have existed, such as the United States during the first half of the 1800s and the USSR during its existence, most present-day economies lie somewhere between these two extremes. Today, the United States, Japan, and Canada, for example, can each be thought of as mixed-market economies; while private ownership and decentralized decision making are the rule, part of each economy's resources are governmentally owned and/or controlled, and certainly part of the national output of each country comes from the public sector. Similarly, although China, North Korea, and Vietnam remain near the pure command end given their pervasive public ownership of property, increasingly each is allowing elements of private property rights and decentralized decision making. For this reason, each is better categorized today as mixed command.

A special class of mixed systems has resulted from the fall of the USSR and its former eastern European allies: the transitional economy. While being mixed in the sense of having elements of both command and market economies, these are systems that have made official commitments to move in the direction of the market orientation. The extent of change and the degree of success from these changes varies from country to country. The one constant seems to be that transition is not immediate or easy. The special problems transitional economies face are discussed later in this chapter.

Economies that combine elements of both the pure market and pure command economies are known as **mixed systems.**

Although most present-day economies do not satisfy fully the criteria of either the pure market or pure command economy, these polar cases are useful in analyzing the way in which resources are allocated within existing mixed economies and the impact these differing allocation mechanisms have on social well-being. The extent to which outcomes of this analysis apply to any particular *mixed system* is dependent on how closely the economy satisfies the conditions of the pure market or pure command classifications. That is, an economy in which individuals own and control most resources and in which most economic decisions are made in a decentralized fashion can be expected to yield results that conform closely to the pure market model. Conversely, when most resources are publicly owned or controlled and most decision making is centralized, expect outcomes that closely mimic those of the pure command economy.

Resource Allocation in a Market Economy

When the buyers and sellers of a product or service interact with one another and engage in exchange, a market is said to exist. The geographic area of any market is simply the area within which the two parties are able to transfer information about and ownership of whatever is being exchanged. Some markets are local, some national, and still others international. Markets within the capitalist economy serve to coordinate the infinite decisions concerning resource allocation made by the owners of those resources. For example, in the last couple of decades, the development and application of digital technology has made possible the compact disc player as a cost-effective substitute for phonographic turntables. And consumers' desire for compact disc players, as you are no doubt aware, has been explosive. Left behind, of course, are turntables that are now viewed by most as being old-fashioned. Clearly, both the existing producers of turntables and the many new compact discs were well-advised to reallocate their efforts to the production of compact disc players and away from turntables. How did this happen? As you will see, this and the infinite other decisions about resource allocation and reallocation are brought together through markets.

Market Structure

The quality of market-based resource allocation decisions is in large part determined by the degree of competition that exists within the market economy. At one end of the spectrum, markets fall into the purely competitive classification. At the other, they are classified as purely monopolistic. The markets of any market economy can be found at or near each extreme, but most tend to fall firmly in between.

In a **purely competitive market,** there are a large number of mobile buyers and sellers of a standardized product. Further, the price of the product is free to move up or down, and there are no obstacles to firms entering or leaving the market.

Purely Competitive Markets.   For a market to be *purely competitive* it must exhibit five important characteristics. First, there must be enough buyers and sellers of the product so that no one of them acting alone can influence its price. To illustrate, consider the individual consumer buying a loaf of bread in a supermarket or an individual farmer selling wheat at a grain elevator. Second, each seller must be offering a standardized product. This condition is met when consumers are as happy to buy the product from one seller as from any other. Third, the product price must be free to move up or down without interference from government or any other party. Fourth, buyers and sellers must be mobile. This means that any buyer is free to move among alternative sellers and buy from whomever will sell at the lowest price. Similarly, sellers must be free to move among all potential buyers and sell to that individual who is willing to pay most for the product. Fifth, sellers must be free to leave the industry if they wish, and potential sellers must be free to enter if they feel they can produce the product more efficiently than existing sellers.

Few markets in the United States are purely competitive in the sense of rigorously fulfilling all five requirements, but some almost do. Perhaps coming closest to pure competition in the United States is agriculture. The market for agricultural products certainly satisfies the first, second, and fourth characteristics of the purely competitive market, although it fails to fulfill the third and fifth. Since 1933, the government has often been actively involved in establishing and maintaining prices in agricultural markets, violating the third characteristic of pure competition. And the extremely large amount of money necessary to effectively enter this market probably poses a significant barrier to entry, violating the fifth characteristic.

Purely Monopolistic Markets.   A *purely monopolistic* selling market, at the opposite end of the spectrum, exists when there is but one seller of a product. The seller is able to manipulate the product price to his or her advantage. Typically, the monopolist is also able to block potential competitors from entering the market—often with government help. When markets are controlled by a single seller, the consuming public usually suffers in the form of higher prices and lower quantities and/or qualities of the good or service. With a little reflection, you may be able to recall an example of the negative effects of monopoly. Perhaps, if you are old enough or come from a small town, you recall a time when there was only one firm offering videotapes for rent in your community. Eventually, numerous competitors opened up shop. How did the new competition change things? If your town is representative, you probably saw greater variety in tapes available, lower rental rates, and perhaps the advent of multinight rentals as the new competitors attempted to gain the allegiance of the former monopolist's captive customers. Competition among sellers typically benefits consumers. Given that consumers, taken as a whole, are society, the existence of monopoly tends to keep the market economy from achieving its maximum level of social well-being. As such, the problems posed by monopoly are significant enough to warrant the thorough treatment given in Chapter 8. Although samples exist, pure monopolies fortunately are rare in the United States.

In a **purely monopolistic market,** there is only one seller of a product. The monopolist has substantial control over price and is often able to prevent potential sellers from entering the market.

Imperfectly Competitive Markets.   Most markets in the United States fall somewhere between the purely competitive and purely monopolistic extremes. These markets are called *imperfectly competitive,* and the performance of such a market is dependent on the degree to which the mar-

Markets that fall between the purely competitive and purely monopolistic extremes are said to be **imperfectly competitive** and may exhibit characteristics of either or both of these extremes.

ket diverges from the extremes. That is, markets that do not fully satisfy the conditions of pure competition but come close to doing so can be expected to perform much the same as those that are purely competitive; those markets that are almost pure monopolies will likely yield outcomes not too dissimilar from those of pure monopoly.

Market Forces

Markets bring together or coordinate all the decisions that economic factors make within the capitalist economy. You may have heard this referred to as the *forces of demand and supply*. To fully understand the market economy, you must have a solid understanding of how demand and supply interact to answer the question of how a market economy's scarce resources are allocated. Before we enter into that discussion, however, it is vitally important to bear in mind that the description of markets that follows assumes a very high degree of competition. As alluded to above, the virtue of markets as allocators of scarce resources is not independent of the degree of competition that exists in individual markets. For the remainder of this chapter, we present the market model in its ideal form. Circumstances in which the performance of markets is less than optimal are the basis for much of the remainder of this book.

The **demand** for a good or service refers to the quantity of the product that consumers are willing to purchase at various prices, other things being equal. The other things that must remain equal are (1) the consumers' incomes, (2) the prices of goods related in consumption, (3) the consumers' tastes, (4) the consumers' expectations, and (5) the number of consumers.

Demand.   The *demand* for a product refers to the maximum quantities of the product that consumers are willing to purchase at various prices, other things being equal. Consider the demand for Pepsi in your town, Collegetown, USA. Suppose that during 1 week, the consumers of Pepsi in Collegetown are willing to purchase 1,500 six-packs if the price is $1.50 per six-pack; 1,000 six-packs if the price is $2.00; or 500 six-packs if the price is $2.50. Each of these price-quantity combinations is listed in the demand schedule in Table 2–1 and then plotted as a demand curve in Figure 2–1. The demand schedule and curve each have several characteristics that are vitally important.

First, it is incorrect to refer to any of the individual price-quantity combinations listed above as demand. The quantity of a product that consumers are willing to purchase at a specific price, reflecting one point on a demand curve, is properly referred to as the quantity demanded at that price. That is, demand refers not to a specific price-quantity combination but to all the price-quantity combinations taken together. In this way, the demand for Pepsi in Collegetown is properly reflected in the entire demand curve or schedule.

Second, demand relates to the quantities of the product that consumers are actually willing to purchase at various prices, not merely the quantities of the product that consumers would like to consume. Each of us probably desires an expensive, oceanfront home, but unless we are actually willing to purchase such a house at its market price, we do not demand it in the economic sense of the term.

Table 2–1	A demand schedule for Pepsi in Collegetown	
	Price (Dollars)	**Quantity (Six-Packs per Week)**
	$1.50	1,500
	2.00	1,000
	2.50	500

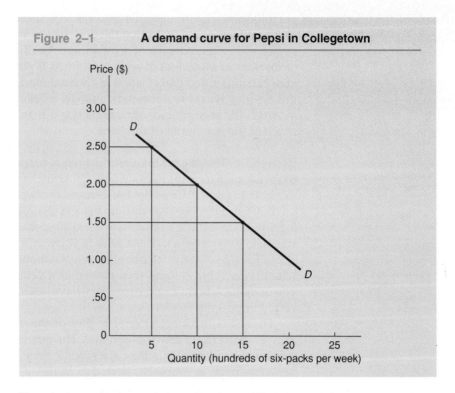

Figure 2–1   **A demand curve for Pepsi in Collegetown**

The price-quantity demanded combinations of Table 2–1, plotted graphically, form the demand curve for Pepsi, *DD*. The demand curve shows the quantities of Pepsi that the consumers are willing to purchase at various prices, other things being equal.

Third, demand reflects the quantities of the product that consumers are willing to purchase during some specific period of time. For example, the demand schedule and curve presented accurately depict the demand for Pepsi in Collegetown during 1 week. It makes little sense to discuss the quantity of Pepsi demanded at a specific price unless the period of time in which the purchases may take place is specified.

Fourth, it is assumed that customers will desire more of a product when its price is low than when it is high. Although this may seem to be nothing more than common sense, it serves as the often-overlooked basis of much that is done in economics. Formally, this inverse price-quantity demanded relationship is called the *law of demand* and states that the lower the price of a product, the larger will be the quantity demanded; and the higher the price, the smaller will be the quantity demanded, other things being equal. It is the law of demand that gives the demand curve its negative slope.

It is important to note that the law of demand does not simply state that the quantity demanded is greater when the price is low than when the price is high. The law states that this inverse price-quantity demanded relationship holds *only with other things being equal.* Although many factors could be listed as the other things that must be equal or held constant, the five most important are (1) the consumers' incomes, (2) the prices of goods related in consumption, (3) the consumers' tastes, (4) the consumers' expectations, and (5) the number of consumers.

Changes in the Quantity Demanded Versus Changes in Demand.
From the information given previously, we know that the consumers of Collegetown are willing to purchase 1,000 six-packs of Pepsi per week when its price is $2.00 per six-pack. This quantity demanded is identified as Point A on the original demand curve DD in Figure 2–2.

Should the price of Pepsi increase to $2.50, the consumers would reduce the amount they wish to purchase to 500 six-packs per week. That is, when the price rises to $2.50, the consumers move to the left on their demand curve to point B, which reflects a quantity demanded of 500 six-packs per week. Such a movement along one demand curve, brought about by a change in the price of the product, is called a *change in quantity demanded.* It is important to understand that this movement is not a change in demand. The consumers are merely moving from one price-quantity combination, or quantity demanded, to another in response to a change in the price of Pepsi.

A *change in demand* is said to occur when the entire demand schedule and curve change. For example, Figure 2–2 includes the original demand curve of Figure 2–1 (labeled DD) and two new curves, D_1D_1 and D_2D_2. Along demand curve D_1D_1, the consumers desire less Pepsi at each price than is the case along demand DD. Thus, a shift in demand from DD to D_1D_1 is referred to as a decrease in demand. Demand curve D_2D_2 indicates just the opposite, so a shift from DD to D_2D_2 is called an increase in demand. You should note that in each case the entire demand curve shifts, and this is what distinguishes a change in demand from a change in quantity demanded.

The **law of demand** states that the lower the price of the good, the larger will be the quantity demanded; and the higher the price, the smaller will be the quantity demanded, other things being equal.

A movement along one demand curve, brought about by a change in the price of the product, is called a **change in quantity demanded.**

A shift to an entirely new demand curve, brought about by a change in one or more of the factors assumed to be held constant, is called a **change in demand.**

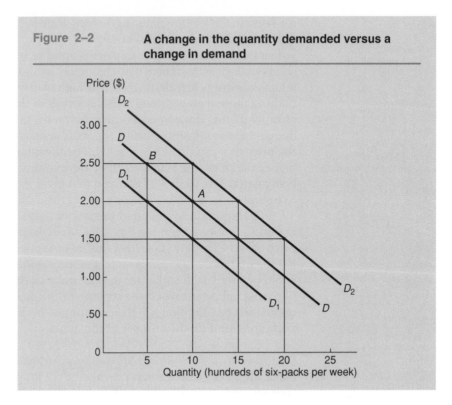

Figure 2–2   **A change in the quantity demanded versus a change in demand**

The movement along *DD* from *A* to *B* is brought about by a change in the price of Pepsi and is called a *change in the quantity demanded.* A shift in the entire demand curve to either D_1D_1 or D_2D_2 is called a *change in demand* and is brought about by a change in one of the factors assumed to be held constant when the demand curve is drawn.

Changes in demand occur when one or more of the five factors assumed to be held constant changes. Before proceeding to the discussion of how changes in the constants lead to changes in demand, however, you must fully understand the distinction between a change in quantity demanded and a change in demand. If the price of the product rises or falls, consumers will adjust the quantity demanded per unit of time. Graphically, this adjustment is represented by a movement along one demand curve and is called a change in the quantity demanded. By contrast, if one or more of the five factors assumed to be held constant changes, consumers move to an entirely new demand curve, and this is called a change in demand. Do not confuse the two.

Changes in Consumers' Incomes.   A change in demand may come about due to a change in the incomes of consumers. Suppose that initially demand curve *DD* in Figure 2–2 applies and the price of Pepsi is $2.00 per six-pack. At this price, the quantity demanded is 1,000 six-packs per week. Now suppose that the incomes of consumers rise. With incomes on the increase, it is likely that consumers will be willing to purchase more Pepsi, even if the price remains $2.00. Perhaps now they are willing to buy 1,500 six-packs. Similarly, had the initial price been $1.50, the increase in incomes might have caused consumers to increase the amount they wished to buy from 1,500 to 2,000 six-packs per week. Thus, when incomes rise, demand increases from DD to some higher level such as D_2D_2. Conversely, had incomes fallen, demand would have decreased to some lower level such as D_1D_1. In this example, an important assumption is implicitly made. Specifically, it is assumed that Pepsi is a *normal good*. A good is said to be a normal good if its demand increases as incomes rise and decreases as incomes fall. Although most goods satisfy this condition and are considered to be normal, there are goods for which the demand-income relationship is just the reverse. Such goods are known as *inferior goods* and exhibit demands that decrease as incomes rise and increase as incomes fall. Examples of inferior goods might include hot dogs, generic goods of all sorts, public transportation, and rabbit-ear antennae for television sets.

Changes in the Prices of Goods Related in Consumption.   Regarding the demand for a particular good, the prices of two types of related goods are important. First, the prices of *substitute goods* must be considered. In simplest form, goods are considered to be substitutes if they satisfy the same consumer need or desire. More formally, goods are substitutes if an increase in the price of one leads to an increase in the demand for the other. Assuming that Pepsi and Coke are substitutes and starting from an initial position at point A in Figure 2–2, what would be the impact on the demand for Pepsi of a doubling in the price of Coke? Given that the two are substitutes, the rising price of Coke could be expected to increase the demand for Pepsi to some higher level such as D_2D_2 as consumers substitute Pepsi for the now more expensive Coke. Just the opposite would occur if the price of Coke were to fall.

Another type of related good whose price must be held constant is *complementary goods*. Complementary goods are used in combination, such as hot dogs and hot dog buns or cars and gasoline. The impact of a change in the price of a complement is just the opposite of that for substitutes. With complementary goods, the demand for the good in question decreases as the price of the complement rises. Again, returning to Collegetown, suppose that Pepsi and potato chips are complements. A decrease in the demand for Pepsi might be caused by an increase in the price of chips, but why? When the price of chips increases, the quantity of chips demanded must, of necessity, decline. Since consumers use the two products in combination, and it is known that they are purchasing fewer bags of chips, it follows that they will demand less Pepsi as well. Just the opposite can be expected when the price of chips falls.

If the demand for a good increases as incomes rise and decreases as incomes fall, the good is said to be a **normal good.**

If the demand for a good decreases as incomes rise and increases as incomes fall, the good is said to be an **inferior good.**

Two goods are said to be **substitute goods** if an increase in the price of one leads to an increase in the demand for the other.

Two goods are said to be **complementary goods** if an increase in the price of one leads to a fall in the demand for the other.

Changes in Consumers' Tastes.   When a demand curve is drawn, the consumers' tastes must be held constant. The way in which changes in this factor lead to changes in demand requires little discussion. Put simply, when tastes change in favor of a good, its demand increases, while demand decreases when the reverse occurs. Changes in tastes can occur for a variety of reasons, such as advertising or increased information about the product or its substitutes. Pepsi and Coke regularly enlist the services of famous record and film industry stars to advertise their products. To the extent that consumers associate these famous faces with the products, the advertising campaign can be expected to increase demand. At least, this is what the makers of Pepsi and Coke have in mind.

Changes in Consumers' Expectations.   The fourth category of demand controls concerns the consumers' expectations with regard to the future. How would you respond if you believed that the price of Pepsi would double in the next week? You probably would buy more Pepsi this week, that is, increase your demand for Pepsi this week, and store it so that you do not have to purchase as much next week at its higher price. If the consumers of Collegetown exhibit the same degree of common sense as you, an increase in the demand for Pepsi such as that from DD to D_2D_2 might accompany an expected future price increase, whereas a decrease in demand can be anticipated when consumers expect future price decreases.

Changes in the Number of Consumers.   The final factor that must be held constant concerns the number of consumers in the group being considered. For example, an increase in the demand for Pepsi in Collegetown may come about purely due to an increase in the size of the consuming population of the city. Similarly, a decrease in the demand for Pepsi can be expected each summer as many of the students leave the city.

The key to this factor, as with each of the others, is that if the factor changes, the entire demand curve shifts, and such a shift is known as a change in demand.

Supply.   The *supply* of a product refers to the maximum quantities of the product that sellers are willing to sell at various prices, other things being equal. Suppose that the firms that produce and sell cars in the United States are willing to sell 250,000 cars per year when the price of a car is $5,000; 500,000 per year when the price is $10,000; and 750,000 when the price is $15,000. These price-quantity combinations are presented as a supply schedule in Table 2–2 and as a supply curve in Figure 2–3. As was true for demand, the supply schedule and curve have several important characteristics.

First, each of the price-quantity combinations listed in the supply schedule and graphed along the supply curve SS is properly referred to as a quantity supplied at a specific price. For example, the quantity supplied is 250,000 cars per year when the price is $5,000. These individual price-quantity combinations do not by themselves represent the supply of cars;

The **supply** of a product refers to the quantity of that product that sellers are willing to sell at various prices, other things being equal. The other things that must remain equal are (1) the cost of production, (2) the prices of goods related in production, (3) sellers' expectations, and (4) the number of sellers.

Table 2–2	A supply schedule for cars in the United States	
	Price (Dollars)	**Quantity (Cars per year)**
	$ 5,000	250,000
	10,000	500,000
	15,000	750,000

Figure 2–3   **A supply curve for cars in the United States**

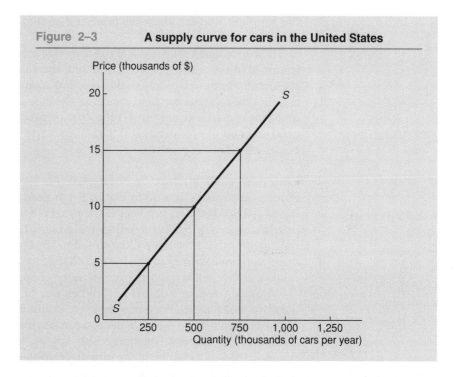

The price-quantity supplied combinations of Table 2–2, plotted graphically, form the supply curve for cars, *SS*. The supply curve shows the quantities of cars that the sellers are willing to place on the market at various prices, other things being equal.

rather, the supply of cars is represented by all of these individual price-quantity combinations taken together. Thus, the supply of cars is represented by the entire supply schedule in Table 2–2 or the entire supply curve in Figure 2–3.

Second, supply refers to the quantities of the good that sellers are willing to sell at various prices during some specified period of time. As was true on the demand side, it makes little sense to identify a specific quantity supplied unless the time period in which the sales are to take place is specified. For this reason, the supply information presented here reflects the sellers' intentions during 1 year.

Third, the positive slope of supply curve *SS* indicates that the quantity of cars offered for sale increases as the price of cars increases. The reason for this is simple: As the price increases, it becomes more profitable to sell cars, which encourages existing sellers to produce and sell more cars. This is a fundamental economic principle known as the *law of supply*, which states that the higher the price of the product, the larger will be the quantity supplied; and the lower the price, the smaller will be the quantity supplied, *other things being equal.*

It is once again the case that the *other things being equal* part of the law is crucial. As was the case with demand, the supply schedule and curve presented above accurately depict the intentions of the car sellers only if certain other factors are held constant. On the supply side, the other factors that must be equal are (1) the cost of production, (2) the prices of goods related in production, (3) the sellers' expectations, and (4) the number of sellers of the product.

Changes in the Quantity Supplied Versus Changes in Supply.
Point *A* on supply curve *SS* in Figure 2–4 indicates that the sellers are willing to sell 500,000 cars per year if the price is $10,000 per car. Should the price increase to $15,000, the sellers will move to point *B* on *SS*, increasing the quantity that they are willing to sell to 750,000 per year. Such a movement along one supply curve due to a change in the price of the product is called a *change in the quantity supplied,* not a change in supply.

A *change in supply* occurs only when one or more of the four factors listed above changes. For example, there might be an increase in the supply of cars from *SS* to S_2S_2 or a decrease in supply from *SS* to S_1S_1 due to a change in the supply constants. The key is, if the price of the good changes, there is a change in the quantity supplied, which is depicted as a movement along one supply curve, whereas a movement to an entirely new supply curve is referred to as a change in supply and is brought about by a change in one or more of the four factors assumed to be held constant.

Changes in the Cost of Production.
Suppose supply curve *SS* in Figure 2–4 accurately reflects the intentions of car sellers and that the price is initially $10,000. At this price, the sellers are willing to sell 500,000 cars per year. What would happen if, for whatever reason, it became more expensive to build cars? Individual sellers would likely find it to be no longer profitable to keep production at previous levels, and some sellers might even choose to cease operations altogether. Regardless, we can be certain

The **law of supply** states that the higher the price of the product, the larger will be the quantity supplied; and the lower the price, the smaller will be the quantity supplied, other things being equal.

A movement along one supply curve, brought about by a change in the price of the product, is called a **change in the quantity supplied.**

A shift to an entirely new supply curve, brought about by a change in one or more of the factors assumed to be held constant, is called a **change in supply.**

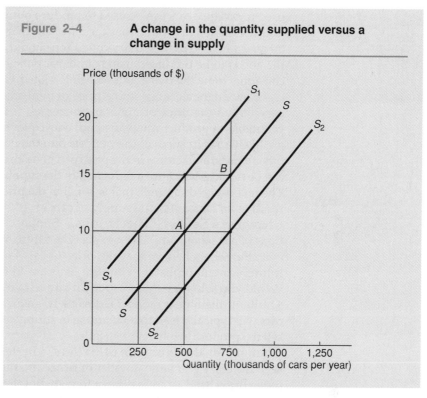

Figure 2–4   **A change in the quantity supplied versus a change in supply**

The movement along *SS* from *A* to *B* is brought about by a change in the price of cars and is called a *change in the quantity supplied.* A shift in the entire supply curve from *SS* to either S_1S_1 or S_2S_2 is called a *change in supply* and is brought about by a change in one of the factors assumed to be held constant when the supply curve is drawn.

that when the cost of producing cars increases, the supply of cars will decrease to some lower level such as S_1S_1. Changes in the cost of production can come about in a variety of ways, two of which deserve special note. First, production cost changes are often due to advances in technology. If a new robot is developed that improves the efficiency of the production process, such an efficiency gain will be translated into a fall in the cost of production. A second common cause of production cost changes concerns input prices. When the price of steel, plastic, or labor increases, the cost of producing cars increases.

Changes in the Prices of Goods Related in Production.   A change in supply may come about due to a change in the price of a good that is related in production. Minivans may be thought of as a good that is related in production to cars since, with only slight modification, the facilities used to produce cars can be used to produce minivans. Similarly, corn and milk are related in production since the land that is used to grow corn can be typically used to raise dairy cows. You should note is needed here is for the goods to be produced using similar inputs; it is not required that the consumer view the two goods as being related.

How might a change in the price of minivans influence the supply of cars? When the price of minivans increases, it becomes relatively more profitable to product minivans and, consequently, the producers of cars are likely to shift some of their efforts into the production of minivans. In other words, an increase in the price of a good that is related in production can be expected to cause a reduction in the supply of the good in question. The reverse holds as well; that is, a fall in the price of minivans will likely result in an increase in the supply of cars.

Changes in Sellers' Expectations.   Supply curve *SS* reflects the intentions of car sellers when they expect the future to be unchanged. If, however, the sellers believe that the price of cars is going to rise in the near future, we will probably witness a decrease in the supply of cars today. Would you sell as many cars today if you felt you could get an additional $1,000 for them next month? Conversely, an expected fall in the price of cars will typically lead to an increase in supply today as sellers attempt to sell the product before its price falls.

Changes in the Number of Sellers.   In the past 20 years, we have seen the entry of a large number of firms into the U.S. auto market. Most of the firms have, of course, been foreign, but their impact has been much the same as it would have been if they were American. Specifically, the increase in the number of sellers has greatly increased the supply of cars. This is the typical case. When the number of sellers increases, supply increases as well. Were we to witness a fall in the number of firms selling cars in the next 20 years, the result would undoubtedly be a decrease in supply.

The key to this factor, just as with the previous three, is that if the factor changes, there is a movement to an entirely new supply curve, and this movement is referred to as a change in supply.

Competitive Market Equilibrium and Social Well-Being

Equilibrium Price and Quantity Purchased.   The price of a product in a competitive market is determined by the interaction of buyers and sellers. To see how this works, return to Collegetown and consider the market for pizza during a typical semester, as detailed in Figure 2–5.

At a price of $6, the sellers are willing to sell 700 pizzas per semester. Why exactly 700 pizzas? The resources used to produce and sell pizza have many other uses. The pizza shops and their equipment might, for example, be used as bakeries, and the employees clearly could offer their employment elsewhere. It can be reasonably assumed that the

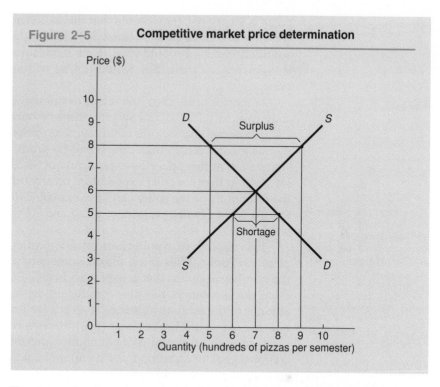

Figure 2–5   **Competitive market price determination**

The demand and supply curves together show how the equilibrium price of a product is determined in the market. If the price is above equilibrium, surpluses occur, and the sellers undercut each other's prices until the equilibrium price is reached. If the price is below equilibrium, shortages occur, and the buyers bid against each other for the available supplies, driving the price up to the equilibrium level. At the equilibrium, there are neither surpluses nor shortages.

owners of these resources will offer them for employment where they receive the greatest return. The quantity of resources devoted to producing pizza, then, and the resulting number of pizzas offered for sale reflect the value to the resource owner of using his or her resources in the production of pizza, relative to all other possible employments. When the price of pizza is $6 per pie, the resources necessary to produce and sell 700 pizzas will be drawn away from other production processes because they yield a greater return to their owners in producing pizza than in any of their other possible employments. As the supply curve indicates, if the price of pizza rises, new resources will be brought into pizza production from other production processes because those resources now offer their owners an increased return if used to produce pizza, given the rising price of pizza.

At the same time, Figure 2–5 indicates that at a price of $6, consumers wish to buy 700 pies per semester. Once again, the consumers have a nearly infinite number of ways to spend their incomes. When the price of pizza is $6 per pie, they decide that the $4,200 necessary to purchase and consume 700 pizza pies ($6 times 700 pies) could not be used to purchase anything else that would give them more satisfaction than the pizzas. If this were not true, they would not be willing to buy 700 pies at this price.

At a price of $6, then, the intentions of the sellers and consumers exactly coincide. That is, the owners of the resources necessary to produce 700 pizzas feel that no other employment of their resources will yield to them a greater return than can be had by producing pizza. And the consumers feel at this price, the expenditure of $4,200 on pizza yields greater satisfaction than a similar expenditure on any other good or goods. When the intentions of the sellers and buyers coincide in this fashion, we say that $6 is the *equilibrium price* of pizza and 700 is the *equilibrium quantity purchased.*

This concept of equilibrium price is particularly important. At this price, and only at this price, the consumers of pizza want to buy exactly the number of pizzas that sellers wish to sell. Put differently, only at this price do consumers feel that producers are using precisely the right amount of the economy's scarce resources to produce pizza. If this were not true, we could not say that their interests coincide with those of the producers. This outcome is of paramount importance in that the generally accepted goal for an economy is the minimization of the effects of resource scarcity, that is, the maximization of social well-being. The market economy leads to this outcome by ensuring that scarce resources are used where they are most highly valued by the consuming public. And who is in a better position to identify the amount of resources that should be used in each production process than the consuming public? Typically then, an equilibrium price, by indicating when consumers are satisfied with a particular allocation of resources, indicates that unique allocation of resources that maximizes social well-being. To see this more clearly, consider what happens when price is not at its equilibrium.

The price at which the sellers of a product wish to sell exactly the same amount as the consumers wish to buy is called the **equilibrium price.** As such, the equilibrium price indicates when consumers feel that precisely the correct share of the economy's scarce resources are devoted to producing the product.

The quantity of the product that is actually exchanged at the equilibrium price is called the **equilibrium quantity purchased.**

Effects of a Price Above Equilibrium.   If the price is not at the equilibrium level, market forces are set in motion that move the price toward that level. Suppose, for example, that the price of pizza rises from $6 to $8. The sellers can be expected to increase the quantity supplied because pizza is not relatively more profitable to produce. That is, sellers can be expected to draw additional resources from other production processes and devote them to producing pizza because these resources can now earn a greater return in producing pizza. This is shown as a movement along SS to the 900-pizza quantity-supplied level.

But how will consumers react to the higher price? As price rises from $6 to $8, individual consumers can be expected to shift some of their purchasing power from pizza to other goods because these other options are now relatively cheaper. As depicted, at the price of $8 per pie, the consumers are willing to purchase only 500 pizzas during a semester. Consequently, when pizza is priced at $8 per pie, there is a surplus of 400 pies per semester.

From a standpoint of resource allocation, what does a surplus of 400 pizzas imply? Consumers are simply saying that when pizza is priced at $8 per pie, the resources necessary to produce the 400 surplus pizzas would be better used (add more to social well-being) in producing some other good or service. A surplus implies that consumers feel that too much of the economy's scarce resources are being devoted to a particular production process and, thus, they would prefer having those resources reallocated to another production process. How will this reallocation take place? When there is a surplus of any product, each seller who is unable to sell all that he or she has produced has an incentive to cut the price a bit below the existing price, because such a price advantage will enable the seller to dispose of his or her own surplus more easily. As long as a surplus exists, each of the pizza makers is likely to undercut his or her competitors in this fashion. Thus, if the price of pizza is above its equilibrium, market forces will cause the price to fall. And the price can be expected to continue falling until the surplus is completely eliminated. Figure 2–5 indicates that the surplus is eliminated when the price again returns to its equilibrium. In other words, the price of pizza can be expected to stop falling when the quantity of pizzas that the sellers wish to sell is equal to the quantity the consumers wish to buy. In this way, the market operating on its own ensures that the consumer's desire to have those resources that were used to produce the surplus pizzas released to be used in another production process is met.

Effects of a Price Below Equilibrium.   Now consider a price below equilibrium. When the price of pizza is $5, the consumers desire 800 pizzas per semester, while the sellers are willing to sell only 600, indicating that a shortage equal to 200 pizzas exists. Shortages of any good or service imply that consumers wish to have a larger share of their economy's scarce resources devoted to producing the product. In this situation, individual consumers have an incentive to offer the seller a bit more than $5 per pie to increase their chances of actually being able to purchase a pizza. For example, you call the local pizza shop to place an order and are told that the price is $5, but unfortunately, due to a shortage, the pizza cannot be delivered until the next day. How do you respond? Given that the friends you have invited for dinner are knocking at the door, you call the pizza shop back and offer $7 if the pizza can be delivered immediately. To your satisfaction, but not surprise, before your friends have time to complain, the pizza arrives.

Whenever a shortage exists, market forces are put into action that tend to drive the price of the product up. As the price edges upward, the shortage becomes increasingly less severe as individual sellers respond to the rising price by increasing their production of the product. This process continues until the shortage is eliminated. That is, until the market once again reaches its equilibrium price.

In this way, the market operating on its own brings about the reallocation of resources that consumers desire because the shortage indicated that consumers felt more of the economy's scarce resources should be devoted to producing pizza. In other words, if left alone, the forces of demand and supply tend to ensure that social well-being, as reflected in consumer preferences, is maximized. This is not to say that market determined outcome always maximizes social well-being. In certain circumstances, which are considered in detail in later chapters, the market fails to maximize well-being on its own. These circumstances, though important, are uncommon enough to be properly considered exceptions to the rule rather than the rule.

Resource Allocation in a Command Economy

As indicated earlier in this chapter, the choice of an economic system is not a choice to have or not have decision making and planning; rather, the particular economic system selected simply indicates who will make resource-use decisions and plans. In the market economy, the consumer is king. That is, consumers decide what allocation of resources between competing production processes maximizes their well-being. Markets then coordinate this information and bring about any needed reallocation. None of this applies in the command economy, as can easily be seen by considering the example of the former Soviet Union.

The Soviet Model

On the heels of the Bolshevik revolution of 1917–1918, Soviet leader Vladimir Lenin instituted War Communism (1917–1920). The key economic features of this system were an aggressive attempt to eliminate all vestiges of market allocation of resources, nationalization of important industries, and forced requisition of agricultural output. In other words, Lenin attempted to eliminate private property rights and markets, the defining elements of market economies. This process left the infant Soviet state in near economic collapse by 1920. Faced with this, a second phase of Soviet economic policy went into effect, known as the New Economic Policy, which remained until 1928. Under the New Economic Policy, the Soviet Union, in many respects, instituted what we might now call a mixed-command economy by allowing a return of private property rights in certain industries and by reintroducing the market as a fundamental mechanism for resource allocation. Interestingly, the near collapse of the economy that had occurred during the War Communism period was reversed, or nearly so, during the New Economic Policy.

One might think that the Soviet experiences during War Communism and the New Economic Policy would have led the Soviet leadership to conclude that economic stability and development would not be enhanced by radical departures from market principles. This was not the case. To the contrary, the lesson taken from this period by Soviet leaders was that market principles could be eliminated but only if an alternative means of resource allocation was put into place. That is, War Communism was thought to have failed not because it eliminated private property rights and the market, but because it did not offer an alternative to market allocation of resources.

Joseph Stalin, in 1928, put this "new learning" into practice by establishing a vast system of centralized economic planning and control that remained in effect until the Soviet Union's collapse. Although overly simplistic in some respects, the Soviet economic system during the period of 1928 to 1991 may be summarized in four words: Centralized planning and control.

Planning and control in the Soviet system took place within a rigidly structured hierarchy of ministries, committees, and agencies. In total, by 1990, there were nearly 100 such groups that promulgated nearly 14,000 pages of *plans* each year concerning the production and distribution of more than 24 million products. The problem for the planners, as mind-numbing as it seems in retrospect, was to determine both the desired quantities of each good or service to be produced and the appropriate production technique to employ for each. These two questions can, of course, be summarized as one by noting the problem is to determine the quantities of resources that each production process will be allocated. This determination was made, in broad, general terms, by the ruling political body, the Communist Party of the Soviet Union, which would formulate directives on resource use between the competing production processes. These general directives were then fleshed out into precise, although tentative, resource allocations and production targets by the State Planning Commission, known as the *Gosplan*. The production targets were then transmitted through the ministries, commissions, and agencies responsible for each production process down to the actual factory or enterprise level. Once down to the production level, the flow of information changed directions and the State Planning Commission received feedback on its tentative production targets from those who had to implement its directives. The commission, operating under the authority of only the Communist Party, prepared a final and binding plan that was then carried out through the ministries. In this way, resource allocation plans were developed both on an annual basis and on a multiyear basis. It is important not to overlook that these plans carried the force of law.

To what extent may we expect that such an allocation mechanism serves to maximize social well-being? This question turns on the answer to a separate question: Who is the best judge of what will give a person satisfaction—the state or the individual? Within the market economy, it is assumed that the individual is in most cases the best judge. In the Soviet mindset, the state is thought to be the better judge. Which is optimal? Perhaps insight can be had by comparing the performance of each system in a hypothetical example.

Social Well-Being: Market Versus Command

Suppose that initially a car can be purchased by citizens of both the United States and the USSR for the equivalent of $10,000 and that at this price there is neither an obvious shortage nor a surplus of cars. That is, suppose that in each economy resources are initially allocated such that the public is satisfied with the quantity of cars available to them. Now suppose that, for whatever reason (perhaps rising incomes), the public of both countries desire more cars at each price? Put in the terms of this chapter, how well does each economic system respond to an increase in demand for cars?

Market Economy Reaction to Changing Demand

Initially, the demand for cars is DD and the supply is SS, as indicated in Figure 2–6. The interaction of demand and supply yields an equilibrium position with Q_0 cars being produced and sold at a price of $10,000 per car. Now assume that perhaps due to rising incomes, the demand for cars increases to some greater level like D_1D_1. At the existing price of $10,000, a shortage of cars develops equal to Q_0Q_1 cars. But what does a shortage indicate? Recall that an equilibrium is said to exist when the public feels that the existing allocation of resources maximizes its well-being. By extension, a shortage indicates that the public feels its satisfaction would be increased if more of the economy's resources were devoted to this production process.

With this as background, how does the market economy react? In the near term, we can expect the price of cars to rise to $13,000 as each potential purchaser bids the price up a bit in order to increase the chances that he or she will be able to buy a car. But the reaction of suppliers is also of much importance. Specifically, as the price is bid up, each supplier finds it to be in his or her interest to increase the output of cars. This increase in the quantity supplied is depicted as the movement from A to B on supply SS. That is, in response to the rising price, the quantity supplied increases in the near term to the new equilibrium of Q_2. Already we can conclude that the market is bringing about what the consuming public wants: more cars.

But the market does not stop here. The new equilibrium at $13,000 is in reality only an immediate reaction. Recall that one of the items held constant when supply is considered is the number of firms offering the product. Given the increasing price of cars, it can be reasonably expected

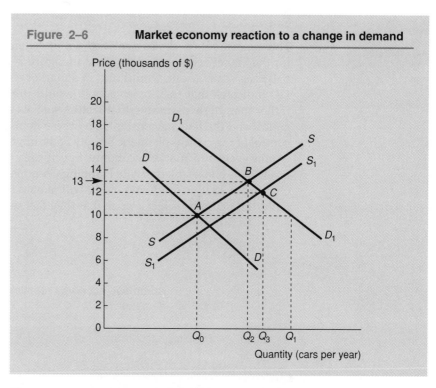

Figure 2–6   **Market economy reaction to a change in demand**

The interaction of the demand for cars *DD*, and the supply of cars *SS*, yields an equilibrium price of $10,000 and equilibrium quantity purchased at Q_0. An increase in demand to D_1D_1 initially causes price to rise to $13,000. In response to this price increase, the quantity supplied and purchased increases to Q_2. In the longer term, the increased profitability of producing cars leads to an increase in supply to S_1S_1. The interaction of D_1D_1 and S_1S_1 yields the final equilibrium price of $12,000 and quantity purchased of Q_3 cars.

that in the longer term (long enough to build new facilities, convert factories that were producing tractors, and the like) new firms will enter the car market leading to an increase in supply to S_1S_1. Given this, a new and final equilibrium is established at point *C* in which Q_3 cars are being produced and sold at a price of $12,000.

To summarize, the increase in demand for cars indicates that the public desires to have more of its economy's scarce resources devoted to the production of cars. And the market, operating on its own, causes a reallocation of resources to the production of cars. In this sense, the market operated to ensure that social well-being was once again maximized following the increase in demand for cars. and it is essential to note that this reallocation of resources to the production of cars took place without the blessing (or curse) of government or any other outside party.

Command Economy Reaction to Changing Demand

The same situation can be analyzed within a demand and supply context for the Soviet economy, as depicted in Figure 2–7. Demand DD is essentially the same as one would find in a market economy. That is, demand DD indicates that the Soviet people would prefer to buy at low prices rather than high, assuming that factors such as income, prices of related goods, and the like are constant. And these items are not under the direct control of the central planners. Supply SS is, however, different from what would exist in a market economy. Specifically, a particular production level, Q_0, is chosen by the State Planning Commission, as discussed above. Once selected, this production level will remain for the life of the plan. Finally, the planners select a price that they feel will clear the market. At a

| Figure 2–7 | Command economy reaction to a change in demand |

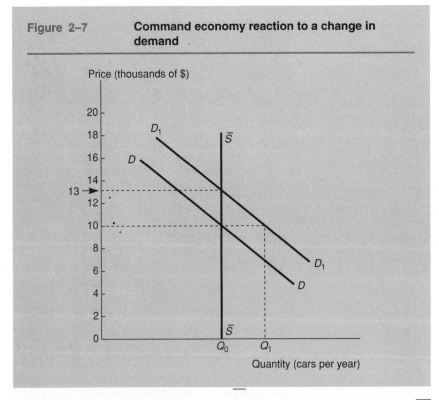

The interaction of demand DD and the administratively determined supply $\overline{SS}$ yields the initial price for cars of \$10,000. An increase in demand to D_1D_1 leads to a shortage of Q_0Q_1. This excess demand is either tolerated, leading to long lines, or simply siphoned off by adding a turnover tax of \$3,000, bringing the price up to \$13,000 per car.

price of $10,000, the planners decide that neither a shortage nor surplus will exist; thus, $10,000 is chosen as the initial price of cars.

It is important to stress that this price is arrived at administratively. That is, the price indicates little about the cost of producing the product as would be true in a market economy. Suppose, for example, that the actual cost of producing cars in the Soviet Union is $8,000. The $2,000 difference between the cost of production and the administered price is not simply left to the producer as profit. In the Soviet model, part of the $2,000 may have been left as a "fair" profit, but the remainder was taken by the central authorities in the form of a tax, known as the *turnover tax*. Price determination in a command economy then worked something like this: The central planners estimated the price at which the quantity demanded would be approximately equal to the quantity it wished to supply. Then the cost of producing the good was estimated, allowing for a modest profit. If the cost of producing the good was less than the market clearing price, the difference was taken through the turnover tax. Conversely, although rare in practice, if the cost of producing the good exceeded the market clearing price, central authorities held price down to the market clearing level and provided a subsidy (or negative turnover tax) equal to the difference between production costs and the market clearing price to the producer.

Now, what happens when demand rises? That is, suppose that incomes are rising in the Soviet Union leading the public to desire that more of the economy's resources be devoted to producing cars. This is shown as a movement to D_1D_1 in Figure 2–7. As was true in the market economy, an excess demand or shortage now exists at the $10,000 price level equal to Q_0Q_1 cars. How do the planners respond? Initially, they typically do not. That is, initially, the shortage is tolerated. And the outcome of such shortages has been well reported in the West: long lines as potential consumers attempt to satisfy their individual needs and desires. In the longer term, if the shortages persisted, the planners simply siphoned off the new demand by allowing the price to rise to $13,000 per car. Note, however, that this rising price does not spur an increase in either the quantity supplied from existing producers or an increase in supply from new producers, as would be the case in a market economy. Rather, the increased revenue from the sale of cars simply is taken by the planners in the form of a higher turnover tax. In this way, while shortages and long lines were tolerated in the near term, the planners could ensure that most markets came close to clearing in the longer term by manipulating the turnover tax.

Although markets in some sense cleared, does this suggest that social well-being was maximized? A bit of reflection clearly indicates that the answer is "no." Assume for the moment that social well-being was at its maximum initially. The public then decided that it wished more of their economy's scarce resources be devoted to the production of cars. That is, well-being was no longer at its peak, but a new higher peak could be

When shortages of goods and services developed within the Soviet economy, the excess demand was often siphoned off by increasing prices through the addition of, or increase in, the turnover tax.

reached by having more cars produced. This outcome, although automatic in a market economy, did not occur in the command economy. Rather than respecting the public's increased desire for cars by ordering an increase in production, the planners simply negated the increased demand by pushing up the turnover tax, that is, by increasing the price of cars.

Within the command economy, then, it is highly unlikely that the public's desire will be taken into account when resource allocation decisions are made. These decisions are driven by whatever is viewed as most important by the central planners. And Soviet central planners had a strong desire not for consumer goods, but for heavy industry and military goods. This is evidenced in Table 2–3, which reports the position of the Soviet consumer relative to consumers in several selected countries in 1985.

Although it is generally accepted that the USSR, with enormous economic resources at its disposal, developed a military that was second to none, the relatively resource-starved consumer sector of the Soviet economy was incapable of providing its people with the quantities or qualities of products that their counterparts in much of the rest of the world enjoyed. For example, as of 1985, the Soviet Union had developed an inventory of only 36 cars per 1,000 persons compared with 552 cars per 1,000 persons in the United States, and, even more telling, 127 cars in the relatively poor Greek economy. The second column of Table 2–3 summarizes the standing of the Soviet public. It indicates that goods available for consumption, per person, in the USSR, was only 28.6 percent of that available

Table 2–3	The relative position of the Soviet consumer, 1985	
Country	Passenger Cars (per 1,000 Persons)	Consumption (per Person, U.S. = 100)
USSR	36	28.6
United States	552	100.0
Germany	412	69.3
France	380	68.1
Japan	226	65.7
United Kingdom	305	65.6
Italy	376	64.6
Finland	315	61.7
Austria	335	59.0
Spain	241	46.1
Ireland	202	37.2
Greece	127	37.0

Source: Abram Bergson, "The USSR Before the Fall: How Poor and Why," Journal of Economic Perspectives, volume 5, number 4, Fall 1991, pp. 29–44.

to the typical American consumer and less than citizens of any other country listed had access to. Does this analysis fit your understanding of the position of Soviet consumers relative to their counterparts in the United States or in other less command-oriented economies?

The Problems and Promise of Transition

Although the preceding sections make it abundantly clear that public well-being in command systems like that in the Soviet Union was relatively low by the time of the collapse of the Soviet state, this should not be taken to suggest that the transition to a more market-oriented system can be quickly or painlessly achieved. For transitional economies, the typical initial economic pattern has included enormous increases in inflation coupled with dramatic falls in national output. For example, data from the International Monetary Fund and the World Bank show that in the countries which made up the former Soviet Union, annual inflation on average reached a peak of more than 4,600 percent in the early transition period, while the output of goods and services declined, on average, by a bit more than half. With respect to both measures of economic performance, however, there is reason for optimism. Specifically, by the end of 1996, in nearly all the transitional economies spawned by the fall of the Soviet Union and its eastern European allies, inflation had fallen into the double-digit range and per capita GDP had begun picking up. Of course, not all the transitional economies have performed equally well. Strong performers include Poland, Hungary, and the Czech Republic, while Russia, Kazakhstan, and Ukraine continue to lag behind. Why has transition been so painful? Clearly there are many answers to this question, and equally clearly, each transitional economy has faced its own unique problems. But two general problems have been common for all transitional economies.

Legal Systems.   Recall that the fundamental characteristics of the market economy are the institution of private property rights and decentralized decision making with respect to the privately held resources. That is, within a market-oriented economy, most of the country's scarce resources are owned and controlled by private parties who are assumed to put those resources to the uses that best serve their interests. In order for this type of allocation mechanism to work, there must be a legal system that provides for both the right of individuals to hold property and their right to make decisions as to how they wish to use their property. Further, it is not enough simply to have such a legal system in place, the general public must have confidence that these rights can and will be protected.

During the Soviet era, there were neither laws providing for private property rights nor respect for individual decision making. The state owned, or at least controlled, nearly all resources, and most important economic decisions were communicated from the leadership down to the people. Further, part of Soviet ideology was a distrust of the pursuit for personal betterment through entrepreneurial activities. Government authorities regularly regarded those who engaged in such activities as shady or as having questionable morals, and in many cases simply treated them as criminals. Finally, the legal system that existed was not designed to protect the rights of the people; it served as little more than a means of justifying whatever the leaders wished to do.

Naturally, this all changed with the onset of transition, but unfortunately, old habits die hard. This is especially true when the old habits developed over two complete generations, as in the Soviet case. And simply enacting market-oriented legislation is not enough to cause people to understand how to effectively function in a market economy, to change people's attitudes about markets, or to cause people to trust that their leaders have their best interests at heart. This lack of familiarity with private property rights and with the legal systems necessary to protect and promote such rights has contributed not only to the poor early economic performance of the transitional economies but also, at least in the Russian case, to the extensive growth of locally developed organized crime syndicates, which are now exporting their loan-sharking and drug-running activities to the United States.

Increasing Government Debt.   The primary method of raising revenue for government operations in the former Soviet state was through the profits of state-owned businesses. With transition came the loss of much of this and other traditional revenue sources. Unfortunately, the lost revenue was not matched by falling demands for spending on the part of everyone from the military leaders who retain oversight of one of the world's largest and most lethal fighting forces, down to the pensioner who had been promised public assistance in his or her old age. Although spending has declined during transition, initially it declined far less rapidly than did revenues leading to an explosion of government debt. To cover the shortfalls, governments from each of the transitional economies cranked up the money printing presses. This, as will be discussed in detail in Chapter 12, inevitably contributed to the inflation discussed above.

Summary

One of the most important economic decisions (if not *the* most important) a country must make in dealing with the fundamental problem of resource allocation concerns the choice of an economic system. Economic systems range from the pure market economy to pure command. The key differences between the two surround the issues of resource ownership and/or control and the mechanism through which resource allocation decisions are made.

Within a market economy, the economy's scarce resources are owned and controlled by private parties. This is referred to as the institution of private property rights. Equally important, within a market economy, resource allocation decisions are made by private owners and then these decisions are coordinated within markets. Within free markets, the forces of demand and supply operate to ensure that equilibrium prices and quantities are established at which neither shortages nor surpluses exist. Put differently, markets operating on their own tend to ensure that production is carried to the point where social well-being is maximized, given that the equilibrium reached is one in which the desires of consumers and producers exactly coincide. Should consumer desires change, indicating that they would prefer either more or less of a given good or service, the market reacts to bring about the desired change. Circumstances in which markets fail to maximize social well-being, treated in detail in the following chapters, occur infrequently enough to be considered exceptions to the rule rather than the rule.

A command economy is one in which resources are owned, or at least directly controlled by the state. Further, decisions about resource allocation are made directly and with the force of law by the state. Put simply, within the command economy, resources are allocated based on the preferences of the planners, rather than the preferences of the public. Given this, social well-being is maximized only if the planners know better than the public what mix of goods and services yields maximum satisfaction.

The history of the Soviet Union argues loudly the benefits of the market form of economic organization. In response to rising demands, the Soviet Union's central planners either allowed long lines to exist or siphoned off the new demand with increasing turnover taxes and thus higher prices. Years of such economic deprivation no doubt played a significant role in the collapse of the Soviet Union. But this is not to say that the transition to a market economy is easy. In fact, during the early part of the transition to a market orientation, most countries encounter severe economic hardship in the form of falling national output and runaway inflation. Fortunately, however, it appears that most of the transitional economies growing from the former Soviet Union and its eastern European allies are turning the corner, as indicated by a rising per capita GDP and falling rates of inflation. Nearly a century of economic mismanagement cannot be overcome instantly, which itself reinforces the importance of the choice of an economic system.

Discussion Questions

1. Compare and contrast the pure market and pure command economic systems. Where does the United States fit on this continuum?

2. The outcomes for consumers are expected to be quite different if a market is purely competitive rather than purely monopolistic. List some of the differences you would expect and explain your choices.

3. Without reference to a diagram, explain the difference between a change in demand and a change in quantity demanded.

4. Discuss: "Recently the price of gas went up, and at the same time the quantity of gas purchased increased. This is a clear violation of the law of demand."

5. List and explain the factors we typically hold constant when drawing a demand curve. What additional factors do you think could be added to the list?

6. List and explain the factors that we typically hold constant when drawing a supply curve. What additional factors do you think could be added to the list?

7. With reference to a supply-and-demand diagram, explain why the equilibrium reached by a market typically reflects a well-being maximizing production level of the good or service.

8. Suppose that during this year there is a very large personal income tax cut. Show and explain the effects you would expect on the market for new cars.

9. Labor unions typically desire both rising wages and job security. Draw a diagram of the demand and supply of labor, and explain why these two goals are to some extent contradictory.

10. Make up an example that shows the ability of a market economy to respond to a change in consumer demand relative to a command economy.

11. Explain why the transition from a command economy to a more market-oriented economy often entails a difficult period of transition.

Additional Readings

Carson, Richard L. *Comparative Economic Systems.* Armonk, NY: M. E. Sharpe, Inc., 1992.

Excellent and accessible text on the topic of economic systems. This book is especially interesting because of its emphasis on the role of government and the institution of private property rights.

Csaba, Laszlo. *Privatization, Liberalization and Destruction: Recreating the Market in Central and Eastern Europe.* Brookfield, VT: Ashgate Publishers, 1994.

Presents and debates in 13 papers the problems and prospects of transforming the command economies of Central and Eastern Europe.

The Journal of Economic Perspectives, Spring 1996.

A thoughtful and accessible symposium on the problems the transitional economies have faced and are continuing to face as they evolve into mixed-market economies.

Kern, William S. *From Socialism to Market Economy: The Transition Problem.* Kalamazoo, MI: W. E. Upjohn Institute, 1992.

This collection of papers presents and analyzes the problems that have plagued the former eastern bloc countries as they moved toward market reforms.

Remnick, David. *Lenin's Tomb: The Last Days of the Soviet Union.* New York: Random House, 1993.

A journalist who spent the crucial period 1987 through 1991 in Moscow, Mr. Remnick offers a fascinating firsthand historical account of the fall of the Soviet state.

Schmookler, Andrew. *The Illusion of Choice: How the Market Economy Shapes Our Destiny.* Albany: State University of New York Press, 1993.

Describes how the market economy affects all aspects of life.

White, Stephen. *Gorbachev and After.* Cambridge: Cambridge University Press, 1991.

Chapter Four, "Reforming the Planned Economy," discusses Gorbachev's economic reform policies.

World Development Report, 1996: From Plan to Market. New York: Oxford University Press, 1996.

A thorough treatment of the problems and promise of transitional economies. Includes a great deal of summary data on transition.

World Wide Web Resources

The CATO Institute
www.cato.org/home.html

A private institution founded to support "public policy based on individual liberty, limited government, free markets, and peace." Provides links to various free market-related sites and publications.

CIA World Factbook 1997
www.odci.gov/cia/publications/factbook/index.html

Gives demographic, environmental, geographic, and governmental information for all the countries in the former Soviet Union, as well as other countries.

Information About Russia and the Former USSR
www.cs.toronto.edu/~mes/russia.html

Illustrated history of Russia, Russia-related servers, and tips for travelers.

The Jerome Levy Economics Institute of Bard College
www.levy.org

A nonprofit institution devoted to the study of market-based public policy. Provides links to economic forecasts and other market-related sites and publications.

The National Council on Economic Education
www.nationalcouncil.org/index.html

Nonprofit organization that promotes economic literacy in the United States and abroad. Major producers of economic education material for grades K through 12. Their "Economics International" program is involved in bringing economics education to the former Soviet republics.

Russia and the Former Soviet Republics Maps
www.lib.utexas.edu/Libs/PCL/Map_collection/commonwealth.html

Gives links to maps on the politics, geography, ethnic groups, defense industries, and land use for the countries of the former Soviet Union.

Russian History
www.departmentss.bucknell.edu/russian/history.html

Breaks the history of Russia into different time frames, with links for every period.

Economics of Higher Education

Who Benefits and Who Pays the Bills?

Chapter Outline

Checklist of Economic Concepts

Human capital
Spillovers in consumption,
  social
Spillovers in production, social
Opportunity costs
Production possibilities curve

Explicit costs
Implicit costs
Demand
Supply
Price, equilibrium

Price elasticity of demand
Surplus
Shortage
Transfer payments
Free riders

The average cost of college tuition rose roughly 4 percent this year, a slightly smaller increase than last year's, according to the annual survey by the College Board.

This year's increase is more than twice the rate of inflation as measured by the Consumer Price Index, as was last year's. The C.P.I. rose 1.6 percent for the 12 months ending in August.

Four-year private institutions raised their prices the most, despite the many news stories in recent years noting how expensive such institutions have become.

- At four-year private colleges, students are paying an average of $14,508, a 5-percent increase.
- Four-year public colleges are charging an average of $3,243, up 4 percent.
- At two-year private colleges, tuition and fees rose 4 percent, to $7,333.
- At two-year public colleges, tuition is $1,633, a 4 percent increase.

Donald M. Stewart, president of the College Board, said at a press conference here last week that for most Americans, paying for college had become "a daunting task." "We must encourage colleges to do even more to hold the line on rising prices, even as we encourage families to plan ahead," he said.[1]

[1]Ben Gose, excerpt from "Average Tuition Rises 4% in a Year, More Than Twice the Rate of Inflation," *The Chronicle of Higher Education*, October 16, 1998, p. A56.

Problems in Higher Education

Colleges and universities are going through troubled times. Since World War II, enrollments have increased greatly, placing tremendous pressure on their personnel and facilities. Enrollments peaked in the early 1990s and are expected to remain flat throughout the rest of this century. University administrators now talk of retrenchment. Although the riots, strikes, boycotts, and other disruptions of the academic processes that were so common in the 1960s have subsided, they remain as potential threats to administrators. Most institutions face serious financial problems. The problem is especially acute in public colleges and universities where government appropriations are failing to grow as in the past. In response, tuition and fees have risen rapidly. Some say too rapidly. Others say too many degrees are being granted—there is no room for new college and university graduates to work in the fields of their choice. Still others say that colleges and universities are too tradition-bound and are not responsive to the needs of society.

All these issues (and more) call for systematic analysis of the higher education system. The economics of such an analysis center around four interrelated questions: (1) What kinds of higher educational services should be provided? (2) How much should be provided? (3) What is the appropriate institutional structure for providing them? (4) Who should pay for them?

What Kinds of Services?

Society expects higher educational institutions to perform multiple roles. Traditionally they have been learning centers, accumulating and transmitting knowledge of all kinds to students. University faculties are expected to engage in research and other creative activities that advance the frontiers of knowledge, and to be at the cutting edge of the intellectual, cultural, social, and technological developments of civilization.

In addition, society has come to expect colleges and universities to provide professional and vocational types of training. These range from the preparation of physicians and lawyers to the training of automobile mechanics and secretaries. In many, if not most, cases, these multiple roles of colleges and universities are inextricably bound together.

How Much Service?

The question of how much college and university educational service the society should provide is a very live issue today. Another name for this problem is the *financial crisis* of higher education. Most administrators, faculty members, and students are convinced that a financial crisis exists, that not enough is being spent for educational services.

Over the years, legislative appropriations to public institutions have not kept pace with growing enrollments and rising costs. In response, tuitions have increased in both public and private schools. Many private schools have been operating with deficits, and a number face the possibility of shutting down their operations. Is all this an indication that society is unwilling to support higher education at present levels or that it believes relatively too much is being spent for higher educational services?

What Institutional Structure?

The present system of higher education is a dual one made up of both private and public colleges and universities. In both components of the system, there are three types of institutions: (1) junior colleges, (2) 4-year colleges, and (3) universities. The public institutions are state-owned and operated, except for a growing number of community colleges and a very few municipal colleges and universities.

Is this structure conducive to providing the appropriate kinds and quantities of higher educational services relative to other goods and services desired by the society? Is it flexible? Or is it tradition-bound and susceptible to being a political football for state politicians?

Who Should Pay?

A related question concerns the extent to which governments (taxpayers) should pay the costs of producing the services of higher education and to what extent the costs should be paid by students and their families. If the government is to pay a substantial part of the cost, how should it go about doing so? Is the state university, with the state appropriations for its capital and operating costs, the best way? Or should the state, instead of making appropriations to institutions, make funds available to students themselves, letting them and their parents choose their schools, paying tuition and fees sufficient to meet the costs of their educations? Should government payments of the costs of higher education favor poor families? These are some of the questions that bother us.

The Economic Basis of the Problems

The basic issues outlined above are primarily economic problems. The economic aspects of providing higher educational services were largely ignored until the 1960s because such services composed a relatively small part of the GDP and used small proportions of the nation's resources. In addition, it was somehow thought that education was above mundane things like analysis of economic benefits and costs.

The burgeoning enrollments since World War II changed all that. Those responsible for decision with regard to higher education—legislators, administrators, faculties, students, and concerned citizens—can no longer ignore the economic consequences of their decisions. The provision of higher educational services requires the use of large quantities of resources, and the resources so used are not available to produce other goods and services. Higher educational services represent one of a great many competing uses for resources.

In this chapter we construct an economic framework of the higher education "industry" that should be useful in the decision-making processes concerning it. The present system of higher education will be evaluated within the context of this framework.

The "Product" of Higher Education

Like other producing units in the economy, institutions of higher education use resources and technology to produce something of benefit to individuals and society. This "something" can probably best be characterized as *educational services.* To get at what constitutes educational services, we can pose the question: Why are you attending a college or university? There are at least three answers to the question. First, you expect higher education to improve your capacity to produce and to earn income, that is, to augment the quality of your labor resources. We call this the development of *human capital.* Second, quite apart from improving the quality of your labor resources, you derive direct, immediate satisfaction from your present participation in college or university processes and activities—it is in this respect a direct consumption service. Third, you may expect that there will be some benefits to the society as a whole in addition to the benefits that accrue to you from your obtaining higher education. We will look at these facets of educational services in turn.

Investment in Human Capital

A large part of educational services must consist of the development of human or labor resources. This is called *investment in human capital* because in an economic sense it is very much the same thing as investing in machines, buildings, or other material capital. We invest in additional nonhuman capital whenever we think that it will generate enough additional product output to more than repay the new investment costs. Similarly, it pays an individual to invest in human capital—additional education—if the increase in education increases the earning power of the person being educated by more than the cost of the additional education. Just as investment in nonhuman capital is expected to increase and expand the capacity of capital resources to produce, so is a large part of the investment in human capital, expected to augment the capacity of labor resources to contribute to GDP.

Investment in human capital is in no sense restricted to the provision of vocational education. Classical education—language and literature, the humanities, the fine arts, philosophy, and the like—broadens and deepens people's capacities to think, act, and enjoy, and thereby increases their productivity in an economic sense. In many cases employers of colleges and university graduates are just as interested in hiring students with broad liberal arts degrees as they are in those trained in specific vocational majors. What they want are bright individuals who know how to think and how to accept responsibility.

Direct Consumption

Some part of the educational services produced by colleges and universities consists of *direct consumption benefits.* Participation in the activities of the institution and interaction with other students in university life yield direct satisfaction to many. Students who have no interest in making their education pay off through increased earning power are prime examples of direct consumers of educational services.

By way of contrast, there are students whose sole purpose in attending college is to enhance their capacities for earning income. Sometimes these are part-time students who are employed by business enterprises. Sometimes they are commuters who attend classes only and do not participate in other aspects of university life. Direct consumption benefits may be zero for them.

For most students the consumption benefits are inextricably mixed with the human capital investment elements of educational services. Classes, discussions, and social life combine to provide personal satisfaction as well as to increase the capacities of the human resource to produce goods and services.

Social Spillovers

Typically when a good or service is produced, the actual producer bears the full cost of production. Similarly, in most circumstances, the actual consumer of a good or service is the only person whose satisfaction is affected as the item is consumed. There are circumstances, however, when this is not the case. Suppose, for example, that my wealthy neighbor hires an orchestra to play at her garden party and I am not invited. She pays for the pleasure of her guests, and their satisfaction is enhanced as they listen to the orchestra. But who is to stop me, a lover of beautiful music, from listening to its haunting strains from my side of the property line? The consumption of the music by my neighbor and her guests yields a *social spillover in consumption,* which in this is positive. That is, not only do my neighbor and her guests find that their satisfaction is enhanced, but so do I. Conversely, the consumption of some goods and services can yield social spillovers in consumption that are negative. A good example is cigarette smoking. Much attention has been paid recently to the problem of secondhand smoke. Presumably people smoke cigarettes for the positive satisfaction they receive, but as a by-product of their smoking, those around them might find their own satisfaction reduced. If so, the cigarette smoking is said to yield a negative social spillover in consumption.

> When the consumption of a good or service causes a change in satisfaction for someone other than the direct consumer of the item, a **social spillover in consumption** exists. Such spillovers can have positive or negative effects on satisfaction.

Social spillovers can also occur in the production process. The most common example is that of pollution, which will be discussed in detail in Chapter 5. As you will see, often when a firm or group of firms pollutes, it causes the cost of production to rise for other firms who must use the polluted environment in their own production processes. In this case, we say that the pollution causes a *social spillover in production* that is negative. Social spillovers in production can also have positive effects. Perhaps the most significant examples of positive social spillovers in production during our lifetimes have come from the production of space exploration. Many firms, having nothing to do directly with space exploration, have had their cost of production reduced due to advances spawned by the exploration of space.

> When the production of a particular good or service causes a change in the cost of producing some other item, a **social spillover in production** exists. Such spillovers can have positive or negative effects on production costs.

The widespread provision of educational services is generally thought to yield positive social spillovers in consumption. Many believe that over and above the direct benefit of satisfaction that accrues to the individual—greater productivity, earning power, and direct consumption benefits—there are additional benefits to the society as a whole. Some of the positive social spillovers commonly cited are a better functioning democratic process stemming from greater voter literacy, more enlightened citizens who make the society a more pleasant place to live, better government services to the community, more rapid technological growth, improved community sanitation techniques and facilities, reduced crime rates, and reduced fire hazards.

The Incidence of the Benefits

When individuals obtain college or university educations, to whom do the foregoing benefits accrue? Suppose we look again at the nature of the "product." The direct consumption benefits are easiest to assign. They very clearly add to the level of well-being of the individual student. There are no obvious widespread social spillovers of these to others in the society as students work their way through the usual 5 or 6 years of undergraduate study.

The development of human capital also provides first-order benefits to individuals and their families. Individuals who develop engineering skills, medical skills, legal skills, or specialized knowledge and teaching skills increase their capacities to contribute to GDP. Society as a whole benefits from this additional productivity since it makes greater supplies of certain goods and services available for consumption. But this increase in output is not, in itself, indicative of a positive social spillover in consumption since it can be expected that the individual in whom the investment in human capital was made will be compensated for this increased productivity through his or her earnings. For a positive social spillover in consumption to exist, society—apart from individuals and their families—must receive the added satisfaction or benefit. Suppose that a group of researchers utilizing the human capital they had developed over decades of study solves the HIV puzzle, relegating the illness to a non-life-threatening status. Clearly, we could expect the researchers to receive first-order benefits in the form of significantly increased earnings. But, wouldn't the value of such a medical advance to society significantly exceed any compensation that the researchers might reasonably receive? This excess of benefits accruing to society at large is the social spillover. in consumption of the treatment. While such benefits clearly exist, it is very difficult to identify them in many instances, and when they are identifiable, it is often very difficult to accurately measure their value. Thus, there is much debate as to their significance for higher education.

Many people argue that the social spillovers in consumption associated with each additional year of education decrease as an individual moves through the educational system. They believe that the greatest positive spillovers come from the achievement of basic literacy—learning to read, write, and do arithmetic. These are associated with primary education. They expect secondary education to develop skills of interacting with others in the society and to provide some measure of sophistication in the administration of the joint affairs of those who constitute the society. They do not believe that higher education provides much more in positive social spillovers. They believe that it benefits society mostly through the benefits it provides to those who obtain its services.

What can be said in summary, then, about the benefits of higher educational services? First, there are very clear benefits to those who receive these services both in the form of higher earning power as compensation for their greater productivity and in the form of the value of direct consumption benefits. Equally clearly, there may be positive social spillovers to society as a whole from higher educational services. The value of these spillovers is open to some debate, however, given the difficulties associated with their identification and measurement.

Economic Concept of Costs

One of the most important principles of economics is summed up in the statement, "There is no such thing as a free lunch." We speak glibly of such things as free medical care, free housing, free food, and free education. What we mean is that those who use the "free" goods and services do not themselves have to pay money for them. All too often our chain of reasoning stops right there. But if we really think that these are free to the society as a whole, we delude ourselves. The production of the "free goods" is costly to someone—perhaps even partly to their users.

The economic costs of a product may or may not be reflected in the direct money outlays that must be made in producing it. The basic concept underlying economic costs is the *opportunity cost principle*.

The Opportunity Cost Principle Revisited

We defined and discussed the nature of the opportunity cost principle in Chapter 1. The concept is particularly useful in identifying the costs of higher education.

Suppose we start with the production possibilities curve of Figure 3–1, which measures units of educational services along the horizontal axis and composite units of all other goods and services along the vertical axis—all these in terms of dollars' worths. The curve TT_1 shows all alternative combinations of other goods and services and of education that the

Figure 3–1   **The costs of education**

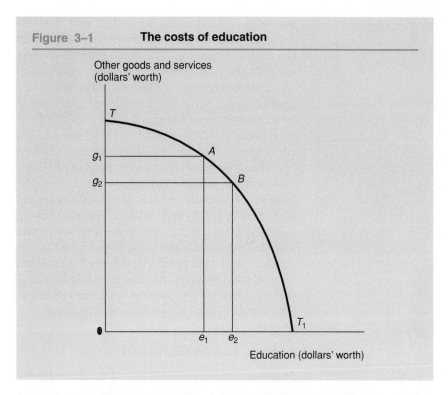

Production possibilities curve TT_1 shows all alternative combinations of other goods and services and education that the economy's resources and technology can produce per year. Two possible alternative combinations are represented by A and B. If the economy is initially producing combination B, it is obtaining g_2 units of other goods and services and e_2 units of education. If e_1e_2 represents one unit of education per year, it becomes apparent that g_2g_1 units of other goods and services must have been sacrificed to obtain it. The value of the g_2g_1 units thus measures the cost of a unit of education at the e_2 level of production.

economy's given resources can produce per year. Suppose that initially combination B, made up of e_2 dollars' worth of education and g_2 dollars' worth of other goods and services, is being produced and the economy's resources are fully employed.

What is the cost to the society of a unit of education when B represents the economy's output mix? Recall, from Chapter 1, that *it is the value of the alternative goods and services which must be forgone to produce that unit.* Let the distance e_1e_2 represent $1 worth of education. If this unit had not been produced, the society could have had more of other goods and services, equal to the amount g_2g_1. Thus, the society had to sacrifice g_2g_1 dollars' worth of other goods and services to produce the one unit of education. The sacrifice of the other goods and services releases just enough resources to produce the additional unit of education. We call the physical amounts of other goods and services sacrificed the *real cost* of producing the unit of education. The value that consumers attach to the goods and services given up is the true *economic money cost*.

Stated in a slightly different way, *the cost of producing a unit of any one good or service is equal to the value of goods and services that those resources could have produced had they been employed in their best alternative way.* A little reflection will show that this statement of the opportunity cost principle is identical to the one developed in Chapter 1.

The opportunity cost principle is capable of general application. In an economy in which resources are fully employed, an increase in the amount of medical services provided draws resources from the production of other goods and services. The value of these other goods and services forgone is the true cost of the increase in medical services. The cost of a bushel of wheat is the value of the corn that must be forgone in order to produce it, if corn production is the best alternative use to which the resources used in wheat production could be put. The cost of a soldier in the society's army is the value of what one could have produced as a civilian. Thousands of such examples could be cited.

Explicit and Implicit Costs

The economic costs to society of producing a good or service do not necessarily coincide with its accounting costs. As an example, consider a small family-owned grocery store for which the labor is provided by the owning family. A large part of the costs of resources used by the store to put groceries in the hands of consumers—costs of grocery stocks, utilities, and the like—is indeed accounting costs, but some resource costs may be omitted from the accounting records. The costs of labor are not likely to be listed. Amortization and depreciation costs on the land, building, furniture, and fixtures also may be omitted. The family may simply take what is left after the out-of-pocket expenses are paid, calling this remainder *profit*.

The costs of resources bought and hired for carrying on the business are called *explicit costs of production*. These are the economic costs that are most likely to be taken into account by the business, since they are usually actual cost outlays.

The **explicit costs of production** are the costs incurred by the producer to buy or hire the resources required to carry on business.

The **implicit costs of production** are the costs incurred by the producer for the use of self-owned, self-employed resources.

The costs of self-owned, self-employed resources (like the labor of the family in the example) are called *implicit costs of production*. They tend to be hidden or ignored as costs. Implicit costs of a resource can be identified by using the opportunity cost principle. What the resource would be worth in its best alternative use is determined; this is its cost to the owner-user. If the family members had used their labor working for someone else, this labor would have produced other goods and services and would have earned income about equal to the value of those other goods and services.

So the cost of self-employed labor is what it could have earned in its best alternative employment.

Given this, the true cost to society of producing a good or service, what we call the opportunity cost, can only be accurately measured if one takes into account both the explicit and implicit costs of the activity. Always recall—although accounting costs are often readily available, they are only reliable measures of opportunity cost if an activity involves no implicit costs. And this is very unlikely.

The Costs of Higher Educational Services

From the point of view of the society as a whole, the services of higher education are not free. Resources used in their production could have been used to produce other goods and services, and the value of these forgone goods and services is the economic cost of higher education. In this section we try to pin down the nature of those costs and identify who pays them.

The Explicit Costs

The explicit costs of the services provided by a college or university are the costs of the resources that it buys and hires to provide those services. These are the costs of capital resources and labor resources. The university uses land, buildings, equipment, and supplies. It also uses professors, maintenance personnel, administrators, secretaries, and clerks.

The institution's annual budget provides a first approximation of the annual explicit costs of its services. The budget should include amortization costs of major capital outlays, depreciation costs, small-equipment costs, maintenance costs, and the costs of hundreds of kinds of supplies. It should also include the wages and salaries of labor resources used.

The true explicit costs are the values of the resources used by the institution in their best alternative uses. This should be interpreted with some degree of caution. The economic cost of a university's buildings is not what the value of the buildings would be if the university were to close its doors. Rather, it is the value of the goods and services that were forgone in order to build and maintain the building. Whether or not the institution's explicit costs are reflected accurately by its accounting records depends upon the accounting procedures it uses.

Additional explicit costs of education to students, apart from the costs of inputs used by colleges and universities in providing educational services, consist of student outlays for various items necessary or desirable in the educational process and unique to it. These include books, notebooks, calculators, pencils, pens, paper, and the like. They also include clothing and entertainment costs that would not have been incurred in nonacademic lifestyles.

The Implicit Costs

The costs to a society of producing higher educational services greatly exceed the explicit costs discussed above. To obtain educational services, most students withdraw their labor wholly or partly from the labor force, thus reducing the amounts of other goods and services available to the society. In order to be students, they sacrifice some of what they could have earned as workers, and society sacrifices the value of the goods and services they would have produced had they been working. These forgone earnings, or the equivalent forgone GDP, are implicit costs to the student and to society of the educational services obtained by the student. They do not show up in the institution's budget or books of account.

Sources of Support

One of the unique economic features in the production and sale of higher educational services in the United States is the diversity of the sources tapped to pay the costs. Those who have taken on the responsibility of providing higher educational services have traditionally not been willing—or able—to leave them subject to market forces. Neither public nor private universities charge their customers the full explicit costs of the educational services provided, but the extent to which they approach full costing of those services is a key difference between the two types of institutions.

Public Institutions.   State and community colleges and universities depend heavily on *government sources* to meet their explicit costs. For the academic year 1994–1995, governments provided 69 percent of their current funds revenues. Almost four-fifths came from state governments, almost one-fifth came from the federal government, and local governments supplied the rest.[2]

   Tuition and *fees* as a means of meeting explicit costs are relatively low at most public educational institutions. Usually state colleges and universities charge higher tuition rates for out-of-state than for in-state students, indicating that state appropriations are a substitute for tuition to which they believe only the citizens of the state are entitled. About 25 percent of public institution funds came from this source in 1994–1995.[3]

   To a relatively small extent, public institutions depend on *private donors* to help meet their explicit costs. Funds are received from donors as endowment gifts, cash grants, scholarship gifts, and the like. The donors include foundations, corporations, philanthropists, and alumni who can

---

[2]U.S. Department of Education, National Center for Educational Statistics, *Digest of Education Statistics, 1997*, December 1997, Table 328.
   [3]Ibid.

be convinced that they are contributing to a worthwhile cause. To the public institution, funds from donors, rather than being a primary source of support, tend to be the frosting on the cake that enables it to engage in some activities that no-nonsense legislative appropriations will not permit. In 1994–1995, about 6 percent of public institution funds came from private donations.[4]

Even at public colleges and universities, students and their families must pay the implicit costs of educational services. If a student does not work at all, the forgone earnings or forgone goods and services for the society as a whole are implicit costs. If the student works part-time, the implicit costs are the difference between what could have been earned and what is actually earned. If the husband or wife of a student is forced to accept unemployment or less remunerative employment at the college or university site than could have been obtained elsewhere, forgone earnings will be larger than those for the student alone.

Private Institutions.   Private colleges and universities, since they do not typically receive state appropriations, must meet much of their explicit costs from the payment of *tuition* and *fees.* About 53 percent came from this source in 1994–1995.[5] Contributions from *private donors* are also an important source of support—the more they can secure from this source, the less pressure there is to rely on tuition and the better able they are to compete with the low tuition rates of public institutions. Seeking funds from donors is always a major activity of private institutions. They obtained about 17 percent of their explicit costs from donors in 1994–1995.[6]

Government grants to private educational institutions vary widely from school to school. Those that are research-oriented have secured sizable research grants. Many schools receive very little from government sources. For private schools in total, about 21 percent of their funds were obtained from government in 1994–1995.[7]

The implicit costs of educational services are the same for private as for public institutions. They amount to the forgone earnings of students.

The Incidence of the Costs

Where do the costs of producing the services of higher education finally rest? Table 3–1 is a rough estimate of the incidence of costs for a typical good public institution and a typical good private institution. We assume that the kinds and qualities of services provided are the same for each

---

[4]Ibid.
[5]Ibid.
[6]Ibid.
[7]Ibid.

Table 3–1	Estimated per student annual cost of higher education by type of institution and source of support		
		Private	**Public**
Explicit costs			
Tuition and fees (student and family)		$ 4,550	$ 1,500
Government appropriations, grants, and contracts (taxpayers)		2,650	7,000
Private gifts, grants, contracts, and endowment income (donors)		1,800	500
Books and miscellaneous items (student and family)		1,500	1,500
Total explicit costs		10,500	10,500
Implicit costs			
Forgone income (student and family)		13,000	13,000
Total costs		23,500	23,500

Note: We assume equal sizes and qualities of the public and the private institution.

institution and that each is equally efficient in providing them. Three features of the incidence of costs are significant.

First, implicit costs are a very large part of the total costs of the educational services provided a student. They amount to about 55 percent of the total costs. Note that they are the same whether the student attends a public or private institution.

Second, the major source of support for the explicit costs of public institutions is government appropriations, whereas that for private institutions is tuition and fees. Except for scholarship holders, the burden of tuition and fees rests on students and their families. Government appropriations are made from general revenue funds in any given state and consist of money collected from taxpayers of the state; consequently, the incidence of this large part (over one-half) of the explicit costs of public institutions rests on taxpayers rather than on students and their families. Public institutions, then, bring about a shift in the incidence of over one-half of the explicit costs of higher educational services from students and their families to taxpayers.

Third, private institutions rely more heavily on donors as a source of support than do public institutions. To the extent that funds can be obtained from donors and substituted for tuition, the incidence of explicit costs is shifted from students and their families to donors. About 20 percent of the incidence of explicit costs of private institutions is shifted from students and their families to donors.

Economic Evaluation of the Problems

Although the economic framework established in the preceding sections permits the problems of higher education to be approached in a systematic and logical way, it does not always provide clear-cut, correct solutions. Economic analysis helps determine what causes what, and why. It helps determine, once goals have been set, the most efficient way of reaching those goals. However, economic analysis cannot always provide answers as to what the goals or objectives in higher education or any other activity should be. Equally intelligent people often disagree on the goals that should be sought by a particular society.

What Kinds of Services?

Are our expectations realistic with respect to the kinds of services higher education should produce? Of course they are! The industry can produce whatever mix of services we as a society want it to produce. The important economic problem is concerned with how well institutions respond to the society's desires or demands for those services.

Economic analysis generates questions as to how responsive the current structure of higher educational institutions permits them to be in meeting societal demands. By and large, throughout the economic system consumers register their demands for goods and services by the ways in which they dispose of or spend their purchasing power. Suppliers respond to the array of prices that result. Is this the way in which the mix of programs that are offered by colleges and universities is determined? Obviously not.

Colleges and universities make little or no use of the price system or market forces in determining what programs they will offer. Their officials usually try to offer what they think the society wants—business, engineering, computer science, and the like. Of course, the desires of students and their families must be taken into consideration; otherwise, the enrollments would not be forthcoming. In addition, in public institutions that depend heavily on legislative appropriations, the desires of the legislature are of great importance. The legislature can threaten to withhold appropriations that might be used to expand programs of which the majority of its members may disapprove. In private institutions major donors may be able to influence programs offered; however, the interest of students and their families are likely to receive prime consideration because they represent the main source of revenue to private schools.

One wonders why the price system is so completely ignored or snubbed in determining program priorities. Most colleges and universities charge the same price (tuition) to all students, regardless of the program of study pursued. College and university administrators and faculties, legislators, and students themselves seem to believe that this is the equitable way to operate the system. Yet a little reflection will reveal its inefficiency.

Differential Pricing Based on Differences in Demand.   Consider two possible undergraduate programs, say business administration and agriculture. Suppose that initially, student demand for agricultural programs is represented by $D_{a1}D_{a1}$ in Figure 3–2. The price per person per year is a

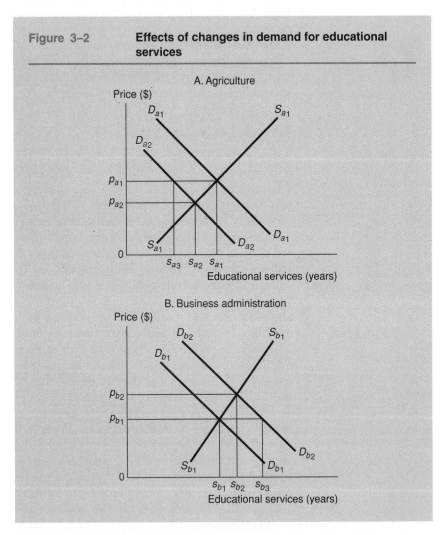

Figure 3–2   **Effects of changes in demand for educational services**

A. Agriculture

B. Business administration

$D_{a1}D_{a1}$ and $S_{a1}S_{a1}$ are the initial demand and supply curves for years of agricultural education, whereas in business administration they are $D_{b1}D_{b1}$ and $S_{b1}S_{b1}$. Now, suppose that demand for business administration increases to $D_{b2}D_{b2}$ and demand for agriculture falls to $D_{a2}D_{a2}$. Maintaining explicit costs (tuition and fees) at p_{b1} and p_{a1} results in a surplus of agricultural education capacity and a shortage of business administration capacity. Letting the tuition and fees for business administration rise to p_{b2} and those for agriculture fall to p_{a2} will result in increasing the efficiency with which both are utilized.

composite of all costs except implicit costs to the student for a year of the program. The demand curve for agricultural programs would be expected to slope downward to the right as do most demand curves—the lower the price of the program, the larger the quantity of years of it students will demand. The supply curve $S_{a1}S_{a1}$ of agricultural programs would be expected to slope upward to the right. The more money per year universities can obtain from the sale of such programs, the more resources they can attract and use to expand them. The demand curve $D_{b1}D_{b1}$ and the supply curve $S_{b1}S_{b1}$ for business administration programs are conceptually the same as those for agricultural programs. Ignore $D_{b2}D_{b2}$ for the time being. Suppose that by some great coincidence, the initial supply and demand curves for both programs are such that the prices are the same for each; that is, p_{a1} equals p_{b1}. The program sizes are s_{a1} and s_{b1}, respectively.

Now, let student demand for business administration programs increase relative to that for agricultural programs. The business administration demand curve shifts to $D_{b2}D_{b2}$, and the agricultural demand curve shifts to $D_{a2}D_{a2}$. What are the effects of maintaining equal prices for the two programs as colleges and universities now tend to do? At price p_{b1}, universities cannot expand business administration programs and cover the costs of doing so. A shortage of business administration faculty and facilities will result. Classes will be larger and rooms will be more crowded. The quality of instruction will deteriorate. In agriculture programs, at price p_{a1} class sizes will decrease and facilities will be less fully utilized. There is a surplus of faculty and facilities. Shortages and surpluses of these types are common in colleges and universities today, representing inefficiencies in the production of educational services as institutions fail to allow the price system to allocate resources efficiently.

If universities were to use a differential pricing scheme for different programs, they could increase both efficiency and responsiveness to customers. Let tuition and fees in business administration rise to p_{b2}. Additional revenue is obtained to expand to s_{b2}, taking care of the increased demand. The price increase also serves to reduce the pressure on facilities by reducing enrollment from s_{b3} to s_{b2}. Let tuition and fees in agriculture fall to p_{a2}. Universities have an incentive to cut programs back to s_{a2}, at which they are once more just covering costs. Additionally, the decrease in the price in agriculture from p_{a1} to p_{a2} will increase the enrollment in agriculture from s_{a3} to s_{a2}.

To make the preceding economic analysis more general, suppose that in universities a demand arises for a program that has previously not existed—say, for ecology studies. Costs of supplying different numbers of years of the program can be determined, and the supply curve can then be matched up with the demand curve. The resulting equilibrium price will reflect the costs of the program and the values of the program to students. It will also generate the correct program capacity, reflecting neither a shortage nor a surplus.

Increases in Tuition and the Price Elasticity of Demand.

Differential pricing schemes in response to differing levels of demand for alternative academic programs clearly would allow school administrations to operate both more efficiently and responsively to their customers. As noted in the introduction to this chapter, and something that you are undoubtedly aware of, many public school systems are increasing tuition and fees rapidly in the face of reduced infusions of money from other sources, primarily government aid. In fact, between 1980 and 1990, tuition and fees as a percentage of current operating funds at public colleges and universities rose in relative importance by 20 percent. While tuition and fees have also been rising in importance at private schools, the increase during the same period has been less than half as great. The rationale is clear—to maintain revenues at the levels perceived to be necessary to fulfill their missions in the face of budget cuts from government appropriations, students in public colleges and universities are being asked to carry more of the burden.

But will this strategy work? That is, will public schools actually take in more revenue from tuition and fees when they increase tuition rates? The answer would seem to be an obvious yes, but recall that the law of demand is not suspended simply because we are discussing higher education. Reconsider Figure 3–2. The law of demand, as expressed through any of the various demand curves of this figure, clearly indicates that, other things being equal, as tuition rises, enrollment falls. That is, if other things remain the same, increases in tuition at public schools will cause some individuals to choose alternative sources of education (private, trade, or whatever) and others to simply discontinue their educations. The amount of tuition revenue taken in is determined not just by the tuition rate, but also by enrollment. Whether tuition revenues rise, fall, or remain unchanged in response to a tuition increase is determined by the relative strengths of the changes in the two key variables: the tuition rate and enrollment. The economic term for the relationship between these two variables is the *price elasticity of demand*, which is defined as the percentage change that occurs in the quantity demanded of a good or service divided by the percentage change in its price. Suppose that tuition increased by 10 percent and in response enrollment fell by 5 percent. The price elasticity of demand for educational services would have a coefficient of negative one-half, which would imply that for each 1 percent increase in tuition, enrollment could be expected to fall by one-half of 1 percent.

Price elasticity of demand is a measure of the responsiveness of consumers to price changes and is equal to the percentage change in the quantity demanded divided by the percentage change in the price of the product.

The law of demand indicates that as tuition rises, enrollment would fall. But will the fall in enrollment be sufficient to offset the tuition increase and actually leave the school or university in a position to take in less tuition than it had prior to the tuition increase? A good estimate of the price elasticity of demand for higher educational services gives an answer to the question.

Consider the two possible situations detailed in Table 3–2. In each we start with an initial enrollment of 5,000 students and tuition of $2,000 per

Table 3–2	Tuition rates, revenues, and the price elasticity of demand				
	Situation One		Situation Two		
	Before	After	Before	After	
Tuition	$ 2,000	$ 2,200	$ 2,000	$ 2,200	
Enrollment	5,000	4,750	5,000	4,250	
Tuition revenue	$10,000,000	$10,450,000	$10,000,000	$9,350,00	

year, yielding tuition revenues to the school of $10 million per year. Now suppose, in response to cuts in other support, the administration increases tuition by 10 percent to $2,200. In situation one, enrollment falls by 5 percent to 4,750, and in situation two, enrollment falls by 15 percent to 4,250. What happened to tuition revenues? The bottom row shows tuition revenues rising in the first case by $450,000 and *falling* in the second by $650,000. What is the reasoning behind these very different outcomes? The answer is found in differing price elasticities of demand. Specifically, the price elasticity of demand in the first situation was −½ while in the second it was 3 times as great, in absolute terms, −1½. (You should confirm these calculations.) Put in less technical terms, the consumers responded much more negatively to the tuition increase in the second situation than the first, leaving tuition revenues actually lower after the tuition increase than before.

Whether tuition revenues increase, remain the same, or fall in response to a tuition rate increase, then, is determined by how responsive students are to that tuition increase. In general terms, if the coefficient of price elasticity exceeds 1, in absolute value, we say that demand is relatively elastic at the current price, and a tuition rise will actually leave the school taking in less revenue than it would without the tuition increase. Intuitively, what is happening in this case is that the revenue-enhancing effect of the tuition increases is more than offset by the revenue-draining effect of the enrollment fall. Such was the case in situation two. Alternatively, when the coefficient is less than 1 in absolute terms, demand is said to be relatively inelastic at the current price, and a tuition increase does lead to the desired increase in revenues from tuition. Completing the picture, a situation might exist where, at a specific price, the coefficient is equal to 1 in absolute terms, and in such a situation, a tuition increase will bring about an offsetting enrollment fall that leads to no change in the school's tuition revenue. In this case, we say that the price elasticity of demand is unitary.

How should schools and universities use this information? Clearly, tuition increases in the face of relatively elastic demand make little sense

if the goal is to increase tuition revenue. There is a more interesting implication, however, which couples the notion of price elasticity with differential tuitions as discussed above. Experience with public schools over the
past decade indicates that administrators feel that when tuition is to be increased, the most effective means of doing so is with a simple across-the-
board increase. Although this approach is, no doubt, based on some
notion of equity, there may be a more efficient, market-oriented approach.

Differential Pricing and the Price Elasticity of Demand.   Consider
a school or university with a strong clinical technician program (from any
of the biological/medical fields) and also a strong accounting program.
Further suppose that, in response to cuts in government funding, the administration is planning to impose a substantial tuition increase. Finally,
suppose that, from past experience, it is known that the demand for these
programs at current price levels is relatively price-inelastic overall; thus,
the proposed tuition increase would achieve the goal of increasing tuition
revenue. Does it follow that the most effective method of increasing tuition is the across-the-board method preferred by most administrations?
The answer depends on the relative price elasticities of demand for the
two programs, clinical technician and accounting. That is, while the overall price elasticity for all the school's students might be relatively inelastic,
there may be extreme differences between the elasticity for accounting
students versus clinical technician students.

Although many factors influence the degree of price elasticity of demand for any good or service, two tend to be most important with respect
to higher education: (1) the proportion of the consumer's income taken by
the good or service and (2) the availability of substitutes. There would
seem to be no reason for elasticity differences based on the first between
accounting and the clinical technician programs. That is, given our tendency toward uniform tuition rates, the proportion of income taken by
tuition is roughly the same for the accounting student as it is for the clinical technician student. The availability of substitutes is quite a different
matter, however. If one wishes to be a professionally certified accountant,
there is but one avenue to proceed and that is through a formal, accredited
accounting program. In fact, certification into the profession explicitly requires a carefully specified course of study. In this type of situation in
which there simply are no good substitutes, demand tends to be very
price-inelastic, and any tuition increase would likely lead to a significant
increase in tuition revenues.

Compare this with the situation for a student with a clinical technician major. Although an academic technician program is an excellent en-
trée into the profession, it is by no means necessary. Numerous vocational
and technical schools offer programs that are, more or less, substitutes for
the clinical technician programs offered by colleges and universities.
When substitutes abound, demand tends to be relatively price-elastic,

and any tuition increase would likely lead to a significant fall in tuition revenues.

Given this, what should an administration do if its goal is to maximize tuition revenue through a tuition increase? It must identify those programs for which demand tends to be highly inelastic and require those programs to bear the brunt of the tuition increase, leaving programs with relatively elastic demands less affected. Can you come up with a list of programs that might fall into the two camps? In any case, the point to be made is that the use of the price system could aid not only in responsiveness to consumer demands, but also in funding decisions. It remains remarkable that this valuable tool is so often neglected.

How Much Service?

Economic analysis provides a conceptual answer to how much educational service the economy should produce relative to other goods and services. The resources used in producing educational services can be used to produce other goods and services, and from the opportunity cost principle, the costs of educational services are the values of those resources in their best alternative uses. Consequently, if the value to society of a unit of educational services is greater than its costs—the resources used in producing it are more valuable in the production of education than in alternative ones—then the output of educational services should be expanded. On the other hand, if the value of a unit of educational services is worth less to the society than it costs to produce it, the output should be reduced.

In terms of demand-supply analysis, let DD represent the demand curve for higher educational services and SS be the supply curve for them in Figure 3–3. If the economy is presently providing a quantity of s_1 years, the value of a unit to demanders (students) is v_1, but the cost of a unit to the society is c_1. The excess of the value of a year's education over its cost indicates that resources needed to produce a year of education are more valuable if they are so used than they would be in their best alternative uses. Educational services should be expanded relative to the production of other goods and services in the economy. The correct amount of educational services for the society is s_2 priced at p_2 per year. What can you say about quantity s_3?

The value of higher education services in relation to their costs is obscured by the way they are provided currently. Higher education services are not priced in the marketplace in a way that will cause the quantity supplied to be adjusted to the quantity demanded. On the demand side, it is difficult, if not impossible, for students in the present system to make known how they value alternative quantities of educational services. The combination of public and private sources of support on the supply side compounds the difficulties of valuing educational services and of determining how much should be produced.

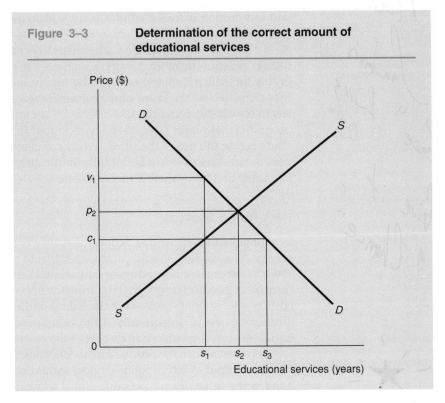

Figure 3–3   **Determination of the correct amount of educational services**

If s_1 years of educational services are provided in the society, the value of a year exceeds its cost, indicating that an expansion of services is in order. At the s_2 level of services, the value of a year is equal to the costs of providing it. The correct amount for the society is s_2.

On the demand side, consider potential students who want educational services in some specific field—say medical training. In medical schools throughout the country, the annual number of openings for students is limited. At current levels of costs per student, many more want training than can be accepted; that is, there is a shortage of medical training services. This is the same thing as saying that potential medical students would be willing to pay more for the services of medical schools than they are now required to pay. However, students are not permitted to bid up the price at which these educational services are offered, and hence the price system cannot express their valuations of them. The same kind of analysis holds true for many other fields of specialization.

The supply of educational services made available by public higher education institutions is not a direct response to student demands. The amounts supplied are determined primarily by the appropriations public institutions receive from state legislatures rather than by what students are willing to pay. Colleges and universities compete with a number of other state-supported activities for the dollars that legislatures have available to appropriate, and since state revenues are limited, they will never receive as much as educational administrators think they ought to have. At the same time, such public institutions are reluctant to supplement the funds received from the state with tuition receipts. Tuition is supposed to be kept low because of state appropriations—this is the purpose of the state-allocated funds. The higher the tuition rates set by the public institutions, the less will be their bargaining power with the legislature for state-appropriated funds.

State colleges and universities can be expected to encounter a continuous financial crisis. The services they can supply are limited by the always inadequate appropriations received from the state, while the demands for their services are augmented as they succumb to the pressure to keep their tuition rates low.

At the same time, the relatively low tuition rates of the public institutions enable them to draw students away from private institutions. The competition of public institutions limits the services that can be provided by private institutions. It also sets upper limits on the tuition rates that private institutions can charge and still remain in business. Pressure on private institutions to obtain gifts, grants, and the like is increased. Competition from public institutions makes it very difficult for some private colleges and universities to stay solvent.

Who Should Pay?

The controversy over who should pay for higher educational services is undoubtedly the key problem faced by higher education. If this problem could be resolved, answers to "what kind?" and "how much?" would be much easier to determine. At one extreme of the controversy are those who maintain that educational services should be *above* market forces. Education is seen as the great equalizer, providing opportunities for self-development and self-realization. Everyone is entitled to as much education as one is able to absorb, and, consequently, educational services should be free. At the other extreme are those who believe that each student and family should bear the full costs of that student's education.

"Free" Education.   What is meant by "free" education? The economic aspects of higher education discussed in this chapter make it clear that there is no such thing from society's point of view. Neither is education free, from the individual student's point of view—unless, of course, both explicit and implicit costs are covered by scholarships. Ordinarily education is said to be free if state appropriations to state colleges and universities are large enough so that no tuition is charged. In most states, public colleges and universities are not tuition-free; state appropriations simply permit them to charge substantially lower tuition than do private institutions.

The differences in costs between what is generally called a free education in a state college or university and what is called a full-cost education in a private college or university are nowhere near as great as tuition differentials would lead us to believe. In the example in Table 3–1, the annual costs borne by the student and family in a public institution would be about $16,000, while in the private institution they would be about $19,000.

State Support of Higher Education.   In terms of economic analysis, state support of higher education means that some part of the costs of obtaining educational services is shifted from the student who receives the services to taxpayers. State appropriations to the college or university decrease the tuition that students are required to pay. Funds appropriated to the institution by the state are obtained from taxpayers. Thus, state support constitutes a *transfer* of purchasing power from taxpayers to college and university students.

Under what circumstances do such transfers seem to be in order? They appear defensible: (1) to the extent that positive social spillovers in consumption are generated by higher education and (2) as a means of enabling children of the poor to develop their human resources.

When the consumption or utilization of some good or service by one or more people results in positive social spillovers, those who receive the spillovers are in a good position to be *free riders.* Direct consumers of an item pay for the direct benefits they receive; otherwise, they will not be able to obtain whatever it is they want to consume. Those who receive the positive social spillovers do so whether they pay anything or not; their tendency is to be free riders and pay nothing. Direct consumers are in no position to force the free riders to pay, but what they cannot do as individual private citizens they may be able to accomplish collectively through their government. The government can levy taxes on the free riders, thus coercing them to pay for the positive spillovers they receive. The government is a unique and logical agency to accomplish this purpose.

> Those who receive the benefits of a positive social spillover in consumption are said to be **free riders** since they do not pay any part of the production costs of the good or service.

To the extent that positive social spillovers in consumption from higher educational services exist, the use of state taxing powers and state support of higher education sufficient to pay for those spillovers would seem to be reasonable. Several questions arise. Most importantly, remember that there is much controversy as to the value of social spillovers from higher educational services in consumption, given the difficulties associated with their identification and measurement. Further, to the extent that such spillovers exist, they are undeniably generated by private colleges and universities as well as by public institutions. On these grounds, should not the higher education provided by private universities be subsidized to about the same extent as that provided by state universities?

The other major argument for state support of higher education is that it enables capable but poor students to obtain a college or university education. Education serves to increase the capacities of human resources to produce and to earn income. Since poor families do not have the means to pay for higher education for their children, and this is not the fault of the children, the state can do much to enable them to escape from poverty by providing them with the same kind of educational opportunities that are available to the children of middle- and upper-income families.

The case has much merit. One of the generally recognized functions of government in the modern world is that of mitigating poverty. In the United States, very substantial parts of both state and federal budgets are geared to this purpose. Welfare programs, along with income taxes that are intended to take larger proportions of the incomes of the rich than of the poor, provide examples. It seems reasonable that state support of higher education for the poor should be an integral and important part of any antipoverty program.

Although state support looms large in meeting the explicit costs of educational services in public institutions, the implicit costs that still must be met by the student and the student's family are a very substantial part of the total costs. The inability of a poor family to meet the implicit costs— the need for children to go to work and earn income—discourages the children of the poor from attending any college or university, public or private. For the most part, state-supported colleges and universities are not devices for transferring purchasing power from taxpayers to children of the poor. Most college and university students do not come from poor families; they come from middle- and upper-income families. For the academic year 1997–1998, for example, it is estimated that about 65 percent of incoming freshmen were from families earning more than $40,000.[8] Most of the transfer, then, is from taxpayers in general to middle- and upper-income families. If legislatures are serious about using higher educational services as part of an antipoverty program, they must be prepared to use tax revenues to offset the implicit costs of these services as well as the explicit.

Student Self-Support.   Many people believe that students and their families rather than the state should bear the costs of higher education. This does not necessarily mean abandonment of state institutions. A state-owned college or university can recover the full costs of education through tuition and fees levied on students just as a private one can. There are two main arguments why students should pay for their own education. These are that (1) those who benefit are the ones who should pay and (2) economic resources would be used more efficiently; that is, some waste would be avoided.

---

[8]*The Chronicle of Higher Education*, August 28, 1998, p. 22.

The argument that those who benefit should pay is an equity argument. It asks why one group of persons—taxpayers—should be forced to pay a part of the educational costs of another group—students and their families. To be sure, there will be overlapping of the two groups; students and their families are also taxpayers. However, a much larger proportion of taxpayers are not college and university students, and neither are their children. Many of these are poor families. Is it equitable for the state to levy taxes that rest partly on poorer nonstudent families to help pay for the education of children from middle-income and wealthy families?

The argument maintains further that investment in human capital is essentially comparable to investment in material capital. Suppose a high school graduate has a choice of investing in an education or investing in a business. One considers the payoff of each in terms of future well-being and makes the choice that one (and one's family) thinks will yield the highest return on the investment. This is the way that intelligent economic decision making should be accomplished. Ordinarily we do not expect taxpayers to bear a part of the investments of high school graduates in businesses. Why should we expect them to bear a part of such investments in higher education?

Another argument for student self-support is that people tend to waste whatever is free to them and to economize or conserve whatever they have to pay for. The greater the cost of a purchase relative to one's income, the more incentive one has to use the item carefully in order to increase the possible returns from it. This is said to be the premise underlying high charges made by psychiatrists for their services. The argument is used extensively by those who think students should pay for their own education.

If higher educational services are provided at reduced or free tuition costs to students, the incentive to economize on or make the best possible use of the resources providing those services is weakened—so the argument runs. Low tuition induces students who have no interest in learning to attend the university, whereas higher tuition charges would make them or their parents think more carefully about whether or not they should do so. Further, those who do attend would be inclined to make more of their opportunities if they cost more.

Which Way?   Which of the arguments is correct? If the student and family reap the benefits of higher education—that is, if the benefits of higher education are primarily private human capital development and direct consumption—then a strong case can be made that the student and family should pay its full costs. If substantial social spillover benefits result from putting some part of the population through the processes of higher education, or if higher education is used effectively as a campaign against poverty, a strong case can be made for shifting a part of its costs to taxpayers.

An Alternative Institutional Structure

When an activity such as higher education has been pursued over a long period of time, a set of institutions is developed to carry on the activity. The structure of the set that evolves becomes very difficult to change. First, people think in terms of the structure to which they have become accustomed and find it hard to think in terms of alternatives. Second, the performance of the present structure is known; the alternative might not work. Third, many people build up vested interests in the existing structure and can be expected to resist changes that would affect them.

The possibility that the institutional structure of higher education in the United States is outmoded is worth considering. Nearly 80 percent of college and university students in the United States are enrolled in public institutions that receive the bulk of their support from legislative appropriations. The rationale for the state-supported system is that (1) it makes higher education available to the children of poor families and (2) it increases the social spillovers in consumption from higher education by encouraging large enrollments. As we have argued, it does not appear to serve either of these purposes very well. The implicit costs of higher education are so great that even with the low tuition rates of public institutions, few children of the poor find it possible to attend. It seems likely that the most important effect of the low tuition rates of public institutions is to divert students from private to public institutions rather than to bring about any substantial increase in enrollment in all institutions. In addition, the present system does not enable society to place accurate demand values on the services being provided, nor does it provide the mechanism for colleges and universities to be responsive to the demands of the society.

An alternative to the present higher education institutional structure is one that would make greater use of the price system in the production of higher educational services. A key feature of such an alternative is that students obtaining educational services would pay tuition to the colleges and universities they attend sufficient to cover the full explicit costs of the services obtained. There would be no differentiation between private and public institutions in this respect. If public institutions were to remain in operation, they would be required to pay their own way without obtaining direct appropriations from legislatures.

If society desires to help the children of the poor to obtain educational services, it could do so easily and directly. Instead of allocating money to public colleges and universities, legislatures could make grants directly to the children of the poor, letting them choose for themselves the institutions they would attend. Presumably they would attend the institutions that best meet their needs. The antipoverty aspects of state support would be realized directly and efficiently. The state would not be supporting those who are not in need; with the present system, many of those it supports are not in need since state appropriations to public schools hold tuition levels down for all students.

If, because of positive social spillovers in consumption, the state desires to encourage larger enrollments than would occur if all students were required to pay the full costs of the services they obtain, this also can be done easily and directly. By raising the minimum income standards used to define what constitutes a poor family, the state can increase the number of students eligible for state support. Besides tuition scholarships to meet explicit costs, various devices now in use can continue to assist students from low-income families in meeting their implicit costs. These include access to loan funds and part-time employment.

Such an institutional structure could go far toward solving the problems that confront higher education. It would attack the problem of who should pay, moving toward a structure in which those who receive the benefits are the ones who pay the costs. But note that this *does not* preclude using the system of higher education as a part of an antipoverty program, nor does it preclude government (taxpayer) support of higher education. Government support would contribute more directly and more efficiently to making higher education available to the children of the poor.

Such a structure would also move toward a solution of the perpetual financial crisis of higher education. Government support of higher educational services—whatever the amount of support the society desires—would be provided to students and not to institutions. This would eliminate the primary cause of the crisis—the support of public institutions by the state, which, although usually thought to be inadequate, entails low-tuition competition and attendant financial problems for private institutions.

Further, it would tend to induce the education industry to supply the quantity of educational services the society wants relative to the quantities of other goods and services produced in the economy. Tuition would be the main source of revenue for institutions; it would cover the full explicit costs of services supplied. Colleges and universities would supply services to as many persons as are willing to pay that tuition. Persons not willing to pay the full tuition are saying in effect that alternative ways of spending that amount of money yield greater satisfaction to them.

Finally, the proposed institutional structure should be responsive to its clientele—students and their families. Institutions not responsive to the wants of students and their families would lose students to those that are. Competition among institutions for students' tuition should generate greater efficiency and a variety of innovations in programs and in the techniques of providing educational services.

Summary

Colleges and universities face many problems, most of them stemming from four fundamental issues: (1) what kinds of services they should provide, (2) how much service should be provided, (3) what is appropriate institutional structure, and (4) who should pay for it. These are issues about which economic analysis has much to say.

Institutions of higher education use resources to produce educational services. These services provide (1) investment in human capital, (2) direct consumption benefits, and (3) social spillovers in consumption. By far, the greatest part of educational services appears to be composed of investment in human capital. There is controversy over the extent to which positive social spillovers in consumption exist, but these are not likely to be a large part of the total. The first-order benefits of educational services accrue mainly to the student who obtains them, although society gains from secondary benefits just as it does from investment in material capital.

Higher educational services, like other goods and services, have economic costs. All economic costs are measured by the opportunity cost principle. Some costs are explicit in nature, while others are implicit. The explicit costs of higher education services are the costs of the capital and labor resources used by colleges and universities. Most people view these as the total costs. However, to students and their families there are implicit costs that are greater in amount than the explicit costs. Most important of these are the forgone earnings of students and their families.

Sources of support (payment of explicit costs) for higher educational institutions in the United States are different for public than for private institutions. Structurally, the system of institutions consists of public institutions, which receive the bulk of their revenues in the form of state legislative appropriations, and private institutions, which receive the bulk of their revenues from tuition. The implicit costs to students do not enter into college and university budgets and are the same whether they attend public or private institutions. The incidence of the costs of higher educational services rests most heavily on the student and family, even in public institutions, despite their relatively low tuition levels.

An economic evaluation of the fundamental problems involved in the provision of higher educational services highlights several shortcomings of the present institutional structure of higher educational facilities. Public institutions, supported primarily by legislative appropriations, are likely to be more responsive to the demands of legislators than to the demands of students in the determination of what kinds of services should be provided. The amounts of services provided also are determined by legislative appropriations rather than by the economic factors of demand and costs. As a device for making educational opportunities available to the children of the poor, public institutions leave much to be desired.

An alternative structure for higher educational institutions that appears worthy of serious consideration is one in which the tuition rates charged are sufficient to cover all the explicit costs of providing educational services. This would tend to make institutions more responsive to the demands of students and their families. It would tend toward the production of the *correct* amounts of higher educational services, as compared with other goods and services. It would also provide a structure in which state (taxpayer) support of the educational costs of the children of the poor could be met directly and efficiently.

Discussion Questions

1. Based on your own experience, develop a list of the explicit and implicit costs of higher education. From this list, explain why government appropriations to public colleges and universities do relatively little to bring the children of the poor into higher education.
2. At any college or university, certain courses or programs of study are overcrowded but others are not. Explain how this situation could be corrected if administrators made use of market principles.
3. Explain the concept of price elasticity of demand. How might college and university administrators use the concept in deciding whether to increase tuition?
4. Develop a list of programs at your college or university that you think might have relatively price-elastic demands and a list of programs that might have relatively price-inelastic demands. How might administrators use this information?
5. When you purchase a burger and eat it, no one other than you benefits. As such, we expect that you will pay the full cost of producing the burger. Does this logic apply to higher educational services? That is, should the student pay the full cost?
6. A main justification for government support of higher education is positive social spillovers in consumption. Develop a list of the positive social spillovers you think are part of the higher educational process.
7. If positive social spillovers in consumption exist with respect to higher educational services, don't they exist equally for public and private colleges and universities? If so, shouldn't states provide direct funding to private as well as public institutions?
8. Public support of higher education is often defended on grounds of it making college affordable to the children of relatively poor families. Does the current approach to funding seem to achieve this goal effectively?

Additional Readings

Breneman, David W., and Alton L. Taylor. *Strategies for Promoting Excellence in a Time of Scarce Resources*. New Directions for Higher Education, 94. San Francisco: Jossey-Bass Publishers, 1996.
    Seven essays on strategies to improve spending in higher education while maintaining high standards in teaching, research, and service.

Facts About Public Universities: Looking to the Future. Washington, DC: National Association of State Universities and Land Grant Colleges. *Research in Education (RIE),* item ED393356.

Provides a section on the economic advantages of having a college education and discusses key issues that public universities must address in the next years.

Heller, Donald E. "Tuition Prices, Financial Aid, and Access to Public Higher Education: A State-Level Analysis." Paper presented at the annual meeting of the American Educational Research Association (New York: April 8–13, 1996). *Research in Education (RIE),* item ED394469.

Shows the correlation between tuition, financial aid, and access to public higher education through economic analysis of data from states, 1976 to 1993.

Massey, William F., ed. *Resource Allocation in Higher Education.* Ann Arbor: The University of Michigan Press, 1996.

Presents key concepts in resource allocation for colleges and universities.

Psacharopoulos, George, ed. *Economics of Education: Research and Studies.* New York: Pergamon Press, 1987.

Excellent and thorough treatment of the issues raised in this chapter. Especially interesting are the essays concerning the cost-benefit analysis of investment in higher education.

World Wide Web Resources

College and University Home Pages
www.mit.edu:8001/people/cdemello/univ.html

Search college and university home pages alphabetically by state and/or name.

CollegeNET
www.collegenet.com

Links to financial aid and scholarships, virtual campus tours, and colleges and universities in the United States.

National Educational Association (NEA)
www.nea.org

NEA focuses on the advancement of public education. Members of the NEA range from preschool to college and university educators. Provides links to information on teacher salaries, educator resources, the English-only debate, and other sites.

Peterson's Education & Career Center
www.petersons.com

Gives links to colleges and universities, graduate study, summer programs, and financial aid.

United States Department of Education
www.ed.gov

Some of the most requested sites include Title IV School Codes, Direct Loans, NCES (Education Statistics), and Student Guide to Financial Aid.

4

Economics of Crime and Its Prevention

How Much Is Too Much?

Chapter Outline

Checklist of Economic Concepts

Opportunity costs
Individually consumed goods
   and services
Collectively consumed goods
   and services
Semicollectively consumed
   goods and services

Spillovers in consumption,
   social
Spillovers in production, social
"Free rider" problem
Public goods
Cost-benefit analysis

Marginal social benefit
Marginal social cost
Equimarginal principle
Psychic income
Psychic costs

On Thursday, March 17, 1988, at 10:45 P.M., in the Bronx, Vernia Brown was killed by stray bullets fired in a dispute over illegal drugs. The 19-year-old mother of one was not involved in the dispute, yet her death was a direct consequence of the "war on drugs." By now, there can be little doubt that most, if not all, "drug-related murders" are the result of drug prohibition. The same type of violence came with the Eighteenth Amendment's ban of alcohol in 1920. The murder rate rose with the start of Prohibition, remained high during Prohibition, and then declined for 11 consecutive years when Prohibition ended. The rate of assaults with a firearm rose with Prohibition and declined for 10 consecutive years after Prohibition. In the last year of Prohibition—1933—there were 12,124 homicides and 7,863 assaults with firearms; by 1941 these figures had declined to 8,048 and 4,525, respectively.

Vernia Brown died because of the policy of drug prohibition. If, then, her death is a "cost" of that policy, what did the "expenditure" of her life "buy"? What benefits has society derived from the policy of prohibition that led to her death? To find the answer, I turned to the experts and to the supporters of drug prohibition.

In 1988, I wrote to Vice President George Bush, then head of the South Florida Drug Task Force; to Education Secretary William Bennett; to Assistant Secretary of State for Drug Policy Ann Wrobleski; to White House drug policy adviser Dr. Donald I. McDonald; and to the public information directors of the Federal Bureau of Investigation, Drug Enforcement Administration, General Accounting Office, National Institute of Justice, and National Institute on Drug Abuse. None of these officials was able to cite any study that demonstrated the beneficial effects of drug prohibition when weighed against its costs. The leaders of the war on drugs are apparently unable to defend on rational cost-benefit grounds their 70-year-old policy, which costs nearly $10 billion per year (out of pocket), imprisons 75,000 Americans, and fills our cities with violent crime. It would seem that Vernia Brown and many others like her have died for nothing.[1]

[1]James Ostrowski, "Thinking About Drug Legalization," *Policy Analysis*, number 121, May 25, 1989, The Cato Institute.

Criminal activities create an important set of social problems in the United States. They affect our general well-being by threatening the loss of property and by generating concern for our physical safety. In addition, a large share of national output is devoted to crime prevention activities, and resources so used become unavailable for other production processes. As crime rates have increased over the years, public support for "getting tough on crime" has grown as well; as evidenced by the fact that most candidates for political office above the level of city dogcatcher have made crime and its prevention a primary part of their campaigns in recent years.

While there is near unanimity on the importance of the topic, we too often seem to approach it with emotion rather than reason. When increases in the crime rate are reported, we immediately demand increases in the budgets of police forces so that the criminals can be apprehended, without considering whether it might be more beneficial to devote the additional resources to ensuring quick trials and certain incarceration. When we feel that too many crimes are being committed by repeat offenders, we demand long mandatory minimum sentences, without reference to the potentially more violent offenders who must be released to make room for the those with mandatory minimum sentences. When we conclude that we would be better off without certain goods or services in society, we simply outlaw their production, distribution, and use, without reference to any potentially negative side effects that outright prohibition might bring.

While our approach to crime and its prevention is typically rooted in emotion, it is unlikely that we will ever be successful unless we begin to look at these issues in a systematic, analytical way. To do so requires the use of economic analysis along with input from other disciplines—especially the social sciences. In this chapter, we focus on the economic aspects of crime and its prevention, addressing six interrelated questions: (1) What is crime? (2) What role should government play in crime prevention? (3) What is the optimal level of crime prevention activities? (4) How should the resources devoted to crime prevention be allocated among the police, courts, and penal system? (5) What are the overall effects of prohibition? (6) What are the causes of criminal activity?

What Is Crime?

It seems almost silly to raise such a question as "What is crime?" However, if we are to look at crime analytically, we must have a solid base from which to work. The concept of what constitutes criminal activity is often not clear in the mind of any one person and may be ambiguous from one person to another. Some people think of crime in terms of that which is immoral; others think of it in terms of that which is illegal.

Immorality?

Are immoral acts criminal? It is not easy to answer this question. In the first place, many acts do not fall clearly into a moral-immoral classification. In modern societies, some acts are generally considered immoral— murder and most kinds of theft, for example. But the morality of many other acts depends on what group in the society is evaluating them.

Examples of such acts include marijuana smoking, drinking alcoholic beverages, betting on horse races, homosexual activities, and adultery. It is clear from these simple examples that the moral-immoral classification helps little in determining whether or not specific acts are criminal.

Illegality?

A definition that seems to be meaningful and useful analytically is that a criminal act is one the society (or one of its subdivisions) has decided it is better off without and which it has therefore made illegal through laws, ordinances, and the like. It may or may not be immoral. For example, is it immoral to drive 30 miles an hour along a deserted street that is posted for 20 miles an hour, or to run a stop sign at an intersection where there are no other cars, or to catch a fish in a mountain stream before you have obtained a fishing license? As you quickly discover when you are caught, these acts may very well be criminal in nature. On the other hand, if gambling, drinking, and prostitution are immoral, there are many places where they are not illegal and are therefore not criminal.

Acts that are illegal or criminal are designated as such by legislative bodies, such as city councils, state legislatures, and Congress. There are a number of reasons for making certain acts illegal. Some acts may indeed be offensive to the moral standards of a majority of legislators and their constituents. Murder, rape, and theft are cases in point. Others may lead to consequences (in the minds of legislators, at least) of which the doer is ignorant. The consumption of alcohol, cocaine, or heroin thus may be made illegal because legislators fear that those who try them may become addicted, with disastrous consequences to the users. Still other acts are designated illegal in order to prevent chaos or to promote order—violation of established traffic rules, for example. Further, some acts may carry no taint of immorality but may be made illegal because they are considered contrary to the general welfare of the society. Acts of pollution, such as burning your trash within the city limits, illustrate this point.

Classification of Criminal Acts

For purposes of reporting crime rates, the Department of Justice classifies criminal acts as (1) violent crimes and (2) crimes against property. We can add to the classification (3) traffic in illegal goods and services and (4) other crimes. Violent crimes are crimes against persons. They include murder, rape, aggravated assault, and armed robbery. Crimes against property include such things as fraud, burglary, theft, embezzlement, forgery, arson, vandalism, and the like. Traffic in illegal goods and services is made up of dealings in such things as gambling, narcotics, loan-sharking, prostitution, and alcohol. The "other crimes" classification is of course a catchall for everything from nonpayment of alimony to speeding.

Crime is generally thought to be a very serious problem in the United States. In every large city, and in many small ones, people are reluctant to go out at night for fear of being robbed, raped, beaten, or even murdered. Table 4–1 reports the rates of violent, property, and total crime for the period 1977–1995. The data show a pronounced cyclical pattern both for the total crime rate and the violent and property crime subcategories. Although the turning points are not precisely the same for each category, we can roughly summarize by saying that crime increased during the late 1970s, began declining in the early 1980s, and continued to fall until about 1985, at which time it increased again until the early 1990s, and has declined since. Even though the trend suggests a cyclical pattern of crime with periodic ups and downs, it is important to note that the longer-term trend, at least for violent crime, is upward. For example, the most recent peak in violent crime occurred in 1992, when the United States suffered through 758 violent crimes for every 100,000 citizens. The previous peak in violent crime occurred in 1980, when the rate reached 597 per 100,000 citi-

Table 4–1	Crime rate per 100,000 inhabitants, 1977–1995		
Year	Total	Violent Crime	Property Crime
1977	5,080	476	4,602
1978	5,140	498	4,643
1979	5,566	549	5,017
1980	5,950	597	5,353
1981	5,858	594	5,264
1982	5,604	571	5,033
1983	5,175	538	4,637
1984	5,031	539	4,492
1985	5,207	556	4,651
1986	5,480	617	4,863
1987	5,550	610	4,940
1988	5,664	637	5,027
1989	5,741	663	5,078
1990	5,820	732	5,089
1991	5,898	758	5,140
1992	5,660	758	4,903
1993	5,484	747	4,738
1994	5,374	714	4,660
1995	5,278	685	4,593

Source: U.S. Department of Commerce, Bureau of the Census, Statistical Abstract of the United States, 1997, p. 201.

zens. Thus, the general public's continued concern about crime seems well-founded.

The Costs of Crime

That crime has economic costs is certain. The measurement of those costs, however, is at present very inaccurate. First, many criminal activities go unreported. Second, an accurate dollar value cannot be attached to the cost of those crimes that are reported. Nevertheless, estimates of the costs of crime are necessary if decision making regarding the level of crime prevention activities is to have any degree of economic soundness. The better the estimates, the better the decisions that can be made.

The basis for measuring the cost of crime is the opportunity cost principle. The net economic cost of crime to the society is thus the difference between what the gross domestic product (GDP) would be if there were neither criminal nor crime prevention activities and what GDP currently is, given present criminal and crime prevention activities.

Current reports on crime are concerned solely with the number of crimes committed, not with dollar estimates of their costs. To estimate correctly the cost of violent crime, we would start with the loss of earnings (or value of production services rendered) of the victims and of those close to the victims. Obvious costs of crimes against property are the values of property destroyed or damaged. It is not at all clear that there is a comparable direct cost to the society of traffic in illegal goods and services—the production and the sale of these *adds* to the well-being of their consumers but may at the same time impose negative spillovers on the society as a whole. Thus, traffic in illegal goods and services imposes a direct cost on society whenever the production and negative social spillovers in consumption exceed the addition to consumer well-being, whereas the reverse would indicate that such traffic actually provides a direct benefit to society. Additional costs of the whole range of criminal activities consist of the costs of prevention, apprehension, and correction since resources used for these purposes could have been used to produce alternative goods and services valuable to consumers. Many items thought to be costs are really transfers of purchasing power to the perpetrators of the crimes from their victims. In the case of theft, the thief is made better off at the same time that the person from whom the item is stolen is made worse off. Reprehensible as theft may be, it is difficult to conclude that it represents a large net economic cost to society. It may, however, represent sizable costs to the individual victims.

Criminal activities in the aggregate lower GDP below what it would be without them. *Crime prevention activities* should, if effective, raise GDP above the level that it would be in their absence. Crime prevention activities can thus be considered an economic good or service since GDP is

Table 4–2	Expenditures on criminal justice in the United States by level of government, 1992	
Level of Government	Direct Expenditure ($ Millions)	Percent
Federal	$17,423	17.8
State and local	80,247	82.2
Total	97,670	100.0

Source: U.S. Department of Commerce, Bureau of the Census, *Statistical Abstract of the United States, 1997,* p. 213.

higher with them than it would be without them. We can think of crime prevention activities as using productive resources—labor and capital—going into the production process. The costs of these services are measured by applying the opportunity cost principle: The costs of resources used in crime prevention are equal to the value these resources would have had in their best alternative uses. From Table 4–2, we see that the expenditures of federal, state, and local governments for law enforcement and justice were an estimated $97,670 million for 1992, the latest year for which data are available.

In summary, satisfactory measures of the costs of crime, in terms of GDP lost because of it, have not yet been devised. The costs of crime prevention activities can be estimated with a fair degree of accuracy; however, these figures leave out a substantial part of the total costs of crime.

Individually and Collectively Consumed Goods

Would a 5 percent increase in the police force of your city be worth anything to you personally? Would an increase in the number of patrol cars on the city's streets affect you directly? Would it benefit you if there were an increase in the number of courts and judges in the system of justice? Your answers to these questions will be "no," "I don't know," or "possibly."

Such questions lead us logically to a useful threefold classification of the economy's goods and services. The first includes those that are *individually consumed*. The second includes those that are *collectively consumed*. The third is made up of *semicollectively consumed* goods and services.

Individually Consumed Goods

Any good or service that gives satisfaction only to the consumer of it is said to be **individually consumed**.

The concept of individually consumed goods and services is straightforward. It includes those that only directly add to the satisfaction of the person who consumes them. Much of what we consume is of this nature—hamburgers, suntan lotion, pencils, and the like. The person doing the consuming is able to identify the satisfaction received. For example, eating a hamburger gives the eater pleasure and reduces hunger pangs. Finally, individually consumed goods and services are said to be exclusive in that once they are consumed by one person, they are unavailable for others to consume.

Collectively Consumed Goods

Collectively consumed goods and services yield benefits to each person within a group, and no one person in the group can identify the specific part of the benefit he or she receives. In addition, once provided, the benefits of a collectively consumed good or service cannot be excluded from any member of the group.

Collectively consumed goods and services lie at the opposite extreme from those that are individually consumed; in this case, the individual is not able to isolate or identify a specific personal benefit. Consider national defense services. What part of the total defense services provided by the economy can you identify as being consumed by you, and what is your estimate of the resulting increase in your satisfaction or well-being? Services such as these contribute to the welfare of the group to which we belong, but it is not possible to pick out the part of the benefit that accrues specifically to any one person. An additional characteristic of a collectively consumed good is that once it is provided, no individual can be excluded from its benefits. Can the government exclude you from the benefits of national defense?

Many kinds of services produced and consumed by a society are collectively consumed. They include national defense, crime prevention, space exploration, some aspects of public health, and most antipollution measures.

Semicollectively Consumed Goods

Semicollectively consumed goods and services yield satisfaction both to the individual doing the consuming and to others.

Semicollectively consumed goods and services yield identifiable satisfaction to the one who consumes them, but their consumption by one person yields social spillovers in consumption to others as well. My neighbors' consumption of the various items that lead to beautiful landscaping on their property yields satisfaction to me as well as them. When other people in a democratic society consume the services of primary education—learn to read, write, and do arithmetic—they benefit directly, and I benefit, too, because a literate population improves the functioning of democratic processes. When other people purchase sufficient medical care to avoid epidemics, I benefit from their purchases of health care.

A great many items that people consume and that yield direct satisfaction to them also cause the satisfaction of others to rise as the consumption occurs. These benefits to persons other than the direct consumers were identified in Chapter 3 as positive *social spillovers* in consumption. We also noted that the consumption of some semicollectively consumed goods may yield negative *social spillovers in consumption* to persons other than the direct consumers. Cigarette smoking in a restaurant or workplace in which there are nonsmokers may be a case in point.

The "Free-Rider" Problem

An individual who consumes benefits from a collectively consumed good but who pays no part of its cost is said to be a **free rider**.

A society may have difficulty in getting collectively consumed goods produced because of a tendency for some of the beneficiaries of the goods to be *"free riders."* The nature of the free-rider problem can be illustrated by an example from the Old West. On the plains of Oklahoma, Texas, Kansas, and other frontier cattle-raising states, cattle rustling was a serious problem. To deal effectively with the problem in one area (say, the Dodge City environs), it was advantageous for the cattle raisers of the area to band together. They organized vigilante groups of sufficient size to make rustling in the area an exceedingly dangerous business—as a few who were caught and hanged would have testified, if they had been able. All the cattle raisers of the area contributed to the cost of organizing and maintaining the vigilante group.

As the problem was brought under control, however, it became difficult to meet the costs of holding the vigilante group together. Any one rancher was inclined to think that if the others maintained the group, they could not keep the one from benefiting from its activities. If rustlers were afraid to operate in the area, *everyone* benefited, even those who did not help pay the costs. Each rancher, therefore, had an incentive to withdraw support from the group and to become a free rider since no producer, even one who did not pay a part of the costs of protection it provided, could be excluded from its benefits.

Government Production of Collectively Consumed Items

Historically, groups of people have found that in banding together they can do things collectively that they are not able to do as individuals. One of the first things discovered was that the group provides better protection from outsiders than individuals can provide on their own. They also found that group action is well-suited to protecting the members of the group from predators in their midst.

Group action on a voluntary basis is technically possible, of course. The vigilante group of the Old West is an excellent example. But voluntary associations to provide collectively consumed goods have a tendency to fall apart because of the incentives that induce some people to become free riders and because free riders cannot be excluded from the benefits of the good. Thus, the voluntary association is a tenuous mechanism for this purpose.

Supplanting the voluntary association with the coercive association that we call *government* can effectively remedy the free-rider problem. A coercive government unit (and the power of coercion is an essential feature of government) simply requires that all who receive the benefits of a collectively consumed good or the service it provides should pay appropriate taxes for it. Thus, the provision of national defense, crime prevention, pollution prevention and cleanup, and other collectively consumed goods and services becomes a government function. These items are often referred to as *public goods*.

Most modern governments do not confine their production of goods and services to collectively consumed goods. Name any good or service, and there probably is a government somewhere that produces it. As pointed out in Chapter 2, a major difference between the market and command economic systems is that the government of the latter is responsible for the production of individually consumed as well as collectively consumed and semicollectively consumed items. The government of the former leaves the bulk of individually consumed goods to private business, although it may play a relatively important role in the provision of such semicollectively consumed goods as education.

> Collectively consumed goods and services are sometimes referred to as **public goods**.

The Economics of Crime Prevention Activities

The "Optimal" Level

What is the appropriate, or optimal, level of expenditures on crime prevention activities by governmental units in the United States? Is the $97 billion level currently being spent roughly optimal? The same question can and should be asked about any category of government activity and expenditure. We gain an important insight when we realize that this is very much the same question that must be addressed regarding the production of any good or service, whether individually, semicollectively, or collectively consumed. Recall from Chapter 1 that we identified the fundamental goal of an economy as being the maximization of social well-being. Thus, in principle, the optimal level of production for any good or service is that level where the well-being of society is maximum. But how do we find this level of production? Chapter 1 also discussed *cost-benefit analysis*. This widely useful economic tool can help us identify the optimal level of expenditures on crime prevention activities, but it requires good estimates of the benefits and costs of these activities. Once benefits and costs are carefully estimated, cost-benefit analysis indicates that well-being will be enhanced through an increase in crime prevention activities so long as the benefit society derives from the increase is at least as great as the cost of the increased activities.

The framework for such a problem is set up in Table 4–3. Suppose the annual benefits and costs to society of crime prevention at various levels

> **Cost-benefit analysis** is a technique for determining the optimal level of an economic activity by considering the relationship between the costs and benefits of the activity. In general, an economic activity should be expanded so long as the resulting increase in benefits is at least as great as the resulting increase in costs.

		Table 4–3 Estimated benefits and costs of crime prevention, typical U.S. community (thousands of dollars)			
(1)	(2)	(3)	(4)	(5)	(6)
Units of Crime Prevention per Year	Total Benefit to Society	Marginal Social Benefit	Total Cost to Society	Marginal Social Cost	Net Benefit to Society
0	$ 0		$ 0		$ 0
		$ 200		$60	
1	200		60		140
		180		60	
2	380		120		260
		160		60	
3	540		180		360
		140		60	
4	680		240		440
		120		60	
5	800		300		500
		100		60	
6	900		360		540
		80		60	
7	980		420		560
		60		60	
8	1,040		480		560
		40		60	
9	1,080		540		540
		20		60	
10	1,110		600		500

have been investigated thoroughly and the estimates have been recorded in columns 1, 2, and 4. A "unit" of crime prevention is a nebulous concept, a composite of police personnel, patrol cars, courthouses, judges' services, prison costs, and the like. We avoid the problem of defining physical units by using arbitrary $60,000 units of crime prevention, assuming that each $60,000 chunk is spent in the best possible way.

The money expense of crime prevention to society is met by levying taxes. The *economic cost* to society is the value of the goods and services that resources used for crime prevention activities could have produced if they had not been used for crime prevention. The *benefit* to society of crime prevention is society's best estimate of how much better off the suppression of crime will make them—the value of the extra days they can work as a result of *not* being raped, maimed, or murdered, plus the value of property *not* destroyed, plus the value of the greater personal security they feel, and so on. Obviously, the benefits will be much more difficult to estimate than the costs. In fact, the most difficult and vexing part of the problem is the estimation of the benefits that ensue from various kinds of crime prevention activities.

If the benefits and costs are known, and we assume in Table 4–3 that they are, determination of the optimal level of crime prevention is relatively simple. Consider first whether there should be no crime prevention at all or whether one unit would be worthwhile. One unit of prevention yields benefits to society of $200,000—keeps $200,000 worth of GDP from being destroyed by criminal activities—and it would cost society only $60,000 to obtain it. Obviously, this is better than no prevention; the net benefit to society (total benefit minus total cost) is $140,000.

Now consider two units of prevention versus one unit. The total benefit yielded to society is $380,000. But note that the increase in total benefit yielded in moving from one to two units is $180,000, somewhat less than the increase in total benefits resulting from a movement from zero to one unit. Using the terminology of Chapter 1, the increase in total benefit to society resulting from a one-unit increase in the amount of crime prevention is called the *marginal social benefit* of crime prevention. As the number of units of prevention is increased, marginal social benefit can be expected to decline because each one-unit increase would be used to suppress the most serious crimes outstanding. The more units of prevention used, the less serious the crimes to which they are applied and, therefore, the less the increase in the benefit to society from each one-unit increase in prevention.

The increase in total benefit to society due to a one-unit increase in an economic activity is referred to as the **marginal social benefit** of the activity.

It pays society to move from the one-unit level to the two-unit level of prevention because the marginal social benefit yielded by the second unit exceeds the marginal social cost of the increase. Again drawing on the terminology of Chapter 1, the *marginal social cost* of crime prevention is defined as the increase in total cost to society resulting from a one-unit increase in prevention. Marginal social cost of prevention is constant in the example because we are measuring units of prevention in terms of $60,000 chunks. Therefore, the net benefit to society will be increased by $120,000 ($180,000 − $60,000) if the level of prevention is increased from one to two units. As such, we can be sure that social well-being is increased when the second unit of crime prevention is added. (Make sure you understand this before you go any further.)

The increase in total cost to society due to a one-unit increase in an economic activity is referred to as the **marginal social cost** of the activity.

Using the same kind of logic, we can determine that it is worthwhile for society to use the third, fourth, fifth, sixth, and seventh units of crime prevention. For each of these increases, the marginal social benefit is greater than the marginal social cost—that is, each adds more to total benefit than it adds to total cost. Therefore, each brings about an increase in net benefit to society. Net benefit to society, our measure of social well-being, reaches a maximum of $560,000 at the seven-unit level. If the level of prevention is raised to eight units, no harm is done. Marginal social benefit equals marginal social cost and there is no change in net benefit. But if the level is raised to nine units., the net benefit to society will fall to $540,000.

As citizens, we *must* understand the logic underlying determination of the optimal amount of government activity in crime prevention—or in anything else. It is very simple, very important, and usually overlooked. If a small increase in the level of an activity yields additional benefit to society worth more than the additional cost to society of providing it, it should be expanded. On the other hand, if its marginal social benefit is less than marginal social cost, the activity should be contracted. It follows that the optimal level is that at which marginal social benefit equals marginal social cost. (Study Table 4–3 until you understand this thoroughly.)

The foregoing economic analysis suggests something about dealing with increasing crime rates. If, when crime prevention activities are stepped up, the cost of in increase in prevention is less than the benefit it realizes, we ought to engage in more crime prevention activities. We are irrational if we do not. However, if a unit of prevention is not worth to us what it costs, then it is irrational to attempt to further suppress crime at present levels of crime prevention activities. Complete suppression of crime is never logical from the point of view of economics alone. There will be some level of crime prevention at which the benefits of an additional unit of prevention are simply not worth what they cost. (What about 10 units of prevention in Table 4–3?)

The economic analysis developed above, as important as it is, fails to touch on a very large part of the problems of crime. It does not consider, for example, such questions as: What gives rise to crime in the first place? What causes children to become delinquent and to grow up to be criminals? What causes adults to turn to criminal activities? Can criminals be rehabilitated, or should they simply be punished? These and many other questions are *psychological*, *social*, and even *political* in nature. Given the social milieu in which crime takes place, however, economic analysis is valuable in determining the level at which prevention activities should be pursued.

Allocation of the Crime Prevention Budget

Economic analysis also has something to contribute in determining the efficiency of different facets of crime prevention activities. There are several facets to any well-balanced government crime prevention program. Ideally, it should deter people from engaging in criminal activities. Failing in this—as it surely will—it must first *detect and apprehend* those engaging in criminal activities. This is primarily a police function. To *determine the guilt or innocence* of those charged with criminal acts, the legal system utilizes courts, attorneys, judges, and juries. Those convicted are fined and/or put in prison to *rehabilitate and/or punish* them. Reference to the prison system as a corrections system indicates hope that those incarcerated will somehow be rehabilitated and deterred from engaging in further criminal activities. In practice, the sentences of those convicted of crimes usually take on at least some aspects of punishment.

How much of a governmental unit's crime prevention budget should be allocated to police departments? How much for courts, judges, and prosecutors? How much for corrections, rehabilitation, and punishment? Detection and apprehension of persons thought to be committing criminal acts are of little value unless there are adequate court facilities for trying them. Trying persons apprehended and sentencing those convicted presuppose an adequate system of corrections or punishment. No one facet of crime prevention can contribute efficiently unless the others are there to back it up.

The allocation of government expenditures for control and prevention of crime in 1992 is shown by function and by the level of government making the expenditure in Table 4–4. Note that state and local governments make the greatest total expenditures in all functions.

The **equimarginal principle** states that an efficient allocation of a budget exists when the last dollar spent on any one facet of the budget yields the same marginal social benefit as the last dollar spent on any other facet of the budget.

The most efficient mix of the different facets of crime prevention is determined logically by what economists call the *equimarginal principle*. The crime budget should be allocated among police, courts, and corrections so that the last dollar spent on any one facet yields the same addition to the benefits of crime prevention as the last dollar spent on the others. Another way of saying this is that the budget should be allocated so that the marginal social benefit from a dollar's worth of police efforts equals the marginal social benefit of a dollar's worth of judicial effort and a dollar's worth of corrective effort in the overall suppression of crime.

As an example, suppose that the crime prevention system is relatively overloaded in the area of detection and apprehension. The courts cannot handle all those who are being arrested, so many of them must be set free without trial or, in the case of plea bargaining, sentenced for a lesser crime than the one committed. The mere fact of arrest will have some crime-deterring effects, but the deterrent effect will be much less than would be the case if there were adequate court facilities to try the persons apprehended. The contribution to crime prevention of an additional dollar's worth of police activity at this point is low. On the other hand, an expansion of court facilities would increase the likelihood of trial and conviction of those apprehended. We would expect the crime-deterring effect of a dollar's worth of such an expansion to be greater than that of a dollar spent on detection, apprehension, and subsequent freeing of those apprehended. Suppose that taking $1 away from police work brings about enough of a crime increase to cause a 75-cent loss in GDP to society. Now suppose that court activity was increased by $1, and the increased activity deters criminal activity enough to make society better off by $3. Under these circumstances, society will experience a net gain of $2.25 in GDP by a transfer of

Table 4–4	**Allocation of criminal justice expenditures by function and by level of government, 1992**					
	Federal		**State and Local**		**Total**	
	Amount (Millions)	**Percent**	**Amount (Millions)**	**Percent**	**Amount (Millions)**	**Percent**
Police protection	$ 7,400	42.5	$34,624	43.1	$42,024	43.0
Judicial and legal	7,377	42.3	16,573	20.7	23,950	24.5
Corrections	2,646	15.2	29,050	36.2	31,696	32.5
	17,243	100.0	80,247	100.0	97,670	100.0

Source: U.S. Department of Commerce, Bureau of the Census, Statistical Abstract of the United States, 1997, p. 213.

$1 from police activities to court activities. Such net gains are possible for any dollar transfer among police activities, court activities, and corrections activities when the marginal social benefit of $1 spent on one is less than the marginal social benefit of $1 spent on either of the others. No further gains are possible when the crime prevention budget is so allocated that the marginal social benefit of $1 spent on any one activity equals the marginal social benefit of $1 spent on any one of the other activities.

Changing the Legal Status of Goods and Services

Economic analysis can also be applied to advantage when evaluating the effects of changing the legal status of goods and services. The provision and sale of goods and services in some cases can change, from being generally legal to generally illegal, or vice versa. Good examples include certain drugs, abortion services, certain types of gambling, and prostitution. But the classic example, no doubt, concerns alcohol. Early in this century, a great deal of controversy surrounded the production, sale, and consumption of alcoholic beverages. Those opposed to alcohol use were even able to change the Constitution of the United States when the Eighteenth Amendment ushered in the prohibition era. The legal treatment of alcohol changed again in 1933 with the passage of the Twenty-First Amendment, which repealed prohibition. In many such controversies, the primary arguments turn on issues of morality. Clearly, economists are in no position to offer much insight into the moral issues surrounding the legal status of goods and services. Economic analysis can, however, provide valuable insights into the effects that changing the legal status of goods and services will have on the conditions of sale and use of the products.

Over the past few decades, the legal status of drugs such as marijuana and cocaine has come up for a great deal of public debate. And in general referendums during recent election cycles, the people of California, Arizona, and Washington, among others, voted in favor of allowing the medicinal use of some previously illegal drugs. Opponents, which include the Clinton administration's drug policy advisers, see such moves as misguided and as inevitably leading to outright legalization of what they view to be very dangerous drugs. Such opponents usually argue that the production, traffic in, and use of illegal drugs lead to much of the criminal activity that we see in society today and, furthermore, lead to severe personal consequences, often unexpected, for the users. Proponents of some form of legalization counter that the criminal activity associated with illegal drugs today is not a consequence of the drugs per se but simply a consequence of the drugs being considered illegal. Further, they argue that any unintended consequences to users are again due to the drugs being illegal since it is the illegality that limits reliable information about the products being readily available to consumers. This issue is obviously quite complex. However, some important insights can be had when economic analysis is applied to the issue. To do so, let's consider the possible legalization of a physically nonaddictive substance such as marijuana.

In Figure 4–1, suppose that D_1D_1 and S_1S_1 represent the demand and supply curves for marijuana with its current illegal status. Under this circumstance, the interaction of consumers and producers leads to an equilibrium price of p_1 per ounce and an equilibrium quantity exchanged of M_1 million ounces per year. What can we expect to happen in this market if marijuana production, distribution, and use are all legalized? On the demand side, we can expect to see some increase to a level such as D_2D_2. As shown, the increase in demand is quite modest. The drug's current widespread use—a 1996 survey of tenth graders found that more than 20 percent had used marijuana in the previous 30 days and about 30 percent had used the substance in the previous year—would seem to confirm the supposition of only a modest increase in demand following legalization. That is, apparently rather few individuals currently avoid using marijuana solely due to its illegality.

The real dramatic effect on the market can be expected on the supply side. We show this as the increase to S_2S_2. Why such a dramatic increase in supply? Recall that the first thing we hold constant when drawing a supply curve is the cost of production. Consider the cost to produce and distribute marijuana when it is illegal versus when it is legal. When the substance is illegal, the grower must either cultivate indoors and lose the productivity of the outside environment or run the added risk of growing outdoors. Given the risk of discovery, outdoor growers must choose remote locations for cultivation and often have to "pack in" supplies such as water. Once harvested, the drug has to be shipped, without detection, to every corner of the country. And, at every step in the process, the producer has to be aware of the legal implications, and the costs, of the operation being discovered. None of this would be necessary were the drug legal.

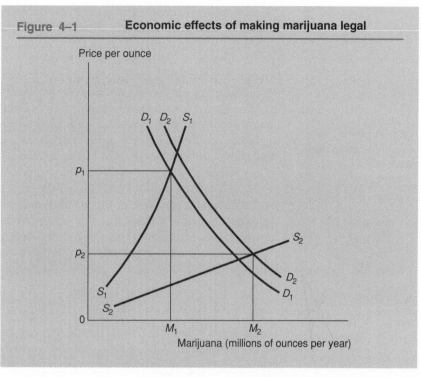

Figure 4–1   **Economic effects of making marijuana legal**

When marijuana is illegal, the interaction of demand D_1D_1 and supply S_1S_1 leads to an equilibrium price of p_1 and an equilibrium quantity exchanged of M_1. Legalization would lead to a modest increase in demand to D_2D_2 and sharply increased supply to S_2S_2. The result would be a large fall in equilibrium price and a large increase in the quantity exchanged.

Clearly, then, legalization of marijuana would lead to greatly reduced production costs and, consequently, greatly increased supply.

Taken together, the new demand and supply would lead to a new equilibrium price of p_2 per ounce and an equilibrium quantity exchanged of M_2. That is, we can expect that legalization will lead to a great fall in price and a significant increase in the quantity of the good exchanged and consumed. But, are there other outcomes that might reasonably be expected? Experience with other goods and services suggests that additional outcomes should be expected from legalization. These outcomes might include a significant increase in the quality of marijuana available as suppliers are forced to compete for business, less criminal activity associated with the good since violence rarely is associated with the production and sale of legal goods, and a significant freeing up of resources within the government's crime prevention budget that would then be available for other uses.

Should we legalize drugs such as marijuana then? Again, keep in mind that economic analysis alone does not provide an answer to this question, especially if the drug in question is highly physically addictive, such as heroin or crack cocaine. With these types of drugs, the analysis presented above really does not hold since it assumes that the user is making a voluntary choice—is not addicted—when he or she purchases and uses the drug. When we are considering a nonaddictive drug such as marijuana, however, what economic analysis provides is a clear understanding of the economic aspects of the market for a good or service given its legal status. To summarize that analysis, when a good or service is legal, we can expect relatively low prices, high product quality, large quantities available for consumption, and limited illegal activity associated with the production, sale, and use of the good or service. That is, we can expect that, as is generally true, the market will work to the benefit of the consuming public. Should there be moral issues associated with the analysis, these issues, as is appropriately the case, must be left for individual consideration.

Causes of Criminal Activity

Thus far we have looked at the issue of crime and crime prevention from society's perspective. Economic analysis is also helpful in looking at crime from the perspective of the criminal or potential criminal. Specifically, why do some people choose to participate in criminal activities? Clearly the reasons are nearly infinite, and many have little or nothing to do with economics. In many cases violent crimes are the result of unrestrained passions or emotions. Most murders, for example, result from deep-seated, highly intense feelings of some sort between the murderer and victim. The victim may be a wife, a husband, a lover, or the guy who drives too aggressively on the highway. The level of the murderer's emotion pushes aside the constraints of conscience and law that society has established. While this is often the case, a great deal of criminal activity no doubt has roots that are economic in nature, especially in cases such as trafficking in illegal substances. For these types of criminal activities, economic analysis can offer important insights into the motivations of the individuals involved.

To see the value of economic analysis in understanding why people commit certain crimes, consider the supply side of the market for marijuana as presented above. What are the motivations that lead individuals into the business of growing marijuana even though it is against the law? The key word in this question is "business." That is, marijuana is grown as a business venture, and as such the motivations to enter this business are much the same as those which exist for any other business—whether legal or illegal. There are, no doubt, many different motivations. Some people enter a particular business because that business offers a lifestyle they greatly value. In other cases, decisions to enter a particular business are the result of a desire to live in a certain area of the country or world. While these and other motivations exist, it is undeniable that in many instances the fundamental reason that someone enters into a business is the pursuit of profit—the difference between income and cost. But does the pursuit of profit as a motivation for entering a particular business necessarily conflict with other motivations such as desiring to live and work in a beach community? Not necessarily. If we broaden our notion of income to include what is known as *psychic income* as well as money income, there is no conflict between these various motivations. That is, while one might be willing to sacrifice money income that could be earned as a big-city public accountant to operate a bicycle shop at a beach, presumably the lost money income is more than offset by the psychic income he or she receives from living and working at the beach. Taking both money and psychic income into account then, we assume that the decision to enter a particular business is driven by a desire to earn profit. And if this seems reasonable when considering opening a bicycle shop at a beach, why should we believe the situation to be any different for the potential marijuana grower?

In order for the operation to make a profit for the grower, total income, or revenues, from the sale of marijuana must be greater than the production costs. If this is true, we might conclude that "crime does pay." The revenue side of the operation is quite straightforward; it is simply the price at which the grower can wholesale his or her produce times the quantity that is sold, plus any psychic income that he or she derives from being in the business. The cost side is a bit more complex. Recall from Chapter 3 that economists measure costs in opportunity cost terms. The opportunity cost of operating the marijuana growing business is made up of both explicit and implicit costs. The explicit costs are likely to include the money paid to secure the property used to grow the product and the costs of electricity, lighting systems (assuming indoor growth), and fertilizers and pesticides needed to actually bring forth a harvest. As is often the case, however, there are going to be implicit costs borne by the marijuana grower. Chief among these is the cost created by the fact that the garden will need tending, and time spent tending cannot be used to earn income in some other way. That is, if the grower spends 20 hours a week tending plants, the income that could have been earned during the 20 hours is an implicit cost of growing marijuana. Equally important, the grower must take into account the implicit cost of getting caught—lost liberty, especially in an environment of mandatory minimum prison sentences. Of course, the cost of getting caught is difficult to estimate. Suppose the penalty for getting caught is highly severe, say, life imprisonment. This would seem to create an extremely significant implicit cost of growing marijuana. But, this might not be the case. Whether or not the existence of a severe penalty imposes a great implicit cost depends on the risk of being caught. If the risk is high, the implicit cost imposed is equally

When an individual receives benefits from a business endeavor in the form of personal satisfaction rather than in the form of money, he or she is said to be earning **psychic income**.

high. On the contrary, if the risk of being caught is low or nonexistent, the cost of being caught is proportionately low. Finally, an additional implicit cost to the grower is the loss of social standing. If there is some degree of social stigma attached to being known as a criminal grower, this loss of social standing must be added to the cost side of the marijuana grower's ledger. In this way, the stigma attached to growing marijuana can be thought of as negative psychic income or simply as a *psychic cost* of the business.

When an individual incurs costs in pursuing a business in the form of negative personal satisfaction rather than in the form of money, he or she is said to be bearing **psychic costs**.

Once potential revenues (including both money and psychic income) and potential costs (including all explicit and implicit costs) are estimated as accurately as is possible, the decision to enter the business of marijuana growing becomes a simple application of cost-benefit analysis. If the revenues are reasonably expected to be greater than costs, the individual increases his or her level of well-being by becoming a marijuana grower, that is, by becoming a criminal. If the reverse is true, the individual finds another line of work.

Although this analysis seems straightforward, we must discuss a couple of other factors. Specifically, let's look more closely at the implicit costs of growing marijuana from an opportunity cost perspective. The most important implicit costs for the grower are likely to be the income that he or she forgoes from other employment in order to grow marijuana and the potential cost of incarceration should the operation be busted. But what if the individual, prior to entering the business, is unemployed and, because of local economic conditions, sees little likelihood of becoming a gainfully employed legally? For such a person, the cost side of the equation is much smaller than would be true for someone who is employed in a high-paying job. This is not to say that all, or even most, poor people will enter into a criminal activity such as marijuana growing. But this application of the opportunity cost principle does, for example, seem to explain the widespread growth of marijuana in highly depressed areas of Appalachia, which produce such a large share of the domestically grown marijuana in the United States. When the possibility of earning even a minimal living by legal methods seems dim, at best, the field is ripe for criminal activity. But, on the contrary, this does not suggest that the opportunity cost principle is applicable only to criminal activities of the poor. Although the opportunity costs are much greater for someone who is in a good-paying job than for someone who is unemployed or who has a low-paying dead-end job, even someone from the highest strata of society may be tempted to enter into a criminal enterprise if the potential income is great enough—this is, no doubt, the primary cause of white-collar crime.

Thorough consideration of the implicit costs of entering a particular illegal endeavor from the standpoint of the opportunity cost principle provides insights into the causes of certain criminal activities. And these insights can be useful to society in its attempt to reduce criminal activity. That is, to the extent that those in dire economic circumstances turn to criminal activities because their desperate plight lowers the opportunity cost of the activities, many of these individuals may be deterred from turning to crime through improved educational opportunities that can be expected to increase earning power from legal jobs as well as programs such as job training and counseling, community economic development, and relocation in some instances. Similarly effective might be public provision of recreational activities for young people in depressed areas. Each of these types of programs, to the extent that they are successful, tend to increase the opportunity cost of pursuing a criminal activity and, thus, make it less likely that the individual will so choose. Also important is the implicit cost created by being caught and punished. As pointed out, this cost approaches zero if the risk of capture is very low. In this way, an application of the equimarginal principle might suggest that some people could be convinced not to enter into a particular illegal activity if relatively more resources are put into the quick and certain arrest and conviction of criminals, and relatively fewer resources are put into longer, but less certain, prison terms.

Summary

Criminal activities are defined as activities that are illegal. They may or may not be immoral. They are usually classified as (1) crimes against persons, (2) crimes against property, (3) traffic in illegal goods and services, and (4) other crimes.

Crime constitutes a serious problem in the United States; crime rates generally have been increasing over the years.

Good information on the costs of crime is not available because many criminal activities go unreported and because it is difficult to place dollar values on the results of some kinds of these activities. Some reported "costs" of crime are not really economic costs to the society as a whole but are transfers of income from the victim of the crime to its perpetrator.

In an economic analysis of crime, it is useful to classify goods and services into three categories: (1) individually consumed, (2) collectively consumed, and (3) semicollectively consumed items. Governments, with their coercive powers, are in a unique position to efficiently produce such collectively consumed items as crime prevention. Consequently, collectively consumed services of this type are usually provided by governments.

Cost-benefit analysis can be used to advantage in determining the optimal level of crime prevention activities in a society. The cost of crime prevention can be easily determined, but the benefit—much of which is intangible—is hard to estimate. Conceptually, it is the difference between what GDP would be *with* crime prevention and what it would be *without* such activities. On the basis of the best estimates that can be made, society should seek that level of crime prevention at which the net benefit to society is greatest. This will be the level at which the marginal social benefit of crime prevention is equal to marginal social cost.

Once the level of the government's crime prevention budget is determined, it should be efficiently allocated among the different facets of crime prevention activities. These include detection and apprehension of violators, determination of their guilt or innocence, and corrections. The most efficient allocation of the crime prevention budget among these facets is determined by applying the equimarginal principle. The most efficient allocation will be such that the marginal social benefit from a dollar's worth of detection and apprehension is equal to the marginal social benefit from a dollar's worth of each of the other two facets of crime prevention.

Economic analysis is also helpful in determining whether goods or services should be considered illegal. Typically, when an illegal activity is made legal, both supply and demand increase, although in most cases the increase in supply can be expected to be greater in degree than the increase in demand, leading to a fall in the equilibrium price of the activity and an increase in the equilibrium quantity purchased. Additionally, it is reasonable to expect the quality of the good or service to increase. In each case, just the reverse may be anticipated if a currently legal activity is made illegal.

Economic analysis is also useful in understanding the motivations of individuals to commit certain crimes. A rational individual can be expected to enter into a criminal activity if the revenue generated from the activity is perceived as being greater than the cost. It is important that all revenues (from both money income and psychic income) and all costs (both explicit and implicit) be taken into account. With the balance sheet properly understood, society can make more effective use of the equimarginal principle in its attempt to protect itself from crime.

Discussion Questions

1. Some people think of crime as that which is immoral. Explain why morality helps little in determining whether specific acts should be considered criminal.
2. Goods and services can be assigned to one of three categories: individually consumed, semicollectively consumed, or collectively consumed. Explain the differences, and provide examples of each category.
3. What are free riders, and how do they influence the ability of markets to allocate resources effectively?
4. Markets have difficulty in providing collectively consumed goods and services. Explain why. Be sure to use the free-rider concept.

5. From a standpoint of the free-rider problem, discuss the likely effectiveness of group assignments. Does the economic analysis based on the free-rider problem seem to match your experiences?

6. Explain how the optimal level of government expenditure on a collectively consumed good or service can be arrived at.

7. Suppose the end of the semester is approaching and you have exams to prepare for in economics, calculus, and history. Further suppose that your primary goal is to maximize your grade point average. Explain how the equimarginal principle might be used to help you allocate your study time.

8. Using abortion services as the example, describe the effects that you would expect were the services to become illegal.

9. Explain how economic analysis can assist in understanding why individuals commit crimes. What does this analysis have to say about attempts to reduce crime?

10. Political pressure remains high for mandatory minimum sentences for those convicted of certain crimes. Based on the analysis of this chapter, discuss the likely consequences of such sentences.

11. Discuss: "The crime associated with the drug trade is due to the illegality of the drugs, not due to drugs per se. As such, if you want to bring down crime in the United States, you should legalize drugs such as marijuana and cocaine."

12. The city of Boca Raton, Florida, recently opened a publicly financed skateboard facility. Using the analysis developed in this chapter, explain this facility's likely impact, if any, on juvenile crime in the city.

Additional Readings

Bayer, Ronald, and Gerald M. Oppenheimer, eds. *Contemporary Drug Policy.* New York: Cambridge University Press, 1993.

A set of essays about drug decriminalization.

Boaz, David, ed. *The Crisis in Drug Prohibition.* Washington, DC: The Cato Institute, 1990.

Taken together, these essays offer an in-depth, thoughtful, and balanced analysis of the question of legalizing drugs.

Eide, Erling. *Economics of Crime: Deterrence and the Rational Offender. Contributions to Economic Analysis.* New York: North Holland, 1994.

Thorough analysis of the economics of criminal activity, although the figures on crime are from Norway.

Federal Bureau of Investigation. *Crime in the United States.* Washington, DC: U.S. Government Printing Office, annual.

Sums up all reported crimes in the United States on an annual basis, providing the most complete statistical data available on the different types of crimes and the people who commit them. Also provides trend data for key types of crime statistics. There is very little analysis of the data.

Miller, Roger L., Daniel K. Benjamin, and Douglass C. North. *Economics of Public Issues*. 10th ed. New York: HarperCollins College, 1996.

Discusses the economic gains from legalizing prostitution, the economic nature of criminal activity, and other issues. The authors argue that to reduce crime, the price paid (punishment) by the criminal must be increased.

Myers, Samuel L., Jr., and Margaret C. Simms, eds. *The Economics of Race and Crime*. New Brunswick, NJ: Transaction Books, 1988.

Combination of historical and contemporary articles discussing blacks, crime, unemployment, and other issues.

World Wide Web Resources

Bureau of Justice Statistics
www.ojp.usdoj.gov/bjs

Provides latest national statistics on crimes and victims. Links to information about the U.S. justice system and other justice-related databases.

The Cato Institute
www.cato.org

Offers numerous public addresses and policy analyses concerning drug policy matters.

Federal Bureau of Investigation
www.fbi.gov

Provides access to *Uniform Crime Reports* and gives statistics on crime rates, violent crimes, and other figures.

National Archive of Criminal Justice Data
www.icpsr.umich.edu/NACJ

Provides links to over 550 data collections of statistics, prevention, specialized training sites, and more.

United States Department of Justice
www.usdoj.gov

Has links to the Department's press room, publications, employment, fugitives and missing persons, and justice for kids and youth.

World's Most Wanted
www.MostWanted.org

World's Most Wanted, Inc., a not-for-profit corporation, provides a home page to help law enforcement agencies use the Internet more effectively. Provides links to child support, bail jumpers, U.S. listings by state, and other sites.

Pollution Problems
Must We Foul Our Own Nests?

Chapter Outline

Checklist of Economic Concepts

Biologist Nancy Rabalais fights nausea as she struggles into a wet suit and scuba gear on the pitching deck of the *R. V. Acadian* about 15 miles off the Louisiana coast.

She is preparing to descend along the metal leg of an abandoned oil rig to the shallow bottom of the Gulf of Mexico, where she will replace a meter that measures the amount of oxygen in the water.

It's not the most pleasant of chores for a marine biologist prone to seasickness. But Rabalais considers a little nausea a small price to pay to gain another clue to the Gulf of Mexico's biggest, most alarming mystery:

How do we stop the dead zone?

A 7,000 square mile swath of Gulf water stretching from the mouth of the Mississippi River to the Texas border, the zone becomes so devoid of oxygen each summer that it kills the clams, crabs, worms and other organisms that live on and in the sediment, destroying the food chain from bottom up.

It begins in the spring, when the Mississippi River is swollen by rains and melted snow that wash a rich mixture of agricultural fertilizers and municipal sewage from 40 states downstream into the Gulf.

The lighter fresh water floats on top of the denser salt water of the Gulf, creating layers. As spring turns to summer, the sun combines with the pollution from fertilizers and sewage to fuel huge blooms of algae.

When the algae dies, it sinks to the bottom, where its decay uses up oxygen in the saltier water. Oxygen from the surface can't get past the freshwater layer at the top to replenish the water below. By midsummer, all the oxygen in a vast area of the Gulf may be gone.

"The effect can be akin to taking Saran Wrap and placing it over [an area the size of] Connecticut and Rhode Island, slowly pulling it down and suffocating everything beneath it," said Melissa Samet, a lawyer and wildlife biologist with the Sierra Club Legal Defense Fund."[1]

[1]Mark Schleifstein, "Fertilizer, Sewage Brew Dead Zone," *The Times-Picayune,* Mar. 25, 1996, p. A-7. Permission granted by The Times-Picayne Publishing Corporation. All rights reserved.

Most of us are concerned about environmental problems, but we are not quite sure what we can do about them. As individuals, we seem to believe that we can do little. In fact, we are likely to add to the problems by thinking that our own bit of pollution is just a drop in the bucket.

Public reaction to pollution varies a great deal. At one extreme are those who object to everything that decreases the purity of the air and water or that mars the natural beauty of the landscape. At the other extreme are those who seem not to value clean air, water, and natural beauty at all. Most of us are between these two extremes.

A sensible attack on pollution problems requires the use of economic analysis along with inputs from other disciplines—especially the natural sciences. In particular, economic analysis can help us (1) understand why and under what circumstances economic units pollute; (2) determine the impact of pollution on resource allocation and social well-being; (3) determine the extent to which pollution control should be exercised; and (4) evaluate alternative antipollution activities of the government. Before we can fully apply economic analysis to the problem of pollution, however, two additional steps are needed. First, we must come to a clear understanding of what constitutes pollution. Having done this and since one of our primary goals concerns determining the impact of pollution on resource allocation and social well-being, we must pull together and extend what we have learned about these topics thus far.

What Is Pollution?

We will not make much progress in an economic analysis of pollution until we are familiar with both the nature of the environment in which we live and what it is that constitutes pollution of that environment. Let's consider these two concepts in turn.

The Environment and Its Services

The environment is easily defined. It consists of the air, water, and land around us. These elements provide us with a variety of important services, including a habitat in which to live and resources with which to produce goods and services.

The services of the environment are used by production units and household units as they engage in activities of various kinds. Production units lay heavy claims on the environment's resources, but they may also make use of its habitat and amenity characteristics.

As production units engage in the process of transforming raw and semifinished materials into goods and services that will satisfy human wants, there are at least three ways in which the environment can be affected. First, some of the environment's stocks of exhaustible resources may be diminished. These include coal, petroleum, and many mineral deposits. Second, it is called upon for replaceable resources like timber, grassland, oxygen, and nitrogen. Third, it is used as a place to dispose of the wastes of the production and consumption processes—as a gigantic garbage disposal.

Recycling of Wastes and the Concept of Pollution

The pollution problem arises primarily from the use of the environment by producers and consumers as a dumping ground for wastes. We litter the countryside with cans, paper, and the other residues of consumption and production. We dump the emissions from our automobiles and factories into the atmosphere. We empty sewage and residue from production directly and indirectly into streams, rivers, and lakes.

As wastes from production and consumption are dumped into the environment, nature sets recycling processes in motion. Animals use oxygen, giving off carbon dioxide wastes. But plants use carbon dioxide, giving off oxygen wastes. Dead plant and animal life are attacked by chemical elements that decompose them, restoring to the soil elements that the living organisms had withdrawn from it. Living organisms frequently contribute to the decomposition process. Iron and steel objects rust and disintegrate over time. So do wood and other matter. Wastes that can be decomposed in air, water, and soil are said to be biodegradable. But some wastes are not biodegradable, for example, aluminum containers such as beer cans.

Recycling—the transformation of wastes into raw materials that are again usable—requires variable lengths of time, depending on what it is that is being recycled. It takes many years for a steel pipe to rust away. Wood varies a great deal in the time it takes for its complete disintegration. But many plant and animal products require only a very short time to decompose.

Pollution consists of loading the environment with wastes that are not completely recycled, are not recycled fast enough, or are not recycled at all. It involves a diminution of the capacity of the environment to yield environmental services. Pollution occurs when recycling processes fail to prevent wastes from accumulating in the environment.

Common Forms of Pollution

Pollution is as old as civilization itself. Wherever people have congregated, their wastes have tended to pile up more rapidly than the forces of nature can digest them. As long as the world was sparsely populated and no permanent cities existed, no great problems were created. When the extent of pollution in one locale imposed costs on the people living there that outweighed the costs associated with moving, they simply moved away from it. Then, given time, natural recycling processes could in many cases take over and restore the excess wastes to usable form.

When towns and cities came into existence, pollution raised more serious problems. How could body wastes from humans and animals, as well as refuse from the daily round of living, be disposed of? Until fairly recent times it was not disposed of in many instances—levels of sanitation were unbelievably low, and levels of stench were unbelievably high. As the density of the world's population has increased and as it has become more difficult to move away from pollution problems, the human race has increasingly turned its attention toward the development of control measures. But in order to control pollution, it must be identified as accurately as possible in its various forms.

Air Pollution.   In the processes of production and consumption, five major kinds of wastes are dumped into the atmosphere. Most result from combustion and have caused local problems for a long time. Since there are millions of cubic miles of atmosphere to absorb these wastes, however, air pollution has not caused great concern until the last few decades. These wastes are carbon monoxide, sulfur dioxides, nitrogen oxides, hydrocarbons, and particulates.

Carbon monoxide, an odorless, colorless gas, makes the atmosphere a less hospitable habitat for animal life. In concentrated amounts, it causes dizziness, headaches, and nausea in humans. Exposure to a sufficiently high concentration for a few hours can be fatal. In 1995, 81 percent of the carbon monoxide emissions into the atmosphere in the United States came from transportation sources, and another 6 percent came from industrial sources of one kind or another.[2]

Sulfur dioxides constitute a second major source of atmospheric pollution. Where they are heavily concentrated, they cause damage to both plant and animal life. Dioxides result largely from the combustion of fuel oils and coal. Consequently, high levels of concentration are most likely to occur where these are used for the generation of electricity and for residential heating.

A third atmospheric pollutant is nitrogen oxides. These can cause lung damage in human beings and may also retard plant growth. The main sources of the pollutant are automobiles and stationary combustion processes such as those used in generating electric power.

Hydrocarbons constitute a fourth kind of waste emitted into the air. At their present concentration levels, no direct harmful effects have been attributed to them. However, they combine with nitrogen oxides and ultraviolet rays of the sun to form petrochemical smog. The smog may produce breathing difficulties and eye irritation for human beings. In addition, it speeds up the oxidation processes to which paints and metals are subject, resulting in substantial damages to industrial plants and equipment. Almost 50 percent of hydrocarbon emissions in the United States comes from industrial sources, and another 40 percent comes from automobiles.

A fifth air pollutant consists of a heterogeneous mixture of suspended solids and liquids called particulates. These are largely dust and ash, along with lead from automobile exhausts. The major source of particulates, however, is fuel combustion in stationary sources and in industrial processes. Open fires used to burn trash and garbage also make their contributions. Particulates lower visibilities. Some, such as lead from automobile exhausts, may be directly harmful to human beings.

---

[2]U.S. Department of Commerce, Bureau of the Census, *Statistical Abstract of the United States, 1997,* p. 234.

Water Pollution. Water pollution is ordinarily measured in terms of the capacity of water to support aquatic life. This capacity depends on (1) the level of dissolved oxygen in the water and (2) the presence of matter or materials injurious to plant and animal life.

The level of dissolved oxygen is built up through aeration of water and through the photosynthetic processes of plant life living in the water. It is destroyed in the decomposition of organic matter that originates in or is dumped into the water. The oxygen needed for decomposition purposes is referred to as biochemical oxygen demand (BOD). The level of dissolved oxygen available for supporting aquatic life, then, depends on the balance between aeration and photosynthesis on the one hand and on BOD on the other.

The level of dissolved oxygen is affected by several factors. First, it tends to be higher the greater the amount of a given volume of water exposed to the atmosphere. In nature, fast-running streams, rapids, and waterfalls contribute to aeration. Artificial aeration is frequently accomplished by shooting streams of water through the air. Second, it tends to be higher the greater the amount of photosynthesis that occurs in the water. In some instances, the amount of photosynthesis that occurs in aquatic plant life may be reduced by air pollution. In this way, air pollution may be a source of water pollution. Third, it tends to be higher the lower the temperature of the water—use of the water for cooling by firms such as steel mills, oil refineries, and electricity-generating plants raises the temperature of the water and lowers its capacity to hold dissolved oxygen. Fourth, organic wastes that create BOD come from both domestic and industrial sources, so the level of dissolved oxygen varies inversely with the amounts that are dumped. The decomposition of such wastes can be greatly facilitated, and BOD can be correspondingly reduced by chemical treatment of such wastes before they are discharged into streams, rivers, lakes, or oceans.

The capacity of water to support aquatic life is reduced when various kinds of materials and matter are dumped into it. Among these are toxins that do not settle out of the water and are not easily broken down by biological means. Mercury is a toxin that has created problems of contamination in various types of fish. Phenols, herbicides, and pesticides have also contributed greatly to the water pollution problem. There have been heated discussions in recent years over the propriety of using them in large quantities. Questions have been raised also as to whether the oceans should be used for the dumping of nuclear wastes and for undersea nuclear explosions.

Land Pollution. Land pollution results from the dumping of a wide variety of wastes on the terrain and from tearing up the earth's surface through such activities as strip mining. Highways are littered with refuse thrown from passing automobiles. Junkyards grow as we scrap millions of automobiles per year, to say nothing of the prodigious amounts of other machinery and appliances that are retired from use. Garbage dumps and landfills grow as towns and cities dispose of the solid wastes they collect and accumulate. Even more troubling are hazardous waste sites, many of which are located in densely populated states. Examples include New Jersey with 108 sites, Pennsylvania with 102, New York with 79, and California with 94.[3] All these reduce the capacity of the terrain to render environmental services.

Markets, Resource Allocation, and Social Well-Being: A Recap and Extension

Before we can fully appreciate the economic effects of pollution, we must summarize and extend what we have learned about markets, resource allocation, and social well-being. Thus far, we have examined social well-being from two different perspectives. In Chapter 2, we considered social well-being within the context of the market model of supply and demand. From this perspective we conclude that a market equilibrium occurs when consumers feel that producers have used precisely the correct portion of society's scarce resources in a particular production process. And since we believe the consuming public to be the best judge of what yields well-being, their satisfaction with the market outcome leads us to conclude that the market-determined equilibrium reflects that allocation of resources which maximizes social well-being. Were this not true, consumers would not be satisfied with the outcome.

A second perspective on the issue of maximizing social well-being was first introduced in Chapter 1 and has been used regularly since. From this perspective and relying on cost-benefit analysis, we say that social well-being is enhanced when an increase in the production of a good or service benefits society at least as much as it costs. Consequently, social well-being is as high as is possible when production of all goods or services is carried to the point where marginal social benefit (MSB) equals marginal social cost (MSC).

Now, we must bridge these two ways of looking at resource allocation and social well-being. To do so, we must bring the cost-benefit analysis comparison of marginal social benefit and marginal social cost into the demand-supply analysis of the market model.

---

[3]U.S. Department of Commerce, Bureau of the Census, *Statistical Abstract of the United States, 1997*, p. 238.

Demand, Marginal Private Benefit, and Marginal Social Benefit

Consider first the demand side of a market. As consumers, we make purchases for the satisfaction, or benefit, that consumption brings. If our goal in these purchases is to maximize our own well-being, given our income constraints, cost-benefit analysis suggests that we should not make a particular purchase unless the benefit to us from the purchase is at least as great as its cost.

Is this logic found in a demand curve? Typically we think of a demand curve as indicating the maximum quantity of a good or service that consumers will buy at various prices, other things being equal. An equally valid way of looking at demand is as the maximum price that consumers would be willing to pay for each successive unit of a good or service, other things being equal. For simplicity, consider one person's individual demand for a good such as pizza. Suppose Jim's demand curve for pizza indicates that the maximum he is willing to pay for one pizza during a given week is $10. Why $10? Jim could spend his $10 on a pizza or anything else that $10 would buy. If he chooses to buy a pizza for $10, based on the logic of cost-benefit analysis, we can conclude that the expected satisfaction, or benefit, from eating the pizza is at least as great as the satisfaction that any other $10 purchase would bring. Were this not so, Jim would simply buy something else with his $10. The benefit to Jim then of the first pizza is roughly worth $10. We call this Jim's marginal benefit of the first pizza.

Having consumed the first pizza, what's a second pizza worth to Jim? The downward, to the right, slope of his demand curve indicates that the maximum price he is willing to pay for a second pizza is less than $10, perhaps only $8. That is, having eaten one pizza during the week, the marginal benefit Jim anticipates from consuming a second pizza falls. Does this make sense to you? Consider which gives you more satisfaction, the first glass of orange juice at breakfast or the second? the first mug of cold beer after a difficult day of exams or the second? And so on. Experience suggests, and Jim's demand curve points out, that typically marginal benefit, as measured by willingness to pay, declines as more of something is consumed.

This of course applies to market demand curves as well as to that of an individual. For each successive unit of a good or service, the market demand curve indicates the maximum price consumers are willing to pay. And the maximum price of necessity will be dictated by the benefit in terms of added satisfaction, or simply the marginal benefit, that consumers anticipate from consuming each unit of the good or service. Consequently, a market demand curve can correctly be thought of as a marginal benefit curve for the consumers of a good or service.

Recall that we are trying to bridge the market model of supply and demand with the notions of marginal social benefit and cost. We are nearly halfway there. That is, we now know that the market demand is a marginal benefit curve. But, is it the marginal *social* benefit curve? That is, are the benefits to the direct consumers of a good or service as reflected in the demand curve the same as the benefits to society from the item? Under most circumstances they are. Usually, there are no benefits from consuming a particular good or service other than the benefits that accrue to the direct consumer. Unfortunately, this will not always be the case. Recall that in the case of social spillovers in consumption, individuals other than the direct consumers of a good or service find their satisfaction either increased or reduced when the item is consumed. For example, it was argued in Chapter 3 that the consumption of higher educational services gave benefits to society as a whole, over and above the benefits to the student. In this case, marginal social benefit will be greater than the marginal benefit of the direct consumers. Conversely, cigarette smoking reduces the satisfaction of those negatively affected by secondhand smoke. In this case, the marginal social benefit of cigarettes is less than the marginal benefit of the smokers. To be safe then, we will call the marginal benefit to the direct consumers of a good or service *marginal private benefit (MPB)*. This convention will allow us to distinguish it from marginal social benefit in those cases in which social spillovers in consumption occur. Consequently, market demand curves are both marginal private and marginal social benefit curves only in those instances in which there are no social spillovers in consumption.

Marginal private benefit (MPB) is the benefit that accrues to the direct consumers of a good or service resulting from a one-unit increase in consumption and is reflected in the demand curve for the good or service.

Supply, Marginal Private Cost, and Marginal Social Cost

Now consider a standard supply curve. As presented in Chapter 2, a supply curve shows us the maximum quantity of a good or service that sellers are willing to offer for sale at various prices, other things being equal. Once again we can turn this around to say that supply indicates the minimum price necessary to induce sellers to offer each unit for sale, other things being equal. Suppose, for example that to induce an individual seller to offer a first pizza for sale, a customer must be willing to pay at least $5. Why is $5 the minimum that the seller will take? Again, apply cost-benefit analysis. The benefit side of the transaction is the $5 the seller will take in as revenue if the sale is made. The cost side is simply the cost to produce the pizza. If the seller wishes to make as much profit as possible, he will produce and sell the first pizza only if it brings in at least as much revenue as it cost to produce. If the seller is willing to take no less than $5 for the first pizza, we can conclude that the cost to produce it is $5. That is, we can conclude that $5 is the marginal cost to produce the first pizza. Consequently, the supply curve, by showing the minimum price necessary to induce the seller to offer each successive unit of the good or service for sale, can correctly be thought of as the producer's marginal cost curve.

Consider a second pizza. Supply curves slope upward to the right; thus, in order to induce the seller to offer a second pizza for sale, a price greater than $5 must be offered. In other words, the marginal cost to produce must be rising. Why? Recall from Chapter 1 the concept of increasing opportunity costs. That is—just as is true for society as a whole—as the firms of an individual industry attempt to increase output they must eventually begin to pay more for additional resources since these resources have to be attracted from increasingly valuable alternative employments. That is, perhaps initially, a pizza maker in a college town can hire labor very cheaply since there is a pool of student workers to draw from who have limited alternative earning power. As production expands, eventually the pizza maker will run out of relatively cheap labor to hire, and the marginal cost to produce rises. The same will occur for all other resources used as well.

Consequently, whether you are looking at the supply curve of one seller or the combined supply curve of a group of sellers, supply can correctly be thought of as a marginal cost curve. But is the marginal cost borne by producers necessarily the same as marginal *social* cost? Typically, there are no significant social spillovers in production processes. They do occur, however, and they can be positive or negative. An example of a positive social spillover in production exists in raising cattle for human consumption. Although most parts of the cow find their way into food uses, the hides typically do not. Cowhides do, however, find their way into the production of leather products. The availability of such large supplies of cowhides leads to a very large reduction in the cost to produce these leather products. In cases such as this, the marginal cost to the cattle producer will be greater than the marginal social cost since the reduced cost of other producers is not taken into account. Conversely, strip mining operations may make it more difficult and expensive to prepare a particular piece of land for other uses. In this case, the marginal cost of extracting the minerals through strip mining will understate the true marginal social cost of the operation. Whenever social spillovers in production exist, whether positive or negative, the producers' marginal cost will not be the same as marginal social cost. To be safe then, we will call the producers' marginal cost of production, *marginal private cost (MPC)*. When no social spillovers in production exist, this marginal private cost curve, or supply curve, is also the marginal social cost curve.

Marginal private cost (MPC) is the increase in total cost that producers incur when output is increased by one unit and is reflected in the supply curve for the good or service.

The Market and Social Well-Being

With demand and supply curves redefined as marginal private benefit and marginal private cost curves, what can we say about the equilibrium that a market reaches? By equating demand and supply, the market leads to an equilibrium at which the marginal private benefit to consumers is exactly equal to the marginal private cost of producers. And if there are no social spillovers in either consumption or production, the market outcome also gives an equilibrium where marginal social benefit equals marginal social cost, the condition necessary for proving that social well-being is maximized. Given this, when we, as in Chapter 2, conclude that a market equilibrium of necessity leads to the resource allocation that maximizes social well-being, we are implicitly making the assumption of no social spillovers in consumption or production. Fortunately, such spillovers are either rare or, at least, of such modest size as to be unimportant. When they exist in significant size, however, the equilibrium outcome of the market will not embody an allocation of resources which maximizes social well-being. We refer to such situations as cases of *market failure*. With this in mind, let's return to the case of pollution and see how it is an example of market failure.

Market failure exists when markets, operating on their own, do not lead to a socially optimal allocation of resources.

Economics of Pollution

No one likes pollution. Almost everyone would like to see something done about it. Toward this end, we consider in this section the fundamental economics of the pollution problem. First we will examine the reasons pollution occurs, analyze the effects of pollution on resource allocation, look at the costs of pollution control, and identify its benefits. Then we will attempt to establish criteria for determining the appropriate level of control.

Why Polluters Pollute

Why is it that pollution occurs? What is there about the environment that causes consumers and producers to use it as a dumping ground? Ordinarily, pollution results from one or both of two basic factors: (1) the fact that no one has property rights or enforces them in the environment being polluted and (2) the collectively consumed characteristics of the environment being polluted.

If no one owns a portion of the environment or if an owner cannot police it or have it policed, then it becomes possible for people to use a river, a lake, the air, or an area of land as a wastebasket without being charged for doing so. Because no one owns the air above city streets and highways, automobile owners can dump combustion gases into it without paying for the privilege of doing so. Similarly, a paper mill can dump its wastes into a river without charge because no one owns the river. But even ownership of the environment may not be enough to keep pollution from occurring. How many times have you seen litter accumulate on a vacant lot or junk dumped in a ditch in a pasture away from town because the owner was not there to prevent the dumping?

In addition, many environmental services are collectively consumed or used. It is hard to single out and determine the value of the air that one person—or an automobile—uses. Similarly, it is often difficult to attach a value to the water deterioration caused by one industrial plant when thousands dump their wastes into a river. Would any one person be willing to pay someone not to take an action that would destroy a beautiful view across the countryside? When values cannot be placed on the amounts of environmental services used by any one person, it is difficult to induce people not to pollute by charging them for doing so.

Pollution and Resource Allocation

Supply curves indicate the marginal private cost of producing a good or service. This would include both the explicit and implicit costs that the producers bear. That is, the marginal private cost curve, or supply curve, includes the costs for all the resources firms hire to produce their product plus the costs associated with any resources used in production that are owned by the firms. As such you can expect to find in an economic accounting of firm costs entries for wages and salaries, mortgages and leases for plant, equipment and land, outlays for materials, and implicit cost entries for things such as the value of the owners' labor used by the firms. What would not be included in the private costs would be entries for resources used that firms do not pay for, either explicitly or implicitly. For example, if firms use a local river or stream for waste disposal and do not pay for the right to do so, no charge is incurred by the firms.

Although the use of the river for waste disposal does not show up on the firms' cost ledger, society as a whole is not so lucky. The use of the river for waste disposal creates a negative social spillover in production; thus, the marginal social cost of production will be greater than the marginal private cost. To see this more clearly and to fully appreciate the implications, suppose that two industries are located along a riverbank. An industry producing paper is located upstream and downstream there is an industry producing electric power. Further, suppose that the paper producers discharge a great deal of waste into the river and that this is particularly problematic for the power-generating firms since they need large quantities of clean water for cooling purposes. What impact does the pollution from paper production have on resource allocation and social well-being?

Consider first the paper-producing market as shown in Figure 5–1. The demand curve D_rD_r is also labeled MPB_r, for the reasons discussed above. Further, let's suppose that there are no social spillovers in consumption so that $MPB_r = MSB_r$; that is, the demand curve is both the MPB and MSB curve. The supply curve S_rS_r reflects the marginal private cost to the producers of paper, so we label it MPC_r. This curve indicates the cost that the firms producing paper incur for the resources they use in the

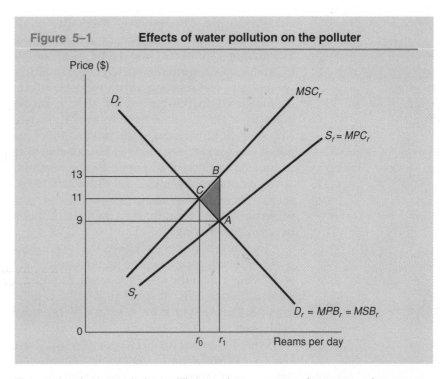

Figure 5–1   **Effects of water pollution on the polluter**

The market for paper is in equilibrium when r_1 reams of paper per day are produced and sold for \$9 per ream. At this level of production, *MSC* is greater than *MSB*; thus, social well-being would be enhanced if production were reduced to the r_0 level. The value of well-being lost by the overproduction of paper is equal to the area of the shaded triangle *ABC*.

production of paper. These costs are therefore part of the marginal social cost to produce paper. But society also bears the burden of the negative social spillover created by the firms' use of the river as a sewer since so using the river reduces its value to other users. Thus, MSC_r exceeds MPC_r, with the difference being the value of the social spillover in production. As shown, we assume that the damage done to the river, and thus to society, grows at an increasing rate as the production of paper is expanded.

Markets bring together producers and consumers to create an equilibrium at which the price of paper is \$9 per ream and resources necessary to produce r_1 reams are employed. But is this market outcome socially optimal? Recall that social well-being is maximized when marginal social cost equals marginal social benefit. What does the market give? At equilibrium, $MSB_r = MPC_r$, but due to the social spillover, MSB_r is not equal to MSC_r. In fact, at equilibrium, while the marginal benefit to society of paper is \$9 per ream, the cost to produce it, from society's perspective is \$13. But what do these numbers tell us? The marginal social benefit side is straightforward: The resources needed to produce the r_1 ream of paper will yield $9 of benefits to society if used to produce that ream of paper. The marginal social cost side is a bit more complex. The resources needed to produce the r_1 ream cost society $13 if used to produce paper. But recall, we measure cost in an opportunity cost context. Thus, when we say that the marginal social cost to produce the r_1 ream of paper is $13, what we are in reality saying is that if the resources were used in their best alternative employment rather than in the production of paper, they would produce goods and/or services worth $13 in benefits to society. In other words, by producing the r_1 unit of paper, the paper producers use resources that have an opportunity cost of $13 but which yield only $9 of satisfaction to society. Society's well-being, then, falls by $4 from what it could have been when the r_1 ream is produced. Graphically, this is the vertical distance between A and B in Figure 5–1.

The same reasoning suggests that when each unit of paper from r_0 to r_1 is produced, social well-being is sacrificed. The total value of the lost well-being due to the overproduction of paper is equal to the area of the shaded triangle ABC. If social well-being is to be maximized, production of paper should stop at the r_0 level with the price—which covers all costs of all resources used—being $11 per ream.

What happened here? That is, why did the market outcome not maximize social well-being? The problem came about because the private paper producers were not required to bear the full cost of their production. They were able to shift some of their cost onto society as a whole. And this artificial reduction in the cost to produce paper induced all overproduction of paper. You should see this as an application of the *law of supply*. For this reason we say that polluters face an incentive to overproduce, that is, to use relatively too much of society's scarce resources. This overproduction causes social well-being to be restricted below its maximum potential level.

This, as bad as it is, is not the end of the story. Consider the market for electric power, as depicted in Figure 5–2. Once again, the supply curve S_eS_e (or MPC_e curve) reflects the total explicit and implicit cost that the power producers bear. Note, however, that MSC_e is less for each unit of output than is MPC_e. The difference is that, from society's perspective, the cost of cleaning the river's water before it can be used for cooling by the power generators is properly considered a cost of producing paper, not a cost of producing power. As such, the true cost to society of producing electric power is best measured as the cost that would exist were the river not polluted by the paper producers. While society as a whole has the luxury of looking at cost in this light, the power producers do not. They have to clean the river's water before using it, so this cost is part of MPC_e.

The market equilibrium occurs at a price of 12 cents per kilowatt-hour, and resources necessary to produce e_0 kilowatts per day are hired. But, from society's perspective, each unit of power between e_0 and e_1 should be

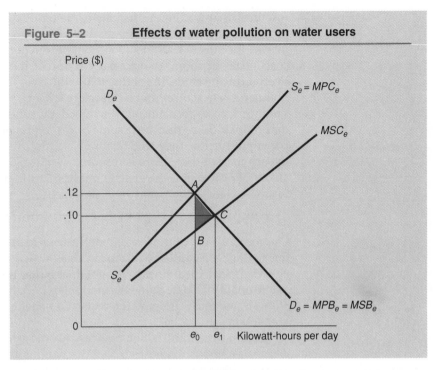

Figure 5–2   **Effects of water pollution on water users**

The market for electric power is in equilibrium when e_0 kilowatt-hours per day are produced and sold for 12 cents per kilowatt-hour. At this level of production, *MSB* is greater than *MSC*; thus, social well-being would be enhanced if production increased to the e_1 level. The value of well-being lost by the underproduction of power is equal to the area of the shaded triangle *ABC*.

produced because the benefit to society, MSB_e, is greater than the cost, MSC_e. Once again, well-being is restricted by the market outcome. In this case, the area of shaded triangle *ABC* shows the added well-being that society could enjoy if power production were carried to the socially optimal e_1 level. At this level of production, the price that power users would have to pay in order to cover all the legitimate costs of producing power would be 10 cents per kilowatt-hour.

Why did the market get it wrong? Because the power producers had to bear the added cost of the negative social spillover, artificially increasing their cost of production, they faced an incentive to underproduce. Again, this is an application of the *law of supply*. Any time the cost of production rises, whether artificially or not, the rational firm reaction is one of reducing supply.

In summary, when social spillover costs are created by the use of the river for waste disposal by the upstream paper producers, the outcomes in both the markets for paper and for electricity do not reflect an allocation of resources that maximizes social well-being. For both the polluting paper producers and the power generators who bear the burden of the pollution, market incentives lead to suboptimal production levels. For the polluter, costs of production are artificially reduced; thus, an incentive exists to overproduce. That is, the ability to use the river without charge causes the polluter to attract too much of society's scarce resources. For the power producers, costs are artificially increased; thus they face an incentive to underproduce. Since they bear some of the legitimate costs associated with paper production, they tend to attract too few of society's scarce resources. In each market then, there is resource misallocation. And when resources are misallocated, it is the general public that suffers lost well-being.

The Appropriate Level of Pollution Control

Our reactions to pollution often motivate us to say, "Let's wipe it out!" We feel that we are entitled to clean air, clean water, and clean land. But, how clean is clean? Cleanliness, like goodness, is a relative rather than an absolute quality. To determine the amount of pollution, if any, that should be allowed, we must compare the costs and benefits of keeping the environment clean.

Pollution control is not costless. An industrial plant that scrubs or cleans its combustion gases before discharging them into the atmosphere must use resources in the process. Labor and capital go into the making and operation of antipollution devices, and resources so used are not available to produce other goods and services. The value of the goods and services that must be given up is the cost of the plant's pollution control activities.

The benefits of pollution control consist of the increase in well-being that members of society feel when they have the opportunity to experience a cleaner environment. To measure the benefits of a pollution control activity, the value of the increase in well-being that it generates must be accurately estimated. Suppose that smog permeates a particular metropolitan area but that pollution control activities can reduce it or perhaps even eliminate it. To determine the benefits of, say, a 50 percent reduction in smog, we can ask each individual living in the area how much a reduction would be worth to him or her personally. By totaling the replies, we would arrive at a dollar value of the expected benefits.

Once the costs and benefits of pollution control are determined, it becomes possible to establish the appropriate level of control. If the marginal social benefit of additional control—what cleaner air, for example, is worth to the citizens of the society—exceeds the marginal social cost of the additional control, then pollution control should be expanded. Pollution control should therefore be expanded up to the point where the marginal social benefit just ceases to exceed marginal social cost. Once again, cost-benefit analysis in action.

As an illustration, consider a community of 10,000 persons that is pervaded by a nauseating stench from an incinerator used to dispose of the community's garbage. Suppose that the odor can be completely eliminated by an expenditure of $100,000 per year for an alternative method of garbage disposal (carrying it away and burying it in a landfill outside the town) and that it can be partially controlled by using various combinations of burning and burying.

Suppose that the costs of different levels of partial control are those of columns 1, 2, and 3 of Table 5–1. For simplicity, suppose that each unit of pollution control costs $10,000. By spending $10,000 on carrying and burying, the community can eliminate 10 percent of the stench; each additional $10,000 expenditure eliminates another 10 percent of the original total stench, until with a $100,000 expenditure the pollution is entirely eliminated.

Column 3 in Table 5–1 lists the marginal social cost of pollution control. The concept is essentially the same as the marginal social cost of crime prevention: It shows the change in total cost per unit change in the amount of pollution control. Since each increment in pollution control (an increment is defined as 10 percent of the control needed to eliminate the odor) adds $10,000 to the total social cost of pollution control, the marginal social cost of pollution control at each control level is $10,000. The assumption of constant marginal social cost of pollution control is used here

Table 5–1	Annual costs and benefits of pollution control					
(1) Pollution Control or Eliminated Stench	(2) Total Social Cost of Control ($000)	(3) Marginal Social Cost of Control ($000)	(4) Per Person Marginal Benefit of Control	(5) Marginal Social Benefit of Control ($000)	(6) Total Social Benefit of Control ($000)	(7) Net Social Benefit of Control ($000)
1st 10%	$ 10	$10	$10.00 ea.	$100	$100	$ 90
2nd 10	20	10	8.00	80	180	160
3rd 10	30	10	6.00	60	240	210
4th 10	40	10	4.00	40	280	240
5th 10	50	10	2.00	20	300	250
6th 10	60	10	1.60	16	316	256
7th 10	70	10	1.20	12	328	258
8th 10	80	10	0.80	8	336	256
9th 10	90	10	0.40	4	340	250
10th 10	100	10	0.20	2	342	242

merely to facilitate the analysis. The more typical case is for marginal social cost to rise as pollution control is expanded. This case is discussed later in this chapter.

The benefits of pollution control to the community are shown in columns 4, 5, and 6. Before any control is undertaken, each person in the community is asked for an opinion of what a 10 percent reduction in the stench is worth. Suppose each person indicates a willingness to pay $10 for it. We conclude that $100,000 measures the total social benefit yielded by the first 10 percent reduction. Since the benefit exceeds the cost by $90,000, the first 10 percent reduction is clearly warranted.

The question now arises as to whether a second 10 percent reduction in the stench is worthwhile. Since the pollution is not as intense as it was with no control, a second 10 percent reduction is of less value than was the first. Suppose each person values the move from 10 percent control to 20 percent control at $8 so that the community valuation of the extra control—or the marginal social benefit of it—is $80,000. Since the marginal social cost of the additional control is only $10,000, putting it into effect adds $70,000 more to the net social benefit of control and is therefore a good investment for the community.

Column 5 shows the marginal social benefit at different levels of control. Marginal social benefit of pollution control, like the marginal social benefit of crime prevention, is defined as the *change* in total social benefit per unit *change* in whatever it is that yields the benefit. Note that the total social benefit at any given level of control is obtained by adding up the marginal social benefit as the level of control is increased unit by unit up to that level.

Marginal social benefit, as shown in Table 5–1, declines as the level of pollution control is increased (the level of the stench is decreased). This is what we would expect to happen in the case at hand. The greater the amount of control, or the lower the level of the stench, the less urgent additional control becomes. This will be the usual situation in controlling pollution.

The level of pollution control yielding the maximum net social benefit is that at which the marginal social benefit just ceases to exceed the marginal social cost. The marginal social benefit of the first two 10 percent increments in the total amount of control needed to eliminate the stench exceed the marginal social cost of making them. Thus, net social benefit is increased by increasing control at least to the 20 percent level. The third, fourth, fifth, sixth, and seventh 10 percent increments also yield marginal social benefit exceeding their marginal social cost, and they increase the net social benefit of control. Now consider the eighth 10 percent increment. Marginal social benefit is $8,000, and marginal social cost is $10,000. Extending pollution control from the 70 percent level to the 80 percent level *reduces* net social benefit by $2,000. The eighth 10 percent increment is not worth to the community what it costs.

The principle is perfectly general. Net social benefit, or social well-being, will always be enhanced by increasing control if the marginal social benefit of the increase is greater than the marginal social cost of making it. Net social benefit will fall following an increase in the control level if the marginal social benefit of that increase is less than its marginal social costs. The appropriate level of control is the one that approaches as closely as possible the level where the marginal social benefit equals marginal social cost.

What Can Be Done About Pollution?

Human beings often react to problems with their emotions rather than with the capacity for logic with which they are endowed. Policies recommended to control pollution reflect this human characteristic. A typical recommendation calls for direct control of pollution by the state. But this is only one of the possible avenues of reducing pollution problems. Others include indirect control by the state through a system of incentives encouraging potential polluters not to pollute or to limit their pollution, and the creation by the state of markets for the right to pollute.

Direct Controls

An appealing, simple way to control pollution is to have the government ban polluting activities or agents. If phosphates contaminate water, then ban the use of phosphates in detergents. If DDT pollutes water and land, ban the use of DDT. If the burning of fuel oil and coal increases the sulfur dioxide content of the atmosphere, prohibit their use. Require industrial plants to clean the pollutants from whatever it is they discharge into the atmosphere or water. The method is straightforward and, on the face of it, seems eminently fair.

Government agencies, notably the Environmental Protection Agency (EPA) at the federal level, use direct controls to reduce many kinds of polluting activities. They set and attempt to enforce emission standards for such polluters as automobiles, power plants, and steel mills. State regulation of polluters, to the extent that it is accomplished, is, in general, supervised by the EPA.

The case of the city with the terrible stench shows that complete prohibition of pollutants is not likely to be worth its costs. Pollution control uses resources that could have produced goods and services, and the value of the goods and services forgone is the opportunity cost to society of controlling the pollution. If the damage done by an additional unit of pollution is less than the costs of preventing it from occurring, social well-being is greater if it is allowed to occur. Consequently, direct controls usually should aim at a less idealistic goal than a pollution-free environment.

They may take the form of controlling the level of pollution by such devices as setting emissions standards or limits for industrial plants, automobiles, and other polluters.

One problem raised by the use of direct controls to limit the amount of pollution is that it presupposes the regulatory body can determine what the economically desirable levels of pollution are. This is not an insurmountable problem. Tolerance limits on the amount of pollution to be allowed can be reasonably well established. Within those limits, overall costs can be weighed continually against benefits to establish an approximation of the desirable levels of pollution.

A second problem is the difficulty facing a regulatory body in achieving an efficient allocation of the permissible pollution among different polluters. For example, it may be more costly for a steel mill to eliminate a unit of sulfur dioxide from its emissions than it is for a power plant. In the interests of economic efficiency, it is best to eliminate pollution where it is least costly to do so. Thus, the power plant should be required to reduce its sulfur dioxide emission before the steel mill is required to do so. This is a difficult kind of decision for a regulatory body to make because it is responsible to a political body for which economic efficiency is not a primary goal. In addition, it is unrealistic to suppose that the regulatory body has a working knowledge of the nature of costs for every polluter.

A third problem is that of enforcing the standards of emissions once it has been determined what those standards should be. Direct controls fail to provide polluters with an economic incentive not to pollute. In fact, it will pay them to seek ways and means to evade the pollution standards set for them. But we should not overstate the enforcement problem. Almost any prohibition of activities that individuals and business firms want to engage in creates enforcement problems.

Indirect Controls

It is possible for the government to control many types of pollution by placing taxes on polluting activities. Where the amounts of polluting discharges can be measured for individual polluters, a tax can be placed directly on each unit of discharge. This will induce the polluter to reduce the amount of pollution that is discharged. In some cases where such measurement is not possible, polluters may be taxed indirectly—for example, automobiles not equipped with pollution control devices can be subjected to a tax on a mileage basis. This would induce their owners either to install pollution control devices or to drive less.

Figure 5–3 illustrates the use of a tax to control the amount of pollutants discharged into the environment. Consider all industrial concern that discharges its polluting wastes into a river. Processes for cleaning the wastes to control the extent of pollution are available, but are not free. For

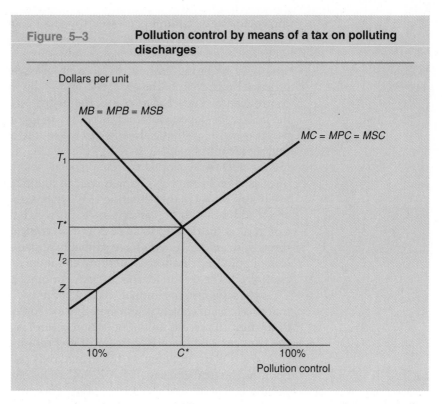

Figure 5–3   **Pollution control by means of a tax on polluting discharges**

When the tax exceeds the marginal cost of control, a firm will choose to eliminate its polluting discharge and avoid the tax. If the cost and benefits of pollution control can be accurately estimated, a tax can be established that will cause the firm to voluntarily produce the appropriate level of pollution control. In this case, a tax of T^* per unit of polluting discharge will bring about the optimal level of pollution control C^*.

simplicity, suppose there are no social spillovers in producing pollution control; thus the marginal cost curve of Figure 5–3 is both the *MPC* and *MSC* curve. As shown in Figure 5–3, as more of the pollution is suppressed, that is, as we approach 100 percent control, the marginal cost of additional control rises. This is simply the rational firm's response to the problem of eliminating its discharge. For example, suppose that the polluting discharge is a composite of a number of chemical wastes. If the firm is left on its own to clean up the discharge, what strategy will it follow? Given that a number of chemical wastes are involved, the rational firm will choose to first eliminate those wastes that it can eliminate most cheaply. The waste that can only be eliminated with extreme cost will be saved until last. In other cases, the polluting discharge may involve only one offending substance. Here we can also expect the marginal cost of control to rise as control is pressed toward 100 percent. For example, minor adjustments in the production process might yield modest increases in pollution control, while complete elimination of the polluting discharge may only be brought about by a complete overhaul of the production process. Regardless of the exact reasoning, the marginal cost of pollution control can be expected to rise as the degree of control increases, giving the positively sloped marginal cost curve of Figure 5–3. From the opposite perspective, as we have already discussed, the marginal social benefit of pollution control is likely to fall as the degree of control is increased, giving the negatively sloped marginal social benefit curve of Figure 5–3. As discussed earlier in this chapter, we can identify the appropriate level of pollution control in this situation as C^*, that is, that level at which the benefit of additional control just ceases to outweigh the cost of additional control. If C^* is the desired level of pollution control, how can it be achieved through taxation? As you have probably already guessed, a tax of T^* per unit of polluting discharge will bring about the desired degree of pollution control, C^*. The reason for this is clear: For units of pollution control below C^*, it pays the firm to eliminate its discharge and avoid the tax because the marginal cost of control is less than the tax. For example, the marginal cost of the first 10 percent unit of pollution control is Z dollars. Put differently, the firm can eliminate 10 percent of its polluting discharge if it incurs a cost of Z dollars. In doing so, the firm avoids paying the tax of T^*. Consequently, the firm can save $T^* - Z$ dollars by eliminating the first unit of pollution. Savings of this nature to the firm exist for each unit of pollution control up to the C^* level. Beyond this level, the firm will choose to pay the tax because it is less than the cost of control.

It is equally important to realize that such a tax regimen can lead to less than optimal outcomes. For example, a tax of T_1 per unit will result in too much pollution control effort and, thus, too much of the economy's scarce resources devoted to pollution control, whereas a tax of T_2 per unit will result in too little control and too little of the economy's resources devoted to this purpose. Can you explain why?

The use of taxes to control pollution has its advantages. A major one is that it provides an incentive to the polluter to seek improved ways and means of avoiding or cleaning up its discharge. Another advantage is that it prevents the polluter from shifting some of its production costs (pollution costs) to others; it reduces the incentive to overproduce.

There are also disadvantages. First, it usually is difficult to determine the benefits—total and marginal—to society of cleaning the discharge. The criticism should not be carried too far, however, since it applies to any attempt to control pollution. Second, enforcement of such a tax is not easy. Policing is necessary to determine that the discharge is indeed properly cleaned. Third, taxes are levied by political rather than economic bodies, and politics may well get in the way of the enactment of appropriate tax levels.

Creation of Pollution Rights Markets

As was discussed earlier in this chapter, the absence of well-defined property rights to the use of the environment's services is the primary source of pollution problems. Recall the example of the upstream paper industry and the downstream power industry. Since neither owns the river, that is, since neither has a property right to use the river, the paper industry is able to use the river as a sewer for its polluting wastes. And the cost of cleaning the wastes falls on the power industry.

In many such instances, it is possible to bring about the optimal level of pollution control in a cost-efficient manner through the establishment of a *pollution rights market*, in which firms buy and sell government-issued licenses to pollute. Specifically, the state can determine how much discharge it wishes to allow based on marginal social benefit and marginal social cost analysis, print licenses or permits that in total grant the holders the right to discharge the optimal amount, and then allocate to the polluting firms a share of these licenses.

When firms are allowed to buy and sell government-issued licenses granting the holder the right to create a certain amount of pollution, the resulting market is called a **pollution rights market**.

To see how this might work, suppose that after the market for pollution rights on the river has been in operation for some time, an equilibrium price is established such that a firm can purchase the right to dump 100,000 gallons of discharge into the river for $1,000. Any paper producer capable of making a 100,000-gallon reduction in its discharge for less than $1,000 could increase its profits by making the reduction and then selling a license to dump 100,000 gallons of waste that it holds to another firm. And any firm that could only reduce its discharge by 100,000 gallons at a cost greater than $1,000 would be happy to purchase this license because the difference between the license price of $1,000 and the cost of the reduction in discharge would be directly added to profits. If a decision is made that the overall level of pollution must be reduced, the government would need only to *buy back* some of the licenses it had previously made available to the market. In this way, the state can achieve any particular level of pollution control it wishes and it can be sure that any needed reductions in pollution will be made where it is cheapest to do so. Put differently, through the establishment of a pollution rights market, the state can make certain that any desired level of pollution control can be accomplished in the way that places the least burden on the economy's scarce resources.

Interestingly, the use of pollution rights licenses and the resulting creation of a pollution rights market is not just an academic aside. In the Clean Air Act of 1990, the federal government took its initial steps in this direction by allowing electric companies to trade in sulfur dioxide licenses. Specifically, the act allowed roughly 100 utilities operating principally in the Midwest to produce a certain amount of sulfur dioxide discharge each year. Firms that could reduce their discharge cheaply were allowed to sell their licenses to others. Those could not reduce their discharge as cheaply could then purchase the right to continue to pollute. While the full program has only been in effect for about 5 years, it appears clear that it will not only lead to the targeted reduction in sulfur dioxide emissions, but it will do so in a cost-effective manner. That is, the early evidence indicates that the 1990 Clean Air Act's creation of a market for pollution rights is working in textbook fashion.

Summary

The environment provides environmental services that are used by both household units and producing units of the economy. In the processes of consumption and production, wastes are generated. If the ecological system cannot recycle these wastes as fast as they are generated, wastes accumulate. This constitutes pollution.

Economic analysis of pollution provides a perspective on its causes and its effects, along with the costs and benefits of controlling it. Incentives to pollute stem from (1) an absence of property rights in the environment and (2) the collectively consumed nature of whatever is being polluted. Polluters, by polluting, transfer a part of their costs to others. Cost-benefit analysis is useful in determining how much pollution should be allowed. It indicates that it is seldom in the common interest to forbid pollution altogether.

There are three main avenues that government pollution control policies can take. First, certain polluting activities may be controlled directly through prohibitions or limitations on polluting activities. Second, they may be controlled indirectly by providing polluters with incentives not to pollute—say, through taxation of polluting activities. Third, in some cases, pollution may be efficiently controlled by allowing for the creation of markets for pollution rights, in which firms buy and sell government-issued licenses to pollute.

Discussion Questions

1. Recent research indicates that secondhand smoke from cigarettes endangers the health of those who are in sustained contact with smokers. Show graphically and explain why the market, operating on its own, will lead to an overproduction and overconsumption of cigarettes.
2. From an economic perspective, explain why pollution takes place.
3. Show graphically and explain why polluters face an incentive to overproduce their product.

4. Show graphically and explain why those who bear the burden of pollution face an incentive to underproduce their product.

5. Explain how polluting firms effectively force other firms to bear part of their legitimate production costs.

6. The equilibrium reached by a market typically reflects a resource allocation that maximizes social well-being. Explain why this will not be the case when social spillovers in production exist.

7. Discuss: "The goal for pollution control should be the complete elimination of all polluting discharges."

8. Show graphically and explain how taxes can be used to cause polluting firms to voluntarily cut their polluting discharges to the socially optimal level.

9. Under what circumstances would it make economic sense to eliminate all of a particular type of pollution?

10. Explain how the creation of a pollution rights market might work. Suppose, after a few years, it was decided that too much pollution was being allowed under the plan. What could be done?

Additional Readings

Constanza, Robert, Charles Perrings, and Cutler J. Cleveland. *The Development of Ecological Economics.* The International Library of Critical Writings in Economics 75. Brookfield, VT: Edward Elgar Publishing Company, 1997.
Readings on the history, principles, theories, and assessment of ecological economics.

Garbage: The Practical Journal for the Environment. Various issues, monthly.
A wealth of well-balanced information about the various problems of and proposed solutions to pollution.

The Journal of Economic Perspectives, Summer 1998.
A thorough and accessible treatment of the 1990 Clean Air Act's creation of a sulfur dioxide pollution rights market.

Markandya, Anil, and Julie Richardson, eds. *Environmental Economics: A Reader.* New York: St. Martin's Press, 1992.
Collection of essays that covers all aspects of environmental economics, from an overview to valuation methods and applications and on to international and global environmental problems.

Taylor, Jeffrey. "Smog Swapping: New Rules Harness Power of Free Markets to Curb Air Pollution." *The Wall Street Journal,* Apr. 14, 1992, p. 1.
Describes ways many companies are beginning to acquire and trade pollution rights following the Clean Air Act of 1990.

Tietenberg, Thomas H. *Economics and Environmental Policy.* Brookfield, VT: Edward Elgar Publishing Company, 1994.
Collection of articles discussing theories and applications of economic incentives in environment policy.

World Wide Web Resources

Environmental Organization Web Directory-Recycling
www.webdirectory.com/Recycling

Recycling icons for chemical recycling, recycled glass, metals, paper products, petroleum plastics, computer products, and links to other sites.

The Internet Consumer Recycling Guide
www.obviously.com/recycle

Provides links to guides for curbside materials and hard-to-recycle material, an index to local recycling centers, and ways of reducing unwanted mail.

National Pollution Prevention Center for Higher Education
www.snre.umich.edu/nppc/index.html

A compendium of education materials designed for university instruction in pollution prevention.

Sierra Club
www.sierraclub.org

"The Sierra Club is a nonprofit, member-supported, public interest organization that promotes conservation of the natural environment by influencing public policy decisions." Provides links to their clubhouse, the global environment, the great outdoors, and environmental quality.

United States Environmental Protection Agency
www.epa.gov

Gives links to U.S. laws and regulations, projects and publications, programs, and other resources.

CHAPTER

6

Discrimination
The High Cost of Prejudice

Chapter Outline

What Is Discrimination?
The Public View
A Working Definition

Economic Analysis of Discrimination
Sources of Market Discrimination
Labor Market Discrimination
Product Market Discrimination
Economic Costs of Discrimination

Nonmarket Discrimination
Social Discrimination
Educational Discrimination

What Can Be Done About Discrimination?
Reduce Tastes for Discrimination
Reduce Market Imperfections
Reduce Discrimination in Development of Human
    Capital
Reduce Occupational Segregation

Continuing Controversies
Affirmative Action Programs
Comparable Worth

Summary

Checklist of Economic Concepts

Labor market discrimination
Product market discrimination
Derived demand
Marginal revenue product of
    labor
Law of diminishing returns

Substitution effect
Income effect
Wage discrimination
Employment discrimination
Occupational discrimination
Price discrimination

Nonmarket discrimination
Monopoly power
Exploitation
Affirmative action
Comparable worth

A study by a University of Maryland researcher shows that gay men make 11% to 27% less than heterosexual men in comparable jobs. Lesbians earn 5% to 14% less than heterosexual women, the study says. "Lesbians and gay men are experiencing discrimination that actually hurts them economically," said University of Maryland economics professor Lee Badgett, author of the study. "They are losing money just for being gay."

The study comes barely a month after a Yankelovich Partners Inc. report on consumer attitudes shot holes in the oft-repeated notion that gays have a much higher disposable income than heterosexual consumers. The Yankelovich study found that gay couples have roughly the same household incomes as heterosexual couples.

Badgett found that lesbians make less, and are more likely to wind up in low-income, blue-collar jobs where tolerance for their sexual orientation is often low. Gay men are more likely to hold professional jobs, according to the study, but they are less likely to be promoted into managerial ranks. While 17.9% of heterosexual men surveyed were managers, only 12.8% of gay men were managers.[1]

[1] "Gays Earn Smaller Salaries," *Rocky Mountain News,* August 18, 1994, p. 48-A.

Discrimination shows its ugly face through varied expressions. At its worst, discrimination takes away freedom and rights, robs people of human dignity, and, in the end, enslaves them. In its milder form, discrimination is an unintentional by-product of decision making. For example, a famous restaurant in the French Quarter in New Orleans will not take a reservation unless there are at least four people in the party. Parties of three or less are denied access to a service because of the decision of the restaurant to exclude or discriminate. However, the decision of the restaurant to restrict reservations to parties based on size was undoubtedly motivated not by the desire to discriminate but by the desire to use its facilities efficiently. Also, this form of discrimination leaves open access to the restaurant to everyone in a party of four or more.

What Is Discrimination?

The Public View

Most people relate discrimination to what they consider to be unfair treatment of some sort. Discrimination is viewed as the opposite of social justice. A person who is discriminated against is one who is treated unjustly.

There is nothing wrong in relating discrimination to unfair treatment. The shortcoming of this view is that it does not go far enough. It leaves unanswered the vital question: What is unfair treatment?

A Working Definition

Discrimination The term means that equals are treated unequally or unequals are treated equally.

Discrimination as we use it means that equals are treated unequally or that unequals are treated equally. More specifically, discrimination exists in a labor market when people with equal productivity are paid different wages or people with differences in productivity are paid equal wages. Discrimination exists in the product market when consumers pay different prices for the same product.

Market discrimination exists, then, when the terms on which market transactions are based are not the same for all. A seller who charges different prices to different consumers for essentially the same product or service is practicing price discrimination. An employer who pays different wages for identical units of labor provides another illustration. Sellers who cannot sell in a certain market and buyers who cannot buy in a certain market for reasons other than price provide examples of complete market discrimination.

Economic Analysis of Discrimination

Sources of Market Discrimination

Market discrimination may be traced to two primary sources. These are the *power* to discriminate in the market and the *desire* to discriminate.

Monopoly Power. Monopoly power may exist on the selling and buying sides of markets. A monopolistic market is one in which the seller is able to manipulate the product price to his or her own advantage and can keep potential competitors out of the market. A similar problem exists on the buying side of the market when one firm or a group of firms acting as a cartel hires all or most of the available labor in a particular area and of a particular type. An example might be a mill town in western North Carolina or, as discussed in Chapter 9, professional sports leagues. In this case, the firm or firms are said to be labor market monopolists or simply *monopsonists.* A monopsonist has the power to control the price at which labor is hired. The existence of monopoly power on the buying and selling sides of the market makes it possible for consumers and workers to be exploited. Consumers are exploited when the price of a product is above the cost per unit of producing it, and workers are exploited when the wage rates paid are below their marginal revenue product, that is, below their contributions to the receipts of their employer.

Exploitation may exist without discrimination. For example, both blacks and whites with the same productivity may be paid equal wages that are below their productivity. However, monopoly power is a source of discrimination. In the exercise of monopoly power, a seller may segregate the market and charge consumers different prices for the same product. A monopsonistic buyer may segregate the job market and practice discrimination by paying workers on bases other than merit or productivity.

Desire to Discriminate. Some people have a taste for discrimination and strive to satisfy this taste or desire. An employer who desires to discriminate acts as if nonmonetary costs were connected with hiring those whose skin color, religion, age, gender, or sexual orientation, among other factors, differ from the employer's subjective ideal.

The primary source of an individual's desire to discriminate is personal *prejudice*. Prejudice refers to the biases and unfavorable attitudes that people hold against others who do not share their own personal characteristics or beliefs. Prejudiced individuals may or may not engage in discrimination. However, when unfavorable actions based on personal prejudices are taken against others, discrimination occurs. From an economic perspective, discrimination motivated by prejudice results in resources being allocated on a basis other than productivity. Thus, employment opportunities and incomes of the adversely affected groups are reduced.

Labor Market Discrimination

Market discrimination can take different forms and occur in a variety of situations. Three major types of discrimination are found in labor markets. These are wage, employment, and occupational discrimination. Labor market discrimination may create significant economic costs for those who experience it and, in some cases, for those who practice it. In order to understand the effects of labor market discrimination, we must first understand how wages and employment are determined in competitive labor markets. As we will see, an employer in a competitive labor market will treat workers of equal productivity equally.

Market Demand for Labor. The demand for unskilled labor by the employers of the economy is given in Figure 6–1. It should be noted that whereas the horizontal axis is labeled in the standard way, the vertical axis measures the wage rate since the wage rate is the price of labor per hour. There is an important difference, however, between the demand for labor by employers and the demand for a good or service by consumers. Specifically, consumers demand a good like orange juice because they receive satisfaction directly from consuming the product. Employers do not demand labor for the same reason. Employers demand labor not because they directly receive satisfaction from labor but because they indirectly receive satisfaction from labor, in the form of increased revenues, when they sell the products that are produced by labor. For this reason, the demand for labor is said to be an indirect or *derived demand*. In other words, the demand for labor is derived from the demand for the product being produced.

The demand curve for labor in Figure 6–1 is downward-sloping, just as the demand for a good such as orange juice would be. Such a negatively sloped demand curve for orange juice would suggest that the value placed on an additional unit of orange juice by the consumer declines as more orange juice is consumed. The demand for labor is downward-sloping for exactly the same reason. The negative slope of the demand for labor

> The demand for labor is said to be dependent on, or derived from, the demand for the product being produced. In this sense, the demand for labor is a **derived demand**.

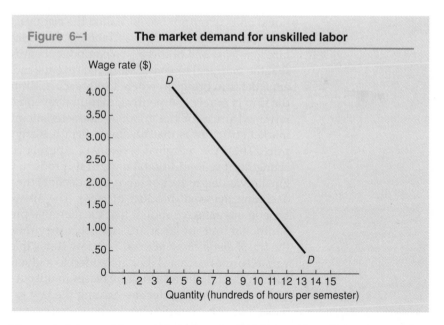

Figure 6–1   **The market demand for unskilled labor**

The market demand for unskilled labor shows the quantities of labor that employers in the economy are willing to hire at various wage rates. It is important to note that the law of demand holds for labor. That is, the quantity of labor demanded by employers falls as the wage increases, other things being equal.

indicates that, in terms of extra revenues, the value of an additional worker to the employer declines as more labor is hired.

It seems reasonable to argue that a fifth quart of orange juice consumed during a week yields less satisfaction than the fourth, but why would the same be true for units of labor? That is, why would a fourth unit of labor add less to the satisfaction (revenues) of the employer than the third? To answer this question, detailed consideration must be given to the way in which a firm's revenues change as the firm's employment level changes. Thus, we must shift away from the demand for unskilled labor by all employers, as presented in Figure 6–1, and consider the demand for unskilled labor by one employer.

The Demand for Labor by One Employer.

When a unit of labor is hired by a firm, a certain amount of additional output is produced, which is converted into additional revenue for the firm once the output is sold. The increase in revenue due to hiring one additional unit of labor is called the *marginal revenue product of labor* and indicates the value the firm places on the additional unit of labor. Our goal, then, is to determine why the marginal revenue product of labor declines as more labor is hired. The marginal revenue product of labor has two parts: (1) the increase in output due to hiring the additional unit of labor, called the *marginal product of labor*, and (2) the increase in revenue for the firm when each of the additional units of output is sold, called the *marginal revenue*. Given this, if the marginal revenue product of labor is to decline as additional labor is hired, at least one of these two components must be declining. Consider first the marginal revenue. Marginal revenue indicates the amount of revenue the firm brings in when it sells each additional unit of its product. If the firm is purely competitive, marginal revenue is simply the market determined price for the good. A characteristic of the purely competitive market structure is that no single firm has any control over the market price. Thus, the marginal revenue of a purely competitive firm does not change as it sells additional units of its product. Consequently, if the marginal revenue product of labor is to decline, the decline must be due to a declining marginal product of labor. The answer has now been found. Economists are so confident that the marginal product of labor declines as additional units of labor are hired that they refer to this phenomenon as the *law of diminishing returns*. This law states that as additional units of a variable input such as labor are added to a given amount of a fixed input such as capital, the resulting increases in output (the marginal product of labor) will *eventually* decline. Stating the law as fact, of course, does not make it so. An example should, however, convince even the most skeptical reader.

Table 6–1 details a typical situation for a firm that sells hamburgers when various quantities of labor per hour are hired. Labor is the variable input for this firm, and its capital consists of its building, tools, and

The increase in revenue that accrues to the firm when an additional worker is hired is called the **marginal revenue product of labor** and, as such, indicates the value of the worker to the firm.

The increase in output due to hiring an additional worker is called the **marginal product of labor**.

The increase in revenue from selling an additional unit of the product is called the **marginal revenue**.

The **law of diminishing returns** states that as additional units of a variable input are added to a given amount of a fixed input, the resulting increases in output eventually will decline.

(1) Units of Labor	(2) Total Production	(3) Marginal Product	(4) Marginal Revenue	(5) Marginal Revenue Product (MRP) = (3) × (4)
0	0			
		5	$.50	$2.50
1	5			
		20	.50	10.00
2	25			
		25	.50	12.50
3	50			
		20	.50	10.00
4	70			
		10	.50	5.00
5	80			
		5	.50	2.50
6	85			
		1	.50	.50
7	86			

Table 6–1 Total production, marginal product, marginal revenue, and marginal revenue product for the hamburger shop

equipment. When the firm hires no workers, total production is, of course, zero hamburgers, as given in column 2. When the first worker is hired, total production rises to five hamburgers per hour. Thus, the first worker contributes five units of production, which is given as that worker's marginal product in column 3. The firm operates in a purely competitive market, so the marginal revenue or price is constant at 50 cents per burger, as indicated in column 4. Finally, column 5 reports the marginal revenue product of each unit of labor. The first worker increased production by five units, each of which sold for 50 cents. Thus, the first worker's marginal revenue product is $2.50.

Suppose now that a second worker is hired. Total production rises to 25 burgers, indicating that the second worker's marginal product is 20 units. Why does the second worker add more to production than the first? Think about the way in which the firm would have to operate were it to have only one employee. This worker would have to be a "jack of all trades," first taking a customer's order, then scrambling to the supply area for the needed ingredients, then scrambling to the preparation area and to the grill. Once the "beef" patty is cooked, the worker must assemble the burger and scramble (now short of breath) back to the counter to serve the customer. Put simply, with only one worker (or perhaps only a few workers), there is too little labor for the amount of capital that the firm has at its disposal. In other words, the firm's capital is underutilized. When the second worker is hired, the available capital can be used much more efficiently through the specialization of labor. For example, perhaps one worker concentrates on taking customer orders and gathering ingredients, while the other worker actually prepares the burger. Such specialization of labor often yields increasing returns to labor initially and serves as the justification for modern assembly line processes.

Returning to Table 6–1, you see that the same situation holds true for the third worker. Eventually, however, just the opposite occurs. Experience teaches that just as capital can be underutilized, leading to the possibility of increasing marginal returns to labor, capital eventually becomes overutilized. When this occurs, diminishing returns to labor follow. For the hamburger shop, this occurs with the addition of the fourth worker. When this worker is hired, total production rises from 50 burgers per hour to 70. The marginal product of the fourth worker is 20 units, which is five less than the marginal product of the third worker. Diminishing returns of this nature come about for a variety of reasons, the most obvious being that the hamburger shop itself is equipped to accommodate only a certain number of workers comfortably. As more workers are hired, they may have to share their tools with other workers or wait their turn to use capital equipment. Common sense dictates that regardless of the size of the firm, if additional workers are continually hired, eventually a new worker will do little more than get in the way. Just as your mother probably told you, "Too many cooks spoil the soup."

Diminishing returns for labor may also come about due to the over specialization of labor. Although requiring each worker to be a "jack of all trades" is clearly inefficient, specialization can go too far. If specialization goes to the point where the extent of a particular worker's job is squirting ketchup on buns all day, the worker will likely become bored, easily distracted, and perhaps even a bit resentful. The result is clear—reduced efficiency or, in other words, diminishing returns to labor.

Regardless of the exact cause of the fall in efficiency, we can be sure that it will eventually occur. The outcome of diminishing returns is equally clear: The value to the firm of additional units of labor falls. Consider the hamburger shop. The third worker has a marginal revenue product of $12.50; thus, this worker is worth $12.50 to the firm. When the fourth worker is hired, the marginal revenue product and, therefore, the value of the fourth worker falls to $10.00. The same will be true for each unit of labor hired beyond the third. As additional units of labor are hired by a firm, the value placed on each new worker eventually declines due to the law of diminishing returns.

Now that the question of why an additional unit of labor may be valued less highly by the firm than a previously hired unit has been answered, the firm-level discussion of the demand for labor must be tied into the discussion of the demand for labor by all employers as presented in Figure 6–1. This requires two steps. First, as you have probably guessed, the marginal revenue product of labor is the firm's demand for labor. A demand curve simply indicates the value placed on each unit of a good or service by the purchaser. Marginal revenue product (*MRP*) is the firm's valuation of labor; thus, it is the firm's demand curve for labor. Plotting the data on the marginal revenue product of labor from Table 6–1 gives the demand for unskilled labor for the hamburger shop in Figure 6–2. It should be noted that the data for only the third through seventh workers are included. The reason for this is that if the hamburger shop is managed rationally, it would never hire fewer than three workers. Why? The third worker is more valuable than either of the first two workers. Thus, if it is rational to hire the first and second workers, it *must* be rational to hire at least three.

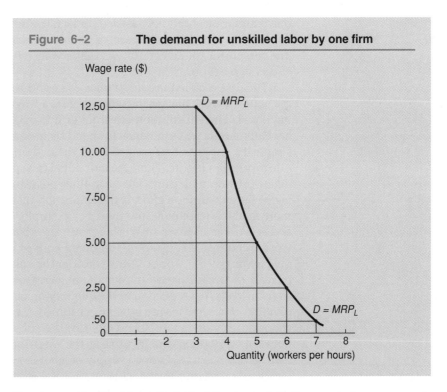

Figure 6–2   **The demand for unskilled labor by one firm**

The demand for labor for an individual firm is given by the marginal revenue product of labor, which measures the increase in firm revenues due to hiring additional units of labor.

The second step requires a tie between one firm's demand for labor and the demand by all firms. That is, there may be 100 or even 1,000 firms similar to the hamburger shop. In such a case, how is the demand for labor by one firm linked to the demand for labor by all firms? If your common sense suggests that all that must be done is to sum the individual firm demands, then you are right. The procedure is quite simple; for each wage, each individual firm's quantity demanded is added to the quantity demanded by all of the other firms to form the quantity demanded of labor by all firms. In this way, the demand for labor by all employers, as represented by Figure 6–1, may be thought of as the summation of the individual demands for labor by the individual employers in the economy.

Market Supply of Labor. The supply of labor refers to the quantities of labor, in terms of hours, that workers are willing to offer at various wage rates, other things being equal. As such, the supply of labor curve indicates what happens to the hours of work offered by an economy's workers when there is a change in the wage. For example, suppose there is a general wage increase. In such a situation, what will happen to the number of hours that workers are willing to work? There is a temptation to conclude that the number of hours increases as the wage increases, but this temptation should be resisted. In fact, the number of hours offered by workers may increase, decrease, or remain the same as the wage increases. The reason for the uncertainty is that a wage change puts two offsetting effects into action.

> The **substitution effect** of a wage change refers to the change in the hours of work that occurs in response to a wage change, other things being equal.

The first is called the *substitution effect* and is defined as the change in the hours of work that occurs when there is a wage change, other things being equal. The substitution effect takes into account the fact that people have numerous ways in which to spend their time other than working. For simplicity, suppose that we group all these alternative uses of time into a category called leisure. Thus, the individual can spend his or her time working or consuming leisure. The only other point needed for an understanding of the substitution effect is the realization that the wage rate is nothing more than the price of leisure time. For example, if the wage is $5 per hour and a worker chooses to work 1 hour less than normal—that is, if the worker chooses to consume 1 additional hour of leisure—the worker must give up or pay $5 to do so. Now consider the substitution effect of a wage increase. A wage increase amounts to an increase in the price of leisure and, as such, leads to a reduction in the quantity of leisure demanded by the individual. Since less leisure is being consumed, the individual of necessity is choosing to work more. Consequently, the substitution effect causes the hours of work offered to increase as the wage increases and would, on its own, give a positively sloped supply of labor curve.

Before drawing the conclusion that the supply of labor is positively sloped, however, recall that a second and offsetting effect is put into action when there is a wage change. This is called the *income effect* and is

The **income effect** measures the change in the hours of work that occurs when there is a change in income, other things being equal.

defined as the change in hours of work that occurs when there is a change in income, other things being equal. The income effect treats leisure as a normal good. Recall that a normal good is one for which demand rises as income rises. Given a wage increase and the accompanying income increase, the demand for leisure can be expected to increase. With the demand for leisure increasing, the hours of work offered tend to decline in response to the income effect of a wage increase. Thus, the income effect of a wage increase, on its own, gives a negatively sloped supply of labor curve.

Which of the two effects dominates? If the substitution effect is dominant, the supply of labor is positively sloped, while a dominant income effect gives a negatively sloped supply. Clearly, this is not a question that can be answered theoretically. Fortunately, a great deal of research has been conducted on the issue, resulting in a general conclusion that suggests the supply of labor is very slightly positively sloped. When there is a general wage increase, then, the number of hours offered will increase, but only slightly. Such a supply of labor curve is drawn in Figure 6–3.

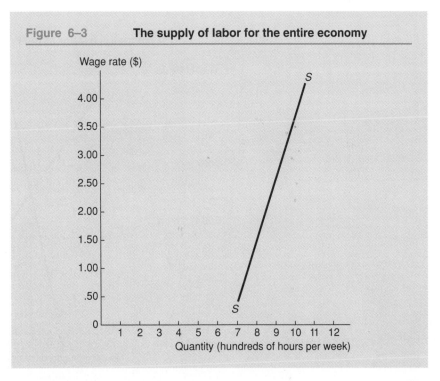

Figure 6–3   **The supply of labor for the entire economy**

The supply of labor shows the number of hours of labor that individuals are willing to offer at various wage rates. The steep positive slope indicates that a wage increase will coax some additional hours but not a great increase in the number of hours offered.

The Labor Market. Figure 6–4 brings together the demand for and supply of unskilled labor in the economy. Once this is done, it becomes clear that the labor market behaves much like any other market. For example, if *DD* and *SS* are the initial market demand and supply curves, there is an equilibrium wage and quantity hired of $5 and 900 hours per week, respectively. Note that at this wage there is neither a surplus of labor (unemployment) nor a shortage. Just as in any other market, the equilibrium indicates that the intentions of the buyers (firms) are the same as the intentions of the sellers (workers). In other words, at this wage the firms are willing to hire exactly the number of hours of labor that the workers desire to offer.

Before we continue, it is important to understand why the employers desire 900 hours of labor at the equilibrium wage of $5. A rational employer will hire a worker only if the worker adds more to revenue than to cost. The addition to revenue is given by the marginal revenue product or the demand for labor curve. The addition to cost, on the other hand, is

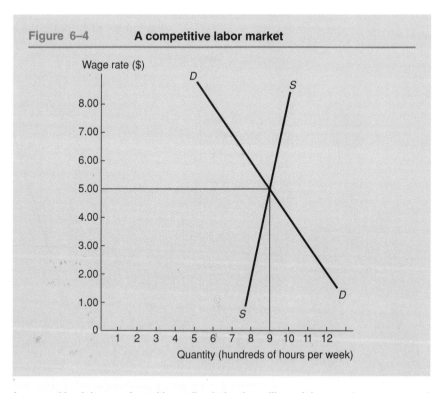

Figure 6–4   A competitive labor market

A competitive labor market without discrimination will result in a market wage equal to the workers' marginal revenue product. In this case, marginal revenue product is $5 per hour, and 900 hours of labor will be hired.

given by the wage rate. Thus, the rational firm increases employment up to the point where the wage rate equals the demand for labor. Figure 6–4 indicates that this occurs at the 900-hour level of employment. For each unit of labor up to the 900-hour level, the marginal revenue product is greater than the wage, indicating that these workers are profitably hired. Were employment to be carried even one unit beyond 900, however, the firms would be losing money on the additional worker since the worker would be adding more to cost than to revenue.

Wage Differentials. In our complex market economy the wages of workers vary widely between industries and firms. Even workers hired by the same employer to perform similar jobs are often paid different wage rates. Given what we've learned about how wages are determined, it is easy to see why wage differentials exist. Remember, the demand for labor reflects a worker's productivity and the ability to generate revenue for the employing firm. More productive workers can command higher wages because they are more valuable to employers than less productive workers. Workers who differ in skill and ability will not be treated as equals by the labor market. Thus, it is not surprising that today the average college graduate earns approximately 75 percent more than the average high school graduate. Wage differentials between workers that result from different levels of productivity should not be labeled as discrimination.

Another important point to recall is that labor is a derived demand. The demand by consumers for the product or service that workers produce influences the employer's demand for labor. Everything else being the same, product markets with relatively strong demand will result in higher prices than product markets with relatively weak demand. Higher product prices, in turn, imply higher wages for the workers who produce the product. This is true because higher product prices, which increase revenue, make each worker more valuable to the employer. Thus, wage differentials may exist between industries or firms due to differences in the demand for their products. Once again, when workers vary in their contribution to a firm's revenue, nondiscriminatory wage differences may result.

Wage Discrimination. Full-time working women earn, on average, about 70 percent of what full-time working men earn. The situation is only slightly better for blacks, with the typical full-time black worker earning about 80 percent of the earnings of full-time white workers. These statistics do not, however, suggest that there is a 30 percent discrimination gap in earnings by gender or a 20 percent discrimination gap by race. To determine the importance of discrimination in earnings, we need a better understanding of what constitutes wage discrimination.

The meaning of wage discrimination can be elucidated by the slogan "equal pay for equal work." Suppose a man and woman complete their accounting degrees at the same time and place, have identical records and recommendations, are hired by the same accounting firm as entry-level staff accountants, and differ in only one respect—the man is paid $30,000 a year and the woman is paid $26,000 a year. This is a case of discrimination. Two workers contribute equally to their employing firm but are paid unequal wages.

It is often difficult to be sure that wage discrimination exists because the person who discriminates typically denies it, and the relative productivities of labor may be difficult to measure. A discriminator may say that qualified blacks cannot be found or that females are paid less than males because their productivity is less. In some instances, discriminators may be right; in others, they may only be trying to hide discriminatory behavior.

The meaning of wage discrimination is clear enough—unequal pay for equal contributions. But proving discrimination depends on being able to distinguish among individuals on the basis of individual efforts and productivity. Generally speaking, human resources, like any other resources, are paid approximately what they are worth in a competitive economy. Thus, wage differences where competition exists reflect differences in labor productivity. Wage discrimination that does exist in the economy means that the market is not working properly in allocating resources among alternative uses.

What can we conclude with regard to the importance of discrimination in earnings gaps according to race and gender? Some part of these gaps is no doubt due to "legitimate" factors such as differences in productivity and occupations. If we were able to determine the part of the earnings gaps that is due to these factors, the part of the gap that remained would serve as a rough estimate of the degree of discrimination in earnings. Researchers have spent much time doing just this. A general conclusion of this research is that legitimate factors explain only about half of the earnings gaps. In other words, if women were comparable to men with regard to productivity, occupation, and other legitimate factors, they would still earn only about 85 percent of what men earn, while blacks, under the same conditions, would earn about 90 percent of what whites earn.

Employment Discrimination. Employment discrimination means that some people are not hired because of noneconomic characteristics such as race or gender. Two individuals with the same training, education, and experience apply for a job. One is black and one is white. If both do not have the same chance of getting the job, discrimination has entered into the decision-making process.

Employment discrimination, like wage discrimination, is difficult to identify positively. Differences in unemployment rates among whites and minority groups and between males and females may suggest discrimination but do not prove that it exists. However, when you consider all low-productivity families and discover that unemployment rates are much higher among blacks than whites, or when you look at families with identical education levels and find unemployment rates higher among black families than white families, the evidence of employment discrimination becomes more conclusive. For example, in 1996 the unemployment rate of white high school graduates was 4.0 percent, while the unemployment rate of black high school graduates was 9.1 percent. Similarly, the unemployment rate of black college graduates was about 50 percent greater than that of white college graduates.[2] Although not absolutely conclusive, evidence of this nature certainly is suggestive of employment discrimination.

Occupational Discrimination. There is a growing belief that discriminatory differences in pay, especially gender differences in pay, occur largely because of occupational segregation. In general, men work in occupations that employ very few women, and women work in occupations that employ very few men. The economic results of occupational segregation for women are low wages. Women are often relegated to occupations where productivity and experience have little to do with their status and where opportunities for overtime and premium pay are limited.

Why do women fail to enter higher paid male-dominated occupations? It is widely believed that women are socialized into roles that minimize the importance of establishing a career. Women are frequently taught from an early age that their primary roles are as housewives and mothers. In our culture, the division of labor within households often leaves women at home to produce domestic services, such as raising children, whereas men pursue work in the marketplace to provide income for the family. However, the traditional economic roles of men and women have changed dramatically during this century. Two-income households are now the norm, but a woman's job is still most often considered "secondary." Some economists argue that because of our cultural division of labor between the sexes, women *choose* occupations that allow them to simultaneously work and pursue domestic activities. Such occupations generally require less education and training and are therefore lower-paid.

There is some evidence to suggest that women have made major gains in several male-dominated occupations in the last several decades. For example, in 1960, only 3.4 percent of lawyers in the United States were women. By the late 1990s, women accounted for more than one-fourth of all lawyers. However, such dramatic changes have not occurred in all occupations, and very little movement of men into traditionally female jobs has been observed. More than 90 percent of registered nurses, secretaries,

---

[2]U.S. Department of Education, Office of Educational Research and Improvement, National Center for Education Statistics, *Digest of Educational Statistics 1997* (Washington, DC: 1997), p. 421.

and child care workers continue to be female. Clearly, a large degree of occupational segregation still exists in our economy.

Product Market Discrimination

Price Discrimination. In 1990, a shopping study in Chicago revealed that white males were systematically offered new cars at lower prices than were blacks and females.[3] The study involved 90 new car dealerships and nearly 200 "customers" who had been trained to bargain in the same fashion so as to minimize differences in offered prices that might simply be due to differences in bargaining abilities. The author reported that white females on average had to pay about $150 more than did white males to purchase identical cars. The situation was even worse for blacks. Black males on average could only purchase the vehicle if they were willing to pay an additional $425, while the premium for black females averaged $950.

In other cases, price discrimination may take the form of preventing a person, because of race, from having access to a given market. The housing market is a market in which some sellers may not sell at any price to certain buyers. Another illustration is the refusal to allow blacks equal access to the capital or credit markets. The purchase of real capital—equipment, machinery, buildings—is usually financed from borrowed money. The complete or partial barring of blacks from the credit market may result in low ratios of capital to labor for blacks and, consequently, low productivity. Blacks' production efforts are thus limited to those products and services where high ratios of labor to capital are required.

Economists have identified other forms of price discrimination that result from sellers having a degree of control over the marketplace. For example, a theater owner can control the time of the day during which movies are shown. It is common practice at most theaters to charge a higher price for evening shows than for afternoon matinees. Theater owners recognize that the demand for tickets on Friday night is more inelastic than on Saturday afternoon, and charge accordingly. Although the intent of such behavior is to increase profits and not to injure or harm a specific population group, given our definition, this is a form of price discrimination based on monopoly power.

Some forms of price discrimination in product markets are not overtly intended to harm or injure specific population groups. In fact, price discrimination often occurs specifically to *benefit* a target group of consumers.

---

[3]Ian Ayers, "Fair Driving: Gender and Race Discrimination in Retail Car Negotiations," *Harvard Law Review,* February 1991, pp. 817–874.

A classic example is the retailer who offers a discount to customers who are elderly. In recent years, such "senior citizen discounts" have become commonplace in the restaurant, lodging, and entertainment industries. When a business offers a different price to one group of customers based on their age, clearly discrimination (as we have defined it) occurs. However, rarely do younger customers, who are charged a higher price, cry foul and protest this form of discrimination. Why? Because this form of discrimination is not motivated by negative prejudices or exercised through monopoly power. Retailers may offer senior citizen discounts as a form of advertising to attract and maintain sales. Further, the general public may view such discriminatory discounts as "fair" in the sense that many who qualify are retired and living on fixed incomes.

Economic Costs of Discrimination

The economic costs of discrimination are both individual and social in nature. The individual costs of discrimination are those imposed on individuals or groups who lose one way or another because of discrimination. The social cost of discrimination is in the form of a reduction in total output in the economy due to discrimination.

Individual Losses and Gains. Individual losses and gains flow from discrimination. Individuals discriminated against, or the discriminatees, suffer losses in the form of reduced living standards. They tend to be paid less for what they sell, to pay higher prices for what they buy, to have fewer employment opportunities, and to be segregated in low-paying occupations. Individuals who discriminate, the discriminators, may gain and may lose. An employer-discriminator may gain if a female worker can be hired at a lower wage than a male worker, assuming both are equally productive. The wages of whites may be kept artificially above blacks if blacks are shut off from jobs and occupations because of race. Discriminators, however, may lose by having to forfeit income in order to satisfy their taste for discrimination. For example, an individual who refuses to sell a house to a black may end up selling the house at a lower price to a white person. As another example, an individual who refuses to hire a woman may end up paying a higher price for a man with the same productivity.

Output Reduction. We have said that the cost to society of discrimination is the reduction in the nation's output of goods and services (GDP) resulting from discrimination. We concluded that monopolistic elements within the economy reduced GDP by about 1 percent per year. One study estimates that the loss in GDP due to racial discrimination is about 4 percent per year.[4] Another older study, but more analytical in nature, places the loss due to gender discrimination at about 3 percent of GDP per year.[5] Taken together, race and gender discrimination reduced the nation's output of goods and services by more than $500 billion in 1998. Add to this discrimination against homosexuals, the aged, the physically challenged, and others, and you have an annual loss of goods and services to the American society that could easily exceed one-half of a trillion dollars per year.

Discrimination causes losses of goods and services to society because it results in unnecessarily low levels of economic efficiency. Without discrimination, resources would tend to be allocated on the basis of their productivities. Units of any given resource would tend to be used where their productivity is the greatest. Consider, for example, the case of a young female college student studying biology with the intention of attending medical school. Suppose further that this young woman has all the intellectual and emotional tools necessary to become a fine physician but, due to discrimination, is routed into nursing school instead. Society must have nurses and nursing is a profession of distinction, yet society loses in the exchange. Why and how much does society lose? Had the young woman attended medical school her annual contribution to GDP (her income) would, no doubt, be 5 or even 10 times greater than it will be as a nurse. This income gap for her is an output gap for society that grows with each passing year.

The production possibilities curve shown in Figure 6–5 illustrates the impact of discrimination on the production of goods and services in the economy. Point D represents the combination of goods X and Y produced in the economy when discrimination exists, with its resultant inefficiency. Without discrimination, the quantities of goods X and Y may be expanded to such points as B and C.

Discrimination prevents the efficient use of resources, causing the combination of goods and services that is produced to lie below the production possibilities curve. The elimination of discrimination makes possible the production of those combinations of goods and services that lie on the curve. The social cost of discrimination is equal to the difference between the gross domestic product represented at point D and that represented by points on the production possibilities curve, such as points B and C.

---

[4]Joint Economic Committee, *The Cost of Racial Discrimination* (Washington, DC: U.S. Government Printing Office, 1980), p. 2.

[5]Estelle James, "Income and Employment Effects of Women's Liberation," in *Sex, Discrimination, and the Division of Labor,* ed. Cynthia B. Lloyd (New York: Columbia University Press, 1975), p. 406.

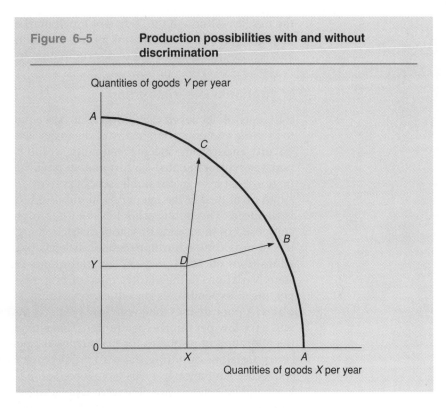

Figure 6–5   **Production possibilities with and without discrimination**

Quantities of goods *Y* per year

Quantities of goods *X* per year

Point *D* = Combination of *X* and *Y* with discrimination
Points *B* and *C* = Combination of *X* and *Y* without discrimination
Line *AA* = Production possibilities curve

Nonmarket Discrimination

Social Discrimination

Social tastes and attitudes, customs, and laws are the bases for social discrimination. Social discrimination may take the extreme form of preventing certain individuals or groups from engaging in social interaction. A Little League rule that prohibits girls from playing baseball in Little League games provides an illustration. Fraternities and sororities that have rules limiting membership to certain races provide another. Segregated schools are examples of discrimination based on customs and laws.

Social discrimination is difficult to root out, since it is based on deep-seated beliefs and customs often supported by law. In contrast to market discrimination, it is difficult to associate monetary costs with social discrimination. Members who may with joy vote to keep certain people from joining their country club often with the same joy sell products to them in the market. Although the source of much market discrimination is social discrimination, the self-interest motive in the market tends to overcome and reduce the effectiveness of discrimination in the marketplace.

Educational Discrimination

It is generally believed that if everyone had equal access and opportunity to training and education, many of the major issues in our society, such as poverty and extreme income inequality, would be significantly alleviated, perhaps even eliminated. Unfortunately, however, inequality and discrimination exist even in our public school system.

A great deal of the inequality in public education is due to the way it is financed. The public school system is a highly decentralized system composed of thousands of school districts charged with the responsibilities of providing education. School districts pay for education with revenues from the local property tax and grants-in-aid, primarily from the state. Variations in the market value of property give rise to variations in per pupil expenditures on education within a given state and among states. A poor district (one with low property values) within a poor state will have low per pupil expenditures. This regional and state inequality in the allocation of resources for the purpose of public education has led to court decisions opposing the way public education is financed. Several court cases in the early 1990s have forced some states to change the way local public schools are financed. The result has been the passage of "Robin Hood laws," whereby the states have reallocated tax revenues from richer school districts to poorer ones in an effort to provide greater equality of resources.

What Can Be Done About Discrimination?

Markets and humans are not perfect. Perfection may be beyond reach. However, movements in the direction of perfection are possible. What courses of action can be taken to move in the right direction? What policy implications can be drawn from our analysis?

Reduce Tastes for Discrimination

If tastes for discrimination are to be reduced, people must be persuaded that they should alter their views and behavior. These tastes and desires may be reduced by education, by legislation, and by the use of government subsidies to discourage discrimination.

Education.   A task of education is to teach people to understand one another so they will not be prejudiced. Unfortunately, this task of education is hampered by discrimination in education itself, especially in regard to the allocation of resources for primary and secondary education. Although not a panacea, a more equal distribution of resources for public education would reduce inequality in per pupil educational services, and it could contribute toward reducing tastes for discrimination.

Legislation. It is difficult to change the tastes of people by coercion, that is, by passing laws. Laws are usually only effective when they are supported by or coincide with people's beliefs. However, the framework for reducing tastes for discrimination can be established by laws. The Equal Pay Act of 1963 was the first major federal attempt to control discrimination. The act makes it illegal for employers to pay different wage rates for "equal work." Since the Equal Pay Act applies only to wage discrimination, it is quite limited. To broaden the impact on discrimination, the Civil Rights Act of 1964 was enacted.

The Civil Rights Act covers discrimination against workers based on race, color, gender, religion, or national origin. Additional antidiscrimination laws have been enacted since the mid-1960s to include other minority groups. The Age Discrimination in Employment Act covers older workers, and the Americans with Disabilities Act (ADA) protects "qualified" workers with physical or mental disabilities. The federal laws that protect workers from discrimination are administered by the Equal Employment Opportunity Commission (EEOC), which has the power to pursue court action on behalf of workers.

Federal law now requires not only equal treatment in wages but also equal treatment in hiring, promotion, and ultimately firing. The law may reduce discrimination by imposing greater risks and higher costs on discriminators. For example, a person who satisfies a taste for discrimination by refusing to sell a house to a black breaks the law and risks prosecution.

Government Subsidies. If the sole goal is to eliminate discrimination, government subsidy payments may be used to encourage employers not to discriminate. Subsidy payments would be made to employers who do not practice discrimination in hiring, wages, and promotions. Employers who discriminate would be sacrificing subsidy payments. Thus, an incentive is provided not to discriminate. Government subsidy payments will reduce discrimination if the subsidy payments are equal to or greater than the nonmonetary gain the discriminator receives from discrimination. Although no direct subsidy payment program currently exists, an implicit subsidy occurs when the federal government grants preferences to contractors who meet equal employment opportunity standards.

Reduce Market Imperfections

Market defects such as scarce labor market information, imperfect competition, and immobility of labor constitute a major source of market discrimination. Some people receive low wages, that is, wages below what they could earn in alternative employments, because they are unaware of other job openings. Better access to job information would make it less likely for a person to receive income below what he or she would be paid on a similar job.

The market for goods and the market for resources may not work well at all if there is little competition in these markets. In imperfect markets, discrimination may be prevalent. A seller or a buyer has control over the price of what he or she sells or buys in highly monopolized markets. Other potential sellers or buyers are shut out of the market. Price, wage, employment, and occupational discrimination may remain unchallenged in the absence of competitive forces and in the presence of monopolistic controls. Antitrust action to strengthen competition and reduce barriers to entry into markets would be an important way to eliminate or at least lessen discriminatory market behavior.

The government has an important role to play in the elimination of discrimination when it is due to the use of monopoly power. It is the responsibility of the government to reduce monopoly power and restore competition in markets where competition is lacking through the vigorous use of antimonopoly laws. In Chapter 8 we more closely examine how markets operate when sellers have monopoly powers, and in Chapter 9 we explore the behavior of monopsonistic employers of labor.

Reduce Discrimination in Development of Human Capital

Investment in human capital, that is, spending on education, training, and health, provides a high rate of return in the form of increased productivity and income. Blacks and other minority groups generally do not and cannot invest enough in human capital, and public investment in human capital is unequally distributed. The elimination of human capital discrimination would tend to make most forms of market discrimination, such as wage and employment discrimination, less effective. The reason is that it is difficult to treat human resources unequally if they are productive and have access to other jobs.

Reduce Occupational Segregation

Occupational segregation results in women, blacks, and other minorities being overrepresented in the low-wage sectors of the economy. The effect of segregation by occupations is twofold. First, the supply of labor is increased in those occupations restricted to minority groups, depressing wages in those occupations. Second, the supply of labor is decreased in those occupations closed off to minority groups, thus increasing wages in those occupations. The result of these effects is to create a wider gap between low- and high-wage occupations.

In addition, if a member of the minority group crosses over into segregated occupations usually closed to members of the group, he or she has typically not received equal pay for equal work. For example, a black male with a Ph.D. in chemistry who works as a research chemist for an oil company may be discriminated against in wages and opportunities for advancement because he has a position typically reserved for whites. In recent years this situation has been reversed in many cases by the Equal Employment Opportunities Act. Employers are virtually required to bid for minority group personnel. The small supplies available of these workers who are qualified assure that they will receive salaries above those of white employees.

However, segregation by occupations would be difficult to maintain if minority groups were relatively well-educated and well-trained. Education and training open up job opportunities. Those who have job opportunities cannot easily be forced into designated occupations; they are mobile and can cut across occupations. Providing improved job opportunities for minority groups is one way to break up segregation by occupations.

Continuing Controversies

Frustration over the slow progress toward equality that economic minorities have experienced has led to a call by some for more aggressive approaches to reducing discrimination. Legislation like the Equal Employment Opportunities Act and the Civil Rights Act reduce discriminatory behavior in the labor market by making it illegal and by imposing fines and punishment on offenders. Laws such as these may be effective in discouraging discriminatory activity, but they do not remedy the effects of existing and past discrimination. Laws and regulations that require employers to take a *proactive* approach to reducing discrimination and its adverse effects are referred to as *affirmative action* programs. From their inception, affirmative action programs have been politically controversial and have even been openly opposed by organizations representing the interests of economic minority groups. The public debates on affirmative action concern the fairness of implicit hiring quotas, the possibility of "reverse discrimination," and the sensibility of comparable worth programs.

Affirmative Action Programs

Affirmative action programs began as a result of Executive Order 11246 issued in 1965 by President Lyndon Johnson. This order was designed to prevent discrimination by employers holding contracts with the federal government. Specifically, the order applies to all federal contractors who employ 50 or more workers and have contracts valued at $50,000 and higher. The order requires contractors to undertake actions to remedy any underrepresentation of minority groups within their labor force. The Office of Federal Contract Compliance (OFCC) was established to enforce the regulations. In 1968, the OFCC began requiring contractors to develop formal plans including target goals and timetables to remedy any deficiencies in equal opportunity employment. Standardized procedures were introduced to identify underrepresentation of protected groups, and contractors were required to issue progress reports on actions taken to meet their goals.

A common element of the affirmative action plans filed by federal contractors is the establishment of specific numerical goals for the hiring of economic minorities in designated job categories. This has led many to charge that the result of affirmative action has been the establishment of hiring *quotas*. It is important to note that Executive Order 11246 does not establish quotas as a means of satisfying its requirements. However, legal pressures and the threat of losing federal contracts may cause some employers to treat minority employment goals as if they were hiring quotas. Supporters argue that affirmative action plans are virtually unenforceable without numerical standards and goals. Opponents contend that affirmative action results in de facto quotas that do not result in more equal *opportunity* but in more equal *representation* on the workforces of federal contractors. It is argued that affirmative action plans create incentives for employers to hire workers based on their minority status and not on their qualifications and productivity.

After implementation of Executive Order 11246, several states and local governments enacted laws and regulations that also required the development of formal affirmative action plans. These laws vary in their scope and coverage. In some states, affirmative action programs also apply to the admission of students in public colleges and universities. One primary goal of these programs is to reduce discrimination in education and human capital development and thereby generate more equal opportunities in the labor market for economic minorities.

Today, affirmative action programs are under fire from two fronts. On one front, traditional opponents of affirmative active claim that numerical hiring goals promote reverse discrimination against whites and males. It is argued that qualified white and male candidates are often not hired (or admitted to school) ahead of less qualified black and female candidates. On the other front, minorities claim that affirmative action has sheltered them from competitive forces of the market and has removed the economic incentives for hard work, professional growth, and personal development. Various political and social organizations that support the interests of blacks and women argue that, in practice, affirmative action does not promote the long-run welfare of economic minorities but rather uses them in a manner to meet the short-run objectives of managers. They claim that minorities are often hired (or admitted) only "to fill the slots" in order to comply with the law and maintain federal or state funding.

Furthermore, these groups argue that affirmative action programs create a social stigma for *all* minority workers, including those who are highly qualified and succeed in the labor market without the benefits of affirmative action. Such arguments have garnered widespread political support in recent years.

Intense public debate led California voters in 1996 to repeal that state's affirmative action laws. Nationally, the issue remains unsettled and public policy makers continue to look for proactive antidiscrimination programs that eliminate the possibility of reverse discrimination opened by traditional affirmative action plans. One possible alternative is the implementation of *comparable* worth pay systems.

Comparable Worth

The **comparable worth** proposal would replace market determination of wages with a pay system based on the skill, effort, and responsibility requirements of individual jobs.

Comparable worth programs primarily address the issue of discrimination based on gender. The essence of such programs is a realization that women and men do not do the same work. As discussed earlier in this chapter, women are concentrated into relatively few low-paying occupations, whereas men are disproportionately represented in the higher-paying occupations. Given this, laws such as the Equal Pay Act can do little to improve the economic position of women since they only require "equal pay for equal work." The comparable worth doctrine would extend the "equal pay for equal work" principle to require "equal pay for similar or comparable work." Would such an approach be desirable? Strong arguments are made on each side of the debate.

Comparable worth advocates argue that the occupations dominated by women (nursing, elementary and secondary school teaching, clerical, and so on) are low paying not due to "market forces" but purely because they are jobs held by women. That is, in a male-dominated society, the work done by women is of necessity valued less than comparable work done by men. A logical extension of this argument suggests that if a job currently dominated by females (such as nursing) switches and becomes primarily male, the average pay of nurses would increase substantially.

The remedy proposed is to require employers not only to pay equal wages for equal work but also to require equal wages for jobs of comparable worth, where the comparability of jobs is determined by factors such as the skill, effort, and responsibility requirements of the jobs. For example, suppose that it is determined that secretaries (primarily female) and truck drivers (primarily male) do jobs that are comparable in terms of skill, effort, and responsibility. The comparable worth doctrine would require that employers pay secretaries and truck drivers the same salaries. Although comparable worth pay systems have not made significant inroads in the private sector, a number of state and local governments have started the process of evaluating jobs, determining their "intrinsic value," and paying workers accordingly.

Although the arguments of the comparable worth adherents are logical and to some extent consistent with evidence concerning occupational segregation and the pay of women, comparable worth may not be the panacea its advocates hope for. A number of fundamental policy questions have been raised in regard to comparable worth. Overlooking the difficulties involved with determining the "intrinsic value" of a job, opponents suggest three shortcomings of comparable worth. First, the essence of comparable worth is to increase the pay of women relative to men. To the extent that the program is successful, the outcome must be to reduce the employment of women relative to men. Although some women will gain (those who remain employed), a significant number of women may lose. Second, opponents suggest that what is truly needed is for women to move into the higher-paying male occupations and that comparable worth, by making the female occupations more attractive, will do just the opposite. Thus, the policy would serve to reinforce occupational segregation rather than reduce it. Finally, opponents argue that comparable worth treats a symptom of a disease rather than the disease itself. Specifically, opponents argue that women are low paid because they work in low-paying jobs, and to the extent that this occupational segregation is due to discriminatory hiring and promotion factors, the appropriate remedy is more strict enforcement of existing law rather than comparable worth legislation.

Although no definitive conclusion may be reached with regard to the comparable worth controversy, the debate points out several things of importance with regard to discrimination and attempts to deal with it. First, even when problems of discrimination are perceived, the development of remedial actions that generate widespread support is very difficult. Second, before policy actions are undertaken, careful consideration must be made of all the possible effects of the policy. In many cases, those we wish to help most may end up being harmed.

Summary

Market discrimination means that people with the same economic characteristics are not treated equally. For example, workers who have the same productivity receive different wages, and consumers are charged different prices for the same product.

Discrimination comes from two sources—market and human imperfections. Market imperfections are due to imperfect knowledge, immobility of resources, and imperfect competition. Human imperfections are revealed in the tastes and preferences that some people have for discrimination.

Competitive labor markets will result in workers of equal ability being treated equally by an employer. The demand for labor is determined by the workers' marginal revenue product. Workers who contribute more to their employer's output and revenues will command higher wages than those who contribute little. Wage differentials in competitive markets reflect differences in worker productivity. Such wage differentials should not be confused with labor market discrimination. Labor market discrimination exists in the form of wage, employment, and occupational differentials due to factors unrelated to differences in worker productivity.

Discrimination is costly both to individuals and to society. There are individual welfare gains and losses from discrimination. It is difficult to say who gains and who loses. Sometimes the discriminator can lose. It is certain that there is a loss to society from discrimination, in the form of a reduction in output.

The economic analysis of market discrimination stresses two related points: (1) the observed differences in wages and prices may reflect differences in productivity, and (2) market discrimination exists only to the extent that wage and price differences cannot be explained on the basis of productivity. Competitive markets tend to minimize the extent and degree of discrimination. Occupational segregation explains to a large extent differences in wages and income, and social discrimination, especially in the field of public education, is the source for much inequality.

Several policy conclusions may be drawn from our analysis. One, tastes for discrimination have to be reduced. This can be done by changing the tastes of people concerning discrimination through education, preventing by law the fulfillment of tastes for discrimination, and encouraging people not to discriminate by the payment of subsidies to employers who refrain from discrimination. Two, the source of much discrimination—the exercise of monopoly power—has to be reduced. The way to reduce the use of monopoly power is to reduce that power itself through vigorous enforcement of antimonopoly laws. A great deal of market discrimination is primarily due to human capital discrimination. If there were no discrimination in regard to investment in human capital (education, training, and health), segregation by occupations would be dealt a serious blow. It is difficult to discriminate in the market against people who are productive and have job choices.

Discussion Questions

1. Define discrimination. What are the two primary sources of market discrimination? Provide an example of each.
2. Define the term *marginal revenue product of labor*. What are the two components of the marginal revenue product of labor? Illustrate with a graph.
3. Explain why the marginal revenue product of labor curve slopes downward to the right. Why is the marginal revenue product of labor curve also the demand for labor curve?

4. Explain the concepts known as *income* and *substitution effects*. How do these effects relate to the supply of labor?

5. Most truck drivers earn a greater salary than bank tellers. Is this discrimination? Explain.

6. On average, male workers earn about 30 percent more than female workers. Does this entire gap represent the effect of gender discrimination? Explain.

7. Are wage differentials a natural outcome of a market economy? Explain. Under what circumstances do wage differentials reflect discrimination?

8. How can discrimination against specific groups affect the GDP of an entire economy? Illustrate your answer with examples.

9. Discuss the economic costs of discrimination to individuals and society. Does anyone benefit from discrimination? Explain.

10. Identify forms of discrimination that occur outside the market yet have an economic impact on its victims.

11. How has the government attempted to reduce the incidence and effects of market discrimination in our society? In your opinion, have these efforts been successful? Why or why not?

12. Explain how government action may result in "reverse discrimination." Is this a fair price to pay to reduce traditional forms of market discrimination? Why or why not?

Additional Readings

Baily, Martin Neil, Gary Burtless, and Robert E. Litan. *Growth with Equity*. Washington, DC: The Brookings Institution, 1993.

Discusses earnings inequality, improving labor market efficiency, and promoting investment in the economy to stimulate growth.

Braun, Denny. *The Rich Get Richer*. Chicago: Nelson-Hall Publishers, 1991.

Discusses theories of income inequality, the role of multinational corporations on income inequality, and other issues.

Clayton, Susan D., and Faye J. Crosby. *Justice, Gender, and Affirmative Action*. Ann Arbor: The University of Michigan Press, 1992.

Argues for affirmative action as a solution to sexual discrimination in the workplace.

Danziger, Sheldon, and Peter Gottschalk, eds. *Uneven Tides*. New York: Russell Sage Foundation, 1993.

Series of essays on labor market changes and the distribution of earnings, demographic changes and the distribution of family income, and public policy changes and the distribution of family income.

England, Paula. *Comparable Worth: Theories and Evidence*. New York: Aldine DeGruyter, 1992.

Perhaps the most thorough treatment of the economic problems women face and the proposed comparable worth remedy available today.

Hartman, Heidi I., and Donald J. Treiman. *Women, Work and Wages: Equal Pay for Jobs of Equal Value.* Washington, DC: National Academy Press, 1981.

Provides evidence regarding wage differentials and introduces wage-adjustment approaches to overcome discrimination.

Herrnstein, Richard J., and Charles Murray. *The Bell Curve: Intelligence and Class Structure in American Life.* New York: Free Press, 1994.

Controversial book purported to claim that many economic differences between groups in American society may be explained by differences in measured intelligence, and not overt discrimination.

Jain, Harish C., and Peter J. Sloane. *Equal Employment Issues: Race and Sex Discrimination in the United States, Canada, and Britain.* New York: Praeger Publishers, 1981.

Examines the complex human resources problems policymakers face regarding minority employment. Uses economic analysis to point out where we might expect discrimination to be more extensive.

Journal of Economic Perspectives, volume 12, number 2, Spring 1998, pp. 23–117.

This issue presents six articles by leading economists from a symposium titled "Discrimination in Product, Credit and Labor Markets." These very readable articles review the latest evidence and theories concerning discrimination in the American economy.

Thurow, Lester C. *Poverty and Discrimination.* Washington, DC: Brookings Institution, 1969.

A classic that covers the economic theories of discrimination. In Chapter 7, various kinds of market discrimination are presented and analyzed.

Twomey, David P. *Equal Employment Opportunity Law.* Cincinnati: Southwestern Publishing, 1990.

Concise overview of federal regulations and laws pertaining to discrimination in the workplace.

Vanderwaerdt, Lois. *Affirmative Action in Higher Education.* New York: Garland Publishing, 1982.

Demonstrates how affirmative action has changed employment practices regarding faculty and staff on college and university campuses.

Wolff, Edward N. *Economics of Poverty Inequality and Discrimination.* Cincinnati: Southwestern Publishing, 1997.

Complete textbook covering the major theories of discrimination and its effects on the economy.

World Wide Web Resources

American Association for Affirmative Action (AAAA)
www.affirmativeaction.org

Provides links to articles and commentary on affirmative action, including a history of antidiscrimination legislation. Also provides links to other related sites.

American Civil Liberties Union Freedom Network
www.aclu.org/index.html

Gives links to rights for immigrants, lesbians and gays, students, women, voting, and the workplace.

Americans with Disabilities Act (ADA) Home Page
www.usdoj.gov/crt/ada/adahom1.htm

Provides information to new or proposed regulations, a toll-free ADA information line, the Technical Assistance Program, and other services.

Office of Equal Employment Opportunity Home Page
www.gsa.gov/eeo

General Services Administration. Explains what EEO is, who the regional EEO officers are, and gives links to EEO sites and other information.

U.S. Employment Discrimination Law
www.law.cornell.edu/topics/employment_discrimination.html

Provides an overview of the law and a menu of sources.

Poverty Problems

Is Poverty Necessary?

Chapter Outline

Checklist of Economic Concepts

Income inequality
Demand for labor
Marginal revenue product of
    labor
Supply of labor

Wage rate determination
Determinants of income
    distribution
Ownership pattern of resources
Price floors

Price ceilings
Unemployment
Negative income tax
Lorenz curve
Tax policy

Athens, Ohio. For April Rupe and her son, it's a time of big adjustments. For two years, she was a welfare mother at home. Two months ago, she started work full time as an assistant at a nursing home. Ms. Rupe is delighted she can now pay her bills on time. But to do that, she often works 12- and 18-hour shifts, and goes in on her days off. "It's hard when you've got a four-year-old and he's saying, 'Mommy, stay home,'" says Rupe. But there's one adjustment this family won't have to make. They were poor when they were on welfare, and they're poor now. Like thousands of other former welfare families in these coal-mine-scarred hills of rural Appalachia, a full-time job hasn't meant a ticket out of poverty.

"Back in the 1960s we declared war on poverty. This is a war on welfare," says Jack Frech, director of the Athens County Department of Human Services. Rupe and others like her represent one of the Clinton administration's best successes and, in the eyes of some, one of its most prominent failures. In 1992, then-candidate Clinton pledged, "No one who works full time and has children at home should be poor anymore. And no one who can work should be able to stay on welfare forever."

"[Mr. Clinton] delivered the second sentence; he's not yet delivered the first," says Sheldon Danziger, a professor of social work at the University of Michigan at Ann Arbor. While still in its early stages, welfare reform has already been judged a great success in many states—at least in getting people off welfare. It's estimated that more than 2 million people have left the rolls since 1994. But in terms of lifting families out of poverty and improving the quality of their lives—the gauge Athens County's Mr. Frech says should be used to judge success—the jury is still out.

In the past four years, welfare rolls in Athens County have been cut in half. But 70 percent of the people who left in the past two years took jobs that paid less than $6 an hour. The result: The Athens County poverty rate stubbornly remains at more than 30 percent—twice the national average. For advocates for the poor, that's an indication much more needs to be done.

"More people are getting jobs, but it's not making their lives any better," says Kathy Lairn, a policy analyst at the Center on Budget and Policy Priorities in Washington. A center analysis of US Census data nationwide found that between 1995 and 1996, a greater percentage of single, female-headed households were earning money on their own, but that average income for these households actually went down. But for many, the fact that poor people are able to support themselves almost as well without government aid as they did with it is in itself a huge victory.

"Welfare was a poison. It was a toxin that was poisoning the family," says Robert Rector, a welfare-reform policy analyst at the Heritage Foundation, a conservative Washington think tank. "The reform is changing the moral climate in low-income communities. It's beginning to rebuild the work ethic, which is much more important." Mr. Rector and others contend that once "the habit of dependency is cracked," then the country can make other policy changes aimed at improving living standards.

But advocates for the poor say the problem is not so simple, particularly in an economy where real wages have held steady and low-wage jobs are paying less now in real terms than they did 20 years ago. In other words, a good job is hard to find, let alone one with benefits. Just ask Dave Smith, a Vietnam veteran who also lives in Appalachia, in The Plains, Ohio. He says it's been more than 25 years since he's had a good-paying job with benefits. "There's jobs, but the jobs they got don't pay enough to live on," says Mr. Smith. "And the way they talk to you don't build self-esteem. They're more like slave drivers."

Several years ago, Smith was on general assistance and joined the Appalachian People's Action Coalition. Created by low-income people to improve their lives and job prospects, APAC started a used-furniture store where Smith now works. "Athens is a hotbed of grass-roots efforts to create sustainable development and jobs that are 'Appalachian,'" says APAC director Kathryn Lad. "But the bottom line is, the capital isn't here to get it going."

That's one reason advocates for the poor still see a role for the US government. They cite things like creating seed money for business development in low-income areas, expanding child-care subsidies, and boosting the minimum wage. They also want to build on the already-expanded earned income tax credit for the working poor.

"America still has a high poverty rate relative to that of other industrialized countries," says Professor Danziger. "It will take more government policies designed to make work pay to fulfill the first part of Clinton's campaign soundbite."[1]

[1]Alexandra Marks, "Less Welfare, Same Poverty in Heart of Appalachia," *The Christian Science Monitor*, May 6, 1998, p. 1. 1998. The Christian Science Publishing Society. Reproduced with permission. All rights reserved.

"Poverty amidst plenty" exists in America. In the world's richest nation millions are poor, and millions more not in poverty are *relatively* poor. Not the American dream, this is the American paradox.

Poverty may be a more serious problem in our society than in less affluent societies. Poverty amidst poverty is easier to understand and even condone. But in a land of abundance, it is difficult to comprehend why some people are inadequately fed, clothed, and sheltered.

We approach our study of poverty in the United States in two ways. First, we examine poverty in reference to *absolute* income levels, which permits the identification of people who live below a designated poverty level of income. Second, we study it in terms of income distribution, that is, the share or percent of national income that people receive.

Poverty in Terms of Absolute Income Levels

In today's American economy, poverty is essentially an income distribution problem. The U.S. economy generates enough income to go around so that no one really has to live in poverty. But enough income does not go to everyone, and some people do live in poverty.

Figure 7–1 illustrates the incidence of poverty in our economy between 1959, when the federal government first began measuring poverty, and 1997. The first official poverty count for 1959 revealed that 22.4 percent of the American population lived in poverty. This statistic meant that almost 40 million people in the world's richest economy suffered from poverty. At the time, these numbers shocked many people, and poverty became one of the major social issues of the turbulent 1960s. The challenge the Kennedy and Johnson administrations took up was to eradicate poverty through a vigorous "war on poverty." Although the ultimate goal was not fully met, new social programs were developed and new initiatives were taken by the federal government that significantly reduced the rate of poverty throughout the 1960s. By 1969, the poverty rate stood at 12.1 percent of the population, a reduction in the rate of 46 percent. This is the legacy of the period that is often referred to as the Great Society. Unfortunately, the downward trend in poverty did not continue into the

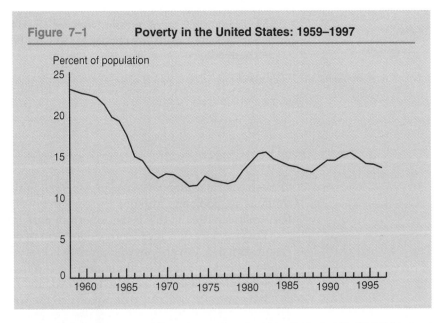

Figure 7–1   **Poverty in the United States: 1959–1997**

Percent of population

Source: U.S. Department of Commerce, Bureau of the Census, *Statistical Abstract of the United States*, various issues.

following decades. As can be seen in Figure 7–1, the poverty rate has fluctuated in narrow range since the 1970s. After reaching a low of 11.1 percent in 1973, the poverty rate has in general trended upward, peaking above 15 percent in 1983 and 1993. Understandably, these peaks roughly correspond to economic recessions and periods of relatively high unemployment. However, the poverty rate has never fallen back to the levels experienced in the early 1970s, even though the 1990s saw the overall economy grow for an unprecedented period of time and the economy record the lowest rates of unemployment in more than 20 years.

What Is Poverty?

Poverty is not easily defined. Yet, a precise definition has been implied in the statement that many Americans are poor. We shall use the definition of poverty developed by the government.

Poverty is concerned with the relationship between the minimum needs of people and their ability to satisfy those needs. The difficulty with any definition of poverty involves the meaning of "minimum needs" and the amount of money required to satisfy these needs. The federal government's approach is a two-step process. First, the monetary cost of a nutritionally sound minimum diet is determined. Second, the cost of the minimum diet is multiplied by 3 to allow for expenditures on all other goods and services. The multiplier value of 3 was chosen because the cost of food represented about one-third of the average family's aftertax money income when the poverty definition was formulated more than 40 years ago. Each year, the monetary cost of the minimum diet is adjusted for price changes using a price index. (Recall from Chapter 1 how price index numbers can account for the effect of inflation.) Using this process, a set of poverty lines, or thresholds, are calculated for various family sizes and compositions. Separate poverty thresholds are calculated based on the number of adults and children in the household, and for some households, the age of the family head. A person is officially counted as living in poverty when their household's annual pretax income is less than the threshold for their household's size and composition. Poverty thresholds as defined for different household sizes are listed in Table 7–1 on page 176.

Since the 1960s, the government's method of calculating poverty thresholds has been criticized. For example, some critics argue that the definition of income should be expanded to include the value of in-kind benefits such as health insurance and day care services received by families. Others argue that changes in living standards call into question the legitimacy of defining poverty based on the relative size of what an average family's food budget was more than 40 years ago. Studies indicate that households today spend less than one-third of their income on groceries. Furthermore, the current poverty definition does not account for different costs of living in different regions of the country. Although numerous

Table 7-1	Poverty threshold levels in 1997
Family Size	**Threshold Level**
1	$ 8,183
2	10,473
3	12,802
4	16,400
5	19,380
6	21,886
7	24,802
8	27,593
9 or more	32,566

Source: U.S. Department of Commerce, Bureau of the Census, Current Population Reports, Series P-60, No. 201, *Poverty in the United States: 1997*, p. A-4.

refinements and alternatives to the current process of defining poverty have been proposed over the years, none has been officially adopted.

Who Are the Poor?

In 1997, 7.1 million families, or 10.3 percent of all families, lived in poverty (Table 7–2). The incidence of poverty is much higher than this among certain family groupings. You would expect the poverty rate to be very high among very young families and very large families. You would expect the same among families headed by a person who has a low level of education and families headed by an unemployed person. However, the highest rates of poverty are found among families headed by females with children under the age of 18. The situation is even more critical if the female householder (no husband present) is black. Almost one out of every two families headed by a female with dependent children lives in poverty. If the female householder is black, 46.9 percent of these families live below the poverty threshold level (Table 7–2). Extremely high rates of poverty are traced, then, to broken homes, and are gender- and race-related, with children the major victims.

The Upward Struggle of the Poor

It is often stated that a person living in poverty today will likely live in poverty in the future. The main argument is that a poor person becomes "trapped" and has little chance of breaking out of the economic conditions that put him or her there in the first place. Furthermore, some believe that a poor person does not have the motivation to advance and is even

Table 7–2   **Selected characteristics of families below the poverty level, 1997**

Characteristics	Total Families (000)	Families Below Poverty Level	
		Number (000)	Percent
All families	70,884	7,324	10.3
Married couple families	54,321	2,821	5.2
With children under 18	26,430	1,863	7.1
Male householder—no wife present	3,911	508	13.0
Female householder—no husband present	12,652	3,995	31.6
With children under 18	8,822	3,614	41.0
White families	59,515	4,990	8.4
Married couple families	48,070	2,312	4.8
With children under 18	22,783	1,516	6.7
Male householder—no wife present	3,137	373	11.9
Female householder—no husband present	8,308	2,305	27.7
With children under 18	5,502	2,069	37.6
Black families	8,408	1,985	23.6
Married couple families	3,921	312	8.0
With children under 18	2,275	205	9.0
Male householder—no wife present	561	110	19.6
Female householder—no husband present	3,926	1,563	39.8
With children under 18	3,060	1,436	46.9

Source: U.S. Department of Commerce, Bureau of the Census, Current Population Report, Series P-60, No. 201, *Poverty in the United States: 1997.*

encouraged to retain a low economic status by low-income support programs of the government. There has been little research on the upward mobility of the poor. The exception to this is a 10-year longitude study of family status conducted at the Survey Research Center of the University of Michigan. The findings of this study are reported in a book entitled *Years of Poverty, Years of Plenty.*[2]

---

[2]Greg J. Duncan, *Years of Poverty, Years of Plenty* (Ann Arbor: Institute for Social Research, University of Michigan, 1984).

A major finding in the Michigan study is that there is an amazing amount of turnover in the low-income population. "Only a little over one-half of the individuals in one year are found to be poor in the next" year.[3] In addition, only a minority of people who live in poverty remain in poverty over a long period of time. It is concluded, also, that attitudes are not the causal explanation why some people live and remain in poverty.

The study referred to above covered a period of time (1968–1979) when the poverty rate was staying about the same or declining. It would be expected that the upward mobility of the poor would be reduced in recent years with the increase in the number of people living in poverty. However, Greg J. Duncan, the major author of *Years of Poverty, Years of Plenty*, is confident that findings of the Michigan study will prevail in the future.[4] Assuming this is so, a high turnover among the poor does not resolve the poverty issue, although it does provide a more hopeful outlook concerning this important issue.

Poverty in Terms of Income Distribution

The second approach to poverty considers the distribution of income in the United States. We have said that the poverty problem in this country is mainly one of income distribution. This means that the level of income in our country is high enough so that a more equal distribution of income should mitigate the poverty problem and reduce its significance.

Income Equality

A **Lorenz curve**, which shows the cumulative percentage of total family income that is going to the lowest percentiles of families, is a way of measuring the degree of income inequality in a country.

Economists usually explain income equality and income inequality by reference to a curve called a *Lorenz curve*, after M. O. Lorenz. Income equality among families means that any given percent of families receive an equal percent of family income: 10 percent of families receive 10 percent of income, 20 percent of families receive 20 percent of income, and 100 percent of families receive 100 percent of income. In Figure 7–2, equal percentages of families and incomes can be measured along the two axes. Income equality is shown by a 45-degree line starting at the origin. At any point on the 45-degree line, the percent of families shown receive an equal percent of total family income.

Income Inequality

Income inequality can be illustrated graphically by lines that deviate from the line of income equality. A Lorenz curve derived from actual data on

[3]Ibid., p. 3.
[4]Ibid., p. 7.

income distribution will usually lie to the right of the line of income equality (the 45-degree line). The farther to the right of the 45-degree line it lies,
the greater the inequalities in income distribution. Lorenz curves are useful in making income distribution comparisons in a given year among different countries or in the same country over time.

Table 7–3 (next page) divides U.S. families into five numerically equal
groups, or quintiles, and indicates the distribution of personal income
among these groups. The table also shows the income share of the top 5
percent of families. It can be observed that income is very unequally distributed. The highest 20 percent of families received 46.5 percent of income in 1995, and the lowest 20 percent received 4.4 percent. The top 5
percent of families received 20.0 percent of income. These data on income
inequality are shown by the Lorenz curve in Figure 7–2.

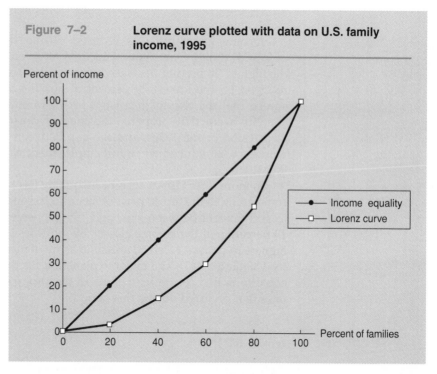

Figure 7–2   **Lorenz curve plotted with data on U.S. family income, 1995**

The Lorenz curve shows the degree of income inequality. The horizontal axis
measures the percent of families, starting with the poorest. Thus, 20 percent represents the lowest fifth of the families. In 1995, the lowest 20 percent earned 4.4
percent of the total income, and the lowest 40 percent earned 14.5 percent. This
means that the second quintile (the families between the 20 percent and 40 percent marks) earned 10.1 percent of the total income (14.5–4.4). If perfect income
equality existed, the Lorenz curve would be a 45-degree line.
Source: U.S. Department of Commerce, Bureau of the Census, *Statistical Abstract
of the United States, 1997,* p. 470.

Table 7-3	Percentage of income received by each fifth and the top 5 percent of families, 1960–1995			
Quintile of Families	**1960**	**1970**	**1980**	**1995**
Lowest fifth	4.8%	5.4%	5.2%	4.4%
Second fifth	12.2	12.2	11.5	10.1
Third fifth	17.8	17.6	17.5	15.8
Fourth fifth	24.0	23.8	24.3	23.2
Highest fifth	41.2	40.9	41.5	46.5
	100.0	100.0	100.0	100.0
Top 5 percent	15.9	15.6	15.3	20.0

Source: U.S. Department of Commerce, Bureau of the Census, *Statistical Abstract of the United States, 1997*, p. 470. *Note:* Column totals may not sum to 100% due to rounding.

Income inequality was reduced during the 1930s and the years of World War II. The share of income received by the top 5 percent of the highest 20 percent decreased between 1929 and 1944, while the share received by the lowest 20 percent of families increased. It is generally agreed that the two main reasons for this trend toward greater income equality were that property income fell drastically during the Great Depression of the 1930s, and the gap between low-paid and high-paid workers was reduced when full employment was reached during World War II.[5]

In more recent times, income inequality has increased. The share of income going to the top 20 percent income class increased from 41.5 percent to 46.5 percent between 1980 and 1994, a percentage increase of almost 13 percent. All the income classes by quintiles with the exception of the highest 20 percent received a smaller share of income in 1995 as compared to 1980 (Table 7–3). The major explanation for this increase in income inequality is tied to the reductions in the progressive federal income tax rates that occurred during this period.

The Economic Causes of Poverty

Determinants of Resource Prices and Employment

Family incomes depend on the quantities of resources that families can place in employment and the prices received for those resources. To understand poverty, then, it is important to understand what determines the

---

[5]Joseph A. Pechman, "The Rich, the Poor, and the Taxes They Pay," *The Public Interest*, Fall 1968.

prices paid for human and capital resources and what determines the quantities that can be employed.

Wage Rate Determination.

Under competitive market conditions, the basic principle of wage rate determination is that units (person-hours) of any kind of labor tend to be paid a price equal to any one worker's (hourly) contribution to an employer's total receipts. In other words, workers are paid about what they are worth to employers. What a worker is worth to an employer is referred to by economists as the *marginal revenue product of labor*.

> The **marginal revenue product of labor** is the change in the firm's total revenue resulting from adding or subtracting a unit of labor, say, adding an hour of work or adding another worker. Thus, it indicates the value of a unit of labor to the firm.

Suppose the marginal revenue product of the worker is $4 per hour; that is, an hour of labor is contributing $4 to the receipts of the employer. Then the worker is worth $4 an hour to the employer and would be paid that amount under competitive conditions. If a worker were paid less than what she or he is worth to an employer, the worker would also be paid less than she or he would be worth to *other* employers. Consequently, other employers would bid for the worker's services, driving the worker's wage rate (hourly wages) up to what she or he *is* worth. On the other hand, rather than pay $5 an hour, an employer would lay a worker off.

This principle can be seen more clearly with reference to Figure 7–3. The demand curve for labor (*DD* in the figure) shows what employers are willing to pay at different quantities of labor (worker-hours per month), or alternatively, how much a unit of labor is worth at different possible employment levels. The supply curve for labor (*SS* in the figure) shows the quantity of labor that will be placed on the market at different wage rates. Labor is paid less than it is worth at the wage rate w_0. Only q_0 units of labor want to work at this wage rate. However, at this employment level, labor is worth w_2 to any employer. Thus, a shortage exists; that is, at the wage rate w_0, the quantity of labor demanded is greater than the quantity supplied, and the wage rates will be driven up to w_1. Labor is paid about what it is worth at w_1. At a wage rate above w_1, however, the quantity of labor supplied is not worth that wage to employers. A surplus exists; that is, the quantity of labor supplied is greater than the amount demanded. Thus the wage rate will return again to w_1.

The Price of Capital.

In a competitive market the price of a unit of capital, say a machine, is determined in a way similar to the price of a unit of labor. The price of any kind of capital depends on the demand for and supply of units of capital, and, at market equilibrium, the price of capital equals what that capital is worth to its employer.

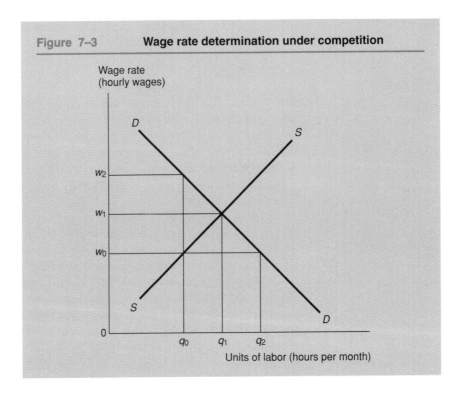

Figure 7–3   **Wage rate determination under competition**

Determination of Individual or Family Income

The income of a person depends on the *price* he or she receives for his or her resources, labor and capital, and the *quantities* of resources he or she can place in employment. For example, the monthly family income from labor equals the quantity of its labor employed, multiplied by the wage rate. From capital, its income equals the quantity of capital employed, multiplied by the price of each unit of capital. Total monthly family income, then, is a summation of the two monthly income flows.

Determinants of Income Distribution

The distribution of income among individuals and families depends on the distribution of resource ownership and the prices paid for resources of different kinds in different employments. The ownership pattern of resources is unequally distributed among individuals and families. This unequal ownership pattern of resources gives rise to an unequal distribution of income in our society. People at the bottom of the income ladder own a small share of the nation's resources on which the market places a high value.

Causes of Differences in Labor Resource Ownership

Brains and Brawn. The inheritance of mental and physical talents is not equally distributed among people. Some people have greater capabilities than others. Some families' labor resources have exceptional learning abilities; others' labor resources have special talents—acting, singing, playing baseball or football. Other families are not so fortunately endowed.

Skill Levels. Skill levels vary among individuals. Differences in skills among people are primarily due to differences in inherited capabilities, training opportunities, and discrimination. Some inherit specific abilities to do certain tasks better than others. Most often people with high skill levels have acquired them from their training and education. In some instances, people have low skill levels because they have been discriminated against and have not had equal opportunities for training and education. Even with the same training, certain groups, say women, may not receive the same pay as others, although they perform the same tasks. In general, those with highly developed skills are worth more and, therefore, are paid more in the market than are unskilled or semiskilled workers.

Capacity Utilization Rate. The capacity utilization rate is the ratio of actual earnings to earnings capacity. Utilization rates differ among people for many reasons. Among these reasons are differences among people with respect to their preferences for income and leisure, and with respect to their responsiveness to changes in their income due to, say, taxes and government transfer payments. Also, some people, such as working wives, may have low utilization rates because of certain labor supply barriers. Garfinkel and Haverman found that the major cause of income inequality is due to differences in earnings capacity among people and that not more than 20 percent of income inequality can be explained by differences in capacity utilization rates.[6]

Causes of Differences in Capital Resource Ownership

Inheritance. Some individuals and families inherit real property and claims on real property such as stocks and bonds. These people have a head start on those who do not begin with inherited capital resources.

Luck. Luck is not evenly distributed among the population. Some families may be at or near the bottom of the income pyramid because of bad luck. A business failure caused by a depression, a prolonged illness, a fatal

---

[6]Irwin Garfinkel and Robert H. Haverman, *Earnings Capacity, Poverty, and Inequality* (New York: Academic Press, 1977), p. 39.

accident, or a natural disaster may leave persons and families without income or the ability to earn an adequate income.

Propensities to Accumulate. People vary as to their propensities or tendencies to save and accumulate capital resources. Those who are strongly motivated are willing to forgo consumption today in order to enjoy greater income in the future. Others are more concerned about their current consumption standards. They do not save and do not accumulate capital resources.

Summary of the Causes of Poverty

Several things are clear about the poor and about low-income families. They have small quantities and low qualities of resources. The market places a low value on the services they provide in the market. The low productivity and, therefore, the low pay of the poor are due to low levels of training and education, misfortune, relatively small inheritances, and discrimination. The poor are in a vicious circle that is difficult to escape. What they need in order to move out of poverty, they do not have and cannot afford to acquire. So they remain poor.

Government Attempts to Alleviate Poverty

Two approaches to poverty are suggested by the foregoing analysis. First, the productivity of the employable poor can be increased. This can be accomplished through subsidized education of the children of the poor, adult training and education programs, counseling and guidance, job placement programs, and the elimination of discrimination. Second, a minimum annual income can be guaranteed. Some people, such as the very young, the very old, the disabled, and the ill, are poor because they cannot produce at all, and others are poor because they cannot produce enough. Income-support programs are required to aid those who are unproductive and those who have low productivity.

Although the federal government continues to fight poverty using both approaches, a close examination reveals an emphasis on income support rather than comprehensive human capital development. The government programs designed to alleviate poverty and to help the poor are often referred to as "public welfare." However, it is important to realize that there has never been just one federal welfare program, but rather a loose system of programs, each targeted to those people with specific characteristics and needs. For example, some programs subsidize the income needs of single-parent households, while others address the health care requirements of the aged and disabled. Many targeted welfare programs have attempted to address the various aspects of poverty during the past 35 years. Even though some of the programs have been success-ful, in recent years the voting public has called for welfare reform to re-duce the federal government's role in assistance to the poor. In the next sections we briefly examine some of the major federal antipoverty pro-grams as they existed prior to 1997 and some of their inherent problems. Following that we turn our attention to an analysis of the ongoing welfare reform that places a new emphasis on work.

The Old Federal Welfare System

Since the "war on poverty" began in the 1960s, numerous federal pro-grams have been designed and undertaken specifically to benefit low-income groups in our society. Most welfare programs prior to 1997 were to a large extent centralized by the federal government. Although the daily operation of the programs may have been handled by state or local agen-cies, everyone followed the rules established by the federal government. Thus, eligibility requirements and degrees of assistance were generally set according to national guidelines. The most important of these centralized programs were those that provided income support to poor female-headed households and the disabled. Others included health care provi-sion, housing services, and nutritional assistance. Many of these continue under the ongoing welfare reform measures but with new rules and a decentralized administrative structure.

Income Support. The first federal welfare program to provide income support to the poor was the Aid to Families with Dependent Children (AFDC) program, which was introduced in 1935 along with the establish-ment of Social Security. AFDC provided direct income transfers to poor families with only one parent living in the household. In practice, this usu-ally meant female-headed households with children under the age of 18. (Some states severely restricted or prohibited AFDC payments to single male-headed households.) AFDC was a *means-tested* program in which families became eligible only if family income and assets fell below some predetermined level. Federal guidelines allowed each state to set its own needs standards for families of different sizes and living locations. Fund-ing for AFDC was shared by the federal government and the states.

Members of families receiving AFDC were allowed, but not required, to work. AFDC benefits were reduced as family income increased. The re-duction in benefits was less than dollar-for-dollar, which allowed total family income to rise when gainful employment was maintained. Total an-nual AFDC payments varied across each of the 50 states, but no state paid benefits sufficient to bring a family above the established poverty line. In the mid-1990s, the average annual AFDC benefit amounted to only 38 per-cent of the poverty threshold. Because of this, families receiving AFDC were automatically eligible for other federally supported assistance pro-grams, including Medicaid and food stamps.

A second major income support program was enacted in 1972 with the signing of the Supplemental Social Insurance Act by President Richard Nixon. Benefits under this program, known as supplemental security income (SSI), were originally targeted to the elderly who do not qualify for Social Security and the blind and disabled whose income and assets fall below specified thresholds. The federal act provided for uniform national guidelines and benefit levels. This program continues to exist under the welfare reform provisions of 1996, with stricter requirements for continuing eligibility.

Health Care Support. The major health care support program targeted toward the poor was, and continues to be, Medicaid. Under the old welfare system, all families who qualified for AFDC or SSI were automatically entitled to Medicaid benefits. In addition, Medicaid was designed to pay the major costs of both hospital care and physician services for low-income pregnant women and children who were not otherwise eligible for public assistance. Prior to the recent welfare reform provisions affecting Medicaid, more than 32 million persons were annually served by the program.

Funding for Medicaid is shared by the federal and state governments. States with lower average incomes receive more federal dollars than high-income states. The federal government's share of Medicaid funding averages between 50 and about 80 percent of the total program cost. The rising cost of health care accounted for more than one-half of the growth in all federal dollars directed toward the poor during the early 1990s.

Food and Nutrition Assistance. Historically, the primary program providing food and nutrition assistance to the poor has been the federal Food Stamp program. Families receiving food stamps are able to redeem vouchers for the purchase of food in order to maintain a nutritious and healthy diet. Interestingly this program was, and continues to be, administered by the Department of Agriculture as a program to support the demand for food and agricultural products produced by American farmers. Under the old welfare system, recipients of AFDC automatically qualified for food stamps, with the level of support being determined by a means test. By the mid-1990s, more than 25 million people received the benefits of food stamps at an annual outlay of almost $30 billion. In addition to the Food Stamp program, the federal government has maintained programs to support lunches for low-income public school children and meals in other institutionalized settings.

Housing Assistance. Housing assistance for the poor has most commonly been provided in the form of rent subsidies. Over the years, a number of federal programs provided direct subsidies for the construction and rental of housing units for the poor in both rural and urban areas. More recently, emphasis has been on housing assistance in the form of rent vouchers. The major problem most low-income families face is not the lack of available housing but a lack of income to afford decent housing. Rent vouchers address this problem directly by giving low-income families the opportunity to choose among publicly and privately owned rental units.

Other Social Services. A number of federal programs provide a variety of social services for the poor. These programs target low-income groups such as the elderly, the disabled, dependent children and youths, and Native Americans. The mix of social services provided include day care, foster care, child abuse intervention, job placement, health counseling, and emergency shelter. The recent welfare reforms have significantly reduced funding for such services, and greater emphasis is being placed on private charities to meet these needs.

Training and Employment. A number of federally sponsored training and employment programs have been undertaken since the 1960s. These programs generally take the form of grants to states for the purpose of assisting people who have difficulties in the job market. Target groups include workers displaced by technology, teenagers, and those on other forms of public assistance. The most comprehensive current training and employment program was established by the Job Training and Partnership Act (JTPA), which encourages local businesses to become involved in delivering training and support. Although each state has responsibility for running their JTPA projects, the federal government requires that a major portion of the funding be used for training the economically disadvantaged. Other federal programs include support for each state's Employment Service (job banks) and subsidized summer employment projects for youths.

Problems with the Old Welfare System

Over the years, economists, social workers, and the general public alike widely criticized the old welfare system. This criticism was grounded in the frustration of growing budget requirements for programs that did not appear to reduce the rate of poverty. The inability of the welfare system to significantly lower the incidence of poverty, even during periods of economic expansion, led many to conclude that the system was flawed. It was argued that most of the programs placed an emphasis on financial support and did not encourage recipients to remedy the causes of their poverty. Furthermore, many argued that the programs were structured in ways that created a "welfare dependency" that resulted in a permanent culture of poverty. These criticisms eventually led to the welfare reform initiatives of the mid-1990s.

The most important criticism of the old welfare system is rooted in basic economic theory. In Chapter 6 we discussed the *income effect* of a wage change. Recall that the income effect measures the change in hours of work supplied by an individual when there is a change in income, other things being equal. Because leisure is a normal good, a person will demand more leisure time, and therefore work fewer hours, when income rises—if everything else remains the same. Under the old welfare system, recipients were provided income (in the form of cash, food stamps, rent vouchers, etc.) without a work or training requirement. This tended to create a pure income effect. When receiving welfare, recipients increased their income while everything else remained the same. Thus, the income effect reduced the hours of work supplied to the labor market by those receiving welfare benefits. Numerous empirical studies have demonstrated that programs such as AFDC did generate significant reductions in hours of work by recipients. However, because of the low wages available to most workers on welfare, it is problematic to conclude that this disincentive to work kept large numbers of people on the welfare rolls.

The most controversial criticism of AFDC and its related programs was that they created an economic incentive for those on welfare to establish and maintain single-parent households and to have babies. Under the old system, the highest levels of benefits were available only to unmarried, separated, or divorced women with dependent children. In most states the benefit levels increased directly with the number of children present in the household. Critics of the system viewed this as public support for unwed motherhood and single-parent families. Although there has been an alarming increase in the number of unwed births and female-headed households, economic studies have not found strong evidence to correlate this trend with the availability and level of welfare payments. Contrary to popular perceptions, the marginal increase in welfare benefits to a single mother who has an additional child were far less than the expected marginal costs of caring for the child. Thus, it was not "profitable" to continue having babies while on welfare.

Most welfare programs were designed to provide temporary stopgap relief for those who found themselves in an economic emergency due to some event outside their control. However, studies indicate that only about one-quarter of welfare recipients left the welfare rolls within a year, and many of these returned at a later date. Furthermore, the probability of leaving the welfare system was found to decrease with the amount of time spent on welfare. In other words, the longer a person remained on welfare, the lower the likelihood that they would exit. Long-run studies of AFDC indicated that as many as one-fourth of the recipients spent at least 10 years on welfare. Results such as these pointed to a permanent welfare class and led policymakers to conclude that the old system needed to be reformed.

Welfare Reform and the New System

When President Bill Clinton signed The Personal Responsibility and Work Opportunity Reconciliation Act during the fall of 1996, he claimed that it would "end welfare as we have known it." This piece of legislation made broad, sweeping changes in the organizational structure and daily operations of our public assistance system. Most importantly, the bill eliminated the open-ended AFDC program and replaced it with block grants to the states for time-limited income support programs. It also modified various aspects of SSI, Food Stamps, and other social service programs targeted to the poor. Based on the criticisms of the old welfare system, two important themes are reflected throughout the 1996 welfare reform legislation: (1) the act places time limits on how long a person, or family, may receive benefits, and (2) the act requires those who receive public assistance to work.

The major differences between the old welfare system and the new are highlighted in Table 7–4 on page 190. Some of the most important aspects of the new system are reviewed below, followed by a brief discussion of some potential problems.

Income Support. In 1997 the old AFDC program was phased out and replaced by state-designed and state-operated Temporary Assistance for Needy Families (TANF) programs. These programs are financed by block grants from the federal government and state revenues. To qualify for the federal money, each state program must adhere to specific guidelines concerning time limits for assistance and work requirements for able-bodied adults. With these two exceptions, states have a nearly free hand in setting their own eligibility requirements and level of support.

Under the TANF programs, adults who are not working must participate in community service within 2 months of receiving benefits. All adults in families receiving income support must work, or be engaged in training, after 24 months or lose their eligibility for assistance. Also, TANF recipients are subject to a lifetime limit of 60 months (5 years) of benefits. To ensure that each state designed a TANF program that encouraged work, the 1996 legislation set minimum standards for annual work participation rates of families receiving assistance. These minimums increase over time, and states that fail to meet the mark are penalized through reductions in their block grants. Figure 7–4 on page 191 illustrates the annual work participation targets as stated in The Personal Responsibility and Work Opportunity Reconciliation Act. States that meet or exceed the goals are eligible for performance bonuses in the form of additional financial support.

Medicaid. Under the old system, all recipients of AFDC automatically qualified for Medicaid benefits. The welfare reform legislation of 1996 severs this automatic link and allows states to set their own eligibility

Table 7-4	Major changes in the welfare system due to The Personal Responsibility and Work Opportunity Reconciliation Act of 1996	
At Issue	**Old System**	**New System**
Cash assistance	AFDC* had no limits on how long income support could be received.	TANF† allows no more than 2 years of assistance without working and sets a 5-year lifetime limit for adults.
	No work requirement to remain eligible for AFDC.	Adults in families receiving TANF are required to participate in work activities after 24 months of assistance.
Medicaid	AFDC recipients automatically qualified for Medicaid.	States may set their own eligibility requirements within specified guidelines.
Food stamps	No time limit for those who qualified.	Able-bodied adults may receive food stamps for only 3 months in every 36-month period unless they work.
SSI	Developmentally disabled children qualified.	Stricter diagnosis of developmentally disabled children required, and behavioral disorders no longer qualify.
Citizenship	Noncitizens qualified for a wide variety of programs.	New immigrants cannot receive benefits in their first 5 years; no food stamps or SSI for those who have not paid taxes for 10 years or served in the military; illegal immigrants ineligible for most benefits.
Child support	Female recipients not required to name father of their children.	Female recipients required to cooperate in identifying father and seeking child support.

*AFDC: Aid to Families with Dependent Children.
†TANF: Temporary Assistance for Needy Families.

requirements within a set of guidelines. States also have the option of denying Medicaid to persons who are not citizens of the United States and those denied income support because of refusal to work. States are required to provide coverage to needy pregnant women and minor children.

Food Stamps. The welfare reform measures retain the basic structure of the Food Stamp program. However, new work requirements have been established for those receiving benefits under the program. Able-bodied adults between 18 and 50 years of age may receive food stamps for only

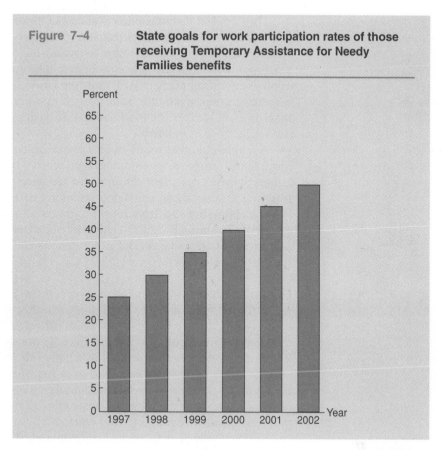

Figure 7–4   **State goals for work participation rates of those receiving Temporary Assistance for Needy Families benefits**

The Personal Responsibility and Work Opportunity Reconciliation Act of 1996 established these work participation goals to be met by each state. States that do not meet these goals are subject to reductions in their block grants, and states that beat the goals are eligible for bonus grants.

3 months during every 36-month period unless they are engaged in work or are training for work. Special exemptions can be made only on a limited basis for hardship cases. Recipients who work at least 20 hours per week can continue to receive benefits for an uncapped period of time.

Supplemental Security Income and Other Social Services. The welfare reforms established new disability standards for those receiving and applying for SSI benefits. Changes in the criteria used to establish disability make it more difficult to qualify for income support. For example, under the new system, children with developmental maladaptive behavior problems are no longer considered handicapped and are not eligible for assistance.

The Personal Responsibility and Work Opportunity Reconciliation Act also addresses the issue of citizenship. Most programs in the old welfare system did not give consideration to citizenship or even legal resident status. Programs under the new system may take these factors into consideration. New immigrants must live in the United States for 5 years before benefits become available from most programs. The residency requirement is even stricter for food stamps: 10 years of paying taxes or some service in the U.S. military.

A number of other requirements are included as part of the welfare reform. For example, single mothers who receive benefits must identify the fathers of their dependent children and assist in seeking child care support from them. Also, those convicted on felony drug charges are prohibited from receiving benefits from most programs. In addition to these changes, a variety of training programs, child nutrition programs, health care counseling, and other social service programs were affected by the welfare reform legislation.

Potential Problems with the New System. Experts estimate the welfare reforms discussed above will force roughly 1.5 million adults off the welfare rolls during the first few years. Another 800,000 will likely lose their Food Stamp program benefits. Even before the new reforms were put into place, critics began questioning whether the labor market can absorb such an influx of new workers. The work requirements of the new system pose a major obstacle to its success. Some economists claim that the economy cannot grow fast enough to create enough new jobs for those on welfare who are now required to find work.

In 1996, New York City had approximately 470,000 adults on welfare. If the New York economy grew at its historic rate, it would take 21 years for enough new jobs to be created for so many. This problem is not limited to New York. Growth rates in most major cities fall well short of being able to provide enough new jobs in the near future. According to one city official in New York, "In the short term it logically leads you to understand that a massive job creation effort beyond anything the government has done since the Great Depression would have to go on to provide work for all these people."[7]

The number of jobs available is just one problem. Perhaps even more complex is the problem concerning the *types* of jobs available. Most workers on welfare do not possess the same training and skills that are in demand by employers. Low-skill jobs, such as those in manufacturing and agriculture, have declined in importance over the years and no longer offer an easy entry into the world of work for untrained individuals.

---

[7]Alan Finder, "As Welfare Limits Loom, New York Recipients Outnumber Jobs They Might Fill," *The New York Times*, Sunday, August 25, 1996, p. 17.

Although the TANF grants encourage states to offer education and training programs to welfare recipients, experience has shown that it is difficult to overcome the mismatch in skill requirements.

Given such hard problems, it will be difficult for states to meet their work participation goals (Figure 7–4). One solution is to place welfare recipients on the public payroll. This is a highly controversial issue. Some believe that this approach results in "make work" jobs or may lead to a substitution of welfare workers for current civil servants. Others argue that such programs can provide needed training and experience that will help workers land jobs in the private sector. All parties agree that it is in everyone's best interest if welfare workers can be placed in private sector jobs. To encourage private firms to hire welfare workers, President Clinton proposed a $1 billion subsidy program for companies that made such hires. Whether such a program will assist a significant number of welfare workers and help the states meet their work participation goals is yet to be determined.

Using Tax Policy to Fight Poverty

For a long time, many economists have argued that the most efficient way of transferring dollars to the poor is to use the national income tax system. As our national tax collector, the Internal Revenue Service (IRS) has in place an elaborate system that tracks household income and distributes checks, and by carefully designing our tax policy, it is possible to take advantage of these characteristics in a way that will improve the economic position of the poor. In fact, we have been doing just that for about 25 years. The major program that accomplishes this is the Earned Income Tax Credit (EITC), and as we shall see, its principles are very similar to a more comprehensive approach that policymakers have debated and considered for several years: the negative income tax proposal.

The Earned Income Tax Credit

The EITC was originally established in 1975 as a modest program designed to offset the negative effects of the Social Security and Medicare payroll taxes paid by the working poor. Because Social Security and Medicare taxes are levied from the first dollar earned and because there are no personal deductions or exemptions, low-wage workers tend to bear a greater burden from these taxes than from other income taxes. (An economic analysis of taxes is presented later in Chapter 13, and Social Security and Medicare taxes are discussed in more detail in Chapter 14.) The basic idea of the EITC is to reduce the total taxes paid by poor workers by providing them a refundable credit against their annual federal income tax liability. By reducing the total tax liability of the poor, the EITC increases the annual take-home pay of low-income workers and creates a stronger incentive for them to remain active members of the labor force. Because of these positive aspects of the EITC, Congress has expanded the program several times, most recently in 1993.

The EITC is administered by the IRS as part of the federal income tax system. Individuals and families with modest earned incomes, up to a specified limit, are eligible to claim the credit. Since the EITC is a *refundable* tax credit, if a family's tax liability is less than the credit, it will receive a check from the IRS for the difference. For example, if you owe the federal government $1,000 in income taxes but you are also eligible for a $1,500 tax credit, then you could claim a $500 refund from the IRS. For people in this circumstance, the EITC is like cash—it increases their disposable income.

Unlike more traditional income assistance programs that reduce benefits for every dollar earned by the recipient, the EITC increases in value as earnings rise up to some point and then it is phased out once an earnings threshold is reached. Figure 7–5 illustrates the 1998 EITC structure for a family with two or more dependents. Such families are eligible for a 40 percent tax credit on all wages and salaries up to an income of $9,390. Thus, the maximum EITC is 0.40 × $9,390, or $3,756. This amount can be claimed by families earning up to $12,260 where the phase-out threshold has been established. Families earning more than $12,260 have their EITC reduced by a rate of 21.06 percent for every dollar of earnings. Therefore, as can be seen in Figure 7–5, the value of the EITC falls until $30,095 is reached. Families earning more than this are not eligible to receive the tax credit.

As a result of the legislative expansions of the program, more than 20 million American households now receive the EITC benefit. Comparison of Figure 7–5 with the poverty thresholds shown earlier in Table 7–1 reveals that the largest tax credits will go to those working families with earnings below the poverty line. This fact makes it more likely that the EITC will lift families out of poverty than programs that target families with little or no income. Proponents of the EITC point out that its design is consistent with the recent welfare reform measures in that it increases the net earnings of those who leave the welfare rolls to take jobs in the private economy. In fact, because the EITC is refundable, it can be considered a wage supplement for the working poor. However, once the phase-out threshold is reached, this wage supplement begins to decline at a relatively high rate. The current rate of reduction in the phase-out range, 21.06 percent, is higher than the ordinary income tax rate of 15 percent, which is applied to the lowest levels of taxable income. Critics have suggested that this element of the EITC may create disincentives to work for those who find themselves in the phase-out range. To date, however, research into

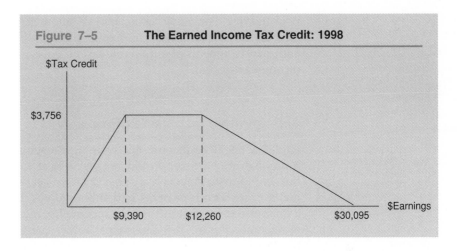

Figure 7–5   The Earned Income Tax Credit: 1998

Families with two or more children may claim a refundable tax credit of 40 percent on earnings up to $9,390. This results in a maximum credit of $3,756. Once earnings exceed $12,260, the tax credit is reduced by 21.06 percent for each additional dollar earned. The tax credit is thus exhausted at an earnings level of $30,095.

this facet of the program has not revealed a significant reduction in work effort for the affected group of beneficiaries.

Even though the EITC plays an important role in lifting families above the poverty threshold, its impact is not reflected in the official poverty statistics because of the way the government measures household income. Recall that a household's poverty status is determined by comparing its *pretax* income to the appropriate poverty threshold based on family size. Thus, income is measured before any tax credits are applied. Because this approach overlooks the effect of tax credits, economists have devoted considerable research into determining the impact of the EITC on poverty. A recent study published by the Center for Budget and Policy Priorities found that in 1996 more than 4.6 million people were lifted out of poverty status by the EITC. Furthermore, the researchers found that families were more likely to be pushed above their poverty threshold by the EITC than by other more traditional income transfer programs.

Clearly, the EITC has become an important component in our nation's policy to fight poverty. However, some experts argue that the EITC is too complicated and that its cumbersome eligibility rules encourage families with modest incomes to cheat the system. Indeed, the IRS has estimated that in recent years more than 20 percent of EITC benefits were paid in error. For many years, some economists and policymakers have advocated that the way to avoid such problems yet maintain the antipoverty benefits of refundable tax credits is to institute a true negative income tax system.

The Negative Income Tax Proposal

The **negative income tax** is a government subsidy or cash payment to households who qualify because of having income below a minimum or guaranteed level.

Under a negative income tax system, households with income below a predetermined level would not be subject to an income tax liability but would instead receive a subsidy based on their income and the normal tax rate. This type of tax structure involves three important variables: a guaranteed level of income, an income tax rate, and a break-even level of income. Figure 7–6 illustrates how a negative income tax structure works.

In Figure 7–6, a household's income is measured on the horizontal axis and its income tax liability on the vertical axis. Thus, the amount of income taxes owed the government is shown as the upward-sloping line. The slope of this line is determined by the income tax rate. With a negative income tax structure in place, all households are guaranteed a minimum level of income equal to the absolute value of point G. Households with zero income therefore have a negative tax liability equal to G. This means that instead of paying income taxes, the government sends to the household a check equal to G. As seen in Figure 7–6, this subsidy declines by the rate of the income tax as household earnings rise. At point B the subsidy is exhausted. Point B is the break-even level of income above which households face a positive tax liability. In other words, after point B is reached, households no longer receive a check *from* the government; rather, they must pay an income tax *to* the government.

The negative income tax proposal has several attractive features. It is based on the idea that when a household has income above its poverty threshold, the household pays positive taxes; and when a household has income below its poverty threshold, the household owes negative taxes and receives a subsidy check from the government. Because the subsidy check increases total household income, people are always better off if they earn income than they are if they do not earn it; and the more they earn, the better off they will be. In this way, the negative income tax encourages low-income beneficiaries to work. This scheme is designed for individuals and families that have one and only one characteristic: They live in poverty. It is not necessary to be old and poor or blind and poor. To be eligible, you need only be poor. Thus, a negative income tax system is much simpler and probably easier to administer than the vast array of current antipoverty programs. Because of these positive attributes, the negative income tax proposal has been advocated by many influential economists, such as Nobel Prize winner Milton Friedman.

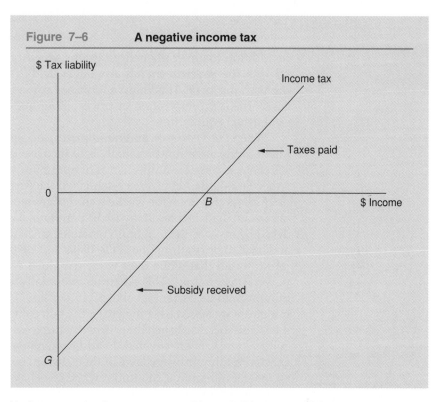

Figure 7–6   **A negative income tax**

Under a negative income system all households are guaranteed a minimum level of income. This is shown as point G. Households with no income would receive a subsidy check from the government equal to that amount. As household income rises, the amount of the subsidy declines at a rate equal to the normal tax rate. Point B represents the level of income where the subsidy is exhausted. Beyond this break-even level of income, households are subject to a positive tax liability.

It is important to note that the refundable EITC incorporates some of the same features of the negative income tax proposal into our existing tax structure. Just as under a negative income tax system, low-income households may receive a check from the federal government. However, the EITC program is not a true negative income tax because to qualify a household must have earnings. Families with no one working, perhaps due to disability or other reasons, cannot apply for the EITC. Today, families without earnings must rely on other welfare programs for support. With a true negative income tax system, however, these families would receive cash benefits. Thus, many of the more traditional income transfer programs could be downsized or even eliminated if the negative income tax proposal were adopted.

Price Floors and Ceilings

In addition to governmental programs specifically designed to alleviate poverty, the government has also intervened in the marketplace to assist the working poor. This intervention has come in the form of price controls—the legal imposition of prices either above or below the market-established equilibrium.

A **price floor** is a minimum allowable price for a good or service. Price floors are typically set by a governmental unit or a group of sellers.

When *price floors*, or minimum prices, are set for particular items, the intent of the government usually is to increase the incomes of those who sell them. A classic example is that of minimum-wage legislation. The Fair Labor Standards Act of 1938 established the first federal minimum wage of 25 cents per hour for workers in designated industries. By 1981, the minimum had increased to $3.35 per hour. For the remainder of the decade, however, the minimum remained unchanged. Given a rising general level of prices throughout the 1980s and 1990s, those earning the minimum found that while their wage remained constant, their purchasing power was eroding. This situation eventually led to an increase in the minimum to its current level of $5.15 per hour. Further, not only has the minimum increased over the years, the percentage of workers covered by it has also increased such that currently in excess of 80 percent of nonagricultural workers are covered. In addition, many state governments have enacted minimum-wage laws of their own to cover workers not covered by federal minimums. Minimum-wage laws have had wide support from the general public. They apply, of course, to workers at the lower end of the income scale and were enacted to combat what Congress identified as "labor conditions detrimental to the maintenance of the minimum standard of living necessary for health, efficiency, and general well-being of workers."

Governmental units often set a maximum allowable price for a good or service, which is called a **price ceiling**.

Price ceilings, or maximum prices, have been put into effect from time to time in the United States for two primary purposes. They have been established across the board in attempts to hold inflation in check. They have also been used on a selective basis to keep the purchase of certain items within reach of those at the lower end of the income scale. This latter purpose may also have an anti-inflationary intent. Across-the-board ceilings in the United States have been confined largely to wartime periods except for the 90-day wage price freeze of August 1971, but selective price ceilings have been used in specific markets at other times. We shall concern ourselves in this chapter with selective price ceilings, using as an illustration rent controls.

Rent controls have been used in metropolitan areas as a device to hold housing costs in check for low-income groups. During the 1970s alone, more than 200 U.S. cities enacted some type of rent control. The most well-known example of such controls is undoubtedly that of New York City, which has had rent controls in effect since World War II. On a much smaller scale, it is common for a university to set rental rates on university apartments at relatively low levels to help alleviate problems encountered by low-income students.

Minimum Wages

The establishment by law of minimum hourly wage rates is looked upon favorably by a large majority of those in our society. Most see minimum-wage rates as a means of helping those at the lower end of the income scale raise their wage rates and thereby raise their incomes. There is apparently a philosophical belief in our society that those who work should not find themselves living in poverty. Yet at its current level, the minimum wage fails to keep even a family of three (one working for the minimum) out of poverty. What are the economic effects of the minimum? Is it a good means of improving the lot of the working poor? Does the minimum serve to improve the distribution of income in the economy?

The Effects of a Minimum Wage. Starting from the equilibrium wage of $5 in Figure 7–7, suppose a well-meaning Congress, concerned with the low incomes of unskilled workers, enacts a minimum wage of $6 per hour. What is the impact of the program? Consider the impact of the program on the demand for and supply of labor separately. Employers must now pay $6 for each unit of labor hired. Given that a rational employer will only hire a worker if the worker's marginal revenue product is greater than the wage, we can be sure that the quantity of labor demanded will fall in response to the wage increase. Recalling that the demand for labor represents the marginal revenue product of labor, Figure 7–7 indicates that the quantity of labor demanded will fall to 800 hours when the wage rises to $6. The reason for this is clear—for each unit of labor between the 900-hour and 800-hour levels of employment, the wage rate is greater than the marginal revenue product of labor.

This situation is further complicated by the supply reaction to the minimum wage. Specifically, the effect of the minimum is to increase the quantity of labor supplied from 900 hours to 925 hours.

At the minimum wage of $6, then, there is a surplus of labor equal to 125 hours per week. That is, at this wage, there are 125 hours of employment that workers wish to provide but are unable to provide. This is the inevitable conclusion of government-established price floors. Whenever such minimum prices are established, they result in a surplus, which in this case is called *unemployment*.

Theoretically, it is clear that the establishment of a minimum wage leads to some unemployment, but what about increases in an existing minimum wage? A bit of insight suggests that the analysis just presented is equally applicable to a minimum-wage increase as it is to the initial establishment of a minimum. For example, suppose that the existing minimum of $6 were increased to $7. What would be the result of such a

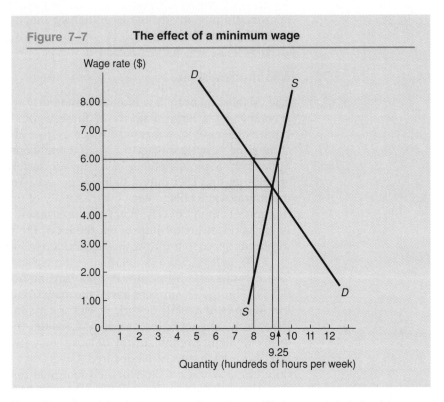

Figure 7–7   **The effect of a minimum wage**

The effect of a minimum wage set above the equilibrium wage is to lead to a surplus of labor. In this case, a minimum established at $6 leads to a surplus of 125
hours per week. This surplus is, of course, known as unemployment.

policy? The quantity of labor demanded would fall further, the quantity of
labor supplied would increase further, and the two taken together would
lead to even more unemployment.

   Given the unemployment effect of the minimum, may it be concluded
that minimum wages fail to make economic sense? Such a decision must
rely on an analysis of the benefits and costs of the program. The costs are
clear, but what are the benefits? Returning to Figure 7–7, it can be noted
that the minimum generated a good deal of unemployment, yet not all
workers lost their jobs. In fact, 800 hours of labor remained employed.
These workers clearly benefited from the establishment of the minimum,
given that they earn more for their labor. Further, if these workers are from
the lower end of the income distribution, the fact that they are earning
more suggests that the minimum may tend to improve the distribution of
earnings in the economy as a whole.

   Given that the minimum wage involves costs and benefits, to properly
evaluate the minimum wage or any increases in the minimum, we must

answer three questions: How many people gain, and by how much do they gain, when a minimum is established or increased? By how much does the unemployment rate rise when the minimum wage is increased? And, to what extent does the minimum improve the distribution of income in the economy? Relatively little research has been conducted on the first of these questions. An exception is the study by the Department of Labor concerning the 1981 increase in the minimum from $3.10 to $3.35 per hour. Its estimates suggest that 5.5 million workers stood to gain from the increase in the minimum. Further, the study indicates that the increase in the minimum added about $2 billion to the incomes of workers in the economy.

In contrast, a great deal of research has been directed toward considering the unemployment impact of increasing the minimum wage. Although the outcomes of these studies differ in some regards, two results are commonly found. First, in terms of increased unemployment, teenagers appear to be more commonly harmed by the minimum than any other group of workers since they work in disproportionate numbers for the minimum wage. In fact, increases in the minimum appear to have little or no effect on the unemployment rate of adult workers. Beyond this, the research suggests that a 10 percent increase in the minimum is associated with an increase in the teenage unemployment rate of about ½ of 1 percent. For example, if the teenage unemployment rate is initially 12 percent and the minimum wage is increased by 10 percent, teenage unemployment can be expected to rise to about 12.5 percent.[8]

Research into the third question is also quite informative. Specifically, the evidence suggests that the minimum wage has little impact on the distribution of income in our society.[9] The primary reason for this outcome is that many of the individuals benefiting from the minimum wage are teenagers from middle- and upper-income families. As a policy designed to help the working poor, then, the minimum wage may be poorly targeted.

What may we now conclude about the minimum wage? First, some individuals clearly benefit from the minimum. The primary beneficiaries are those who remain employed and have their earnings increased in response to the minimum. Second, however, it is equally clear that other individuals lose when a minimum wage is established or increased. Especially hard hit are the many teenagers who lose their jobs in response

[8]Charles Brown, Curtis Gilroy, and Andrew Kohen, "The Effect of the Minimum Wage on Employment and Unemployment," *Journal of Economic Literature,* June 1982, p. 487.

[9]William Johnson and Edgar Browning, "The Distributional Effects of Increasing the Minimum Wage," *American Economic Review,* March 1983, p. 204.

to the minimum. Third, it appears that the minimum wage is a poor means of improving the distribution of income in the economy since many of its recipients are not poor. At this point, a final decision concerning the desirability of the minimum wage must be left to each of us. It does appear obvious, however, that these outcomes are not exactly what Congress had in mind when it enacted the minimum wage.

Rent Controls

Almost everyone looks with disfavor on slums. In certain areas of any city, one sees housing conditions that are distressing to say the least. Several families may be using the same bath and toilet facilities. Some families live in units that are not well-lighted or well-ventilated. Two or more families may be living in the same apartment. The buildings and apartments may be in various states of disrepair. Why do people live in them? Usually these are as much as lower income families can afford. Or, if you have tried to find an apartment in Manhattan recently, you know that they may be all that is available. Why do these problems occur? Do the rent controls that have been operative in places such as New York City serve the best interests of lower-income groups? An examination of housing demand, supply, and pricing will help us evaluate the housing problems of the poor.

Demand. The demand for housing originates in households—families and unattached individuals living in the economic system. Within the constraints of the incomes available to them and the prices they must pay for different goods and services, households make their choices as to what goods and services they will buy and how much of each they will purchase. Presumably, each household moves toward an allocation of its income among different goods and services that will yield it the highest level of total satisfaction. Any given household will try to allocate its income among various goods and services in such a way that a dollar's worth of housing contributes the same to consumer well-being as a dollar's worth of anything else the household buys. If a dollar's worth of something else, say food, were more valuable to the household than a dollar's worth of housing, the household would gain satisfaction by shifting some of its expenditure away from housing toward food. On the other hand, if a dollar's worth of housing were more valuable to a household than a dollar's worth of food, the household would gain in well-being by purchasing less food and more housing with its more or less fixed income.

How does this translate into a demand curve for housing? In Figure 7–8, suppose that the rental rate is r dollars and that when households are spending their incomes so that a dollar's worth of housing makes the same contribution to household well-being as a dollar's worth of anything else, they purchase h units of housing per year. What would happen to the

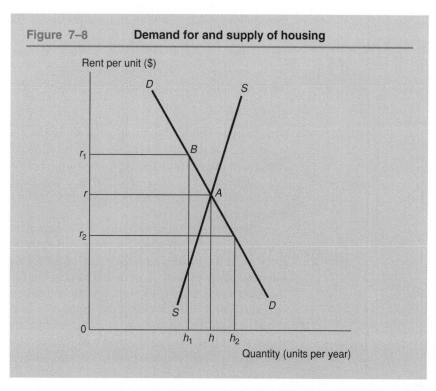

Figure 7–8   **Demand for and supply of housing**

The demand curve for housing *DD* shows the value of a unit of housing to households at various alternative quantities. If the quantity available were *h* units per year, the value of a unit to households is *r* dollars per year. If the quantity available were *h*, the value of a unit to households is r_1 dollars. If h_2 units were available, the value of a unit becomes r_2.

quantity of housing if rent rises to r_1 and the other factors that influence demand remain unchanged? At the higher rent level, a dollar's worth of housing is a smaller quantity of housing than before; consequently, the contribution that a dollar's worth of housing makes to household well-being is smaller than it was before the rent increase. The contribution of a dollar's worth of any other item to household well-being thus is greater than that of a dollar's worth of housing. Households will shift dollars from housing to other items, reducing the amount of housing consumed to some level h_1. The entire demand curve *DD* is made up of such points as *A* and *B*, at which households consider that the are buying the correct amounts of housing relative to other goods and services at various prices for housing.

One more point should be made before we leave the concept of the demand for housing. The demand curve *DD* shows that when households take *h* units of housing, a unit of housing is worth *r* dollars to them; that is, they believe the amount a unit contributes to their total well-being is the same as the contribution of r dollars' worth of any other good or service they consume. Similarly, if only a smaller amount h_1 were available to them, they would value a unit of housing at r_1 dollars. In general terms, the less we have of any given item, the more we value a unit of it.

Supply. The supply of housing available is not very responsive to price and/or rent levels over relatively short time spans. The supply curve tends to be sharply upward-sloping, as shown by SS in Figure 7–8. The reason for this is quite evident. Most of the housing supply in any given year consists of the stock of already existing units. In the course of a year, the amount by which this stock is likely to be increased or decreased is relatively small.

Nevertheless, some variation in the quantity supplied will occur in response to price changes. Consider, for example, the entire complex of housing units in New York City. The space they occupy is highly valuable for business purposes. A decrease in housing rental rates relative to what the space could earn if converted to business uses would cause some conversion to occur and decrease the number of housing units available. This can also work the other way around. An increase in housing rental rates relative to what the space could earn in business uses may result in conversion of some business space to housing units. It may also result in some construction of new housing units.

Price. Suppose that in New York City the demand curve for housing is DD and the supply curve is SS, as in Figure 7–9. The equilibrium rental rate is r, and the number of housing units occupied is h. Over time, economic growth and rising household incomes increase the demand for housing to D_1D_1. In the absence of rent controls, the short-run impact of the increase in demand is a rise in rental rates to r_1 and an increase in the units made available to h_1.

The rise in rental rates will make investment in housing units more profitable, and in the long run—say a period of 5 years or more—such additional investment will shift the supply curve for housing to the right. Rental rates will fall to some value r_2, and the number of units rented will rise to h_2. In New York City, because of space limitations and because of the alternatives of using property for business purposes, it is highly unlikely that increases in supply can keep pace with increases in demand, so the rental rate r_2 will undoubtedly exceed the original rental rate r. In other localities in which space is a much smaller problem and in which business competition for space is much less, r_2 may be very close to r.

The Effects of Rent Controls. Following World War II, New York City elected to continue rent controls established during the war. These controlled rates were maintained to some degree, although over time they

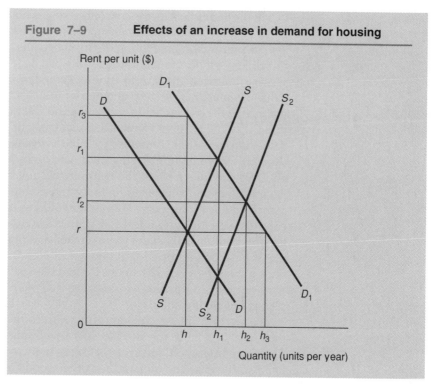

Figure 7–9   **Effects of an increase in demand for housing**

If the demand curve for housing units is *DD* and the supply curve is *SS*, the equilibrium level of rent is *r* and the equilibrium quantity occupied is *h*. An increase in demand to D_1D_1 increases the rent level to r_1 and the quantity occupied to h_1. The increased profitability of providing housing causes the supply curve to shift to S_2S_2 over time, increasing the units occupied to h_2 and lowering rents to r_2. If, however, rent controls had been enacted at level *r*, the long-run increase in housing would not take place. A shortage of hh_3 units would persist over time.

have crept gradually upward. The purpose of the controls has been to keep the price of housing within the reach of lower income groups. What are the *actual* effects of the controls?

In the first place, they generate a housing shortage. In Figure 7–9, as demand increases from *DD* to D_1D_1 with the supply curve at *SS*, if rents are not allowed to rise above *r*, a shortage of hh_3 units develops. Not all households looking for apartments are able to find them. Not all households desiring to add to their living space are able to do so. Much time is wasted in futile searches for apartments. Those whose employment is in New York City and who cannot find housing there are forced to outlying areas from which they must commute. This is the inevitable outcome of price ceilings. Whenever price ceilings have been instituted, shortages have quickly become apparent.

In the second place, the cost of housing is not kept down for everyone. In the normal turnover of housing units—some households vacating their apartments and others renting them—it becomes common to make under-the-table payments to landlords for the privilege of a new lease. For those seeking housing, the search time is extended by the shortage, and the value of the extra search time required is a cost to the searchers. Many, if not most, of those forced to commute find their costs increased in at least three ways: (1) higher rents, (2) direct costs of commuting, and (3) the value of time lost in commuting. Only those ensconced in housing before the controls were put into effect and who did not move after they became effective can be sure that the controls will not raise their housing costs. Such protection from rising rents for those who have lived in controlled apartments for long periods of time would seem to be exactly what the controls were put into effect for. Unfortunately, many who receive these benefits could hardly claim them on the basis of financial need. For example, it has been reported that a judge in New York City's housing court rents a two-bedroom apartment for less than $100 per month, which, if it were not rent-controlled, would bring well over $1,000 per month. Examples of this nature abound.[10]

In the third place, the long-run profit inducements that would shift the supply curve to the right to S_2S_2 are eliminated by the rent controls. The rising household incomes that serve to increase the demand for housing also increase the demand for other goods and services produced in New York City. These are not subjected to price controls. The industries producing them become relatively more profitable than the housing industry in which investors cannot capture higher returns from households. Consequently, investors in real estate are provided with profit inducements to increase the space available for business relative to the space available for housing. It is even possible that rent controls may cause the supply curve for housing to decrease in the long run, leaving even fewer housing units available than existed before rent controls were put into effect. This, no doubt, leads to an increase in the population of the homeless, as discussed in the introduction to this chapter. It is no fluke that, of major U.S. cities, 6 of the 10 with the highest rates of homelessness also have rent controls in effect.

In the fourth place, landlords faced with rent controls tend to allow the quality of their properties to deteriorate. For any given type of good or service, lower quality sold at the same price per unit is equivalent to an increase in the price when the quality is not decreased. So quality deterioration is a disguised means of securing at least some price relief. The enactment of minimum housing standards by a municipality may block

---

[10]William Tucker, "Moscow on the Hudson," *American Spectator,* July 1986, pp. 19–21.

landlords from this escape route; however, omnipresent slums indicate they are not always a resounding success.

Finally, the enforcement of rent controls means that for present housing supplies, the rental level of housing units is held below households' valuation of those housing units. For example, in Figure 7–9, after the increase in demand to D_1D_1, the quantity of housing supplied with rent controls at r is h units. But for this quantity of housing, the value of a unit to households is r_3. The price of housing is not allowed to reflect the value that households place on a unit of it.

Summary

The number of people living in poverty in the United States was significantly reduced by the war on poverty during the 1960s. This downward trend in poverty did not continue in the following decades. It is somewhat understandable that the number of poor persons and the poverty rate were not reduced in the 1970s for the economy was essentially stagnant and confronted with other problems during the period. However, this was not the situation after the early 1980s. The economy was in a record-breaking period of expansion. Under these conditions, it would be expected that the incidence of poverty would have been reduced.

Poverty rates vary a great deal among different family groupings. The poverty rate among all families was 10.3 percent in 1997. The poverty rate, however, was very much higher than this among families with a female head of the household—approximately 3 times higher. And if the female householder was black, the poverty rate was almost 5 times higher. Another important factor closely associated with very high family poverty rates is the presence of children under 18. The odds then increase considerably that a family will live in poverty. For example, all married-couple families with children under 18 had a poverty rate of 7.1 in 1997, as compared to 5.2 percent for married-couple families with and without children. The highest possible poverty rates are found when these factors positively related to high poverty rates are put together—a white female householder with children under 18 and a black female householder with children under 18. In the first case, the poverty rate is 37.6 percent, and in the second case, it is 46.9 percent. To deal with problems of poverty and low income, programs should be designed to (1) increase the upward mobility of the poor and near-poor and (2) guarantee a minimum annual income to families and individuals who cannot work and those who cannot earn a minimum income when they do work.

Over time, the government has undertaken a wide variety of efforts to reduce poverty, including direct assistance for the needy and market price controls. Many of the federal programs developed piecemeal, and some were not originally designed strictly for the poor. Critics of the old welfare system claimed that the government programs created negative work incentives for the poor and created a culture of poverty. Welfare reform measures in the mid-1990s established a new system of assistance that ties benefits to work and training and places time limits on eligibility. Whether the economy can successfully create enough jobs for welfare workers is yet to be seen. Given the inherent problems of traditional antipoverty programs, a negative income tax scheme appears to offer the taxpayer greater efficiency and cost savings.

Discussion Questions

1. What is the difference between "absolute poverty" and "relative poverty"? Provide examples of each.
2. Discuss the issues that determine the distribution of income in an economy. What has been the primary trend in the U.S. income distribution in recent years? Explain why we see this trend.
3. What factors explain why some people earn very low incomes? Who controls these factors? Can governments through public policy influence all the factors that result in poverty?
4. Explain why some critics claimed that the old welfare system created a "culture of poverty." Using economic reasoning, explain the negative incentive to work that results from cash assistance.
5. Is it possible to provide someone with income support without also creating a negative effect on their hours of work? Explain.
6. How do the welfare reform measures address the criticisms of the old system? What problem confronts the new system?
7. How does the Earned Income Tax Credit (EITC) help alleviate the problems of poverty for low-income families? Can the effect of the EITC be seen in the official poverty statistics? Explain.
8. In what ways are the EITC and the negative income tax proposal alike? In what ways are they different? Do you think the United States will ever have a negative income tax system? Why or why not?
9. Explain how a negative income tax differs from more traditional antipoverty programs.
10. Explain (1) how the minimum wage adds to the problem of unemployment, (2) what type of worker benefits from the minimum wage, and (3) what type of work is hurt by the minimum wage.
11. What effect do rent controls have on the quality of apartments in a rent-controlled district? Do the poor benefit from rent controls in the long run?
12. Why are price controls such as the minimum wage and rent controls popular even though they create inefficiency in the market?

Additional Readings

Duncan, Greg J. *Years of Poverty, Years of Plenty.* Ann Arbor: Institute for Social Research, University of Michigan, 1984.

Reports on the findings of a longitudinal study of family status conducted by the Survey Research Center of the University of Michigan. The introduction and Chapters 1 and 2 are recommended. The major finding is that there is upward mobility among the poor.

Garfinkel, Irwin, and Robert H. Haverman. *Earnings Capacity, Poverty, and Inequality.* New York: Academic Press, 1977.

Concept of earnings capacity is developed and used as a measure of poverty to explore many important poverty issues.

Levitan, Sar A. *Programs in Aid of the Poor.* 5th ed. Baltimore: The Johns Hopkins University Press, 1985.

Thorough analysis of programs in aid of the poor. Especially recommended for further reading are chapters on programs for the next generation and strategies to combat poverty.

Levitan, Sar A., and Isaac Shapiro. *Working but Poor.* Baltimore: The Johns Hopkins University Press, 1987.

Many Americans work but live in poverty. As a matter of fact, it is pointed out in this reference that 9 million Americans work in poverty. The working poor is an often-overlooked poverty group. This is a complete coverage of the plight of the working poor and the reforms that are needed to eliminate or reduce significantly poverty among Americans who work.

Murray, Charles. *Losing Ground.* New York: Basic Books Inc., 1984.

Provocative book examining the effects of traditional antipoverty programs. The author has become a leader in the conservative approach to "welfare reform" in the 1990s.

National Research Council. *Measuring Poverty: A New Approach.* Washington, DC: National Academy Press, 1996.

This book reviews the problems and flaws with the current methodology the federal government uses to determine the extent of poverty in our economy. Alternative conceptual and practical measures of poverty are evaluated, and proposals for a new system are presented.

Robbins, Philip K., Robert G. Spiegelman, and Samuel Weiner, eds. *A Guaranteed Annual Income: Evidence from a Social Experiment.* New York: Academic Press, 1980.

The focus of this selection of essays is on the issues of welfare reform and the effects of welfare reform alternatives based on experiments, especially experiments with negative income tax plans.

Rodgers, Harrell R., Jr. *Poor Women, Poor Families.* New York: M. E. Sharpe Inc., 1985.

Good account of the economic plight of families headed by females.

World Wide Web Resources

American Public Human Services Association
www.aphsa.org

Provides an in-depth analysis of new federal and state welfare reform legislation. Links to other welfare-related sites and the latest news concerning public policy debates.

Center on Budget and Policy Priorities
www.cbpp.org

The Center on Budget and Policy Priorities is a nonpartisan research organization and policy institute that conducts research and analysis on a range of government policies and programs, with an emphasis on those affecting low- and moderate-income people. The Web site provides links to reports concerning welfare reform legislation and the Earned Income Tax Credit.

ESA—The Minimum Wage
www.dol.gov/dol/esa/public/minwage/main.htm

Sponsored by the U.S. Department of Labor. Describes the minimum wage, employees' rights, what employers need to know, the legislative history of minimum wage, and other information.

Health and Human Services Poverty Guidelines
www.aspe.os.dhhs.gov/poverty/poverty.htm

Provides explanations for two versions of the federal poverty measure: poverty thresholds and poverty guidelines.

Institute for Research on Poverty
www.ssc.wisc.edu/irp

IRP is a nonprofit national center for research into the causes and consequences of poverty and inequality in the United States. Site provides links to research reports and other poverty study resources.

Joint Center for Poverty Research
www.jcpr.org

Produced by Northwestern University and the University of Chicago, this site supports academic research into poverty. Has links to the federal guidelines for determining the poverty level and to federal publications, programs, and research events.

United States Census Bureau
www.census.gov

Click on *Subjects A–Z*, type in **poverty**, and a screen about poverty will appear. Gives statistics on poverty by year, historical data, poverty measurements, and other data.

U.S. Department of Housing and Urban Development's Homes and Communities
www.hud.gov

Gives links to housing options for people with low incomes, fair housing and equal opportunity, and other sites.

8

The Economics of Big Business

Who Does What to Whom?

Chapter Outline

Checklist of Economic Concepts

October 15, 1996. Archer Daniels Midland Co. today has agreed to plead guilty and pay a $100 million criminal fine—the largest criminal antitrust fine ever—for its role in two international conspiracies to fix prices to eliminate competition and allocate sales in the lysine and citric acid markets worldwide, the Department of Justice announced today.

"This $100 million criminal fine should send a message to the entire world," said Attorney General Janet Reno. "If you engage in collusive behavior that robs U.S. consumers, there will be vigorous investigation and tough, tough penalties."

The Department said that feed companies, large poultry and swine producers—and ultimately farmers—paid millions more to buy the lysine additive. Also, the Department said that manufacturers of soft drinks, processed foods, detergents, and others, paid millions more to buy the citric acid additive, which ultimately caused consumers to pay more for those products.

These are the Department's second round of charges brought as a result of its ongoing antitrust investigation into the food and feed additives industries. In August, two Japanese and one U.S.-based Korean subsidiary and their executives agreed to pay more than $20 million in criminal fines for their participation in the lysine conspiracy.

"These fines should send a signal to corporations throughout the world that they had better take a hard look at their own behavior," said Joel I. Klein, Acting Assistant Attorney General in charge of the Antitrust Division. "We have reason to believe that international cartels are by no means rare. We will vigorously pursue such violations on our own as well as in cooperation with law enforcement authorities in other countries."[1]

[1] *www.usdoj.gov/atr/public/press_releases/1996/508at.htm*

Americans seem, by nature, to be suspicious of concentrations of power. Whether it's rapid expansion of government, the role played by special interest groups in the political sphere, the growing dominance of a particular religion or sect in everyday life, or the consolidation of markets by large firms, one can expect at least apprehension on the part of the general public and, in extreme cases, outright hostility. This is not to suggest that our innate fear of concentrations of power is generally misplaced; it is often fully justified. A case in point is in the introduction to this chapter, which summarizes the Justice Department's investigation of the food and feed additives industries. This investigation concluded that, among other firms, the large American agribusiness concern Archer Daniels Midland conspired to set the price for two major food additives, lysine and citric acid, above competitive levels. Other recent investigations of this sort by the Justice Department have uncovered similar price-fixing conspiracies in various industries. In total, between 1997 and mid-1998, the Justice Department's investigations resulted in fines totaling nearly $500 million.

In this chapter, our focus is on the economic performance of big businesses. While conspiracies like those noted above can easily be found, care should be taken before concluding that big businesses of necessity lead to negative outcomes for the consuming public for two important reasons. First, firms need not be large to engage in such actions. For example, the price-fixing conspiracy in cattle wholesaling involved what would be called very small firms. Conversely, many truly enormous firms with long histories have never even been accused of such wrongdoing. Second, recall that a large share of the innovations and inventions which yield great satisfaction to the consuming public results from large and powerful firms. Given this, the primary questions we wish to consider in this chapter are: (1) Should we fear bigness in the business world? (2) What role, if any, should government play in counteracting the growth of bigness?

The Economics of Monopoly Power

As such, it is commonly assumed that if a firm grows very large, it must have monopoly power which will eventually be exercised against the public. Unfortunately, the two terms are not synonymous. The first step in evaluating the performance of big business is then to understand what distinguishes big business from monopoly. Having more carefully identified the source of the problem, we turn our attention to the actual performance of firms that possess monopoly power.

What Is Monopoly Power?

As we noted in Chapter 2, *monopoly* in its strictest sense means there is a single seller of a good or service. Not many big businesses fit the full condition of this definition, however. Most large enterprises operate in markets in which there are several other firms producing and selling the product. In Chapter 2, we labeled such a market structure one of *imperfect competition*. It is the monopoly power exercised by firms in imperfectly competitive as well as monopolistic markets that people worry about and to which we address ourselves in this chapter.

The monopoly power of a firm refers to the extent of its control over the supply of the product that is produced by the industry of which it is a part. The more firms there are producing and selling a given product, the less control any one of the firms can exercise over industry supply. If there are enough firms in an industry so that one firm's output and its control over industry supply are insignificant, we have a market that should tend to be competitive. On the other hand, if there is only one firm producing and selling the product, we have a market of pure monopoly. The monopoly power of a firm in an imperfectly competitive market is greater the larger the firm's output is relative to the output of the industry as a whole. It is less the smaller the firm's output is relative to the output of the entire industry. As such, it is not the absolute size of the firm that gives it monopoly power, but rather its size relative to its rivals that is important.

Defined as the percent of industry sales accounted for by the four (or eight) largest firms in an industry, **concentration ratios** provide a measure of monopoly power.

In order to determine the degree of monopoly power in imperfectly competitive markets, we often use *concentration ratios*. The most common is the four-firm concentration ratio, which indicates the percentage of industry sales controlled by the four largest firms in an industry. Thus, an imperfectly competitive industry with four or fewer than four firms would have a concentration ratio of 100 percent and would be thought to have a very high degree of monopoly power. However, an industry with a large number of small firms might have a concentration ratio of 10 or 20 percent and would be thought to have very little monopoly power. Typically, one might suspect a significant degree of monopoly power when the concentration ratio reaches 70 or 80 percent. Table 8–1 shows four-firm concentration ratios for selected industries. As an example, consider the cereal breakfast foods industry. The concentration ratio of 85 percent indicates that 85 percent of the sales of cereal breakfast foods is controlled by the industry's four largest firms. Consequently, this industry probably resembles the pure monopoly model more closely than the pure competition model.

The rather high degrees of concentration indicated in Table 8–1 might suggest that the economy is composed of highly monopolistic markets. However, we should be careful before drawing such a conclusion. Although concentration ratios are valuable and do indicate the potential for monopoly power, they have some limitations. Consider the motor vehicles and bodies industry. The concentration ratio for this industry is 84 percent. In reality, however, the industry is not quite so concentrated because the ratio does not take into account the sales of imported cars. With the sales of imports included, this industry might have a four-firm concentration ratio slightly less than 70 percent. As an example of an opposite limitation, consider the cement industry. The concentration ratio is 35 percent, indicating that 35 percent of cement sales nationally is controlled by the four largest cement firms. The problem with this number is that due to the product's inherent characteristics, cement producers compete only with other cement producers who are located in the same geographic area. That

Table 8–1	Selected four-firm concentration ratios	
Industry	**Concentration Ratio**	
Cigarettes	93	
Malt beverages	90	
Cane sugar refining	85	
Cereal breakfast foods	85	
Motor vehicles and bodies	84	
Glass containers	84	
Household refrigerators	82	
Aircraft engines	77	
Soap and other detergents	63	
Primary aluminum	59	
Synthetic rubber	48	
Blast furnaces and steel mills	37	
Cement	35	
Petroleum refining	30	

Source: U.S. Department of Commerce, Bureau of the Census, *Census of Manufacturers, 1992, Concentration Ratios in Manufacturing,* MC 82-S-2 (Washington, DC: U.S. Government Printing Office, 1997).

is, for cement, we should be interested in the percentage of cement sales in one geographic area controlled by the four largest cement producers in that area. If this were done, the cement industry would appear much more concentrated than Table 8–1 suggests.

How then should the data in Table 8–1 be interpreted? Bearing in mind the limitations of concentration ratios, perhaps a reasonable conclusion might be that there is some evidence of monopoly power in the U.S. economy. We turn our attention now to identifying the impact of monopoly power on firm performance and, ultimately, on the overall performance of the economy.

Outputs and Prices

What impact does monopoly power have on the price a firm charges and on the output level it produces and sells? A useful approach to this question is to contrast the price and output of a firm that exercises monopoly power with those of a firm that does not—that is, with that of a competitive firm.

Demand. We look first at demand for the product being sold. Figure 8–1 illustrates a typical market demand curve. It can be established immediately that with any market structure—competitive, monopolized, or

Figure 8–1 A market demand curve

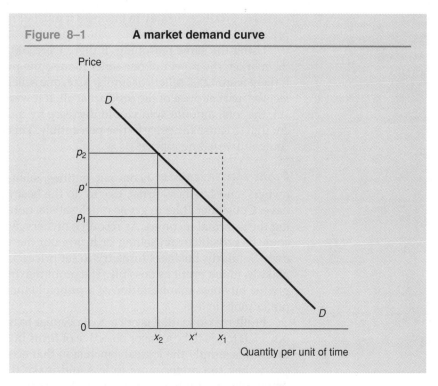

A market demand curve is downward-sloping to the right like DD. Consumers will not pay more than p_1 per unit for an output of x_1 per unit of time. In order to sell at a price of p_2 the total sales level must be reduced to x_2 per unit of time. If four firms of equal size were producing output level x_1, one of the four could cause the product price to rise to p' only by cutting its output and sales to zero.

imperfectly competitive—sellers must take into account what buyers will do. For quantity x_1 per unit of time, buyers will pay a price not higher than p_1. If sellers try to raise the price above p_1, say to p_2, they cannot sell quantity x_1. At the higher price they can sell quantity x_2 only. Consequently, we conclude that the price which sellers are able to charge is always limited by what buyers are willing to pay. Sellers cannot escape the *law of demand*.

The more sellers there are in the market for a product, the less control any one seller has over the price that it can charge. Suppose, for example, that in Figure 8–1 four sellers of approximately equal size are selling a total quantity of x_1. By how much can any one of the four raise product price? If one firm reduces its output and sales to zero, the other three firms would be selling a total of approximately x' per unit of time, and the price would be p'. Price p', then, is the highest level to which any one of the four firms acting independently can force the price, and it can do this only if it ceases to produce. To stay in business it must of necessity charge less than price p'.

Using the same reasoning, if there were 100 sellers of similar size in the market, the power of one seller to raise the price would be much less. If there were 1,000 sellers of similar size, one seller would not be able to affect the market price of the product at all. If it were to drop out of the market, the total amount sold would decrease by only $\frac{1}{1,000}$ of x_1, which is not enough to cause the price to rise perceptibly. This latter case is typical of a competitive selling market.

Profit Maximization. Economic entities, such as consumers, resource owners, and business firms, like to do the best they can with what they have. Consumers like to get as much satisfaction as possible from spending their annual incomes. As resource owners, we like to get as much income as possible from selling or hiring out the labor and the capital we own. Similarly, business firms try to set prices and output levels so as to make as much profit as possible. The profit maximization principle is simply the business manifestation of a principle that affects most of us—we prefer more to less.

Profit maximization is not a goal peculiar to firms that have monopoly power. It tends to be a major objective of firms in all types of market structures. It is simply the logical conclusion that economic entities reach because they too prefer more to less and make their choices accordingly. Although profit maximization is undoubtedly a major goal of business firms, it is not necessarily the only goal. Firms may also want to build up goodwill in a community, to do right by their employees, or to be known for a quality product. They may also want to get rid of their rivals, collude to raise prices, or block entry into the industry.

In any case, prices and outputs tend to be set so as to maximize profits (or minimize losses) regardless of whether firms producing and selling the product are competitive or have monopoly power. But monopoly power, as we shall see, has important implications for what those prices and outputs will be.

Price and Output in a Competitive Market. How does a firm in a competitive market determine what price to charge and what output to produce? Consider the market diagram in Figure 8–2. This is an ordinary market demand-supply diagram. The market price is p_x and the market output is X. But one individual firm selling this product has *no price-setting capabilities whatsoever* since it supplies an insignificant part of the total market supply. The individual competitive firm can determine only the quantity per unit of time to sell at the market price p_x.

The competitive firm thus faces the *horizontal demand curve dd* for its possible outputs. Its level is determined by the market price of the product. Suppose the market price is $14. In Table 8–2 (page 220) columns (1) and (4) represent the demand schedule facing the firm, and column (5)

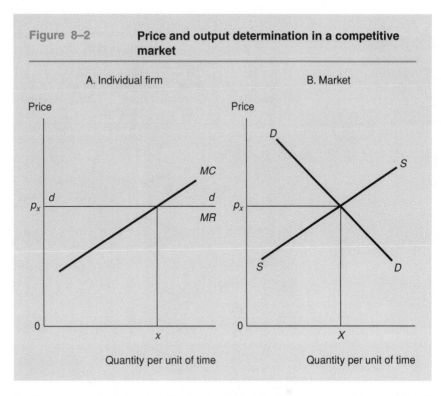

Figure 8–2   **Price and output determination in a competitive market**

A. Individual firm

B. Market

Product price p_x is determined in the market by the interaction of all buyers and all sellers. The individual firm faces the horizontal demand curve *dd*, which is also the firm's *MR* curve. The firm maximizes profits by producing output level *x*. Altogether the many firms in the market produce output *X* in the market diagram. The market quantity scale is highly compressed relative to the firm quantity scale. The price scale is the same in both diagrams.

shows the firm's total revenue (*TR*) at output levels up to 10 units per day. Although the numbers in column (6) are the same as those in column (4), the concept of marginal revenue for the firm differs from the concept of price. *Marginal revenue* (*MR*) is defined as the change in total revenue resulting from a one-unit change in the output level. The significance of this concept will become apparent shortly.

The increase in revenue accruing to the firm from selling an additional unit of its product is called **marginal revenue**.

On the cost side, let column (2) in Table 8–2 represent the firm's total costs (*TC*) at different daily output levels. Marginal cost (*MC*), what we referred to as marginal private cost in Chapter 5, is the change in the firm's total cost resulting from a one-unit change in the output level.

Profits, equal to the difference between total revenue and total cost, are maximized by producing the output at which marginal revenue equals marginal cost.

Determination of the output level that maximizes the firm's profits is easy once we know its *TC* and its *TR* at each possible output. *Profits* are the difference between *TR* and *TC* at any given output level and are listed in column (7). Profits are maximum at either six or seven units of output per day.

Table 8–2   **Outputs, revenues, costs, and profits for a competitive firm**

(1) Output (X per Day)	(2) Total Cost (TC)	(3) Marginal Cost (MC)	(4) Price (Pₓ)	(5) Total Revenue (TR)	(6) Marginal Revenue (MR)	(7) Profits
0	$ 0		$14	$ 0		$ 0
		$ 8			$ 14	
1	8		14	14		6
		9			14	
2	17		14	28		11
		10			14	
3	27		14	42		15
		11			14	
4	38		14	56		18
		12			14	
5	50		14	70		20
		13			14	
6	63		14	84		21
		14			14	
7	77		14	98		21
		15			14	
8	92		14	112		20
		16			14	
9	108		14	126		18
		17			14	
10	125		14	140		15

An alternative means of identifying the firm's profit-maximizing output is to find the output at which MR equals MC. Consider any output below the six-unit level, say three units. A one-unit increase in output would increase TR by $14, or by the amount of MR. It would increase TC by $11, or by the amount of MC. Therefore, it would increase profits by $3, the difference between the MR and the MC of the fourth unit of output. Check the accuracy of this computation in the profit column. We have discovered an important principle: When MR is greater than MC, an increase in the output level will increase profits. (Do you see how this is yet another application of cost-benefit analysis?) Further increases in output through five and six units also increase profits since MR is greater than MC for each of the increases. An increase in output from six to seven units per day adds nothing to profits since MR = MC = $14. However, it does not cause profits to decrease. If output is increased from seven to eight or more units per day, MR is less than MC, and profits decrease—another important principle. But the most important principle of all is that profits are maximized by producing the output level at which MR equals MC. In Table 8–2 profits are maximum at an output level of seven units per day. To be sure, profits are also maximum at six units of product per day, but it will be easier to remember—and always correct—to settle on the output level at which MR equals MC.

The individual firm diagram of Figure 8–2 shows output x as the firm's profit-maximizing output. Note from Table 8–2 that if a firm's MR is plotted for each output, it will be a horizontal line coinciding with the firm's demand curve dd. The firm's MC curve can be thought of as column (3) of Table 8–2 plotted against output. The output level at which profits are maximum is the one at which MR equals MC.

Recall from Chapter 5 that the MC curve of the firm is the *firm's supply curve* for x, showing how much the firm will place on the market at alternative possible prices, other things being equal. In Figure 8–3 ignore for the present the market diagram and consider the individual firm diagram only. At a price of $14, seven units per day will be produced and sold by the firm. What would the firm do if the price were $10 instead of $14? The firm's demand curve and MR curve become d_1d_1 and MR_1, respectively. The profit-maximizing output level falls to three units per day. Since the firm seeks to maximize its profits, whatever the market price happens to be, the firm will try to produce the output at which MC equals MR. For a competitive firm, MR and p_x are always equal, so in producing the output level at which MC equals MR, the firm is also producing the output level at which MC equals p_x. Thus, the outputs that will be produced at alternative price levels are shown by the MC curve, making it the firm's supply curve for the product.

By adding the quantities that all firms in the market will place on the market at each possible price, we get the *market supply curve*. For example, in Figure 8–3 if one of 1,000 identical firms in the market will place seven units of product per day on the market at a price of $14, all firms together will place 7,000 units per day on the market. In Figure 8–3 at the $14 price, the firm would be at point a on its supply curve. The market as a whole would be at point A. Similarly, at a $10 price level the firm would be at point b, and the market as a whole would be at point B. The market SS curve is said to be the *horizontal summation* of the individual firm MC or ss curves. It is really a market marginal cost curve for all firms together.

The simultaneous determination of the market price of a product, the individual firm level of output, and the market level of output for a competitive market now fall neatly into place. In Figure 8–3 let the market demand curve be DD and the market supply curve be SS. The price of $14 is determined by the interaction of buyers and sellers in the market as a whole. It is this price that any one firm in the market takes as given and cannot change. To maximize profits, the firm chooses the output level at

Figure 8–3   Marginal costs and supply in a competitive industry

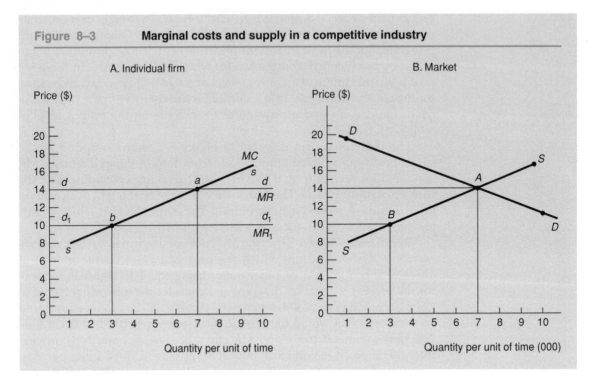

Since an individual firm produces the output at which $MC = MR = p_x$ in order to maximize profits, the firm's MC curve shows how much it will place on the market at alternative price levels like $10 and $14. The market supply curve shows the combined quantities that all firms in the market will supply at each alternative price. It is the horizontal summation of the MC curves of all the individual firms and is thus a market MC curve for the market as a whole.

which MC equals MR—seven units in this case. The market output level of 7,000 units is, of course, the sum of the output levels of all firms producing the product when they are confronted with a $14 product price.

Pricing and Output in a Monopolized Market. To show the effects of monopoly power on the price and the quantity produced of a product, we will suppose that the purely competitive market just discussed becomes monopolized. Consider first the competitive market. The market demand curve DD of Figure 8–3 is listed as a demand schedule in columns (1) and (4) of Table 8–3. Similarly, the horizontal summation of the MC curves of the 1,000 individual competitive firms, which comprises the supply curve SS in Figure 8–3, is listed in columns (1) and (3) of Table 8–3. This information is presented again as DD and SS in Figure 8–4 (page 224). As noted in the preceding section, the market price of producing X is $14, and the quantity produced and sold is 7,000 units per day.

Table 8–3   Outputs, revenues, costs, and profits for a monopolized firm

(1) Output (X per Day) ($000)	(2) Total Cost (TC) ($000)	(3) Marginal Cost (MC)	(4) Price (P_x)	(5) Total Revenue (TR) ($000)	(6) Marginal Revenue (MR)	(7) Profits ($000)
0	$ 0		$ 20	$ 0		$ 0
		$ 8			$ 20	
1	8		20	20		12
		9			18	
2	17		19	38		21
		10			16	
3	27		18	54		27
		11			14	
4	38		17	68		30
		12			12	
5	50		16	80		30
		13			10	
6	63		15	90		27
		14			8	
7	77		14	98		21
		15			6	
8	92		13	104		12
		16			4	
9	108		12	108		0
		17			2	
10	125		11	110		− 15

Now let the 1,000 competitive firms be merged into one gigantic monopoly. Suppose that all the production facilities of the 1,000 firms are taken over in their entireties and that they can be operated by the monopolistic firm with no loss in efficiency. What happens to the output of the industry and the price of the product?

Keep in mind the quantities the competitive firms were producing as they maximized their profits. Each firm found itself looking at a $14 product price that it could not change. Each firm saw a horizontal demand curve for its own output at the $14 level. Each firm viewed marginal revenue as constant at the $14 level—equal to the product price. Each firm produced an output level at which its MC was equal to MR *and product*

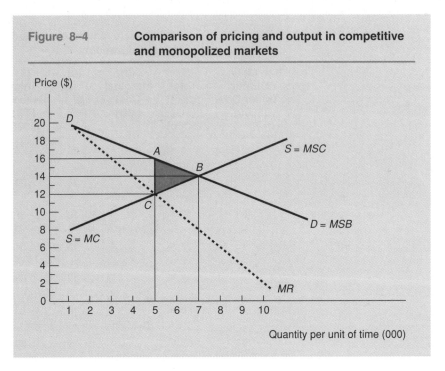

Figure 8–4   **Comparison of pricing and output in competitive and monopolized markets**

If the market is competitive, the market price will be $14 and the output will be 7,000 units. Each of the 1,000 firms in the market faces a horizontal demand curve and marginal revenue curve at the $14 level and maximizes profits by producing the output at which its *MR* equals *MC*. Monopolization of the market causes the firm to see *DD* as the demand curve it faces. Since *DD* slopes downward to the right, *MR* lies below *DD*. The profit-maximizing output for the monopolistic firm becomes 5,000 units, which will be sold at a price of $16 per unit.

price. Each firm's output level was seven units per day, and the total industry output was 7,000 units per day

All of that is changed by monopolization of the industry. The monopolist faces the market demand curve *DD*, which is downward-sloping to the right instead of horizontal. This fact has important implications for marginal revenue. Any firm that faces a demand curve that is sloping downward to the right will find that its *marginal revenue is less than product price* at any given output level. We demonstrate this principle in Table 8–3. If the monopolist were to sell 2,000 units of product per day and were to increase sales from 2,000 to 3,000 per day, total revenue of the firm would increase from $38,000 ($19 × 2,000) to $54,000 ($18 × 3,000). Since the 1,000-unit addition to output increases total receipts by $16,000, each one-unit increase in output has increased *TR* by $16. So marginal revenue for the firm in moving from the 2,000-unit to the 3,000-unit level of output is $16 and is less than the price of $18 at which each of the 3,000 units is sold. Marginal revenue in column (6) is computed in the same way for each output level listed in column (1). Compare price and marginal revenue at each level of output. Marginal revenue is plotted as the *MR* curve in Figure 8–4.

If you were the monopolist, what output would you produce and at what price would you sell if your objective were to maximize profits? You would reduce output and sales from 7,000 units per day to 5,000 units per day. You would raise the price from $14 to $16. You would do this because it would increase your profits from $21,000 per day to $30,000 per day as column (7) indicates. At the 5,000-unit output level, *MC* equals *MR* for the monopolist.

To recapitulate the analysis, in a monopolized market the price of the product tends to be higher and output tends to be less than it would be if the industry could be and were competitive. This is not because the managements of monopolized firms are inherently evil while those of competitive firms are not. The managements of firms in both types of markets seek the same general goal—profits. The monopolistic firm restricts output and charges a higher price because its managers see a different relationship between marginal revenue and price than do the managers of competitive firms.

Refer back to Figures 8–3 and 8–4. These figures show that managers of competitive firms face demand curves horizontal at the market price of the product. Consequently, they see marginal revenue curves that are also horizontal and that coincide with the demand curves. To maximize its profits, the competitive firm chooses the output level at which $MC = MR = p_x$. In the diagrams this occurs at the seven-unit output level for each firm. Since all firms in the market maximize profits in the same way, the market output is 7,000 units.

If the market is monopolized and the monopolist continues with the 7,000-unit output level, the monopolist's *MC* would be equal to the product price of $14. But *MR* for the monopolist at that output level is only $8 because the monopolist faces a downward-sloping demand curve. To maximize profits, the monopolist cuts the output back to 5,000 units per day and raises the product price to $16. The monopolist's $MC = MR = \$12$ at that output level.

Since the monopolist causes the output of the product to fall below the competitive level, resources are misallocated. Here, the resources that should be used to produce the 2,000 units between the monopolistic and competitive production levels are forced to be used where they yield less satisfaction to society or, perhaps, are even forced into temporary unemployment. And as we saw previously, when resources are misallocated, social well-being is restricted. For this reason, monopoly is included along with social spillovers such as pollution in the list of possible market failures that can plague the market economy. To see this clearly, we must apply the tools that we developed in the analysis of pollution in

Chapter 5. Specifically, we need to bring the cost-benefit analysis of social well-being maximization into Figure 8–4. Consider first the market demand curve *DD*. This demand curve indicates the maximum price that consumers are willing to pay for each unit of the good or service. And as discussed in Chapter 5, since it can be reasonably assumed that the maximum price consumers are willing to pay for a particular unit is dictated by the satisfaction they anticipate from consuming the item, the market demand curve is also the marginal private benefit curve. For simplicity, let's suppose that the good being considered is individually consumed; that is, let's suppose that there are no social spillovers in consumption. Given this, the demand curve of Figure 8–4 is both the marginal private benefit and marginal social benefit curve, and so we label it *MSB*.

Now consider the market supply curve, *SS*, in Figure 8–4. This curve reflects the marginal cost of production borne by the producers, and so it is labeled *MC*. In the terms of Chapter 5, this curve is the marginal private cost curve. And if we assume that this good is produced without social spillovers in production, this curve also reflects the marginal social cost of producing the product. For simplicity, we make this assumption, and so we also label the supply curve as the marginal social cost curve (*MSC*).

We now have in Figure 8–4 curves indicating both the marginal social benefit from consuming this product and the marginal social cost of producing it. What quantity of the good should be produced? By now you know that the answer is that production should be carried to the point where social well-being is maximized, that is, to the point where *MSB* = *MSC*. In Figure 8–4, *MSB* = *MSC* at the 7,000-unit output level. As has been pointed out, this is the quantity that the market would cause to be produced if it were competitively structured. However, if the industry is monopolized, output is restricted to the 5,000 level. Now consider each unit of output between the monopolistic and competitive levels. For each of these 2,000 units, the benefit to society (*MSB*) of consuming the unit is greater than the cost to society (*MSC*) of producing it. As such, if these units are produced, social well-being would be enhanced by the difference between *MSB* and *MSC*. The total value of this enhancement in social well-being is given by the area of the shaded triangle *ABC* in Figure 8–4. Since these units are not produced by the monopolist, social well-being is restricted by the area of this triangle. We call this the *deadweight welfare loss due to monopoly*.

The exercise of monopoly power generates a reduction in social welfare known as the **deadweight welfare loss due to monopoly**.

Entry Restrictions

Prices, costs, profits, and losses in a market economy provide the incentives for a continuous reallocation of resources from uses where they contribute less to uses where they contribute more to social well-being. In industries where demand is falling or costs are rising, investors will eventually receive less-than-average returns on their investments. Firms in these industries are said to be incurring economic *losses*. As it becomes possible for them to do so, investors and the firms producing those products will leave the industry, reducing supplies and raising prices relative to costs, until the returns to remaining investors are average for the economy as a whole.

In areas where demand is increasing or costs are falling, investors receive higher-than-average returns, or economic *profits*. New investment and new firms have incentives to enter the industry. If they are successful in doing so, product supplies increase, and prices fall relative to costs until the return on investment is again average. The profit-and-loss mechanism is thus the prime force for contracting productive capacity and output where these are not so urgently desired and for expanding them where they are more urgently desired.

Monopoly power tends to throw sand in the gears of the reallocation mechanism. Over time, firms with monopoly power in profitable industries, those that yield higher-than-average rates of return to investors, may be able to impede or block the entry of new investment and new firms into those industries. To the extent that they are able to do so, outputs will be lower, prices will be higher, and profits will be greater than they would be if entry were open, free, and easy. Such *barriers to entry* can be classified conveniently into (1) private barriers and (2) government barriers.

Monopolists are often able to protect their favored positions from potential competitors through **barriers to entry** such as product differentiation and government licensing.

Private Barriers. Private entry barriers arise from the nature of markets themselves or from marketplace actions of the firms that enjoy their fruits. There are many privately imposed restrictions on entry into specific industries. We shall list some of the more important ones—not necessarily in the order of their importance. First, consider a situation in which a firm or the firms already in a market own or control most of some key raw material needed for making the product. All they must do to restrict entry is deny potential entrants access to it. Second, suppose that when new firms are in the process of entering, the existing firms threaten to lower prices to the extent that the newcomers would experience substantial losses. This threat tends to discourage entry. It is also difficult on those already in the market, but they may be able to withstand temporary losses better than the potential entrants can. Third, product differentiation may be successful in retarding entry in some instances.

Firms often try to differentiate their products from those of their rivals. Once the products are differentiated, firms then attempt to convince the public that their products are not just different, but superior. Consumers tend to prefer the old tried-and-true brands and to be skeptical of new entrants. Product differentiation reinforces this attitude and makes it tougher for potential entrants to actually enter certain markets. This is no doubt one factor that discourages entry into the automobile industry. A similar barrier to entry can be created through product proliferation. Perhaps the best example of this practice is found in the cereal aisle of your local grocery. As pointed out earlier in this chapter, the four largest cereal producers control 85 percent of the breakfast cereal market. Yet a walk through the cereal aisle will certainly turn up dozens of different products. Why do the "big four" offer so many varieties? One answer might be that they are attempting to respond to consumer tastes. A more skeptical answer is that by offering so many versions of their product, any potential entrant's job is made more difficult since, to effectively compete, the newcomer must also offer a wide variety. Product proliferation, then, can have either positive or negative effects on social well-being. To the extent that it exists to serve the varied tastes of consumers, proliferation enhances well-being. When it exists to protect monopoly power, its impact is negative. The list of private barriers could go on and on since it is limited only by the imagination of the firms that wish to protect their monopoly positions.

Government Barriers.   The firms already in specific industries have difficulty in policing and enforcing restrictions on entry. Consequently, they frequently turn to the government for help. They get city councils, state legislatures, and Congress to pass legislation restricting entry into their markets. Often those government units seem not at all reluctant to take actions that confer monopoly power on certain special interest groups and help them to maintain it over time.

First, in some industries such as railroads, trucking, airlines, and communications, regulatory commissions have established entry-blocking rules that have all the force of law. Initially, regulatory commissions such as the Interstate Commerce Commission, the Civil Aeronautics Board, and the Federal Communications Commission were established to "protect" customers from certain practices of monopolistic firms. Over time, however, the range of commissions' activities has expanded to include control of entry into the industries they are regulating. In recent years one could well suspect that their primary function is to protect the firms from consumers. Fortunately, in many of these cases, the regulatory apparatus has been dismantled through deregulation. We discuss the issues of regulation and deregulation in detail later in this chapter.

Second, there are many occupational licensing laws on the books of individual states licensing plumbers, undertakers, physicians, barbers, and a host of other occupations. Whatever else such laws may do, one thing is certain—they restrict entry into the licensed occupations. Licensing standards and licensing examinations usually are controlled by licensed members of the occupation concerned, that is, by those who are already in it and who have a vested interest in keeping the number of new entrants relatively low.

A number of other forms of government-imposed entry barriers exist. Import duties and import restrictions limit the entry of foreign firms into many of our markets. Patent and copyright laws impede entry. Exclusive franchises to taxicab companies and casinos block the entry of new firms. Zoning ordinances and building codes are used to restrict entry into certain housing markets. Like that of private barriers, the list of government-imposed barriers to entry is a lengthy one.

Nonprice Competition

In industries containing only a few firms, it is common practice for firms to compete on grounds other than price. Each such firm in a given industry can increase its profits if it can increase its monopoly power at the expense of its rivals—that is, if it can increase its own share of the total market for the product. One very obvious way for a firm to increase its market share is to reduce the price at which it sells its brand of the product relative to the prices charged by the other firms in the industry. But price-cutting presents dangers to the firm that does it. The other firms can cut their prices, too, thus preventing the firm from accomplishing what it set out to do. Worse yet, all firms could end up with lower prices, a larger industry output, and smaller profits. So firms in imperfectly competitive markets are reluctant to use price-cutting to increase their individual market shares. Usually they attempt to increase their degrees of monopoly power through nonprice competition.

Advertising is a major form of nonprice competition. Although it may provide consumers with important information about a firm's product, its major objective is to increase the market share or the monopoly power of the firm that does it. Unlike a price cut by the firm, a successful advertising campaign is hard for other firms to duplicate. Other firms will try to duplicate or match the advertising campaign of the first firm, but it takes time for them to do so. Meanwhile, the first firm reaps the rewards of its efforts. Eventually, if other firms succeed with effective campaigns of their own, all may end up with approximately the same market shares they had before. Much of the advertising effort will have been wasted, and since the resources used for advertising purposes are not available to produce other goods and services, consumers receive a smaller total output from the economy as a whole.

Periodic change in the design and quality of the product is another major form of nonprice competition. Annual model changes fall into this category. Model changes may incorporate new technological developments, and to the extent that they do so, they enable given quantities of resources to make greater contributions to consumer satisfaction. But they may also simply rearrange or change the chrome and the shape, making old models obsolete and new models no better. Successful design and quality innovations by one firm, like successful advertising, may be hard for other firms to imitate immediately and may increase the market share and monopoly power of the firm for a time. However, if other firms are successful over time with their own design and quality changes, all may again end up with approximately the same market shares or with some re-arrangement of market shares.

Should We Fear Bigness?

Does bigness of business enterprises put our economic future in jeopardy? The economic analysis we just completed leads to the conclusion that in industries in which monopoly power is exercised, outputs will be lower and prices will be higher than they would be if the industries were more competitive. Profitable firms with monopoly power also may be able to successfully block the entry of additional investment and new firms into their industries. Thus, monopoly power may cause the resources or productive capabilities of the economy to be allocated poorly among alternative uses, with too little of the economy's resources allocated to the production of products made by industries in which monopoly power exists and too much allocated to products that are produced competitively. In addition, monopoly power in imperfectly competitive markets may result in some waste of resources on nonprice competition.

Bigness and Monopoly Power

Before turning our attention to identifying the extent of the economic problems caused by the exercise of monopoly power in the United States, it is essential to bear in mind the difference between the terms big business and monopoly. In particular, it must be recalled that monopoly power is not determined by a firm's absolute size but rather by its ability to control the output of the industry of which it is a part. As such, a firm that is truly enormous in terms of assets or sales may have comparatively little monopoly power if it happens to operate in a market along with numerous other very large firms. On the other hand, a very small firm might have a great deal of monopoly power if it has few significant rivals.

It all depends on the position of the firm in the market in which it operates. For example, Chrysler Corporation is a very large firm in terms of its assets and annual sales volume, yet it likely has very little monopoly power. If it drops out of the market, other firms will easily take up the slack. If it raises its prices relative to those of other firms in the auto industry, it will very quickly price itself out of the market. It has much actual and potential competition. On the contrary, Stillwater Power and Light Company in Stillwater, Oklahoma, is a small firm in terms of assets and annual volume of sales, but it comes very close to being a pure monopolist. It has no direct rivals, with the possible exception of the local gas company. We must therefore be careful not to confuse bigness with monopoly power. In assessing monopoly power of firms, we must look at specific industries and at individual firms within each industry to see whether they are able to affect significantly market outputs, prices, and buyers' access to the kind of product produced and sold by the industry.

Outputs and Prices

When imperfectly competitive firms restrict output and increase prices, they impose an economic cost on society in the form of reduced social well-being. This reduction in well-being is the deadweight welfare loss due to monopoly. We can better understand the issue of "fearing bigness" if we have a definitive estimate of this loss. While no definitive estimate exists, a consensus estimate places the loss at about 1 percent of gross domestic product per year.[2] That is, monopolistic elements within the economy serve to reduce economic well-being, as measured by GDP, by about 1 percent of GDP per year. And it must be recalled that this loss in well-being comes not from pure monopolists, since pure monopoly is typically illegal, but rather from firms operating in highly concentrated markets. A case in point is provided in the introduction to this chapter, which details the Justice Department's investigation into the food and feed additives industries. While no firm in these industries is even close to being a pure monopolist, several of the industry's otherwise competing rivals entered into criminal conspiracies designed to allow them the benefits of being monopolists. That is, they reached agreements with one another which had the effect of allowing them to charge prices close to the monopoly price without fear of being undercut by rivals. (Similar examples of what might be called a shared or joint monopoly are addressed in Chapter 9, which focuses on professional sports.)

While the consensus places the deadweight welfare loss due to monopoly at about 1 percent of GDP, how significant is this loss?

This decision is for each of us to make. However, we must bear in mind three points while making the decision. First, a basic economic truth is that while the economy's ability to produce is limited, society's desires for goods and services are unlimited. Consequently, any economic factor that tends to reduce the economy's ability to produce goods and services must be viewed as making an already difficult situation worse. Second, although 1 percent of GDP may not seem significant, 1 percent of GDP amounted to just over $81 billion in 1997.[3] In other words, if all vestiges of monopoly power had been eliminated prior to 1997, during that year society could have consumed $81 billion in additional goods and services. For example, if the increased production due to the elimination of monopoly were equally distributed, during 1997 each individual in the United States would have received just over $300 in additional goods and

---

[2]William G. Shephard, *The Economics of Industrial Organization* (Upper Saddle River, NJ: Prentice-Hall, 1997), p. 109.

[3]Table 1–2.

services. Finally, it must be noted that a deadweight loss of 1 percent of GDP is the cost to society of monopoly when monopoly is illegal and would be, no doubt, much greater were it not for government attempts to limit the exercise of monopoly power through legal action of the type discussed in the introduction to this chapter.

Entry Restrictions and Resource Allocation

While the estimation of the loss to society of monopoly power in terms of outputs and prices is rather straightforward, identifying the loss caused by *private* barriers to entry is not. In fact, there is no consensus as to the extent of private barriers at all. This does not mean that private barriers do not exist, just that they are very difficult to measure with any precision. A useful informal approach might involve addressing why firms seek to erect barriers to entering their markets in the first place. They do so to protect what they see as their favored relative positions. Any firm successful enough to enjoy significant profits will, of necessity, attract rivals. This is the role profits play in the market economy. In a competitive environment, above-normal profits serve as a signal to resource owners that the consuming public wishes to have the output of industry expanded, which is exactly what new rivals would cause to happen. The existing firms, of course, would prefer to block the entry of the new rivals so that they might continue to enjoy above-normal profits. As such, one can conclude that significant barriers to entry must exist if both concentration levels *and* profits remain high within a given market for an extended period of time. As an example, consider the cereal breakfast foods industry. As noted in Table 8–1, the four largest firms in this market control 85 percent of that industry's output. Equally importantly, these same firms have controlled a similarly large share of this market since the 1940s *and* have enjoyed relatively great profits since that time. Why have there been no significant new entrants? At least part of the answer must be that there exists substantial private barriers to entry in this market, with the most likely culprits being the extensive advertising done by the dominant cereal makers and their tendency to proliferate differing brands of their products. Consequently, while not scientific, the combined existence of concentrated markets and relatively high profits over an extended period of time provides at least circumstantial evidence of the existence of significant private barriers to entry.

Where entry to markets is blocked by law, it is easier to find evidences of resource misallocation. One of the more glaring instances of resources being used in quantities that are relatively too small is the medical profession. Physicians' average net incomes are at the top of the list for professions or occupations. Shortages of medical doctors have been publicly proclaimed for years. Yet, with their tight legal control of entry into medical training programs and into the profession itself, medical doctors continue to deter almost half of the annual qualified applicants to medical schools from entering training. In many local building markets, housing costs have soared, and profits to builders have been high because building codes have inhibited the introduction and use of new technology and pre-fabrication. In still another industry, try getting a taxicab in any large city during the morning and evening rush hours.

Nonprice Competition

The impact of nonprice competition on the public is far less clear. The total expenditure on advertising for 1996 ran about $173 billion[4]—somewhere in the neighborhood of 2.3 percent of GDP. However, about a fifth of the total was for advertising in local newspapers, a type of advertising that provides information to consumers on what is available, where, and at what price. Another $40 billion was spent for television advertising and is not a total loss to consumers. It is payment—perhaps an overpayment—for the "free" television programs that we see.

We also cannot be sure whether or how much the public loses from product design and quality changes. Many useful innovations are introduced in this way—the self-starter on the automobile, no-frost freezers and refrigerators, word processors, and thousands of other items that make our lives more comfortable. But there are many others whose only purpose is to make the previous years' models obsolete.

The Peculiar Case of Natural Monopoly

The **average cost** of production, sometimes called the *per unit cost*, is found by dividing total costs by the number of units being produced.

The analysis of monopoly presented thus far leaves little to commend it. But if we are to be thorough, we must consider evidence of any positive effects of monopoly as well as the negative. And in one circumstance monopoly can actually be defended economically. To see this, we need to add a new concept of firm costs to the total cost and marginal cost concepts that we have been using so far. This concept is the *average cost* of production, which is found by simply dividing the firm's total cost by the number of units being produced. For example, if a firm is incurring total costs of $500 to produce 50 units of its good, then its average cost is $10 per unit ($500/50 = $10). Assuming that both of the firm's inputs, labor and capital, may be varied, Figure 8–5 presents a typical long-run average cost (*AC*) for a firm.

The most important characteristic of a long-run average cost curve is its U shape, which indicates that average cost declines initially as output

---

[4]U.S. Department of Commerce, Bureau of the Census, *Statistical Abstract of the United States, 1997,* p. 578.

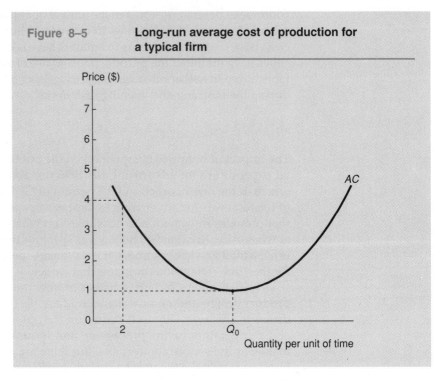

Figure 8–5   **Long-run average cost of production for a typical firm**

The long-run average cost of production for a typical firm is U-shaped. For production levels less than Q_0, an increase in production lowers average cost. This is the range of economies of scale. Production increases beyond Q_0 lead to an increasing average cost; thus, this range is referred to as the range of diseconomies of scale.

per unit of time increases but eventually turns and increases. When the firm is on the downward-sloping portion of the curve (production levels less than Q_0), it is said to be enjoying *economies of scale*. In this situation, the average cost of production may be reduced simply by increasing the firm's size or scale and producing more of the product. Suppose, for example, that General Motors was constrained to produce only 1,000 cars per year rather than the 3 to 4 million cars it now produces. In such a circumstance, assembly lines would be out of the question. Each car would have to be produced essentially by hand. Also ruled out would be bulk-buying discounts for inputs and any benefits that might be derived from the division and specialization of labor. That is, as Henry Ford realized, producing such a small number of cars rules out the use of numerous production techniques that are capable of radically reducing average cost. Thus, a GM producing only 1,000 cars per year would be clearly operating at a much smaller output level than Q_0. It could enjoy significantly reduced average cost simply by increasing the scale of its operation.

When long-run average cost can be reduced simply by increasing the firm's size and producing more of the product, the firm is said to be enjoying **economies of scale.**

Beyond a certain size and production level, average cost can be expected to rise as production is increased. This outcome is caused by **diseconomies of scale**.

Such "economies" of large-scale production do not continue over the entire range of output possibilities. As certain as we are that economies of scale exist over some range of output, we are equally certain that if the scale of operation continues to grow, eventually, long-run average cost will turn and go up. When average cost starts increasing (output levels greater than Q_0), we say the firm is encountering *diseconomies of scale*. The most obvious explanation for this phenomenon is that the firm simply becomes too large to be effectively managed, with each increase in size adding an additional layer of bureaucracy to the production process. Elliott Estes, former president of General Motors, said it best: "Chevrolet is such a big monster that you twist its tail and nothing happens at the other end for months and months. It is so gigantic that there isn't any way to really run it.[5]

Another factor that might lead to diseconomies of scale is worker boredom. The division and specialization of labor inherent in modern production processes narrows the scope of each worker's job so that the worker is capable of becoming very adept, that is, very efficient at the job. This sort of job narrowing can go too far, however. When it does, boredom is likely to set in and the outcome is reduced, rather than increased, productivity.

A typical situation for a firm, then, is to initially enjoy falling average cost as its size and production level are increased due to economies of scale. Beyond some production level, however, diseconomies of scale arise, which cause average cost to turn and go up. These forces taken together give the long-run average cost curve its U shape.

Now back to the case of natural monopoly. The average cost curve of Figure 8–5 shows that the average cost of producing the product reaches a minimum of $1 per unit when the level of production is Q_0 per unit of time. Suppose that this level of production is 10 units per week. Now consider three separate cases. In the first case, the market for the product is such that 1,000 units may be sold during a week. Here, the market could support 100 firms (1,000/10 = 100), each producing at the minimum possible average cost of $1. In this market, we could expect a high level of competition among a large number of firms, each of which is small relative to the market.

As a second case, suppose the market is such that only 100 units of the product may be sold per week. Here, only 10 efficient firms could be supported. We would say that the concentration and thus the potential for monopoly power is greater in this case than in the first.

Now consider an extreme third case in which only 10 units per week may be sold in the market. In this case, only one efficient firm, a natural

---

[5]J. Patrick Wright, *On a Clear Day You Can See General Motors* (Grosse Pointe, MI: Wright Enterprises, 1979), pp. 114–115.

When the industry's average cost of production is minimized by having only one firm produce the product, the industry is a **natural monopoly**.

monopolist, could be supported. This case is referred to as a *natural monopoly* because no matter how many firms are initially in operation in this market, the largest will have an undeniable average cost advantage over its smaller rivals and should eventually push each of them out of business. That is, when the cost structure of an industry is such that the average cost of production is minimized when only one firm operates, the industry is a natural monopoly.

As discussed above, society's interests are well-served when markets are composed of many relatively small firms in competition with one another. When natural monopoly is present, this is not the case. To see this point, return to Figure 8–5 and assume that output level Q_0 occurs at 10 units of production per week. Would society be better served by having the 10 units of output produced by one firm or by five firms? With one firm, a natural monopolist, the average cost of production is $1. With five firms, each producing two units per week, the average cost is $4 per unit. Thus, requiring "competition," that is, insisting on the existence of five firms rather than a monopolist, causes the product to be produced at an average cost four times greater than necessary. In an opportunity cost sense, this implies that it takes four times the value of resources to produce 10 units of the good when production is distributed among five firms than is required when production is concentrated in the natural monopolist. In this case, there are clear benefits to society in allowing the monopolist to exist.

Although these benefits are undeniable, as we have seen, monopolists tend to impose costs on society as well in the form of reduced output and increased prices. Thus it appears that resource misallocation is inevitable. If we allow the market to operate on its own, natural monopoly will result and we reap a deadweight welfare loss due to the monopolist's tendency to reduce output below the socially optimal level. Conversely, if we choose through government intervention to require numerous firms to exist, we cause the product to be produced at an average cost above that which is possible. For most of this century, we in the United States have chosen a third policy option, government regulation.

When Should Government Regulate Business?

Numerous justifications have been offered for government regulation of business. Although most of these have economic aspects, they are often primarily an outgrowth of social and political forces. Experience with various attempts at regulation has taught that regulation works best, and is most likely to be successful, when it is limited to those cases in which its primary justification is economic. In general, government regulation of business may be called for when two conditions exist in the private market. First, there must be market failure; that is, a situation must exist where the market, operating on its own, fails to provide a well-being maximizing allocation of resources. Second, and perhaps more importantly, there must be reason to believe that the market outcome can be improved through some degree of government control over the market in a cost-effective manner. This second condition is particularly crucial. Regulation is not cheap. Regulatory agencies, commissions, inspector services, and other bureaucracies must be established. And the firms being regulated must also expend much energy in complying with the regulations. In each case, resources are used, and being so used, they become unavailable for other production processes. Consequently, in a given case, although some degree of market failure may be present in a market, regulation may not be appropriate if the cost of regulation outweighs the benefit to society of correcting the failure.

Consider again natural monopoly. If the market is left to its own devices, monopoly results—inevitably leading to a deadweight welfare loss due to the monopolist's tendency to restrict output. And forcing competition, which in this case would increase the average cost of production, is no bargain for society either. It is this trade-off that might justify government regulation. That is, regulation might be designed to allow the monopolist to exist (yielding the benefit of a low average cost of production), while attempting to force the monopolist to produce at the competitive output level and charge the competitive price (to avoid the cost imposed by the deadweight welfare loss). Thus there is no guarantee that the process of regulation will work in terms of increasing social well-being above the level that the market would provide. Potential pitfalls include the problems associated with estimating the competitive output and price levels as well as the costs associated with administering and complying with the regulation. Social well-being is certainly not enhanced if the cost of the regulation outweighs the benefit of correcting the market failure. Fortunately, relatively few markets have cost structures that yield economies of scale sufficient to justify their being viewed as natural monopolies. Examples might include local distribution of natural gas and electricity and, perhaps, local telephone and cable television service.

If natural monopoly is so rare, you might wonder why we have had so much government regulation of business in the United States. Without doubt, the primary answer to this question is that much of government regulation was inappropriately applied originally. For this reason a strong deregulation movement began in the 1970s that has led to the dismantling of the existing regulatory apparatus in industries such as airlines and trucking. And, in general, since these regulations were never economically justified, the outcomes for consumers from deregulation have been positive. But this is not to say that all regulation of business is inappropriate and should be eliminated. The rare case of natural monopoly shows that, in some instances, regulation can work to the benefit of society. And we implicitly addressed two other cases in previous chapters.

The first of these concerns circumstances in which consumers lack significant information about a particular good or service. That is, beginning with Chapter 2, we have assumed that consumers have the information necessary to make informed, well-being maximizing decisions when they purchase goods and services. When this information is lacking, consumers can make choices that maximize neither their nor society s well-being. Suppose, for example, that the rear door of a certain minivan has an unreasonably high tendency to fly open if hit from behind, and this fact is unknown to consumers. The market demand curve would reflect the benefits that consumers anticipate from the minivans, but their anticipations would prove incorrect. In such cases, appropriate regulation might take the form of requiring or actually providing safety testing of all automobiles so that consumers can make informed decisions. In other cases of deficient information, appropriate regulatory tools might include the labeling of specific product ingredients, health and safety codes for products and workplaces, or in extreme cases, the outlawing of items deemed inherently too unsafe for general consumption.

A final circumstance that might prompt economically defensible regulation concerns poorly defined property rights, the classic case of which is the social spillover of pollution in a production process. Recall that it is the collectively consumed nature of the environment and the absence of property rights to it that cause economic units to pollute. And we indicated that appropriate government responses to the problem might take the form of taxes, direct controls on emissions, outright prohibitions on the use of particular substances, or in some cases, the establishment of markets for pollution rights. A similar problem exists with respect to airwave communications since no individual or group has a property right to broadcast exclusively on a particular frequency. For this reason, the Federal Communications Commission gives radio stations what amounts to a property right to broadcast on a specific frequency within a given geographic area.

In some cases, government regulation may be a useful tool to improve the functioning of failing private markets. Care must be taken, however, before concluding that regulation is appropriate. It must be kept in the forefront that regulation is not free: It takes resources to administer and comply with regulations. Thus, prior to embarking on a regulation, society must be certain that the benefit of regulation is worth its cost. And even if there is strong reason to believe that regulation will be cost-effective—and, as a consequence, regulation is entered into—the process must be closely monitored to ensure that the outcomes actually serve the interests of the general public. Numerous students of regulation have suggested that in a typical scenario, the regulatory agency is "taken captive" by the industry it was established to control. The reasons for this are unclear. Perhaps the firms of an industry are able to use their political influence to ensure that "friendly" regulators are appointed. Or maybe it

The belief that regulatory agencies, regardless of their initial intentions, eventually come to serve the interests of the firms being regulated rather than the interests of the general public is called the **capture theory** of regulation.

occurs simply as an outgrowth of the fact that regulatory bodies have to rely on the firms being regulated for the data they need to carry out their tasks. Regardless, the outcome of this *capture theory*, as it is called, is that the regulatory agency decides on policy based on the interests of the firms being regulated rather than on the interests of the consuming public. Again, the capture theory does not suggest that regulation should be abolished, but simply that it must be very carefully entered into and then closely monitored.

Summary

Most members of the general public seem to believe that, regardless of how consumer-friendly firms' origins might have been, as firms grow large in size, eventually they will exercise the strength that comes from their bigness to hold back output, raise prices, and waste society's scarce resources. That is, in economic terms the general public fears the monopoly power of large firms. As such, accounts of conspiracies to raise prices such as those noted in the introduction to this chapter come as no surprise. In this chapter, we addressed the issue of fearing bigness in the business world from a systematic, analytical perspective. One of the most important conclusions from this analysis is that bigness, by itself, is not a very good predictor of the types of behavior one might expect from monopolies. Specifically, it was determined that for a firm to have and exercise monopoly power, it need not be large in absolute terms. Rather, monopoly power exists when a firm is large relative to the total output of the industry in which it operates. Thus, an enormous firm like Chrysler Corporation may have rather little monopoly power since it is surrounded by numerous equally large rivals. At the same time, your local cable company, although only a tiny fraction of the size of Chrysler, enjoys the position of being nearly a pure monopolist. Consequently, the question we addressed is whether the public is correct in fearing the monopoly power of firms, regardless of their absolute size.

From a theoretical perspective, there is little to commend with respect to monopoly power. Monopoly power induces firms to produce smaller outputs and charge higher prices than would be the case if the markets in which they operate were competitive. Further, firms with monopoly power are frequently able to restrict entry into their industries, thus compounding the output restriction and higher-price problem and inhibiting movement of resources from less valuable to more valuable uses. Finally, they may also engage in nonprice competition that results in the waste of some of the economy's scarce resources.

Empirically, there is evidence that monopolistic elements within the U.S. economy have imposed, and continue to impose, an economic cost on society in terms of reduced social welfare. Much of the loss in well-being may come from rather small firms. Estimates of the deadweight welfare loss due to monopoly place it at about 1 percent of GDP per year. In terms of 1997 GDP, this implies that monopolistic elements within the economy were responsible for an $81 billion reduction in GDP during that year. Consequently, it is important to keep a close watch on existing and potential monopoly problems. The more competition the market economy can sustain, the better the price mechanism will operate in allocating the economy's scarce resources among their many uses. The primary procompetition tools at government's disposal are the existing antitrust laws. Of particular importance are the Sherman Act and the Clayton Act, which effectively outlaw both monopoly and anticompetitive behaviors deemed injurious to public well-being.

In the unusual case of natural monopoly, however, the impact of monopoly on social well-being is mixed. This circumstance and the problems caused by poorly defined property rights and consumers having deficient information about products can lead to calls for government regulation of private business. Care must be taken prior to entering into regulation to ensure that the benefit of the regulation is at least as great as its cost. Further, even in those cases where regulation seems cost-effective, the regulatory process must be closely monitored to avoid the problems associated with the capture theory of regulation.

Discussion Questions

1. Explain what a concentration ratio measures and how it can be used to indicate whether a firm is operating in a competitive industry or an industry that is close to the monopolistic model. What shortcomings do concentration ratios have?
2. The profit-maximizing condition for a competitive firm requires production to be carried to the point where marginal revenue is equal to marginal cost. Explain why. Is this condition the same for firms with monopoly power?
3. What are barriers to entry, and how do they inhibit the proper functioning of a market?
4. A merger of formerly competing firms forming a monopoly invariably leads to a fall in industry output. Why?
5. Using the deadweight welfare loss diagram, compare and contrast the outcomes of competition and monopoly.
6. Explain why bigness and monopoly power are not necessarily the same.
7. What is natural monopoly, and what dilemma does it pose for public policy? Give examples of natural monopoly.
8. The typical firm's long-run average cost curve is U-shaped. Why?

9. List and discuss the three economic justifications for government regulation. If one of these exists, does that mean that regulation should be imposed?

10. Define and explain the capture theory of regulation.

Additional Readings

Adams, Walter, ed. *The Structure of American Industry*. 8th ed. New York: Macmillan, 1990.

A thorough economic analysis of various industries. Although this title has been in print for some time, it remains a classic.

Adams, Walter, and James Brock. *The Bigness Complex*. New York: Pantheon. 1986.

The most thorough analysis of bigness available today. Includes a thoughtful critique of both conservative and liberal approaches to bigness.

Berg, Sanford V., and John Tschirhart. *Natural Monopoly Regulation: Principles and Practice*. Cambridge Surveys in Economic Literature. New York: Cambridge University Press, 1988.

In-depth analysis of the regulation of natural monopolies, from the history of regulatory economics, to how natural monopolies should be regulated, to how and why they are regulated.

Carson, Robert A. "Monopoly Power: What Should Be Our Policy Toward Big Business?" In *Economic Issues Today: Alternative Approaches*. 4th ed. New York: St. Martin's Press, 1987, Chapter 4.

Presents the liberal, the conservative, and the radical answer to the question asked in the chapter title.

Goodman, Marshall R., and Margaret T. Wrightson. *Managing Regulatory Reform: The Reagan Strategy and Its Impact*. New York: Praeger Publishers, 1987.

Thorough analysis of Ronald Reagan's plan to deregulate many social and economic programs and to move regulatory authority from the federal to the state and local level. Implications and impacts for today are also outlined.

Krueger, Anne O., ed. *The Political Economy of American Trade Policy*. National Bureau of Economic Research Project Report. Chicago: University of Chicago Press, 1996.

Collection of papers discussing protectionism of several industries. Comments by other authors appear at the end of each paper.

Lo, Andrew W., ed. *The Industrial Organization and Regulation of the Securities Industry*. National Bureau of Economic Research Project Report. Chicago: University of Chicago Press, 1996.

Collection of papers from an NBER conference, discussing the regulation of the securities industry. Comments by other authors appear at the end of each paper.

World Wide Web Resources

Antitrust Policy
www.antitrust.org

Gives links to price fixing, mergers, vertical restraints, industry links, and other information.

Federal Communications Commission (FCC) Home Page
www.fcc.gov

"The mission of this independent government agency is to encourage competition in all communications markets and to protect the public interest." Has links to the Telecommunications Act of 1996, a daily digest, consumer information, and other issues.

Federal Trade Commission
www.ftc.gov

Provides links to consumer protection, antitrust/competition, economic issues, and regional offices.

United States Securities and Exchange (SEC) Commission
www.sec.gov

Search the EDGAR database for financial information on publicly owned companies.

The Economics of Professional Sports

What Is the Real Score?

Chapter Outline

Checklist of Economic Concepts

Markets, imperfectly
   competitive
Product markets
Resource markets
Cartel

Antitrust laws
Demand and supply
Marginal revenue
Marginal costs
Monopsony

Supply of labor
Marginal cost of labor
Marginal revenue product
Monopsonistic profit
Profit maximization

Gerald W, Scully, a professor of management at the University of Texas at Dallas, is in the middle of the debate over the issue. His new book, *The Business of Major League Baseball,* just published by the University of Chicago Press, challenges what he calls *time-honored myths* about the economics of sport:

- Team owners are losing money and staying in the game for the love of it. Instead, Scully writes in his book, "Major league baseball has entered a golden era of wealth and prosperity."
- Exemption from U.S. antitrust law, which has allowed baseball to function for years as a self-regulating cartel, is necessary to balance teams and provide competitive play. Not so, Scully says.
- The baseball park is a haven for ordinary fans. No longer, says Scully; it is increasingly the preserve of upper-income patrons.
- Players are overpaid.

In recent decades, scholars such as Scully have increasingly moved the study of sports beyond departments of physical education and physiology, where it originated, and into the humanities and the social sciences. Today, more than 100 interdisciplinary programs in sports studies are to be found on college and university campuses, along with numerous specialized journals and book series.

"A lot of the new work has been pioneered by economists, who see professional sports as a great place to apply economic theory to a particular industry," said Scully in an interview.

Professional sports provide not only the opportunity to study basic economic issues, such as the behavior of companies, the bidding process for talent, and racial discrimination in salary, but they also provide a rare look at a restricted market dominated, as in baseball, by a cartel.[1]

[1]Karen J. Winkler, "Challenging the Time-Honored 'Myths' of Baseball: A Book Examines the Economies of 'American Sport,'" *The Chronicle of Higher Education,* October 18, 1989, p. A10.

The Professional Sports Business

Does the sports page in your favorite newspaper often resemble the business section? Articles concerning labor disputes, ticket prices, television contracts, club relocations, changes in ownership and management, and, of course, player salaries can easily outnumber reports concerning the latest games and scores. Why do the happenings in the boardroom gather as much attention as the happenings on the field or the court? Examination of the economics of professional team sports reveals why following the business of athletics has itself become a major spectator sport for many people.

Professional sports in the United States is a multibillion dollar business that provides entertainment to millions of fans each year. As do all business firms, professional sports clubs face a myriad of economic decisions in their quest to earn profits. And many sports clubs are very profitable. For example, the Dallas Cowboys of the National Football League have earned as much as $24 million annually in recent years. However, professional sports clubs are unlike most other business firms in at least two important ways: The organizational structure of the professional team sports industry, and the unique relationship between the sports clubs and their most important employees, the players, have created a number of economic and social issues that have captured public attention.

Organizational Structure

Today, four major team sports are played professionally in the United States: baseball, basketball, football, and hockey. Each of these sports has a long and colorful history. Although details vary somewhat between sports, a similar organizational structure has evolved within each of the four professional team sports.

In most cases, individual teams, or clubs, are owned and operated for profit by private individuals or partnerships. The team owners are entrepreneurs who hire and fire the managers, coaches, and players; rent or build the stadium; and sell the tickets and broadcast rights to games. The owners of a sports club are ultimately responsible for the economic decisions necessary to the daily operation of the organization.

The spirit of all sports is competition. To attract ticket-buying fans, a sports club must compete on the field or the court against other teams. Thus, sports clubs cannot operate independently but must cooperate with one another in order to sell their entertainment services to the public. The necessary cooperation is institutionalized through the professional sports leagues—the American League (AL) and National League (NL) in baseball [collectively known as Major League Baseball (MLB)], the National Basketball Association (NBA), the National Football League (NFL), and the National Hockey League (NHL). The leagues are formal organizations of individual clubs.

All the major sports leagues currently have more than two dozen member clubs. Sports clubs are located in major metropolitan areas scattered throughout the country. The baseball, hockey, and basketball leagues also have clubs located in Canada. The professional sports leagues serve as the mechanism for the cooperation that is necessary between the geographically dispersed teams.

Teams that are members of a professional sports league are contractually obligated to one another. Member clubs agree to abide by the rules and guidelines of the league. Among other things, the league determines the annual schedule of games, makes and enforces the game rules, and sets the guidelines for hiring new players. Because the league also determines when a new team will be admitted to the league and allowed to compete with its members, clubs are often referred to as *league franchises*. In general, the professional sports leagues are controlled by the club owners who hire an outside (nonowner) "commissioner" and staff to oversee the league's operations. The decisions made by the commissioner of a professional sports league are intended to be made in the best interest of the sport, and not to favor any individual owner or group of owners.

The rules and guidelines adopted by a professional sports league have important economic implications for the individual member clubs. For most clubs, the rules with the greatest consequences on operating costs and revenues are those that govern the relationship between the teams and their players.

Teams and Players

The relationship between professional sports clubs and their players is perhaps unlike any other employer-employee relationship in our economy. Nowhere else is a worker's productivity so visible to so many and so easily measured. Productive workers in most firms do not receive the cheers of tens of thousands for a job well done or have the quality of their work publicly reviewed in the press. Likewise, most workers who make a mistake on the job (and who hasn't made a mistake?) do not hear the boos and catcalls of an upset crowd. The productivity of a professional athlete is constantly monitored by fans through a myriad of statistics—runs batted in, touchdowns scored, field goal percentage, and so on. Although the performance of professional athletes may be objectively measured and compared by the vast quantities of statistics compiled by sports analysts, controversy still surrounds the salaries earned in professional sports.

The general public is still shocked when a star player signs a multi-million dollar contract to play baseball or basketball, yet many professional athletes claim they are underpaid by the team's owners. Further, it is not uncommon for one player to earn 10 or even 20 times more than other players on the same team. Ironically, rules imposed by each of the major sports leagues to promote competition on the playing field contribute to the seemingly inconsistent economics of players' salaries.

Each of the major professional sports leagues has very specific and detailed rules that govern the employment of players by the member clubs. Competition on the field would diminish if any club had the ability to hoard the best athletic talent. Thus, league rules are designed to ensure that each club has the opportunity to employ and retain quality players. In essence, the leagues establish the procedures whereby member clubs acquire the "property rights" to contract with specific players. Because specific clubs may hold the exclusive right to contract with a player, athletes are not always free to work for the highest bidder.

Economic Analysis and Professional Sports

Economic analysis provides a means of understanding the issues and controversies surrounding the business of professional team sports. Likewise, professional sports can serve as an example of how market structures and institutional arrangements can influence the economic behavior of firms in an industry.

The preceding discussion suggests that professional sports teams operate in imperfect markets. In fact, sports clubs sell their services in an imperfect *product market* and hire their players in an imperfect *resource market*. A product market exists when buyers and sellers engage in the exchange of final goods and services. When a sports club sells you a ticket for a game or a jacket emblazoned with the team logo, the transaction takes place in a product market. On the other hand, a resource market exists when buyers and sellers engage in the exchange of the factors of production. Thus, when a sports club hires a new player or builds a new stadium, the transaction takes place in a resource market. (Later, in Chapter 11, we will see how product and resource markets are related in the overall aggregate economy.)

A closer examination of the product and resource markets in professional team sports can help us to better understand many of the economic issues discussed daily in sports columns across the nation. But perhaps even more important, our study of professional sports will provide us with general conclusions about how imperfect markets affect consumers and employees.

> **Product markets** exist when buyers and sellers engage in the exchange of final goods and services.
>
> **Resource markets** exist when buyers and sellers engage in the exchange of the factors of production.

The Product Market

Cooperation Among Teams

As we noted earlier, the essence of sports is competition. However, it is in the best interest of professional sports clubs that this competition occurs on the playing field and not in the marketplace. The reason is easily observable. Imagine that sports clubs competed for fans in purely competitive markets. The more successful clubs would sell more tickets and team merchandise and would naturally earn higher profits, which, in turn, would allow these clubs to attract the best players through higher salaries. Over time, these clubs would become so much stronger than the less successful teams that competition on the playing field would deteriorate and become boring for spectators. Weak teams would eventually be forced into bankruptcy, and strong teams would lose fans. Thus, a professional sports club's economic decisions are inherently interdependent with those of its rivals.

In order to remain in business and earn profits for their owners, professional sports clubs must avoid the above scenario. How are they able to do this? The answer is through coordination of economic decisions through league rules and guidelines. The alliance of teams through league organizations coordinates and restrains economic competition among member clubs. In many ways, professional sports leagues resemble market cartels. A *cartel* is a group of firms that formally agrees to coordinate its production and pricing decisions in a manner that maximizes joint profits. Thus, a cartel can be viewed as a group of firms behaving as if they were one firm—a shared monopoly.

In the United States, antitrust laws make it illegal, in most cases, for firms to monopolize an industry through the formation of a cartel. The business of professional sports is a unique exception. In 1922, the U.S. Supreme Court ruled that major league baseball did not meet the legal definition of interstate commerce and was therefore not subject to the restrictions of antitrust law (*The Federal Baseball Club of Baltimore v. The National League of Professional Baseball Clubs*). This precedent has been upheld by the courts in numerous cases since then. Although the antitrust exemption for baseball has not been fully extended to the other professional sports leagues, a variety of cases and legislative acts have granted limited protection to the collective action of clubs in other sports. (As examples, the Sports Broadcasting Act of 1961 allows professional sports leagues to sell the broadcast rights of games as a "package deal" in lieu of individual teams competing against one another for airtime, and the Football Merger Act of 1966 paved the way for the upstart American Football League to be absorbed into the NFL's established cartel.) The law implicitly recognizes that a professional sports team can profitably survive only as long as its league survives.

A **cartel** is a group of firms that formally agrees to coordinate its production and pricing decisions in a manner that maximizes joint profits.

Cartels

The unique status of the professional sports leagues helps them avoid many of the problems faced by illegal cartels in other industries. Professional sports leagues have been able to maintain economic cooperation between member teams over long periods of time. For any cartel to be successful, several requirements must be met.

First, the cartel members must be responsible for most of the output produced in their market. The greater the proportion of total market output generated by the cartel members as a group, the greater the cartel's degree of monopoly power. Further, in order to maintain monopoly power, the cartel must be able to prevent new competitors from entering the market, or be able to integrate new competitors into the cartel. Each of the major sports leagues has been successful in eliminating competition from teams outside their cartel. By controlling the contracts of star players and holding exclusive contracts to play in major stadiums and arenas, the existing leagues have restricted the ability of newly formed rival leagues to compete for the fans' attention. In several instances, new competitors have been driven out of the market. A recent example was the demise of the United States Football League (USFL) after only three seasons of competition. In other cases, rival leagues were successful in finding new market territories that had been overlooked by the established leagues. When this occurred, the established leagues found it beneficial to invite the upstarts to join their cartel. Over the past 30 years, we have witnessed the mergers of the American Football League (AFL) with the NFL, the American Basketball Association (ABA) with the NBA, and teams from the World Hockey League (WHL) with the NHL. These mergers helped the leagues maintain their shared monopoly power in their respective sports.

A second requirement of a successful cartel is the production of fairly homogeneous outputs by the member firms. That is, each firm in a cartel should produce outputs that are substitutes for the outputs produced by the other member firms. Pricing and output agreements are easier to enforce and maintain if all member firms are producing the same goods and services. If each cartel firm produced different products, special agreements would have to be made for each output. Within a professional sports league, all clubs do produce the same primary output—entertainment for fans who watch the games. The league structures ensure that all the games played by member clubs are fairly homogeneous. All teams must follow a common set of game rules and regulations enforced by referees and umpires hired by the league. Further, some leagues like the NFL determine the schedule of games whereby each club plays other clubs based on the competitive strength of the teams. This is done in a manner to promote greater parity on the playing field. Thus, common game rules and league-determined schedules help reinforce the appeal of sports and help the leagues maintain their cartel arrangements.

A third requirement for a successful cartel is the ability to divide the market into territories controlled by each member and to establish production quotas. In essence, the cartel members must agree on how their combined monopoly power will be shared among themselves. In professional sports, the market territories and output quotas are determined through the league structure. Each club's territory is protected from inside competition by the league. The location of new expansion teams and the ability of established teams to relocate are determined through league rules and normally require the agreement of a majority of the clubs' owners. Likewise, the production of games is controlled by the league offices, which set the schedule for each season. All teams are given an equal share of the total output during normal seasons by playing an equal number of games. These actions by the professional sports leagues grant local monopoly power to each team and help maintain the shared monopoly of the cartel.

Fourth, in order to succeed, the cartel must have the power to prevent "cheating" by member clubs. In many cartel situations, an incentive to cheat on the agreement exists for member firms. Some firms may find it profitable to break production quotas or enter another member's sales territory in an effort to capture more than the agreed-upon share of the monopoly. Because most nonsports cartel arrangements are illegal, it is virtually impossible for members to enforce their agreements. However, in professional sports the league offices have the contractual power to enforce league rules and guidelines. In each of the major sports, the league's commissioner is empowered to sanction and levy fines against member clubs that do not adhere to the rules. Again, the unique legal status of professional sports leagues reinforces the ability of clubs to maintain monopoly power through the enforcement of cartel agreements.

Coordinated Behavior

The most obvious forms of cartel behavior among a league's member clubs involve various methods of joint marketing and revenue sharing. A professional sports club receives revenue from three major sources: ticket and concession sales, merchandising rights for team souvenirs and novelties, and radio and television broadcast rights. Professional sports clubs cooperate with one another in each of these three areas through their respective league organizations.

Each of the sports leagues has specific rules for dividing the revenue generated through ticket sales between the host home team and the visiting team. Although the formulas vary between leagues, in most circumstances each team is guaranteed a percentage of the gate receipts for the games in which they play. For example, in the NFL the home team receives 60 percent and the visiting team receives 40 percent of ticket sales.

The league organizations also regulate the business of merchandizing products that carry team logos and trademarks. One reason for doing so is to discourage counterfeiters, but it also allows the league to promote entire lines of merchandise for all the member clubs and to minimize interclub competition in this area. If you look hard enough, you can find almost anything from T-shirts to toilet bowl lids in your favorite team's colors with their name and logo on it. The NFL has been very successful in promoting their teams' merchandise. In 1998, the gross retail sales of products promoting NFL teams exceeded $3.6 billion.

In recent years, the primary source of revenue for most sports clubs has been the sale of broadcast rights to television and radio. This is the area in which sports clubs have been most successful in jointly selling their entertainment services through their respective leagues. Each league sells the national television and radio broadcast rights to all the games played by its members as "package deals" to the highest bidder. The revenue raised from selling all the league's games as a package is then evenly divided among the member clubs. Thus, teams in large media markets do not gain an economic advantage over the clubs in smaller cities. The practice of teams pooling their broadcast rights dates back to 1964 when the NFL sold its games to network television for $14.1 million. The revenues raised from selling the broadcast rights to professional sports has dramatically increased over the years. In 1998, the NFL signed a media broadcasting deal with ABC, CBS, Fox, and ESPN that will pay the league a combined $18 *billion* over 8 years.

Pricing and Output for Broadcast Rights

To see the effect of cartel behavior on the pricing and output of broadcast rights to professional sporting events, consider Table 9–1 and Figure 9–1. The hypothetical data reflect the output, revenue, and cost figures a sports

Table 9–1		Monthly broadcast output, costs, revenues, and profits for a professional sports league				
(1) Units of Output	(2) Total Costs ($000)	(3) Marginal Costs ($000)	(4) Price ($000)	(5) Total Revenue ($000)	(6) Marginal Revenue ($000)	(7) Profit ($000)
0	$ 0		$100	$ 0		$ 0
		$40			$100	
1	40		100	100		60
		45			90	
2	85		95	190		105
		50			80	
3	135		90	270		135
		55			70	
4	190		85	340		150
		60			60	
5	250		80	400		150
		65			50	
6	315		75	450		135
		70			40	
7	385		70	490		105
		75			30	
8	460		65	520		60
		80			20	
9	540		60	540		0
		85			10	
10	625		55	550		−75

league faces in the provision of broadcast rights over a period of time, in this case, 1 month. The league faces the demand schedule reported in columns (1) and (4) of Table 9–1, which is shown as demand curve *DD* in Figure 9–1. *DD* represents the summation of the downward-sloping demand curves for broadcast rights faced by each club in the league. Given its monopoly power, the league's marginal revenue curve, *MR*, lies below the league's demand curve. The league's marginal cost curve, *MC*, is the horizontal summation of the marginal cost schedules each team would face if it individually and competitively provided broadcast rights to its games. Thus, columns (1) and (3) in Table 9–1 list the total marginal cost schedule for the league as a whole.

If a cartel agreement did not exist and teams competed against one another in the market for broadcast rights, each club would maximize its profits by selling up to the point where its own *MC* equaled its own *MR*.

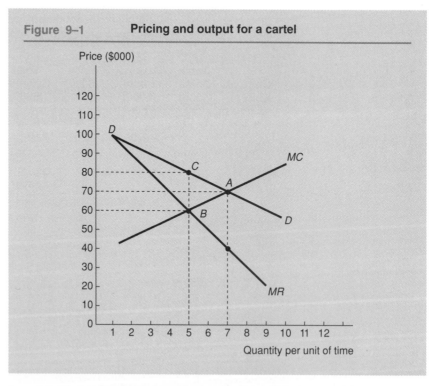

Figure 9–1   Pricing and output for a cartel

As a shared monopoly, cartel members collectively face demand *DD* and marginal revenue *MR*. Just like a single monopoly firm, the cartel can maximize market profits by producing output such that marginal cost *MC* equals *MR*. In this case, the cartel output is 5, with a price of $80,000. If cartel members competed with one another, the market would reach equilibrium at an output of 7 and an average price of $70,000.

Because each individual club is a local monopoly facing its own unique demand and costs schedules, it is likely that the profit-maximizing level of output will vary among clubs. But how many total games would be broadcast across all clubs without a cartel agreement? Recall from Chapter 8 that the *MC* curve can be considered the supply curve for an individual competitive firm. Thus, in Figure 9–1, because *MC* represents the summation of marginal costs across all clubs, *MC* can be thought of as the competitive market supply schedule. Likewise, *DD* represents the market demand schedule. Without a cartel agreement, the market would reach equilibrium at point *A* where *DD* intersects with *MC*. The market equilibrium price for the rights to broadcast a game would be $70,000, and seven games would be broadcast in total each month. On average, each broadcast would generate marginal revenue of $70,000 for the team selling the game. Examination of Table 9–1 reveals that the competitive solution would result in $490,000 of total revenue and $105,000 in average profits each month for the clubs that sold games.

It is important to note that this analysis does not indicate how the profits would be distributed among the clubs in the absence of a cartel agreement. In the short run, teams of poorer quality might find it difficult or impossible to sell the broadcast rights for their games. In this case, the quality of athletic competition would decline as teams that were successful in selling their broadcast rights earned more profits and could afford to hire the best players. Thus, in the long run, less successful clubs would be forced to shut down, leaving the league with fewer teams.

By agreeing to collectively sell their broadcast rights as a league, and not as individual firms, the clubs effectively enter an agreement to share their monopoly power and behave as if they were one firm. Each team would no longer examine its own demand and costs schedules to determine its profit-maximizing output, but would accept a share of the overall market profits. As a cartel, the teams in the league collectively face demand curve *DD* and marginal revenue curve *MR* in Figure 9–1. Just like a single monopolistic firm, the cartel can maximize profits by producing the level of output where marginal revenues equal marginal costs. Table 9–1 reveals that marginal revenue is equal to marginal cost when the broadcast rights to five games are provided each month. Marginal revenue and marginal cost are $60,000 at this level of output. This can be seen in Figure 9–1 as point *B* where the *MR* curve intersects with the *MC* curve. The demand schedule in Table 9–1 indicates that buyers will pay $80,000 per game for five games (point *C* in Figure 9–1). Profit maximization can therefore be achieved by selling the rights to five games each month for $80,000 per game. This is verified in column (7) of Table 9–1, which shows that this output and price combination maximizes the cartel's collective profit at $150,000 per month.

The cartel agreement to sell broadcast rights as a league affects both price and quantity. In this example, the cartel will provide five games for broadcast at $80,000 per game, whereas individual teams in competition with one another will provide seven games for $70,000 each. Given the costs of producing additional games for broadcast, the cartel agreement increases total profits across all the league members from $105,000 to $150,000. Without the cartel agreement, the distribution of profits favors the teams of relatively greater athletic success. With the cartel agreement, the distribution of profits is determined by the league's rules and guidelines. Today, most revenue from the sale of broadcast rights is equally divided among a league's member clubs. Even teams that rarely appear on national television or radio receive the same share of revenues from the sale of the league's broadcast rights.

Through the formation of a cartel, professional sports clubs have found it in their best economic interest to cooperate in the competition for the fans' dollars. By restricting output below competitive levels and raising price, overall profits for cartel members can be increased and a degree of stability in the number of teams can be achieved.

The Number and Location of Teams

Today another of the most controversial issues in professional sports concerns the number and location of teams within each league. Recall that a successful cartel must be able to divide the market between its members and to share joint profits. Thus, from each cartel member's perspective there is an incentive to restrict the number of new members. By limiting cartel membership, each existing cartel member will be guaranteed a larger slice of the profit pie. This is clearly seen in professional sports, where, compared to other industries, expansion has been relatively slow. For example, during the past 25 years, Major League Baseball has added only four new teams. All four of the major sports leagues stick to a very strict and rigorous process in allowing new members to enter the market. When expansion franchises are granted entry, they are required to pay the existing teams an entry fee that compensates these teams for lost market share.

One consequence of limited expansion in professional sports is the incentive for existing teams to relocate to new markets. Over the past several decades, the demand for sports entertainment has grown dramatically in the United States and Canada. Economists have estimated that approximately 50 major metropolitan areas in North America are capable of profitably supporting professional sports teams. However, the largest professional sports league, the NFL, has only 31 teams. There are more cities with fans who want their own teams than teams in each league. Clearly, a shortage of teams exists.

As we learned earlier, whenever a shortage occurs, the market price will rise; this is also true of professional sports. Prospective owners and tax-paying fans in cities without teams will often offer attractive financial deals to teams that are willing to relocate. These deals take the form of publicly built and supported stadiums and arenas, tax abatements, loans, and outright financial payments. In some cases, cities have openly bid on teams that have indicated their willingness to move. Recent examples include the relocation of the NFL's Los Angeles Rams to St. Louis and the Houston Oilers to Nashville (where they became the Tennessee Titans). Of course, teams that relocate must receive league permission and must share their new-found profits with the cartel membership. Other teams have been successful in garnering new public facilities and tax breaks by simply indicating that they are willing to move elsewhere. Tax-paying fans who were afraid of losing their hometown teams have recently financed new stadiums in Tampa Bay, Seattle, and Milwaukee.

The wave of relocations, and threats of relocations, in the 1990s resulted in a booming market for the construction of professional sports stadiums and arenas. In fact, some cities (like St. Petersburg, Florida) built facilities before securing a team. According to *USA Today*, the decade saw the construction of $9 billion worth of new professional sports facilities across North America.[2] An astonishing $4 out of every $5 in financing came from public sources. This taxpayer support for profit-making enterprises is openly debated in cities trying to attract a new team or to hold on to an existing team.

Why are taxpayers and elected public officials willing to financially support a professional sports franchise? The most obvious answer to this question is the desire to satisfy the local public's demand for sports entertainment. However, this is most likely secondary in importance. The primary reason cities seek to attract and maintain a professional sports team is the "major league" status that it brings to the community. A sports team places a city "on the map" and generates national publicity and public relations opportunities for other businesses located there. City officials often claim that a professional sports franchise will generate jobs and tax revenue as new businesses are attracted to the area. After its expansion team had completed only two seasons in the NFL, a spokesperson for the Jacksonville Chamber of Commerce said, "What the Jaguars are doing for us is worth millions, maybe tens of millions of dollars in advertising and exposure."[3]

Undoubtedly the Jacksonville Jaguars did improve the image and visibility of their city, but is a professional sports team a wise investment for economic development? Maybe not. According to economist Andrew Zimbalist, a professional sports team has about as much economic impact

---

[2] Erik Brady and Debbie Howlett, "Ballpark Construction's Booming," *USA Today*, September 6, 1996, p. 13C.

[3] Jason Cole, "Jags Well on Road Toward Recognition," *ESPNET*, January 8, 1997, pp. 1–2.

as a new Macy's department store.[4] The average revenue for an NFL team is approximately $65 million. In the case of Jacksonville, the metropolitan area's disposable income is about $11 billion. Therefore, the NFL is contributing only about 0.6 percent to the community's purchasing power. (The figure is even less for other cities because Jacksonville is the smallest NFL market.) Further, most of the jobs directly created by a professional sports franchise are low-paying service sector jobs that are often seasonal. Most of the high-paying jobs are held by small groups of players and management who may not live in the local community year-round. Finally, when a new sports team arrives in town, a substitution effect will occur with respect to consumer spending. Local fans who purchase tickets, concessions, parking, and souvenirs will have less to spend on other forms of entertainment. Thus, fewer dollars are available for spending at businesses such as local restaurants, theaters, and bowling alleys.

Because the primary benefits of a professional sports team to its local community are intangible and hard to measure (how much is civic pride worth?), the debate concerning the use of public funds to support professional sports is likely to continue. However, many economists would argue that public investments in new factories would generate greater and longer term economic returns to the community than investments in new stadiums and arenas.

The Resource Market

The Employment of Players

Perhaps one of the most controversial economic aspects of professional team sports involves the leagues' rules that govern the hiring and employment of players. Each of the major professional leagues strictly controls the methods by which teams hire and fire their player-employees. The employment contracts between clubs and players must meet the very specific guidelines imposed by the league. The rules are rigidly enforced to ensure that no club can gain a competitive athletic advantage due to its employment practices.

The most visible of a league's employment rules involve the procedures used to allocate new players among the league's member clubs. In an effort to generate a competitive playing balance among teams (sometimes referred to as *parity*) and to prevent any single club from hoarding quality players, each sport conducts an annual "draft" of the new players who enter the market. Although the specific procedures are different in

---

[4]Federal Reserve Bank of Atlanta, "Does the Bouncing Ball Lead to Economic Growth?" *Regional Update* 8, No. 3 (July/August 1996), pp. 1–8.

each sport, the basic design of each league's draft is the same. In a prede-termined order, clubs take turns choosing ("drafting") players from the available pool of new players. The drafting order is normally determined by the previous season's league standings. In general, teams with rela-tively poor records choose first, and relatively strong teams choose last. Under league rules, when a club drafts a player, that club has exclusive rights to sign the player to a contract. No club can hire a player drafted by another team unless that team first sells or trades away its exclusive rights to hire the player. In most cases, league rules dictate that once a drafted player signs a contract with a club, that club maintains its exclusive right to the player's services for a specified number of seasons. Thus, new play-ers become the "property" of their employing clubs and do not have an open opportunity to offer their skills to the highest bidder. League rules also forbid a team from "tampering" with a rival team's players by offer-ing them employment opportunities while they are still under contract.

For decades, professional athletes who were drafted had virtually no ability to choose the team for which they played. Players could change teams only if their employing club chose to trade their contract for the contract of a player owned by another club, or if another club purchased their contract. If an athlete wished to play professional sports, he had to agree to these terms as imposed by the leagues. Thus, players had little, if any, real bargaining power when salaries were determined. Obviously, this situation provided owners with the opportunity to pay their players relatively low wages.

Even though professional sports league employment rules are de-signed to increase the quality of competition on the playing field, it is clear from the description above that drafts and hiring restrictions reduce the quality of competition in the market for ballplayers. When league rules allow the member clubs to own the property rights to new player con-tracts, an imperfect factor market called a *monopsony* is created.

Monopsony

A **monopsony** is a market with only one buyer, or employer.

A *monopsony* is a market with only one buyer, or employer. When only one club, according to league rules, has the right to contract with a specific player, that club becomes a pure monopsony from the player's perspec-tive. In an even broader sense, the leagues themselves can be considered joint monopsonies. For example, if you want to play professional football in the United States, you must play in the NFL. There are no other buyers for the specific athletic talents of football players. A league's draft and em-ployment rules reinforce and strengthen the monopsony powers collec-tively held by its member clubs.

Two major factors create monopsony power for professional sports clubs and leagues. The first factor is the immobility of new players who have been drafted. New draftees who wish to play professional sports are required to sign contracts that bind them to their teams for a specified number of years as determined by league rules. Once a player has entered the league and signed a contract, he does not have the option of negotiating with other clubs. In fact, because of the draft structures, new players who are drafted often never have the option of offering their services to the highest bidder. Thus, from a legal perspective, the mobility of players is severely limited. New players become "locked in" to their teams for the period specified in the contracts sanctioned by the leagues. Because new players are contractually obligated, the employing clubs become the only potential buyer of the players' athletic talents in the league.

The second factor that generates monopsony power in professional sports is the highly specialized athletic talents and skills possessed by the players. Athletes who are qualified to play a professional sport have invested many years in training and instruction to learn their craft. The athletic skills and knowledge acquired during this preparation by a professional athlete are in most cases very specific to their sport and are not readily transferable to other sports or employment situations. Very few athletes have the ability to excel at more than one professional sport. (Deion Sanders and Bo Jackson are rare exceptions.) Recall that basketball great Michael Jordan failed to advance beyond the minor leagues in his attempt to play professional baseball. Players who possess only very specialized skills have employment opportunities limited to only those employers who require such skills. The talents of a player who has trained and studied to be a professional quarterback are demanded by only 31 NFL clubs. Since each club employs only two or three quarterbacks, less than 100 individuals in the United States earn their living in this highly specialized occupation. Compare this with the nearly 4 million people who are schoolteachers or even the 125,000 people who are professional economists! Teachers and economists are more generally trained than quarterbacks and have many more options in the labor market. It is easy to see that the specialized talents of professional athletes contribute to the monopsony power of their employers.

Wages and Employment in a Monopsony

The effects of monopsony power on wages and employment are illustrated in Table 9–2. Because a monopsony is the single buyer of labor in its market, it faces a positively sloped market supply curve of labor. (The market supply curve of labor was previously discussed in Chapter 6.) Thus, in order to attract additional workers, a monopsony must increase its wage offer as it hires additional employees. This is seen in column (2) of Table 9–2. The monopsony baseball club in this example can hire two pitchers for an average wage of $400,000 each, but to hire three pitchers it must pay a wage of $500,000 each. Columns (1) and (2) are plotted in Figure 9–2 (page 260) as the market supply curve SS.

Table 9–2		Wages, costs, and the marginal revenue product of professional baseball pitchers		
(1) Number of Players	(2) Wage ($000)	(3) Total Cost of Labor ($000)	(4) Marginal Cost of Labor ($000)	(5) Marginal Revenue Product ($000)
0	$ 0	$ 0		
			$ 300	$1,500
1	300	300		
			500	1,300
2	400	800		
			700	1,100
3	500	1,500		
			900	900
4	600	2,400		
			1,100	700
5	700	3,500		
			1,300	500
6	800	4,800		

Because a monopsony firm must raise the wage along the market supply of labor schedule in order to hire additional workers, the monopsony firm will experience a change in its total labor costs that is in excess of the wage. This fact can be seen in Table 9–2. Columns (2) and (3) report that when two pitchers are hired at $400,000 each, the total cost of labor is $800,000. However, in order to hire a third pitcher, the wage of $500,000 must be paid to each. This raises the total cost of labor to $1,500,000. By hiring a third pitcher, the club experiences a change in its total labor cost of $700,000. The change in the total labor cost of a firm due to hiring an additional worker is known as the *marginal cost of labor (MCL)*. The *MCL* is reported in column (4) of the table. Notice that the *MCL* is greater than the wage beyond the first player hired. This is because a monopsony must pay a higher wage to the additional worker as well as all workers previously hired. The *MCL* curve is plotted in Figure 9–2 using the numbers from columns (1) and (4) of Table 9–2. Graphically, the *MCL* curve lies above the supply of labor curve and is more steeply sloped.

The **marginal cost of labor** is the change that occurs in a firm's total labor costs due to hiring an additional worker, per unit of time.

Column (5) of Table 9–2 reports the marginal revenue product *(MRP)* for the pitchers hired by the ball club. Recall that *MRP* is the change in revenue experienced by a firm when it employs an additional worker. As additional pitchers are hired by the ball club, the team can produce more

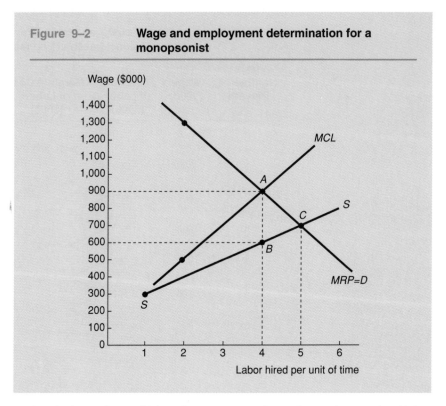

Figure 9–2   **Wage and employment determination for a monopsonist**

As the single employer of labor, the monopsony faces the market supply of labor curve *SS*. The marginal cost of labor curve *MCL* reflects the addition to costs the firm experiences by hiring an additional worker. The monopsonist will hire workers up to the point where *MCL* equals *MRP*. In this case, the firm will hire four workers at a wage of $600,000.

games and other entertainment services that generate revenue for the club. However, just like any other business firm, the ball club experiences diminishing returns from hiring additional workers. Thus, as more pitchers are added to the team's roster, team output and revenue increase at a declining rate. This is seen in column (5), which shows *MRP* falling as the number of pitchers hired increases. Recall from Chapter 6 that the *MRP* schedule represents the demand for workers.

How many pitchers will the ball club's management decide to hire, and what wage will they be paid? To answer these questions, first compare columns (4) and (5) of Table 9–2. When the *MCL* in column (4) is less than the *MRP* in column (5), the ball club adds less to its labor costs by hiring an additional pitcher than it adds to its revenues. In this case, it is obviously profitable to go ahead and hire. However, when the *MCL* in column (4) is greater than the *MRP* in column (5), the ball club adds more to its labor costs by hiring an additional pitcher than it adds to its revenues. In this case, the ball club would reduce its profits by hiring. Thus, the ball club will continue to hire pitchers up to the point where $MCL = MRP$. In our example, this occurs when four pitchers are hired and MCL and MRP are both equal to $900,000. Note that if the ball club hired more than four pitchers, MCL is greater than MRP and the club would experience a loss of profitability.

As our example illustrates, for a monopsony, the optimum quantity of labor to hire is found at the point where $MCL = MRP$. This is shown in Figure 9–2 as point A where the MCL curve intersects with the MRP curve. Point A indicates that MCL and MRP are equal at $900,000 when four pitchers are hired. However, according to the market supply schedule, the ball club can attract and hire four pitchers for a wage of $600,000 each. This occurs at point B on the supply curve SS in Figure 9–2. Thus, even though a pitcher's contribution to the club's revenues *(MRP)* is $900,000, each pitcher will be paid a wage of only $600,000. In a monopsony, the difference between a worker's contribution to the firm's receipts and the

Monopsonistic profit is the difference between the workers' contribution to a monopsonistic firm's receipts and their wages.

wage is known as *monopsonistic profit*. In our example, the ball club earns a monopsonistic profit of $300,000 for each of the four pitchers hired for a total of $1,200,000. This is the additional profit earned by the ball club because of its monopsony power.

Recall from Chapter 6 that, in competitive labor markets, additional workers are hired up to the point where the wage is equal to MRP. If the ball club in our example operated in a competitive labor market, it would hire more than four pitchers. According to Table 9–2, the wage rate is equal to MRP when five pitchers are hired. This is seen in Figure 9–2 as point C where the supply curve SS intersects with the MRP curve. If the labor market was competitive, five workers would be hired for $700,000 each and their MRP would also be $700,000. Thus, in a competitive labor market, a firm does not earn a monopsonistic profit.

As our example illustrates, a monopsony hires fewer workers than a competitive firm and pays a lower wage than a competitive firm. Because of these two economic outcomes, it is often said that monopsonies "exploit" their workers. If firms with monopsony power are made to purchase labor under more competitive conditions, we should expect to see more workers hired and wages rise. In fact, in recent years, professional sports leagues have been forced to give up some of their monopsony powers and we have seen dramatic increases in player salaries.

Free Agency

For many years, all professional baseball players were asked to sign a basic playing contract that included what came to be known as the reserve clause. This part of the contract reserved the right of the employing ball club to perpetually hold exclusive rights to the player's services. Players could not move freely among clubs. A player could change teams only if his employer traded or sold the rights to his contract to another team. The reserve clause arrangement gave baseball clubs monopsony power over the players they hired.

Realizing that the reserve clause kept salaries below what could be obtained in a competitive market, baseball players organized and fought the owners in antitrust court. In 1975, an independent arbitrator overturned the reserve clause in Major League Baseball. The players and owners eventually reached a compromise whereby the employing club can hold exclusive rights to a player's contract for a specified number of years after which the player can declare "free agency" and sell his services to the highest bidder. A free agent is a player whose contract is no longer exclusively held by one club.

Each of the major sports leagues has very specific rules concerning when a player can declare free agency. In baseball, a player must have at least 6 years of playing experience and not be under contract with any ball club. In 1993, football players entered into an agreement with the owners of the NFL that gives unrestricted free agency status to uncontracted players with 5 years of experience. In both the baseball and football leagues, some clubs have openly opposed free agency and players have accused team owners of secretly agreeing not to hire certain free agents. However, the advent of free agency has greatly reduced the degree of monopsonistic exploitation in professional sports.

The impact of free agency on player salaries has been dramatic. Figure 9–3 reports the increase in the average salaries for baseball players since the inception of free agency. In 1976, the average Major League Baseball player earned $51,501. By the late-1990s, the average player was earning almost $1.5 million! Wages and prices in the overall economy also increased during this time, but not to the same extent. For example, the average weekly earnings of a full-time worker in the U.S. economy increased by about 135 percent while the average salary of a major league baseball player increased more than 25-fold.

As another point of comparison, consider the "plight" of professional football players. Until 1993, football players had very limited access to free agency status. In 1992, before the new free agency rules, the average NFL starting player's salary was $660,092—about half of the average comparable salary in baseball at that time. Free agency clearly reduces the degree of monopsonistic exploitation in professional sports.

Labor Disputes

Professional athletes have fought for many years against monopsonistic employment rules, such as the reserve clause, enforced by the leagues. In opposing the restrictive employment practices of team owners, players in all four major sports have united to form labor unions. A *labor union* is a

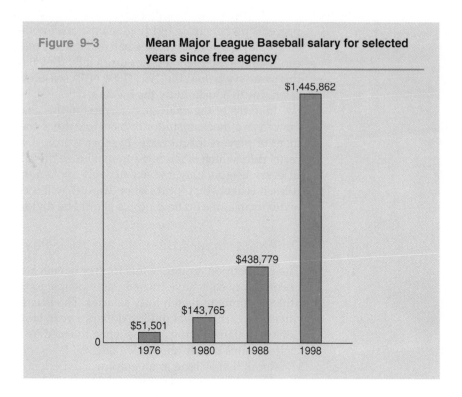

Figure 9–3   **Mean Major League Baseball salary for selected years since free agency**

$1,445,862

$438,779

$143,765

$51,501

0

1976   1980   1988   1998

A **labor union** is a formal organization of workers that bargains on behalf of its members over the terms and conditions of employment.

A **strike** is a work stoppage initiated by labor; a **lockout** is a work stoppage initiated by management.

formal organization of workers that bargains on behalf of its members over the terms and conditions of employment. Player unions negotiate with team owners to determine the standards that are applied to all player contracts.

Disagreements between the team owners and the players' unions have resulted in a number of labor disputes in the past several years. In 1994, the Major League Baseball Players Association (the players' union that represents baseball players in both the American and National Leagues) called a *strike* that forced the cancellation of hundreds of games, including the World Series. Later in the same year, the team owners of the NHL canceled half a season by enforcing a *lockout* against professional hockey players. In both cases the major points of disagreement concerned the mechanics of how players would be paid and the conditions necessary for players to become free agents.

The shortened baseball and hockey seasons of 1994 resulted from the players' resistance to the owners' proposed "salary caps." A salary cap is a rule that limits the amount of money that any team can spend on player compensation. The owners argued that player salaries were too high for them to make a "fair profit" on their investments and that limits needed to be placed on their spending to ensure parity. However, a salary cap also prevents owners from bidding against one another for the services of talented players. Therefore, baseball and hockey players argued that a salary cap would keep their salaries artificially low. Basketball players took up this same cry before the 1998–1999 NBA season, which was partially canceled due to a lockout by the owners.

In terms of the analysis presented in this chapter, a salary cap can be viewed as a mechanism for owners to enforce the monopsonistic employment of players leaguewide. In other words, a salary cap is just another cartel rule, which is intended to maximize the joint profits of the leagues. In every league, players have actively spoken out against the salary cap rules. It is likely that future labor disputes will occur unless the players and owners can agree on how profits should be divided among themselves.

Do Professional Athletes Earn Their Pay?

The competition among teams for free agents and the insistence by owners on salary caps have caused many people to wonder why professional athletes command such lofty salaries. The premier players in each sport can easily earn several million dollars a year. How can someone earn millions of dollars playing a game when the median household income in the United States is only about $37,000?

Recall that as long as an employer experiences an increase in revenue that is greater than the increase in costs due to hiring an additional worker, the employer can increase profits with a new hire. Stated another way, profits increase as long as the marginal revenue product is greater than the marginal cost of labor. Therefore, a club can make a profit and pay its players millions of dollars if those players generate even more millions of dollars in revenues. For example, in 1988, the Los Angeles Kings of the NHL paid $15 million to the Edmonton Oilers for the right to hire Wayne Gretzky. The Kings then signed Gretzky to an 8-year, $20 million contract. Was this a good deal? It has been estimated that Gretzky increased the Kings' revenues over the 8 years by as much as $52,150,000 through increases in season ticket sales, game attendance, and cable television rights.[5] Thus, due to Gretsky's contract, the Kings experienced a change in total costs of $35 million, but revenues increased by even more. The Kings made more than $17 million from the deal.

The salaries of professional athletes reflect their contribution to the club's revenue. The same is true for all workers in a market economy. The more a worker contributes to an employer's revenues, the more that worker can be paid. Workers with relatively large *MRPs* will command higher wages, and those with relatively small *MRPs* will command lower

---

[5]Robert J. Downs and Paul M. Sommers, "Is the Great One Slipping? Not on the Ice," *Journal of Recreational Mathematics* 23, no. 1 (1991), pp. 1–5.

wages. Why doesn't the average doctor or teacher have a multimillion dollar contract? Because they do not generate millions of dollars in revenues for their employers. Salaries in a market system are not determined by a worker's contribution to the public's health or overall well-being but by the worker's contribution to his or her employer's revenues. Professional athletes earn their salaries because fans are willing to pay to enjoy their performances.

Summary

The business of professional team sports provides an example of imperfect market structures. A unique characteristic of professional sports is the interdependence of teams. A professional team can be successful only if its competitors are successful. Each team must have rivals to play games and attract fans. To ensure their mutual success, ball clubs are organized into professional leagues. These leagues have important economic implications in both the product and resource markets.

Professional sports leagues are economic cartels. Through the leagues, teams formally agree to behave as if they were one firm—a shared monopoly. By forming cartels, sports clubs can increase the joint profits for all members of the league by restricting output and increasing price relative to a competitive market. By sharing the joint profits from the sale of their output, leagues can ensure the long-term survival of member teams.

In the resource market, professional sports leagues enforce employment rules that grant member clubs exclusive rights to player contracts. When a club holds the exclusive rights to contract with an athlete, the club is a monopsony—the single buyer of labor in the market. A monopsony is able to employ workers at wages below what would be observed in a competitive market. In recent years, professional athletes have won the right to free agency, which reduces the monopsony power of the clubs. In response to free agency, the average salaries of professional athletes have dramatically increased. The size of a professional athlete's paycheck reflects the player's contribution to his club's revenue.

Discussion Questions

1. Explain why professional sports teams must cooperate with one another in order to produce competitive games for fans.
2. What is a cartel? What industry characteristics are necessary for the successful formation and operation of a cartel?
3. Professional baseball enjoys a special legal exemption in the United States. What is this exemption, and why does it exist? Does it apply to other sports leagues?

4. Explain how professional sports leagues maximize joint profits through coordinated behavior in the product market. Will each team earn the same amount of profit under a cartel agreement as it would if market competition prevailed?
5. Why does a cartel's marginal revenue curve lie below its demand curve? Explain with a numerical example and a graph.
6. Discuss the economic pressures and incentives for professional sports teams to relocate. Are professional sports teams an important tool for a city's economic development? Explain why or why not.
7. What is a monopsony? What conditions give rise to a monopsony? How can professional sports teams be considered monopsonies?
8. What is free agency? How has it eroded the monopsonistic power of professional sports teams?
9. For many years professional football players earned on average about half of what professional baseball players earned. Using economic reasoning, how can this fact be explained?
10. What is the difference between a strike and a lockout? Why are labor disputes so common in the professional sports industry?
11. Define what is known as monopsonistic profit. How is it different from normal profit? If an employer is earning monopsonistic profit, are workers being "underpaid?" Why or why not?
12. From an economic perspective, are professional sports players worth their million dollar salaries? Explain.

Additional Readings

Danielson, Michael N. *Home Team.* Princeton: Princeton University Press, 1997.
  Excellent book that details the impact professional sports has on urban areas, with one chapter devoted to how stadiums affect where teams play.

Euchner, Charles C. *Playing the Field: Why Sports Teams Move and Cities Fight to Keep Them.* Baltimore: Johns Hopkins University Press, 1993.
  Explores the competition between major cities to attract and keep professional sports franchises. Examines the economics and the politics of team relocation.

Lupica, Mike. *Mad as Hell: How Sports Got Away from the Fans and How We Get It Back.* New York: Putnam, 1996.
  Irreverent and sometimes sarcastic examination of the business of professional sports from the fans' perspective.

Quirk, James, and Rodney D. Fort. *Pay Dirt: The Business of Professional Team Sports.* Princeton: Princeton University Press, 1992.
  Inside look at the modern business of professional sports. Includes a detailed bibliographic reference section.

Rosentraub, Mark S., *Major League Losers.* New York: Basic Books, 1997.
  Discusses subsidizing sports, how governments make money from sports, how sports affect economic development in Canada, and other issues.

Scully, Gerald W. *The Business of Major League Baseball*. Chicago: University of Chicago Press, 1989.

In-depth economic analysis of the many facets of major league baseball.

Scully, Gerald W. *The Market Structure of Sports*. Chicago: University of Chicago Press, 1995.

Examines the market structure of professional sports leagues in the United States and provides an overview of the historical and current context of anti-competitive practices in the industry.

Sheehan, Richard G. *Keeping Score: The Economics of Big-Time Sports*. South Bend, IN: Diamond Communications, 1996.

In-depth and critical economic analysis of almost every major facet of modern professional sports. Also examines major college sports and the NCAA. Lots of numbers and statistics.

Staudohar, Paul D. *The Sports Industry and Collective Bargaining*. Ithaca, NY: ILR Press, 1986.

Examination of the relationship between players' unions and team owners.

Weistart, John C., and Cym H. Lowell. *The Law of Sports*. Indianapolis: Bobbs-Merrill, 1979.

Detailed historical analysis of the antitrust controversy in professional sports.

World Wide Web Resources

American League Baseball
sports.yahoo.com/al

Provides access to standings, statistics, news, and team pages.

CNN/SI
www.cnnsi.com

Created by CNN and *Sports Illustrated*. A Web-based sports page with links to professional and college sports, top stories, features, and *Sports Illustrated* for kids.

ESPNet SportsZone
www.espn.go.com

Provides daily sports news and commentary on the sports industry.

ILSR's Community-Owned Sports
www.ilsr.org/newrules/sports.html

The Institute for Local Self Reliance (ILSR) is a nonprofit research and educational organization to assist politicians and citizens with economic development strategies. Their "Community-Owned Sports" page has links to stadium economics, community ownership, and other resources.

Laboratory for Leisure, Tourism and Sport
www.sp.uconn.edu/~YIAN/frl/08econ.htm

Researched and compiled by Aminuddin Yusof, this "Economics Aspects of Sport" is an exhaustive bibliography of journal articles, books, and proceedings.

National Basketball Association
www.nba.com

League home page, which provides access to standings, statistics, news, and team pages.

National Football League
sports. yahoo. com/nfl

Provides access to standings, statistics, news, and team pages.

National Hockey League
sports.yahoo.com/nhl

Provides access to standings, statistics, news, and team pages.

National League Baseball
sports.yahoo.com/nl

Provides access to standings, statistics, news, and team pages.

CHAPTER

10

Protectionism Versus Free Trade

Can We Restrict Ourselves into Prosperity?

Chapter Outline

Checklist of Economic Concepts

Imports
Exports
Production possibilities curve
Consumption possibilities curve
Comparative advantage
Comparative disadvantage
Terms of trade

Demand
Supply
Exchange rates
Current account transactions
Capital account transactions
Balance of trade (merchandise)
Balance of payments

Tariffs
Quotas
Voluntary restraint agreements
Dumping
Customs union
Free trade area

Whether we see it or not, our daily lives are touched everywhere by the flows of commerce that cross national borders as inextricably as the weather. Capital clearly has become global. Some $3 trillion of capital race around the world every day. And when a firm wants to build a new factory, it can turn to financial markets, now open 24 hours a day, from London to Tokyo, from New York to Singapore. Now if you buy an American car, it may be an American car built with some parts from Taiwan, designed by Germans, sold with British-made advertisements, or a combination of others in a different mix. Services have become global. The accounting firm that keeps the books for a small business in Wichita may also be helping new entrepreneurs in Warsaw. And the same fast-food restaurant that your family goes to—or at least I go to—also may well be serving families from Manila to Moscow and managing its business globally with information, technologies, and satellites. And most important of all, information has become global and has become king of the global economy. In earlier history, wealth was measured in land, in gold, in oil, in machines. Today the principal measure of our wealth is information: its quality, its quantity, and the speed with which we acquire it and adapt to it.

The truth of our age is this, and must be this: Open and competitive commerce will enrich us as a nation. It spurs us to innovate. It forces us to compete; it connects us with new customers. It produces global growth without which no rich country can hope to grow wealthy. It enables our producers, who are themselves consumers of services and raw materials, to prosper. And so I say to you in the face of all the pressures to do the reverse, we must compete, not retreat.

We have got to focus on how to help our people adapt to these changes, how to maintain a high-wage economy in the United States without ourselves adding to the protectionist direction that so many of the developed nations have taken in the last few years. These barriers, in the end, will cost the developing world more in lost exports and incomes than all the foreign assistance that developed nations provide, but after that they will begin to undermine our economic prosperity as well.

It's more than a matter of incomes, I remind you. It's a matter of culture and stability.

Trade, of course, cannot ensure the survival of new democracies, and we have seen the enduring power of ethnic hatred, the incredible power of ethnic divisions, even among people literate and allegedly understanding, to splinter democracy and to savage the nationstate. But as philosophers from Thucydides to Adam Smith have noted, the habits of commerce run counter to the habits of war. Just as neighbors who raise each other's barns are less likely to become arsonists, people who raise each other's living standards through commerce are less likely to become combatants.

So if we believe in the bonds of democracy, we must resolve to strengthen the bonds of commerce.[1]

[1]Taken from President Bill Clinton's address on international trade given at American University, Washington, D.C., February 26, 1993.

The Controversy over International Trade

During the 1981–1983 and 1990–1991 recessions we saw a growing tide of resentment against the importation and sale of foreign goods into the United States. Actually, the resentment was nothing new; it was merely augmented, as it always is, by recession. Historically, since the human race has organized itself into geographic groups and engaged in trade among those groups, conflict has emerged between those wanting to suppress trade relationships and those wanting to promote them. The U.S. government severely restricted product imports right up to the end of World War II. Since the late 1940s, import restrictions have tended to fall slowly and steadily. The pace of the fall in the United States and the rest of the world, for that matter, has recently increased with the enactment of various multinational trade accords, such as the North American Free Trade Agreement and the General Agreement on Tariffs and Trade. Opposition remains keen, however. What underlies this conflict between *protectionists* and *free traders?* It is useful to consider the polar positions, recognizing that within the U.S. one finds all shades of intermediate positions—people who are free traders in some respects and protectionists in others.

The Protectionist Viewpoint

First, protectionists want to reduce foreign competition against U.S. goods and services. They see the importation and sale of foreign goods crowding U.S. goods out of the markets in such areas as stereo and video equipment, automobiles, steel, footwear, and textiles. They note that shrinking markets for U.S. goods means less demand for U.S. labor and higher domestic unemployment rates. Our industries cannot compete successfully, in the protectionists' view, against those in other countries that pay only a fraction of the wage rates that U.S. producers pay. The argument usually gains force during recession periods as unemployment increases. It also received much attention during the debates surrounding the North American Free Trade Agreement because that accord leads to the elimination of tariffs on imports from the notoriously low-wage economy of Mexico.

A second argument advanced by protectionists is that import restrictions are necessary to remedy balance of trade and balance of payments problems. They point to the continuing deficits in the U.S. balance of trade, noting how much more we pay out for our imports than we receive for our exports of goods. Sometimes, as was the case in the first half of the 1970s, these deficits are viewed as driving the dollar prices of foreign currencies up, making the dollar worth less. In this case, if we were to reduce our imports, the dollar demand for foreign currencies would also be reduced, decreasing the balance of trade deficits and protecting the value of the dollar. At other times, as during the early 1980s, the causal relationships are turned around. A strengthening dollar is seen as causing balance of trade deficits because it encourages imports and discourages exports. Protectionism is then advocated to block foreign competition from merchandise sales in the United States.

Still another protectionist argument is that there are certain key industries in the United States that are vital to our security and to our economic welfare. Among such industries we find automobiles, aerospace, steel, petroleum energy, and nuclear energy. We cannot depend on foreign suppliers during times of war. To be superior to other countries in technology of key industries, we must encourage their development and growth by restricting imports of those products from other countries.

The Free Trade Viewpoint

Free traders generally maintain that it is in the best interests of consumers worldwide if economic units in all countries are free to engage in whatever voluntary exchanges they believe will be advantageous to them. They see trade among nations conferring the same benefits on the exchanging parties as trade among individuals in any one country. If all parties to a potential voluntary exchange fail to see gain for themselves in it, then it will never be consummated. So, why inhibit economic activity—voluntary exchange—that takes place only if all participants gain? We are all made better off, they argue, through specialization and voluntary exchange.

The Economics of International Trade

What can economic theory contribute toward resolving the conflict of viewpoints? It is useful to learn and apply to the problem (1) the underlying mechanics of international trade, (2) the production and consumption possibilities of a country, without trade and with trade, (3) the principle of comparative advantage, (4) the financing of international trade, and (5) the economics of international trade restrictions. The world is increasingly becoming a global marketplace, and it is vitally important to understand how international trade affects our economy and our own standard of living.

How Trade Takes Place

It takes two to tango. A country cannot unilaterally import unless it also exports goods. Neither can it export unless it also imports goods.

Suppose the *only* potential international transaction that exists, now and forever, between the United States and the rest of the world is the importation by me of a German BMW automobile. This assumption is ridiculous, but it illustrates an important point. Where would I get the marks to make the purchase? The answer is obvious. There are and will be none available. Or, looking at it from the other side of the water, if I want to pay in dollars, what would the Germans do with dollars? They would have no use for dollars and, consequently, would not accept them. The transaction would never take place.

Suppose now that I want to import a BMW, and Cessna Aircraft wants to export a Cessna to a German citizen. If Cessna can sell the airplane for marks, then I can buy marks from Cessna for dollars, using the marks in turn to purchase the BMW. In order for people in one country to import, it is also necessary that they export. There is no escape from this fundamental proposition.

Production and Consumption Possibilities

In general, why do people in different countries want to engage in exchange? The underlying reason is that it enables them to increase the levels of well-being they can get from their resources. Recall from Chapter 1 that an economy's production possibilities curve shows the maximum quantities of goods and services that can be produced when the economy's resources are used efficiently. Given this, the production possibilities curve may also be thought of as a *consumption possibilities curve* because, in the absence of trade, the economy can consume no more than it produces. With trade, however, it becomes possible to consume more than is produced domestically. That is, trade can cause the consumption possibilities curve to shift outward, beyond the production possibilities curve. Thus, trade enables the totality of consumers in each country to achieve higher satisfaction levels with the complement of labor, capital, and technology available to them. Let's see how it works for two countries, Alpha and Omega, that can engage in trade with each other and with other countries of the world.

> The **consumption possibilities curve** represents the maximum quantities of two goods and/or services that can be consumed in an economy when its resources are used efficiently.

Without Trade. Consider the production and consumption possibilities of Alpha in the absence of international trade. Given Alpha's resources and techniques, suppose its economic system can produce either 100 million loaves of bread or 200 million gallons of milk. Assuming that its resources are unspecialized to either product, the trade-off between the two products is one for two. By giving up 1 million loaves of bread, the resources released can always be used to produce an additional 2 million gallons of milk. So Alpha alone can produce and consume any combination of bread and milk on line *AB* in Figure 10–1. Thus, *AB* is both Alpha's production possibilities curve and its consumption possibilities curve in the absence of trade. Suppose its people select combination *C*, containing 50 million loaves of bread and 100 million gallons of milk.

Let Omega's resources differ somewhat from those of Alpha, but consider that they, too, are unspecialized. Suppose that Omega's economy can produce, without trade, either 100 million loaves of bread or 50 million gallons of milk. The trade-off in production between the two products is a half million gallons of milk for 1 million loaves of bread, or 2 million

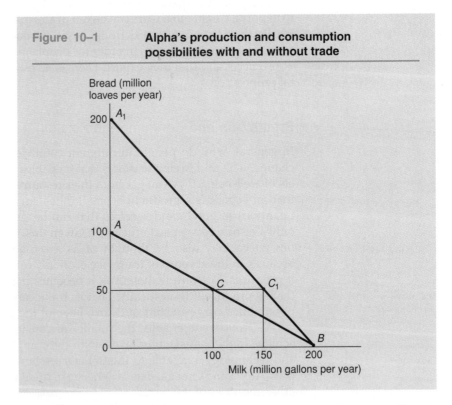

Figure 10–1   **Alpha's production and consumption possibilities with and without trade**

In the absence of trade, Alpha's resources will produce 100 million loaves of bread, or 200 million gallons of milk, or any combination of the two products as shown by *AB*. Given this, *AB* is both the production and consumption possibilities curve for Alpha when there is no trade.

If terms of trade are one for one, with trade Alpha's production possibilities curve remains *MN*, but its consumption possibilities curve rotates outward to A_1B. Alpha can concentrate on milk production and can trade for bread at less than it would cost to produce it in Alpha.

loaves of bread for 1 million gallons of milk. Thus, Omega's production possibilities curve is *MN* in Figure 10–2. Likewise, since there is no trade, *MN* is also Omega's consumption possibilities curve. Suppose its population settles on combination *P*, containing 50 million loaves of bread and 25 million gallons of milk.

With Trade.   What would happen if Alpha and Omega were now able to enter into international trade relationships? Under what circumstances would Alpha and Omega be willing to trade bread for milk? Or milk for bread? First, we determine the limits within which the terms of trade must fall if the countries are to engage in trade. Second, we show what trade within the terms of trade limits will do for each country.

Figure 10–2

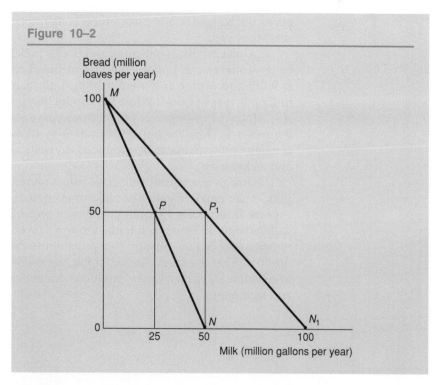

In the absence of trade, Omega's resources will produce per year 100 million loaves of bread, or 50 million gallons of milk, or any combination shown on the line *MN*. Given this, *MN* is both the production and consumption possibilities curve for Omega when there is no trade.

If terms of trade are one for one, with trade Omega's production possibilities curve remains *MN*, but its consumption possibilities curve rotates outward to MN_1. Omega can concentrate on bread production and trade for milk at less than it would cost to produce it in Omega.

Alpha would refuse to enter into any trade relationships in which the cost of importing 1 gallon of milk exceeds a half loaf of bread, or in which the cost of importing a loaf of bread exceeds 2 gallons of milk. A gallon of milk produced domestically costs Alpha only a half loaf of bread. Why import it if the cost per gallon of the import is greater? A loaf of bread produced domestically costs 2 gallons of milk, so Alpha would not be willing to pay more to import it. We summarize these results in Table 10–1.

Omega would not voluntarily engage in trade if the terms of trade exceed two loaves of bread for the importation of a gallon of milk or a half gallon of milk for the importation of a loaf of bread. It could do better producing both domestically. These limits are shown in Table 10–1.

Suppose now that as the countries consider engaging in trade, the terms of trade between bread and milk settle at a gallon of milk for a loaf of bread. Both Alpha and Omega can gain from trade. The reason each can gain is that while trade leaves each country's production possibilities curve unchanged, trade causes their consumption possibilities curves to rotate outward.

If Alpha produces only milk and trades milk for bread, the population of the country can import one loaf of bread for each gallon of milk it is willing to export. If it were to export all its milk, it could import 200 million loaves of bread. While the production possibilities curve remains AB, Alpha's consumption possibilities curve rotates outward to A_1B in Figure 10–1. Thus, the impact of trade is to allow the citizens of Alpha to consume more than can be produced domestically, given their resources and technology.

If Omega concentrates all its resources on breadmaking and trades for milk, it can import a gallon of milk for every loaf of bread it produces and exports. If it exports 100 million loaves of bread, it can import 100 million gallons of milk. Thus, with trade, Omega's production possibilities curve remains MN, but its consumption possibilities curve becomes MN_1 in Figure 10–2. That is, as was true for Alpha, trade allows the citizens of Omega to consume more than can be produced domestically, given their resources and technology.

Table 10–1	Limits to terms of trade between bread and milk, Alpha and Omega	
	Alpha	Omega
Bread	1	2
Milk	2	1

Country Alpha will concentrate on the production of milk, and Country Omega will produce bread. Producing milk only, Alpha's people are not limited to combination C of milk and bread, which contains 50 million loaves of bread and 100 million gallons of milk. They can produce 200 million gallons of milk and trade 50 million gallons for 50 million loaves of bread, leaving themselves with combination C_1, containing 150 million gallons of milk and 50 million loaves of bread. They are 50 million gallons of milk better off than they were before the trade.

Country Omega's people will be better off producing only bread and trading for milk. Before trade they chose combination P, containing 50 million loaves of bread and 25 million gallons of milk. By specializing in bread, they can produce 100 million loaves, trade 50 million loaves for 50 million gallons of milk, and end up with combination P_1, containing 50 million gallons of milk and 50 million loaves of bread. Trade enables them to obtain a net gain of 25 million gallons of milk.

The Principle of Comparative Advantage

A country has a **comparative advantage** in the production of a good when it has a lower opportunity cost of producing the good than any other country.

A country has a **comparative disadvantage** in the production of a good when it has a higher opportunity cost of producing the good than another country.

Clearly, specialization and exchange help both Alpha and Omega increase the volumes of goods and services available for their people to consume. It pays any country to specialize in producing those things in which it has a *comparative advantage* and to trade for goods in which it experiences a *comparative disadvantage.*

A country has a comparative advantage in the production of any good that it can produce with a smaller sacrifice of some alternative good or goods, that is, at a lower opportunity cost, than can the rest of the trading world. Note that there is no presumption that the country can produce that good at a lower *absolute* cost than can other countries. In terms of the number of units of labor and capital necessary to produce a million gallons of milk, Alpha may use 3 times (or 10 times) more of each than other countries. Yet if Alpha must give up a half million loaves of bread for 1 million gallons of milk and can trade the million gallons of milk for *more* than a half million loaves of bread, Alpha has a comparative advantage in producing milk. Use this same reasoning to determine Omega's comparative advantage product, if any.

Symmetrically, a country has a *comparative disadvantage* in the production of any good that requires a greater sacrifice of some alternative good or goods, that is, it produces at a higher opportunity cost, than is required in the rest of the trading world. Country Alpha in our example has a comparative disadvantage in the production of bread. It must sacrifice 2 gallons of milk for a loaf of bread if it produces bread domestically. But it can import a loaf of bread by giving up only 1 gallon of milk to the international market. In which product does Omega have a comparative disadvantage?

Look again at the complete examples of Alpha and Omega, without and with trade. Note that if a country has a comparative advantage in the production of one good (and it most certainly will have in the real world), it must have a comparative disadvantage in the production of some other good or goods. Usually a country will have comparative advantages in the production of several goods and comparative disadvantages in the production of several others.

The reasons that every country has comparative advantages in the production of some goods and comparative disadvantages in the production of others is that countries differ in their respective resource endowments and in their states of technology. Some countries are short on certain mineral deposits such as oil, coal, and copper, but they may have relatively large quantities of good capital equipment and high levels of technological know-how. Such a country, Japan, for example, will likely have comparative advantages in the production and sale of goods embodying high technology and good stocks of capital with which to work. Some countries have vast quantities of good agricultural land while others do not. Some are particularly well-suited in terms of climate, terrain, and soil to grow outstanding wine grapes. Some excel in coffee production and others in growing tea. A beef industry seldom thrives in densely populated, mountainous countries. Some countries have high literacy rates. In others the bulk of the population may be illiterate. All these differences, and many more, confer on each country or region of a country certain comparative advantages and disadvantages that make specialization and exchange worthwhile.

How International Trade Is Financed

International trade has two important characteristics that set it apart from trade within the boundaries of any given country. First, each country has its own currency. Producers in any given country want to be paid in that currency, and buyers want to use it to pay for goods and services. Second, nationalism and political objectives are invariably injected into trade relationships among nations. All sorts of impediments to trade are enacted by governments to further political ends even though the trade, if allowed, would have been in the best economic interests of the trading parties. Remember that voluntary exchange will occur only if *all* parties to the exchange expect to gain. In this section we concentrate mostly on the problems arising from the different currency units used by different countries.

The link between the currencies of any two trading countries is the exchange rate. An *exchange rate* is the price of one country's currency in terms of the monetary units of another. It is useful for us to think of it as the dollar price of another country's currency. We list a recent sample of such exchange rates in Table 10–2. The dollar exchange rate for the British

An **exchange rate** is the price of one country's currency in terms of the monetary units of another country.

Table 10–2	Dollar exchange rates for selected foreign currencies, December 1, 1998	
Country	**Dollars**	**Foreign Currency Unit**
Argentina	1.0005	1 peso
Australia	0.6287	1 dollar
Britain	1.6495	1 pound
Canada	0.6523	1 dollar
Denmark	0.1552	1 krone
France	0.1761	1 franc
Germany	0.5905	1 mark
Greece	0.0035	1 drachma
Italy	0.0006	1 lira
Japan	0.0081	1 yen
Mexico	0.1001	1 peso
Saudi Arabia	0.2666	1 riyal
South Africa	0.1760	1 rand
South Korea	0.0008	1 won
Switzerland	0.7170	1 franc
Taiwan	0.0308	1 dollar

Source: *The Wall Street Journal*, December 1, 1998, p. C11.

pound of $1.65 is the highest one listed. The lowest one listed is $0.0006 for the Italian lira (this amounts to 6 one-hundredths of a cent).

Exchange rates, in the absence of intervention by governments, are determined in exchange markets that arise from millions of such transactions as the importation of a BMW automobile into the United States or the export of a Cessna to Germany. The existence of exchange markets makes the pairing of individual import transactions with individual export transactions unnecessary. Anyone in the United States can buy foreign currency with dollars and can use it to import that country's goods. Similarly, anyone with excess amounts of a foreign currency on hand from selling goods abroad, or for any other reason, can sell that currency for dollars in the foreign exchange market.

In the absence of government intervention, the exchange rate of any home country currency for a foreign currency is determined, like any other price, by the forces of demand for and supply of the foreign currency. Insight into the demand for and supply of foreign currency is had when it is realized that people in the home country demand foreign currency so that they might purchase goods from the foreign country, while foreigners supply foreign currency through their demand for goods produced in the home country. Specifically, the demand curve for the foreign currency is essentially the same as the demand curve for anything else. That is, it slopes downward to the right, like *DD* in Figure 10–3, since it is derived from the demand for foreign goods, which is itself negatively sloped. Similarly, the supply curve *SS* illustrated in Figure 10–3 usually slopes upward to the right because it is derived from the foreign demand for goods produced in the home country. The exchange rate *r* is the equilibrium price. Quantity *q* is the equilibrium quantity exchanged of the foreign currency.

In order to discuss the demand for and supply of foreign currency more formally, consider the summary of U.S. international transactions for 1997, which is presented in Table 10–3. As noted above, our demand for foreign currency arises from our desire for foreign goods. Thus, our demand for foreign currency may be determined by identifying any payments that we want to make abroad. The largest part of our demand for foreign currencies in 1997 arose from imports of goods, shown on line 2.

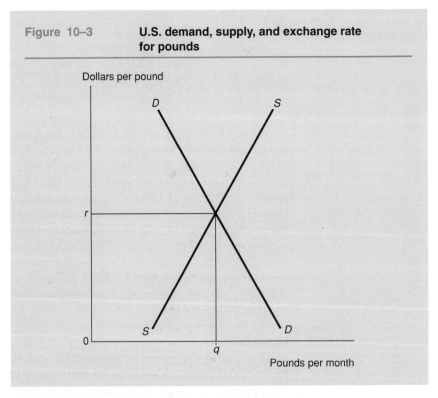

Figure 10–3   U.S. demand, supply, and exchange rate for pounds

Demand for pounds is represented by *DD* and supply is *SS*. The equilibrium exchange rate is *r* dollars per pound and the equilibrium quantity of pounds is *q*.

This demand source is straightforward. During 1997 we needed $877.3 billion worth of foreign currencies to purchase goods imported from other nations. The second largest part of our demand for foreign currency arose from increases in U.S. investments abroad; this is shown on line 6. When American companies invest abroad, they need foreign currencies to purchase land, build plants, and buy equipment. According to Table 10–3, this amounted to $478.5 billion in 1997. Much smaller but third in importance is the transfer of funds by private individuals and organizations shown on line 5. This figure represents the foreign currency needed to support cash gifts and grants made to relatives, friends, and organizations abroad. Finally, line 4 of Table 10–3 reports the demand for foreign currency needed to support interest payments, dividends, and capital gains on investments held in the United States by foreigners. This amounted to $5.3 billion in 1997. Summing all the sources of demand results in a total demand for foreign currency of $1,400.8 billion during 1997.

Supplies of foreign currencies, as one would expect, arise from transactions reciprocal to those generating demand. The largest single source of foreign currency in 1997 was the export of goods. Line 1 of Table 10–3

Table 10–3	U.S. international transactions, summary, 1997 (billions of current dollars)		
Transaction Type	**Demand for Foreign Currency**	**Supply of Foreign Currency**	**Balance**
Current Account			
1. Goods exported		679.3	
2. Goods imported	−877.3		
3. Net services		87.8	
4. Net investments	−5.3		
5. Transfers	−39.7		
Balance on current account			−155.2
Capital Account			
6. Change in U.S. assets abroad	−478.5		
7. Change in foreign assets in the United States		733.4	
Balance on capital account			254.9
Totals	−1,400.8	1,500.5	99.7
Statistical discrepancy			99.7

Sources: U.S. Department of Commerce (Bureau of Economic Analysis) and Department of the Treasury.

indicates that this amounted to $679.3 billion. Next in importance was the change in assets within the United States held by foreigners. This represents new investments here by foreign companies and individuals. Examples of such investments include the Japanese building a new car plant or the Germans buying U.S. property or financial securities. The level of foreign investment in the United States has been increasing in recent years. Line 7 of Table 10–3 reports that $733.4 billion in new foreign investment occurred in 1997. A third source of foreign currency was the net export of services. This includes transactions undertaken by the military abroad, travel and transportation receipts from foreigners, and other services produced by Americans while overseas. In 1997 net services accounted for $87.8 billion in our supply of foreign currencies. Adding together each source of foreign currency results in a total supply of $1,500.5 billion during 1997.

The separation of transactions in Table 10–3 into "current account" and "capital account" categories is simply a classification convenience. Current account items are more or less immediate and short-term in character. A transaction is consummated, and that is the end of it. Other transactions of a similar nature are occurring concurrently and over time. Capital account items are long-term transactions that will persist into the future and yield continuing influence on the demand for and supply of foreign exchange.

Notice the difference between the total demand for and the total supply of foreign exchanges listed in Table 10–3. It amounted to $99.7 billion, a sizable pocketful of change. Our table shows the difference as being owed to foreigners—we used or demanded more foreign exchange than was available. Such an amount is sometimes interpreted as a balance of payments deficit. But actually it is simply a statistical discrepancy: a failure to get all international transactions on record. Suppose that for the year people in the United States end up owing $99.7 billion to foreigners. If *all* transactions were recorded, those in the United States would have issued IOUs of different kinds, and foreigners would have accepted them. Otherwise the extra items would not have been sold to us. Acceptance of ownership of those IOUs by foreigners would increase line 7, change in foreign assets in the United States, by $99.7 billion, making the demand and supply columns balance. The statistical discrepancy is not a cause for concern.

International Trade Restrictions

Despite the strong arguments that favor the free exchange of goods and services between countries, governments often impose restrictions on international trade. Protectionist laws that tax and regulate the flow of goods between nations have a long and colorful world history. International trade has been a controversial social issue for centuries. In fact, the philosophical debates concerning the English "corn laws" of the eighteenth century, which restricted the trade of food grains, were instrumental in the development of classical economics. In today's global economy, international trade restrictions generally fall into one of three broad categories: (1) tariffs, (2) quotas, and (3) voluntary restraint agreements. In this section we briefly describe each category and examine the economic effects of international trade restrictions.

A **tariff** is a tax placed on internationally traded goods, usually imports.

Tariffs. A *tariff* is a tax placed on internationally traded goods, usually imports. Tariffs are the oldest and most common form of international trade restrictions. In the United States, tariffs have been imposed on imported goods since the American Revolution. Throughout much of our history, tariffs were an important source of federal government revenue. Since the Great Depression, tariffs have been imposed primarily to protect domestic jobs and production, not as a means of generating tax revenue. Today, revenue from tariffs represents an insignificant portion of the total U.S. budget.

The economic effects of a tariff are shown in Figure 10–4 (next page). *DD* represents the demand curve for a specific brand of imported Japanese cars, and *SS* represents the supply curve of these cars exported from Japan to the United States. Without a tariff, or other form of trade restriction, 10,000 cars per year will be sold at the domestic market equilibrium price of $20,000. When a tariff of $5,000 is placed on cars imported from Japan, the supply curve shifts back by the amount of the tariff. The new supply curve reflecting the tariff is shown as S_1S_1 in Figure 10–4. In effect, the tariff increases the marginal cost of producing and exporting the Japanese cars to the United States. With the tariff in place, a new market equilibrium will be established at the intersection of the S_1S_1 curve and the *DD* curve. Notice that the tariff results in a higher price for consumers and a lower number of imported car sales. In our example, the tariff raises the price to $22,500, an increase of $2,500, and lowers the quantity sold to 8,000, a decrease of 2,000 cars per year.

Why is the increase in price ($2,500) less than the tariff ($5,000)? The answer is that the burden of the tariff is shared by the consumers and producers. Buyers pay the Japanese car producers $22,500 for each car, but in turn the producers must pay the U.S. government a $5,000 tariff per sale. Thus, the net revenue to the producer is only $17,500 per car ($22,500 − $5,000). Without the tariff, producers would have kept the entire $20,000 original selling price. Thus, in our example, the burden of the tariff is equally shared. Producers receive $2,500 less in revenue, and consumers pay $2,500 more in terms of a higher price. In practice, the relative shares of the tariff burden depend on the relative shapes of the demand and supply curves.

The government will collect revenue from the tariff equal to the amount of the tariff times the number of cars sold. In our example, this would be $5,000 × 8,000 = $4,000,000. Therefore, the government receives $4 million in new revenue from the imposition of the tariff.

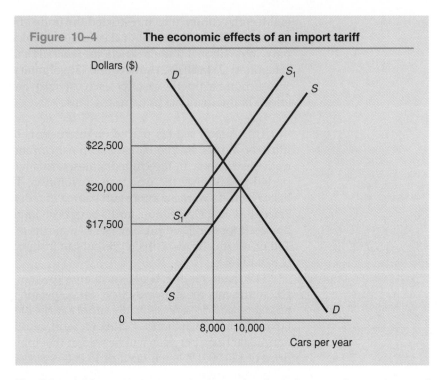

Figure 10–4   **The economic effects of an import tariff**

The *DD* and *SS* curves represent the demand and supply curves for cars imported from Japan. Without a tariff, 10,000 cars will be sold per year at an equilibrium price of $20,000. A $5,000 tariff reduces supply to $S_1 S_1$. With the tariff, only 8,000 cars will be sold per year at a price of $22,500. In this case, the burden of the tariff is shared equally by the Japanese producers and the domestic consumers.

Tariff revenues are often referred to as *import duties* and are generally collected by customs agencies when goods are physically brought into the country.

Tariffs also have an effect on domestic producers. Because tariffs reduce the quantity of foreign-produced goods and raise their price, the demand for domestically produced products increases. In our example, tariffs on Japanese cars will increase the demand for American-made Chevrolets and Fords. As the demand for domestically produced cars increases, so too will their prices. The end result is higher prices for both Japanese and American cars.

Quotas. A second method by which governments can restrict international trade is called a *quota*. A quota limits by law the quantity of specific foreign goods or services that may be imported during a period of time. Quotas are used less often than tariffs, but they are still a common form of

A **quota** limits by law the quantity of specific foreign goods or services that may be imported during a period of time.

international trade restriction. Examples of quotas imposed by the United States include those on peanuts, cotton, and sugar.

Figure 10–5 illustrates the economic effects of a quota. In this example, *DD* represents the demand curve for sugar imported into the United States from Brazil, and *SS* represents the supply curve of sugar exported from Brazil to the United States. Without a quota or other form of trade restriction, the market equilibrium price would be $30 per ton, and 1,000 tons of Brazilian sugar would be purchased by U.S. consumers. Now, assume that a quota of 750 tons per year is imposed. This results in a new vertical supply curve at the quota limit, as shown by the $S_1 S_1$ curve in Figure 10–5. The new supply curve is vertical because only 750 tons of Brazilian sugar can be sold in the United States—regardless of the market price. The quota results in the establishment of a new market equilibrium at the

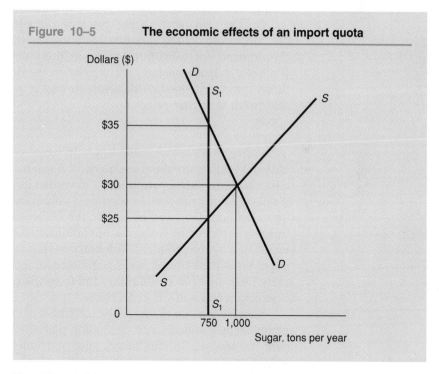

Figure 10–5   The economic effects of an import quota

The *DD* and *SS* curves represent the demand and supply curves for sugar imported from Brazil. Without a quota, 1,000 tons of sugar will be sold per year at an equilibrium price of $30 per ton. A quota of 750 tons per year reduces supply to $S_1 S_1$. This new supply curve is vertical because only 750 tons can be sold per year regardless of price. Given *DD*, the equilibrium price with the quota will be $35 per ton. Because Brazilian suppliers of sugar are willing to sell 750 tons per year for $25 per ton, holders of import licenses will earn an extra $10 per ton in profits due to the quota.

intersection of the DD and S_1S_1 curves. Thus, in Figure 10–5, the price of Brazilian sugar in the United States will rise to $35 per ton.

According to the original supply curve SS in Figure 10–5, Brazilian suppliers of sugar are willing to sell 750 tons of sugar to the United States at a price of $25. What then is the difference between the price that consumers must pay with the quota ($35) and the price received by Brazilian suppliers ($25)? This $10 per ton of sugar is extra profit earned by the holders of the quota rights. Often licenses will be granted to foreign governments or companies that give them the right to export specific quantities of products to the United States. The owners of these licenses therefore receive the profits generated by the quota restrictions. Notice that the source of these profits is divided between the foreign suppliers and American consumers in a manner similar to the shared burden of import tariffs. (Foreign suppliers receive $5 per ton less than what they would receive with free trade, and American consumers pay $5 per ton more than they would with free trade.)

Quotas also increase the price of domestically produced goods. As quotas restrict the quantity of foreign goods and raise their price, the demand for substitutes made in the United States will increase. If all else is held constant, an increase in the demand for these domestically produced goods will result in higher prices. Quotas, therefore, also result in higher prices for both foreign and domestically produced goods.

Voluntary Restraint Agreements. In recent years, a new form of international trade restriction has emerged. A *voluntary restraint agreement* occurs when one nation "volunteers" to restrict its exports of a product that it sells to another nation. In essence, a voluntary restraint agreement is a quota without the effect of law. In the United States, tariffs and quotas must be approved by Congress, but voluntary restraint agreements can be negotiated by the president. Voluntary restraint agreements have become popular since the United States negotiated an agreement with Japan in the early 1980s that places voluntary limits on the number of cars that Japanese companies will sell in America.

A **voluntary restraint agreement** occurs when one nation "volunteers" to restrict its exports of a product that it sells to another nation.

Because they do not have the force of law, voluntary restraint agreements are negotiated when one nation places economic or political pressure on another. In this sense, such agreements may not always be voluntary. For example, Japan agreed to limit the sales of cars in the United States due to the threat of new heavy tariffs and quotas in other sectors of the economy.

The economic effects of voluntary restraint agreements are similar to those of a quota. Foreign producers must coordinate their export activity, as if they were monopolists, in order to maintain the voluntary limits. The result once again is a restriction in the number of foreign-produced goods and an increase in the price for domestic consumers.

Analysis of the Controversy

In the light of this brief survey of the economics of international trade, what light is shed on the controversy between protectionists and free traders? Should we protect ourselves from imports of Japanese and European automobiles and steel? Is it wise to limit textile imports from South Korea, Taiwan, Hong Kong, and China? Is the importation of Japanese motorcycles a threat to our prosperity? What will happen to us if we reduce the import quotas on sugar and other agricultural products? In analyzing these issues, it is important that we separate economic from political considerations. Economic analysis provides insight primarily into the former.

Protection from Cheap Foreign Goods

The principle of comparative advantage and the economic gains ensuing from specialization and exchange make it reasonably clear that a country's population as a whole will lose from import restrictions. They will have less of all goods and services to consume. Real per capita income and living standards will be lower than they would be if all potential international voluntary exchanges are allowed to be consummated. Foreign goods cannot displace all or even a large part of the domestic production and sale of goods. A country cannot import unless, by selling domestic goods and services or other kinds of domestic assets to foreigners, it earns foreign exchange with which to buy those imports. International trade is a two-way street enabling those countries that engage in it to shift their consumption possibilities curves outward. It serves to *increase* the real per capita income and living standards in the trading countries.

Free trade may indeed injure segments of a country's economy. It is concern for that part of the population investing in and working in the injured segments that prompts most protectionist efforts. Import quotas and/or high tariffs on steel and automobiles keep the demands for the outputs of domestic steel and automobile manufacturers higher than they would otherwise be, thus supporting profits, wages, and employment in those industries. Free trade enables foreign competitors to invade the domestic producers' markets, resulting in lower domestic profits, wages, and employment levels in those industries.

Consequently, the imposition of import restrictions leads to winners (those investing and working in the protected sector) and losers (consumers who must pay higher prices for the protected good). But do the winners "win" by more than the losers "lose"? In other words, do the benefits of the import restrictions outweigh the costs? Considering the case of automobiles will help us see that in the typical case, the costs of import restrictions far outweigh the benefits. In the early 1980s, in response to poor domestic auto sales, the Reagan administration was successful in getting

Japan to voluntarily limit auto exports to the United States. The major benefit of the import restriction was the significant number of jobs saved in the auto sector (at the expense of jobs lost in the export sector). The cost of the program increased the price that consumers had to pay for autos. Which was greater? One estimate suggests that the voluntary import restriction imposed a cost of $160,000 per job saved.[2] That is, in an effort to save a job paying $30,000 to $40,000, we spent $160,000. Similar outcomes have been found for protectionistic practices in areas as divergent as the importation of shoes and citizen's band radios.[3] If the benefits of import restrictions rarely outweigh the costs, why is protectionism so popular? The gains from free trade, because they are spread over the entire consuming population, tend to be unnoticed by the average individual. The same is not true with respect to those injured by free trade. Had the import restrictions on Japanese autos not been in effect, numerous individuals would have lost their jobs. Significant personal losses of this nature are easily noticed by the entire population. Consequently, it is not strange to find that "free traders win the arguments, but protectionists win the elections," as the anonymous saying goes.

Payments Problems

Protectionism for balance of trade problems appears to stem from a less than complete view of the whole set of a country's international transactions. In the United States, we are reminded by the news media every month of the balance of trade deficit for that month. We are warned by many members of Congress of the dire consequences of the continuing trade balance deficits unless we curb our appetites for foreign-made goods. What seems to be overlooked is that the trade deficit doesn't really matter in the overall set of international transactions.

From current account transactions alone, the U.S. population could reasonably expect to import a greater value of goods than it exports for almost as far as one can see into the future. For a great many years, we have earned much larger investment income abroad than foreigners have earned in the United States. Net investment income alone would enable us to import more than we export, even if we were to maintain a current account balance of zero. The merchandise trade balance simply doesn't tell us much.

When we take capital account transactions into consideration, the merchandise trade balance becomes even less important. Foreign investments in the United States provide us with foreign currencies to import

[2]Robert W. Crandall, "Import Quotas and the Automobile Industry: The Costs of Protection," *Brookings Review,* Summer 1984, p. 8.

[3]Keith E. Maskus, "Rising Protectionism and U.S. International Trade Policy," Federal Reserve Bank of Kansas City, *Economic Review,* July–August 1984, pp. 3–19.

goods if we so desire. U.S. investments abroad use supplies of foreign currencies, leaving smaller quantities available for importing merchandise. And, since much trade and investment is done by private economic units without the need of government supervision, blessing, or curse, a great many transactions never get in the official record.

Trade deficits are important only to the extent that they lead to overall balance of payments deficits. A balance of payments deficit means that a country, during a given year, is short of sufficient foreign currencies to meet its obligations. Government setting or pegging of the country's exchange rate would be necessary for such a shortage to occur.

The circumstances creating a foreign exchange shortage are illustrated in Figure 10–6. Let the equilibrium exchange rate be $1.75 for £1 (1 pound sterling). If the U.S. government sets an exchange rate ceiling on the pound at $1.50 each, the British will want smaller quantities of our exports (which are now more expensive to them), and we will want to import

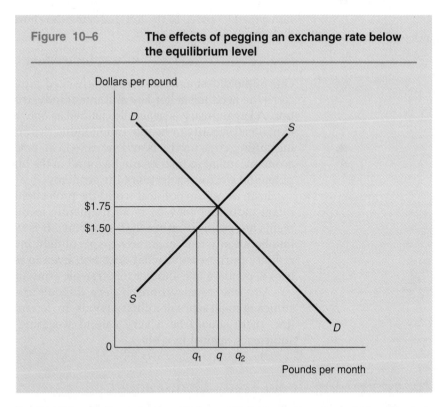

Figure 10–6   **The effects of pegging an exchange rate below the equilibrium level**

If a country pegs its exchange rate for another country's currency below the equilibrium level, the effect is the same as it is for the imposition of any effective price ceiling. There will be a shortage. If the exchange rate is fixed at $1.50 per pound, the shortage is $q_1 q_2$ pounds per month.

more from them (because British goods are now cheaper for us). A shortage of q_1q_2 pounds per month occurs. Such a shortage is generally referred to as a *balance of payments deficit*.

The deficit can persist only if the lid is kept on the price of the pound. The $1.50 ceiling overvalues the dollar relative to the pound. If it is removed, the shortage of pounds will induce buyers of British goods to bid against each other for the available supply of pounds. The price of the pound will move toward its equilibrium level of $1.75, and the dollar will depreciate relative to the pound.

The free trade position and a free exchange rate position go hand in hand. In general, the argument runs that with free trade a freely flexible exchange market will appropriately value the currencies of different countries with respect to each other. Shortages or surpluses of foreign exchange will be short-term transitional phenomena. On the other hand, a fixed exchange rate will result in incentives to restrict trade. In Figure 10–6, for example, with the ceiling of $1.50 for the pound, the shortage of pounds gives Congress an incentive to restrict imports. Import restriction would move the *DD* curve to the left, reducing the shortage of pounds.

Protection of Key and Infant Industries

One of the oldest and most frequently cited protectionist arguments concerns the need to shelter key and infant industries from foreign competition. A key industry is generally defined as one that is important and vital to national security or health. Infant industries are new industries producing cutting-edge products and services in an emerging market. In today's economy, infant industries can be found in the high-tech areas of the computer and electronics sector of the economy.

In an uncertain political world the protectionist viewpoint for key and infant industries may be more frequently recommended. But the arguments are political rather than economic. It is very difficult to draw the line between what constitutes an absolutely indispensable industry for military purposes and what does not. Even in times of war, allied countries depend on one another for strategic arms and other war materiel.

Any one country finds it very difficult and very costly to be self-sufficient in all types of military goods. In determining where to draw the line, there should be a very careful weighing of the benefits of self-sufficiency against its costs.

Today's International Trade Environment

It is often said that the world is fast becoming a "global marketplace." International trade today is more open and free of protectionist restrictions than ever before. In part, this is due to the lessons learned from the past.

During the 1930s the United States and Europe engaged in a devastating trade war. Severe restrictions in the form of high tariffs and strict quotas led to a reduction in world trade of more than 75 percent. This downturn contributed significantly to the worldwide Great Depression of that decade. As a result, following World War II, a treaty was signed by 23 industrialized nations, lowering the barriers to international trade. Known as the *General Agreement on Tariffs and Trade* (GATT), this trade treaty was renegotiated over the years as more countries joined the pact. The GATT treaty was instrumental in lowering world tariffs from an average of 40 percent in the 1940s to about 4 percent today. On January 1, 1995, a new international body, the *World Trade Organization,* took over from GATT, which now oversees international trade relations between member countries.

The World Trade Organization

The World Trade Organization (WTO) is the permanent institutional foundation for the negotiation of trade agreements and settlement of trade disputes between its 132 member nations. The WTO has outlawed most import quota systems, but tariffs and voluntary restraint agreements remain legal. Members of the WTO must offer all other member countries the same trade concessions as any member country. Thus, all members must treat one another as equals at the bargaining table; this is known as the *most-favored nation* clause of the WTO agreement. Under the WTO, average worldwide tariffs are expected to fall even further.

The WTO's Dispute Settlement Body is charged with handling trade disagreements between member nations. This body enforces the WTO's provisions on "unfair competition" and violations of the most-favored nation clause. The most predominant charge of unfair competition involves the practice of *dumping*. Dumping occurs when a producer sells products abroad at a price below cost or below its domestic price. Although dumping charges are frequently filed by domestic producers of products that face strong international competition, such charges are often difficult to prove. In practice, most real dumping occurs during recessions when international producers find themselves with surpluses that cannot be sold at home. Long-term dumping cannot take place unless the producer's economic losses are subsidized. The WTO strictly regulates the practice of export subsidies and treats them as a form of unfair competition.

Dumping occurs when a producer is selling abroad at a price below cost, or below its domestic price.

Additional nations may join the WTO over time. However, each new nation must negotiate its conditions for entry. The WTO provides special concessions for developing countries with emerging economies, but eventually all member nations must adhere to WTO standards and the most-favored nation clause. As the economic importance of international trade increases, so too will the importance of the WTO.

Common Markets

The economic benefits of free international trade have led to the creation of multinational treaties where all or most barriers to trade have been lifted. The primary goal of these treaties is to create a "common market" that is shared among the member nations. The two most important common markets are the *European Union* and the zone created by the *North American Free Trade Agreement.* Although these two alliances of nations share a common ideal, they do differ in significant ways.

A **customs union** is a free trade alliance of nations that share common external tariffs.

The European Union (EU). The European Union is a *customs union* that includes most of the nations in Western Europe. (See Figure 10–7.) A customs union is a free trade alliance of nations that share common external tariffs. Member nations of the EU have dropped all significant trade barriers between themselves and have devised a common set of rules regarding international trade between union and other nonmember nations around the world.

The EU has been successful in increasing the flow of resources and goods between its members. It continues to work toward creating a truly unified single European market, but many nationalistic hurdles still stand in the way. The most ambitious plan is for the creation and adoption of a new European currency. Although all EU members have agreed to a single currency in principle, several countries are reluctant to give up control of their own money supply. The new currency, known as the euro, will be introduced in stages over the next several years.

On January 1, 1999, the euro became a recognized currency in 11 of the 15 EU member nations (Denmark, Sweden, and the United Kingdom postponed their decision to adopt the euro, and Greece failed to meet the qualification deadline). However, European consumers will not be able to make everyday purchases with the euro until January 1, 2002. Until that time, the euro will be used only for paper and electronic financial transactions, record keeping, and the sale of public bonds. The original value of the euro was determined by a weighted average of the participating nations' respective currencies. On the first day of trading, the exchange rate for the euro in U.S. dollars was 1.1747.

During the first 6 months of 2002, new euro coins and paper money will begin replacing the old national currencies. By July 1, 2002, the old national currencies will cease to exist and all transactions must be made using euros. The introduction of the euro is expected to result in an increase in trade between the member nations and to further strengthen Europe's economic standing in the global marketplace. The primary reason for this expectation is very easy to understand: The euro will reduce the costs of trade between member nations. Prior to the introduction of the euro, a French citizen would have to purchase marks before a shopping trip to Berlin, and a German would have to purchase francs before a vacation on the Riviera. Of course, every time a currency conversion is

Figure 10–7   **Countries of the European Union and the North American Free Trade Area**

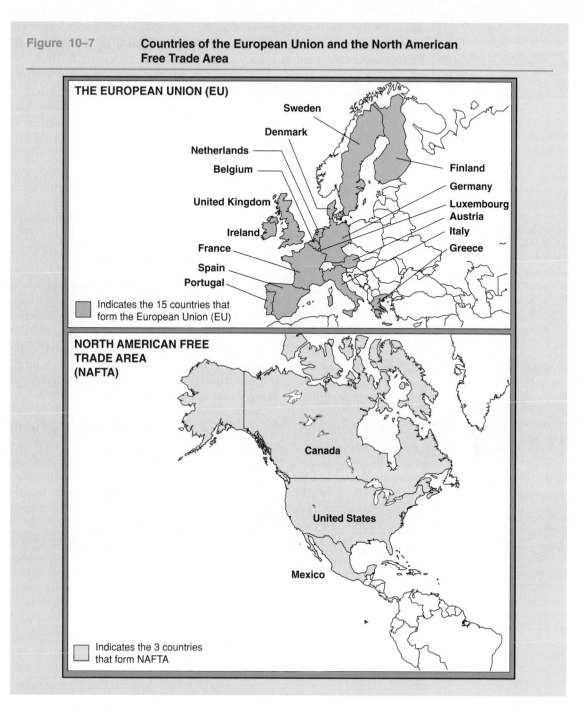

The European Union is composed of the following 15 nations: Austria, Belgium, Denmark, Finland, France, Germany, Greece, Ireland, Italy, Luxembourg, Netherlands, Portugal, Spain, Sweden, and the United Kingdom. The North American Free Trade Area is composed of the United States, Canada, and Mexico.

made, the broker making the exchange demands a fee for this service. With a common currency such as the euro, these transaction costs, and all the time spent making currency conversions, are eliminated. Thus the euro will reduce the costs of trade. In addition, the euro will make it easier for consumers to understand the true prices they are paying for internationally traded products. For example, French shoppers in Berlin will not have to convert marks to francs in their heads before deciding whether to buy a new car there or to wait until they return home. Prices all across Europe will be posted in euros, and since everyone will also be paid in euros, accurate price comparisons will be made easily. Because of this, many expect a greater degree of competition, and therefore efficiency, to emerge in the European economies that use the euro.

Of course, the introduction of the euro does not come without costs. And these costs may be significant. For example, each and every vending machine, cash register, and ATM will have to be modified to accept the new euro coins and paper money, all the financial accounting systems will have to be converted, and every posted price in catalogs, menus, and on department store shelves will have to be replaced. These costs have made some economists concerned about how long it may take before the benefits of the euro begin to outweigh the tremendous costs of introducing the new currency. Since the euro represents the first time that a common currency has been adopted by so many nations representing such a large share of the world's economy, it is difficult to predict the final outcome of this bold experiment at forming a true common marketplace.

The North American Free Trade Agreement (NAFTA). The North American Free Trade Agreement creates a *free trade area* between the United States, Canada, and Mexico. A free trade area is an alliance of nations without trade barriers between its members. Members within a free trade area are allowed to set their own tariffs with nations outside the alliance. Thus, a free trade area agreement does not require the same degree of cooperation as a customs union.

A **free trade area** is an alliance of nations without trade barriers between its members.

Mexican tariffs have historically been twice as high as those of the United States, and American exporters have seized on this opportunity. Sales of American-made products in Mexico have increased dramatically since the inception of NAFTA in 1992. However, many Americans have expressed fear that NAFTA will create domestic unemployment. It is true that some unemployment will result, but it is also true that new jobs will be created. Remember the principle of comparative advantage: All trading partners gain when they specialize. Thus with NAFTA, the United States will gain jobs in the areas in which we specialize and have a comparative advantage and lose jobs in those areas in which Mexico and Canada specialize and have a comparative advantage. Although the *mix* of jobs in each of the three NAFTA nations will change to some extent, all indications are that more jobs will be created in total than are lost.

The perceived benefits of NAFTA have been so great that Chile and other Latin American countries have petitioned to join. As international trade barriers fall we can expect to experience lower prices, greater availability, and more diversity of products in our markets and stores for years to come.

The Spread of Common Markets. In general, most world leaders view the economic alliance of nations through common markets in a positive light, as evidenced by the increasing number of common markets around the globe. For example, Australia and New Zealand recently amended the Australia New Zealand Closer Economic Relations Trade Agreement (ANZCERTA) to establish a bilateral free trade zone between them, and 10 nations of southeast Asia are now members of a free trade area allied through the Association of Southeast Asian Nations (ASEAN). Other common markets and trading blocks closer to home now exist in Latin America (through the Latin American Integration Association, or LAIA), South America (through Mercado Comun del Cono Sur, or MERCOSUR), Central America (through the Central American Common Market, or CACM), and the Caribbean (through the Caribbean Community and Common Market, or CCCM). In fact, treaties establishing either custom unions or free trade areas are in effect in every populated continent of the world. Virtually every member of the WTO is a participant in one or more common market agreements.

Why have we experienced a proliferation of common market treaties? Clearly, the nations which sign such agreements must expect that membership in a common market yields economic and political benefits. In most cases, almost without exception, the establishment of a common market is a hotly debated issue among the citizens of the participating countries. The traditional protectionist arguments outlined in this chapter have been argued and debated countless times in public forums around the world. However, the promise of economic growth and improved living standards through freer international trade has caused many of the world's citizens to abandon their protectionist points of view and support the common market concept.

Given the trend toward common markets, it seems fair to inquire into the actual effects of such treaties on the economies of member nations. Such an inquiry appears at first straightforward, yet an empirical analysis of a free trade pact is fraught with difficulty. For example, if we are interested in NAFTA's effect on employment patterns, we can observe the employment patterns that exist today now that NAFTA is in place, but we cannot observe what the employment patterns would have been today if NAFTA had not been signed. Thus, researchers must make assumptions about the economic conditions that would have existed in the absence of a common market environment. Of course, different assumptions will lead to different conclusions. This is illustrated in two studies of NAFTA's effect on U.S. jobs that were published only 2 months apart. A report from the Brookings Institute concluded that NAFTA had created more jobs than it destroyed, while a report published by the Economic Policy Institute concluded that during its first 3 years NAFTA had eliminated almost 400,000 jobs.[4] Obviously, when conflicting empirical results are published by well-respected policy research institutions, the protectionist versus free trade debate will continue. However, we should note that most economists agree that free trade in the long run is beneficial to both trading partners and that many of the debatable issues concerning common markets lay in the details of the agreements which may give one nation an advantage over another in specific situations. Therefore, as long as common market agreements lead to freer international trade, they will undoubtedly continue to spread around the globe.

Summary

Recent recessions, along with the creation of the North American Free Trade Agreement and the World Trade Organization, stepped up the controversy between protectionists and free traders. Protectionists argue that imports should be limited to reduce foreign competition with goods produced in the United States, to remedy balance of trade and balance of payments problems, and to encourage U.S. industries vital to national security and economic welfare. Free traders maintain that economic welfare of a country is enhanced by voluntary free exchange among countries.

A country's consumption possibilities are usually greater when it trades with other countries than when it does not. By concentrating on the production of goods in which it has a comparative advantage and trading for goods in which it has a comparative disadvantage, the population of the country will have a larger GDP to consume and/or invest.

International exchange markets arise from international transactions. A country's demands for foreign exchange are generated by imports of goods, investments in other countries, and any other transactions that result in payments made abroad. Supplies of foreign exchange are created by exports, foreign investments in the country, and by any other transactions that cause payments to be made to the country. Exchange rates are determined by the forces of demand for and supply of currencies used in international trade.

Trade restrictions generally take the form of tariffs, quotas, or voluntary restraint agreements—all three of which result in higher prices for

---

[4]For an overview of these two reports, see David Ensign, "NAFTA: Two Sides of the Coin," *Spectrum: The Journal of State Government*, vol. 70, no. 4, September 22, 1997, p. 1.

imports as well as domestically produced goods and services. Further, trade restrictions reduce the availability of products at the consumer level. Governments can raise revenue through the imposition of tariffs, but quotas result in extra profit for holders of import licenses. Recently, voluntary restraint agreements have become more widespread, but they are difficult to enforce and are often influenced by international political relations.

Economic analysis indicates that a country's population as a whole usually loses as a result of import restrictions. Gains to the protected industries come at the expense of export industries and consumers. Balance of payments problems are essentially exchange rate problems arising when countries attempt to peg exchange rates. It appears that the preferred solution to such problems is exchange rate adjustment rather than protectionism. Protection of key industries may have some merit—if only we could determine which industries fall into this category.

In recent years, nations have sought the benefits of free trade by reducing international trade restrictions worldwide. The GATT treaty and the WTO have been instrumental in minimizing the barriers to trade between member countries. The nations of Western Europe formed the EU, and the United States entered into NAFTA in order to reap the benefits of free trade. Other groups of nations around the world have followed suit, forming their own regional custom unions and free trade areas. Many people still support protectionist policies, but the trend is toward more open markets and global economies.

Discussion Questions

1. Why do some people fear international trade? Defend the protectionist viewpoint using sound economic reasoning.
2. Explain the principle of comparative advantage. In what areas do you have a comparative advantage over your classmates? How can this be used to improve your current economic position?
3. Verbally discuss how international trade can improve the social welfare of two nations engaged in exchange. Provide an example.
4. Use diagrams to illustrate how international trade affects both the production possibilities and consumption possibilities of a trading nation.
5. What is today's exchange rate for the British pound? Convert the price of lunch in your school cafeteria to British pounds.
6. Discuss the differences between tariffs and quotas. How are they the same, and how are they different?
7. What is the balance of payments deficit? Is it a major problem? What can be done about it?
8. Discuss the differences between the European Union and the North American Free Trade Agreement. In what ways are they similar?

9. Should American workers fear the long-term effects of NAFTA? Provide a solid economic argument using the economic analysis discussed in this chapter.

10. How do international trade restrictions hurt the American consumer? Provide an example.

11. What is the WTO? Discuss the role that it serves in promoting international trade between participating nations.

12. Why have common market agreements between nations become so prevalent in today's global economy? Have such agreements been successful? Explain why or why not.

Additional Readings

Artis, Mike, and Norman Lee. *The Economics of the European Union: Policy and Analysis.* Oxford: Oxford University Press, 1997.

Volume of 15 articles that provide a comprehensive account of the economics of the European Union. Papers cover the gamut of economic topics, including monetary integration, international trade, environmental policy, and social development.

Bhagwati, Jadish. "The Case for Free Trade." *Scientific American.* November 1993, pp. 42–49.

Excellent response to those who claim that trade agreements come at the expense of environmental standards.

"The Consumer: A Force Against Protectionism." *OECD Observer* 129 (July 1984), pp. 22–25.

Explains who gains and who loses from protectionism and weighs the gains against the losses.

Gonnelli, Adam. *The Basics of Foreign Trade and Exchange.* New York: Federal Reserve Bank of New York, 1993.

This short book offers an excellent introduction to the basics of international trade and exchange.

Heilbroner, Robert L., and Lester C. Thurow. *The Economic Problem.* 7th ed. Englewood Cliffs, NJ: Prentice-Hall, 1984, Chapters 36 and 37.

Good discussion of the protectionist as well as the free trade point of view.

Irwin, Douglas A. *Managed Trade.* Washington, DC: American Enterprise Institute, 1994.

Provides an argument against trade restrictions and for free international trade.

Miller, Henri, ed. *Free Trade Vs. Protectionism.* The Reference Shelf, vol. 68, no. 4. New York: The H. W. Wilson Company, 1996.

Excellent reference source that discusses all the major economic and political aspects of global trade in today's world.

World Wide Web Resources

Europa—The European Union's Server
europa.eu.int
Europa, the European Union's Web server, provides access to press releases from EU institutions, basic information about and policies of the EU, and other links.

The European Union in the U.S.
www.eurunion.org

This is the Web home in the United States for the European Union. Provides comprehensive information on the history and status of European integration, including plans for the introduction of the euro.

National Law Center for Inter-American Free Trade
www.natlaw.com

This nonprofit research and educational institution provides the full text of major international trade treaties through its "Inter-Am Database."

North American Free Trade Agreement (NAFTA)
the-tech.mit.edu/Bulletins/nafta.html

Provides the complete text of the agreement on the Web.

Organization of American States (OAS)
www.oas.org

OAS is the world's oldest regional organization. It provides links to public information, programs and issues, member states and observers, and current international issues.

United States Foreign Trade Statistics
www.census.gov/foreign-trade/www

Part of the Census Bureau. Gives links to foreign trade statistics, who's who in foreign trade, and other trade data.

United States Trade Representative Home Page
www.ustr.gov

Provides links to reports, agreements, mission of the department, history of the department, and other information.

CHAPTER 11

Unemployment Issues
Why Do We Waste Our Labor Resources?

Chapter Outline

Costs of Unemployment
Economic Costs
Noneconomic Costs

What Is Unemployment?
The Labor Force
Unemployment in a Market Economy

Analysis of the Unemployment Problem
Types of Unemployment
Further Dimensions of the Unemployment Problem

What Causes People to Lose Their Jobs?
Circular Flow of Economic Activity

Aggregate Demand
Aggregate Supply
Aggregate Demand and Supply
Reasons for Deficient Aggregate Demand
Reasons for Weak Aggregate Supply

Combating Unemployment
Aggregate Demand Policies
Aggregate Supply Policies and the Economy in the 1980s
The Decade of the 90s: Recession, Recovery, and Expansion

Summary

Checklist of Economic Concepts

Labor force
Discouraged workers
Frictional unemployment
Structural unemployment
Cyclical unemployment
Full-employment unemployment rate

Circular flow of production and income
Aggregate demand
Marginal propensity to consume
Marginal propensity to save
Psychological law of consumption

Investment multiplier
Aggregate supply
Leakages
Injections
Aggregate demand policies
Aggregate supply policies

I'd get up at five in the morning and head for the waterfront. Outside the Spreckles Sugar Refinery, outside the gates, there would be a thousand men. You know dang well there's only three or four jobs. The guy would come out with two little Pinkerton cops: "I need two guys for the bull gang. Two guys to go into the hole." A thousand men would fight like a pack of Alaskan dogs to get through there. Only four of us would get through. I was too young a punk.

So you'd drift up to Skid Row. There'd be thousands of men there. Guys on baskets, making weird speeches, phony theories on economics. About 11:30, the real leaders would take over. They'd say: OK, we're going to City Hall. The mayor was Angelo Rossi, a dapper little guy. He wore expensive boots and a tight vest. We'd shout around the steps. Finally, he'd come out and tell us nothing.

I remember the demands: We demand work, we demand shelter for our families, we demand groceries, this kind of thing. . . .

I remember as a kid how courageous this seemed to me, the demands, because you knew that society wasn't going to give it to you. They'd demand that they open up unrented houses and give decent shelters for their families. But you just knew society wasn't yielding. There was nothing coming.[1]

[1]Studs Terkel, *Hard Times* (New York: Random House, 1970), p. 30.

Costs of Unemployment

Two kinds of costs are related to unemployment. The first is the economic cost, which can be measured rather precisely. The second is the social, or noneconomic, cost, which is just as real as the economic cost but more difficult to assess and measure.

Economic Costs

The economic cost of unemployment to the person unemployed is the loss in income and the resulting decrease in consumption and saving. The economic cost of unemployment to the economy, as explained in Chapter 1, takes the form of a decrease in the production of goods and services because the economy is not operating on its production possibilities curve. It is operating instead inside the production possibilities curve, and the full potential of the economy is not being realized. The sum of the losses in income of the unemployed equals the losses in production and therefore the total economic cost of unemployment.

Another interesting thing to keep in mind regarding the production possibilities curve and the economic cost of unemployment is that the opportunity cost of decreasing unemployment may be low, or even zero. Production can be expanded for a given product without a decrease in the production of other products when the economy is operating inside the production possibilities curve. However, if unemployment is reduced below a certain rate, inflation rears its ugly head. This problem is discussed in the next chapter.

Noneconomic Costs

Unemployment threatens the stability of the family as an economic and social unit. Without income or with a loss of income, the head of the family cannot play the role in which he or she was cast. Family wants and needs are not fulfilled, and family relationships suffer as a consequence. Economic and social dependency and important family ties may be in jeopardy and eventually may be severed by prolonged unemployment. High unemployment rates have been found to be associated with drug abuse, higher divorce rates, and higher crime rates generally.

Human relationships outside the family are also seriously affected by unemployment. An unemployed person loses self-respect and influence among those who are employed, faces possible rejection by working companions, and experiences a possible loss of pride and confidence. In the end, the unemployed may become emotionally disabled.

Some families may be economically and socially prepared for unemployment. Perhaps they have savings they have set aside just in case of a rainy day, or maybe they can receive financial support from other family members. However, unemployment generally has a profound effect on families the least prepared and capable of withstanding either its economic or social effects. The incidence of unemployment, for example, is high among low-income groups.

What Is Unemployment?

It would seem that unemployment could be easily defined. However, there are many complexities and ramifications concerning its meaning. The first thought about unemployment may be that the unemployed are people without jobs. This may be true, but many people without jobs are not considered unemployed. What about a person who prefers leisure to work? Are persons over 65 to be considered unemployed? Is a full-time college student included in the unemployment count?

Our approach to unemployment in this section is, first, to give the official definition of the labor force and, second, to elucidate the importance of the unemployment problem. The subsequent sections probe deeper into the sources of unemployment.

The Labor Force

To understand how employment is defined and measured, we must first become familiar with the concept of an economy's labor force. A labor force consists of all the human resources currently engaged in, or available for, productive economic activity in an economy. A nation's culture and legal institutions determine which human resources will be included in the force. In the United States we define the *labor force* as including all noninstitutionalized individuals 16 years of age and older who are either employed for pay, actively seeking employment, or awaiting recall from a temporary layoff. This definition is used by the U.S. Department of Labor to measure the size and growth of our labor force over time. Other nations use slightly different definitions, which sometimes make international comparisons difficult.

There are several aspects of the official labor force definition that are important to understand. First, note that individuals who are institutionalized are not included in the labor force. Institutions include jails, prisons, mental hospitals, and long-term nursing homes. Second, members of the labor force must be at least 16 years of age. In the United States, children under the age of 16 are subject to child labor laws and are not legally available for many types of paid work. Third, note that the labor force includes those who are employed and those who are unemployed. The employed members of the labor force consist of those who are working for pay. Anyone who works at least 1 hour per week and receives pay is considered to be an employed member of the labor force. Unemployed members of the labor force include those who are actively seeking employment and those waiting to be called back from a layoff.

It is crucial to realize that being without work is not a sufficient condition to be counted as unemployed in the United States. An individual must be actively seeking employment or available for work during a temporary layoff. Someone who is actively seeking employment undertakes the normal job search activities such as responding to want ads, submitting resumes and job applications, and taking interviews with prospective employers. When someone stops actively searching for a job, he or she no longer satisfies the labor force definition and is therefore not counted as being unemployed. The unemployed who give up their job search activities and officially leave the labor force are called *discouraged workers*. Some economists believe that the official measures of unemployment may underestimate the problem during downturns in the business cycle due to the existence of discouraged workers.

The **labor force** includes all noninstitutionalized individuals 16 years of age and older who are either employed for pay, actively seeking employment, or awaiting recall from a temporary layoff.

Discouraged workers are not included in the official measures of unemployment because they have stopped actively searching for work and are no longer in the labor force.

Today the labor force in the United States is approaching 137 million members. The vast majority of the labor force is employed. Still, every month there are millions of Americans who are counted as being unemployed. Why does unemployment occur and what can be done about it?

Unemployment in a Market Economy

The economic aspect of unemployment originates from a situation in which the quantity of labor demanded is less than the quantity supplied at the market wage rate. This results in unemployment. Unemployment occurs when wage rates are too high, that is, above competitive levels. The solution to unemployment is to expand demand or, if competitive forces are operating, to rely on automatic market forces to drive wage rates down to the level at which the amount of labor demanded equals the amount supplied.

Figure 11–1 clarifies the meaning of unemployment in a competitive economy. DD and SS are the demand and supply curves for labor. The wage rate is w_1. The amount of labor demanded at this wage rate is e_0, and the amount supplied is e_1. This difference between e_0 and e_1 is the unemployment at the wage rate of w_1. In a purely competitive situation, wage rates would be forced down to w, and unemployment would disappear.

Analysis of the Unemployment Problem

Types of Unemployment

The meaning of unemployment may be elucidated further by distinguishing between different types of unemployment. Three major types are frictional, structural, and cyclical unemployment.

Frictional unemployment usually originates on the labor supply side of the market, is transitional, and is often in the form of people changing and searching for new jobs.

Frictional Unemployment. *Frictional unemployment* is transitional or short-run in nature. It usually originates on the labor supply side; that is, labor services are voluntarily not employed. A good illustration is the unemployment that occurs when people are changing jobs or searching for new jobs. The matching of job openings and job seekers does not always take place smoothly in the economy, and, as a consequence, people are without work.

The important thing about frictional unemployment is that it does not last. Frictional unemployment may exist at all times in the economy, but for any one person or family it is transitional. Therefore, frictional unemployment is not considered a significant economic problem, and it can be reduced by improvements in the flow of information concerning job openings.

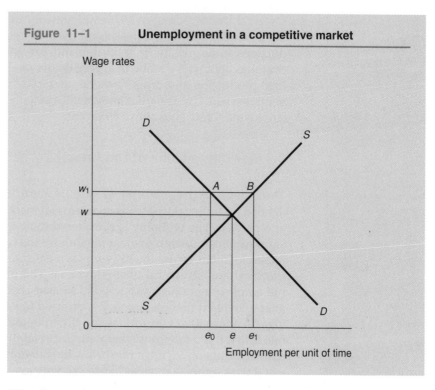

Figure 11–1   **Unemployment in a competitive market**

DD = Demand curve for labor
SS = Supply curve for labor
e_0 = Amount of labor demanded at w_1
e_1 = Amount of labor supplied at w_1
$e_1 - e_0$ = Unemployment

Structural unemployment is unemployment that is caused by fundamental changes in demand for certain kinds of labor due to, say, technological changes or changes in consumers' tastes and preferences.

Structural Unemployment. *Structural unemployment* is usually long-run in nature and usually originates on the demand side of labor. Structural unemployment results from economic changes that cause the demand for specific kinds of labor to be low relative to the supply in particular markets and regions of the economy.

A relatively low demand for labor in a given market may be due to several factors. Technological change, although expected to reduce costs and expand the productive capacity of the overall economy, may have devastating effects in a particular market. Changes in consumer preferences for products expand production and employment in some areas but reduce them in others. Immobility of labor prolongs the period of unemployment that may have originated due to technological change and changes in consumers' tastes. A reduction in job opportunities should induce the unemployed to move, but immobility may prevent this from taking place.

Cyclical unemployment is unemployment caused by a contraction in aggregate demand or total spending in the economy.

Cyclical Unemployment. Unemployment caused by economic fluctuations is called *cyclical unemployment.* Cyclical unemployment is due to reductions in aggregate or total demand for goods and services in the overall economy. A decline in aggregate demand in the economy reduces total production and causes general unemployment throughout the economic system. Cyclical unemployment is usually the culprit when the unemployment rate goes above 6 percent.

Further Dimensions of the Unemployment Problem

The **full-employment unemployment rate** is the rate that reflects frictional and structural unemployment, and is consistent with price stability.

The Full-Employment Unemployment Rate. Full employment is often defined for policy purposes as an unemployment rate of, for example, 4, 5, or 6 percent. The economy is considered to be operating at less than full employment at unemployment rates above the full-employment rate. The unemployment below the full-employment rate is supposed to measure frictional and structural unemployment. The unemployment above the full-employment rate is supposed to measure cyclical unemployment, the unemployment that fiscal policy is directed toward reducing or eliminating. An alternative way of viewing the full-employment unemployment rate is that it is a rate consistent with price stability. Any policy attempt to reduce the unemployment rate below the full-employment rate, or the *natural rate,* as some economists like to say, will accelerate the rate of inflation. In the 1950s and 1960s, full employment was defined in reference to a 4 percent unemployment rate. In the 1970s, the rate was increased to 5 percent, and in the early 1980s it was increased to a range between 5 and 6 percent. Presently, there seems to be a general consensus among economists that a rate of unemployment of 5.5 percent is consistent with a nonaccelerating inflation rate. The basic reasons for defining full employment in terms of a higher unemployment rate are the increasing probability of higher inflation rates when unemployment rates fall below a certain rate and a recognition of structural changes in the labor force such as the increasing number of women and teenagers in the labor force and the restructuring of industries in response to technological advances.

Unemployment Rates over Time. Figure 11–2 shows unemployment rates in selected years from 1961 to 1998. The selected years are the high and low unemployment rates during this period. Unemployment rates follow the ups and downs in the economy and are generally above the unemployment rate officially targeted for policy purposes as full employment. The high unemployment rate in the 1960s centered in 1961 when the rate was 6.7 percent. This occurred during the 1960–1961 recession. After 1961, the unemployment rate declined steadily as the economy expanded, reaching a low rate of 3.5 percent in 1969. For 4 years, 1966 through 1969, during this decade the unemployment rate was under the

Figure 11–2   **High and low unemployment rates during the period 1961–1998***

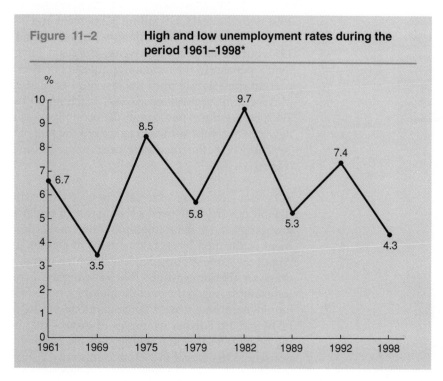

*The unemployment rate in 1998 is the unemployment rate for the months of April and May.
Source: Economic Report of the President, February 1998, p. 330; and *Economic Trends,* Federal Reserve Bank of Cleveland, July 1998, p. 11.

full-employment target rate of 4 percent. The unemployment rate rose steadily during the first half of the 1970s, reaching a high of 8.5 percent in 1975, which was the last year of the 1973–1975 recession. The rate of unemployment decreased somewhat between 1975 and 1979, falling to 5.8 percent in 1979. With the exception of 1 year, 1970, the unemployment rate stayed above the rate of 5 percent, which was established as the rate consistent with full employment during this decade. The 1981–1982 contraction in the economy sent the unemployment rate soaring to almost 10 percent in 1982, the highest since the Great Depression of the 1930s. Job opportunities began to improve in 1983 as the economy embarked on a record-breaking economic expansion. The result was a steady decrease in the unemployment rate to 5.3 percent in 1989. The economy began to show signs of a recession in the summer of 1990, and the unemployment rate began to increase. The recession officially began in the third quarter, of 1990, when the real GDP fell about 1 percent. This downward trend in the economy continued in the fourth quarter and in the first quarter of

1991 with the real GDP falling 3.2 percent and 2.4 percent, respectively, in these two quarters. The economy turned around in the second quarter of 1991, but the recovery was weak. The real GDP grew at a slow rate of less than 2 percent in the remaining quarters of 1991 and did not exceed a 3.5 percent growth rate until the last quarter of 1992. As a result, the unemployment rate continued to rise, reaching a peak of 7.7 percent in June 1992, before the expansion in the economy was rapid enough to provide new jobs at a pace sufficient to reduce the rate of unemployment. Between 1992 and 1998, the unemployment rate fell from 7.4 percent to 4.3 percent (Figure 11–2).

Who Are the Unemployed? Just as we learned in Chapter 7 that the overall poverty rate masks the degree of poverty faced by certain family groupings, the general unemployment rate hides the degree of unemployment confronted by certain persons in a given unemployment grouping. About the same groups that have a much higher poverty rate than the average are the same groups that have higher unemployment rates. In 1997 for example, when the overall unemployment rate was 4.9 percent, the unemployment rate was 14 percent among young persons between the ages of 16 and 19. Further examples of groups that have much higher unemployment rates than the average rate are families with a female head of the household (8 percent in 1997 and minority groups (8.8 percent in 1997).

What Causes People to Lose Their Jobs?

People lose their jobs in a recession when production in the economy is failing. But what causes the recession? What causes a decline in production? Economists have searched for a single answer and have found many: not enough spending, too much saving, or relatively high wages. Thus, the answer is neither simple nor single. There are many contributory causes; we shall try to explain those that seem to be the most important.

Circular Flow of Economic Activity

To understand why people lose their jobs, it is necessary to understand how jobs are created. This is not difficult in terms of the forces of supply and demand pertaining to products in individual markets. We have established an understanding of equilibrium prices and quantities demanded for individual commodities such as wheat, automobiles, dresses, televisions, ice cream, necklaces, and all other commodities produced in our economy. We now move from demand and supply curves for individual products to a demand-supply curve representing all commodities. Thus, we present an overview of the operation of the economy, which economists call the *circular flow of economic activity*.

The circular flow is illustrated in Figure 11–3. The relationships it shows are important in understanding the operation of the economy. (Study this figure carefully.)

Income and jobs are created in a society when goods and services are produced. Owners of resources—labor, capital, and natural resources— sell their productive services to producers who, in turn, pay them money in the form of wages, interest, rent, and profits. The flow of productive services to producers represents the supply of resources, and the flow of money payments from producers represents the demand for resources. Producers transform productive services or resources into goods and services through the production process and sell the goods and services to households. They receive a flow of money payments from households in exchange. The flow from producers to households represents the aggregate supply of goods and services, and the flow of money payments from households to producers represents the aggregate demand for them.

There are several points to remember about the circular flow. First, there are two markets: a resource market and a product market. The prices of resources and employment are determined in the resource market, and the prices of goods and production are determined in the product market. Second, the resource and product markets are interrelated. The demand

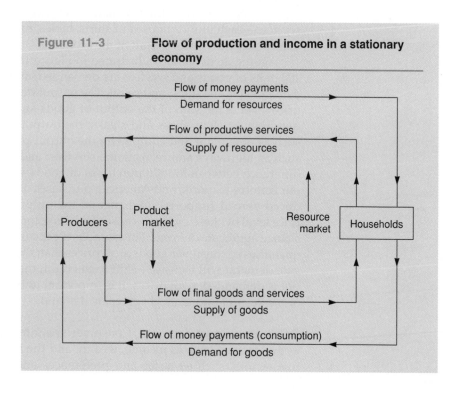

Figure 11–3   **Flow of production and income in a stationary economy**

Flow of money payments
Demand for resources

Flow of productive services
Supply of resources

Producers   Product market   Resource market   Households

Flow of final goods and services
Supply of goods

Flow of money payments (consumption)
Demand for goods

for goods creates a demand for the resources that are used to produce goods. The costs of producing goods depend on the prices paid and the quantities of resources used in production. Third, there are two circular flows involved in the economy—a real flow of productive services (labor, capital, and natural resources) and products (autos, dresses, medical services) and a flow of money payments to owners of resources for productive services and to producers for goods and services. Fourth, real income is determined by the physical goods and services produced, and money income is the money value of the physical goods and services produced.

The circular flow of economic activity shows in a simple way how the overall economy operates. It emphasizes the interdependency of economic variables—the dependency of income on production, production on spending, spending on income, demand for resources on the demand for products, and so on. Now we shall turn to the product market in order to find possible reasons why people lose their jobs.

Aggregate Demand

Aggregate demand is a schedule showing output demanded at different price levels.

Aggregate demand is a schedule showing total output demanded in the economy at different prices. Since we are concerned with the prices of all goods and services, we must view prices as an average, or as a price level. Since we are also concerned with the quantities of all goods and services, we must view the quantities demanded as composite units of goods and services—each unit composed of shirts, tables, food, fuel, and other items that constitute the real output of the economy.

Aggregate demand is illustrated in Figure 11–4. At the price level p_1, 200 units of goods and services are demanded; at the price level p, output demanded is 400 units, and so on. The output demanded of goods at any price level is the sum of the output of goods and services purchased by *consumers*, such as shoes and steaks; the output purchased by *investors*, such as new plant and equipment; the output purchased by *government*, such as highways and recreational services; and net exports, that is, the difference between foreign purchases of goods and services produced in our country (exports) and American purchases of goods and services produced abroad (imports). A change in the output demanded at a given price level by these groups—consumers, investors, and government—will change aggregate demand. For example, if consumers begin to buy greater quantities of consumer goods at all prices than they did previously, aggregate demand will increase—shift to the right, indicating that greater output is demanded at all prices. It is important at this time to discuss some of the key determinants of aggregate demand.

Consumer Spending (*C*). Consumer spending is determined by objective factors, such as income, wealth, and the interest rate, and subjective factors, such as tastes and preferences and consumer confidence.

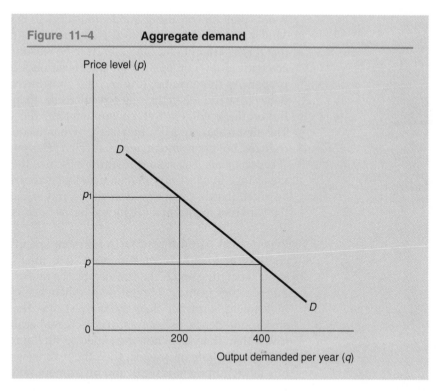

Figure 11–4   **Aggregate demand**

DD is an aggregate demand schedule that shows the output demanded at differ-ent price levels. For example, at price level p_1, 200 units of goods and services are demanded.

Consumer spending is positively related to income and wealth, and nega-tively related to the interest rate; that is to say, we expect that the output demanded by consumers at every price level would be greater when their income and wealth rise due to the increased ability to buy and that it would be lower when the interest rate increases because it would be more costly to buy on credit. Tastes and preferences—and consumer confi-dence—play an important role because these variables influence the propensity of consumers to spend and save given the income and wealth of consumers. Among all these variables that determine C, the income of consumers is generally considered the most important variable. A more logical way of saying this is that C depends upon income (Y), given these other variables. To extend the relationship between C and Y further, an im-portant concept to understand is the *marginal propensity to consume (MPC)*. The *MPC* is the change in consumption divided by the change in income. Assuming the *MPC* is ⅘, then an increase in Y of $100 billion will increase C $80 billion and increase saving (S) $20 billion. In this instance, the *mar-ginal propensity to save (MPS)* is ⅕, for any part of an increase in income that

Marginal propensity to consume is the change in consumption divided by the change in income.

Marginal propensity to save is the change in sav-ing divided by the change in income.

is not spent on consumer goods and services is saved. The *MPC* plus the *MPS* is always, then, equal to 1. Two general characteristics of the *MPC* are that it is less than 1 and that it tends to be reasonably stable. This last characteristic does not mean that all consumers have the same marginal propensity to consume; low-income consumers will have a higher tendency to spend when their income increases than high-income consumers. But on the average for all consumers the *MPC* does not vary over time. This first feature of *MPC* means that when income changes, consumption changes, but not as much, which is often referred to as the *psychological law of consumption.* The second feature indicates that when income changes, the change in consumption can usually be accurately predicted. It should be noted that in the discussion above and in the discussion to follow, all the variables mentioned are in real terms or constant prices.

Psychological law of consumption states that when income changes, consumption changes, but by less than the change in income.

Investment Spending (*I*). Investment spending is primarily the purchase of new equipment and plant. It is much more volatile than consumer spending and is determined by the rate of interest and the expected rate of return from new investment. When the expected rate of return from investment is greater than the interest rate, the inducement to invest is strong, and hence, investment will increase because it is more profitable to invest than to lend. When the expected rate of return from investment is less than the rate of interest, then the reverse is true—the inducement to buy new equipment is weak and investment will fall. It follows, then, that when the expected rate of return or the expected profit rate is equal to the interest rate, the level of investment is determined; that is, investment spending will not increase or decrease under these circumstances. Expectations play a strategic role in the determination of investment spending. It is not the current profit rate that determines investment but the "expected" profit rate. New investment has to compete with old investment. The fact that the current rate on some existing investment is greater than the rate of interest does not ensure that new investment will be profitable. An increase in the supply of apartments for rent, for example, will tend to decrease the rent that may be charged for apartments and reduce the net income flow from such an investment. Under such circumstances, the profit rate from investments in rental apartments would be expected to be reduced, and, depending upon the rate of interest, may result in a decision not to invest. It is the role of expectation in making investment decisions along with the state of confidence of investors that causes the output demanded by investors to follow a cyclical pattern over time.

Investment Multiplier. There is another aspect of investment spending that calls for special analysis. An increase in investment of $1 will increase income or output demanded by more than $1. This is easy to understand. Suppose an automobile plant was constructed in your town with the cost of the plant and equipment at $100 million. In addition to the output demanded by this investment, a chain of consumer spending will be set off by this investment, resulting in an increase in output demanded or income greater than the cost of the investment. The connecting link between a given change in investment and the resulting change in income is the *investment multiplier.* The multiplier is a numerical coefficient such as 3, 4, or 5. It is the reciprocal of 1 minus the marginal propensity to consume, or simply the reciprocal of the marginal propensity to save. For an example, if the *MPC* is ⅘, the multiplier is 5 [1/ (1 − ⅘)]. The investment multiplier times the change in investment spending will equal the change in income. In the illustration of the investment in the auto plant, income will increase $500 million as a result of an investment of $100 million, assuming an *MPC* of ⅘. The increase in income or output demanded of $500 million will be composed of an increase in output demanded by investors of $100 million and an increase in output demanded by consumers of $400 million. The increase in income, assuming an *MPC* of ¾, would be $400 million (4 × $100 million), assuming again an increase in investment of $100 million. The breakdown between the increase in investment spending and consumer spending in this instance would be an increase in investment spending of $100 million and an increase in consumer spending of $300 million. The increase in consumption, resulting from increase in investment, will always be the marginal propensity to consume times the change in income.

> **Investment multiplier** is the reciprocal of 1 minus the marginal propensity to consume.

Government Purchases (*G*). Government purchases are the final output of goods and services demanded by government. Government purchases have an impact on income or output demanded similar to the impact of investment; that is, an increase in *G* will have a multiplier effect on income. With respect to the multiplier, it is necessary to distinguish between government spending in the form of purchases of final goods and services and in the form of transfer payments. Government transfer payments such as Social Security payments are payments to individuals and do not directly increase output demanded. Income or output demanded is indirectly affected by transfer payments, for the recipients of the transfer payments will have an increase in their disposable income and will increase their consumption as a consequence. Thus, an increase in government transfer payments will set into action a higher flow of consumer spending, but the multiplier effect will be smaller than an equal increase in *G* due to the fact that transfer payments per se do not increase output demanded. More specifically, the transfer payment multiplier is the regular multiplier minus 1. For example, if the regular multiplier is 5, the transfer payment multiplier is 4. Government lump-sum taxes (taxes that do not vary with income) have an impact on income exactly the same as transfer payments, except that the impact is in the opposite direction. An increase in transfer payments, then, financed by an equal increase in lump-sum taxes, will not change output demanded. On the other hand, an increase in *G* financed by an equal increase in the same kind of taxes will increase output demanded. The increase in output demanded is equal to the increase in *G* because the difference between the government purchase multiplier and the tax multiplier is equal to 1.

Exports and Imports.   The final two variables that influence output demanded in the economy are exports and imports. Exports increase output demanded and imports reduce output demanded. The net effect of international trade on output demanded, therefore, can be measured by the difference between our exports and imports, or net exports. When net exports are increasing, the effect is to increase output demanded, and when net exports are decreasing, the effect is to decrease output demanded. A so-called *trade deficit* means that net exports are negative or that exports are less than imports. A *trade surplus* means the reverse—that exports are greater than imports.

Aggregate Supply

Aggregate supply is a schedule showing the output supplied at different price levels.

Aggregate supply is a schedule showing the output supplied at different price levels. It is generally shown as an upward-sloping curve, reflecting increasing marginal costs of producing higher levels of national output. It is profitable to produce higher levels of national output only at higher price levels when higher marginal costs are associated with higher levels of national output.

The determinants of aggregate supply are the same as the determinants of individual supply curves, namely, resource prices and techniques of production. Aggregate supply varies inversely with resource prices; that is, higher resource prices decrease aggregate supply, and lower resource prices increase aggregate supply. Improvements in production techniques that increase the productivity of resources increase aggregate supply.

Two aggregate supply curves, SS and S_1S_1, are shown in Figure 11–5. Both these supply curves indicate the positive relationship between output supplied and the price level. At the price level p, output supplied is q, given SS, and q_1, given S_1S_1. In reference to aggregate supply SS, aggregate supply S_1S_1 indicates an increase in aggregate supply. The output supplied at q_f is full employment.

Aggregate Demand and Supply

Employment and job opportunities depend on both aggregate demand and supply. Figure 11–6 (page 316) shows three aggregate demand curves and two aggregate supply curves. Beginning with aggregate demand DD and aggregate supply SS, the equilibrium price level is p, and output demanded and supplied is q. The economy is experiencing unemployment at this equilibrium level of national output, as indicated by the difference between q and q_f, the full-employment level of output. Given aggregate

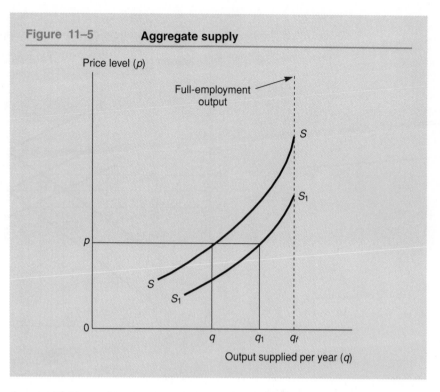

Figure 11–5   **Aggregate supply**

Aggregate supply shows the output supplied at different price levels. At the price level p, output supplied is q, given aggregate supply SS, and q_1, given aggregate S_1S_1. Aggregate supply S_1S_1 represents a greater aggregate supply.

supply SS, the economy could reach full-employment output only with a greater aggregate demand as represented by D_2D_2. At this level of aggregate demand, the equilibrium price level is p_2—much higher than it was at the lower level of aggregate demand. However, given the higher level of aggregate supply S_1S_1 and the higher level of aggregate demand D_1D_1, full employment could be reached at the price level p.

It can be said that at price level p and at the output level q, both aggregate demand and aggregate supply are deficient, for the economy is not operating at full employment when DD and SS represent the strength of aggregate demand and supply. What are some of the reasons for a relatively weak aggregate demand and supply?

Reasons for Deficient Aggregate Demand

Aggregate demand may not be high enough to provide for a full-employment economy for many reasons. A deficient aggregate demand may be due to an inadequate level of output demanded by consumers. Consumers may reduce their rate of spending for the many reasons that

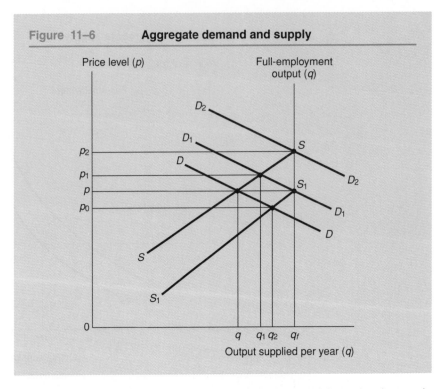

Figure 11–6   Aggregate demand and supply

Starting with *DD* and *SS*, the equilibrium price level is *p* and the national output is *q*. Full-employment output q_f can be reached by an increase in aggregate demand to D_2D_2. Full-employment output can be reached at a lower demand D_1D_1 if aggregate supply can be increased to S_1S_1.

have been discussed, such as changes in tastes, reductions in real income and wealth, and rising interest rates. The weakness in aggregate demand may be traced to the level of investment spending that falls short of the investment spending that would be required for a full-employment economy due to a fall in the expected profit rate and/or a rise in the interest rate. The deficiency in aggregate demand may be related to reductions in government purchases or increases in taxes that discourage private spending. Finally, aggregate demand may be deficient because of a high level of imports relative to exports. All or any of these reasons may explain why the economy may not operate at its full potential.

In order to understand more thoroughly why the economy may not operate at full employment, let's return to the circular flow of economic activity. The circular flow of economic activity shows that income is created in the process of production and that income created in production may return to producers in the form of spending for the products produced. However, there may be breaks in the circular flow.

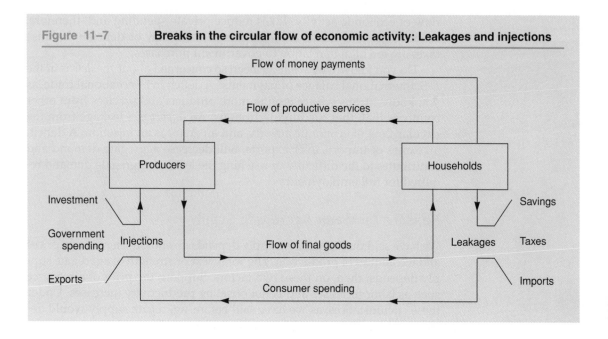

Figure 11–7   **Breaks in the circular flow of economic activity: Leakages and injections**

These breaks are called *leakages* and *injections*. Figure 11–7 shows the leakages and injections in the circular flow of economic activity. Leakages, or withdrawals from the flow of economic activity, may be offset by injections to the flow of economic activity. An example of a leakage is *saving*, and an example of an injection is *investment*. Saving means that people are not spending part of the income created in production on the purchase of consumer goods such as radios, apples, cigarettes, ties, or refrigerators. This may turn out all right. Saving is required for the economy to invest in new plant and equipment and to grow. If the rate of saving at full employment returns to the circular flow of economic activity through investment (that is, the purchase of investment goods such as plant and equipment), aggregate demand will be sufficient to buy all the goods and services produced. If full-employment saving is greater than full-employment investment, then aggregate demand will be deficient unless other injections into the circular flow are greater than other leakages by the amount of difference between saving and investment. When aggregate demand is deficient, part of the income created by production does not return to producers in the form of spending. This results in surpluses at current market prices and employment levels. Producers respond to a surplus market situation by reducing production (and, therefore, income), causing people to lose their jobs.

Another example of a leakage is government taxes, and the corresponding example of an injection is *government purchases*. Taxes are similar to saving in the sense that they represent a withdrawal from the circular flow of economic activity. Taxes reduce private spending and, therefore, reduce aggregate demand. Aggregate demand may be deficient because taxes are too high in relation to government purchases.

Do you know why we have been so concerned about the *deficit* in the U.S. international balance of payments? A deficit in international trade, as you know, means we are buying more products and services from other countries than they are buying from us. An *import* is a leakage from the circular flow of economic activity, and an *export* is an injection. A deficit, an excess of imports over exports, will decrease aggregate demand and contributes to the difficulty of reaching the level of aggregate demand required for full employment.

Reasons for Weak Aggregate Supply

We have said that aggregate supply depends essentially on resource prices and techniques of production. The weakness or strength of aggregate supply depends, then, on these two factors. Suppose the price of a resource such as labor increases and is not offset by productivity increases. Under these circumstances, as we have said before, aggregate supply would decrease and cause unemployment. As we have also said previously, the weakness in aggregate supply may be attributable to the low productivity of labor.

The motivating force behind aggregate supply in a market economy is the profit motive. Producers are not going to expand output if it is not profitable to do so. The relationship between employment and wages and productivity may be extended further. It is profitable to expand employment out to the point where the real wage equals the marginal productivity of labor. In Figure 11–8, with the demand or the marginal product of labor shown by DD and the real wage equal to w, the equilibrium or profitable level of employment is equal to n. There are two ways in which it would be profitable to expand output and increase employment to n_1. One way is for the real wage to decrease to w_1. The second way is for the marginal product of labor to increase to D_1D_1. Again, the weakness of aggregate supply is closely linked to wages and productivity.

The weakness of aggregate supply can be related to incentives to save and work. The stock of real capital assets in the economy cannot increase unless there is an adequate flow of savings to finance real investment. It is the stock of real capital assets that determines the general productivity of the economy. If incentives to save are seriously reduced, say, by taxes, saving could be inadequate to provide for the replacement, modernization, and additions to the economy's capital stock. Certain taxes and certain government expenditure programs may reduce incentives to work by lowering the relative price of leisure. As a consequence, people may work less and take more leisure, resulting in a decrease in the supply of labor and a weaker aggregate supply.

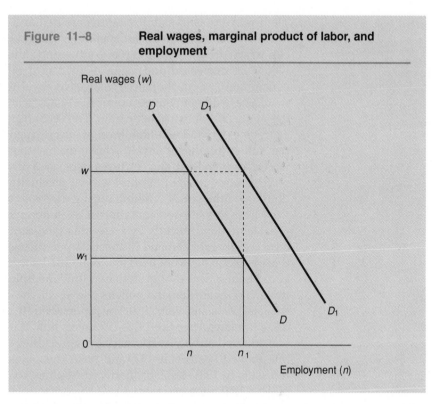

Figure 11–8   **Real wages, marginal product of labor, and employment**

Given the demand or marginal product of labor *DD*, and the real wage *w*, the level of employment is *n*. There are two ways to increase employment to n_1. One way is to reduce the real wage to w_1. The second way is to increase the marginal product of labor to D_1D_1.

Combating Unemployment

Unemployment has to be approached from both sides of the market since it may arise from the demand side or the supply side of the market. In the 1950s, 1960s, and 1970s, an aggregate demand approach was taken to cope with unemployment. More attention has been given to the supply approach in recent years because of some aggregate demand policy failures and because unemployment appears to stem more from the side of supply than in the past.

Aggregate Demand Policies

Aggregate demand policies are based on aggregate demand theory. This theory develops and explains the determinants of private consumer and investment spending. Two policy views have emerged from this theory.

The first view is to stabilize aggregate demand over the business cycle. This means that government spending would be increased and/or taxes cut when private spending is contracting, and government spending would be decreased and/or taxes increased when private spending is expanding. The effect of these changes in government spending and taxes would be to smooth out economic fluctuations in the economy by stabilizing aggregate demand over time. The second policy view is to stabilize aggregate demand at a high level of employment and production, say, at the full-employment level, which means that government spending would be increased and/or taxes decreased any time the economy was not operating at the full-employment production level. This latter view dominated the policy thinking during the 1960s and most of the 1970s.

The aggregate demand approach to unemployment is to increase aggregate demand directly by increasing government purchases and to increase aggregate demand indirectly by reducing taxes. Policies based on this approach have not been an unqualified success. The economy experienced a long period of growth and low unemployment rates in the 1960s under aggregate demand policies. However, the inflation rate increased in the late 1960s and very little was done about it, and what was done was done too late. After the 1973–1975 recession, the economy expanded but encountered strong inflationary pressures that erupted into an inflation rate above 10 percent in 1979 and 1980. Then, the economy fell into a sharp recession in 1981–1982, primarily in response to contractionary economic policies that were necessary to rid the economy of inflationary forces that were permitted to build up in the latter part of the 70s. This set the stage for the introduction of aggregate supply policies to cope with the problem of unemployment.

Aggregate Supply Policies and the Economy in the 1980s

Aggregate supply policies are based on aggregate supply theory. This theory provides the framework for analyzing the determinants of aggregate supply. The implication of the theory is that an alternative approach to unemployment is to pursue policies that would increase aggregate supply. The drawback in the supply-side approach is not in the theory but in the difficulty of designing a policy that will increase aggregate supply. What sort of economic policy will reduce resource prices and increase productivity in the economy?

The Reagan administration did set into action, beginning in 1981, policies that were at least inspired by supply-side thinking, even though the policies had an impact on aggregate demand as well as aggregate supply. The most significant policy from a supply-side viewpoint was the reduction in federal tax rates, especially the reduction in the marginal income tax rate from 70 to 50 percent, and then (in 1986), to 28 percent. The stated purpose of these marginal tax rate reductions was to increase aggregate supply by increasing incentives to save, work, and produce.

The economy responded well to the above policy incentives (and to other underlying forces in the market) and started to expand in 1983. The real growth rate in the gross domestic product (GDP) was 3.9 percent and 6.2 percent in 1983 and 1984, respectively. The expansion continued during the rest of the 1980s but at a slower growth rate. The growth rate was 2.5 percent in 1989. Figure 11–9 shows the role that the different component parts of the GDP have played in the expansion.

Consumer spending played an important role in bringing the economy out of the 1982 recession and in sustaining the expansion into 1990. Consumption was maintained, even during the recession, and increased steadily from 1982 to 1990. Investment, as usual, was more volatile in nature, decreasing and contributing to the recessionary forces in 1982 but increasing and contributing to the rapid real growth in the economy during 1983 and 1984. Between 1984 and 1990, investment remained at about the same rate. Government (federal, state, and local) purchases of goods and services were a stimulating force throughout the expansionary period from 1983 to 1990, increasing in real terms $263 billion over this time span.

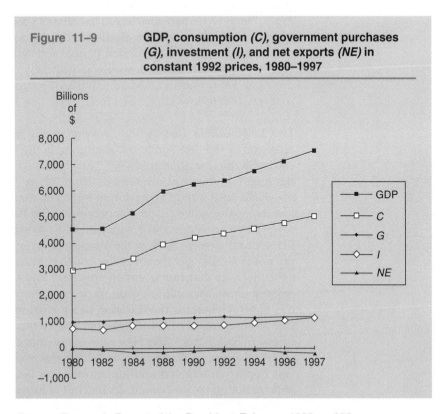

Figure 11–9   **GDP, consumption *(C)*, government purchases *(G)*, investment *(I)*, and net exports *(NE)* in constant 1992 prices, 1980–1997**

Source: Economic Report of the President, February 1998, p. 282.

On the other hand, net exports (exports − imports) were a contractionary force during the first part of the period. Export deficits increased from $63 billion in 1983 to $164 billion in 1986. The export deficit was reduced over the remaining expansionary period to $62 billion in 1990. Even though there were trade deficits in each year from 1986 to 1990, exports increased faster than imports during these years, contributing to the expansion.

What role did federal economic policy play in the economic expansion that began in 1983? The cut in income tax rates and the increase in federal purchases of goods and services together stimulated both aggregate demand and supply. However, the private sector not only had to respond to these policies and other market forces, such as the decline in oil prices, but it also had to introduce new products and services and efficiently supply them in order for the economic expansion to have been as long-lasting.

The Decade of the 90s: Recession, Recovery, and Expansion

The 1983–1990 economic expansion came to an end in 1990. There have been 11 expansions in the last 60 years. The 1983–1990 expansion was second only to the 1961–1969 expansion as the longest expansion in recent times. Only two expansions lasted less than 3 years, and only one less than 2 years (1980–1981). A sharp decline in the economy might have been anticipated after such a long period of economic growth in the 1980s. However, the recession that followed was relatively mild and was of average duration. There were some distinctive features of this recession and of the recovery that followed.

The 1990–1991 Recession. As previously mentioned, the 1990–1991 recession lasted three quarters, beginning in the third quarter of 1990 and ending in the first quarter of 1991. During this contraction in the economy, the unemployment rate increased from 5.1 to 7.1 percent. This did not seem like such a mild recession to the more than 3 million persons who lost their jobs; however, in comparison to the 1981–1982 recession when unemployment soared to 9.7 percent, the recession was mild. A striking feature of the recession was the absence of an aggregate demand or supply policy to alleviate the recession and to stimulate the economy. The policy belief was that the recession was mild and that the economy would recover on its own. There were some encouraging factors in support of this belief. Generally, the duration of a recession is closely related to the size of the increase in inventories because of the depressing effects that a recession has on final sales. The ratio of inventories to sales did not change significantly with the beginning of the recession because the recession was in part anticipated and inventories had been allowed to fall on the anticipation that sales would decline in the future. In addition, consumer and business confidence, which had dropped to low levels, was expected to rise with the success of the coalition forces in the Persian Gulf and with the return of American troops.

The 1991–1992 Recovery. As it turned out, the 1991–1992 recovery was among the weakest recoveries on record. After most recessions, the economy bounces back with a real growth in the GDP of 4 to 5 percent in the first quarter. Instead, in the second quarter of 1991, the first quarter after the recession, the rate of growth in the nation's real income was only 1.7 percent. This slow pattern of growth continued during the rest of the year and into the first part of 1992. During this five-quarter recovery period, the real GDP growth rate averaged 1.6 percent and exceeded 2 percent only in one quarter. As a result, the rate of unemployment not only did not decrease but increased during this early recovery period. The unemployment rate reached 7.7 percent before the rate of growth in the economy in 1992 began to exceed 3 percent and created enough new jobs to reduce the unemployment rate.

The 1991–1998 Expansion. At the beginning of 1998, the current expansion was 82 months long, making it the third longest expansion in recent times. It was reported in the *Economic Report of the President* in 1998 that expansions do not die of old age but come to an end because of economic reasons like rising inflation, financial troubles, and excessive inventories.[2] This expansion is unique in that inflation has been kept under control. There is some concern about the growth in consumer debt, and some financial woes may appear to be on the horizon. However, inventories do not appear to be excessive at the moment because of the strong consumer demand for goods and services. Consumer spending has been a strong force behind the expansion, increasing at an annual real rate of 3.5 percent between 1992 and 1997. In comparison, the real rate of annual growth in investment spending was only 1 percent, and government purchases remained at about the same annual level during this same period. Imports increased relative to exports during the period and therefore played a negative role with respect to the level of aggregate demand spending in the economy. The real GDP continued its merry way in the upward direction at a growth rate of 5.5 percent in the first quarter of 1998 and then slowed down to a 1.6 percent rate of growth in the second quarter of the year. As a result, the unemployment rate fell to a 28-year low of 4.3 percent in April and May but then increased to 4.5 percent in July and August of 1998.[3] The reality is that this growth in the economy and the creation of jobs are likely to continue to slow down in the second half of 1998

---

[2]Economic Report of the President, February 1998, p. 87.
[3]Economic Trends, Federal Reserve Bank of Cleveland, July 1998, p. 11.

because of the repercussions on the U.S. economy of economic problems beyond our direct control, namely, the unsolved economic problems facing Japan, the Asian economies, and other countries in the world. The forecast of the Clinton administration is that the real GDP will grow at an annual rate of 2 percent in 1998 and 1999, and the unemployment rate will stay around the full-employment rate of 5 percent in these years.[4] This forecast is likely to turn out to be too optimistic. There are already (October 1998) some warning signs appearing, such as decreases in exports and corporate earnings, which suggest that the current expansion may soon be coming to an end and that the unemployment rate may soon be above the full-employment rate.

Summary

There are both economic and social effects of unemployment. The economic effect involves the waste and loss of goods and services when resources are unemployed. The social effect involves the breaking up of human relationships within the family and outside it.

There are three types of unemployment—frictional, structural, and cyclical. Frictional unemployment is transitional in nature and is not a major economic issue. Structural and cyclical unemployment are major economic issues. Structural unemployment results from fundamental changes in demand and supply for products in specific sectors of the economy. Cyclical unemployment is associated with the ups and downs in the overall economy.

Aggregate demand and supply theories are developed to explain why people lose their jobs. Aggregate demand is composed of the output demanded by consumers, investors, and government. The determinants of consumer spending are prices, income, wealth, and rate of interest. At a given price level, the output demanded by consumers will vary directly with income and wealth, and inversely with the rate of interest. The determinants of investment spending are the expected profit rate and the rate of interest, with investment spending related directly to the expected profit rate and inversely with the interest rate. Government purchases, the final part of aggregate demand, depend on social priorities and policies.

A deficient aggregate demand or a weak aggregate supply may explain why the economy may operate at less than full employment. An aggregate demand approach to unemployment would pursue fiscal policies that would increase aggregate demand, namely, increase government expenditures related to taxes. An aggregate supply approach would

---

[4]Economic Report of the President, February 1998, p. 86.

pursue policies that would increase aggregate supply, namely, policies that would increase the productivity of resources and decrease the price of resources. The best possible approach is to pursue consistent aggregate demand and supply policies because unemployment may be caused by both a deficient aggregate demand and a weak aggregate supply.

The decade of the 90s commenced with the economy in a recession that was mild and of average duration. The recession began in the third quarter of 1990 and ended in the first quarter of 1991. The economy started moving upward in the second quarter, but the pace was so slow that the unemployment rate continued to increase in 1991 and 1992. After reaching a high of 7.4 percent in 1992, the economy began to grow fast enough to lower the unemployment rate. The expansion was a slow but steady one without serious inflationary forces operating to accelerate it. As a result of the expansion, jobs were created at a faster pace, and the unemployment rate was below 6 percent in 1995 and 1996 and below 5 percent in 1997 and into 1998. It is difficult to predict the unemployment rate in the future, but it will be reflecting as usual what is happening in the economy.

Discussion Questions

1. Discuss the economic and noneconomic costs of unemployment.
2. Explain the meaning of *labor force*. Are the unemployed included in the definition of the labor force? What about discouraged workers?
3. Discuss the different types of unemployment. Include in your discussion the type of unemployment that may be reduced without causing inflation.
4. Draw the circular flow of economic activity diagram. In reference to the diagram, explain the relationship between the product market and the resource market.
5. What are the components of aggregate demand? Discuss the marginal propensity to consume and save and the investment multiplier principle.
6. Explain the causes for increases in aggregate demand and supply.
7. Explain why the economy will contract when leakages from the circular flow of economic activity are greater than the injections into the flow of economic activity.
8. Compare and contrast aggregate demand policies and aggregate supply policies with respect to attempting to maintain a full-employment economy without inflation.
9. Discuss the 1990–1991 recession, the 1991–1992 recovery, and the 1992–1998 expansion.

Additional Readings

Froyen, Richard T. *Macroeconomics Theories and Policies.* 5th ed. Upper Saddle River, NJ: Prentice-Hall, 1995.

Chapter 5 develops aggregate demand theory in detail and discusses aggregate demand policies.

Hyman, David N. *Economics.* 3rd ed. Burr Ridge, IL: Irwin, 1994.

The circular flow diagram is presented and discussed in Chapter 24. Also, there is a thorough discussion of the kinds of unemployment in Chapter 25.

Layard, Richard, Stephen Nickell, and Richard Jackman. *The Unemployment Crisis.* New York: Oxford University Press, 1994.

Addresses the rise in unemployment over the last few years and the reasons behind the fluctuations.

Reducing Unemployment. Symposium by the Federal Reserve Bank of Kansas City. Jackson Hole, Wyoming, August 25–27, 1994. Kansas City, MO: Federal Reserve Bank of Kansas City, 1994.

Alan Greenspan, Martin Feldstein, John P. Martin, and others contributed to this symposium on the causes of and the policies to reduce unemployment.

Schiller, Bradley R. *The Macro Economy Today.* New York: Random House, 1983.

Supply-side policies are examined in Chapter 13. This chapter and Chapter 15, "Reagan Economics," are recommended.

Walton, Gary M., and Frank C. Wykoff, *Understanding Economics Today.* 5th ed. Burr Ridge, IL: Irwin, 1996.

Chapter 17, which discusses the causes of unemployment, is highly recommended.

World Wide Web Resources

Best Jobs in the USA Today
www.bestjobsusa.com

Provides links to job ads all over the country.

Bureau of Labor Statistics
www.bls.gov

An agency within the U.S. Department of Labor. Provides data on unemployment and other statistics.

Current Population Survey (CPS) Main Page
www.bls.census.gov/cps/cpsmain.htm

CPS is a joint project between the Bureau of Labor Statistics and the Bureau of the Census. Provides links to unemployment figures.

Economic Report of the President
www.access.gpo.gov/eop

Sponsored by the Executive Office of the President. Use the *search terms* box to find statistical information on unemployment.

United States Department of Labor
www.dol.gov

Provides links to labor related data and information on the Department's programs and activities.

Welcome to the White House
www.whitehouse.gov/WH/Welcome.html

Push the *The Briefing Room* icon to take you to the latest federal statistics, including unemployment figures.

Inflation

How to Gain and Lose at the Same Time

Chapter Outline

Checklist of Economic Concepts

We had sold out almost our entire inventory and, to our amazement, had nothing to show for it except a worthless bank account and a few suitcases full of currency not even good enough to paper our walls with. We tried at first to sell and then buy again as quickly as possible—but the inflation easily overtook us. The lag before we got paid was too long; while we waited, the value of money fell so fast that even our most profitable sale turned into a loss. Only after we began to pay with promissory notes could we maintain our position. Even so, we are making no real profit now, but at least we can live. Since every enterprise in Germany is financed in this fashion, the Reischsbank naturally has to keep on printing unsecured currency and so the mark falls faster and faster. The government apparently doesn't care; all it loses in this way is the national debt. Those who are ruined are the people who cannot pay with notes, the people who have property they are forced to sell, small shopkeepers, day laborers, people with small incomes who see their private savings and their bank accounts melting away, and government officials and employees who have to survive on salaries that no longer allow them to buy so much as a new pair of shoes. The ones who profit are the exchange kings, the profiteers, the foreigners who buy what they like with a few dollars, kronen, or zlotys, and the big entrepreneurs, the manufacturers, and the speculators on the exchange whose property and stocks increase without limit. For them practically everything is free. It is the great sellout of thrift, honest effort, and respectability. The vultures flock from all sides, and the only ones who come out on top are those who accumulate debts. The debts disappear of themselves.[1]

[1]*The Black Obelisk* by Erich Maria Remarque. Copyright © 1957 by Erich Maria Remarque. Copyright renewed © 1985 by Paulette Goddard Remarque.

Most people consider inflation as equal to or second only to unemployment among the nation's major aggregate economic problems. In almost every presidential campaign, candidates call inflation a bad thing and vow to control it once elected. The rising cost of groceries, auto repairs, medical services, clothes, travel, and everything else is a main topic of conversation among consumers. Business firms realize that higher prices for materials, labor, equipment, and other things they buy will reduce business profits unless they are successful in passing these higher costs on to the consumer in the form of higher consumer prices. Inflation is a prime bargaining consideration in labor union negotiations. A stated national goal of government economic policy is to stabilize the price level. All groups composing the population—consumers, unions, business firms, and government—are concerned about inflation.

Meaning and Measurement of Inflation

Most people have a good idea of what is meant by inflation. They know that it causes a sack full of groceries to cost more money. They know that buying Christmas presents costs more. They know that it is more expensive to eat out, to go to a movie, to take a vacation, or to buy a car. They know they will be generally worse off in the future unless their pay can keep up with inflation.

Inflation Defined

Inflation is a continuing rise in the general level of prices.

Inflation is a continuing rise in the general level of prices. This is in sharp contrast to a simple one-shot increase in the price level to a higher equilibrium level. An equilibrium price level is not reached when there is inflation since forces are continuing to move prices upward. During inflation some commodities may be falling in price and some may be rising, but the commodities that are rising are dominant, and they exert an upward force on the general price level.

Further Aspects of Inflation

Dynamic Aspects. Inflation has dynamic and self-sustaining properties. Increases in the price level induce economic groups to react to rising prices, causing further increases in prices. For example, consumers expecting increases in prices may increase current consumer spending, causing current market prices to rise. During periods of rising prices, producers are not inclined to resist increases in wages and other costs, since higher production costs may be shifted forward to consumers in the form of higher prices. These increases in prices, however, become the basis for further increases in production costs and still higher prices.

Inflation Without Rising Prices. Inflation is not always observable in the form of rising prices. It may be suppressed; market prices may not always reflect the inflationary forces operating in the economy. *Suppressed inflation* is usually associated with an attempt on the part of government to control prices. During the control period, market prices remain the same. Inflationary forces, however, persist because the government is not doing anything to alter the underlying inflationary forces in the market. Under these circumstances, it is difficult to keep prices under control, and prices in general will rise rapidly when price controls are lifted.

Measurement of Inflation

Inflation is measured by price index numbers. Price index numbers indicate the general level of prices in reference to the base year. For example, the consumer price index in 1997 was 161, using 1982–1984 as the base period. This means that consumer prices on average increased 61 percent between the base period (1982–1984 = 100) and 1997. The consumer price index was 131 in 1990. What was the rate of inflation between 1990 and 1997? The answer is 23 percent. This was derived as follows:

$$\text{Inflation rate} = (161 - 131)/131$$

Price Indexes. The consumer price index, sometimes referred to as the *cost-of-living index,* includes commodities that city wage earners and clerical workers buy, such as food, housing, utilities, transportation, clothing, health services, and recreation. The wholesale price index includes hundreds of commodities such as farm products and processed foods, as well as industrial commodities such as textiles, fuel, chemicals, rubber, lumber, paper, metals, machinery, furniture, nonmetallic minerals, and transportation equipment. Another price index that is used often by economists is the implicit price deflator. The implicit price deflator includes the components of the GDP—consumer services, durable and nondurable goods, residential and nonresidential fixed investment, exports and imports, and goods and services purchased by governments.

Construction of a Price Index. Since inflation is measured by price index numbers, it is important to understand how price index numbers are derived. A simple illustration can point out the essential principles underlying the construction of the consumer price index. Suppose a family spends $20,000, $21,000, and $22,000 in 1996, 1997, and 1998, respectively, for identical baskets of goods. If 1996 is used as the base year, the index number for the goods for that year is 100. It is 105 for 1997, calculated by dividing the cost of the basket in the base year ($20,000) into the cost in 1997 ($21,000) and multiplying by 100 in order to remove the decimal. By the same procedure, the index number in 1998 is 110, or

$$\frac{\text{Cost of market basket (1998)}}{\text{Cost of market basket (1996)}} \times 100 = \frac{\$22,000}{\$20,000} \times 100 = 110$$

The basket of goods used to compute price index numbers is a representative sample of the quantities of each good in the basket—the number of dresses, shirts, loaves of bread, gallons of gasoline, movie tickets, television sets, autos, and so forth—bought during the year specified. The sum of the price times the quantity of each good in the basket gives the value of the basket. After the value of the basket is calculated, the final step in the construction of a price index is to select the base year and compute the index numbers as illustrated.

A set of price index numbers is not a perfect measure of inflation. Only a sample of commodities is included in the index. What constitutes a representative sample is difficult to determine, and it changes over time in response to changes in tastes and preferences of people. It is also difficult to account for changes in the quality of goods that occur over time; for some goods and services, higher index numbers reflect higher costs for a better commodity rather than higher costs for the same commodity. Despite these imperfections, price index numbers are still useful indicators of trends in the level of prices.

A more accurate measure of the cost of living is needed. An advisory committee to study the consumer price index (CPI), chaired by a professional economist, Michael J. Boskin, reported that the CPI has an upward bias. According to this study, the CPI is overstating the inflation rate by 1.1 percentage points each year. The report identified several biases in the calculation of the cost-of-living index. All these biases reflect the failure of the represented "basket" of goods and services to account for, or do not account soon enough for, the changes that are taking place in the consumption and production of goods and services in the economy. A 1.1 percent annual overstatement in the CPI does not sound like much, but it is significant because a 3 percent rate of inflation instead of 2 percent is a 50 percent higher rate. Even more important, a 1.1 higher percentage point per year has a significant impact on government expenditure programs that are adjusted annually based on the official inflation rate. The Congressional Budget Office estimates that this overstatement in the inflation rate could contribute $148 billion to the federal budget deficit over a 10-year period.

Rate of Inflation

Figure 12–1 shows the average inflation rate over selected time periods from 1960 to 1998. The first half of the 1960s was a period when prices were almost stable, with consumer prices on average increasing only 1.3 percent each year. The inflation scenario was different in the last half of the decade. The economy reached full employment in 1965, and inflationary forces began to mount. The result was an average annual inflation rate between 1965 and 1970 of more than three times the rate of the earlier period (4.6 percent). The decade of the 1970s started with a high rate of inflation of about 6 percent and ended with a much higher rate of over 10 percent. What happened? How did the policymakers let inflation get out of control? First, nothing was done to stem the inflationary forces in the late 1960s. The most effective way to control a serious inflation is to not let it happen in the first place. Second, wage and price controls were enacted in the early 1970s to cope with the inflationary problem. Wage and price controls treat only the symptoms of inflation, not the basic cause of inflation. The year controls were removed, 1974, the inflation rate was 11 percent. A final factor that has to be taken into consideration in the assessment of the rampant inflation of this period is the increase in energy prices. An increase in an important input like energy increases the cost of producing most goods and services. In part, then, the high annual rate of

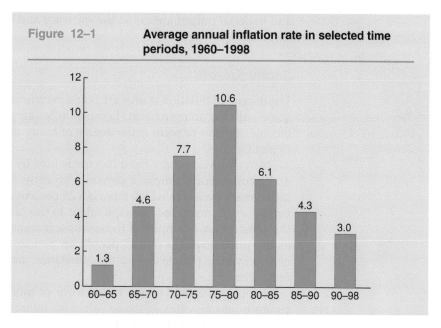

Figure 12–1   **Average annual inflation rate in selected time periods, 1960–1998**

Sources: Economic Report of the President, February 1998, p. 354; and *Economic Trends,* Federal Reserve Bank of Cleveland, July 1998, p. 7.

inflation of 10.6 percent between 1975 and 1980 reflects the higher costs of producing goods and services.

Inflationary forces were brought under control in the 1980s. It took a serious recession in 1981 and 1982 to do so. A recession after a long period of inflation can usually be expected, for in order for inflationary forces to be eliminated, the economy must slow down or decline. The average annual inflation rate was 6.1 percent between 1980 and 1985. However, this average rate of inflation was heavily influenced by the 13.5 percent inflation rate in 1980. The annual rate of inflation was reduced to 4.3 percent in the 1985–1990 period, and fell further to 3 percent in 1990–1998. The lesson to be learned from history is that very high inflation rates reflect the failure of resolving the problem of inflation when it first arises in the economy. Inflationary forces feed upon themselves and can cause people to expect inflation and behave in a way that causes inflation. The causes and cures of inflation will be discussed in subsequent sections.

Economic Effects of Inflation

Inflation affects the distribution of income, the allocation of resources, and the national output. The effects of inflation on the distribution of income are referred to as the *equity effects,* and the effects on resource allocation and national output are called the *efficiency* and *output effects* of inflation, respectively.

Equity Effects

The impact of inflation is uneven. Some people benefit from inflation, and some suffer economic harm. Because inflation alters the distribution of income, a major concern is the degree of *equity* or fairness in the distribution of income.

Anyone who is on a fixed income is hurt by inflation since it reduces real income. For example, a person who earns $20,000 a year during an inflationary period in which there is a 25 percent increase in the price level suffers a cut in real income equivalent to the rate of inflation—$5,000 in this illustration. Examples of those whose incomes often do not rise as fast as the price level are retired people on pensions, white-collar workers, civil servants, people on public assistance, and workers in declining industries.

People who hold assets in the form of money and who have fixed claims on money may be made worse off by inflation. Suppose a person deposits $1,000 in a savings account and receives a 5 percent interest rate, or $50, during the year. If the rate of inflation is in excess of 5 percent, the real value of the original savings of $1,000 plus the $50 earned on the savings for a year is reduced to less than the original $1,000. Creditors and owners of mortgages and life insurance policies are hurt by inflation, since the real value of their fixed money claims is reduced. People who bought government savings bonds for $18.75 and were paid $25.00 at maturity 10 years later have sometimes discovered that the $25.00 would not buy the same quantity of goods and services that the $18.75 would have bought 10 years earlier.

The prices of some goods and resources, due to inflation, may rise faster than the general level of prices. Wages and salaries of workers in rapidly growing industries are likely to rise faster than the price level. Strong unions are sometimes successful in bargaining for wage increases that are greater than the increases in the price level. People who depend on income in the form of profits—owners of stocks and business enterprises—may have increases in real income, depending upon the rate of increase in profits in comparison to prices. The value of land and improvements on land may rise during inflation; if they rise in value faster than the rate of inflation, the owners of land will be relatively better off.

In summary, inflation alters the distribution of income and wealth.[2] Inflation is like a tax to some people and like a subsidy to others. People whose real incomes are reduced by inflation are those who have fixed

Equity effects of inflation are the effects of inflation on the distribution.

---

[2]It is assumed that inflation is unanticipated. A fully anticipated inflation may not alter the distribution of income and wealth.

incomes and hold assets in the form of money. People whose real incomes are increased by inflation are those who have money income that increases faster than prices and hold real assets that appreciate in value faster than inflation. The arbitrary manner in which inflation may change the pattern of income distribution gives support to the claim that inflation is inequitable.

Efficiency Effects

Efficiency effects of inflation are the effects of inflation on the pattern of
resource allocation.

Inflation tends to change the pattern of resource allocation. In a competitive market, the prices of different goods and services reflect differences in consumer valuations of the quantities made available. Inflation causes demands for different goods and services to increase, but demands for some increase more rapidly than those for others. Increases in demands evoke supply responses, the extent of which varies from product to product. Thus, inflation changes relative demands, relative supplies, and relative prices of different goods and services. The pattern of resource allocation, then, is not the same pattern that would exist in the absence of inflation. It is not certain that the pattern of resource allocation with inflation is less efficient (that is, results in lower economic welfare) than the pattern without inflation.[3] However, many economists argue that inflation distorts the pattern of resource allocation, implying a less efficient allocation of resources.

Inflation encourages economic groups to spend time and resources in an attempt to adjust to inflation. Since inflation reduces the purchasing power of money, it encourages everyone to economize or minimize their money balances, that is, assets held in the form of money. The time spent and the resources used in adjusting to inflation could have been used to produce goods and services. Inflation, by encouraging everyone to make adjustments and divert time and resources away from production, reduces economic efficiency.

Output Effects

Output effects of inflation
are the effects of inflation
on the level of production.

The preceding discussion of the equity and efficiency effects of inflation assumes that the levels of real output and production lie on the economy's production possibilities curve. This assumption is made in order to focus attention on how inflation may alter the distribution of real income among people (equity effects) and the allocation of resources (efficiency effects). Simply stated, a certain-size pie is assumed in the previous discussion, and the concern is the way inflation alters the slices of pie and affects the use of resources in making the pie. Now we consider the effects of

---

[3]Frank G. Steindl, "Money Illusion, Price Determinancy and Price Stability," *Nebraska Journal of Economics and Business*, Winter 1971, pp. 26–27.

inflation on the size of the pie. What are the effects of inflation on the level of output of goods and services?

Inflation may have a stimulating effect on production and employment in the economy. The argument in support of this proposition can be presented as follows. During inflation, money wages lag behind price increases. Real profit income is increased. Under the stimulus of higher profits, producers expand production and employ more people.

The argument that inflation may stimulate production and employment should be qualified. Runaway or hyperinflation may depreciate the value of money so drastically that it loses its acceptability as a medium of exchange. Under these circumstances, a barter economy develops, accompanied by lower production levels and higher unemployment. If the economy is operating at full capacity and full employment, then, of course, inflation cannot stimulate them further. Inflation at full employment is usually referred to as *pure inflation.*

The impact of inflation differs depending on whether or not inflation is associated with increases in production and employment. As long as production is rising, there is a check on inflation because, although lagging behind demand, supply is increasing and inflationary forces are mitigated. The equity effects of inflation are also minimized if production and employment are rising. However, as the economy approaches full employment, the seriousness of inflation increases. The possibility of an accelerated rate of inflation is nearer, and the possible beneficial effects of inflation on production and employment are remote.

What Is Money?

It is sometimes stated that inflation is a situation in which "too much" money is chasing "too few" goods. As a first step to understanding inflation, we need to be able to answer the question: What is money?

Money is anything that is generally accepted as a means of payment for goods, services, and debt. Many things have been used for money such as seashells, bullets, and metals. Money is much more than just cash. There are several measures of money, and what is included in the money supply and the functions of money are the points of interest in this section.

Functions of Money

Medium of exchange function of money is the use of money for the payment of goods and services and for the payment of debt.

Money serves three basic functions: a medium of exchange, a measure of value, and a store of value. Goods and services are paid for in money, and debts are incurred and paid off in money. Without money, economic transactions would have to take place on a barter basis, that is, one good traded for another good. Thus, the use of money as the *medium of exchange* simplifies and facilitates the exchange process. Second, the values of economic

Measure of value function of money is the use of money to measure the value of goods and services.

Store of value function of money is the use of money as an asset to hold.

goods and services are measured in money. Money as a *measure of value* makes possible value comparisons of goods and services and the summation of quantities of goods and services on a value basis. It is not possible to add apples and oranges, but *it is possible* to add the *values* of apples and oranges. Third, wealth and assets may be held in the form of money. Money serves as a *store of value*.

The Money Supply (M1 and M2)

Money is an asset that is completely liquid; that is, you do not have to sell money in order to buy goods, services, and other assets. The money supply, then, is composed of assets that are 100 percent liquid or come so close to meeting this liquidity criterion that they are considered to be money. Several definitions of the money supply exist. The narrowest, called M1 for short, includes currency and coins in circulation, nonbank traveler's checks, demand deposits at commercial banks, and other checkable deposits such as NOW accounts, ATS accounts, credit-union share drafts, and demand deposits at mutual savings banks. NOW accounts are negotiable orders of withdrawal, and ATS accounts are automatic withdrawal of savings accounts. NOW and ATS accounts are similar to a regular checking account in the sense that goods and services can be paid for by writing checks on these accounts. In the case of ATS accounts, a bank will automatically transfer from savings to checking accounts when it is necessary to cover checks that have been written. The effect is the same as if all balances were held in a regular checking account. Credit-union share drafts and demand deposits at mutual savings banks are also the same as regular checking accounts at commercial banks.

M1 definition of money includes currency and coins in circulation, nonbank traveler's checks, demand deposits, and other checkable accounts such as NOW accounts.

M2 definition of money includes M1 plus savings and time deposits of small denomination, and money-market mutual funds.

The second definition of the money supply, M2, is broader and includes M1 plus savings and time deposits of small denomination (less than $100,000), and money-market mutual funds. A phone call or a trip to the bank is often the only difference between a demand deposit and a time deposit, especially a time deposit of a small denomination. Some savings accounts may have more stringent conditions placed on them, such as the loss of interest if they are withdrawn early, but, in general, savings accounts are like money. Many people find it convenient and can earn more interest by buying shares of money-market mutual funds. These funds are invested in almost riskless, interest-yielding assets, namely, U.S. Treasury bills. Money-market mutual funds are easily accessible and, under certain conditions, checks can be written against these funds.

There are still broader definitions of money referred to as M3 and L. Time deposits of $100,000 and over plus M2 are included in the definition of M3, and L includes M3 plus other liquid assets such as commercial paper, banker's acceptances, and Treasury bills. The major purpose of these broader measures of money is to have a measure of money and near money and, therefore, a measure of the overall liquidity in the economy. The money supply M2 is the definition of the money supply that is the generally more acceptable definition, especially from a policy viewpoint. This definition of the money supply includes assets that are 100 percent liquid for all practical purposes and is a broader definition than the restrictive M1. For example, the dollar value of M2 in December of 1997 was $4,019.3 billion, while the value of M1 was $1,068.7 billion. Although the Federal Reserve keeps track of the growth rate of M1 and the broader definitions of money, the Federal Reserve has officially announced that the growth rate in M2 is the primary target to watch closely and keep within a stated range of control.

Figure 12–2 shows the growth rate in the money supply in selected years over a 38-year period, 1960–1998. During the 1960s, the rate of growth in the money supply stayed in the range of 4 to 8 percent. The growth rate pattern in the money supply in the decade of the 1970s tended to be upward with wide swings from low to high and from high to low growth rates. For example, the money supply growth rate was 6.5 percent in 1970 and increased to 13 percent in 1972, and then fell to 5.5 percent in 1974. The growth rate in M2 ranged from approximately 8 percent to

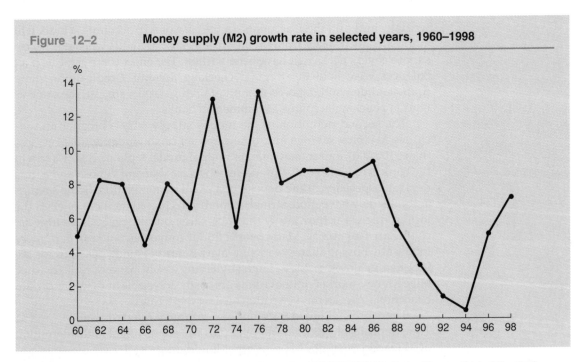

Figure 12–2   **Money supply (M2) growth rate in selected years, 1960–1998**

Sources: *Economic Report of the President*, February 1998, p. 361; and *Economic Trends*, Federal Reserve Bank of Cleveland, September 1998, p. 3.

14 percent between 1975 and 1979. A very high M2 growth rate, above 8 percent, was the trend from 1980 to 1987. During the remaining years of the 1980s, the rate of growth in the money supply varied from only 3.2 to 5.5 percent. Between 1992 and 1994, M2 grew at a very slow pace of between 1 and 2 percent. However, M2 grew at a faster rate in 1996, 1997, and 1998, reaching a rate of 7.2 percent in 1998. The relationship between the growth in the money supply and inflation and how the Federal Reserve can control the growth in the money supply are discussed later in the chapter.

The Process of Creating Money

The major part of the money supply is in the form of demand and other checkable deposits. Checking deposits are held in commercial banks and other depository institutions, namely, savings and loan associations, mutual savings banks, and credit unions. In this section, the focus is on the way these deposits are created and destroyed.

Commercial Banks

There are about 10,000 commercial banks. Banks are private firms that are in business to make a profit by providing a full range of banking services, including checking accounts, savings accounts, loans, automatic transfers from savings to checking accounts, and electronic banking services. Commercial banks are either state banks or national banks. State banks receive their charters to engage in the banking business from the state, whereas national banks receive their charters from the federal government.

Goldsmiths, the original bankers, provided the important service of a safe and convenient place to keep money or gold deposits, generally storing them in a vault. Depositors received a receipt for the gold deposited and used the receipt to buy goods and services. These receipts were the early form of paper money. Goldsmiths discovered early that it was not necessary to have a dollar in gold for each dollar issued in the form of receipts since only a *fraction* of the gold deposited was required to meet gold withdrawals. This discovery led to two more important services. Loans were made to individuals and businesses, and paper money was created in the form of the issue of goldsmiths' receipts. The three main functions of banks today as then are to (1) provide a safe place for depositors to keep money and other assets, (2) make loans, and (3) create money as a group.

Other Depository Institutions

The traditional distinctions between commercial banks and other depository institutions or banks are disappearing. The Monetary Control Act of 1980 allows more flexibility in providing a full range of banking services. Prior to this act, savings and loan associations and mutual savings banks were restricted to offering savings accounts. These institutions now offer checking account services and are expanding other banking services. Historically, savings deposits of savings and loan associations were used primarily to finance the purchase of homes. Now with checking deposits, savings and loan associations will probably make other types of loans as well. Mutual savings banks are very much like savings and loan associations; however, they were originally intended to serve small savers and used their funds for different purposes, such as investment in stocks and bonds.

Another depository institution is the credit union. A credit union is a cooperative banking venture in which members or owners have a common employer or union. Credit unions have savings and checking accounts and use their funds primarily for small consumer loans. The services of credit unions can be expected to expand in the future.

Balance Sheet of a Bank

A balance sheet of a bank shows the relationship among the bank's assets, liabilities, and net worth. The important feature of a balance sheet is

$$\text{Assets} = \text{Liabilities} + \text{Net Worth}$$

When there is a change on one side of the equation, there is an offsetting change either on the same side of the equation or on the other side of the equation. For example, if there is an increase in a liability of $10,000, there is a decrease of $10,000 in another liability or net worth, or an increase in an asset of $10,000.

The major assets of a bank are cash reserves, loans and investments, and fixed investments, such as a building and equipment. The major liabilities of banks are demand or checking deposits and time or savings deposits. The net worth of a bank is the owner's equity or the capital stock of the bank.

The balance sheet of a bank appears as follows:

Assets	Liabilities and Net Worth

Reserves:
    Legal reserves
    Excess reserves
Loans and investments
Fixed investments
	Liabilities:
	    Demand deposits
	    Time deposits
	Net worth

In order to focus on the way money is created, we are concerned only with reserves and loans of banks on the asset side and demand or checking deposits on the liability side.

The Fractional Reserve Banking System

Banks are required by law to keep only a part of their deposits in reserves. These reserves are held primarily in the form of deposits at Federal Reserve Banks but also include the cash that banks have on hand, sometimes referred to as *vault cash*. The legal reserve requirement is expressed in percentage terms and is called the *reserve ratio* since it is the ratio of required reserves to bank deposits. For example, if the reserve ratio for a particular bank with demand deposits of $40 million is 10 percent, this bank must have in legal reserves 10 percent of $40 million, or $4 million. Banks are classified by size into two classes. The reserve ratios are 3 percent and 10 percent for the two classes. Today, most banks are large enough to be subject to the 10 percent reserve ratio.

Banks may have *excess reserves*, that is, reserves above what is required to meet the legal reserve requirement. Banks must have excess reserves to make new loans. When banks as a group expand loans, they create demand deposits; and when banks as a group contract loans, they destroy demand deposits. Now let's turn more specifically to the process of creating and destroying demand deposits or money.

Demand Deposit Creation

Suppose there is a new demand deposit of $10,000, and the reserve ratio is 10 percent. The demand deposits of the bank increase $10,000, and reserves increase $10,000. If the new deposit was made from withdrawing currency in circulation, there is no change in the money supply since the money supply is composed of currency in circulation and demand deposits. Given a 10 percent reserve ratio, the bank has to keep $1,000 in legal reserves and has $9,000 in excess reserves.

Now, let's say you go to the bank and borrow $9,000 in order to buy a car. You sign a piece of paper called a *promissory note* agreeing to pay back the loan plus interest over a period of time in monthly installments. The new auto is used as collateral for the loan. After you sign the promissory note, the bank increases your checking account by the amount of the loan, or $9,000. You write a check for $9,000 to pay for the new auto. Your balance at the bank remains what it was prior to obtaining the loan. Demand deposits at another bank increase $9,000 when the auto dealer deposits your check. A loan of $9,000 to pay for a new auto has created new demand deposits of $9,000 in the banking system.

The process of demand deposit creation does not have to end after your loan of $9,000 creates new demand deposits of $9,000. With the assumed legal reserve ratio of 10 percent, $900 ($9,000 × 0.10) is required to meet the legal reserve requirement. Thus, excess reserves of $8,100 remain in the system. By the same process as your loan, a new loan of $8,100 may be made that creates a new deposit of $8,100. This process may be repeated over and over again until excess reserves become zero.

The multiple expansion of demand deposits from a $10,000 deposit withdrawn from currency in circulation assuming a reserve ratio of 10 percent is shown through four stages in Table 12–1. Could you continue the stages through five, six, seven, and so on? In the final stage, observe demand deposits are $100,000, but the maximum demand deposit *increase* or money supply increase is $90,000, since $10,000 is currency withdrawn from circulation. In a symmetrical way, there may be a multiple contraction in demand deposits and the money supply when demand deposits are reduced in the banking system by a new currency withdrawal of $10,000.

The maximum demand deposit creation possible from a given new demand deposit can be calculated based on the following equation:

Table 12–1	A $10,000 new deposit is made from currency in circulation (legal reserve ratio = 10%)
Assets	**Liabilities**

Reserves:
  Legal + $1,000
  Excess + $9,000
	Stage 1: Bank 1 Demand deposits +
	$10,000

	A $9,000 loan is made Stage 2: Bank 2

Reserves:
  Legal + $900
  Excess + $8,100
	Demand deposits +
	$9,000

	An $8,100 loan is made Stage 3: Bank 3

Reserves:
  Legal + $810
  Excess + $7,290
	Demand deposits +
	$8,100

	A $7,290 loan is made Stage 4: Bank 4

Reserves:
  Legal + $729
  Excess + $6,561
	Demand deposits +
	$7,290

At the end of Stage 4: Sum total of loans + $24,390	

Reserves:
  Legal + $3,439
  Excess + $6,561
	Demand deposits +
	$34,390

Final stage: Sum total of all stages Sum total of loans + $90,000	

Reserves:
  Legal + $10,000
  Excess $0
	Demand deposits +
	$100,000

$$D = E \times \frac{1}{r}$$

The **money multiplier** is a numerical coefficient derived from the legal reserve ratio and equal to the reciprocal of the legal reserve ratio. The money multiplier multiplied by a change in excess cash reserves of banks gives the maximum change in the money supply.

where D = maximum deposit creation
E = excess legal reserves
r = reserve ratio

In our illustration, the $10,000 new demand deposit increases legal reserves $1,000 and excess reserves $9,000. The increase in excess reserves times the reciprocal of the reserve ratio or the *money multiplier* equals the maximum deposit creation possible ($9,000 × 10 = $90,000).

The Issue of Control

It is apparent that with a fractional reserve banking system, the money supply can expand and contract rapidly. The system works well when money growth is controlled. The Federal Reserve Act of 1913 established the Federal Reserve System (the Fed). The main purpose of the Fed is to control the money supply.

The Federal Reserve System

There are 12 Federal Reserve Banks located in various regions of the country. Each Federal Reserve Bank acts as a central bank for private banks in the region. A central bank is a bank for private banks. Just as a private bank provides you with a full range of banking services, the Fed provides private banks with many services. Among these services are the clearing of checks, the holding of bank reserves or deposits, the providing of currency, and the making of loans to private banks.

The Board of Governors manages the Federal Reserve System. The board consists of seven members appointed by the president and confirmed by Congress. The appointments are for 14 years, and reappointments are prohibited after serving a full term. The president selects the chairman of the board, who is the chief spokesperson and architect of Fed policy. The current chairman of the board, Alan Greenspan, was appointed by President Reagan in 1987 and was recently reappointed by President Clinton to a 4-year term.

An influential policy committee is the Federal Reserve Open Market Committee (FOMC). This committee is composed of all seven members of the Board of Governors plus five regional Reserve bank presidents. The FOMC meets about once a month in Washington, D.C., to discuss and determine open-market operations. Open-market operations are the buying and selling of government securities in order to influence the level of bank reserves.

The Monetary Control Act of 1980 brought all banks and depository institutions under the regulations of the Fed. Prior to this act, state-chartered banks could choose whether they wanted to be "members" of the Fed. This distinction between member and nonmember banks no longer has economic significance. All banks are subject to the Federal Reserve legal reserve requirements, and all banks are provided with Fed services.

Federal Reserve Controls

The Federal Reserve has three major policy instruments: the legal reserve requirement, the discount rate, and open-market operations. Each control influences excess reserves and the lending ability of banks. The discount rate is not generally a powerful control but is important because it may indicate the direction of the Federal Reserve policy with respect to interest rates. The legal reserve ratio is a powerful weapon, but changes in the legal reserve ratio are not made frequently. Open-market operations have a direct impact on excess reserves and are the most important way the Fed controls the money supply.

The **legal reserve ratio** is the ratio of cash reserves to demand deposits that banks are required to maintain.

Legal Reserve Ratio. The *legal reserve ratio* is the ratio of reserves that banks are required to maintain to demand deposits. An increase in this ratio reduces excess reserves and the lending potential of banks. Banks that are fully loaned out, that is, banks with zero excess reserves, are required to reduce loans and borrow from the Fed or from other banks with excess reserves in order to meet a higher reserve requirement. A decrease in the legal reserve ratio increases excess reserves and the lending potential of banks. Thus, a contractionary Federal Reserve monetary policy could be in the form of increasing the legal reserve ratio, and an expansionary policy could be in the form of reducing the ratio.

The **discount rate** is the rate of interest that Federal Reserve Banks charge when banks borrow from the Fed.

Discount Rate. The *discount rate* is the rate of interest that Federal Reserve Banks charge when banks borrow from the Fed. The amount that a bank borrows from the Fed counts as legal reserves for that bank. An increase in the discount rate tends to discourage bank borrowing from the Fed, which will lower its reserves, and to increase interest rates on bank loans generally. The Fed increases the discount rate when it desires to tighten credit and slow down growth in the money supply. In contrast, the Fed decreases the discount rate when it desires to ease money and credit. Sometimes, changes in the discount rate are viewed as signals indicating whether the Federal Reserve is pursuing or planning to pursue a policy of monetary ease or monetary tightness. A change in the discount rate not supported by appropriate changes in other monetary weapons may not have much impact on the economy.

Open-market operations are the purchases and sales of government securities by the Federal Reserve Open Market Committee in order to control the growth in the money supply.

Open-Market Operations. The Federal Reserve Open Market Committee (FOMC) buys and sells federal securities in order to influence bank reserves, loans, and demand deposits. An open-market purchase means that the Fed is buying federal securities from banks or from the nonbank public. In either case, banks' excess reserves are increased. The primary impact of the purchase of federal securities from banks is to increase excess reserves and decrease federal securities held by banks. The primary impact of an open-market purchase from nonbanks is to increase demand deposits and excess reserves of banks. The FOMC makes the decision to buy federal securities when it desires to expand the money supply. An open-market sale has the opposite effect. Excess reserves and the lending ability of banks are reduced by open-market sales. Thus, the FOMC makes the decision to sell federal securities when it desires to contract growth in the money supply.

Federal Reserve Targets

The two most often discussed monetary policy targets are the interest rate target and the money growth rate target. Federal Reserve policy has often focused on interest rates. When interest rates were believed to be "too high," the Fed pursued a policy of monetary ease; when interest rates were believed to be "too low," the Fed pursued a policy of monetary tightness. These policy actions are sometimes referred to as a policy of *fine tuning*, that is, pursuing a policy which in effect changes the growth rate in the money supply in order to maintain interest rates at a level that will promote economic stability and growth. This focus on interest rates as the prime basis of Fed policy has at times led to serious inflationary problems. During periods of economic expansion, interest rates generally rise because of the increase in the demand for money and credit. To prevent interest rates from rising in these circumstances, the Fed may pursue a policy that increases the money growth rate. Also, political pressures on the Fed to keep interest rates low or to prevent interest rates from rising tend to increase inflationary expectations and eventually lead to a higher money growth rate and inflation. The major criticism of using interest rates as the main policy target is that the Fed would be relinquishing control over growth in the money supply.

Primarily in response to the high rate of inflation in the late 1970s, the Federal Reserve began in October 1979 to focus on money growth as the prime policy target. Money growth rates were established for the various measures of money. In the early 1990s, the target growth rate set for M2 was a range between 2½ and 6½ percent. The target range for the growth rate in M2 was changed to 1 to 5 percent in the mid-1990s. The actual growth rate in M2 was above this new target range in 1997 and 1998, with the M2 growth rate exceeding 6 percent in 1998 (Figure 12–2).

A growing number of economists support the money growth rate target. They make two major points: First, they argue that it is the growth in the money supply that ultimately determines the inflation rate. Second, they argue that erratic movements in the money growth rate are primarily responsible for the economic instability in the economy. For these reasons, a Fed policy that concentrates on a stable money growth rate is favored by these economists.

Another policy issue related to the money growth target is the ability or inability of the Fed to pursue a *stable* money growth rate policy. In some periods, money growth rates vary widely on a monthly basis from the established targets. Critics of Fed policy believed that the Fed was not focusing on controlling the money supply and was basing policy on other considerations. It may be that this criticism was in part justified. It may also be that money growth rates cannot be precisely controlled in the very short run.

In summary, the issue of the appropriate monetary policy target is not resolved among policymakers. Among economists, there is somewhat more agreement that monetary stability can be best accomplished by a Federal Reserve policy that strives to maintain a stable and reasonable money growth rate.

Inflationary Causes and Cures

Two approaches will be taken to explain the causes of inflation and to present possible methods of stopping it. The quantity theory of money is the first approach. This theory stresses the importance of money in the inflationary process. Aggregate demand-supply analysis provides a framework for approaching the causes of inflation.

Quantity Theory of Money

The **equation of exchange** is an identity. On the left-hand side of the equation, the money supply times velocity equals total spending, and on the right-hand side of the equation, the price level times the quantity of final goods and services produced equals the value of these goods and services produced.

The starting point for the quantity theory of money is the *equation of exchange:*

$$MV = PQ$$

where M = money supply

V = income velocity of money or number of times, on average, a dollar is used to buy final goods and services in a year

P = price level or average price of final goods and services

Q = quantity of final goods and services produced during year

The left-hand side of the equation, the money supply (M) times the velocity or turnover of money (V), measures total money spending in the economy. The right-hand side of the equation, the price level *(P)* times the national output *(Q),* equals the money value of the national output or nominal income. The two sides of the equation are equal since the total spending for goods and services is the same as the total sales value of goods and services.

The quantity theory of money states that increases and decreases in *M* cause increases and decreases in *P* and *Q,* respectively. The assumption of this theory is that *V* is relatively constant. If it is further assumed that the nation's output is fixed, it follows that the price level will rise or fall at the same rate that *M* rises or falls. More relevant than this extreme assumption concerning output is that, given a constant or relatively constant *V,* the inflation rate is closely connected with the growth rate in the money supply as the economy expands and nears full employment.

An increase in the money supply will certainly increase prices unless either velocity of money decreases and/or output increases. In the event of no changes in *V* and *Q,* the price level is the equilibrium variable that moves the economy toward a new equilibrium where the increase in *M* is offset by an increase in *P.* That is to say, when there is "excess money" created by an increase in *M,* the excess money (assuming a constant *V*) flows into the final goods market, resulting in inflation. A decrease in *V* or an increase in *Q* could partially or wholly eliminate the excess money and, therefore, could partially or wholly offset the inflationary pressure. The quantity theory of money teaches, however, that growth in the money supply is the basic cause of inflation, and the cure for inflation is to control the growth in the money supply. The control can be achieved, of course, through appropriate use of Federal Reserve controls over the money supply.

In view of the quantity theory of money, let's examine again the growth rates in inflation and the money supply over 5-year time periods between 1960 and 1998. The average annual inflation rate exceeded the money supply growth rate in every time period (Figure 12–3, next page). This is what you might anticipate based on the quantity theory of money. In the first four time periods between 1960 and 1980, the average rate of inflation increased in every time period from 1.3 percent in the 1960–1965 period to 10.6 percent in the 1975–1980 period. The money supply growth rate was much higher than the inflation rate except in the last time period, 1975–1980, when the inflation rate was over 10 percent and the money supply growth rate was over 11 percent. After reaching a peak in 1975–1980, the inflation rate started on a downward trend, reaching only a 3 percent average rate during the most recent time period, 1990–1998. What was happening to the growth rate in the money supply? The quantity theory of money appears to be substantiated. The average growth rate in the money supply was 6 percent, almost on the target rate of 5 percent during this most recent time period.

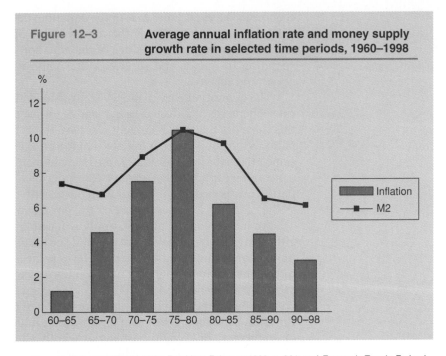

Figure 12–3   **Average annual inflation rate and money supply growth rate in selected time periods, 1960–1998**

Sources: Economic Report of the President, February 1998, p. 361; and *Economic Trends,* Federal Reserve Bank of Cleveland, July 1998, p. 7, and September 1998, p. 3.

Demand-Pull Inflation

An alternative approach to the quantity theory of money is the aggregate demand approach. In this approach, the stress is on excess demand as the major cause of inflation. The two approaches are similar in most important respects, but there are some differences in points of emphasis and in policy recommendations. The aggregate demand approach places more emphasis on total consumer, investment, and government spending in the economy *(MV)* and less emphasis on growth in the money supply. The money supply is viewed primarily as an *accommodating* variable instead of an *initiating* variable. According to aggregate demand analysis, *demand-pull inflation* is initiated by an increase in aggregate demand and is self-enforcing by further increases in aggregate demand. A demand-pull inflation is associated with increases in production and employment until the economy reaches full employment. Once full employment is reached, further increases in demand increase prices only.

    Figure 12–4 depicts demand-pull inflation. Beginning at the price level p and production q, an increase in aggregate demand to D_1 means that all of demand cannot be satisfied at p. Thus, the price level rises to p_1, and

Demand-pull inflation stems from increases in total consumer, investment, and government spending that cause rightward shifts in the aggregate demand curve.

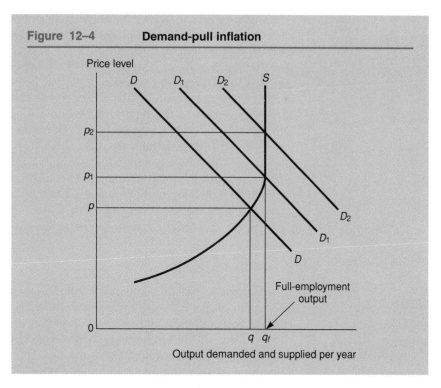

Figure 12–4   **Demand-pull inflation**

Demand-pull inflation is due to increases in aggregate demand from *DD* to D_1D_1 to D_2D_2.

production rises to q_f. An increase in demand to D_2 causes the price level to rise further to p_2. This inflationary process continues as long as aggregate demand increases, since all of demand can be satisfied only at higher prices. Pure inflation, an increase in the price level without an increase in output, is shown when aggregate demand increases to D_2.

Cures for Demand-Pull Inflation

Demand-pull inflation can be stopped by the appropriate use of Federal Reserve monetary policy and federal fiscal policy. We know now that demand-pull inflations are caused by "excess money" leading to excess spending or that they are caused by "excess demand" accommodated by expansions in the money supply. In either case, this type of inflation can be slowed down or stopped completely by Federal Reserve policy that slows down the growth in the money supply: namely, a policy employing a combination of Fed controls that reduce excess reserves in the banking system and the ability of banks to expand loans and create money.

The appropriate federal fiscal policy in periods of demand-pull inflations is some combination of government expenditure cuts and tax increases; that is, federal budget deficits should be reduced. A decrease in
government purchases directly reduces total spending in the economy. A
decrease in government transfer payments or an increase in taxes indirectly reduces aggregate demand by decreasing private spending. In addition, increases in the federal debt brought about by budget deficits
should be financed in a way that does not create money.

Demand-pull inflations are difficult to stop without causing unemployment. The same economic forces causing inflation also increase production and employment. The secret to controlling demand-pull inflation
is not to let it develop in the first place. Once inflation develops and is out
of control, as in the late 1960s and 1970s, it seems almost inevitable that the
opportunity cost to stop inflation is rising unemployment.

Cost-Push Inflation

It is difficult to explain some of the inflationary periods in the 1960s and
1970s only on the basis of demand-pull inflation. The economy has experienced both inflation and recession together at certain times. How can
this be? Demand-pull inflation is characterized by rising prices and rising
production until full employment is reached. Inflation and recession at the
same time mean rising prices and falling production.

The only way the economy can experience simultaneous inflation and
recession is for inflation to be initiated by a decrease in aggregate supply.
This type of inflation is called *cost-push inflation*. Increases in costs cause
aggregate supply to decrease, reducing the quantity of goods produced
and increasing prices.

Figure 12–5 illustrates cost-push inflation. Beginning at price level p
and production q_f, aggregate supply decreases to S_1. Now all of demand
cannot be satisfied at p; that is, aggregate output demanded is greater than
aggregate output supplied. As a consequence, the price level rises to p_1.
Aggregate supply decreases further to S_2. Again, all of demand cannot be
satisfied, and price rises to p_2. This inflationary process continues until
there are no further decreases in aggregate supply. In Figure 12–5, cost-
push inflation is characterized by rising prices and falling production.

Cost-push inflation occurs because of decreases in aggregate supply.
But what causes aggregate supply to decrease? The answer is an increase
in resource prices not offset by productivity increases. If a resource, such
as energy, increases in price, it is not profitable to produce the same levels
of output at the same price levels unless the higher energy costs are offset.
For another illustration, an increase in the price of labor increases labor
unit costs and, therefore, decreases output supplied at every price level.
Sometimes the blame for cost-push inflation is placed on monopoly
power—the power of unions to negotiate successfully for wage gains in

Cost-push inflation stems
from increases in the costs
of producing goods and
services that cause leftward
shifts in the aggregate supply curve.

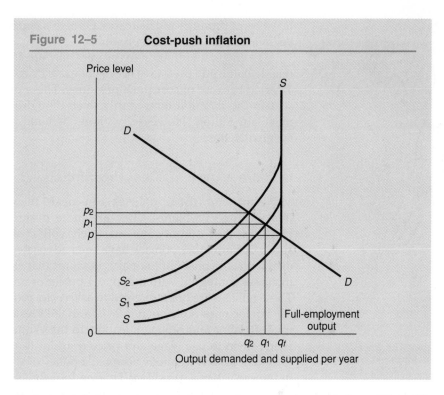

Figure 12–5   **Cost-push inflation**

Cost-push inflation is due to a decrease in aggregate supply from *SS* to *SS₁* and *SS₂*.

excess of productivity gains and the market power of monopoly firms to restrict output and increase prices. In the absence of inflationary demand pressures, the monopoly powers of unions and producers to bring about cost-push inflations are exaggerated. The major point to remember about cost-push inflations is that they are caused by resource price increases or productivity decreases regardless of the reason or reasons why these things may occur.

Demand-Pull and Then Cost-Push Inflation

It may be misleading to look on demand-pull and cost-push as two separate inflationary processes. In fact, a single inflationary period may result from both demand-pull and cost-push pressures. Increases in aggregate demand start the inflationary process. Prices, production, and employment rise in response to the pull of demand. Money wages rise, but with a lag behind prices. Unions realize eventually that wages have lagged behind prices and begin to try to catch up by demanding wage increases

Stagflation

a stagnic economy and high inflation-

in excess of productivity increases. Once this happens, cost-push pressures begin to reinforce demand pressures.

The end of an inflationary process may not coincide with the moment that demand-pull pressures no longer exist. Prices may continue to rise for a period because of cost-push pressures. These pressures operating alone sustain the inflation temporarily, even though production and employment are falling. However, without demand-pull pressures, inflation eventually stops.

Is There a Cure for Cost-Push Inflation?

Monetary and fiscal policies can deal, theoretically anyway, with demand-type problems. They are more designed for these purposes. However, they cannot cope effectively with cost-push inflationary pressures. Certain other policies have been advocated by some economists to deal with cost-push inflationary pressures that stem from wage and price increases connected with monopoly power of unions and business firms. These policies are often referred to as *incomes policies.*

Incomes policies are government policies designed to deal with cost-push inflationary pressures associated with imperfect labor and product markets by establishing wage and price ceilings, and some mechanism for their enforcement.

An incomes policy may range from the President of the United States inviting labor and business leaders to the White House in order to persuade them to use wage and price restraint to wage and price controls. President John F. Kennedy adopted a policy of wage and price guidelines in the early 1960s. President Lyndon Johnson abandoned guidelines for jawboning when inflationary pressures mounted in the late 1960s. President Richard Nixon resorted to wage and price controls between 1971 and 1974. President Jimmy Carter announced voluntary wage-price standards in 1978. Presidents Ronald Reagan and George Bush did not have to deal with cost-push inflationary pressures during their terms of office. There were no strong cost-push forces operating in the economy during the 1983–1990 economic expansion.

Incomes policies have been far from successful thus far. The main criticism of almost any incomes policy is that it does not eliminate the cause of inflation. Assuming that the monopoly power of unions and business firms is the major cause of cost-push inflationary pressures, these pressures do not disappear unless this cause is eliminated. Also, the monopoly power of unions and business firms cannot be effectively used anyway unless there are inflationary pressures caused by expansionary monetary and fiscal policies.

An incomes policy that has not been tried but has support among some economists is called a *tax-based incomes policy (TIP).*[4] The general

---

[4]Sidney Weintraub, *Capitalism's Inflation and Unemployment Crisis* (Reading, MA: Addison-Wesley, 1978), pp. 121–144.

economic thinking behind a tax-based incomes policy is that prices are determined by an average markup of prices over labor unit costs. When labor unit costs rise, say, because of wage increases in excess of productivity increases, prices generally rise in the economy. In the TIP proposal, incentives are provided to discourage "excess wage" increases.

The TIP proposal would work simply as follows. A wage increase guideline would be established, say, 5 percent, at the beginning of the year. At the same time, the government would announce a TIP tax schedule. Suppose the tax schedule is that for each percentage point a corporate firm grants over the wage guideline, 4 percentage points are added to the corporate income tax rate. A firm giving a 6 percent increase in wages, then, would be subject to a 4 percent added tax to its income tax rate.

There are variants to the TIP proposal. One variant is to reward firms that give wage increases less than the wage guideline. Another alternative is to apply the reward-and-penalty system to prices or to both wages and prices. The innovating feature of the TIP proposal and its variants is the use of an incentive system that would tend to foster noninflationary wage and price behavior. However, it remains uncertain as to how effective a tax-based incomes policy would be if implemented sometime in the future.

Summary

Inflation means that the general level of prices is rising, and it takes more money to buy the same quantity of goods and services. Inflation may be suppressed. This occurs when output demanded is greater than output supplied at the current price level, but the price level does not rise because of government price controls.

The three effects of inflation are the equity, efficiency, and output effects. The equity effects are the results of inflation on income distribution. The people who lose during inflation are those who receive fixed incomes and have fixed money claims. The people who gain during inflation are those whose money incomes rise faster than prices and who hold assets that rise in value more than the increase in prices of goods and services.

The efficiency effects of inflation are the results of inflation on the allocation of resources. Inflation changes the allocation of resources, since inflation alters relative commodity prices. It is not certain that this change in resource allocation is a less efficient allocation. However, some economists argue that the allocation of resources is distorted by inflation and results in a less efficient allocation.

The impact of inflation on the national production of goods and services may be to encourage production. Before the economy reaches full employment, rising prices tend to go hand in hand with rising production. The same forces that cause prices to rise cause production to rise. However, the continuation of inflationary forces at full employment leads to pure inflation—that is, rising prices not associated with rising production.

Money plays an essential role in the economy. Money is anything that is generally accepted as a means of payment for goods, services, and debt. Money serves three functions: First, money serves as a medium of exchange; second, the value of goods and services is measured in money; and third, money serves as a store of value. The supply of money in the economy includes currency and coins in circulation, traveler's checks, demand deposits at banks, saving and time deposits of small denominations, and other checkable deposits. There are broader measures of the money supply that include other near-money assets.

The money supply expands when banks as a group expand loans, and contracts when banks as a group contract loans. The Federal Reserve System, which has the responsibility of controlling the money supply, attempts to fulfill this responsibility through the use of policy controls over excess cash reserves of banks. The three policy controls are the legal reserve ratio, the discount rate, and open-market operations. When the Federal Reserve thinks it is desirable to slow down growth in the money supply, the Fed can increase the legal reserves ratio, increase the discount rate, and increase open-market sales of government securities. These policy actions decrease excess cash reserves and reduce the lending ability of banks. The opposite policy actions can be taken if it is desirable to increase the growth in the money supply—namely, decrease the legal reserve rate, decrease the discount rate, and decrease open-market purchases of government securities. These actions increase excess cash reserves and increase the lending ability of banks.

Two approaches are taken to explain the causes of inflation and the cures to inflation. The first approach is the quantity theory of money. This theory stresses the importance of money in the inflationary process. The second approach is an aggregate demand-supply approach. The central message of the quantity theory of money is that behind every inflation there is a rapid growth in the money supply, and the way to stop inflation is to control the growth in the money supply. In a demand-pull inflation, it is excess aggregate demand that initiates and causes inflation. In a cost-push inflation, aggregate supply decreases, resulting in upward pressures on prices. The cure for demand-pull inflation is the appropriate use of monetary and fiscal policies. There is no certain solution to cost-push inflationary pressures other than restoring competitive markets and making sure that inflationary pressures do not exist because of an excessive growth in the money supply. An incomes policy that provides incentives to foster competitive wage and price behavior has been recommended as a possible solution to cost-push inflation but has not yet been implemented.

Discussion Questions

1. Discuss the meaning and measurement of inflation. Include in your discussion the reasons for the upward bias in the consumer price index.
2. Explain the differences in the equity, efficiency, and output effects of inflation. Why do the output effects of inflation encourage inflationary policies?
3. What are the functions of money? Discuss the different definitions of money.
4. Assume a new demand deposit of $1,000 and a legal reserve requirement of 10 percent. Explain in detail how money is created, and show the final balance sheet of the banking system, assuming the maximum increase in the money supply.
5. Discuss the major policy controls of the Federal Reserve. Include in your discussion the relative effectiveness of open-market operations, the discount rate, and the legal reserve requirement.
6. Explain the quantity theory of money. What is the starting point for the theory? Is this theory supported by empirical data? Discuss.
7. Explain the differences between a demand-pull inflation and a cost-push inflation.
8. Discuss the most effective way to cure a demand-pull inflation and a cost-push inflation.

Additional Readings

Anderson, W. H. Locke, Ann Putallaz, and William G. Shepherd. *Economics*. Englewood Cliffs, NJ: Prentice-Hall, 1983.

Chapter 26 is recommended for its good coverage of cost-push and demand-pull inflations.

Mishkin, Frederic S. *The Economics of Money, Banking, and Financial Markets*. 4th ed. Glenview, IL: Scott, Foresman, 1995.

Chapter 28 is recommended. This chapter includes an examination of the German hyperinflation in 1921–1923 and discusses the different views of inflation.

Mishkin, Frederic S. *Strategies for Controlling Inflation*. NBER Working Paper Series 6122. Cambridge, MA: National Bureau of Economic Research, Inc., 1997.

Examines four basic strategies policymakers use to combat inflation.

Schiller, Bradley R. *The Macro Economy Today*. 4th ed. New York: Random House, 1989.

Chapter 7 thoroughly discusses the different types of inflation, and Chapters 14 and 15 extensively cover supply-side policies and the policies of the Reagan administration, respectively.

Walton, Gary M., and Frank C. Wykoff. *Understanding Economics Today*, 5th ed. Chicago: Richard D. Irwin, 1996.

Chapters 14 and 15 are recommended; both are well-written and interesting.

Weintraub, Sidney. *Capitalism's Inflation and Unemployment Crisis.* Reading, MA: Addison-Wesley, 1978.

Sidney Weintraub is one of the pioneers of the tax-based incomes policy. Chapter 3 presents the underlying theory behind the TIP proposal; Chapter 6 discusses the proposal.

World Wide Web Resources

Consumer Prices Indexes
www.bls.gov/cpihome.htm

Gives links to data, news releases, publications and other documentation, FAQs, and other information.

Economic Report of the President
www.access.gpo.gov/eop

Sponsored by the Executive Office of the President. Enter search terms to find statistical information on banks and banking.

Federal Deposit Insurance Corporation (FDIC)
www.fdic.gov

Gives access to consumer information, banking information, statistical information, and asset information.

Federal Reserve Bank of St. Louis
www.stls.frb.org/index.html

Click on Economic Research from the main page to get more information about U.S. monetary policy.

Federal Reserve Board
www.bog.frb.fed.us

Provides links to the following sites: about the Federal Reserve Board, statistics, publications, the 12 Reserve Banks, the annual report to Congress, and general information.

Government Expenditure and Tax Issues

Who Wins and Who Loses?

Chapter Outline

Checklist of Economic Concepts

Government purchases
Government transfer payments
Collective goods
External benefits and costs
Equal tax treatment doctrine
Horizontal equity

Vertical equity
Relative tax treatment doctrine
Ability-to-pay principle of
    taxation
Progressive tax rates
Proportional tax rates

Benefits-received principle of
    taxation
Tax efficiency
Forward and backward tax
    shifting
Tax incidence

I am reminded of the mythical Midwestern farmer retired Senator Stephen M. Young (D-Ohio) used to tell about.

He rode free to public school on free buses, studied agriculture under the GI bill, bought his home with a VA loan, got his power through Rural Electrification Administration lines and sent his kids to government-subsidized colleges on government loans.

He eventually made it big in the farming business, joined the John Birch Society and finally, disgusted with his high taxes, wrote to his senator, one Stephen Young:

"I believe in rugged individualism. People should stand on their own two feet, not expect government aid. I stand on my own two feet. I oppose all those socialistic trends you have been voting for and demand return to the free enterprise system of our forefathers."[1]

[1]William Raspberry, " 'American Way' OK, for the Other Guy," *Tulsa Word*, Section A-13, February 16, 1979.

What Are People Afraid Of?

A great concern of people seems to be related to the involvement of government in their daily lives in the forms of questionable government services, regulations and controls, and the payment of taxes. As is apparent from the introductory quote, many people do not object when they receive government services free or below the market price, but they do object when others are on the receiving line and when they have to pay taxes to support government. On a broader, more philosophical plane, people fear that the increasing scope of government narrows their individual choices and reduces their individual rights.

Most fears of people are related to the *size of government* and to the *distribution of taxes*. Issues connected to government size and tax distributions are the focal points of this chapter.

Size of Government

There appears to be a growing feeling among people that government is too big. If this is so, it could certainly be argued that government services and taxes should be cut. Is there a basis for this feeling?

Some of the fears of people concerning government size are well-founded. Government activities have extended into areas of society not deemed necessary many decades ago. Taxes have risen to pay for these activities until today almost all families have to part with a significant amount of their income in order to pay taxes. The worry that people have about government waste and the abuse that is connected with government expenditures is not imaginary. People have found out about these things through the various means of communication. A day, a month, and certainly a year rarely pass without a report on unnecessary government expenditures or on abuse of some sort in the operation of one or more government expenditure programs.

Some fears of people concerning government size are not well-founded. Although the history of many government expenditure programs is a story of growth, waste, and some abuse, there is also the other side that shows at least in part the success of many government expenditure programs, including the provision of benefits to many people and the fulfillment of the needs of people living in a changing society. For example, since the beginning of the Social Security program in 1936, Social Security taxes have grown rapidly and have become a heavy tax burden to many taxpayers. At the same time, however, this program has been enlarged in scope and coverage and now includes not only retirement income and unemployment benefits to those covered but also health care benefits. More, not less, public debate and scrutiny of government activities are needed, if unneeded programs are to be eliminated and needed programs are to be improved.

The source of some fears is not specific and concrete but more general and philosophical. Fear of too much government is an important aspect of the American heritage. The idea that "the least government is the best government" encourages individual choice and problem solving in the marketplace. In a market-oriented economy, the supposition is that the market will solve problems impersonally and efficiently. It is this belief that underlies the concerns of people when the government interferes in the market.

Tax Inequities

A major concern of people involves the question of tax equity, that is, tax justice. Tax equity refers to the way taxes are distributed among people. Even if tax collections were exactly the right amount to pay for government goods and services demanded by people, there could be concern that tax distributions were not fair. Some taxpayers may be paying more than what they believe is a fair amount, and some may be paying less than what others believe is a fair amount. So, in addition to the fear that government is too big and taxes too high generally, there is the fear that taxes are "too low" for certain taxpayers and "too high" for certain others.

There is ample evidence that there are tax inequities in the tax system at all levels of government. The concept of equity will be developed, and illustrations of tax inequities are presented later in the chapter. It may suffice here to point out that the fears that people have concerning the fairness of tax distributions are in part justifiable.

The Problem of Size

Our approach to the problem of size is, first, to provide background information concerning this problem and, second, to analyze the problem of size in reference to the economic criteria of efficiency and equity.

Government Expenditures

People's concern over the size of government is understandable if you just look at the absolute level and growth in government expenditures. Over the 1960–1997 period, government expenditures increased from $121 billion to $2,511 billion. This is an astounding increase. However, a better prospective of the size of government is revealed if the growth in government spending is compared to the growth in the overall economy as measured by the gross domestic product (GDP). Figure 13–1 shows this pattern of growth. Total government expenditures (federal, state, and local government) grew from 23 percent of the GDP in 1960 to 31 percent in 1997. The federal government expenditure share of the GDP grew from 17 percent to 22 percent, and total state and local government expenditure share grew from 6 percent to 9 percent over the same time period.

Two interesting and somewhat surprising trends are revealed in Figure 13–1. First, total government expenditures have just barely kept up with the growth in the economy since 1980, increasing from 30 percent of the nation's income in 1980 to 31 percent in 1997. Second, this 1 percent relative growth in total government expenditures is due strictly to the relative growth in total state and local government expenditures. It appears then that the size of government is a justifiable concern people should continue to have; however, in recent decades the relative size of government hasn't changed, especially the relative size of the federal government.

Transfer payments are government expenditures in the form of money payments to people who have not contributed to the current production of goods and services.

Government **purchases of goods and services** are expenditures for currently produced goods and services and are a part of the nation's income.

Another matter of interest to some people is the relative importance of the type of government expenditure. Government expenditures may be classified as *transfer payments* or government *purchases of goods and services*. Transfer payments are payments to people who have not made a contribution to the current production of goods and services, whereas government purchases are expenditures for currently produced goods and services. Figure 13–2 (page 362) shows government purchases (G) and transfer payment (Tr) as a percentage of the GDP over the 1960–1997 period. Both government purchases and transfer payments as a percent of

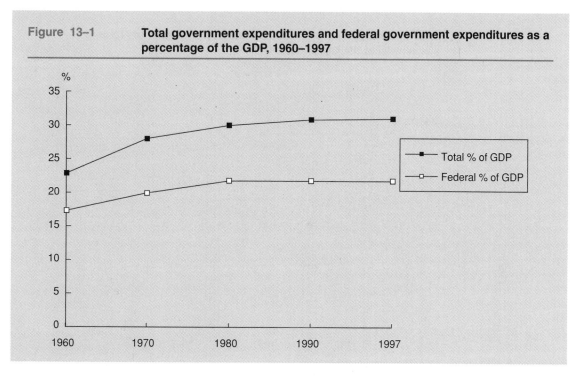

Figure 13–1

Total government expenditures and federal government expenditures as a percentage of the GDP, 1960–1997

Source: Economic Report of the President, February 1998, p. 378.

the nation's income increased in the decade of sixties. Since the sixties, government purchases have not grown as fast as the overall economy, decreasing from 23 percent of the GDP in 1970 to 18 percent in 1997. In contrast, transfer payments have grown slowly but steadily faster than the economy, generally increasing from 8 percent of GDP in 1970 to 14 percent in 1997. This is because of the relative expansion in government transfer programs such as the Social Security and Medicare programs, which are discussed in detail in Chapter 14.

Government Receipts

The other side of the government expenditure-revenue system, receipts, shows a similar pattern with respect to the GDP as government expenditures in the 1960s and 1970s. As Figure 13–3 (page 363) shows, government receipts grew faster than the GDP in these periods, increasing from 26 percent in 1960 to 30 percent in 1980. Government receipts were the same percentage of the GDP in 1990 as it was in 1980 but increased to 32 percent in 1997. As a percentage of the GDP, government receipts were 1 percentage point above government expenditures in 1997.

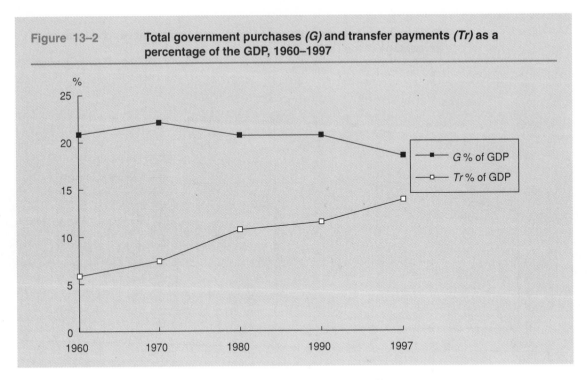

Figure 13–2   Total government purchases *(G)* and transfer payments *(Tr)* as a percentage of the GDP, 1960–1997

Source: Economic Report of the President, February 1998, pp. 281, 379.

Economic Analysis of the Problem of Size

Economic efficiency and equity are two concepts that have been used to analyze many issues previously discussed. Efficiency was the major consideration in the discussion of resource allocation in Chapter 2. It was the basis for evaluation in the examination of the energy problem, the economics of crime, and pollution problems. Equity came directly into play in the treatment of poverty and discrimination. Efficiency in the use of scarce resources of society causes society to produce as many goods and services and to satisfy as many human wants as possible. Equity is concerned with the distribution of goods and services among people. Both equity and efficiency considerations are involved in an analysis of the size of government, for the size of government is determined by expenditure programs aimed at redressing the unequal distribution of income and at providing goods and services that would not be provided at all, or at least would not be provided in efficient quantities, in the marketplace.

Figure 13–3   **Total government receipts and federal government receipts as a percentage of the GDP, 1960–1997**

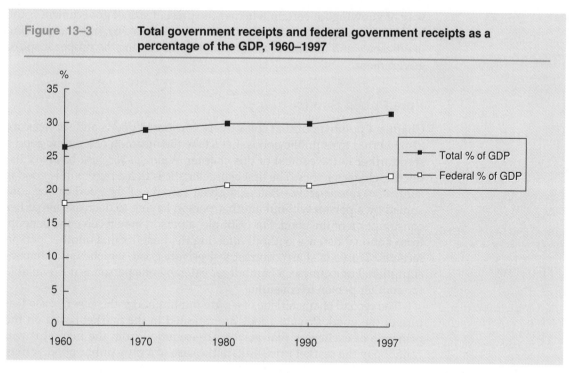

Source: Economic Report of the President, February 1998, p. 378.

An Efficient Level of Government Expenditures

An efficient level of government expenditures is that level at which the *net* benefits to society are maximized, that is, the level at which benefits and costs are equal at the margin. The maximization of net benefits and the equation of marginal benefits and costs were illustrated in Chapter 4 in analyzing the correct (efficient) level of crime prevention activities. To move to an efficient level, government expenditures would be increased (decreased) when the marginal benefits per dollar spent in the public sector of the economy is greater (less) than the marginal benefits per dollar spent in the private sector. Finally, the efficient level of government expenditures would be reached when the marginal benefit per dollar spent in the public sector is equal to the marginal benefit per dollar spent in the private sector.

Although cost-benefit analysis has practical application in many instances and is the guide to an efficient allocation of resources, it must be acknowledged that benefits and costs of government expenditures can seldom be precisely quantified, and often government programs are developed without any attempt to estimate benefits and costs. Thus, there is no way of knowing for certain whether the present size of government is too big or too small. Further insight can be gained, however, into the question of efficiency and the size of government by discussing the proper scope of government.

Pure Public Goods

Chapter 4 pointed out that collectively consumed goods and services are also referred to as public goods. Let's take the meaning of a public good a step further in the context of this chapter. A *pure public good* has two distinctive characteristics. The first characteristic is that a pure public good is *nonrival in consumption*—that is, a given amount of the good can be consumed by a person without another person having to decrease his or her consumption of the good. For example, a person may receive the benefits from national defense without affecting the benefits that another person receives. This is in sharp contrast to a private good, which is rival in consumption. For example, a hamburger eaten by one person is not available for another person to consume.

Nonrival in consumption means that a given amount of the good can be consumed by a person without another person having to decrease his or her consumption of the good.

The second characteristic of a pure public good is the *nonexclusion* feature of the good. Private goods are rationed in the market based on the principle of exclusion; that is, you are excluded from the market if you cannot pay the market price. But, in the case of a pure public good, it may not be feasible to exclude people or it may be undesirable to do so. For instance, everyone should receive the benefits from crime prevention activities: No one should be excluded.

The **nonexclusion** feature of a good means that it may not be feasible or it may not be desirable to exclude people from consuming the good.

The nonrival in consumption and the nonexclusion features of public goods, such as defense and crime prevention activities, make it difficult, if not impossible, for these goods and services to be supplied and demanded in the marketplace. It may be worth remembering that (1) the demand for public goods is not generally divisible into small units on the basis of individual quantities demanded and (2) the supply of public goods is not generally divisible into small units. Thus, it is widely accepted that pure public goods fall under the domain of the government to provide.

The main issue in the supply of public goods, then, is for the government to supply an efficient amount of these goods. This means that estimates of marginal benefits and costs have to be made. As you know, the efficient level of defense spending is the level where marginal benefits equal marginal costs. How would you derive the demand or the marginal benefits for a public good? The demand for a private good is simply the horizontal summation of the quantities that consumers are willing to buy at each possible price. Now in the case of a public good, the demand for a public good is derived by vertically summing up the individual marginal benefits at each quantity. It is much more difficult to determine the efficient level of public goods. In contrast to buyers in the private market, buyers in the market for public goods have an incentive not to reveal their preferences since the quantity available for consumption may not be directly affected.

External Benefits and Costs

The line of demarcation between what government should provide and what private producers should provide would be clear if all goods and services were either collective or private goods and services. However, you have already learned that in the production of certain goods there can be social spillover costs, and in the consumption of certain goods and services there can be social spillover benefits. The existence of *externalities,* that is, social spillovers in production and consumption, broadens the scope of government beyond collective goods and services.

Externalities are the social spillover benefits or costs that flow from the private consumption or production of a product.

Market demand indicates marginal private benefits *(MPB),* and market supply indicates marginal private costs *(MPC).* Assuming no externalities, marginal private benefits and costs equal marginal social benefits and costs. However, if either external benefits or costs are present, a divergence will exist between private and social benefits or between private and social costs. This divergence means that government action is required for resources to be used efficiently.

Figure 13–4 shows private demand and supply of good A. Assuming that no external benefits and costs exist, the efficient quantity would be Q, and the price would be P. Suppose, now, that in the consumption of good A, there are external benefits. In Figure 13–4, the demand curve D_T shows both marginal private and external benefits $(MPB + MEB)$; that is, D_T shows the total marginal social benefits. The demand curve that indicates all benefits is the relevant one. Thus, the efficient quantity in Figure 13–4 is Q_E, not Q. What can government do to guarantee that the efficient quantity is provided?

The government could consider two choices. One choice would be for the government to produce good A and attempt to produce the efficient quantity. This type of action presumes that government will be an efficient supplier and can accurately estimate marginal social benefits. The second choice of action does not depend on government's being an efficient supplier but still depends on precise estimates of benefits. Government action could be in the form of subsidies to consumers of good A so that they would be willing to purchase the efficient quantity. In Figure 13–4, consumers would buy the correct amount at P_0 The total subsidy payment would be equal to $[(P_E - P_0) \times Q_E]$. A subsidy payment greater than this would result in too much production of good A, and a subsidy payment smaller would mean that less than the efficient quantity is produced.

The case of external costs in production was examined in Chapter 5 and illustrated in the case of water pollution in the production of paper. In this instance, the market price was too low and the production of paper was too high because external cost in the form of water pollution was not

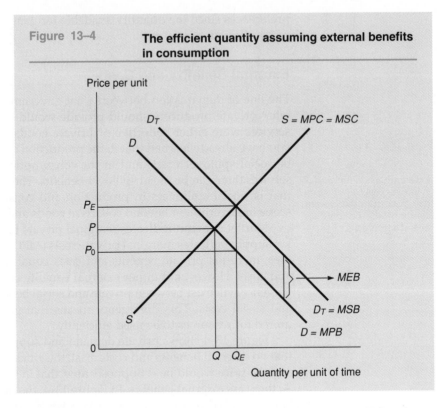

Figure 13–4   **The efficient quantity assuming external benefits in consumption**

D represents marginal private benefits *(MPB)*, and D_T represents *MPB* and marginal external benefits *(MEB)*. Given the supply curve *S*, the optimum or efficient quantity is at Q_E, where *MSB* equals *MSC*. The government could ensure that the efficient quantity would be demanded by giving a subsidy payment to consumers equal to $[(P_E - P_0) \times Q_E]$.

taken into account in the supply of paper. To correct this situation, the government could levy a tax on each unit of paper supplied. The effect of the tax would be to increase the marginal cost of supplying paper and, therefore, to decrease supply. Assuming that the tax equals marginal external costs, an efficient but lower quantity of paper will be supplied at a higher price. The price elasticity of demand for paper will determine how much the price of paper will rise as a result of the tax.

Income Distribution

Government actions thus far have been rationalized on economic efficiency grounds. The scope of government has been greatly extended and defended based on the belief that income inequality needs to be reduced. The distribution of income, and therefore consumption, would be largely based on the productivity of people in a highly competitive economy. A social problem arises because some people have no or low productivity. What should be done to alter the distribution of income so as to help people who cannot work and those who can work little?

Shifting income from those who are relatively productive to those who are relatively unproductive, say through taxes and subsidies, must be based on the values of people as to what constitutes a "fair" distribution. It is not surprising that government programs aimed directly or indirectly at altering the distribution of income are under constant attack. Evidently there is general support for programs aimed directly at helping low-income people, such as public assistance and the food stamp programs, and for programs that only indirectly help certain low-income groups, such as the Social Security program, for these programs have expanded relative to other government programs. Paralleling this growth has been the increased controversy concerning income transfer programs. Although the debate is not likely to end, the responsibility of government in the area of income redistribution is seemingly established. No private institutions could thoroughly cope with the problem.

Summary

The major ideas that have evolved from our discussion thus far are these: (1) pure public goods and services must be supplied by government; (2) government actions are needed to improve the efficiency of the market system, especially where there are externalities; and (3) government may alter the distribution of income in order to move in the direction of an equitable distribution as determined by the beliefs of people in our society.

Tax Principles and Analysis

The first part of this section develops a theoretical framework based on the criteria of equity and efficiency. The second part examines tax principles pertaining to the shifting and incidence of taxes.

Tax Equity

The **equal tax treatment doctrine** states that taxpayers in the same economic circumstances should be treated equally.

Horizontal equity is achieved when people in identical economic circumstances pay an equal amount of taxes.

Everyone agrees that taxes should be "just." Not everyone agrees, however, on the exact meaning of justice or fairness in taxation. An idea that runs strongly through Western thought is that tax justice means that taxpayers in equal economic circumstances should be treated equally. This is called the *equal tax treatment doctrine* and pertains to *horizontal* equity; that is, people in identical economic positions should pay equal taxes.

In the application of the equal tax treatment doctrine, the best indicator or measure of economic circumstances has to be determined.

Generally, economists interpret economic circumstances to mean a person's real income, namely, consumption plus changes in net wealth. Assuming that real income is the best measure of economic circumstances, then horizontal equity is achieved when all taxpayers with the same income pay exactly the same amount in taxes.

What about taxpayers in different economic circumstances? How should they be treated? These questions are related to the idea of *vertical* equity, that is, the tax treatment of taxpayers in different economic circumstances. The *relative tax treatment doctrine* now emerges: Taxpayers in different economic circumstances should be treated differently. But how differently? Two principles of taxation have been developed to shed light on this question—the *ability-to-pay principle* and the *benefits-received principle*.

Vertical equity is achieved when taxpayers in different economic circumstances are treated unequally based on either the ability to pay or the benefits received.

The **relative tax treatment doctrine** states that taxpayers in different economic circumstances should be treated unequally.

The **ability-to-pay principle** of taxation states that taxes should be distributed among taxpayers based on the ability to pay taxes.

Ability-to-Pay Principle. The ability-to-pay principle of taxation suggests that taxpayers with more ability to pay taxes should pay more taxes. Again, using income as the measure of ability to pay, this means that taxpayers with more income should pay more taxes. But how much more? Progressive and proportional income tax rates are always consistent with the ability-to-pay principle because if the rate of taxation (the percentage of income paid in taxes) is rising as income rises (progressive rates) or constant as income rises (proportional rates), the amount paid in taxes will always be higher as income is higher. On the other hand, regressive tax rates can violate the ability-to-pay principle since the percentage of income paid in taxes decreases as income rises.

The **benefits-received principle** of taxation states that taxes should be distributed among taxpayers based on the individual benefits received from government goods and services.

Benefits-Received Principle. Do you recall the way the market distributes the costs of producing private goods and services? The market distributes costs based on marginal private benefits. The benefits-received principle of taxation is an attempt to apply the rule of market and is thus a guide to an efficient allocation of taxes rather than to an equitable allocation. However, efficient and equitable tax distributions are not always in conflict, and when equity in the distribution of income is not a concern, the benefits-received principle of taxation is an important tax standard. This principle is more limited than the ability-to-pay principle because private benefits received from government goods and services are usually more difficult to measure than the ability to pay. Illustrations of taxes that are defended on the benefits-received principle are the gasoline tax and local street assessments. The gasoline tax is used primarily to pay for highways. Thus, the demander of highway services, the automobile user, pays for the benefits received from highway services through a tax levied on gallons of gasoline consumed. It is argued that well-maintained local streets benefit property owners by enhancing the value of property. Thus, it is reasoned that property owners should pay in the form of property taxes for the benefits they receive from streets.

Tax Efficiency

There are two aspects of tax efficiency. First, tax efficiency is concerned with the *administration* and *compliance* cost of taxes. Taxes should be economical to collect and to enforce. They should also be convenient and certain to the taxpayer.

The **excess burden** of a tax is a measure of tax inefficiency; that is, it measures the nonneutral or the distortionary effects of the tax on relative prices and resource allocation.

The second and more important aspect of tax efficiency involves minimizing what economists call the *excess burden* from taxes. The idea of an excess burden from taxes can be grasped easily with an illustration. Suppose the government transfers $10 billion worth of resources from the private sector to the public sector via taxes and provides marginal benefits equal to $10 billion. Further, suppose that in the levy of taxes, tax rates are used that discourage incentives to work so that private production is less than what it would have been by $1 billion. It becomes clear in this example that there is a net loss of $1 billion even though the government is using the resources transferred as efficiently as they would be used in the private sector. This net loss in production resulting from the disincentive effects of taxes is the excess burden that has arisen because of the imposition of taxes.

If there is no excess burden or if the excess burden is small, then it can be said that taxes have *neutral* effects or near-neutral effects on the operation of private economy. Unfortunately, taxes seldom have completely neutral effects. However, certain taxes adhere to the idea of neutrality better than others, and these are the taxes that we are searching for to put into an ideal tax scheme. Taxes that directly alter relative commodity prices or that do so indirectly through altering consumption and income patterns are taxes that have strong nonneutral effects and do not adhere to the concept of tax efficiency. For example, a tax levied on a specific commodity will increase the price of that commodity and result in a shift of spending away from the taxed commodity to nontaxed commodities. Progressive and regressive income tax rates change the pattern of income distribution as well as alter the price of work relative to the price of leisure.

Principles of Shifting and Incidence

Taxes may be levied on one taxpayer and shifted to another taxpayer. A tax that is shifted *forward* is a tax that falls on the consumer in the form of higher prices; a tax that is shifted *backward* falls on the owners of resources in the form of lower resource prices. The *incidence* or burden of a tax that is not shifted, then, remains on the original taxpayer.

Forward shifting occurs when any part of a tax is paid for by consumers in the form of higher prices.

Backward shifting occurs when any part of the tax is paid for by the owners of resources in the form of lower resource prices.

The **incidence** of a tax is the burden or the final resting place of the tax.

Two kinds of taxes are to be considered in the following analysis. The first is an output tax, and the second is a tax levied independent of output.

An Output Tax. An output tax is a tax that is levied on each unit of output produced, such as a tax on each pack of cigarettes or on each gallon of gasoline. An output tax increases the cost of producing each unit and, therefore, decreases supply. Given the demand for the taxed commodity, a decrease in supply will increase the price of the commodity. How much of the tax will be shifted forward?

The extent of the forward shifting of an output tax depends essentially on the price elasticity of demand. If demand is *perfectly* inelastic (Figure 13–5), the entire tax is shifted forward. The incidence of the tax, under these circumstances, is *completely* on the consumer in the form of higher prices. If demand is *perfectly* elastic (Figure 13–6), none of the tax is shifted forward; or, in other words, all the tax is shifted backward to resources in the form of lower prices (lower wages, etc.). The elasticity of demand for most products will not be either of these two extremes. We can generalize, then, by saying that an output tax will normally be shifted forward and backward, with more forward shifting when demand is more inelastic and more backward shifting when demand is more elastic.

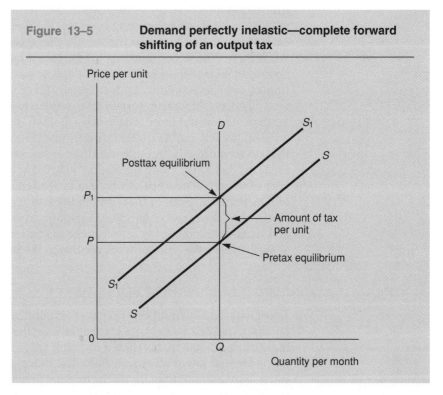

Figure 13–5   Demand perfectly inelastic—complete forward shifting of an output tax

The pretax equilibrium is at a price of P and at a quantity of Q where supply S intersects demand D. An output tax on each unit produced is levied with the amount of the tax shown above. The effect is to decrease supply to S_1. Thus, price rises to P_1, where S_1 intersects D. The full amount of the tax is shifted forward because the rise in price from P to P_1 equals the amount of the tax.

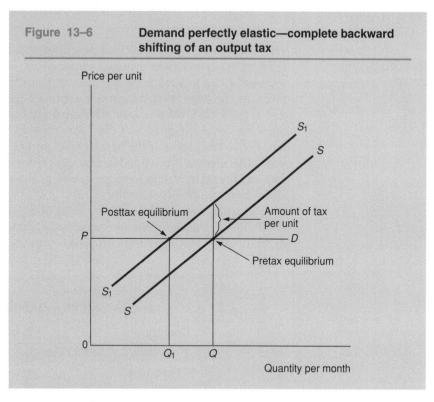

Figure 13–6   Demand perfectly elastic—complete backward shifting of an output tax

The pretax equilibrium is at a price of *P* and a quantity of *Q* where supply *S* intersects demand *D*. An output tax decreases supply to S_1. The posttax equilibrium is at a price *P* and a quantity of Q_1 where supply S_1 intersects demand *D*. There is no forward shifting of the tax because price does not change. Thus, the entire tax is shifted backward to owners of resources.

Independent of Output Tax. A tax levied on income, say the net income or profits of a business, is a good illustration of the tax we are to consider. Suppose a business has selected the best output, that is, the output where profits are maximized, before a 25 percent profits tax is imposed. Now, after the tax, is there a better output? The answer is "no." If the best output is selected before the tax, it remains the best output after the tax. There is no short-run shifting of a tax levied independently of output. The incidence of such a tax is on the owners of the business in the form of a reduction in profits. The difference between an output tax and a tax independent of output is that the former increases costs and decreases supply, whereas the latter does not. For taxes to be shifted, a change in supply has to occur.

The American Tax System

The American tax system is best described as a hybrid system because it relies on taxes levied on income, consumption, and wealth. The major tax sources at the federal level are income taxes, payroll taxes, and excise taxes. At the state level the main tax sources are sales and income taxes, and at the local level property taxes are a vital source of revenue. Two interesting developments over the years have been the increasing importance of payroll taxes at the federal level and of income taxes at the state level. This change has tended to make the federal tax system less progressive and the state system more progressive; however, the federal system is still a more progressive system.

Tax collections in this country were 31.5 percent of the GDP in 1994 (Table 13–1). This is the smallest share of income gleaned by the government of any modern, industrialized country for tax purposes. For

Table 13–1	Tax share of GDP in selected countries, 1994
Country	**% of GDP**
Group of Seven	
United States	31.5
Japan	32.3
Germany	46.5
France	48.9
Italy	44.9
United Kingdom	36.4
Canada	42.2
Australia	32.9
Austria	47.5
Belgium	51.1
Denmark	60.0
Finland	53.1
Greece	35.4
Ireland	41.6
Netherlands	51.4
Norway	55.3
Portugal	45.7
Spain	39.0
Sweden	58.4

Source: Economic Report of the President, February 1996, p. 81.

example, in Canada, the United Kingdom, France, Germany, and many other countries, tax collections are in the 40 to 50 percent range of their respective incomes. Some countries—Belgium, Denmark, Finland, The Netherlands, Norway, and Sweden—have tax collections that exceed 50 percent of the income of the country. The relatively low tax share of GDP in the United States is certainly consistent with the belief in this country in a market-dominated economy.

Federal Tax System

Table 13–2 shows the composition of federal receipts on a fiscal year basis from 1950 to 1998. Approximately 80 percent of federal receipts comes from two tax sources, individual income taxes and social insurance taxes, which pays for Social Security benefits and are sometimes referred to as payroll taxes since they are levied on wages and salaries. Individual income taxes have not changed very much in relative importance over the years, although there have been some major changes in the income tax. Corporate income taxes and excise taxes have declined significantly in relative importance over the past four decades. In contrast, social insurance taxes have increased significantly in relative importance over the same time period. The net effect of these changes has made the federal tax system less progressive.

The federal tax system is a progressive tax rate system, meaning that the ratio of taxes paid to income rises as you move up the income ladder (Table 13–3). The effective federal tax rates projected for 1996 began at 8 percent on the lowest family income bracket (0–$10,000) and ended at 23.7 percent on the highest income bracket ($200,000 and over). On average,

Table 13–2	Composition of federal receipts (% of total receipts)			
Fiscal Year	Individual Income Tax	Corporate Income Tax	Social Insurance Taxes	Excise Tax
1950	39.9	26.5	11.0	19.1
1960	44.0	23.2	15.9	12.6
1970	46.9	17.0	23.0	8.1
1980	47.2	12.5	30.5	4.7
1990	45.3	9.1	36.9	3.4
1998	46.3	11.5	34.4	3.4

Sources: Economic Report of the President, February 1996, p. 83; and February 1998, p. 376.

Table 13–3	Projected effective federal tax rates, 1996
Family Economic Income Class	**Effective Tax Rate, %**
$ 0–$ 10,000	8.0
$ 10,000–$ 20,000	8.8
$ 20,000–$ 30,000	13.3
$ 30,000–$ 50,000	17.5
$ 50,000–$ 75,000	19.5
$ 75,000–$100,000	21.1
$100,000–$200,000	22.0
$200,000 and over	23.7
Total	20.1

Source: Economic Report of the President, February 1996, p. 83.

about 20 percent of the income of a family was sent to the Internal Revenue Service in 1996. This is only a few percentage points higher than what was estimated in 1980 in a study by Joseph A. Pechman.[2]

The federal tax system meets then the ability-to-pay principle of taxation and is generally a fair or equitable tax system. Since the federal tax system is a mildly progressive system, the distribution of income after taxes is more equally distributed; this certainly is true. The Gini coefficient is a measure of income inequality. A number closer to 1 means you have more income inequality. In 1994, the Gini coefficient was .45 before taxes and .39 after taxes. It is interesting to note, however, that both before-tax and after-tax income became more unequal in the 1980s.[3]

Recent Federal Tax Changes

Major income tax reform was undertaken in 1986 that moved the system toward a fairer and a more efficient system. Tax increases in 1991 and 1993 were motivated primarily to reduce the federal budget deficit. Both candidates in the 1996 presidential election proposed tax cuts. Tax cuts appear likely in the future. In what direction will these tax cuts move the system?

---

[2]Joseph A. Pechman, *Who Paid the Taxes, 1966–1985* (Washington, DC: Brookings Institution, 1985).

[3]Ibid., p. 4.

The 1986 Tax Reform Act

Individual income tax rates were drastically cut under the new tax reform act. Instead of 14 income tax rates ranging from 11 to 50 percent under the previous law, there were marginal rates of 15, 28, and 33 percent. However, there were only two effective rates, 15 and 28 percent under tax reform, because the 33 percent marginal rate was phased out on high-income classes when the average tax rate equaled 28 percent. Corporate income tax rates were also reduced under tax reform. The top corporate income tax rate was reduced from 46 to 34 percent. The main benefit from lower marginal tax rates on personal and corporate income was the movement of the federal tax system toward a more neutral and efficient tax system.

The 1986 Tax Reform Act broadened the income tax base. The investment tax credit was eliminated. The long-term capital gains income tax exclusion was repealed. The accelerated depreciation of capital assets was reduced. Losses from tax-sheltered investment could not be deducted from other income. State and local government sales taxes could not be deducted. Interest on consumer loans was phased out as a tax deduction. Mortgage interest was deductible only for the principal and second residence. Investment interest was deductible only against investment income. The dividend tax exclusion, the two-earner couple deduction, and income averaging were disallowed. Many people lost their $2,000 deductible from contributing to an individual retirement account (IRA). Even people who receive prizes and awards for their achievements were no longer permitted to exclude these monetary gifts as income for tax purposes. The list of tax deductions, income exclusions, and credits repealed under the new reform law does not end here, but most of the controversial ones are included in this list. It took a great deal of courage for Congress to eliminate many of these income tax breaks. Tax breaks are politically popular, and sometimes an economic argument can be made for a tax break, such as an investment tax credit to stimulate the economy. However, the temporary benefit that may flow from an investment tax credit should be weighed carefully against other tax policy alternatives and the long-run benefit that flows from a comprehensive income tax base and lower income tax rates.

Every income class gained under the income tax reform. There was a 6.6 percent decrease in taxes for all income classes. The lowest income groups had the greatest percentage of reduction in their taxes. The data clearly indicate the positive impact of a more comprehensive tax base and lower tax rates on the distribution of income taxes among income groups, and the resulting improvement in tax equity. The income tax reform that Congress passed in 1986 was a landmark in the history of tax legislation. However, even at this time many people believed that Congress would revert in the future to the traditional practices of eroding the income tax base by granting tax breaks to certain groups.

Tax Increases in 1991

After much deliberation and several extensions in the deadline date to finalize the 1991 fiscal year federal budget, a highly controversial budget accord was reached. The Bush administration and its supporters in Congress wanted to reduce the capital gains tax rate and reduce the federal budget deficit. The thinking was that a reduction in the capital gains tax rate would stimulate the economy and eventually would increase tax revenues. The Democrats in Congress opposed the cut in the capital gains tax and wanted to increase progressive income rates. The final result was a compromise.

The effective personal income top tax rate was increased from 28 to 31 percent under the new law. The income tax rates of 15 and 28 percent on the lowest income and middle-income groups, respectively, remained unchanged. It was estimated that the increase in the marginal income tax rate will increase income tax collections $11.2 billion over a 5-year period. Additionally, high-income taxpayers lose $300 in deductions for each $10,000 of income above $100,000, and the personal exemption was phased out for taxpayers starting with an income of $100,000 and ending with an income of $225,000. The decrease in deductions and the phasing out of the personal exemption for high-income receivers was estimated to increase income tax collections $29 billion in a 5-year period.

The federal gasoline tax on January 1, 1991, was raised from 9 cents to 14 cents per gallon under the new legislation. This was calculated to increase gasoline tax collections $25 billion over a 5-year period. The cigarette tax rate was increased 4 cents per pack on January 1, 1991, and was increased another 4 cents on January 1, 1993. These two tax rate increases will bring the cigarette tax rate to 25 cents per pack, which was estimated to increase tax collections by $5.9 billion over a 5-year time span. Finally, the increases in tax rates on alcoholic beverages were as follows: increase on liquor by $1 per gallon; increase on beer by 16 cents per six-pack; and an increase on wine by 21 cents per bottle. The increase in taxes on these products was forecasted to raise $8.8 billion over 5 years.

A luxury tax of 10 percent was imposed on autos costing over $30,000, on airplanes over $250,000, and on furs and jewelry over $10,000. The tax on an airplane ticket was increased from 8 percent of the ticket price to 10 percent. The tax on a telephone call of 3 percent was extended, the income ceiling of $51,300 was raised to $125,000 on persons subject to the withholding tax of 1.45 percent for Medicare, and state and local government employees who were not in a retirement system were made subject to Social Security fees. All these tax increases were approximated to bring in $48 billion in tax revenues over a 5-year period.

The major purpose of these tax rate increases was to increase tax collections by about $500 billion in order to reduce the federal budget over a 5-year period. Unfortunately, these tax rate increases went into effect when the economy was in a recession and trying to recover. Thus, the timing of the tax rate increases could not have been worse. There is a justification for tax increases to finance efficient increases in federal spending at a time when the economy is expanding; however, major tax increases when the economy is in a contraction intensifies recessionary forces operating in the economy. With respect to the impact of the tax rate increases on the federal tax system, the personal income system would be more progressive with the increase in the top rate from 28 to 31 percent, and the decrease in tax deductions and exemptions for high-income groups. On the other hand, with the exception of the new tax on luxuries, tax rate increases on gasoline, cigarettes, and alcohol tend to be regressive. The final effect of the tax rate increases on the distribution of taxes, then, may be very small or have no major effect at all. This may be what Congress had in mind.

The 1993 Federal Budget Deficit Reduction Plan

The Clinton administration wasted no time after taking office in 1993 in proposing to Congress major tax increases and expenditure decreases aimed primarily at reducing the federal budget deficit. Congress responded favorably, with the one exception of eliminating the short-run stimulus package that was included in the proposal, and President Clinton signed into law, in August, The Omnibus Budget Reconciliation Act of 1993. This act was guided by three principles. The first principle that has been stated was to reduce the budget deficit. The second principle was to accomplish the deficit reduction goal through a balance of tax increases and expenditure cuts. The third principle was to enact tax increases that would increase the tax burden only on the very highest income class.

This final principle was effectively implemented by increasing the two top marginal personal income tax rates to 36 and 39.6 percent, respectively. As you remember, the top marginal income tax rate was increased from 28 to 31 percent in 1991. Under this new act in 1993, the next to the highest income class ($140,000 to $250,000) is subject to a marginal tax rate of 36 percent and the highest income class (over $250,000) is subject to a marginal tax rate of 39.6 percent. The way this rate of 39.6 percent is calculated is that there is a surtax of 10 percent on all taxable income over $250,000. Thus, for every dollar of taxable income over $250,000 the tax rate is equal to 39.6 percent (36 percent + 10 percent of 36 percent). It was estimated that these income tax rate increases will increase taxes for only about 1.2 percent of the highest income taxpayers.

Other federal tax increases in 1993 included an increase in the corporate income tax rate from 34 to 35 percent, an increase in taxable Social Security benefits from 50 to 75 percent, an increase in the motor fuels tax of 4.3 cents per gallon, and the 2.9 percent payroll tax for Medicare was made subject to all wage earnings instead of the first $135,000 of earnings.

The federal government expenditure cuts in the Act of 1993 include reductions on the discretionary side of the budget and on the mandatory side. Discretionary spending cuts were estimated to be a real cut of about 13 percent, and included a reduction in the federal workforce of 100,000, a delay in the 1994 cost-of-living adjustments for federal employees, and cuts in national defense spending. The largest planned cut in mandatory spending was the cut in Medicare spending, which was estimated to re-duce Medicare spending by $18 billion by 1998. Other mandatory spend-ing cuts included reductions in spending on agriculture and veterans' programs. Total expenditure reductions were estimated to reach $87 bil-lion by 1998.

The 1993–1999 Fiscal Year Period: A New Era?

We stated that the goal of The Omnibus Budget Reconciliation Act of 1993 was to reduce federal budget deficits. Let's take a look at federal budget deficits over the period since fiscal year 1993. Table 13–4 shows federal government receipts and expenditures and the resulting budget deficit (−) or surplus (+) in the fiscal year period 1993–1999. Is this a new era? Fed-eral government receipts grew 51 percent, or at an annual average growth rate of 8.5 percent, while expenditures grew 23 percent, or at an annual av-erage growth rate of 3.8 percent, over the same time period. The results were (1) a budget deficit below $200 billion in 1995, (2) a budget deficit be-low $100 billion in 1997, (3) almost a balanced budget in 1998, and (4) a budget surplus of $10 billion estimated for the fiscal year 1999. This will be the first budget surplus in three decades if it occurs.

The federal reduction budget plan in 1993 certainly contributed to the reductions in the budget deficits over the period. President Clinton, re-elected for a second term, submitted to Congress in 1997 a budget for the fiscal year 1998 that included a 5-year plan which called for a future bal-anced budget. This was to be done by a reduction in the growth rate of some government programs. For example, savings of $100 billion were ex-pected from cutbacks in Medicare spending over the planning period. Both tax cuts and tax increases were proposed by the Clinton administra-tion in the 1998 fiscal year budget plan. Congress was not generally sup-portive of the tax increases. However, the estimate is that the budget deficit will trickle down to $10 billion in fiscal year 1998. There is a great deal of uncertainty with regard to the fiscal year 1999 even though a $10 billion budget surplus was estimated for the year as stated above. Con-gress and the president did manage to get together at the last moment in October 1998 and signed the necessary appropriation bills. The two high-lights covered in the news were the $1.1 billion for education to help local school districts hire teachers and reduce class size, which was promoted by the Clinton administration, and the $9.2 billion worth of tax credits for

Table 13–4	Federal receipts and expenditures during the fiscal year period 1993–1999		
Fiscal Year	Receipts ($ Billions)	Expenditures ($ Billions)	Deficit (−)/Surplus (+) ($ Billions)
1993	1,154	1,409	− 255
1994	1,259	1,462	− 201
1995	1,352	1,516	− 114
1996	1,453	1,561	− 108
1997	1,579	1,601	− 22
1998*	1,658	1,668	− 10
1999*	1,743	1,733	+ 10

*Estimates
Source: Economic Report of the President, February 1998, p. 373.

business supported by Republicans. The two big issues were not resolved. The president wanted the estimated budget surplus in the future to be set aside and used to alleviate the Social Security crisis anticipated in the future, and the Republicans favored using the surplus to make up for the lost revenue from a proposed $80 billion tax cut over 5 years.

In summary, the 1993–1999 fiscal year period is a new era with respect to policies designed to reduce and policies that have successfully reduced the federal budget deficit. A great deal of the credit of federal budget deficit reduction should go to the robust and expanding economy, for a major part of the growth in federal receipts is attributed to the growth in the nation's income. Some people would rightfully argue that the reduction in federal budget deficits decreased the interest rate and increased private investments and therefore has contributed to the growth in the economy. Chapter 15 takes a closer look at this relationship between government budget deficits and private saving and investment. For now, it is important to remember that government policies intended to move toward a balanced federal budget are appropriate in a full-employment and growing economy.

Summary

People are concerned about the size of government and inequities in the distribution of taxes, so this chapter focused on the problems of government size and of tax distributions. After the fears of people were discussed and conclusions were reached that some worries are well-founded and some are not, the problems of government size and tax distributions were approached in the same manner. First, relevant facts were presented; second, an economic framework was developed based essentially on the concepts of efficiency and equity; and finally, policy proposals were discussed to deal with these problems.

In the economic analysis of the problem of size, efficiency considerations justify government expenditures in the form of provisions of collective goods and services, in the form of subsidies to encourage more consumption when external benefits in consumption are present, and in the form of taxes to discourage production when external costs in production are present. Equity considerations justify government programs designed to enhance the economic opportunities of people who do not earn adequate income in the marketplace. The "adequacy" of income as well as the socially accepted distribution of income among people must be based on the beliefs of people.

In the development of tax principles, it was pointed out that an efficient tax is one that has neutral effects on the allocation of resources, and an equitable tax is one that can be defended on the ability-to-pay principle or the benefits-received principle. An equitable system would adhere to the equal tax treatment doctrine and to the relative tax treatment doctrine.

The incidence or burden of a tax is the final resting place of the tax. A tax may be shifted forward to consumers in the form of higher prices or backward to the owners of resources in the form of lower resource prices. The shifting of an output-type tax, such as the gasoline tax, depends on the price elasticity of demand. The more inelastic demand is, the more the tax will be shifted to consumers in the form of higher prices. A tax that is independent of output, such as an income tax, does not increase the cost of producing goods and services; therefore, this type of tax is not shifted, at least in the short run. For a tax to be shifted, supply has to decrease.

The Income Tax Reform Act of 1986 made fundamental changes in the federal income tax system. The income tax base was made much broader by the elimination of many tax deductions, tax exclusions, and tax credits. Many income brackets and tax rates were reduced. The top marginal tax rate was lowered from 50 to 28 percent. Taxpayers in all income classes benefited from the reform, but taxpayers in the lower-income classes benefited the most. The net effect of tax reform was to move the federal income tax system in the direction of a more equitable and efficient tax system.

The top marginal federal income tax rate of 28 percent had a short life. The rate was increased to 31 percent under the Bush administration in 1991 and increased to 39.6 percent under the Clinton administration in 1993 along with other tax hikes in both years. The rationale for all the tax increases in 1991 and 1993 was to reduce the federal budget deficit. The timing for tax increases and budget deficit reductions was much better in 1993 than in 1991 when the economy was trying to emerge from recession. In contrast, the economy was expanding in 1993. The adverse effects on the economy of the tax increases in 1993 were offset by the prospective stimulating effects of reducing federal budget deficits and the resulting lower interest rates. In any event, the economy continued on an expansionary path. This expansionary fiscal year time period 1993–1999 was somewhat of an unusual time period in which government budget deficit reduction policies were associated with a healthy economy.

Discussion Questions

1. Discuss people's fears about the size of government. Include in your discussion an historical account of the growth of government expenditures and government revenues. Are these fears justified?
2. What are the characteristics of pure public goods? Explain why these goods cannot be supplied in the private marketplace. What criterion should the government use in determining the quantity of pure public goods?
3. Discuss why externalities on the demand side or the supply side of the market result in an inefficient quantity of goods produced and sold, even in a perfectly competitive market.
4. Assuming externalities on the demand side, explain how the government may pursue a policy that would lead to an efficient quantity produced and sold.
5. Discuss the meaning of tax equity and tax efficiency. Design a federal income tax system based on the two tax criteria of equity and efficiency.
6. What is meant by the shifting and incident of a tax? Compare and contrast the shifting and incidence of an income-type tax to an output-type tax.
7. Discuss the 1986 Income Tax Reform Act and recent federal income tax changes.
8. Discuss and evaluate the Clinton administration's 1998 fiscal year budget plan.

Additional Readings

Aaron, Henry J., and Michael J. Boskin, eds. *The Economics of Taxation.* Washington, DC: Brookings Institution, 1980.

Collection of essays on the economics, politics, and legal problems of taxation.

Aaron, Henry and Joseph A. Pechman, eds. *How Taxes Affect Economic Behavior.* Washington, DC: Brookings Institution, 1981.

Views of various authors are presented in order to determine the possible effectiveness of tax policy to stimulate economic growth.

Dworak, Robert J. *Taxpayers, Taxes, and Government Spending: Perspectives on the Taxpayer Revolt.* New York: Praeger, 1980.

Examines the results of the taxpayer revolt of 1978 and offers alternatives to higher taxes for all levels of government.

Lindsey, Lawrence B. "Did ERTA Raise the Share of Taxes Paid by Upper-Income Taxpayers? Will TRA 86 Be a Repeat?" In *Tax Policy and the Economy,* ed. Lawrence H. Summers. Cambridge: MIT Press, 1984.

Examines the impact of the Economic Recovery Tax Act of 1981 and the impact of the Tax Reform Act of 1986 on income tax revenue.

Pechman, Joseph A. *Federal Tax Reform.* 4th ed. Washington, DC; Brookings Institution, 1983.

This reference covers the major deficiencies in the federal tax system and discusses various tax reform measures.

Pechman, Joseph A. *Who Paid the Taxes, 1966–85.* Washington, DC: Brookings Institution, 1985.

Shows the distribution of taxes by income groups under various shifting and incidence assumptions. This is the best tax incidence study to date.

Pechman, Joseph A. "Tax Reform: Theory and Practice." In *Readings in Public Sector Economics,* eds. Samuel H. Baker and Catherine S. Elliot. Lexington, MA: Heath, 1990.

Discusses the Tax Reform Act of 1986 and presents the impact of tax reform on the incidence of income taxes.

World Wide Web Resources

Economic Report of the President
www.access.gpo.gov/eop

Sponsored by the Executive Office of the President. Use the *search terms* box to find statistical information on taxes and taxation.

Income Tax Information on the Internet
www.taxresources.com

Provides sites to IRS forms and documents, public tax articles, professional tax articles, tax treaty resources, foreign tax, and other information.

Joint Economic Committee
www.senate.gov/comm/jec/general/flatax.html

Explains the flat tax, and gives links to FAQs, principles of the model tax system, and how the flat tax would benefit individuals and businesses.

TaxResources
www.best.com/~ftmexpat/html/taxsites/law-legi.html

The United States Income Tax Law is available at this site. It also gives links to the most up-to-date U.S. tax codes, a history of the Sixteenth Amendment, and House of Representatives and Senate sites.

United States Internal Revenue Service
www.irs.ustreas.gov/prod/cover.html

Gives tax statistics, electronic services, and taxation relations, forms, and publications.

CHAPTER

14

Social Security and Medicare

How Secure Is Our Safety Net for the Elderly?

Chapter Outline

Checklist of Economic Concepts

Today, 44 million Americans depend upon Social Security, and for two-thirds of our senior citizens it is the main source of income. For 18 percent of our seniors it is the only source of income. But Social Security is more than just a retirement program. More than one in three of the beneficiaries are not retirees. They are the children and spouses of working people who die in their prime. They are men and women who become disabled, or their children. So Social Security is also a life insurance policy, and a disability policy, as well as a rock-solid guarantee of support in old age. That is why we have to act with care as we make needed repairs to the program occasioned by the huge growth in retirees.

When President Roosevelt signed the bill creating the Social Security system, most seniors in America were poor. A typical elderly person sent a letter to FDR begging him to eliminate "the stark terror of penniless old age." Since then, the elderly poverty rate has dropped sharply. In 1959, the poverty rate was over 35 percent for retirees. In 1979, it had dropped to 15.2 percent. In 1996, the poverty rate was down below 11 percent. Even though most seniors need other sources of income in addition to Social Security to maintain a comfortable lifestyle, if Social Security did not exist, today half of all American retirees would be living in poverty—60 percent of all women. Fifteen million American seniors have been lifted out of poverty through the Social Security system.

Today the system is sound, but the demographic crisis looming is clear. The baby boomers—76 million of us—are now looking ahead to their retirement. And people, clearly, are living longer, so that by 2030, there will be nearly twice as many elderly as there are today. All these trends will impose heavy strains on the system. In 1960, which wasn't so long ago, there were over five people working for every person drawing Social Security. In 1997, there were over three people—3.3 people—working for every person drawing. But by 2030, because of the increasing average age, if present birthrates and immigration rates and retirement rates continue, there will be only two people working for every person drawing Social Security.

Now, here's the bottom line. The Social Security Trust Fund is sufficient to pay all the obligations of Social Security—both retirement and disability—until [2032], after which it will no longer cover those obligations. Payroll contributions will only be enough to cover 75 cents on the dollar of current benefits. If we act now, we can ensure strong retirement benefits for the baby boom generation without placing an undue burden on our children and grandchildren. . . .

To the older Americans, let me say, you have nothing to worry about. For you Social Security is as strong as ever. To the younger people here today who may believe that you will never see a Social Security check, indeed, I saw a poll which purported to be serious that said that Americans in their twenties thought it was more likely they would see a U.F.O. than that they would ever draw Social Security. That skepticism may have been well founded in the past, but just as we put our fiscal house in order, we can and must put Social Security in order. And above all, to my fellow baby boomers, let me say that none of us wants our own retirement to be a burden to our children and to their efforts to raise our grandchildren. It would be unconscionable if we failed to act, and act now, as one nation renewing the ties that bind us across generations.[1]

[1]Taken from President Bill Clinton's address to a national forum on Social Security in Kansas City, MO, April 7, 1998.

Social Insurance

"What does the future hold?" "What will happen to my family if I become sick or disabled and unable to work?" "Will I be able to afford a secure retirement?" "Can I obtain adequate health care as I grow older?'

We have all asked ourselves such questions, even though they can never be answered with certainty. The world is full of unexpected events that can dramatically change our lives. Accidents, illnesses, and deaths each year interrupt the lives of millions of families. Because some of these events are more likely to occur than others, people may gain some protection for themselves from the known risks of life through the purchase of insurance. *Private insurance* is a contract whereby individuals agree to make payments, often called premiums, to a company in return for a guarantee of financial benefits in the event that some undesired circumstance occurs. In the modern economy, private insurance is common since most people insure their valuable possessions against damage or loss—their cars, their homes, and even their lives. In addition to the availability of private insurance, today most national governments, including the United States, provide their citizens with a variety of social insurance programs. *Social insurance* programs, financed through tax revenues, guarantee citizens financial benefits from the government for events that are beyond an individual's control, such as old age, disability, poor health, and loss of employment.

A number of U.S. federal programs fall under the definition of social insurance; however, the largest and arguably the most popular is Social Security, with its health care companion, Medicare. Today, most workers and employers in the private economy pay taxes to support the Social Security system. Likewise, millions of Americans each year rely on Social Security and Medicare to maintain their quality of life. The program was

Private insurance is a contract whereby individuals agree to make payments, often called premiums, to a company in return for a guarantee of financial benefits in the event that some undesired circumstance occurs.

Social insurance programs are government programs, financed through tax revenues, that guarantee citizens financial benefits for events which are beyond an individual's control, such as old age, disability, and poor health.

specifically created to reduce the economic insecurity that often accompanied growing old, but over time it has expanded to provide benefits to other at-risk populations.

Although the evidence indicates that Social Security has been successful in improving the plight of the aged, the program has always been controversial, and soon it will face serious economic problems. As President Clinton noted in his address reprinted above, the demographic trends of the late twentieth century have created a number of significant challenges for the long-run economic stability of the Social Security system. Most notable of these trends is the disparity in the sizes of the "baby boom generation" and the younger generations that follow it. The relative sizes of these groups can be seen in the "population tree" reproduced as Figure 14–1 (next page). Notice the "bulge" created by the large number of people between 30 and 50 and the significantly smaller numbers of people at younger ages. As time passes, more and more baby boomers will reach retirement age and become eligible for Social Security pensions. At current tax rates and level of benefits, the smaller younger generations will not be able to support the Social Security demands of the larger older generation.

In this chapter we will explore the nature and possible solutions of this predicament by investigating the economic and financial structure of our major social insurance programs. Furthermore, given that Social Security and Medicare directly affect the income and purchasing power of a large segment of society, we will discover that social insurance has the ability to significantly influence, or perhaps even distort, economic decision making with regard to issues such as the savings rate, the supply of labor, age at retirement, and the demand for health care. Each of these issues has political and social as well as economic dimensions. This chapter will provide a basic framework within which these economic dimensions can be addressed.

Social Security

A Brief History of Social Security

The concept of a national social insurance program did not originate in the United States. That distinction belongs to Germany, where in the late 1880s Chancellor Otto von Bismarck implemented his Prussian Plan to provide retirement pensions and other benefits to German workers. The success of the Prussian Plan led to the adoption of similar programs in other western European nations. Although some states and the federal government did provide pensions for civil servants and veterans, a national social insurance program for all workers was not established in the United States until 1935.

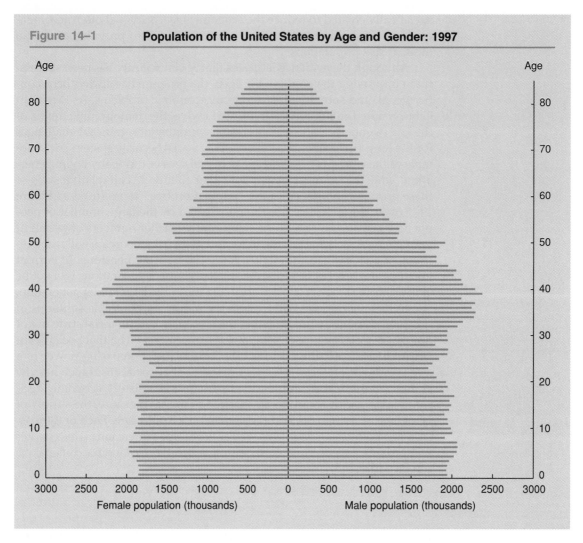

Figure 14–1   **Population of the United States by Age and Gender: 1997**

Source: U.S. Department of Commerce, Bureau of the Census, *Statistical Abstract of the United States,* 1998.1

Throughout the 1930s, American workers experienced the disastrous economic effects of the Great Depression. At some points during this period the national unemployment rate reached almost 25 percent, and most of those lucky enough to hold full-time jobs found that their paychecks purchased very little. Throughout the Great Depression hundreds of commercial banks and financial institutions went bankrupt and were forced to close. Many workers who had saved for personal emergencies and their own retirements lost everything. The future economic security of the average American worker looked very bleak in 1934 when President

Franklin D. Roosevelt recommended to Congress the establishment of a national social insurance program. A year later, on August 14, 1935, the president signed into law the Social Security Act.

The original Social Security Act created a program whereby monthly benefits were to be paid to individual workers upon retirement at age 65. The level of benefits received was to be based on each worker's contribution to the program in the form of a payroll tax collected over his or her working lifetime. The federal government began collecting Social Security taxes in 1937, but before the first regular monthly payments to retirees were issued, Congress significantly modified the program. Amendments to the Social Security Act in 1939 created two new categories of beneficiaries that greatly expanded the scope of the program. First, dependents (spouse and children) of a retired worker were extended benefits upon the death of the retiree. Second, surviving family members became entitled to Social Security benefits in the case of the death of a covered worker. These changes shifted the focus of the Social Security program from the individual to the family.

The program's focus on the family is also evident in the next major enhancement of Social Security. In the 1950s and 1960s, amendments to the Social Security Act created benefits for those who became disabled and could no longer work to support their families. Disability benefits were made available not only for covered workers but also for their dependents. The 1960s also saw the enactment of a new early retirement option, whereby workers could begin receiving reduced Social Security benefits at age 62. The expanded scope of the Social Security Act led to a tremendous growth in the number of Americans receiving benefits. By 1970 Social Security had more than 26 million beneficiaries (see Table 14–1 next page).

Perhaps the most important enhancement to date of the American social insurance system occurred in 1965 when President Lyndon B. Johnson signed the bill that authorized the establishment of Medicare. Medicare is the federal program that provides health care coverage to almost all Americans aged 65 or older. Although many European nations include universal health care coverage as a major element of their social insurance programs, the United States government continues to limit coverage to the elderly and leaves the private sector responsible for providing health care to those below the age of normal retirement. The unique characteristics of the health care industry keep the Medicare program at the forefront of public debate concerning the proper role of government in caring for the welfare of its citizens. (These issues will be discussed later in this chapter.)

Social Security, by any reasonable measure, is one of the most popular and successful federal programs in the United States. By 1997, almost 44 million people received monthly checks from the Social Security Administration, which distributed retirement, survivors, and disability benefits in excess of $360 billion. Many Americans have come to depend on Social Security and view their future benefits as part of their personal wealth.

Table 14–1	The growth of Social Security over time	
Year	**Number of Beneficiaries**	**Total Benefits Paid**
1940	222,000	$35,000,000
1950	3,477,000	$961,000,000
1960	14,845,000	$11,245,000,000
1970	26,229,000	$31,863,000,000
1980	35,585,000	$120,511,000,000
1990	39,832,000	$247,796,000,000
1997	43,971,000	$362,000,000,000

Source: Social Security Administration, various publications. All numbers represent the Old Age and Survivors Insurance and the Disability Insurance programs combined. Dollar figures are reported in current dollars.

Because of this, Social Security is often referred to as an "entitlement" program. The personal importance that most people place on the Social Security system guarantees that its administration and financial soundness is almost always an issue for public discourse and political debate. This has certainly been true in recent years.

The Current Status of Social Security

The Organizational Structure.   Today, the program that most people refer to as Social Security is officially known as the Old Age, Survivors, and Disability Insurance (OASDI) program. OASDI is not only much broader in its scope and coverage than the original Social Security program, it is financed very differently from the way the program was first conceived. Under the original plan, Social Security was to operate in a manner very similar to the way private insurance works. Specifically, individual workers were to make contributions to the program throughout their working lives, and these contributions would be deposited in a fund managed by the government. The fund would accumulate and earn interest over time. Thus, when a worker retired, the interest and principle from the fund would be used to finance the worker's benefits. This type of program, whereby annual benefit expenditures are primarily funded by interest income earned on accumulated payments, is commonly called *a fully funded insurance scheme.* Even though Social Security was originally designed to be a fully funded insurance program, it never operated as such because the immediate pressures to provide benefits to elderly workers who had lost their savings during the Great Depression did not allow the system time to build up an adequate investment fund. In 1939 Social

A **fully funded insurance scheme** provides benefits that are financed from the interest income earned on accumulated payments.

A **pay-as-you-go insurance scheme** provides benefits that are financed from current payments.

Security was converted to a *pay-as-you-go insurance scheme*. Under this type of plan, annual benefit expenditures are financed from current contributions. In other words, the Social Security benefits paid to current recipients are paid from the tax contributions of those presently working. (Notice that one result of this type of financial structure is an intergenerational transfer of income from taxpaying workers to beneficiaries.)

Until recently, OASDI continued to operate as a pay-as-you-go system, whereby one generation's retirees, survivors, and disability beneficiaries were supported by the next generation's workers. During the 1980s and 1990s the baby boom generation swelled the size of the American labor force, and the annual tax contributions the Social Security Administration collected began to significantly exceed the annual amount of benefits paid. The consequence of this action has been the accumulation of a significant surplus that grows each year. This surplus is held in the Social Security Trust Fund, which will be used in the future to help offset the expected increase in benefits payable as the baby boomers reach retirement age. Therefore, at the present time Social Security is neither a fully funded system nor a pure pay-as-you-go system but rather a hybrid combination of the two schemes. Current Social Security taxes are partially used to finance the payments made to current beneficiaries and are partially invested in the Social Security Trust Fund. The Trust Fund will be used to finance the benefits that are payable in the future. At the beginning of calendar year 1998, the Social Security Trust Fund had more than $655 billion in assets, up about 15 percent from the previous year.

The Way Social Security Works.   The vast majority of workers in the private sector of the American economy are now covered by the Social Security system, which is financially supported through the collection of a tax imposed on wages. This payroll tax is a flat percentage of annual gross wages, up to a certain limit, split evenly between the employee and the employer. Although the sharing of the tax bill between the worker and firm was intended to split the cost equally, it is clear that employers may be able to shift all or part of their burden to the workers in the form of lower wages. Both OASDI and Medicare are financed through this form of payroll tax. The current tax rate is 6.20 percent for OASDI and 1.45 percent for hospital insurance under Medicare. Therefore, both employees and employers pay a 7.65 percent payroll tax to support Social Security and Medicare. [Most employees have their share of this tax automatically deducted from their paychecks through the Federal Insurance Contributions Act (FICA).] Workers who are self-employed must pay the combined total of 15.30 percent. In 1998, the payroll tax for OASDI was limited to the first $68,400 in earnings, but there was no earnings ceiling for the tax used to support Medicare's hospital insurance program.

The OASDI benefit structure results in a partial redistribution of income from beneficiaries who earned high wages to those who earned low wages. When a person files a claim with the Social Security Administration, his or her monthly benefits will depend on a number of characteristics, including age, familial status, and most importantly, earnings history. A set of standardized formulas are applied to determine the level of benefits each individual is entitled to receive. (Currently, workers must accumulate 40 "qualifying" quarter years of work to become eligible for pension benefits.) Workers with lower average wages over their lifetimes will receive smaller monthly benefits than those with higher average wages. However, the benefit formulas are designed to provide lower wage workers with a greater percentage of their past earnings than higher wage workers receive. For example, in 1995 it was estimated that Social Security replaced 55.4 percent of earnings for lower wage workers but only 23.5 percent of earnings for higher wage workers. The average earnings replacement rate for Social Security beneficiaries that year was 41.1 percent. Furthermore, the standardized formulas guarantee that recipients with dependents (a spouse and/or children) receive a greater monthly benefit than those recipients who are single. Table 14–2 provides the average monthly Social Security benefits paid to various categories of people in 1997. (If you are interested in the specific rules and formulas used to determine Social Security eligibility and benefit payments, please visit the Social Security Administration Web site referenced at the end of this chapter.)

Under the present rules, workers who retire at age 65 are entitled to full monthly benefits. Workers may choose to retire earlier, beginning at age 62, and receive benefits equal to approximately 80 percent of what they would receive by retiring at 65. Workers may also choose to retire later than 65 and receive an increase in their monthly benefits. Because of

Table 14–2	Average Social Security benefits: 1997
Type of Beneficiary	**Average Monthly Benefit**
Retired workers	$765
Spouses	393
Children (Each)	349
Disabled workers	$722
Spouses	177
Children (each)	201
Survivors	
Nondisabled widows and widowers	$731
Disabled widows and widowers	480
Widowed mothers and fathers	532
Surviving children	500
Parents	636

Source: Social Security Administration, *Fast Facts & Figures About Social Security 1998.*

financial pressures on the system, which we will discuss later, recent amendments to the law will gradually increase the age of retirement at which workers are entitled to full Social Security benefits. By the year 2022, workers will not be able to receive full Social Security retirement benefits until the age of 67.

Another important feature of Social Security for retirees is that their benefits are influenced by their current earnings from work. Retirees are allowed to earn wages and salaries up to some predetermined limit before their benefits are reduced. The earnings limit is determined each year based on national average wages. A penalty is imposed on earnings above this limit—currently benefits are reduced at a rate of $1 for every $3 earned.

Cost of Living Allowances, or COLAs. The Social Security COLA is equal to the amount of inflation experienced within the economy during the previous year as measured by the consumer price index (CPI).

Every year since 1975, Social Security beneficiaries automatically receive increases in their monthly checks to counter the corrosive effects of inflation. These adjustments are known as *Cost of Living Allowances,* or COLAs. The Social Security COLA is equal to the amount of inflation experienced within the economy during the previous year as measured by the consumer price index (CPI). (See Chapter 12 for a discussion of the CPI.) In this respect Social Security is more generous than most private pension plans that seldom incorporate automatic COLAs into their benefit packages. One obvious consequence of this nicety is the growing cost to maintain the program over time.

The Economic Effects of Social Security

Because Social Security touches almost every American family in one way or another, the program has significant social and economic effects. During the past 65 years economists have closely monitored and studied the impacts of Social Security on individuals and the economy. Studies show that both Social Security taxes and Social Security benefits influence a variety of important economic variables, such as disposable income, the labor supply, and savings. It can be easily postulated that the U.S. economy would look very different today if the Social Security system did not exist.

Income

Perhaps the most obvious economic effects of the modern Social Security system are its impacts on disposable income. First, for those working, the Social Security tax reduces take-home pay and thereby lowers their disposable income. However, for those in the elderly, survivors, and disabled populations who receive benefits, Social Security clearly increases their disposable income. As Table 14–1 indicated, more than $360 billion in OASDI benefits were distributed in 1997 to about 44 million recipients. This amount represents a substantial annual contribution of income to households with traditionally high marginal propensities to consume.

Since its inception, Social Security has grown in its importance as a source of income for the aged population. According to the Social Security Administration, more than 90 percent of today's elderly households receive Social Security benefits. (An elderly household is defined as one headed by a person aged 65 or older.) To put this into perspective, consider that only 30 percent of elderly households receive private pensions. Clearly, Social Security payments are widely distributed among the older citizens of this country. Furthermore, the relative size of Social Security benefits, compared to other sources of income, continues to grow over time. In fact, two-thirds of household members aged 65 or older who receive Social Security report that it comprises 50 percent or more of their total income. An astonishing 18 percent of elderly households report that Social Security is their *only* source of income. In the aggregate, Social Security income accounts for 40 percent of senior citizens' income. Figure 14–2 illustrates that Social Security is by far and away the largest single source of disposable income for this population group.

An additional effect of the distribution of Social Security benefits is its impact on poverty. It is estimated that 9 percent of elderly families live below the poverty threshold; without Social Security this number would rise to 50 percent. Thus, Social Security lessens the need for other more traditional antipoverty income transfer programs. (Refer to Chapter 7 for a discussion of these programs.)

Social Security benefits represent a significant source of consumption spending that has an obvious positive effect on aggregate demand. By supporting a higher level of aggregate demand, Social Security benefits tend to stimulate overall economic performance and growth. Social Security and the spending it supports are an integral and vital part of the modern economy.

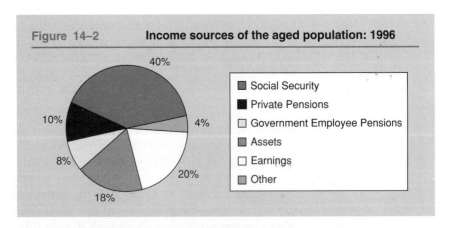

Figure 14–2   **Income sources of the aged population: 1996**

- 40% Social Security
- 10% Private Pensions
- 4% Government Employee Pensions
- 8% Assets
- 20% Earnings
- 18% Other

Source: Social Security Administration, *Fast Facts & Figures About Social Security 1998*

Labor Supply

Both Social Security taxes and Social Security benefits can affect the labor supply decisions of individual workers. The empirical evidence indicates that the overall effect is to cause a net reduction in the size of the labor force. How and why does this happen? The answer is a simple matter of economic incentives that influence the behavior of both the workers who pay Social Security taxes and those who receive Social Security benefits.

First, Social Security is financed through payroll taxes that are unlikely to have a neutral effect on worker behavior. As discussed earlier, the Social Security tax bill is split evenly between workers and their employers. The portion of the tax paid by the worker clearly reduces take-home pay. And this is compounded by the fact that employers could afford to pay higher wages if they were not responsible for their portion of the Social Security tax. Consequently, it is possible for employers to shift all or part of their Social Security tax burden to the worker in the form of lower wages. It seems clear then that the Social Security system tends to lead to lower real wages for workers covered by the program. This reduction in the wage can have an important effect on individual labor supply decisions. Recall that changes in the wage rate result in both a substitution effect and an income effect. The substitution effect turns on the fact that the wage rate is effectively the price of an hour of leisure time. (For example, workers making $10 per hour must give up that amount if they desire an additional hour of leisure.) As such, the reduction in the wage brought about by Social Security's payroll tax tends to reduce the price of leisure and causes the rational individual to choose more hours of leisure, that is, to work less. On the contrary, the income effect turns on the fact that leisure time is a normal good. Recall from Chapter 2 that the demand for normal goods rises as income rises and declines as income falls. The payroll tax in support of Social Security tends to reduce income and, as such, creates an income effect that causes the individual to desire less leisure, that is, to work more. In theory, it is not clear which of these effects dominates. If the substitution effect dominates an individual worker's decision, then the lower wage brought about by the Social Security tax causes the worker to substitute more leisure time for fewer hours of work. On the other hand, if the income effect of the wage reduction dominates, then an individual worker may choose to work more hours and demand less leisure time due to the tax.

While there is no theoretical answer to the question of which effect dominates, a great deal of empirical research has been conducted on the issue. These studies indicate that the substitution effect of the wage reduction appears to be stronger than the income effect for older workers, possibly because the value of leisure time tends to increase with age. Although other factors have undoubtedly influenced the trend, the effect of Social Security on work and retirement decisions can be seen in the changing labor force participation rates for older Americans. In 1930, before the enactment of the Social Security system, about 50 percent of men over the age of 65 were members of the labor force. Today, the percentage has dropped to 20. Even though economists have yet to determine the exact proportion of this decline caused by Social Security, there is considerable agreement that Social Security does reduce the overall supply of labor available to the economy.

Saving and Investment

Social Security also carries with it the potential to distort saving and investment behavior in a way that may be detrimental to the overall performance of the economy. Understanding this requires insight into the economic incentives and disincentives for saving that are created by the Social Security system. In practice, our Social Security system can influence the saving behavior of households at least three ways.

First, as we saw above, the Social Security system creates an incentive for older workers to reduce their supply of labor by retiring earlier. This implies that workers will enjoy longer periods of retirement than they would if Social Security did not exist. And longer retirements necessarily mean that workers have fewer years to accumulate assets to support their nonworking years. Thus, workers who plan for a lengthier retirement have an incentive to save more than otherwise during their working years. This is often referred to as the *retirement effect* of Social Security on saving.

The **retirement effect** is the incentive for workers to increase their saving behavior throughout their working lives because Social Security tends to increase the length of retirement.

A second possible way in which Social Security may increase personal saving is known as the *bequest effect*. This effect is based on the assumption that a major reason people save is to leave financial assets to their children after they die. Under the current operating structure, Social Security transfers income from the younger generation to the older generation. Recognizing this, people who wish to leave something to their children must save more during their working lives to compensate for this loss. Therefore, Social Security's bequest effect reinforces the positive impact of the retirement effect on private personal saving.

The **bequest effect** increases saving among people who wish to leave assets to their children as compensation for the losses incurred due to the burden of Social Security taxes.

The third way Social Security influences personal saving works in the opposite direction of the bequest and retirement effects. Because Social Security provides individuals and their families with a guaranteed retirement income in exchange for payroll taxes, workers may view Social Security as a form of saving. The value of future Social Security benefits is a major portion of many Americans' personal wealth. Thus, there is a tendency for workers to substitute the wealth accumulated through their participation in Social Security for other forms of wealth, such as private saving. Essentially, this *wealth substitution effect* accounts for the fact that many workers feel a diminished need to save because they are part of a Social Security system that guarantees them a future return on their tax dollars.

The **wealth substitution effect** reduces saving as workers substitute the wealth accumulated through participation in Social Security for other forms of private wealth.

If the retirement effect and the bequest effect induce people to save more and the wealth substitution effect induces people to save less, what is the net impact of Social Security on personal saving? This question has been the center of a number of controversial empirical studies. Based on the evidence, many economists today conclude that the wealth substitution effect dominates the other two. Consequently, it appears that Social Security reduces the total pool of savings in the overall economy. Furthermore, the size of this reduction may be quite large. Some studies indicate that total personal saving is less than half of what would exist without our current social insurance safety net.

The importance of a reduction in personal savings should not be ignored. In Chapter 11 we learned that saving is necessary to create the pool of funds available for productive investment. If Social Security reduces aggregate saving, fewer dollars are available for businesses to invest in private infrastructure and capital equipment or for individuals to invest in education and training. In this way Social Security may represent a constraint on both current aggregate demand and future economic growth. This concept may be illustrated with the use of a production possibilities model.

In Figure 14–3, the curve AD represents the production possibilities available to the economy. The axes are labeled to illustrate the trade-off between consumption goods and investment goods that the economy could produce with its available resources. If Social Security causes people to save less, this implies that they also consume relatively more than would otherwise be the case. Therefore, the economy may find itself at a point such as C instead of at a point like B, where relatively more resources would be devoted to investment goods. The short-run cost of the reduction in saving brought about by Social Security is the amount of investment goods given up, the distance $I_B I_C$. However, because fewer resources are devoted to investment good, such as new factories, office buildings, equipment, or educational systems, the economy will not grow as strongly or as quickly as it would if more savings had been available. Thus, the long-run cost is that the economy does not move to a higher production possibilities curve and a point like E, where more of both consumption and investment goods would be available.

Even though Social Security may have some negative economic side effects, the social benefits that the system generates in terms of financial support and economic security for the elderly, survivors, and disabled populations clearly outweigh these costs in the minds of the average American. Social Security is something that eventually touches almost everyone in our nation, and it has become a cherished institution that people are willing to protect. As such, it is important for us to identify and quantify these potential negative economic effects and to attempt to deal with them as effectively as possible as the Social Security system evolves. Of perhaps more immediate importance, however, is the heavy pressure that the changing demographics of the American population has placed on the Social Security system.

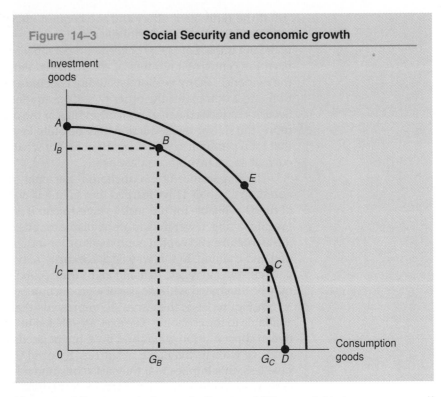

Figure 14–3   **Social Security and economic growth**

The curve AD represents the production possibilities available to an economy. If Social Security causes people to save less and therefore consume more, the economy may find itself at a point such as C, where relatively few resources are available for investment. Thus, one cost of Social Security is that it may not be able to move quickly to a higher production possibilities curve and a point like *E*, where more of both consumption and investment goods would be available.

The Future of Social Security

The Financial Dilemma

It has become apparent in recent years that the Social Security system faces a looming financial crisis. How can a program with billions of dollars in reserve find its future in jeopardy? The answer is ironic. As baby boomers—those of the generation who worked and paid the taxes that built up the large surplus in the Social Security Trust Fund—age and begin to retire, the expected payouts in benefits will exceed the expected inflow of tax contributions. When the Social Security Administration's expenditures become greater than its revenue, the Trust Fund will begin to shrink in size until it is depleted. To make matters worse, once the Trust Fund is empty, the Social Security system cannot revert back to a strict pay-as-you-go program at current tax and benefit levels because the current generation of workers is not of sufficient size to support the large generation of baby boom retirees and beneficiaries.

Figure 14–4 illustrates the projected future fate of the Social Security Trust Fund balance given current tax rates and level of benefits. Recent Social Security Administration forecasts indicate that tax revenues combined with the interest earned on the surplus in the Social Security Trust Fund will continue to exceed expenditures until 2021. In the following year the government will have to begin redeeming Trust Fund assets to cover the difference between income and spending. The Trust Fund balance will thus begin to fall until the year 2032, when the reserves will be exhausted. Before this critical point in time is reached, modifications to the structure of the Social Security system will have to be implemented to avoid significant tax increases and/or benefit reductions.

Possible Solutions

The public debate concerning how to best "fix" the looming financial crisis is not likely to go away anytime soon. Two major approaches have

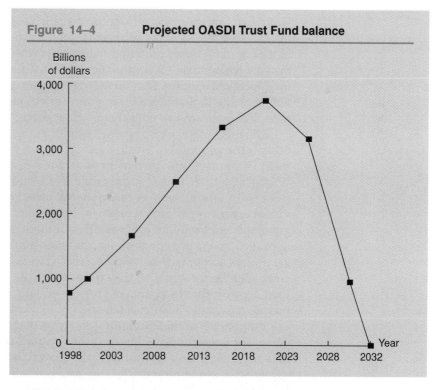

Figure 14–4   **Projected OASDI Trust Fund balance**

Source: Derived form *1998 Annual Report of the Board of Trustees of the Federal Old-Age and Survivors Insurance and Disability Insurance Trust Funds,* Table III.B3, p. 179.

been proposed to solve the problem: either modify the current system or establish a new fully funded system based on private individual accounts. Both approaches have received considerable support, and it is unclear which way, or combination of ways, we will ultimately choose.

The most direct way to address Social Security's financial problems is to simply change some of the current rules and operating policies. The most obvious change would be to increase the payroll tax that finances the system. Even though it has been estimated that modest increases in the current rate of taxation would postpone the shortfall in the Trust Fund by decades, there is very little political support for a tax hike, and therefore a tax increase is not likely to occur anytime soon. Another way to generate more money for Social Security is to transfer more funds from general tax revenues into the system. The federal budget surpluses of the late 1990s have made this a popular option, and President Clinton has proposed such a plan. The amount of the surplus to be transferred must be determined each year by Congress, and as such this should only be viewed as a stopgap measure and not a long-term solution.

If more money cannot be raised for Social Security, the other way to prop up the current system is by reducing its expenditures. Numerous ways have been proposed to do this. In fact, some measures to reduce expenditures have already been put into place, including an increase in the age at which full retirement benefits become available. Most workers now entering the labor force will not be able to receive full Social Security benefits until the age of 67. Other proposed changes not yet adopted include changing the way the annual COLAs are calculated and decreasing the benefits paid for dependent spouses. Undoubtedly, some form of program modifications will be made in the future to slow the growth of Social Security expenditures, but these are also unlikely to yield a lasting long-term solution.

The more innovative approach to addressing Social Security's funding crisis is the proposal to create a new program that would either supplement or replace the current system with personal security accounts (PSAs). The basic idea is to privatize part or all of Social Security. In its most radical form, Social Security payroll taxes would be placed into individual accounts for each worker in the system. Workers would then be given the responsibility to invest these dollars in various financial assets approved by the government, such as stock market funds or money market mutual accounts. When workers reach retirement age, or otherwise become eligible for benefits, they draw upon the savings accumulated in their account. Such a system of PSAs essentially represents a compulsory private retirement insurance scheme.

Proponents of the PSA approach argue that such a system would increase the net savings within the economy and make more dollars available for investment. In this way, the privatized system would encourage greater economic growth and provide beneficiaries with a greater financial return. Of course, one obvious drawback of such a system is that

Table 14-3   **Total return on stocks, bonds, and treasury bills: 1950–1997**

Period	Stocks	Stocks (after Inflation)	Bonds (10-Year)	Treasury Bills
1950–1959	19.28%	16.69%	0.73%	2.02%
1960–1969	7.78%	5.13%	2.42%	4.06%
1970–1979	5.82%	−0.14%	5.84%	6.42%
1980–1989	17.54%	11.87%	13.06%	9.21%
1990–1997	16.63%	13.09%	9.33%	5.03%
1950–1997	13.14%	8.70%	6.05%	5.33%

Source: U.S. Department of Commerce, Bureau of the Census. *Statistical Abstract of the United States,* 1998.

it exposes its participants to greater degrees of financial risk. Worker contributions would earn the market rate of return, which cannot be guaranteed during any period of time. Table 14–3 shows the total return on stocks and bonds experienced during the past five decades. Although the long-run return on these financial instruments may be impressive, notice the wide swings in returns between the decades. Most people do not have the luxury to time their retirement or disability needs to correspond to a strong financial market.

How do the rates of return in Table 14–3 compare to the returns experienced by Social Security beneficiaries who pay into the system throughout their working lives? This is a very complicated question to answer. Due to the benefit structure discussed above, obviously the return varies from person to person according to such factors as age, gender, marital status, and earnings history. Furthermore, analysts disagree about whether the financial return to Social Security should be based solely on a person's payroll contributions to the system or include the taxes paid on his or her behalf by employers. Because of these issues, empirical estimates of the return to Social Security vary widely. For example, one study found that the projected real return to Social Security for someone born in 1975 varied from –0.13 percent (for a single high-wage male) to 4.25 percent (for a one-earner low-wage couple).[2] Although such returns are less than the long-run market averages seen in Table 14–3, keep in mind that defined Social Security benefits are more stable over time because they are not subject to the often wild fluctuations of market activity.

---

[2]Steuerle, C. Eugene, and Jon M. Bakija. *Retooling Social Security for the 21st Century.* Washington, DC: The Urban Institute Press, 1994.

Some economists argue that a Social Security system which relies solely on the market is actually one with less security. That is, what if because of poor investment choices or simply because of significant and continued market declines a large proportion of retirees at some point in time find themselves with little or no income from their PSA? Isn't this the situation that Social Security was designed to eliminate?

A few nations, such as Chile, have adopted privatized social insurance programs with remarkable degrees of success, although it must be noted that they generally have done so during times of market prosperity. It is unclear how successful these programs would have been had they been implemented during a period of prolonged economic stagnation. Regardless, although it is very unlikely that Social Security will be replaced by a private system of compulsory saving, it is possible that elements of the private market will be incorporated into the system at some point in the future. For example, some have advocated that the Social Security Administration be allowed to invest a portion of its trust fund in the stock market or other private financial securities.

Medicare

The OASDI portion of the Social Security program analyzed above is designed to replace earnings lost due to retirement, disability, or early death. This is what most of us think of when we hear the term Social Security. In reality, of course, OASDI is just one part of the overall Social Security program. Another important component of Social Security is Medicare, which is the federal government's health insurance program for those 65 years and older. As discussed above, OASDI faces a funding dilemma created by the demographic shifts resulting from the baby boom generation. The same is true for Medicare since its primary funding source is a payroll tax levied on both workers and their employers. As important as the funding issue is, Medicare also carries with it incentives that have the potential to distort health care markets by contributing to excessive demand. And of course, where there is excessive demand, price increases tend to follow. To fully understand Medicare and how it creates incentives that can lead to inefficiencies in the market for health care, it is useful to be aware of some of the important trends taking place in that market.

The Market for Health Care: A Brief Overview

The Nation's Health Dollar: Where It Came From and Where It Went. Overall spending on health care in the United States reached a mind-boggling $1 trillion in 1996, or about 14 percent of the nation's income. To better understand this statistic, consider Figures 14–5 and 14–6 that, respectively, show where the typical or average health care dollar

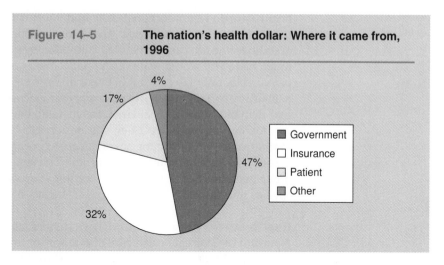

Figure 14–5   **The nation's health dollar: Where it came from, 1996**

Source: Health Care Financing Administration, Office of the Actuary, National Health Statistics, December 22, 1997. www.hcfa.gov

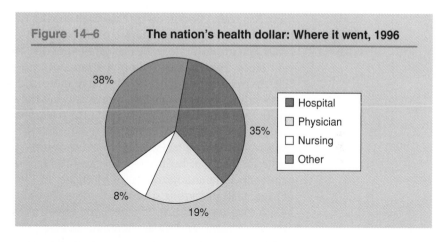

Figure 14–6   **The nation's health dollar: Where it went, 1996**

Source: Health Care Financing Administration, Office of the Actuary, National Health Statistics, December 22, 1997. www.hcfa.gov

came from and where it went in 1996. Figure 14–5 points out one of the most important features of the funding of health care expenditures in the United States. Specifically, only 17 cents of the typical dollar spent on health care comes from the direct consumer, that is, from the patient. On average, 83 cents of each dollar spent on health care in the United States is contributed by third parties—private health insurance (32 cents), public insurance (47 cents), and private donations (4 cents). Of course, consumers of health care do bear additional costs in the form of health insurance premiums and the like. Nevertheless, the impact of third-party payments on the quantity of health care demanded cannot be overstated. Just imagine how much more you would want of any particular good or service if you had to pay directly only 17 cents out of every dollar it costs. Clearly, a primary impact of any sort of third-party payments is to increase the quantity of health care demand by patients at large, as we detail later in this chapter.

As shown in Figure 14–6, the nation's health dollar went, as you might expect, primarily for hospital care (35 cents), physician services (19 cents), and nursing home care (8 cents). The rest of the dollar went for all other personal health services (26 cents) and other spending (12 cents), such as program administration, public health, research, and construction.

Health Care Inflation.   In 1950, we in the United States spent less than 4 percent of GDP on health care of one sort or another. By 1990, expenditures had grown to nearly 13 percent of GDP. While some of that increase purchased more and better care, much of it simply reflects the fact that the prices for health care products and services have often raced ahead at twice the overall rate of inflation. As Figure 14–7 points out, however, there has been good news on this front during the 1990s. Specifically, after rising at an average annual rate of more than 10 percent in the 1970s and 1980s, the growth rate in health care expenditures has decreased in every year since 1990, falling to only 4.4 percent in 1996. Put differently, since 1993, expenditures on health care have increased at roughly the same rate as spending in the overall economy, leaving the share of GDP devoted to health care roughly constant during the middle and late 1990s.

Government Role in Health Care Financing.   The government's role in the financing of health care services has increased steadily and significantly since the inauguration of Medicare in 1965. Prior to the enactment of Medicare, the public sector accounted for only about 25 percent of total health care expenditures. By 1990, the government's share had risen to almost 41 percent, and it has increased in every year since. In 1996, government financed nearly 50 percent of health care services provided in the United States.

The Growth in Importance of Medicare/Medicaid.   The combined spending on the two primary government health care programs, Medicare and Medicaid, came to $351 billion in 1996. (Recall from Chapter 7 that Medicaid is the federal program which provides health care benefits to the poor and economically disadvantaged.) This amounts to more than one-third of all the spending on health care and nearly three-quarters of all public spending on health care. The number of people receiving benefits under the Medicare and Medicaid programs was 38.1 million and 36.1 million, respectively, in 1996.

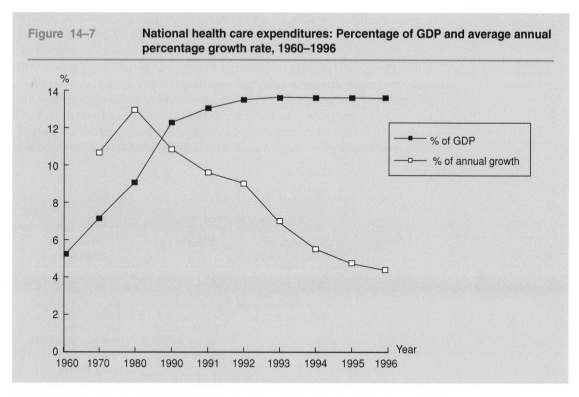

Source: Health Care Financing Administration, Office of the Actuary, National Health Statistics Group, Table 9, January 8, 1998. www.hcfa.gov

The Decline in Importance of Private Health Insurance. Private health insurance premiums amounted to $337.3 billion in 1996 and financed almost one-third of all health care spending in that year. These premiums were paid by employers, employees, and individuals, although the lion's share—over 90 percent—was paid by employers. While private insurance continues to finance a significant portion of overall health care spending, the annual growth rate in employer-sponsored health insurance premiums has decreased substantially in recent years. Effectively, private health insurance is increasingly being replaced with government-sponsored insurance such as Medicare and Medicaid.

The Medicare Program

The social insurance program known as Medicare was established in 1965 under Title XVIII of the Social Security Act and was given the name "Health Insurance for the Aged and Disabled." During its first year, 1966, almost 4 million persons 65 and over received some health care benefits under the new program. Medicare was expanded in 1973 to include persons who had qualified for disability benefits for at least 24 months under either the Social Security or Railroad Retirement programs, persons with end-stage renal disease requiring continuing dialysis or kidney transplant, and certain older persons not covered who decided voluntarily to buy into the Medicare program. The Medicare program consists of three parts: A, B, and C. Although each part differs in terms of what and who is covered, each is essentially a public insurance plan. Table 14–4 shows the coverage,

Table 14–4	Medicare coverage, financing, and payments		
Program	**Coverage**	**Financing**	**Provider Payments**
Part A: Hospital insurance (HI)	Inpatient care, skilled nursing care, home health agency, and hospice care	2.9% tax rate levied on wages and salaries; taxes levied on SS benefits; interest, earned on invested assets; a deductible ($764 in 1998) and a co-insurance payment ($191 per day in 1998) for hospital stay over 60 days	Prospective Payment System (PPS): Payment based on patient's diagnosis within a diagnosis related group (DRG)
Part B: Supplemental medical insurance (SMI)	Physician and non-physician services such as laboratory tests, durable equipment and services, ambulance services, flu vaccinations, some therapy services and prescriptions	Monthly premium ($43.80 in 1998) general tax revenues, an annual deductible (currently $100), and a 20% copayment for covered services	Lesser of submitted charges or a fee schedule based on a relative values scale (RVS); introduction of a prospective payment system in 1997
Part C: Medicare+Choice	Choice among the following plans: Fee-for-service plan, managed care plans, and medical savings accounts	Depends on the plan that is selected. The HI and SMI trust funds are a primary source of revenue. There is some cost sharing depending upon the plan selected.	Provider payments are generally determined by the Capitation Payment Methodology; payments vary by plan depending upon the characteristics of the enrolled population

Source: Health Care Financing Administration, June 25, 1998.

the financing, and the form of provider payments for each part of the Medicare program.

Coverage

Medicare Part A is the basic hospital insurance (HI) program for those who qualify. Part A provides beneficiaries with basic insurance coverage for inpatient hospital care, skilled nursing care, and home health agency and hospice care. Approximately 38 million people were covered under the HI program in 1997 and received benefits totaling $137.8 billion, or about $3,600 per person. Most Medicare enrollees choose to participate in the optional Part B, which provides supplemental medical insurance (SMI) and covers the cost of many physician and nonphysician services (see Table 14–4) not covered under Part A. In 1997, the SMI program cost $72.8 billion and provided benefits to about 36 million people. Medicare Part C provides optional alternatives to the traditional *fee-for-service* coverage of Part A. The Part C program is known as Medicare+Choice because beneficiaries may choose between the traditional plan, a variety of *managed care plans,* and medical savings accounts (MSAs). To date, Part C has not proved very popular.

A **fee-for-service system** is one in which buyers pay the cost of what they receive.

Under a **managed care system,** payments to health care providers are based on a prearranged schedule of fixed fees that has been negotiated between the insurer and the providers.

Financing

Hospital care services and related services under Medicare are primarily paid from revenues collected through the 2.9 percent payroll tax (split evenly between workers and employers as discussed earlier). In addition, the Medicare program receives revenues from *deductibles, co-insurance payments,* taxes on Social Security benefits, and interest income. These sources of funds finance the medical services covered under Part A. Physician and nonphysician medical services covered under Part B are paid mainly from general tax revenues collected by the U.S. Treasury. In addition, Part B is financially supported by a monthly premium ($43.80 in 1998) that covers about 25 percent of the program's costs. Enrollees of Part B must meet an annual deductible and face a 20 percent copayment to defray overall program spending on medical services. The final Medicare plan, Part C, is financed primarily from the revenue generated by the HI and SMI trust funds. There is also some cost sharing under Part C depending on whether the enrollee selects a fee-for-service option, a managed care option, or a medical savings account.

A **deductible** is the portion of a health services bill that is the responsibility of patient, not the health insurer.

Co-insurance is the percentage of the cost above the deductible that the patient is required to pay.

Provider Payments

Medicare pays hospitals for their services under a set of guidelines called the *Prospective Payment System* (PPS). The PPS was established in 1983 in an attempt to slow down the spiraling inflation in the market for hospital

In a **prospective payment system** the prices of health care services are fixed in advance by the insurer at a given amount for a given treatment.

care. Under this system, a hospital is not paid the actual cost of providing care but, rather, is paid based on the patient's diagnosis within a diagnosis-related group (DRG). Historically, Medicare paid physicians based on the idea of a "reasonable charge" for their services. This approach was changed in 1992. Since then, physicians have been paid for their services on the basis of the lesser of the submitted charges or a fee schedule known as the relative value scale (RVS). Recent legislation (1997) has authorized the introduction of the PPS in the Medicare payments made to physicians and other health care providers. The way in which providers are paid under the Medicare+Choice plans varies according to the type of option chosen. Health care providers under the traditional fee-for-service options are paid as just described, but under the managed care options, Medicare makes a predetermined per capita payment each year. More will be said about managed care plans later in the chapter.

The Economic Effects of Medicare

The economic effects of Medicare are felt first and most significantly in the general market for health care. With even a little reflection, it should become clear that the health care market is unlikely to operate like the efficient, purely competitive market describe in Chapter 2. One important difference is that in a competitive market, would-be buyers are excluded from the market if they cannot or will not pay the equilibrium competitive price for a good or service. It is this exclusion from the market, based on a potential consumer's unwillingness to pay, which ensures that goods and services are consumed by those who place the greatest value on them. Contrary to a competitive market, in the market for health care, it is commonly accepted that no one should be excluded from consumption. This proposition is typically defended either on grounds that many aspects of health care goods and services are semicollectively consumed or purely on grounds of equity. But, no doubt, the most important deviation from the competitive market model that exists in the health care market is its reliance on third-party payments.

Third-party payments, primarily in the form of private and public health insurance, have a major influence on the health care market, shown in Figure 14–8, which reflects the market for physical examinations in a given community. In the absence of health insurance, that is, in a more competitive environment, the equilibrium price is $100 per exam, and 10 exams are provided per day. Now suppose that a health insurance plan is implemented which lowers the cost of an exam to the patient to $40. As the law of demand states, if all else remains the same other than a fall in the price of a good or service, the quantity demanded can be expected to rise. In this case, at a price of $40, the quantity of exams demanded doubles to 20 per day. Of course, suppliers are only willing to provide

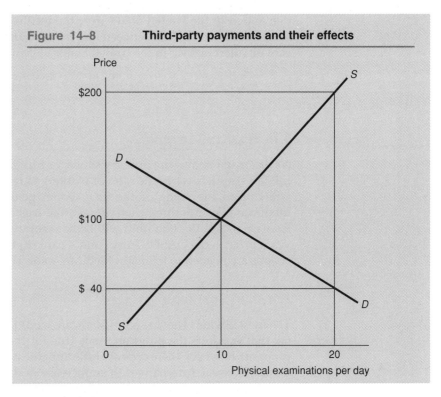

Figure 14–8   **Third-party payments and their effects**

The price is $100 and the quantity demanded is 10 units per day without third-party payments. Third-party payments reduce the price to the patient to $40, and quantity demanded is 20 units per day. The price has to rise to $200 per unit to meet this increase in the quantity demanded. The effect of third-party payments is to increase medical expenditures per day from $1,000 ($100 × 10) to $4,000 ($200 × 20).

20 exams per day if they are paid $200 for each exam. Therefore, third parties—the insurers—pick up the difference between the price the patient pays ($40) and the price paid to physicians ($200). Consequently, in response to the implementation of a health insurance plan, total expenditures on physical examinations rise from $1,000 to $4,000 per day. The impact of health insurance then can be summarized as causing an increase in the quantity of health care demanded, a corresponding increase in health care provided, and an increase in the total cost of providing that care—although the price charged to the patient may decline. Furthermore, it makes no difference whether the insurance is private or social in nature. And remember, the government's two primary health insurance programs, Medicare and Medicaid, provide funding for more than 35 percent of the total expenditures on health care in the United States. As such, the role of Medicare in leading to the explosion in the quantity of health care

demanded in the United States over the past several decades cannot be overstated. And the link between that increase and the high rates of health care inflation that we in the United States have had should be obvious.

The Future of Medicare

The Financial Dilemma

As discussed above, the primary source of funding for Medicare is a payroll tax. As such, when the ratio of workers to retirees declines, as it soon will due to the aging of the baby boom generation, the solvency of Medicare becomes threatened. In fact, the trustees of the HI Trust Fund have predicted that the fund will be bankrupt in the year 2002, some 30 years prior to the OASDI Trust Fund's bankruptcy. Obviously, corrective actions are needed to maintain Medicare's solvency.

Possible Solutions

The most obvious way to secure Medicare would be to increase the payroll tax that supports the program. As is true for the general Social Security program, however, there appears little appetite politically for even a modest tax increase. Alternatives to an increase in the tax rate include (1) increasing the insurance monthly premium enrollees have to pay and (2) increasing required cost sharing by increasing existing deductibles and co-insurance payments. These actions, which are also likely to be unpopular, may carry with them an added benefit by reigning in some of the excess demand for health care created by widespread insurance.

Although each proposal above will have to be considered and some combination will likely be implemented, there are alternatives that attempt to correct some of the inefficiencies created by Medicare. In fact, several of these proposals are already embodied in Medicare's Part C. As was pointed out, Part C allows enrollees to choose among alternatives to Medicare's traditional unrestricted fee-for-service plan. These alternatives include managed care plans and MSAs.

Under a typical managed care plan, payments to providers are based on a prearranged schedule of fixed fees that are negotiated between the insurer (known as the managed care organization) and the various health service providers. There is no incentive under a managed care plan to provide unnecessary medical services since the fees are predetermined. In contrast, Medicare's traditional fee-for-service system tends to encourage providing excessive services since the provider's income rises with the services given.

Managed care plans are not new in the United States, and they have recently experienced very rapid growth. They are especially common when insurance is employer-sponsored. At present, more than 70 percent of all privately insured employees are covered by a managed care plan. A variety of organizational structures provide managed care plans. The most common are health maintenance organizations (HMOs), preferred provider organizations (PPOs), point-of-service (POS) organizations, and physician networks.

A potential benefit of managed care plans to enrollees is that these plans typically require less cost sharing. Under such a plan, a visit to the office of a doctor may only require a modest, fixed fee, say, $10. And, in addition, some medical services, such as preventive care, may be covered that would not be covered under a traditional plan. However, even though an increasing percentage of the enrollees of Medicare are selecting the managed care option, the vast majority have remained with the traditional fee-for-service plan. In 1996, only 4 million (10 percent) persons with health insurance under Medicare were covered by a managed care plan.

Medicare's MSA plan is unique in that enrollment is restricted to the first 5 years of eligibility. Under the MSA option the government purchases for a beneficiary a health insurance policy with a very high deductible and then makes an annual deposit into a savings account that is established by the beneficiary. The beneficiary may then use the money in the savings account to pay for health services received before the deductible is met and for other services not covered by the insurance plan. Unlike other Medicare options there are not limits of what health care providers can charge above the amount paid by the Medicare MSA plan. Also, individuals who enroll in MSAs are locked in for the entire year, with a one-time option of withdrawing by December 15 of the year in which they enrolled.

Each approach has merit, especially since they target the excessive demand for health care created by Medicare insurance, but they have not proven enough among retirees to have a major impact to date.

Expanding Access to Medicare

Another problem facing Medicare concerns access to the program. Medicare is doing an excellent job of providing health insurance coverage to the elderly. However, millions of people, primarily younger than 65, do not have health insurance, private or public. An age group especially prone to insurance coverage problems consists of those between 55 to 64 years of age. As regularly reported in the popular press, many in this group lose their employer-sponsored insurance coverage, because of company downsizing, for example, then find themselves ineligible for government coverage, and are finally confronted with a choice between not having insurance coverage or paying an often prohibitively high price for private insurance coverage. In response to this, the Clinton administration has proposed that this vulnerable age group be given the option of buying into Medicare. The proposal would be self-financing in that the required premiums would be established so as to fully cover the cost of providing the insurance.

Summary

As we saw in this chapter, millions of families rely on Social Security each year to provide income and health care during old age or in the event of disability and death. These social insurance programs have been very successful in providing an economic safety net for the American family. The success of social insurance can be measured by the enormous number of people who are not subjected to the difficulties of poverty or infirmity because they have participated in the system. However, from an economic perspective, the benefits of Social Security and Medicare programs must be viewed alongside their costs. Some costs of social insurance, such as the negative effect of payroll taxes on income, are obvious. Other costs, such as the possible reduction in investment and therefore future economic growth, are not as clearly visible to the average American. The astonishing popularity of Social Security and Medicare indicates that we as a democratic society have decided that the benefits of these programs outweigh their costs.

A major challenge faces us today as we search for a way to restructure our social insurance programs that will guarantee their future financial stability. It is important to recognize that Social Security's financial dilemma has not been caused by an inherent flaw in the concept of social insurance, but rather it is primarily due to the dynamics of changing demographics within the overall population. Although the same factors are at work on the finances of Medicare, the economics of third-party payments for health care services significantly compounds the problem. Given the economics of social insurance, the debate on how to make our programs more financially secure is likely to remain near the top of the public agenda for some time to come.

Discussion Questions

1. What distinguishes private insurance from social insurance? When should governments provide social insurance, and when should insurance be left to private markets?
2. Would the economic effects of a fully funded social insurance program differ from those of a pay-as-you go system? Explain.
3. Evaluate this statement: "The current structure of the American Social Security system results in an intergenerational transfer of income and wealth."

4. Explain how the Social Security system creates economic incentives for early retirement. Is this a positive or negative aspect of the OASDI program? Defend your answer.
5. From a theoretical perspective, explain why Social Security could have either a positive or a negative impact on personal savings.
6. Which current proposal to "save" the Social Security system do you prefer? Defend your answer using economic reasoning.
7. Explain how health insurance, whether public or private, tends to generate excessive demand for health care.
8. Cost-sharing arrangements in Medicare are designed to limit the growth in demand for health care among enrollees. Explain how this works.
9. Many argue that health care is a right and thus should not be denied to anyone. Evaluate this argument.
10. Explain how managed care plans differ from fee-for-service plans.
11. How would you change the Medicare program to make it financially sound? Be specific, and defend your proposals with economic reasoning.
12. Given that both the Social Security and Medicare programs are facing possible financial insolvency, should we continue to rely on social insurance to meet the needs of the elderly and disadvantaged? Why or why not?

Additional Readings

Coll, Blanche D. *Safety Net: Welfare and Social Security 1929–1979*. New Brunswick, NJ: Rutgers University Press, 1995.

Discusses the history of the relationship between American welfare programs and Social Security. Focuses on the role of public policy in addressing the needs of the poor and disadvantaged.

Diamond, Peter A. "Proposals to Restructure Social Security." *Journal of Economic Perspectives* 10 (Summer 1996), pp. 67–88.

Author discusses the economic issues surrounding the most popular proposals to reform Social Security financing. Provides an examination of the Chilean experience with privatizing their social insurance program.

Gramlich, Edward. M. "Different Approaches for Dealing with Social Security." *Journal of Economic Perspectives* 10 (Summer 1996), pp. 55–66.

This article is written by the chair of a federal advisory council appointed to examine alternative plans to reform the Social Security system. The author provides an analysis of the economic impact of the major proposals recommended by the council.

Kingson, Eric, and James Schullz, eds. *Social Security in the 21st Century*. Oxford: Oxford University Press, 1997.

This book is a collection of essays and studies written by leading scholars of social insurance. Emphasis is on the future prospects of the world's social security systems.

Rosen, Harvey S. *Public Finance,* 5th ed. Boston: Irwin/McGraw-Hill Incorporated, 1999.

In this advanced textbook, Rosen devotes two complete chapters to the detailed exploration of the economics of social insurance and its effects on consumers and the economy.

Steuerle, C. Eugene, and Jon M. Bakija. *Retooling Social Security for the 21st Century.* Washington, DC: The Urban Institute Press, 1994.

In-depth look at the economic and financial problems faced by the Social Security system due to the changing demographics and institutional structure of the U.S. economy. Provides analysis and evaluation of potential approaches to solving the problems.

Tynes, Sheryl R. *Turning Points in Social Security: From 'Cruel Hoax' to 'Sacred Entitlement.'* Stanford, CA: Stanford University Press, 1996.

Interesting history of the American Social Security system. Traces the evolution of Social Security from its controversial beginnings to the present time as the most popular federal program.

Waid, Mary O. "Medicare: A Brief Summary." Washington: U.S. Health Care Financing Administration, Office of the Actuary, National Health Statistics Group, 1998.

This report provides an overview of the operating and financial structure of the Medicare insurance program (also available on the World Wide Web through www.hcfa.gov).

World Wide Web Resources

Agency for Health Care Policy and Research (AHCPR)
www.ahcpr.gov

AHCPR is part of the United States Department of Health and Human Services and is charged with conducting research to improve the quality of health care. Gives links to funding opportunities, research findings, clinical information, consumer health, and other issues.

Health Care Financing Administration (HCFA)
www.hcfa.gov

HCFA is the federal agency that administers the Medicare, Medicaid, and Child Health Insurance programs. Has links to the three programs, as well as to publications and forms, laws and regulations, and a search button.

Hot Links to Social Security Resources
sslaw.com/hotlinks.htm

Provides links to the Social Security Administration's home page, the *Code of Federal Regulations,* SSA's regulations, and the National Organization of Social Security Claimant's Representatives.

Social Security Advisory Board
www.ssab.gov

SSAB is an independent, bipartisan board created to advise politician on matters related to the Social Security and Supplemental Security Income programs. Has links to the members of the board, reports, other Web sites, and authorizing legislation.

Social Security Administration
www.ssa.gov

The SSA administers the Social Security and the Supplemental Security Income program. Has links to benefits, online direct services, research and data, the Social Security Law, and other sites.

United States Department of Health and Human Services
www.os.dhhs.gov

HHS has over 300 programs, including Medicare and Medicaid. Provides links to these two agencies, news and public affairs, and other information.

CHAPTER 15

The Big National Debt

Is It Bad?

Chapter Outline

Checklist of Economic Concepts

Mythology distracts us everywhere—in government as in business, in politics, in economics, in foreign affairs as in domestic affairs. . . .

The myth persists that Federal deficits create inflation, and budget surpluses prevent it. . . .

Obviously, deficits are sometimes dangerous—and so are surpluses. But honest assessment plainly requires a more sophisticated view than the old and automatic cliché that deficits automatically bring inflation. . . .

There are myths also about our public debt. It is widely supposed that this debt is growing at a dangerously rapid rate. In fact, both the debt per person and the debt as a proportion of our gross national product have declined sharply.

Moreover, debts public and private are neither good nor bad in and of themselves. Borrowing can lead to overextension and collapse—but it can also lead to expansion and strength. There is no single slogan in this field that we can trust.[1]

[1] Office of the Federal Register, National Archives and Records Service, General Service Administration, *Public Papers of the Presidents, John F. Kennedy, 1962* (Washington DC: Government Printing Office, 1963), pp. 471–473.

The national debt, the debt of the federal government, is big. For every woman, man, and child, the national debt was about $20,000 in 1997. It will be much higher in years to come if history repeats itself.

The Course of the National Debt

People probably became very concerned when the national debt topped $1 billion for the first time. It did this more than 130 years ago when we were fighting each other over the question of slavery. Can you guess when the Civil War national debt high of $2.75 billion was exceeded? It occurred during the First World War. The debt of the U.S. government reached $27 billion in August 1919. During the decade of the 1920s, the national debt was reduced, distinguishing this period for decades to come as the decade to reduce the national debt. The national debt shot upward again during the decade of the 1930s. The cause was another war, but a different kind of war. The war was a fight against a domestic enemy—unemployment. To wage this fight, the government tried spending what seemed at that time to be a lot. The part of the spending not paid for by taxes was paid for by government borrowing. This is the way the national debt was increased then and the way it is increased now.

The $32 billion increase in the national debt between December 31, 1930, and June 30, 1940, was small in comparison to the increase in the debt of over $200 billion during World War II. The highest World War II debt was $280 billion, reached on February 28, 1946. After reductions in the debt for several years after the war, the debt started climbing again during the 1950s. This story was repeated in the 1960s and has continued to the present. The national debt reached $5.4 trillion in fiscal year 1997.

A major point surfaces in this scenario of the history of the national debt: Namely, the growth in the debt is generally associated with wars and economic slumps. The most recent upsurge in the national debt is due to recessionary-induced budget deficits and to structural budget deficits. Structural budget deficits are deficits that occur at high employment levels because of tax cuts and expenditure increases.

The Growth in the Federal Debt Held by the Public

The **federal debt held by the public** is the federal debt held by Federal Reserve Banks and investors, and excludes the federal debt held by federal agencies and trust funds.

The gross federal debt, or the national debt as referred to above, includes all U.S. government securities outstanding—securities held in government accounts and securities held by the public. The federal debt held in government accounts is essentially the debt issued to government trust funds, such as the Social Security trust fund, when trust funds have a surplus. This debt, which is usually about one-fifth to one-fourth of the gross federal debt, does not have an economic impact like the debt that is issued to and held by the public. The absolute and relative growth in the federal debt held by the public, then, will be the federal debt that will now be examined.

The Absolute Growth in the Federal Debt Held by the Public

The federal debt held by the public consists of federal debt held by Federal Reserve Banks and investors, including both domestic and foreign investors. The holdings of U.S. government securities by the Federal Reserve (the Fed) depends on the policy of the Fed with respect to influencing the monetary base and controlling the growth in the money supply. The part of the federal debt the Fed holds varies. For example, the Fed's share of the public-held federal debt in 1970, 1980, and 1997 was 20 percent, 17 percent, and 11 percent, respectively.

The public-held federal debt grew at a rate of 8 percent between 1950 and 1960 and accelerated to 20 percent between 1960 and 1970. This seemed like a rapid growth rate at the time, especially in the 1960s as budget deficits were incurred in every year except in 1960 and 1969. As it happened, however, the federal debt growth rate in the 1960s was small as compared to the growth rates in the 1970s and 1980s of 150 percent and 215 percent, respectively. The public-held federal debt jumped from $283 billion in 1970 to $3,771 billion in 1997, and was projected to remain about the same in 1998 and 1999.

Public-Held Federal Debt as a Percentage of the GDP

A better perspective of the growth in the federal debt held by the public may be gained by comparing this growth to the growth in the economy as measured by the GDP. The federal debt held by the public was very high as compared to the GDP in 1950 (80 percent). This was due primarily to the rapid expansion in the federal debt during World War II. However, after 1950 and until 1980, the public-held federal debt did not grow as fast as the economy. This was especially true during the decades of the 1950s and 1960s (Figure 15–1). The decline in the public-held debt as a percentage of the GDP was from 80 percent in 1950 to 28 percent in 1970. This decline continued in the 1970s, with the federal debt held by the public falling to 26 percent in 1980.

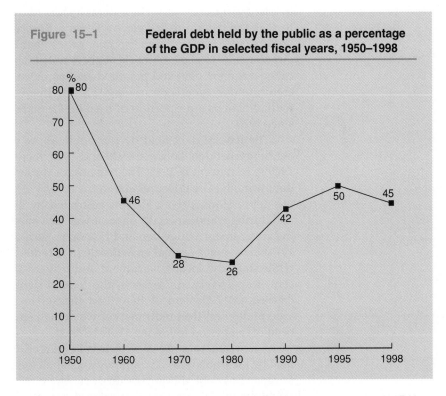

Figure 15–1   **Federal debt held by the public as a percentage of the GDP in selected fiscal years, 1950–1998**

Source: Office of Management and Budget, Budget of the United States Government, *Historical Tables,* fiscal year 1999, pp. 110–111.

The rapidly growing annual federal budget deficits in the 1980s of between $100 billion and $200 billion, and in some years (1983, 1985, and 1986) even greater than $200 billion, brought to a halt the relative decline in the public-held federal debt. From the low of 26 percent in 1980, the debt held by the public increased to 50 percent of the GDP in 1995, but then decreased to 45 percent in 1998. It may be somewhat important to remember that the economy has survived and managed to perform very well when the public-held federal debt as a percentage of the GDP was even higher than what it is today (1998). More important than the changes in the federal debt held by the public as a percentage of the GDP are the changes in this debt as a percentage of total credit market debt. These changes may provide some insight as to the extent to which the growth in the federal debt may be preventing the growth in private debt.

Federal Debt Held by the Public as a Percentage of Total Credit Market Debt

Total credit market debt is the total government debt (federal, state, and local) and the total private debt outstanding in the economy.

Another way to understand the relative importance of the federal debt is to compare the growth in the federal debt held by the public to the growth in *total credit market debt*. The federal debt held by the public, as stated before, is the federal debt held by Federal Reserve Banks and private investors such as individuals, businesses, banks, and state and local government. Total credit market debt is composed of federal, state, and local government debt and private debt—namely mortgage debt, consumer credit, and business borrowing. Figure 15–2 shows the publicly held federal debt as a proportion of total credit market debt in selected years since 1929.

The federal debt held by the public grew much more rapidly than credit market debt between 1929 and 1945, increasing from 13 percent in 1929 to 68 percent in 1945. The reasons for the faster growth in the federal debt were the Great Depression in the early 1930s and World War II. During depressions, private debt is restricted by bad economic conditions, and during wars, especially a major war, private credit is scarce because of the government's huge demand for credit. During the period from 1945 to 1974, the average annual growth rate in federal debt was only 1.1 percent, while state and local government and private debt grew 10 and 9.7 percent, respectively. As a result, the federal debt held by the public decreased to 17 percent of the credit market in 1974. The impact of the federal debt on the credit market was much smaller in 1974 than it had been in the period following World War II.

A new federal debt growth trend emerged in 1975. The federal debt held by the public started to grow faster shall the growth in state and local government debt and in private debt. The new trend in the federal debt started in 1975 because of the increases in federal deficits associated in part with the 1973–1975 recession. Federal budget deficits continued to be incurred in the last part of the 1970s. The public-held federal debt reached

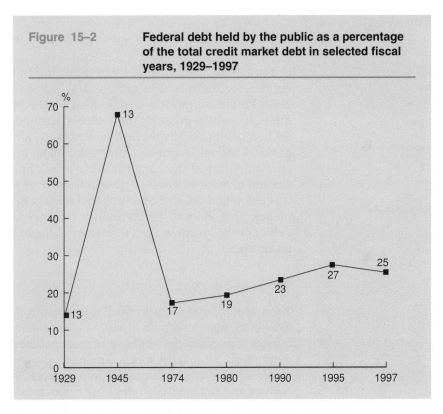

Figure 15–2   **Federal debt held by the public as a percentage of the total credit market debt in selected fiscal years, 1929–1997**

Source: Office of Management and Budget, Budget of the United States Government, *Analytical Perspectives,* fiscal year 1999, p. 245.

19 percent of the credit market debt in 1980. Federal deficits accelerated in the 1980s. During the 14 years between 1980 and 1994, cumulative federal deficits were $2.9 trillion, and, as a consequence, the federal debt held by the public soared from $709 billion in 1980 to $3,603 billion in 1995. Even though the economy and private debt expanded rapidly after 1982, the federal debt held by the public as a proportion of total market debt increased to 27 percent in 1995. However, it should be observed in Figure 15–2 that for the first time since 1974 the federal debt as a percentage of total credit market debt decreased to 25 percent in 1997.

This new federal debt trend is likely to continue. As discussed in Chapter 13, the 1993–1999 fiscal year period is a new era. Federal budget deficits are reduced, and budget surpluses are expected in the years ahead. This means that the total federal debt outstanding is reduced and that the ratio of the federal debt held by the public to total credit market debt is likely to be lower. Assuming all this happens, the effects will be to lower the interest rate and encourage private investment. This will be explained in more detail later in the chapter.

What Is the National Debt?

The national debt, or the gross federal debt, includes all securities issued by the federal government—interest-bearing and non-interest-bearing securities, securities held by citizens of this country, securities held by citizens of other countries, securities held by government agencies and trust funds, those held privately (individuals, businesses, insurance companies, etc.), securities held by the Federal Reserve, and those held by commercial banks. A federal security is a promissory note stating that the federal government will pay the holder or the owner of the note the principal (the amount of money borrowed) plus interest over a specified period of time. It is an obligation of the federal government to pay the holder so much money plus interest for the money borrowed. The government is the debtor or the borrower, and the owner of the federal security is the creditor or lender.

Types of Federal Securities

There are two major types of federal securities. They are marketable securities and nonmarketable securities. Marketable federal securities are bought and sold in the market by investors. The price of these securities is determined by market forces similar to those determining commodity prices, such as wheat, in competitive markets. Nonmarketable federal securities are nonnegotiable debt instruments and cannot be bought and sold in the market. However, they may be redeemed in cash or converted to another security.

Marketable Securities. In 1997, marketable securities represented 64 percent of the interest-bearing debt. Examples of marketable securities are Treasury bills, notes, and bonds. The basic distinction among these securities is the difference in the period of time in which they come due, or mature. Bills are usually of short maturity, less than 1 year, whereas notes range from 1 to 5 years, and bonds mature over longer periods of time. The shorter the maturity of the security, the more liquidity it provides the owner and the more frequent is the need for the federal government to refinance it. Most of the marketable debt is concentrated in bills and notes; bonds represented only 17 percent of the marketable debt in 1997.

Nonmarketable Federal Securities. Nonmarketable securities include convertible bonds, state and local government series, foreign issues, savings bonds, and the government account series. The most important nonmarketable securities are savings bonds and the government account series, which are held almost entirely by government agencies and trust funds. Together, these issues represented 91 percent of the nonmarketable debt in 1997. Savings bonds and notes are generally issued to attract the savings of the public and are redeemable in cash after specified periods of time. An example of nonmarketable securities in the government account series is the securities held by the Social Security Trust Fund. When a tax surplus occurs in the Social Security Trust Fund, the surplus is transferred to the U.S. Treasury in exchange for special issues in the form of nonmarketable securities.

Who Owns the National Debt?

Federal securities are held by U.S. government agencies and trust funds, Federal Reserve Banks, and private investors. Private investors include commercial banks, mutual savings banks, insurance companies, other corporations, state and local governments, and individuals. Private investors hold U.S. government securities because they represent a relatively safe income-yielding asset.

A significant change has taken place in the composition of holders of federal securities. The adage "we owe it to ourselves," meaning that the federal debt is held by U.S. citizens and institutions, is no longer generally true. Foreign holders of federal securities are now the second largest group of private investors. Private investors held $3,389 billion of federal securities in September 1997. This amount of debt held by private investors may be broken down between the public debt held by commercial banks ($260 billion) and nonbanks ($3,129 billion). The distribution of the amount of public debt owned by nonbank private investors in September 1997 was as follows: individuals owned $355 billion; insurance companies, $192 billion; money market funds, $76 billion; other companies, $266 billion; state and local governments, $333 billion; foreign and international accounts, $1,292 billion; and all other private investors, $613 billion. The public nonbank-held debt held by foreign investors grew from about $80 billion in 1976 to $1,292 billion in September 1997. This represents an increase in the percentage of the public nonbank debt held by foreign investors from 25.5 percent in 1976 to 41 percent in 1997.

Problems with a Large National Debt

Now that we know what is meant by the national debt and who owns it, we are perhaps in a better position to identify problems associated with it. Two views will be presented: the views of the general public and the views of economists.

The Views of the Public

Why is the public aroused and alarmed about a large national debt? The public fears that a huge national debt will bankrupt the economy and future generations will have to bear the burden of the federal debt. Are these fears justified?

The Bankruptcy Argument. The argument that a large national debt will lead to bankruptcy is primarily based on an analogy. An individual or a business that has a large debt may go bankrupt. It happens all the time. It is reasoned, then, that like an individual or business, the federal government may become bankrupt.

Unlike individuals and businesses, the federal government cannot go bankrupt in a legal sense. The federal government can always meet its debt obligations. It has the power to tax and the legal right to print money. Individuals and businesses do not have these sources of revenue and therefore are not like the federal government.

Shifting the Debt Burden. Many people are concerned about the national debt because they are worried about its burden on future generations. They would argue that, when the debt is incurred, the current generation is postponing paying for government goods and services and shifting the cost or burden to the future. This is not entirely untrue as far as it goes. The difference between tax financing and debt financing is that in the former case individual taxpayers pay money today for government goods and services today, whereas in the latter case taxpayers pay money in the future for government goods and services today. However, is debt financing, which shifts money costs to the future, necessarily a bad deal for future taxpayers? Suppose the government develops an irrigation project for $1 billion and finances it by selling securities. In the future, the government will have to service the debt by raising taxes to pay $1 billion plus interest. But what about the flow of benefits or income in the future? There is no *net* burden shifted to the future if income from the irrigation project is in excess of the costs of servicing the debt. As a matter of fact, there is a net gain to future taxpayers in this event.

The Concern of Economists

Economists, like the public, are concerned about a large national debt. Economists do not think much of the argument that a large national debt will bankrupt the government and the economy; however, they have had a great deal to say about the primary burden of the national debt. Unlike the public, economists are generally more concerned about the secondary repercussions of a large national debt, that is, the economic impact of the debt on prices, output, and distribution of output.

The Primary Burden of an Internally Held National Debt. Two time periods should be distinguished in trying to locate the primary burden of the national debt: the *present*, when the debt is incurred, and the *future,* when the debt is serviced. Most economists agree that the *primary burden* of an internally held federal debt is in the present in the form of a sacrifice in private production. Assuming full employment, deficit- and tax-financed expenditures withdraw resources from private production. The value of goods and services that could have been produced is the primary burden or real cost. Since these goods are forgone in the present, the burden or real cost is in the present. What about the future, when the national debt is serviced, that is, when interest charges have to be paid? Economists have reasoned that there is no net primary burden in the future since the reduced incomes of taxpayers having to pay higher taxes are offset by the increased incomes of bondholders who receive the interest payments. There is no decrease in private income. Economists realize, of course, that paying interest charges on the national debt may redistribute income. However, the income redistribution effects of servicing the national debt are considered a secondary effect, not a primary one.

> The **primary burden** of the national debt is in the form of the sacrifice in private production that may take place in the present or in the future, depending on whether the debt is held by institutions and citizens of this country or by foreign institutions and citizens.

The Primary Burden of an Externally Held National Debt. Economists do agree that the primary burden of an externally held national debt is shifted to the future. The essential difference is that the sacrifice in private real income and production does not take place until the future in the case of an externally held national debt. For example, suppose the government buys goods and services produced in another country and pays by selling government securities. There is no sacrifice in domestic private real income when the debt is incurred. However, in the future, when the national debt is serviced, a part of domestic private income is reduced since taxes are increased to service the external debt. It is not possible to offset the reduced income of taxpayers with the increased incomes of bondholders as in the case of an internally held national debt, for government securities are held in this case by people outside the country.

Income Redistribution Effects. The secondary effects of the national debt are the *income redistribution effect,* the *output effects,* and the *inflationary effects.* Servicing a national debt redistributes income and, therefore, alters the distribution of the nation's output among people. The income redistribution impact of servicing the national debt depends on the distribution of taxes among people and the ownership pattern of the federal debt. Suppose the federal tax system is less progressive than the ownership pattern of federal securities; or, stated more extremely, suppose only poor people pay taxes and only rich people own federal securities. What happens to the distribution of income if the government pays $10 billion in interest by increasing taxes by $10 billion? The answer is obvious; the distribution of income is shifted away from the poor to the rich. It is generally believed that some shifting of income from lower to upper income groups occurs because of the national debt, although the actual degree of redistribution could be determined only after a thorough examination of the relevant data.

> **Income redistribution effects** are the effects of servicing the national debt on the pattern of income distribution.

Output Effects. Our large national debt may reduce productivity and output. Taxes have to be increased in order to meet interest costs on the national debt. In this instance, the economy would be less efficient. It will not produce as much as it would if the national debt did not exist. These disincentive effects of taxes and other distortion effects that taxes may have are a worry.

The **output effects** are the effects of creating and servicing the national debt on productivity and the stock of real capital.

Real output in the economy may be reduced in still another way by federal debt financing and the ensuing national debt. In the process of creating and servicing the debt, the federal government competes for private saving and, in effect, reduces private saving and private capital formation, that is, the accumulation of real capital assets. The ability of the economy to produce goods and services depends on its stock of capital. A reduced stock of capital—machines, tools, and plants—associated with the national debt, then, lowers the level of national output or income.

Inflationary Effects. There are inflationary woes associated with a large national debt. For one thing, government spending financed from debt is likely to be more inflationary than government spending financed from taxes. This point will be covered more carefully in the next section. In addition, a large national debt like ours gives the economy a great deal of liquidity, that is, assets that are near or like money. This liquidity aspect of the national debt means that people will tend to spend at a higher rate than they otherwise would. The national debt, then, may make it more difficult to control inflation because of the liquidity effect.

The **inflationary effects** of the national debt are in the form of the inflationary pressures created when the debt is incurred, and the increased difficulty that the Federal Reserve has in controlling inflation when large amounts of short-term government securities are held by banks and the public.

Summary in Regard to National Debt Problems

There are problems in connection with the national debt. Some of the fears of the public, however, are unfounded. They are often based on an analogy drawn between an individual and the government—an analogy that is often false. Economists, similar to the public, have their worries about the national debt. But economists differ from the public in that their concerns are more related to the economic effects of the national debt on the operation of the economy. The next section, economic analysis of national debt financing, examines these effects more carefully.

Economic Analysis of National Debt Financing

The following analysis, first, includes a discussion of the different methods of government finance, that is, the different ways in which the federal government can pay for goods and services. Second, the economic effects of government borrowing are presented; and third, the effects of tax and debt financing are compared and analyzed. The analysis draws upon the aggregate demand and supply framework presented in Chapter 11.

Methods of Finance

The U.S. government has three primary ways of paying for goods and services. The government can pay for things out of current tax collections, borrow, or create money.

Tax Finance. The current income of the federal government is primarily derived from its various taxes, such as income taxes, payroll taxes, and excise taxes. Taxes paid out of private income reduce private consumption and saving and, therefore, reduce private demand for goods and services. The government is said to be running a *balanced budget* when tax collections are equal to government expenditures, a *budget surplus* when tax collections are greater than expenditures, and a *budget deficit* when tax collections are less than government expenditures. The net effect of a balanced budget on aggregate demand tends to be neutral, the net effect of a budget surplus tends to reduce aggregate demand, and the net effect of a budget deficit tends to increase aggregate demand. With respect to a balanced budget, we learned in Chapter 11 in the discussion of the multiplier principle that balancing the budget at higher levels of government purchases and taxes may not have a neutral impact on aggregate demand. The positive multiplier effects of an increase in government purchases may be greater than the negative multiplier effects of an increase in taxes since the tax multiplier is the regular multiplier minus 1. Figure 15–3 illustrates the net effect of a budget surplus and deficit on the price level and output.

A **balanced budget** means that tax collections are equal to government expenditures; a **budget deficit** means that tax collections are less than government expenditures; and a **budget surplus** means that tax collections are greater than government expenditures.

Debt Finance. The government incurs debt to finance budget deficits and to pay for goods and services over a period of time. Government debt is incurred by government borrowing, that is, by the government selling securities to private investors who desire to buy them. There are differences between tax and debt financing. People have to pay taxes. People do not have to buy government securities: They do so because government securities are an alternative way of holding interest-yielding assets. Although tax and debt financing both may reduce private consumption and saving, debt financing does not change the total assets of people. It only changes the composition of assets, whereas tax financing reduces the assets of people. Last, tax financing is a way to pay for government goods and services today; and, as mentioned previously, debt financing is a way to pay over a period of time.

Money Creation. The federal government may finance budget deficits and pay for goods and services by creating money. Money is created when the government prints more money and when the government sells securities to banks, assuming banks have excess cash reserves. This latter way is the modern way to create money or to monetize the debt. Let's illustrate how this is done. Suppose the government runs a $5 billion deficit and

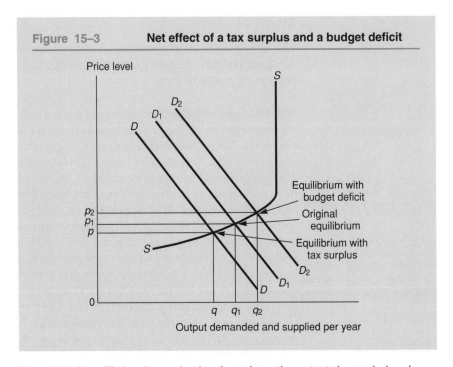

Figure 15–3   **Net effect of a tax surplus and a budget deficit**

The original equilibrium is at price level p_1 where the output demanded and supplied is q_1. The net effect of a tax surplus is to reduce aggregate demand from D_1D_1 to DD. A tax surplus means that the government is taking more away from the income stream than it is putting into the income stream, thereby causing a reduction in the price level and output. The net effect of a budget deficit is to increase aggregate demand to D_2D_2. A budget deficit means that the government is putting more into than it is taking out of the income stream.

covers it by borrowing from banks. The initial effect of the deficit expenditure is to increase demand deposits and cash reserves of banks by $5 billion. The effect of government borrowing from banks is to reduce cash reserves and to increase government securities held by banks. Then the net effect of the whole fiscal operation is to increase demand deposits or the money supply by $5 billion. A budget deficit of $5 billion has given rise to an increase in the money supply of $5 billion. Thus, in this instance, government debt has been monetized. Is the federal debt always monetized? The answer is "no"—only in this case when government securities are sold to banks. The money supply is not increased when government borrowing is from nonbank sources such as individuals, businesses, corporations, and so on. Thus, increases in government debt may or may not lead to increases in the money supply. The method of finance will be referred to as *money creation* when the money supply increases. This terminology stresses the important fact that the debt is monetized.

Economic Effects of Government Debt Financing

Although government debt financing may reduce both private consumption and saving, it is likely to have its major impact on private saving. The part of the nation's income that is not consumed is saved. Saving may flow into low-interest-yielding assets such as demand deposits, interest-yielding assets such as private securities and government securities, and real investments. Government securities compete with private securities and all other alternative uses for saving. Thus, when the government borrows, that is, sells securities to individuals, businesses, corporations, and the like, the government is tapping saving and reducing the amount of saving available for private borrowing and investment. Another way of saying this is that government borrowing increases the demand for saving or loanable funds; and, consequently, upward pressures are exerted on the price paid for loanable funds or the rate of interest. This is shown in Figure 15–4. The effect of a higher rate of interest is to discourage

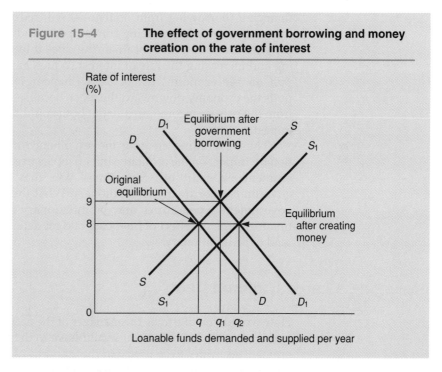

Figure 15–4   The effect of government borrowing and money creation on the rate of interest

Rate of interest (%)

D_1

Equilibrium after government borrowing

S

D

S_1

Original equilibrium

9

8

Equilibrium after creating money

S

S_1

D

D_1

0

q q_1 q_2

Loanable funds demanded and supplied per year

The original equilibrium is at the rate of 8 percent, where loanable funds (saving, etc.) demanded equal loanable funds supplied. Government borrowing increased the demand for loanable funds from DD to D_1D_1, causing the rate of interest to rise to 9 percent. Money creation, that is, government borrowing from banks, increases supply to S_1S_1. In this case, the rate of interest may remain at 8 percent as shown.

private investment. Therefore, increases in government debt may directly reduce private debt and private investment, and indirectly reduce private investment through exerting upward pressures on the rate of interest.

When the government creates money to finance budget deficits, private saving and investment may not be reduced. In this instance, the money supply is increased and the rate of interest may remain unchanged (Figure 15–4). The difficulty here is that, especially at or near full employment, financing the deficit in this way may lead to a demand-pull inflation. The question as to the best way of financing a deficit depends on the state of the economy. Government debt financing is preferable during periods of high production and inflation, and creating money is preferable when the economy is in a deep recession or depression.

Differing Effects of Tax and Debt Financing

The differing effects of tax and debt financing may be known by now. However, several important points can still be stressed. Both tax and debt financing (borrowing from nonbanks) will reduce private demand. Tax financing does it by reducing consumption and saving and leaving people with fewer assets. Debt financing does it by reducing primarily saving and increasing the rate of interest. Which has the greatest downward pull on the economy, tax or debt financing? Tax financing probably pulls the economy downward the most, because taxes are a direct leakage from the private income stream, but both could have a similar downward impact.

Thus, excluding creating money, finance methods have a contractionary impact on the economy and offset the expansionary impact of government expenditures. Sometimes you may hear people say that government borrowing is inflationary. What they probably mean is that government expenditures may be inflationary and, as compared to tax financing, the net effect of financing budget deficits by incurring debt will tend to be inflationary.

Managing a Large National Debt

How would you like to be the manager of the national debt? You would be involved in big business. You would have to determine the kinds of government securities to be used and the amounts of each. You would have to determine how they are to be sold and who is likely to buy them. You would be concerned with the economic effects on the securities market of your decisions, and you would desire to coordinate your decision with decisions made in regard to monetary and fiscal policy, which are closely related.

Debt Management Policy

Debt management policy takes as a given the size of the national debt and the cost and availability of money. The size of the national debt is determined by fiscal policy, and the cost and availability of money and credit are in the domain of monetary policy. *Debt management policy* is essentially concerned with the structural characteristics of the national debt, namely, the types of securities, the ownership pattern, and the maturity distribution of the national debt.

Debt management policy is not concerned primarily with the size of the national debt or the cost and availability of credit but with the types of government securities outstanding, the owners pattern of the debt, and the maturity distribution of the national debt.

Debt Management Principles

Stabilization Role. Economists differ as to what they believe should be the stabilization role of debt management policy. Some economists argue that debt management policy should be neutral; that is, it should be designed to have no appreciable effect on the economy. Others argue that debt management policy should play a positive role in stabilizing the economy. This would mean, during inflationary periods, that the debt coming due should be funded or refinanced into longer term government securities. The effect of this would be to put upward pressures on the long-term rate of interest and thereby discourage private investment spending. It is the long-term interest rate rather than the short-term rate that is relevant in regard to investment decisions. An alternative to investment is to make loans, especially long-term loans. The long-term rate indicates the cost of acquiring long-term funds for investment.

During recessions and unemployment, the stabilization role of debt management policy would consist of funding the debt coming due into shorter term debt or even money. Since the government's demand for long-term funds would be reduced, this would exert downward pressures on the long-term rate of interest and encourage private investment.

Minimizing Interest Cost. A principle of debt management often cited is the idea that debt management policy should be designed to minimize the interest cost of the national debt. This would mean, essentially, funding the debt into short-term securities when the long-term rate is high and funding into long-term debt when the long-term rate of interest is low. The difficulty with this idea is that the effects of such a policy would tend to intensify ups and downs in the economy. The long-term rate of interest is usually low during a recession. If the government increased the supply of long-term securities in a recession, this would tend to drive up long-term interest rates and worsen the recession. Thus, minimizing interest cost on the national debt would be desirable only if it could be done without worsening recessionary and/or inflationary forces.

Lengthening the Debt. A major problem with the national debt is that it is concentrated at the short end of the market. This means that a high percentage of government securities outstanding is in the form of short-term securities such as U.S. Treasury bills that come due within a year. For example, 34 percent of marketable public debt securities held by private investors matured within a year in 1997. The uncertainty and impact on the securities market of the government having to enter the market to fund a huge amount of the existing national debt in this brief time span can be significant. Treasury officials and economists alike agree that the maturity distribution of the national debt should be increased. This would enable the government to better manage and plan its debt management operations and would reduce the frequency and the amount of government securities that would have to be refinanced in a given year. Figure 15–5 shows the impact of refinancing short-term debt into long-term debt on short-term and long-term interest rates.

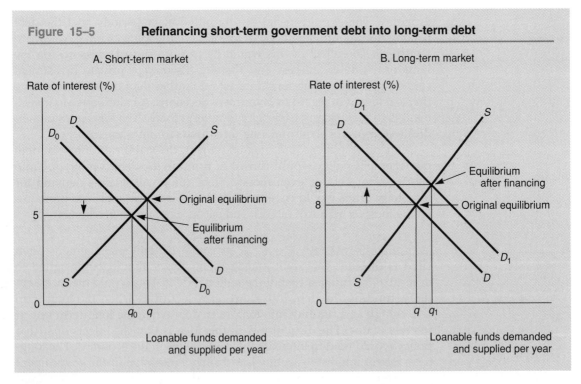

Figure 15–5   Refinancing short-term government debt into long-term debt

A. Short-term market

B. Long-term market

The effect on the rate of interest of refinancing short-term government debt into long-term debt is to put upward pressures on the long-term interest rate and downward pressures on the short-term interest rate because debt management operation increases the demand for long-term loans and decreases the demand for short-term loans. Refinancing, that is, paying off long-term government securities, tends to have the opposite effect—it decreases the long-term interest rate and increases the short-term rate.

When Should the Government Borrow?

The economic effects of government borrowing, and problems associated with a large national debt, have been examined. An important question, however, still remains unanswered. When should the government borrow or, alternatively, when is government borrowing the best or most efficient method of government finance?

Public Investments

Government borrowing may be the efficient way to pay for investment or capital goods. These goods such as bridges, dams, schools, and hospitals provide benefits or real income to society over a period of time. Government borrowing, similar to private borrowing, permits the spreading of the cost of investment goods over a period of time. In this way, costs and benefits can be related over a time span, avoiding the heavy tax claims on private income in a single year.

Government activity of any sort, regardless of how it is financed, should not be undertaken unless it is profitable to do so. In the case of public investments, this means that the present value of the net benefits from the public investment should exceed the present value of the cost of the public investment. After this profitability criterion is met, government borrowing is a legitimate way to distribute the costs of the investment over time.

If government debt is incurred only to pay for profitable public investments, the growth in the national debt would be limited to the growth in public investment goods. Government debt incurred to finance a given public investment project would be paid off over the lifetime of the project. Thus, for the national debt to grow over time, the stock of public investment goods would have to grow.

Economic Instability

If the economy operated at full employment without inflation all the time, the only justification for government borrowing would be to finance public investments. However, this is not the case. The economy experiences ups and downs; that is, the economy experiences economic instability. A responsibility of the federal government is to pursue a fiscal policy that tends to stabilize the economy.

The stabilization responsibility of the federal government suggests three fiscal rules to be followed. First, assuming full or near full employment and a stable or near stable price level, policy designed to stabilize the economy would dictate a balanced budget. In this way, the impact of fiscal operations on the level of aggregate demand would be largely neutral. Second, under the assumption of very high or full employment and inflation, the appropriate fiscal policy would be a budget surplus. The effect of the tax surplus would be to reduce the level of aggregate demand and, therefore, mitigate the inflation. Third, when the economy experiences low levels of production and employment and a decline in the price level, a budget deficit is the appropriate fiscal policy. The effect of the budget deficit would be to stimulate the economy.

Then, the stabilization responsibility of the federal government justifies government borrowing in times of economic recessions. Even if the government does not consciously plan budget deficits, they would likely occur anyway since tax collections automatically decline during recessions.

Is Government Debt Accumulation Necessary During Wartime?

A large part of the national debt arose due to government borrowing during wartime. Can this debt increase be defended on economic grounds? The answer is no. During wars, the economy operates at full employment. The economic problem is to transfer resources from private production to war production. This transfer has to be brought about by a decrease in private disposable income and private demand. The best way to do this is through tax financing. Taxes directly reduce private consumption and saving and are the effective way of releasing resources required to pay for the war.

Next to taxation, the best way for the government to finance war expenditures is to borrow from individuals and businesses by paying interest rates high enough to attract saving and reduce consumption. The worst financing alternative during war periods is money creation. This undermines the wage-price control system, which is usually established during major wars, and causes inflation when the war ends.

A Budget Proposal

A great deal of misunderstanding about budget deficits and the national debt could be clarified by dividing the federal budget into three major accounts—the current account, the investment account, and the stabilization account. The current account would always be kept in balance. This account would include all current costs, including interest costs on the national debt and current revenues exclusive of government borrowing. The investment account would include spending for investment goods and the debt incurred to finance these goods. The stabilization account would include spending programs designed to stabilize the economy and the methods used to finance these programs. The main reason for separating the budget into three major accounts is to make explicit the various responsibilities of government.

The current account recognizes the government's responsibility to manage its current operations based on principles of business and personal finance. Current costs should be met from current revenues. In the case of the government, this means, essentially, that tax revenues should pay for all current or recurrent expenditures such as expenditures for salaries, postal services, recreational services, supplies, interest on the national debt, medical services, welfare services, and so on.

The investment account recognizes that a nonrecurrent expenditure, that is, an investment expenditure, can be financed by government borrowing. This allows for the spreading out of the cost of the investment over a period of time. A $10 billion highway facility could be financed by the government's incurring debt. However, the servicing of this debt and the operation and maintenance of the highway facility are current costs and would be paid from tax collections.

In the past, federal government consumer and investment expenditures were lumped together in budget reports, and there was no way of singling out the annual rate of federal investment spending in the economy. This has changed. In Analytical Perspective's Budget of the United States Government, fiscal year 1997, data are presented on federal investment outlays. Federal investment outlays were $228.8 billion in 1997 and are estimated to be about at this same rate in 1998 and 1999 (Table 15–1). These outlays are divided into three categories. The first category is physical capital investment, which includes direct federal spending on construction and equipment and indirect federal spending in the form of federal grants to states and local governments to assist in the financing of highways and other physical capital projects. The outlays in this category represent about 50 percent of total federal investment outlays. The two other types of federal investment spending are spending for research and development and spending on training and education. The return on these two investment types is in the form of improving the productivity of labor and capital. Even if only physical capital investment spending was set aside in a capital budget ($113.6 billion), the current account budget would be reporting a budget surplus beginning in 1997. The important point here is that the federal government accounting practices do now make a distinction between current and capital expenditures. Therefore,

Table 15–1   Federal investment outlays ($ billions) in 1997 and estimated in 1998 and 1999

Type of Investment	1997	1998	1999
Physical capital investment	$113.6	$108.2	$113.2
Research and development	71.1	71.4	73.7
Education and training	44.0	45.7	50.0
Total	228.7	225.3	236.9

Source: Office of Management and Budget, Budget of the United States Government, *Analytical Perspectives,* fiscal year 1999, p. 125.

the proposal to keep a current account and a capital account can be easily implemented.

The stabilization account recognizes the government's responsibility for economic stabilization. Unemployment represents a waste of human and capital resources. Inflation has undesirable consequences; thus, on the stabilization account, a balanced budget, a tax surplus, or deficit spending would occur, depending upon the state of the economy. The fiscal rule would be (1) a balanced budget when the economy is at full employment without inflation, (2) a budget surplus when the economy is in a serious inflation, and (3) a budget deficit when the economy is in a recession.

In conclusion, any budget position—a balanced budget, a surplus, or a deficit—is neither good nor bad in and of itself. It would be equally inappropriate for the government to incur debt to finance, say, increases in government employee salaries, and not to incur debt to finance a profitable public investment or to promote employment when much unemployment exists.

A Final Comment on the Budget Deficit Issue

More than 1,000 professional economists, including some Nobel prize winners, signed a petition requesting that Congress not pass a constitutional amendment requiring the federal government to balance the budget every year. A vote was taken in 1997 to amend the Constitution and balance the budget in every year, but it was defeated. This is most likely not the last time this vote will be taken. What is paradoxical is that if the federal government simply kept a current account and a capital or an investment account as proposed, the current account would have shown a surplus in 1997 when Congress was voting to amend the Constitution to balance the budget.

The real cost of increasing government spending is independent of the method of finance. This real cost, as you remember, is in the form of the decrease in private spending and production that takes place. The important economic consideration here is whether it is efficient for the government to increase spending. If we assume that it is not efficient, then both tax financing and deficit financing are undesirable from an economic perspective. If we assume that it is efficient, the method of finance should depend on the type of expenditure. As explained earlier, a capital project, such as a bridge, should be financed by government borrowing. On the other hand, recurring expenditures, such as interest on the national debt and salaries of government employees, should be financed from taxes.

A constitutional amendment to balance the budget every year will result in the government's pursuing a policy during an economic recession that will worsen the downturn in the economy. For example, suppose that the economy is operating at full employment and the budget is balanced and then the economy goes into a serious decline. Tax collections will automatically decline, resulting in a budget deficit. Now, the government will have to increase taxes or decrease spending in order to balance the budget. The net effect of this is to worsen the recession. A balanced budget amendment to the Constitution, then, is not a sound economic idea, and hopefully will not be passed by Congress in the future.

Summary

Do you now know the answer to the question, Is the national debt bad? You have studied many pages to probe, to understand, and possibly to answer this question. The organization of your answer could be as follows.

The size and growth of the national debt are closely connected to the way wars are financed and the debt incurred during economic recessions. As big as the national debt is, since 1945 it has declined relative to the nation's income and relative to private, state, and local government debt.

The national debt, or the gross federal debt, includes all the securities issued by the federal government. A federal security is a promissory note stating that the U.S. government will pay the owner its face value plus interest over a specified period of time. There are two types of government securities—marketable and nonmarketable. Federal securities are primarily purchased and owned by private investors, although federal securities are held also by government agencies and trust funds and Federal Reserve Banks. Most of the public debt is held by U.S. investors. However, in recent years, foreign investors have increased the amount they own and in 1997 held 41 percent of the national debt held by nonbank private investors.

There are problems associated with a large national debt, but not all the worries of the public are well-founded. Economists are troubled also about a large national debt, especially with regard to the way the national debt may affect the operation of the economy. A large national debt may redistribute income away from low-income groups, reduce national output and the stock of capital, and increase prices.

The economic analysis of national debt financing focused on the three methods of financing—tax finance, debt finance, and money creation—and the effects on aggregate demand of each method of finance. Taxes exert a strong downward pull on aggregate demand by reducing private consumption and saving. Government borrowing from nonbanks tends to reduce aggregate demand by reducing saving and increasing the rate of interest. Government borrowing from banks (money creation) usually monetizes the national debt; that is, it increases the money supply.

Managing a large national debt is no easy task. Debt management policy takes as a given the size of the national debt (fiscal policy) and the availability of money and credit (monetary policy), and determines the structural characteristics of the debt—types of securities, ownership pattern, and the maturity distribution of the national debt. Some economists believe that the debt management policy should play a positive role with regard to economic stabilization, while some visualize a neutral role. There is general agreement that debt management policy designed to minimize the interest costs on the national debt is not always a desirable policy and that the maturity structure of the national debt should be lengthened; that is, the national debt should be composed of fewer short-term securities and more long-term securities.

Government borrowing is the appropriate method of financing in two circumstances—to finance profitable public investments and to finance programs designed to stimulate employment. Money creation—that is, government borrowing from banks—is the appropriate method of finance when there is much unemployment and no danger of inflation.

Some of the misunderstanding about budget deficits and the national debt could be lessened by dividing the federal budget into three accounts: the current account, the investment account, and the stabilization account. These accounts recognize the various responsibilities of the government, which are to pay for current expenditures out of tax collections, to pay for investment goods over a period of time, and to prevent both unemployment and inflation. Although not a panacea for government inefficiencies, these accounts would possibly provide a better understanding and a basis for evaluating government deficit spending and the ensuing growth in the national debt.

Discussion Questions

1. Discuss the growth in the federal debt held by the public. Include in your discussion the growth in the federal debt by the public as a percentage of the nation's income and as a percentage of total credit market debt.
2. Evaluate the traditional arguments that a large national debt will bankrupt the economy and that the primary burden of the debt will be shifted to future generations.
3. Discuss the income redistribution effects, the output effects, and the inflationary effects of a large national debt.
4. Carefully analyze the effects of tax financing and debt financing. Include in your analysis the differing effects of each.
5. What is debt management policy? Discuss the principles of debt management.
6. Discuss the economic effects of refinancing short-term government debt into long-term debt.

7. Discuss the proposal that the federal government should have three budget accounts: a current account, a capital account, and a stabilization account.

Additional Readings

Aros, J. W., ed. *Balancing the Federal Budget*. The Reference Shelf, vol. 68, no. 2. New York: The H. W. Wilson Co., 1996.

Offers a wide range of opinions on federal budget deficits, balance budgets, and the national debt.

Bernheim, Douglas. "Budget Deficits and the Balance of Trade." In *Tax Policy and the Economy*, ed. Lawrence H. Summers. Cambridge: MIT Press, 1988.

Examines the impact of budget deficits on the U.S. trade deficit. It has been found that budget deficits account for roughly one-third of the U.S. trade deficit in recent years.

Davis, Ronnie J., and Charles W. Meyer. *Principles of Public Finance*. Englewood Cliffs, NJ: Prentice-Hall, 1983.

Chapter 14 discusses some of the same topics concerning the federal debt as discussed in this chapter. Also, state and local government debt are discussed.

Eisner, Robert. " The Federal Budget Crisis." In *The Changing American Economy*, eds. David Obey and Paul Sarbanes. New York: Blackwell, 1986.

Excellent discussion of federal budget deficits. Evaluates the impact of real budget deficits, that is, budget deficits adjusted for changes in interest rates and the price level.

Evans, Gary R. *Red Ink*. San Diego: Academic Press, 1997.

Balanced look at all aspects of the U.S. government's budget, deficit, and debt.

Minarik, Joseph J., and Rudolph G. Penner. "Fiscal Choices." In *Challenge to Leadership*, ed. Isabel V. Sawhill. Washington, DC: Urban Institute, 1988.

Thorough analysis of the federal budget and presents the hard choices that have to be made to reduce the federal budget deficit.

Office of the President, *Economic Report of the President*. Washington: Government Printing Office, 1996.

Most of the data for this chapter is from this reference.

Sharp, Ansel M., and Charles A. Register. "Federal Budget Deficits: A Crisis or a Misunderstanding." *Journal of Business and Economic Perspectives*. Spring 1990, pp. 57-63.

This article presents a framework of discussion concerning federal budget deficits. The framework includes five propositions that lead to a better understanding of deficits.

Shaviro, Daniel N. *Do Deficits Matter?* Chicago: The University of Chicago Press, 1997.

Highlights the historic debates over the budget deficits, the modern deficit debate, macroeconomics issues raised by the deficit, and other issues.

World Wide Web Resources

Bureau of the Public Debt
www.publicdebt.treas.gov

The Bureau of the Public Debt is a small agency within the U.S. Department of the Treasury. It borrows money needed to operate the federal government. Has links to savings bonds, T-bills, notes and bonds, and an up-to-the minute account of the public debt.

Center of Budget and Policy Priorities (CBPP)
www.cbpp.org

The CBPP is a nonpartisan research organization and policy institute that conducts research and analysis on government projects and programs that affect low- and moderate-income people. The home page has links to a budget database, and America's Budget Project, which looks at every line item in the federal budget.

House Budget Committee's Home Page
www.house.gov/budget/welcome.htm

Provides links to the FY 1999 Congressional Budget, the House Budget Committee Minority Home Page, issue papers, committee rules, and other sites.

Institute for Better Education Through Resource Technology
ibert.org

Gives links to the history of the deficit, and America's Budget Project.

The Office of Management and Budget (OMB)
www.whitehouse.gov/WH/EOP/omb

OMB assists the President in overseeing the preparation of the federal budget. The home page is broken into six parts: OMB's Role, Organization of OMB, The Federal Budget, OMB Documents, Employment Information, and Related Information.

16

Economic Growth
Why Is It So Important?

Chapter Outline

Checklist of Economic Concepts

Economic growth
Real gross domestic product
Business cycles
Expansion
Peak
Contraction

Trough
Economic boom
Economic recession
Leading Economic Indicators
    Index
Capital

Labor
Human capital
Technology
Investment
Productivity
Average product of labor

WASHINGTON—The stock market was booming. Companies were fighting their way into fast-growing foreign markets. Technology was transforming many industries. A blue chip panel of business leaders, economists, and government officials hailed "the dynamic equilibrium of recent years," and the "organic balance of economic forces." Their report on the nation's economic outlook concluded: "Our situation is fortunate, our momentum remarkable."

The time was mid-1929.

Economists have never displayed much skill in predicting recessions. But one thing is common, historians have found, to most periods just before a downturn—the emergence of a widespread belief that this time we have found the magic elixir to produce an extended period of prosperity.

So it may be tempting fate now that so many economists, policymakers, and business executives, looking out over an economic landscape defined by years of moderate growth and low inflation, are willing to judge the business cycle tempered if not tamed. But for all the risk of incurring the wrath of the economic gods—and with the important caveat that recessions can never be completely ruled out—it is clear that the economy has undergone such sweeping changes that it is arguably better equipped to maintain its long-run equilibrium.

Still, to the extent that bumps along the economic road have been smoothed over, stability has come at a substantial cost. Improvements in productivity in recent years have come in part from wide-scale layoffs, creating a new level of anxiety in the workforce. And among business and political leaders, there are those who argue that stability has been bought at the price of foregone growth and opportunity.

Moreover, a more moderate business cycle does not necessarily foster progress in dealing with other deep-rooted problems, like income inequality. Most emphatically, it does not mean that individual companies or entire industries will escape upheaval.[1]

[1]Richard V. Stevenson, "Those Vicious Business Cycles: Tamed But Not Quite Slain," *The New York Times*, January 2, 1997. Copyright 1997 by The New York Times Co. Reprinted by permission.

Almost every night on the evening news broadcasts you hear a report about the performance of the economy. The media constantly monitor and report on the economy's health and speculate about where it is headed. Routinely we are provided with the latest statistics on and forecasts of what the economic future will hold. Business leaders, politicians, and professional economists are always eager to offer their views on the economy's performance and what it all means. Why are we so concerned with economic performance and growth? The answer is obvious: A growing economy implies more jobs, greater output, better incomes, and an opportunity for each of us to achieve a higher standard of living. A growing economy gives us more choices and opportunities to better ourselves. Furthermore, the overall performance of the economy is directly related to many of the social issues discussed throughout this book. For example, a healthy, growing economy generally experiences lower rates of unemployment, poverty, and crime. Similarly, these problems are often exacerbated when the economy is in decline. Clearly, economic growth is an important issue to study and understand.

This chapter focuses on economic growth and the factors responsible for it. As we will see, economic growth is not always a smooth ride, and many issues make it difficult to accurately forecast our economy's future health.

The Concept of Economic Growth

A growing economy is a sign of prosperity and the chance to improve our quality of life. Almost everyone agrees that a growing economy is preferred to one that is shrinking. But a number of important questions surround this issue. To begin, how do we measure economic growth, and how fast or slow should the economy grow?

What Is Economic Growth?

Economic growth is a long-run process that results from a compounding of economic events over time.

Economists view *economic growth* as a *long-run process.* It is not the result of a single event but the compounding of many events. For the economy to grow, a number of things must occur. Take, for example, an announcement that the unemployment rate has fallen over the past month. Does this mean that the economy is growing? Maybe, or maybe not. A reduction in unemployment may mean more people are working. However, this increased work must then result in an increase in output and production. In turn, this increase in output must be met by an increase in sales, perhaps through higher levels of aggregate demand. Any break in this chain of events, or an intervention from some other factors that effects the economy's ability to produce, and real economic growth will not occur. Thus, we cannot look at a single monthly or quarterly announcement concerning employment to determine if the economy is growing. We must examine the trends in the events that describe the *overall* level of economic performance over time.

The most commonly used measurement of economic growth is changes in real gross domestic product (GDP). Recall that GDP is the total value of all final goods and services produced in an economy during 1 year. Also recall that *real* GDP accounts for changes in the price level.

Thus, changes in real GDP reflect changes in the economy's actual production of goods and services. A growing economy is characterized by increases in its real GDP over time.

Figure 16–1 is a graphical representation of how the U.S. economy has grown since 1960. Clearly, our economy has experienced dramatic growth over the past four decades. In fact, between 1960 and 1998, real GDP in the United States more than tripled. Notice in Figure 16–1 that the long-run trend in real GDP is clearly upward over time. However, the graph also shows us that the rate of growth is not always constant. Close examination of Figure 16–1 reveals short-run deviations from the long-run trend. In some years the economy appears to grow faster than in others, and in a few instances the economy does not appear to grow at all. In fact, there are years when real GDP actually falls.

Economic growth is sometimes a bumpy ride. Many factors may block the road to continued economic growth. Before we examine these bumps in the road, let's turn our attention to the importance of the *rate* of economic growth.

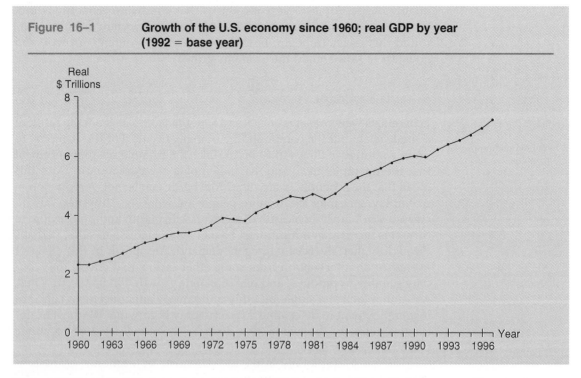

Figure 16–1   **Growth of the U.S. economy since 1960; real GDP by year (1992 = base year)**

Since 1960 the U.S. economy has grown at average annual rate of just above 3 percent. Note that long-run growth is not always steady or even. Recessions occurred in 1970, 1974–1975, 1980, 1982, and 1991. These recessions can be seen as negative deviations from the long-run trend suggested in this graph.

The Rate of Growth

How fast the economy is growing at any point in time is very important. Small differences in growth rates today can translate into significant differences in the level of economic activity in the future because economic growth *compounds* year after year. This concept is easily illustrated by the following example.

Let's assume we have two economies, Nation A and Nation B, and that each economy has a real GDP of $100 billion. However, Nation A's economy is growing at 3 percent per year, and Nation B's is growing at only 2 percent per year. After 1 year, Nation A has a real GDP equal to $103 billion ($100 × 1.03), and Nation B has a real GDP equal to $102 billion ($100 × 1.02). In the next year, Nation A produces a real GDP of $106.09 billion ($103 × 1.03), while Nation B achieves a real GDP of only $104.04 billion ($102 × 1.02). Notice that the gap between the two nation's real GDP is wider in the second year than in the first because each successive year provides Nation A with a higher level of GDP on which to build. Table 16–1 (next page) shows the level of real GDP for Nations A and B over a 25-year span assuming a constant 3 and 2 percent annual growth rate, respectively. Each year Nation B falls further and further behind Nation A. As seen in Table 16–1, after 24 years Nation A's GDP has more than doubled its original $100 billion level, while Nation B's economy is only 1.6 times its original level. (In fact, it will be another 12 years before Nation B's economy will have doubled!)

This example illustrates that the rate of economic growth is of vital importance and that very small changes in the rate can have long-run consequences on the performance of the economy. Given this, you are probably wondering how fast the U.S. economy has been growing. Table 16–2 (page 447) shows the annual rate of growth in real GDP for the U.S. economy over the 1960–1997 time span. (The table also reports the level of real GDP for each year during this period.) Again, we see that economic growth is not constant and that the rate of growth in real GDP varies from year to year. According to Table 16–2, the annual growth in real GDP ranges from more than 6.5 percent in the mid-1960s to a *negative* 2.18 percent in 1982. However, if we average the annual rate of growth over the entire period, we find that the U.S. economy has grown at an annual rate of 3.20 percent. This healthy long-run average rate of economic growth is why the size of real GDP has more than tripled since 1960.

Although the data in Table 16–2 reflect a healthy long-run growth path for the U.S. economy over the past three decades, the numbers also indicate a somewhat disturbing trend. When you calculate the average annual growth rate by decade, the evidence suggests that our rate of economic growth is declining. Based on the data in Table 16–2, the average annual rate of growth in the 1960s was 4.5 percent, in the 1970s it was 3.19 percent, in the 1980s it was 2.77 percent, and in the 1990s economic growth

Table 16–1	Comparison of the effect of different rates of growth on long-run economic performance	
Year	Nation A Real GDP ($ Billions), 3%	Nation B Real GDP ($ Billions), 2%
0	100.00	100.00
1	103.00	102.00
2	106.09	104.04
3	109.27	106.12
4	112.55	108.24
5	`115.93	110.41
6	119.41	112.62
7	122.99	114.87
8	126.68	117.17
9	130.48	119.51
10	134.39	121.90
11	138.42	124.34
12	142.58	126.82
13	146.85	129.36
14	151.26	131.95
15	155.80	134.59
16	160.47	137.28
17	165.28	140.02
18	170.24	142.82
19	175.35	145.68
20	180.61	148.59
21	186.03	151.57
22	191.61	154.60
23	197.36	157.69
24	203.28	160.84

has averaged only 2.30 percent. Given how small changes in growth rates translate into significant long-run differences in economic output, is this downward trend cause for alarm? Before we examine this question, let's look at the short-run fluctuations in economic activity that underlie the long-run trend.

Short-Run Fluctuations in Economic Growth

For almost as long as markets have existed, people have been aware of fluctuations in the level of economic activity over time. Every market-

Table 16–2	Economic growth 1960–1997; real GDP by year (1992 = base year)		
Year	Current GDP ($ Billions)	Real GDP ($ Billions)	Annual Growth Rate
1960	526.6	2260.09	2.04
1961	544.8	2308.47	2.14
1962	585.2	2448.54	6.07
1963	617.4	2551.24	4.19
1964	663.0	2706.12	6.07
1965	719.1	2876.40	6.29
1966	787.8	3065.37	6.57
1967	833.6	3145.65	2.62
1968	910.6	3287.36	4.50
1969	982.2	3386.90	3.03
1970	1035.6	3384.31	−0.08
1971	1125.4	3495.03	3.27
1972	1237.3	3693.43	5.68
1973	1382.6	3905.65	5.75
1974	1496.9	3888.05	−0.45
1975	1630.6	3863.98	−0.62
1976	1819.0	4078.48	5.55
1977	2026.9	4276.16	4.85
1978	2291.4	4492.94	5.07
1979	2557.5	4624.77	2.93
1980	2784.2	4609.60	−0.33
1981	3115.9	4728.22	2.57
1982	3242.1	4624.96	−2.18
1983	3514.5	4807.80	3.95
1984	3902.4	5141.50	6.94
1985	4180.7	5332.53	3.72
1986	4422.2	5486.60	2.89
1987	4692.3	5646.57	2.92
1988	5049.6	5864.81	3.86
1989	5438.7	6063.21	3.38
1990	5743.8	6136.54	1.21
1991	5916.7	6080.88	−0.91
1992	6244.4	6244.4	2.69
1993	6558.1	6404.4	2.56
1994	6947.0	6560.0	2.43
1995	7269.6	6762.4	3.09
1996	7661.6	6997.0	3.47
1997	8110.9	7267.8	3.87
Average annual growth rate			3.20

Source: Bureau of Economic Analysis, 1998.

based economy on record has experienced historical periods of growth and prosperity followed by periods of declining production and incomes. These fluctuations have come to be popularly known as business cycles.

What Are Business Cycles?

A **business cycle** is an erratic short-run fluctuation in economic activity around the economy's long-run growth trend. Every business cycle has four distinct phases: expansion, peak, contraction, and trough.

A *business cycle* is an erratic short-run fluctuation in economic activity around the economy's long-run growth trend. Every business cycle is composed of four distinct phases: expansion, peak, contraction, and trough. These four phases are illustrated in Figure 16–2. During *expansion,* the economy experiences a positive rate of growth. An expansion generally brings the level of economic output above the long-run growth trend for the economy. An exceptionally strong or prolonged expansion is sometimes called an *economic boom.* The end of an expansion or boom is called the *peak,* which occurs when the level of economic output reaches a short-run relative high. The third phase of a business cycle, a *contraction,* is

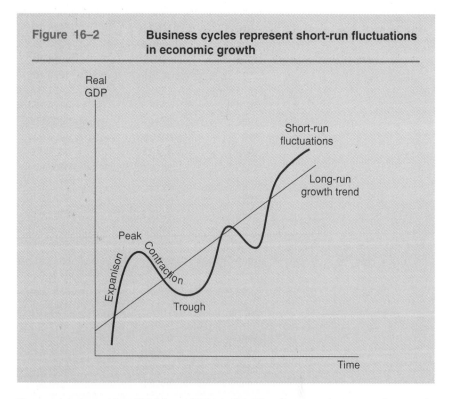

Figure 16–2   Business cycles represent short-run fluctuations in economic growth

Economists have classified four phases of the business cycle: expansion, peak, contraction, and trough. An exceptionally high expansion is sometimes called an economic boom. An exceptionally deep and prolonged contraction is known as a recession. Since 1960, the United States has experienced five recessions.

characterized by a decline in the level of economic activity and output. An exceptionally strong and prolonged contraction is known as a *recession*. The final phase of a business cycle, the *trough*, occurs when economic output hits a short-run relative low. The next cycle begins when the economy grows out of the trough and a new expansion phase begins.

Business cycles are characterized as erratic because no two business cycles are exactly alike. Business cycles vary in duration and the magnitude of their swings around the economy's long-run growth trend. Since 1960, the U.S. economy has experienced five complete business cycles: Recessions occurred in 1970, 1974–1975, 1980, 1982, and 1991. These recessions are shown in Figure 16–1 and Table 16–2 as the negative deviations in the long-run trend of real GDP. These recent recessions have been relatively mild when compared to those of previous generations. The deepest and most severe recession in modern times was the Great Depression of the 1930s. Although there is no formal definition for a *depression*, all economists agree that the United States has not experienced one since the 1930s.

When measured trough to trough, the typical business cycle in the U.S. economy since World War II has averaged approximately 60 months. Historical data suggest that the average length of the business cycle may be increasing, primarily because of longer expansion phases. The 1960s saw an unprecedented expansion of 117 months, and in the 1980s we experienced an expansion that lasted nearly 8 full years. The latest expansion began in mid-1991 and was celebrating its eighth birthday as this book went to press.

The National Bureau of Economic Research (NBER) tracks the performance of the US. economy and announces the official dates for each phase of a business cycle. Because we cannot look into the future to see exactly when an expansion becomes a peak or when a contraction becomes a trough, we generally do not know when the economy moves into the next phase until after it has already begun. Predicting the turning points in the business cycle has become a big business in itself. Many economists earn their living by developing forecasts and predictions about future economic events.

How can you predict what the business cycle will do? Economists have developed a number of techniques to forecast changes in economic growth. The most commonly used tool is the *Leading Economic Indicators Index* developed by the U. S. Department of Commerce and maintained by The Conference Board, a business forecasting organization. As the title implies, this is a composite index of economic variables that tend to move in the same direction as overall economic output but do so *prior* to changes in real GDP. Thus, changes in the index *lead* changes in real GDP. Table 16–3 lists the current 10 components of the Leading Economic Indicators Index. Even though the relationship between this index and short-term economic growth is relatively stable, it has one major drawback: It takes a great deal of time to collect and compile all the data that go into creating

Table 16–3	Components of the Leading Economic Indicators Index

1. Stock market prices
2. Real money supply
3. An index of consumer expectations
4. Average workweek for production workers in manufacturing
5. Interest rate spread (10-year Treasury bonds less federal funds)
6. Initial claims for unemployment insurance
7. New building permits granted
8. New orders for consumer goods
9. Contracts and orders for plant and equipment
10. Vendor's performance index for delivery of inputs

Source: The Conference Board, 1998.

the index. The Leading Economic Indicators Index for a month is generally announced on the last day of the *following* month (for example, the index for January is announced at the end of February). Furthermore, the index is often revised as new data become available. The index tends to lead the turning points in the cycle by 6 months; however, we may not know when we have turned a corner until after it is far behind us.

Theories of the Business Cycle

Historically, economists viewed business cycles as an inherent characteristic of a market-based economy. In a system where all buyers and sellers are free to make their own choices, it seemed reasonable to expect that the level of economic activity would rise and fall as changing situations influenced decision making. Since the Great Depression of the 1930s, economists have closely studied the business cycle and have expounded several theories to explain its occurrence.

Theories of Expectations. Many business cycle theories are based on the belief that economic activity follows general trends of optimism and pessimism. For example, if business owners are optimistic about the future and expect economic growth, they may hire new workers and increase production. This increased employment and output generate higher levels of income, which may then be spent or invested in the marketplace, and the economy grows. When this occurs, the economy will continue to expand as long as people remain confident and optimistic about the future. If business owners begin to worry about how long such an expansion can last, they may begin to reduce their employment and output. This pessimism is self-fulfilling because a lower level of employment reduces income and spending in the economy and growth declines. Thus, actions based on a pessimistic expectation of the future may generate an economic contraction. The next cycle begins when people regain their confidence in the economy and act on their optimistic expectations.

Expectations about the future influence people's economic decisions every day, and these influences can have very important effects in the aggregate. The role of psychological factors that influence economic behavior cannot be dismissed. Notice that one leading economic indicator in Table 16–3 is an index of consumer confidence in the economy.

Theory of Innovations. One of the most widely acclaimed theories of the business cycle was developed by economist Joseph Schumpeter during the early 1900s. Schumpeter believed that the business cycle was based on waves of innovations that changed the structure of the economy over time. According to his theory, new innovations in products and services would start the economy on an expansionary path. New industries would develop to support these innovations, and the economy would grow. Schumpeter believed that this growth inherently led to economic surpluses as imitators entered the market and tried to cash in on the potential profits. A contraction would naturally occur because of this new excess capacity in the marketplace. The next cycle would begin only after the introduction of the next major wave of innovations. Given the length of time necessary for major innovations to have such effects, Schumpeter's theory is often called a "long cycle theory"

Inventory Theories. Inventory theories of the business cycle are based on the relationship between the level of inventories held by businesses and the rate of economic growth. These theories assume businesses have a predetermined level of inventories that they want to maintain. During an economic expansion, the demand for goods and services may increase faster than the businesses' ability to increase production. Because it takes time to expand productive capacity and to hire more workers, business inventories may fall as owners try to meet the rising level of demand for their products. To maintain their desired level of inventories, business owners place orders with their suppliers, who in turn must gear up production to meet this demand. As suppliers increase employment and output, incomes rise and aggregate demand increases, further expanding the economy. Eventually, however, businesses will regain their desired level of inventories and reduce their orders with suppliers. As this occurs, suppliers are forced to cut back their output and employment, and eventually incomes begin to fall. This development begins the contractionary phase of the cycle. The economy will continue to decline until inventories are sold down below the desired level and the cycle begins again.

Monetary Theories. The several monetary theories of the business cycle that have been proposed concern how the monetary authorities react during the various phases of the business cycle. For example, during a period of economic growth, increases in aggregate demand may generate inflationary pressures in the economy. (Recall the discussion of demand-pull inflation in Chapter 12.) In response to this inflation, the Federal Reserve may reduce the growth of the money supply and thereby lower the level of spending in the economy. In addition to reducing inflation, this lower level of spending reduces incomes and output and causes an economic contraction. When the Federal Reserve is satisfied that it has controlled inflation, it may allow the money supply to once again grow at a faster rate. Of course, this action will tend to stimulate aggregate demand, and the economy begins a new round of expansion.

Proponents of the monetary business cycle theories point to the recessions of the early 1980s as support of their argument. In response to historically high rates of inflation, the Federal Reserve significantly reduced the growth rate in the money supply. The results included the minor recession of 1980 and the severe recession of 1982. However, the Fed accomplished its task, and inflationary pressures were abated. When the money supply was later loosened, the economy began an extended period of economic growth.

Real Business Cycle Theories. In recent years new business cycle theories have been developed that focus on economic fluctuations around the level of real potential GDP. [Potential GDP can be considered the level of aggregate output that would exist if the economy operated at its natural rate of unemployment (see Chapter 11).] According to these theories, the business cycle is comprised not only of short-run economic fluctuations around the long-run growth trend but also movements in the long-run growth trend itself around the level of real potential GDP. This perspective of economic fluctuations is known as the real business cycle school of thought.

Real business cycle theorists postulate that economic fluctuations, in both the short and long run, are primarily due to changes in aggregate supply. It is hypothesized that as the growth of an economy's aggregate supply increases or contracts over time, so too does the overall level of economic activity. Furthermore, changes in technology are viewed as being the principal determinant of changes in aggregate supply. Thus, according to the real business cycle perspective, to ensure real economic expansion, an economy should invest in technological advancement and promote other policies that support the growth of aggregate supply. This emphasis on aggregate supply, rather than aggregate demand, is what sets real business cycle theories apart from other theories.

Exogenous Theories. Exogenous theories of the business cycle postulate that factors *outside* the economic system are responsible for short-run economic fluctuations. For example, a war or major international event may set into motion changes in the growth rate of economic output. Certainly, World War II was the major cause of the significant and prolonged economic expansion during the 1940s. Similarly, the international oil embargo by the OPEC nations has been cited as a major determining factor of the 1974–1975 recession. Other exogenous factors credited with influencing the business cycles of economies around the world include natural disasters such as earthquakes, hurricanes, volcano eruptions, and tidal waves. Just about any external event that can significantly disrupt economic activity may influence the erratic pattern of business cycles.

At this point, let us not neglect the first business cycle theory developed by an economist. Nearly 200 years ago, William Stanley Jevons proposed that solar storms were responsible for disrupting economic activity on earth. This exogenous theory became known as the *sunspot theory of business cycles*. The preindustrial economy during Jevons' time was dependent on agriculture, and because sunspots influence weather patterns and therefore crop production, the theory had a minor degree of validity. We no longer study solar storms to forecast the business cycle, but Jevons' ideas are important because they suggest that exogenous factors outside our control can influence economic growth.

Which of these theories is correct? Each has something important to say about how business cycles behave, but no one theory can explain every short-run fluctuation in economic activity. The economy is very complex, and any number of factors may divert us from our long-run growth path. With each business cycle, we need to carefully examine the accompanying economic and social circumstances before choosing a theory to explain what happened.

The Determinants of Economic Growth

In order to understand the long-run process of economic growth, we must look beyond the short-run fluctuations of the business cycle. What primary factors drive the economy forward over the long run? Economists have identified a number of important factors that determine an economy's rate of growth. These determinants of economic growth can be classified into two major groups: (1) availability of economic resources and (2) productivity factors. Let's look closer at each group.

Availability of Economic Resources

Recall from Chapter 1 that an economy's productive resources can be classified as either *labor* or *capital*. Economic production cannot occur without the use of these two types of inputs. All the goods and services that make up an economy's real GDP are produced from labor and capital resources. Without labor and capital, production could not take place. Thus, the availability of resources is essential to economic growth. The greater the availability of resources, the greater the opportunity to produce and grow. Increasing the quantity of labor and the quantity of capital over time are two paths toward economic growth.

The Quantity of Labor. The quantity of labor available for productive uses in an economy is measured by the size of the labor force. In Chapter 11 we learned that the labor force is a specifically defined subset of the population. Remember, not everyone in an economy is available for employment. In the United States, the labor force is defined as those noninstitutionalized individuals 16 years of age and older who are employed for pay, actively seeking employment, or awaiting recall from a layoff. When the number of people who meet this definition increases, the economy has a greater quantity of labor resources to work with. As the labor force increases, the capacity for the economy to produce increases.

The effect of an increase in the availability of labor resources can be shown using a production possibilities graph, such as the one in Figure 16–3. A larger labor force implies that the economy can employ more workers in each production alternative. Thus, in Figure 16–3, the production possibilities frontier shifts outward from *AB* to *CD* in response to an increase in the labor force. The increased availability of labor now provides the economy with a greater set of choices between the two alternative goods. If the economy fully utilizes all its resources, it can produce more of both goods than it did before.

At this point you may be wondering if our labor force has been growing over time. The short answer is a resounding "yes." During the past 50 years, the American labor force has grown dramatically. In 1950, the U.S. labor force was composed of 63.4 million people; by late 1998, this number had increased to 138.3 million. Thus the labor force more than *doubled* during this period. This tremendous increase in the number of American workers has had an important positive impact on our long-run economic growth.

The Quantity of Capital. An economy's capital resources include all the nonhuman elements of production, such as natural resources like land for agricultural production, water, forests, and mineral deposits and manmade tools of production like buildings and equipment. In most cases, the availability of natural resources is determined by a nation's geographical and political boundaries. Some nations have been blessed with a strong natural resource base, while others have not. To increase its availability of natural resources, a nation generally has to expand its physical territory. The quest for additional resources has been the driving force behind many explorations and international wars throughout history. For our purposes,

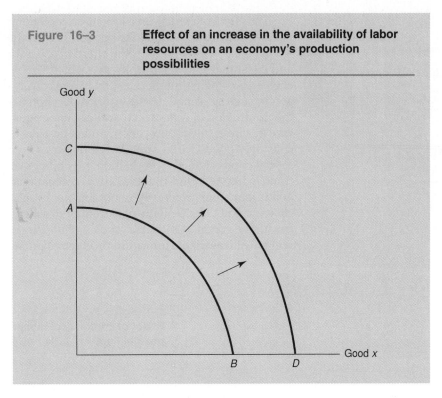

Figure 16–3   **Effect of an increase in the availability of labor resources on an economy's production possibilities**

An increase in the availability of labor resources results in an outward shift of the production possibilities frontier for an economy. If all resources are fully utilized, the economy can produce more of both goods than it did before.

we assume that the quantity of a nation's natural resources are generally fixed by its geographical characteristics and political borders with other nations. Thus, our discussion of capital focuses on the man-made tools of production.

It is important to understand that man-made capital resources such as factories or forklifts are themselves produced through the use of other resources. Spending on capital equipment therefore increases an economy's ability to produce additional tools of production, which in turn can be used to produce more tools, as well as more goods and services. Increases in the quantity of capital tools and equipment today therefore will lead to increases in the capacity of the economy to produce in the future. Because of this relationship between spending on capital and future productive capacity, economists use the term *investment* to describe the purchase of capital by businesses in an economy. (Refer to our discussion of investment in Chapter 12.)

The effect of capital investment on a economy can also be illustrated via the production possibilities model. The production possibilities curve *AB* in Figure 16–4 represents the alternative combinations of capital goods and consumer goods currently available to an economy. If the economy chooses a combination that results in a relatively high quantity of capital goods, such as point *C*, in the future more capital tools will be available for the production of *both* capital and consumer goods. Of course, to undertake this investment the economy must bear the opportunity cost of fewer consumer goods while capital accumulates. Over time, the investment in capital goods shifts the production possibilities curve outward, and a new frontier, like *EF*, offers the economy combinations of capital and consumer goods that were previously unobtainable. Eventually, the economy could choose a point like *G* on the new frontier to satisfy the pent-up demand for consumer goods. (Of course, such a choice implies fewer capital goods will now be available for future productive pursuits.)

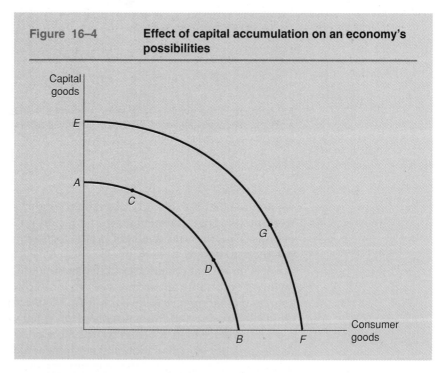

Figure 16–4   **Effect of capital accumulation on an economy's possibilities**

When an economy chooses to produce a relatively large amount of capital, such as at point *C* on production possibilities curve *AB*, over time capital will accumulate, which increases the ability of the economy to produce both capital and consumer goods in the future. This implies that the production possibilities frontier shifts outward, such as to *EF*.

The former Soviet Union and other eastern bloc countries relied on long-run growth strategies that stressed the production and accumulation of capital over the long run. Sometimes the planners of these economies seemed to favor capital goods almost to the exclusion of consumer goods. In fact, this approach was largely successful in making the Soviet Union a world power. However, the tremendous opportunity cost of forsaken consumer goods, and the other inherent problems of a command economy, eventually took their political toll and the system collapsed.

The quantity of capital resources in the U.S. economy has grown at an even faster rate than the labor force. According to data from the Department of Commerce, the real net value of the capital stock held by manufacturers in the United States increased more than fivefold between 1950 and 1998. As the number of productive tools available increases, so too does the economy's ability to generate output. Investment in capital is clearly an important determinant of long-run economic growth.

Productivity Factors

Productivity is measured as the average amount of output that can be produced with a given set of inputs. It can be calculated as the ratio of output to input.

In addition to the availability of resources, factors that affect the productivity of resources are also important determinants of economic growth. *Productivity is* a measure of how efficiently resources are converted into goods and services through a production process. Productivity is usually measured as the average amount of output that can be produced with a given set of inputs. In practice, productivity can be calculated as the ratio of output to input. Thus, the productivity of labor is the output produced per unit of labor, which is calculated as total output produced divided by the total units of labor employed. Economists call this ratio the *average product* of labor. The average product of a resource is a direct measure of its productivity.

Average product of labor is the total output of labor divided by the total number of labor units used in production. The average product of labor is a measure of labor productivity.

The productivity of any resource depends in part on its relationship with other inputs in the production process. For example, a worker equipped with the right set of tools will be more productive than a worker without any tools. Consequently, the productivity of resources can be thought of as being interdependent. Recall that the law of diminishing returns dictates that increases in output will eventually decline as more and more of one input is combined with a given amount of another input. Thus, at some point the provision of additional tools will not significantly enhance a workers' productivity. The productivity of one resource therefore must be evaluated within the context of the availability of other resources.

In addition to these inherent relationships between resources, economists have identified two major factors that influence productivity: (1) human capital and (2) technology. Let's look closer at both factors and examine their impact on economic growth.

Human Capital. Recall that human capital refers to a worker's investment in education and training. Education and training enhance the *quality* of labor. Given the same amount of time and capital equipment, any given number of workers who have been trained and are highly skilled will produce a greater quantity of output than the same number of workers who are untrained and unskilled. In the aggregate, the average product of labor increases due to investment in human capital. Thus, human capital has a positive effect on productivity. Recent studies have shown that human capital investments that improve the quality of an economy's labor force are similar in effect to investments in physical capital that increase the stock of tools and equipment used in production.

American workers have invested heavily in human capital over the past several decades. Between 1950 and 1998, the percentage of adults who completed high school increased from about 35 percent to approximately 82 percent. During this same period, those who attained a college education increased from about 6 percent to more than 24 percent of the adult population. Because they increase productivity, these increases in human capital are a major contributing factor to the long-run growth of the economy.

Technology. Technology refers to the means and methods of production. Normally we think of capital resources when discussing technology because technological change often involves improvements in our tools and equipment. However, technological advances may be more subtle than the latest multitasking automated assembly robot. Technological advances also include changes in the organization or manner in which production takes place. A classic case is the innovation of the assembly line. Henry Ford's workers still used the same tools to build cars, they just built them in a different manner than before. So investments in technology not only include the creation of new "high-tech" tools but also the way we organize production and manage economic resources.

Businesses adopt technological innovations when the new tools or techniques increase productivity. The development of technology allows for the creation of more goods and services from any given quantity of resources. Thus, technological advances can be responsible for outward shifts in an economy's production possibilities frontier over time. (Not unlike an increase in the quantity of resources.) New technologies increase the potential output for an economy. When new technologies become available and are utilized in production, an economy's aggregate supply increases. The link between technology and economic growth is evident.

It is difficult to accurately quantify technological change over time. However, by any standard of measure, technology has dramatically improved productivity in modern times. The tools, equipment, and organizational methods used today are far superior to those of past generations. Obviously, some sectors of the economy have benefited to a greater extent than others, such as agriculture. At the turn of this century, nearly 40 percent of the labor force was devoted to agricultural production. Because modern farming technologies, which are capital-intensive, have so improved agricultural productivity, only about 3 percent of the workforce is employed in this sector today. To some extent, the same story holds true throughout the economy: It requires fewer workers today to produce greater quantities of output than in the past. Technological advances continue to be made and contribute to our overall economic growth.

The Recent Slowdown in Growth

Earlier we determined that the rate of economic growth in the U.S. economy since 1960 has averaged 3.20 percent per year. Official estimates dating back to the last century suggest that the historical rate of growth averages between 3 and 3.5 percent per year. Thus, since 1960 we have been well within the historical trend. However, as we also discovered earlier, if we examine the rate of growth by decade, the U.S. economy appears to be slowing down. In the 1960s, economic growth averaged 4.5 percent per year, but the 1990s have seen an average annual growth rate of only 2.3 percent.

Now that we have examined the factors that determine economic growth, can we identify any reasons that may explain this disturbing trend? There is no straightforward answer to this question. Many factors may have contributed to the recent slowdown in economic growth. Let's look at the major factors economists have identified.

Contributing Factors

Technology Slowdown. According to estimates made by the U.S. Department of Labor, the rate of technology growth has slowed considerably in recent years. In fact, it has been calculated that technological growth during the 1975–1995 period was about one-sixth of that experienced between 1955 and 1975. During the 1950s and 1960s, technological advances were often the result of research and development undertaken to fight the Cold War and space race with the Soviet Union. Although we still devote approximately the same share of GDP to research and development activities, today technological advances appear to be suffering from diminishing returns to production. Some economists have argued that the slowdown in productivity growth due to technology is the primary factor causing the decline in overall economic growth.

Labor Force Factors. As described earlier, the U.S. labor force continues to grow. However, if we examine the characteristics of the new workers contributing to this growth, we notice that a significant proportion of these workers are young and have less experience and on-the-job-training than the rest of the labor force. Furthermore, an increasing number of workers are seeking only part-time employment or temporary jobs. These trends can have a negative effect on productivity and therefore economic growth. On the other hand, many new labor force entrants are bringing more years of formal education to the market. Over the long run, this improvement in the potential quality of labor will offset some of the slowdown in labor productivity.

Saving and Investment.   In the circular flow of the economy, saving is the source of funds for investment in capital resources. As discussed earlier, we must give up current consumption so that we can accumulate capital and achieve greater levels of production in the future. An economy's savings rate thus indicates its willingness to forgo current consumption and determines how many resources are available for investment by businesses. Higher rates of saving contribute to higher rates of capital formation and therefore economic growth. The gross savings rate for the United States has increased slightly in recent years but remains relatively low when compared to other nations. Our savings rate averages about 15–16 percent of GDP, about half the rate of that in Japan. Our tendency to save relatively little may be a contributing factor to the slowdown in economic growth.

The Composition of Output.   Another factor contributing to the recent slowdown in economic growth is the changing composition of our national output. Much has been written about the growing importance of the service-producing sectors in our economy. The U.S. economy has evolved from one dominated by the production of goods to one that relies heavily on the production of services. From a historic perspective, we experienced our highest rates of growth during periods where great strides were made in technology and capital formation in the goods-producing sectors of the economy. Given the nature of most services, technology and capital have not contributed as greatly to productivity in the service-producing sectors. When resources are shifted from a high-productivity sector of the economy to a low-productivity sector of the economy, overall average productivity must fall. This is the effect we are now experiencing as resources shift from the production of goods to the production of services.

In addition, the ongoing growth of the service sector makes it more difficult to measure productivity accurately. Some economists argue that part of the observed slowdown in economic growth is merely a measurement problem. It is easy to calculate output and productivity in the goods-producing sector of the economy: Simply count the number of cars, watches, tennis rackets, bushels of grain, etc. produced by workers employed in that part of the economy. However, it is much more difficult to ascertain the productivity of service workers. For example, how do you measure the output of teachers, lawyers, or doctors? How do you calculate the productivity of the technicians who keep our computer and telecommunications networks functioning? These inherent measurement problems may lead to an underestimation of the quantity and value of services produced in our economy. To correct this potential bias, new and better measurement techniques must be developed.

Government: Regulation and Public Debt. Some economists have argued that our government is in part responsible for the slowdown in economic growth. They cite two primary factors: regulation of business and the growing public debt.

The first argument centers on the belief that government regulation of business diverts economic resources from the production process. Today, most businesses are subject to some form of government regulation, ranging from the Occupational Safety and Health Administration (OSHA) requirements all the way to the formal licensing and oversight regulations public utilities face. In many cases, the businesses must devote resources to ensure that such regulations are met. Obviously, time spent filling out government forms is time not spent producing. However, the net effect of government regulation is not clear-cut. Some regulations, such as OSHA safety guidelines, may have positive impacts on productivity (for example, less work is lost due to injuries on the job). Regardless of the true net effect of government regulation on productivity and growth, this argument has contributed to an ongoing trend to lessen the regulatory burden of business.

Another avenue through which government action may hinder economic growth is the growing public debt. Some economists argue that financing the national debt through borrowing diverts economic resources from the private sector. From this perspective, funds the public loans to the government are funds no longer available for private investment. Thus, when the government borrows to finance the national debt, fewer dollars are left for private businesses to borrow and use to purchase capital and hire labor. Sometimes this is called the "crowding out" effect of government borrowing. To the extent crowding out occurs, productivity and economic growth are diminished. Again, this problem may not be as great as it first appears. Much government spending goes to support social overhead capital expenditures, such as interstate highways, public schools, and health programs, that have a positive effect on productivity and growth. Unfortunately, the proportion of public spending on these items has been falling as the interest on the debt grows.

The total net effect of government action on the recent slowdown in economic growth remains debatable. However, we must note that the government maintains the responsibility for fostering an economic climate that promotes enhanced productivity and long-run economic growth.

Where Do We Go from Here?

What does this recent slowdown in economic growth portend for our future? How will it affect our standard of living as we move into the next century? Can anything be done to enhance economic growth? These important and vital questions concern us all. The concepts and ideas we learned in this chapter give us some insight into answering them.

First, where *is* the American economy headed? Although no one knows for sure what tomorrow holds, economists have learned that the past is the best predictor of the future. History shows us that the economy is capable of sustaining various rates of growth over an extended number of years. Let's forecast the future level of economic activity based on the previous rates of growth witnessed during the past four decades. Recall that the average annual growth rates for the 1960s, 1970s, 1980s, and 1990s (through 1998) were 4.5, 3.19, 2.77, and 2.3 percent, respectively. Figure 16–5 plots the projected level of real GDP from 1999 to 2019 based on these possible average annual rates of economic growth. Notice that this simple forecast technique assumes no short-run fluctuations in the long-run trend. Of course, in reality a business cycle or two could throw us off the path. However, there are some interesting things to note in Figure 16–5.

It is clear that the rate of future economic growth determines the level of economic activity actually achieved at some future date. Figure 16–5 illustrates how the compounding of growth can generate very different outcomes as time progresses. If we continue to grow at the rate established during the 1990s, real GDP will increase from approximately $7.61 trillion in 1998 to $12.25 trillion in 2019. However, if the economy could establish and maintain the same rate of growth that was present in the 1960s, the economy would reach an astonishing $19.15 trillion level of real GDP in 2019. By increasing our rate of growth to 4.5 percent per year, we could increase the size of real GDP almost 1½ times in 20 years!

It is unlikely that the American economy can quickly increase and sustain a rate of growth equivalent to that of the 1960s. Of our four forecasts, perhaps the one based on the 1970s growth rate is most reasonable. The annual average rate of growth in the 1970s was 3.19 percent, almost the same as the average for the entire 1960–1998 time period. Furthermore, this rate is within the 3 percent to 3.5 percent range that history records as the long-run average rate for the economy. According to this projected scenario, the economy would grow to $14.7 trillion by the year 2019. Although this forecast is based on a reasonable assumption, its degree of accuracy depends on the economy reverting to its long-run trend and reversing the recent slowdown in economic growth.

What would these projected rates of growth mean for our standard of living? Recall that one economic measure of our standard of living is per capita real GDP. In Chapter 1 we defined this as real GDP divided by the

Figure 16–5   **Possible future growth paths of the U.S. economy, 1999–2019**

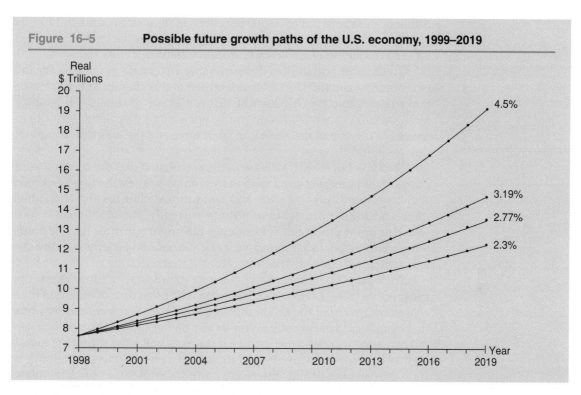

The top line forecasts the potential growth in real GDP, assuming an annual growth rate of 4.5 percent, equal to that experienced in the 1960s. The second line represents the growth path assuming the 1970s growth rate of 3.19 percent. Below that, the third line projects a future growth equivalent to that experienced in the 1980s, 2.77 percent. The bottom line is the forecast, assuming the 2.3 percent annual rate of growth experienced during the 1990s.

population. Therefore, our measure of living standards depends not only on the growth rate of real GDP but also on the growth rate in the population. Most experts agree that the U.S. population will not grow very fast over the next few decades. The current rate of overall population growth is only an approximate 1 percent per year. Thus, all our forecasts suggest that our standard of living will rise because in all four scenarios, real GDP is expected to increase at a faster rate than the expected rate of population increase.

Even though we can almost be assured of higher levels of per capita real GDP in the future, our different forecasts indicate that a set of very divergent outcomes is possible. Assuming a 1 percent rate of population growth, our optimistic forecast based on a 4.5 percent annual growth rate in real GDP results in a per capita real GDP of $57,350 by 2019. The forecast based on the rate of growth experienced during the 1990s (2.3 percent) suggests a per capita real GDP of only $36,684 by that year. That is a difference of more than $20,000 for every man, woman, and child in the economy! Clearly, the rate of economic growth over the next 20 years will have an important effect on our future standard of living.

Given its importance, is there anything we can do to increase the rate of economic growth? The factors identified in this chapter as being important to economic growth suggest that a number of things can be done. First, overall economic growth can be enhanced by promoting future increases in the size of the American labor force and the long-run accumulation of capital.

The slow but steady increase in the population and the continuing increase of labor market participation by women suggest that the labor force will continue to grow. Policy and institutional changes that encourage more and fuller participation of those currently outside the labor force would support this trend. For example, the opportunity for flexible hours, telecommuting, or other attractive work options and benefits may encourage more prospective workers to enter the market. ,

With respect to increasing the rate of capital accumulation, one prospective pro-growth policy has received a great deal of attention in recent years: lowering the tax on capital gains. Proponents of this idea argue that by reducing the tax rate investors pay on the appreciation of their capital investments over time, greater incentives will exist for future investments. In essence, a lower tax rate would increase the profitability of capital investments and, therefore, more investment would take place. Congress has debated this issue a number of times, and it is likely to consider the idea again. Another way to encourage capital accumulation is to promote more personal saving. As the pool of savings in the economy increases, more funds become available for investment. In recent years we have seen a number of public policy initiatives that encourage saving, including individual retirement accounts (IRAs) and 401(k) pension plans. Such policies promote long-run economic growth by providing the economy with the funds necessary for investment.

Another approach to promoting economic growth is to enhance the productivity of labor and capital. Numerous public policies encourage the formation of human capital, which increases the productivity of labor. Public funding for education, at all levels, is a clear example. Congress recently implemented a set of new income tax breaks for those who attend college or receive job training. By lowering the tax liability of those in school, the deductions encourage more people to invest in human capital. This education plan is specifically designed to stimulate labor productivity and enhance long-run economic growth.

The government also promotes productivity growth by encouraging technological innovations. Numerous programs financed by the federal government directly support research and development activities that have commercial applications. Although the U.S. government spends only less than 1 percent of GDP on research and development each year, that amount is more than any other industrialized nation spends. In addition to these direct outlays, a number of additional public programs and tax laws encourage private investments in new technologies.

Obviously, there are many different paths to economic growth. Even though we cannot always predict what the future will bring, history indicates that the American economy will continue on its upward path.

Summary

Economic growth is defined as a long-run process that results from the compounding of economic events over time. To measure economic growth, economists generally examine the rate of change in real GDP from one year to the next. The average annual rate of growth in the U.S. economy averaged between 3 and 3.5 percent during this century. Between 1960 and 1998, the rate of growth averaged 3.20 percent.

Long-run economic growth does not occur at a steady rate over time. Short-run fluctuations in economic activity are commonly known as business cycles, which are composed of four distinct phases: expansion, peak, contraction, and trough. Because they are erratic, business cycles are hard to forecast. Significant expansions are referred to as economic booms, and significant contractions are called economic recessions. Historically, business cycles on average last about 60 months but have been getting longer over time because of prolonged expansions. Since 1960, the U.S. economy has completed five business cycles. A number of theories have been proposed to explain business cycles, including those based on expectations, innovations, inventories, monetary institutions, aggregate supply, and exogenous factors.

Two sets of primary determinants of long-run economic growth have been identified: availability of economic resources and productivity factors. Greater quantities of labor and capital increase an economy's productive capacity and shift its production possibilities frontier outward. Investments in human capital and technology enhance the productivity of economic resources, which in turn leads to economic growth.

Close examination of the recent history of real GDP in the United States indicates that the rate of economic growth has been diminishing over time. A number of factors may be contributing to this slowdown, including a technology slowdown, changes in the makeup of the labor force, a relatively low rate of savings, the changing composition of economic output, and government actions.

Any change in the growth rate of the economy will have a great influence on the level of economic activity and per capita real GDP in the future. Public policies can be designed that enhance the determinants of economic growth identified in this chapter. By increasing the rate of economic growth, we can improve our own future standard of living.

Discussion Questions

1. What constitutes economic growth? How can we distinguish long-run economic growth from short-run fluctuations in economic activity?
2. Define what is often called the business cycle. Why is the business cycle so hard to predict?
3. Based on what is currently occurring in the economy, what phase of the business are we now experiencing? When was the last turning point in the cycle?
4. Which theory of the business cycle do you find most convincing? Defend your answer.
5. Find the latest release of the Leading Economic Indicators Index on the World Wide Web. Based on this information, how do you expect the economy to perform over the next 6 to 12 months?
6. What are the major determinants of long-run economic growth? Which of these determinants do you think has been most important during the past couple of years? Explain.
7. Why do we call formal education an "investment" in human capital? How is it like an investment in physical capital?
8. Use a production possibilities graph to demonstrate an increase in productivity on an economy's productive potential.
9. Explain why economists believe the rate of economic growth has been slowing down. Is this something we should be concerned about? Why or why not?
10. Which of the factors discussed in this chapter do you believe is primarily responsible for the recent slowdown in economic growth? Can you identify any additional factors that were not discussed in this chapter?
11. This chapter presented four projections of economic growth over the next 20 years, each based on historic trends. Which one do you believe is most realistic? Defend your position, and provide specific reasons why the most optimistic projection in unlikely to be met.
12. How is your standard of living related to the overall growth of the economy? Is it possible for the economy to grow "too fast"? Explain.

Additional Reading

Baumol, William J., Sue Anne Batey Blackman, and Edward N. Wolff. *Productivity and American Leadership: The Long View.* Cambridge: The MIT Press, 1991.

This book emphasizes that productivity is a long-term issue. Discusses the factors that affect productivity: savings, investment, education, depletion of natural resources, etc.

Farley, Reynolds. *The New American Reality: Who We Are, How We Got Here, Where We Are Going.* New York: Russell Sage Foundation, 1996.

Chapter 3, "The 1970s: A Turning Point in the Nation's Economy and Whom It Rewards," discusses the effects that changes in productivity, the labor force, and industrial policy had on the economic growth and prosperity from World War II to the 1970s.

Frumkin, Norman. *Guide to Economic Indicators.* 2nd ed. Armonk, NY: M.E. Sharpe, Inc. 1990.

Provides descriptions, backgrounds, and interpretations of more than 50 economic indicators used to measure and forecast economic performance.

Frumkin, Norman. *Tracking America's Economy.* 2nd ed. Armonk, NY: M.E. Sharpe, Inc. 1992.

Written for students and the general public, this book is a great way to understand all the issues discussed in this chapter, with easy-to-understand graphs and tables.

Krugman, Paul. *The Age of Diminished Expectations.* 3rd ed. Cambridge: The MIT Press, 1997.

Discusses such issues as income distribution, the trade deficit, inflation, the budget deficit, free trade and protectionism, and the savings and loan scandal with respect to their effects on economic growth.

Rogers, R. Mark. *Handbook of Key Economic Indicators.* Chicago: Irwin Professional Publishing, 1994.

This book thoroughly reviews the economic indicators that analysts use to construct forecasts and projections of economic growth. Tables and graphs illustrate the dynamic relationships between key variables and economic performance.

Stein, Herbert, and Murray Foss. *The New Illustrated Guide to the American Economy.* 2nd ed. Washington, DC: The AEI Press, 1995.

Very accessible guide to the many ways of measuring economic performance over time. Various trends and issues are explored and illustrated with colorful graphs and charts. Fun book for browsing.

Zarnowitz, Victor. *Business Cycles: Theory, History, Indicators, and Forecasting.* NBER Studies in Business Cycles, vol. 27. Chicago: The University of Chicago Press, 1992.

Excellent source that incorporates all aspects of business cycles, from the trends to the theories to the indicators to forecasting.

World Wide Web Resources

Bureau of Economic Analysis
www.bea.doc.gov

The Bureau of Economic Analysis collects and analyzes national data to measure the current state of the economy and its long-run growth. This site provides access to some of this data and numerous publications, news releases, and links to other related sites.

The Conference Board
www.tcb-indicators.org

This is the home of the Leading Economic Indicators Index. The Conference Board provides the latest estimates and a wide range of articles and other sources of information about business cycles and economic forecasting.

Economic Report of the President
www.gpo.gov/eop/index.html

This annual publication, prepared by the President's Council of Economic Advisers, reports on the current state of the national economy. Short articles on the current and long-term economic climate are provided, along with a number of the most important economic data series that measure the economy's performance.

Economic Time Series Page
bos.business.uab.edu/data/data.htm

This site, maintained by the University of Alabama–Birmingham, provides links to hundreds of data series of economic activity. In addition to a comprehensive listing of time series for the U.S. economy, links are also available for other nations.

National Bureau of Economic Research
www.nber.org

This is the home site for the organization that produces the Leading Economic Indicators Index and determines the "official" dates of U.S. business cycles. The site provides access to a variety of national economic data as well as a table indicating the dates for all U.S. business cycles since 1854.

QM&RBC Data Online
www.er.uqam.ca/nobel/r14160/rbc/data.html

The initials stand for Quantitative Macroeconomics and Real Business Cycle theory. The "real business cycle" theory asserts that the long-run trend in economic growth is not necessarily stable, and therefore the business cycle should not be viewed as merely short-run fluctuations around the long-run trend. This site provides links to research on this perspective as well as links to data and other relevant sites.

Technology Administration
www.ta.doc.gov/TA1.HTM

The Technology Administration is the branch of the U.S. Department of Commerce charged with promoting technological competitiveness in the private sector. One of its primary objectives is to enhance economic growth through the adoption of new technologies in American industry. Links are provided to publications and data sources.

Glossary

Ability-to-pay principle of taxation.   The concept that taxpayers with higher incomes should pay more taxes than those with lower incomes.

Aggregate demand.   The total quantities of goods and services demanded per unit of time by the economy at various price levels, other things being equal.

Aggregate demand policies.   Policies based on aggregate demand theory. The goal of such policies is to stabilize aggregate demand at high levels of production and employment.

Aggregate supply.   The total quantities of goods and services supplied per unit of time in the economy at various price levels, other things being equal.

Aggregate supply policies.   Policies based on aggregate supply theory. The goal of such policies is to increase the level of employment through increases in aggregate supply.

Average cost.   The ratio of total costs to units of output of a good or service. Also known as *per unit cost.*

Average product of labor.   The total output of labor divided by the total number of labor units used in production. The average product of labor is a measure of labor productivity.

Backward tax shifting.   Shifting the burden of a tax to the owners of resources, usually in the form of lower prices paid for their resources.

Balance of payments.   The relationship between a country's total monetary obligations per unit of time to other countries and other countries' obligations to the home country.

Balance of trade.   The relationship of the value of a country's imports to the value of its exports of goods and services per unit of time. It is in *deficit* when more is owed for imports than is earned by exports; it is in *surplus* when less is owed for imports than is earned by exports.

Balanced budget.   A governmental budget is balanced when its total receipts, mainly taxes, are equal to its total expenditures.

Barriers to entry.   The various impediments to the entry of new firms into a market, usually classified as (1) private barriers and (2) government barriers.

Benefits-received principle of taxation.   The concept that taxpayers should pay taxes in accordance with the benefits they receive from the government.

Bequest effect.   The increase in lifetime saving experienced by people who wish to leave assets to their children as compensation for losses incurred due to the burden of Social Security taxes.

Budget deficit.   The situation that exists when a government's total receipts, mainly taxes, are less than its total expenditures.

Budget surplus.   The situation that exists when a government's total receipts, mainly taxes, are greater than its total expenditures.

Business cycles.   Erratic short-run fluctuations in economic activity around the long-run growth trend of the economy. Every business cycle has four distinct phases: expansion, peak, contraction, and trough.

Capital account transactions.   International trade transactions that are long-term in character, usually investment types of transactions.

Capital resources.   All nonhuman ingredients of production. Capital resources can be further divided into natural and man-made categories.

Capture theory of regulation.   The belief that regulatory agencies often come to serve the interests of the firms they were established to regulate rather than the interests of the general public.

Cartel.   A group of firms which formally agree to coordinate their production and pricing decisions in a manner that maximizes joint profits.

Catastrophic health insurance.   Health insurance coverage of long-term and acute-cost illnesses.

Circular flow of production and income.   The concept that expenditures of one group are the incomes for others, who in turn spend and provide income for still others.

Co-insurance.   The percentage of the cost above the deductible that an insured patient is required to pay.

Collectively consumed goods and services.   Goods and services that are consumed by a group or groups as a whole and that yield benefits to the group or groups. No individual can single out and value his or her specific benefits.

Comparable worth.   A proposal designed to reduce wage discrimination against women by extending the "equal pay for equal work" principle to require "equal pay for similar work." The similarity or comparability of jobs would be determined by factors such as the skill, effort, and responsibility the job requires.

Comparative advantage.   The ability of a country to produce a good or service with a smaller sacrifice of alternative goods and services than can the rest of the trading world.

Comparative disadvantage.   The inability of a country to produce a good or service except at greater sacrifice of alternative goods and services than is necessary for the rest of the trading world.

Comprehensive insurance coverage.   A wide range of health care services that are covered under a health insurance program.

Concentration ratio.   A measure of potential monopoly power, defined as the percent of an industry's sales (or assets or output) controlled by the four (or eight) largest firms in the industry.

Consumption possibilities curve.   A curve showing the maximum quantities of two goods or services that may be consumed in an economy, given the economy's resources and technology. In the absence of international trade, the consumption possibilities curve is identical to the production possibilities curve.

Cost of living allowances (COLAs).   Automatic annual increases to insurance benefits or wages equal to the amount of inflation experienced within the economy during the previous year (usually as measured by the consumer price index (CPI).

Cost-benefit analysis.   A technique for determining the optimal level of an economic activity. In general, an activity should be expanded as long as the expansion leads to greater benefits than costs.

Cost-push inflation.   Increases in the average price level initiated by increases in costs of production.

Current account (budgetary).   One of the three major accounts into which a governmental budget can be divided. It represents all current costs, including interest costs on the national debt, and all current revenues exclusive of government borrowing.

Current account transactions.   International trade transactions that are more or less immediate or short term in character.

Customs union.   A free trade alliance of nations that share common external tariffs.

Cyclical unemployment.   Unemployment caused by economic fluctuations. It results from inadequate levels of aggregate demand.

Deadweight welfare loss due to monopoly.   The reduction in social satisfaction, or welfare, due to the tendency of monopolists to restrict output below the socially optimal level.

Debt management policies.   Policies to determine the structural characteristics of the national debt, that is, the types of securities, ownership pattern, and maturity distribution of the debt, given the size of the debt and the availability of money and credit.

Deductible.   The portion of a health services bill that is the responsibility of the patient, not the health insurer.

Demand.   The set of quantities of a good or service per unit of time that buyers would be willing to purchase at various alternative prices of the item, other things being equal.

Demand, changes in.   Shifts in the entire demand schedule or curve for a good or service, resulting from changes in one or more of the "other things being equal." Should not be confused with a movement along a given demand schedule or curve.

Demand, law of.   The general rule that at lower prices, buyers will purchase larger amounts per unit of time than they will at higher prices, other things being equal; that is, demand curves slope downward to the right.

Demand curve facing a firm.   A curve showing the quantities per unit of time the firm can sell at alternative price levels, other things being equal.

Demand-pull inflation.   Increases in the average price level initiated and continued from increases in aggregate demand.

Developed countries.   Countries with relatively higher labor quality, relatively large accumulations of capital, and relatively higher levels of technology, all leading to relatively high living standards.

Diminishing returns.   The principle that increments of a variable resource used with a fixed resource will lead to smaller and smaller increments in product output.

Discount rate.   The rate of interest the Federal Reserve Banks charge commercial banks when commercial banks borrow from the Fed.

Discouraged workers.   Those who have stopped actively searching for work are not considered to be part of the labor force. As such, they are classified as discouraged workers rather than unemployed.

Discrimination, employment.   Failure of an employer to hire because of such noneconomic characteristics of potential employees as race or sex.

Discrimination, market.   A situation in which the terms on which market transactions are based are not the same for all economic units in the market. Different consumers are charged different prices for identical product units. Employers pay different wage rates for workers with identical productivities.

Discrimination, nonmarket.   Social discrimination based on social tastes, attitudes, customs, and laws. Unlike market discrimination, it is difficult to associate monetary costs with nonmarket discrimination.

Discrimination, occupational.   Discrimination in the form of concentrations of minority groups in low-paying occupations.

Diseconomies of scale.   A situation that occurs when the average cost of producing a good or service rises as output is increased.

Dumping.   An "unfair" international trade practice that occurs when a producer is selling abroad at a price below cost, or below its domestic price.

Economic growth.   A long-run process of economic expansion that results from a compounding of economic events over time.

Economies of scale.   A situation that occurs when the average cost of producing a good or service falls as output is increased.

Efficiency.   The extraction of the greatest possible value of product output from given inputs of resources.

Elasticity of demand, price.   The responsiveness of the quantity demanded of a product to changes in its price. Measured by the percentage change in quantity divided by the percentage change in price.

Elasticity of supply, price.   The responsiveness of the quantity offered of a product to changes in its price. Measured by the percentage change in quantity divided by the percentage change in price.

Equal tax treatment doctrine.   The concept that taxpayers in equal economic circumstances should be treated equally; that is, people in identical economic positions should pay the same amounts of taxes.

Equation of exchange.   The truism that the money supply (M) times the velocity of circulation (V_1) equals quantities of goods and services sold in final form (Q) times the average price level (P).

Equimarginal principle.   The allocation of spending among different inputs in such a way that the marginal benefits of a dollar spent on any one input is the same as for that spent on any other input.

Equity in distribution.   The subjective notion of what constitutes fairness in the distribution of income and the output of the economy.

Excess tax burden.   The distortionary effects of a tax on relative prices and resource allocation.

Exchange rates.   The costs of units of other countries' currencies in terms of units of the home country's currency.

Explicit costs.   Costs of production incurred by the purchase or hire of resources by the producing unit.

Exploitation, consumer.   Circumstances in which consumers pay a higher price for a product than its costs of production.

Exploitation, resource owner.   Circumstances in which resource owners receive a lower price for a resource than the value of marginal product of the resource.

Exports.   Goods and services that economic units in one country sell to other countries.

Externalities.   Benefits or costs incurred in the production or consumption of goods and services that do not accrue to the producing or consuming unit, but rather accrue to the remainder of the society.

Fee-for-service system.   A health care program in which buyers pay the cost of what they receive.

Fiscal rules.   Rules governing taxation and expenditures when the federal government is pursuing stabilization policies. Examples include (1) a balanced budget during periods of full employment and price stability, (2) a budget surplus during periods of inflation, and (3) a budget deficit during periods of recession.

Forward tax shifting.   Taxes shifted to consumers in the form of higher product prices.

Free riders.   Those who receive positive social spillovers in consumption benefits without paying the costs of producing the goods or services that yield them.

Free trade area.   An alliance of nations without trade barriers between its members.

Frictional unemployment.   Brief periods of unemployment experienced by persons moving between jobs or into the labor market; it is not related to basic aggregate demand or aggregate supply problems.

Full-cost pricing.   A situation in which the price of a product is equal to its average cost of production.

Full-employment rate of unemployment.   The full-employment rate of unemployment is the rate that exists when there is no cyclical unemployment. The full-employment rate of unemployment is consistent with price stability.

Fully funded insurance scheme.   Insurance programs designed to provide benefits financed from the interest income earned on accumulated payments.

Good, inferior.   When an increase in income leads to a fall in demand, other things being equal, the good in question is said to be inferior.

Good, normal.   When an increase in income leads to an increase in demand, other things being equal, the good in question is said to be normal.

Goods, complementary.   Two goods or services are complementary if an increase in the price of one leads to a fall in the demand for the other, other things being equal.

Goods, substitute.   Two goods or services are substitutes if an increase in the price of one leads to an increase in the demand for the other, other things being equal.

Government purchases.   Government expenditures for currently produced goods and services.

Government transfer payments.   Payments made by governments to persons who have made no contributions to current production of goods and services.

Gross domestic product, current.   The market value of all final goods and services produced within an economy during 1 year. GDP ignores the issue of whether the resources used for the production are domestically or foreign owned.

Gross domestic product, per capita.   Gross domestic product, either current or real, divided by the economy's population.

Gross domestic product, potential.   The level of real GDP the economy could produce at full employment.

Gross domestic product, real.   Gross domestic product corrected for changes in the price level relative to a base year price level.

Gross domestic product gap.   The difference between an economy's potential GDP and its actual GDP.

Gross federal debt.   The total of all outstanding securities of the federal government, including interest- and non-interest-bearing securities, U.S. and foreign held securities, privately and publicly held securities, and securities held by both central and commercial banks.

Horizontal equity.   The notion that people in the same economic circumstances should receive the same economic treatment.

Human capital.   That part of the productive power of human or labor resources resulting from investment in education and training.

Implicit costs.   Costs of production incurred by the use of self-owned, self-employed resources.

Imports.   Goods and services purchased and brought into a country from abroad.

Incomes policies.   Governmental restraints placed on wages and prices intended to reduce cost-push inflation thought to result from the monopolies of labor unions and business firms.

Increasing opportunity costs.   As more of a particular good or service is produced, the cost in terms of other goods or services that are given up grows.

Individually consumed goods and services.   Goods and services that benefit directly, and only, those persons who consume them.

Inflation.   A rising average price level of goods and services.

Injections.   New spending in the circular flow, including new investment, new government expenditures, and new exports.

Investment.   The purchase by economic units of such real assets as land, buildings, equipment, machinery, and raw and semifinished materials.

Investment account (budgetary).   One of the three major expenditure classifications into which a governmental budget may be divided. It includes spending for investment goods and the debt incurred to finance such spending.

Investment multiplier.   The reciprocal of 1 minus the marginal propensity to consume.

Involuntary unemployment.   The situation in which persons qualified for jobs, willing to work, and willing to accept the going wage rate are unable to find jobs. It occurs when the quantity of labor demanded is less than the quantity supplied at going wage rates.

Labor force.   The labor force includes all noninstitutionalized individuals 16 years of age and older who are either employed for pay, actively seeking employment, or awaiting recall from a temporary layoff.

Labor resources.   Human resources, all efforts of mind and muscle, that are ingredients in production processes. They range from unskilled common labor to the highest levels of professional skills.

Labor union. A labor union is a formal organization of workers which bargains on behalf of its members over the terms and conditions of employment.

Leakages. Withdrawals from spending in the circular flow, including taxes, savings, and imports.

Lesser developed countries. Countries with relatively low living standards, usually the result of relatively low labor quality, relatively scarce capital, and relatively low levels of technology.

Living standards. The level of economic well-being of a population, usually measured in terms of its per capita real income.

Lockout. A work stoppage initiated by management.

Lorenz curve. This curve shows the cumulative percentage of total family income that is going to the lowest percentiles of families. It is a way of measuring the degree of income inequality in a country.

Losses. The difference between a firm's total costs and its total revenues when total revenues are less than total costs, including as a part of total costs returns to investors in the firm sufficient to yield an average return on their investments.

Managed care system. A health care program whereby payments to providers are based on a prearranged schedule of fixed fees that has been negotiated between the insurer and the providers.

Marginal benefits. The increase or decrease in the total benefits yielded by an activity from a one-unit change in the amount of the activity carried on.

Marginal costs. The change in total costs resulting from a one-unit change in the output of a good or service.

Marginal private benefit (*MPB*). The benefit that accrues to the direct consumers of a good or service resulting from a one-unit increase in consumption. The *MPB* is reflected in the demand curve for the good or service.

Marginal private cost (*MPC*). The increase in total cost that producers incur when output is increased by one unit. The *MPC* is reflected in the supply curve for the good or service.

Marginal product of labor. The change in production that occurs in response to hiring one additional worker.

Marginal propensity to consume. The change in consumption divided by the change in income.

Marginal propensity to save.   The change in saving divided by the change in income.

Marginal revenue.   The change in the total revenue of a seller resulting from a one-unit change in the quantity sold of a good or service.

Marginal revenue product of labor.   The change in revenue that occurs in response to hiring one additional worker. Serves as the firm's demand curve for labor.

Marginal social benefit (*MSB*).   The true benefit to society of a one-unit increase in the production of a good or service.

Marginal social cost (*MSC*).   The true or opportunity cost borne by society when the production of a good or service is increased by one unit.

Market.   The area within which buyers and sellers of a good or service can interact and engage in exchange.

Market, competitive.   A market in which there are many sellers and many buyers of a good or service. No one buyer or seller is large enough to be able to affect the price of the product.

Market, imperfect competition.   A market that falls between the limits of a competitive market on the one hand and a monopolistic market on the other. It contains elements of both.

Market, monopolistic.   A market in which there is a single seller of a good, service, or resource.

Market failure.   Occurs when markets, operating on their own, do not lead to a socially optimal allocation of resources.

Minimum wages.   Wage rate floors set for specific occupations or groups of workers by governmental units or by labor unions.

Mixed systems.   Economies that combine elements of both the pure market and pure command economies.

Monetizing the federal debt.   Financing deficits with newly created money. The additional money may be created through the sale of government securities to banks or through printing money.

Money creation.   The expansion of demand deposits when banks and other financial institutions, as a group, expand loans.

Money multiplier.   A numerical coefficient equal to the reciprocal of the legal reserve ratio.

Money supply (*M*).   Currency held by the public plus checkable accounts.

Monopoly power.   The degree to which sellers can control the supply and hence the price of what they sell.

Monopsony.   A market with only one buyer or employer of a factor of production.

Monopsony power.   The degree to which buyers can control the demand and hence the price of what they purchase.

Natural monopoly.   When the average cost of producing a product is minimized by having only one firm produce the product, the industry is said to be a natural monopoly.

Near money.   Assets that are easily convertible to cash; they are similar to money because they are very liquid.

Negative income tax.   A government subsidy or cash payment to households that qualify because of having income below a minimum or guaranteed level.

Nonprice competition.   Competition among firms in matters other than product price. It usually takes the form of (1) advertising and (2) changes in design and quality of the product.

Open-market operations.   Federal Reserve purchases and sales of government securities for the purpose of increasing or decreasing commercial bank reserves.

Opportunity cost principle.   The true cost of producing an additional unit of a good or service is the value of other goods or services that must be given up to obtain it.

Pay-as-you-go insurance scheme.   Insurance programs designed to provide benefits financed from current payments.

Pollution rights market.   When firms are allowed to buy and sell government-issued licenses granting the holder the right to create a certain amount of pollution, the resulting market is called a pollution rights market.

Price ceiling.   A maximum price set for a product, usually by a governmental unit. Sellers of the product are not permitted to charge higher prices.

Price, equilibrium.   The price of a product at which buyers are willing to purchase exactly the quantities per unit of time that sellers want to sell.

Price discrimination.   The sale of the same product to different persons or groups of persons at different prices.

Price floor.   A minimum price set for a product, usually by a governmental unit or a group of sellers. Sellers are not permitted to resell at lower prices.

Price index numbers.   A set of numbers showing price level changes relative to some base year.

Primary burden (of the national debt).   The present and future decrease in private production brought about by the national debt.

Private insurance.   A contract whereby individuals agree to make payments, often called premiums, to a company in return for a guarantee of financial benefits in the event that some undesired circumstance occurs.

Production.   The process of using technology to combine and transform resources to make goods and services.

Production possibilities curve.   A graphical representation of the maximum quantities of two goods and/or services that an economy can produce when its resources are used in the most efficient way possible.

Productivity.   The average amount of output that can be produced with a given set of inputs. The productivity of any resource can be calculated as the ratio of the units of output to the units of input.

Profit-maximizing output.   The output per unit of time at which a firm's total revenue exceeds its total cost by the greatest possible amount. It is the output at which the firm's marginal cost equals its marginal revenue.

Profits.   The difference between a firm's total revenue and its total cost when total revenue exceeds total cost, including as a part of total cost returns to investors in the firm sufficient to yield an average rate of return on their investments.

Progressive tax rates.   A tax rate schedule that results in an increase in the ratio of tax collections to income as income increases.

Proportional tax rates.   A tax rate schedule that results in a constant ratio of tax collections to income as income changes.

Prospective payment system.   A health care program whereby the prices of services are fixed in advance by the insurer at a given amount for a given treatment.

Psychic costs.   Costs in the form of negative personal satisfaction, rather than monetary loss, that an individual incurs from pursuing an endeavor.

Psychic income.   Benefits in the form of personal satisfaction, rather than monetary gain, that an individual receives from pursuing an endeavor.

Psychological law of consumption.   A law stating that when income changes, consumption changes but by less than the change in income.

Public goods.   Goods and services of a collectively consumed nature, usually provided by governmental units.

Public investments.   Government spending for capital goods such as roads, bridges, dams, schools, and hospitals.

Pure command economy.   The pure command economy is characterized by state ownership and/or control of resources and centralized resource-use decision making.

Pure market economy.   The pure market economy is based on private ownership and control of resources, known as private property rights, and on coordination of resource-use decisions through markets.

Quantity theory of money.   The theory that changes in the money supply (M) will tend to cause changes in the same direction of total output (Q) and price level (P).

Quota.   A regulation that limits by law the quantity of specific foreign goods or services that may be imported during a period of time.

Rationing.   The allocation of given supplies of a good, service, or resource among its users.

Recurrent expenditures.   Expenditures that the government must make on an ongoing basis, for example, salaries, interest on the national debt, postal services, and welfare services. Public investments are excluded.

Relative price.   The price of a good or service relative to the prices of all other goods and services.

Relative tax treatment doctrine.   The theory that taxpayers in different economic circumstances should pay different amounts of taxes.

Retirement effect.   The increase in a worker's lifetime saving because Social Security tends to extend the length of retirement.

Reserve ratio, legal (or required).   The ratio of reserves to deposits that banks are required by law to maintain.

Resources.   The ingredients that go into the production of goods and services. They consist of labor resources and capital resources.

Secondary repercussions (of the national debt).   The income distribution, output, and inflation effects of the national debt.

Semicollectively consumed goods and services.   Goods and services that yield direct benefits to the consumers of them but that also yield social spillover benefits to others.

Shortage.   A situation in which buyers of a product want larger quantities per unit of time than sellers will place on the market. It may be caused by the existence of an effective price ceiling.

Social insurance. Government programs, financed through tax revenues, that guarantee citizens financial benefits against events which are beyond an individual's control, such as old age, disability, and poor health.

Social overhead capital. Capital used by the economy as a whole rather than being limited to use by specific firms. Examples include transportation and communications networks as well as energy and power systems.

Social spillover in consumption. Occurs when the consumption of a good or service causes a change in the satisfaction for someone other than the direct consumer of the item. Such spillovers can have positive or negative effects on satisfaction.

Social spillover in production. When the production of a particular good or service causes a change in the cost of producing some other item. Such spillovers can have positive or negative effects on production costs.

Stabilization account (budgetary). One of the three major categories into which a governmental budget may be divided. It includes spending programs designed to stabilize the economy, together with the methods used to finance them.

Strike. A work stoppage initiated by labor.

Structural budget. The level of federal outlays and revenues that you would have, assuming the economy is operating at a predetermined high level of production and employment.

Structural unemployment. Unemployment caused by a mismatch between the skills (or locations) of job seekers and the requirements (or locations) of available jobs.

Substitution effects. The effects of a price change of a good or service on the quantity of it purchased because of the substitution of relatively lower priced goods for it when its price increases and the substitution of the item for now relatively higher priced other goods when its price decreases.

Supply. The set of quantities of a good or service per unit of time that sellers would be willing to place on the market at various alternative prices of the item, other things being equal.

Supply, changes in. Shifts in the entire supply schedule or curve for a good or service, resulting from changes in one or more of the "other things being equal." They should not be confused with movements along a given supply schedule or curve.

Supply curve of a firm. A curve showing the quantities per unit of time a firm will place on the market at alternative price levels, other things being equal. The concept is valid for a competitive firm only, and coincides with its marginal cost curve.

Surplus. A situation in which sellers of a product place larger quantities per unit of time on the market than buyers will take. It may be caused by the existence of a price floor.

Tariff. A tax placed on internationally traded goods, usually imports.

Tastes and preferences. Buyers' psychological desires for goods and services—one of the determinants of demand for any one product. A change in consumers' tastes and preferences for a product will shift the demand curve for it.

Tax efficiency. The extent to which a tax has a neutral impact on resource allocation and is economical to collect and enforce, thus minimizing the total tax burden.

Tax incidence. The final resting place or burden of any given tax—who actually pays it.

Technology. The know-how and the means and methods available for combining resources to produce goods and services.

Terms of trade. The cost, in terms of the home country's goods and services, of importing a unit of goods or services from other countries.

Transfer payments. Payments made to persons or economic units that are *not* for services currently performed. They do not result in new output but simply transfer purchasing power from some persons or units to others.

Transformation curve. *See* Production possibilities curve.

Turnover tax. Within the Soviet economy, excess demand for goods and services was often "siphoned off" through the addition of, or increase in, the turnover tax.

Universal coverage. This means that the entire population is covered under a national health insurance program.

Vertical equity. The notion that persons in different economic circumstances should receive different rewards from the economic system.

Voluntary restraint agreement. An international treaty whereby one nation "volunteers" to restrict the exports of a product that it sells to another nation.

Wage discrimination. Payment of unequal wage rates to persons with equal values of marginal product.

Wants. The unlimited or insatiable desires of humans that generate economic activity.

Wealth substitution effect.   The reduction in lifetime saving by workers who substitute the wealth accumulated through participation in Social Security for other forms of private wealth.

Index

From the reviews

'This lively book should be read by all physicians and scientists who plan to put pen to paper in the interests of communicating with their peers. My copy remains close to hand.'

European Science Editing

'...a pleasure to read. It is quite remarkable value for money, and every aspiring author should have his own copy. There should also be a spare (hardback) copy in every medical library.'

Medicine Digest

'Clear, sensible, and often entertaining advice is given about how to plan publication of research findings, how to select an appropriate journal, how to prepare drafts, tables and figures, how to overcome writer's block...'

European Science Editing

'The book is comprehensive. There is a great deal of detailed, practical information in it, especially for the beginner writer, and the experienced contributor will also find up-to-date advice.'

Infection

OTHER TITLES FROM E & FN SPON

Studying for Science
A guide to information, communication and study techniques
Brian White

Study!
A guide to effective study, revision and examination techniques
Robert Barrass

Brain Train
Studying for success
Richard Palmer

Scientists Must Write
A guide for better writing for scientists, engineers and students
Robert Barrass

Effective Writing
Improving scientific, technical and business communications
2nd Edition
Christopher Turk and John Kirkman

Effective Speaking
Communicating in speech
Christopher Turk

Good Style for Scientific and Technical Writing
John Kirkman

Write in Style
A guide to good English
Richard Palmer

For more information about these and other titles please contact:
The Promotion Department, E & FN Spon, 2–6 Boundary Row, London, SE1 8HN

Writing
successfully
in science

MAEVE O'CONNOR

Secretary-Treasurer,
European Association of Science Editors

With cartoons by Jenny Gretton

CHAPMAN & HALL

London · Glasgow · New York · Tokyo · Melbourne · Madras

Published by Chapman & Hall, 2-6 Boundary Row, London SE1 8HN

Chapman & Hall, 2-6 Boundary Row, London SE1 8HN, UK

Blackie Academic & Professional, Wester Cleddens Road,
Bishopbriggs, Glasgow G64 2NZ, UK

Chapman & Hall, 29 West 35th Street, New York NY10001, USA

Chapman & Hall Japan, Thomson Publishing Japan, Hirakawacho
Nemoto Building, 6F, 1-7-11 Hirakawa-cho, Chiyoda-ku, Tokyo 102,
Japan

Chapman & Hall Australia, Thomas Nelson Australia, 102 Dodds
Street, South Melbourne, Victoria 3205, Australia

Chapman & Hall India, R. Seshadri, 32 Second Main Road, CIT East,
Madras 600 035, India

First edition 1991
Reprinted 1992, 1993

© 1991 Maeve O'Connor

Typeset in 10/12pt Palatino by Computape (Pickering) Ltd, North
Yorkshire
Printed in Great Britain at The University Press, Cambridge

ISBN 0 412 44630 8

A catalogue record for this book is available from the British Library
Library of Congress Cataloging-in-Publication Data available